The King James Version of the

Holy Bible

of

JESUS CHRIST

THE WHY OF THIS BIBLE?

A number of years ago the spirit of God spoke to my heart, challenging me to study specific words of the New Testament, and how many times these words were used. Below is a list of these words with a number of times they were spoken in the New Testament.
faith 245, love 180, grace 127, believe 124, hope 53, trust 27, salvation 43, forgive 28, repent 24, spirit 261, holy 181, truth 119, sin 112, These are just some of the words I looked up and studied!

Then the Lord spoke to me very specific. The Holy Spirit encouraged me to look up every time **Jesus Christ** was mentioned, not just by name, but in a personal way! By the time I accomplished this task, I was completely flabbergasted and amazed! This king James version of the Bible is the result of that study! **Christ is revealed to us in a personal way over 9000 times within these 163 pages! Within this Bible you will discover that which describes Jesus Christ will be emphasized in bold letters, and highlighted in gray!**

NEW TESTAMENT STATISTICS:

Number of books: 27
Chapters: 260
Verses: 7,957
Words: 180,552
Letters: 838,380

Jesus revealed personally: over 9000 times

As you read this New Testament, my prayer for you is that **Jesus Christ** will become more alive and real to you then **He** has ever been before! **He** is the very center, heart, soul, mind and message that **God** the **father** has given to the human race. There are Scriptures that clearly declare that there is a transformation, metamorphosis that takes place in the human heart when they look upon, recognize, and have a revelation of **Jesus Christ**, and what He has accomplished for his beloved bride!

Sincerely: doc Yeager

----

1 John 3:2 Beloved, now are we the sons of God, and it doth not yet appear what we shall be: but we know that, when he shall appear, we shall be like him; for we shall see him as he is.

2 Corinthians 3:18 But we all, with open face beholding as in a glass the glory of the Lord, are changed into the same image from glory to glory, even as by the Spirit of the Lord.

1 Corinthians 13:12 For now we see through a glass, darkly; but then face to face: now I know in part; but then shall I know even as also I am known.

2 Peter 1: 2 Grace and peace be multiplied unto you through the knowledge of God, and of Jesus our Lord,................**4** Whereby are given unto us exceeding great and precious promises: that by these ye might be partakers of the divine nature, having escaped the corruption that is in the world through lust.

2 Peter 3:18 But grow in grace, and in the knowledge of our Lord and Saviour Jesus Christ. To him be glory both now and for ever. Amen.

Colossians 3:4 When Christ, who is our life, shall appear, then shall ye also appear with him in glory.

Romans 8:29 For whom he did foreknow, he also did predestinate to be conformed to the image of his Son, that he might be the firstborn among many brethren.

Psalm 17:15 As for me, I will behold thy face in righteousness: I shall be satisfied, when I awake, with thy likeness.

Philippians 3:21 Who shall change our vile body, that it may be fashioned like unto his glorious body, according to the working whereby he is able even to subdue all things unto himself.

Hebrews 9:28 So Christ was once offered to bear the sins of many; and unto them that look for him shall he appear the second time without sin unto salvation.

Revelation 22:4 And they shall see his face; and his name shall be in their foreheads.

1 John 2:28 And now, little children, abide in him; that, when he shall appear, we may have confidence, and not be ashamed before him at his coming.

Philippians 3:8 Yea doubtless, and I count all things but loss for the excellency of the knowledge of Christ Jesus my Lord: for whom I have suffered the loss of all things, and do count them but dung, that I may win Christ,

2 Corinthians 4:6 For God, who commanded the light to shine out of darkness, hath shined in our hearts, to give the light of the knowledge of the glory of God in the face of Jesus Christ.

PS: This task was difficult in some regards, because of the oneness of Christ and his Father. There were many times, especially in the epistles when it was hard to discern who it was speaking about. Whether it was the **Heavenly Father**, or His Son the **Lord Jesus Christ**! I'm sure you would discover that I have missed the proper emphasis at times. And yet the word of God itself has not been changed in the least.

By the way the Gospel and Mistry is Jesus Christ!

Table of Contents

New Testament

Of

JESUS CHRIST

by Dr Michael H Yeager **(King James Version)**

The Gospel According to St. Matthew [total 1169]

{1:1} The book of the generation of **Jesus Christ**, the Son of David, the Son of Abraham. {1:2} Abraham begat Isaac; and Isaac begat Jacob; and Jacob begat Judas and his brethren; {1:3} And Judas begat Phares and Zara of Thamar; and Phares begat Esrom; and Esrom begat Aram; {1:4} And Aram begat Aminadab; and Aminadab begat Naasson; and Naasson begat Salmon; {1:5} And Salmon begat Booz of Rachab; and Booz begat Obed of Ruth; and Obed begat Jesse; {1:6} And Jesse begat David the king; and David the king begat Solomon of her [that had been the wife] of Urias; {1:7} And Solomon begat Roboam; and Roboam begat Abia; and Abia begat Asa; {1:8} And Asa begat Josaphat; and Josaphat begat Joram; and Joram begat Ozias; {1:9} And Ozias begat Joatham; and Joatham begat Achaz; and Achaz begat Ezekias; {1:10} And Ezekias begat Manasses; and Manasses begat Amon; and Amon begat Josias; {1:11} And Josias begat Jechonias and his brethren, about the time they were carried away to Babylon: {1:12} And after they were brought to Babylon, Jechonias begat Salathiel; and Salathiel begat Zorobabel; {1:13} And Zorobabel begat Abiud; and Abiud begat Eliakim; and Eliakim begat Azor; {1:14} And Azor begat Sadoc; and Sadoc begat Achim; and Achim begat Eliud; {1:15} And Eliud begat Eleazar; and Eleazar begat Matthan; and Matthan begat Jacob; {1:16} And Jacob begat Joseph the husband of Mary, of whom was **born Jesus, who** is called **Christ**. {1:17} So all the generations from Abraham to David [are] fourteen generations; and from David until the carrying away into Babylon [are] fourteen generations; and from the carrying away into Babylon unto **Christ** [are] fourteen generations. {1:18} Now the birth of **Jesus Christ** was on this wise: When as **His** mother Mary was espoused to Joseph, before they came together, she was found with **child** of the Holy Ghost. {1:19} Then Joseph her husband, being a just [man,] and not willing to make her a publick example, was minded to put her away privily. {1:20} But while he thought on these things, behold, the angel of the Lord appeared unto him in a dream, saying, Joseph, thou Son of David, fear not to take unto thee Mary thy wife: for **that** which is conceived in her is of the Holy Ghost. {1:21} And she shall bring forth a **Son**, and thou shalt call **His name JESUS**: for **He** shall save **His** people from their sins. {1:22} Now all this was done, that it might be fulfilled which was spoken of the Lord by the prophet, saying, {1:23} Behold, a virgin shall be with **child**, and shall bring forth a **Son**, and they shall call **His name Emmanuel**, which being interpreted is, **God** with us. {1:24} Then Joseph being raised from sleep did as the angel of the Lord had bidden him, and took unto him his wife: {1:25} And knew her not till she had brought forth her **firstborn Son**: and he called **His name JESUS**.   {29}

{2:1} Now when **Jesus** was born in Bethlehem of Judaea in the days of Herod the king, behold, there came wise men from the east to Jerusalem, {2:2} Saying, Where is **He** that is born **King** of the Jews? for we have seen **His** star in the east, and are come to worship **Him**. {2:3} When Herod the king had heard [these things,] he was troubled, and all Jerusalem with him. {2:4} And when he had gathered all the chief priests and scribes of the people together, he demanded of them where **Christ** should be born. {2:5} And they said unto him, In Bethlehem of Judaea: for thus it is written by the prophet, {2:6} And thou Bethlehem, in the land of Juda, art not the least among the princes of Juda: for out of thee shall come a **Governor**, that shall rule my people Israel. {2:7} Then Herod, when he had privily called the wise men, enquired of them diligently what time the star appeared. {2:8} And he sent them to Bethlehem, and said,

Go and search diligently for the **young child**; and when ye have found [**Him**,] bring me word again, that I may come and worship **Him** also. {2:9} When they had heard the king, they departed; and, lo, the star, which they saw in the east, went before them, till it came and stood over where the **young child** was. {2:10} When they saw the star, they rejoiced with exceeding great joy. {2:11} And when they were come into the house, they saw the **young child** with Mary **His** mother, and fell down, and worshipped **Him**: and when they had opened their treasures, they presented unto **Him** gifts; gold, and frankincense, and myrrh. {2:12} And being warned of God in a dream that they should not return to Herod, they departed into their own country another way. {2:13} And when they were departed, behold, the angel of the Lord appeareth to Joseph in a dream, saying, Arise, and take the **young child** and **His** mother, and flee into Egypt, and be thou there until I bring thee word: for Herod will seek the young child to destroy **Him**. {2:14} When he arose, he took the **young child** and **His** mother by night, and departed into Egypt: {2:15} And was there until the death of Herod: that it might be fulfilled which was spoken of the Lord by the prophet, saying, Out of Egypt have I called **my Son**. {2:16} Then Herod, when he saw that he was mocked of the wise men, was exceeding wroth, and sent forth, and slew all the children that were in Bethlehem, and in all the coasts thereof, from two years old and under, according to the time which he had diligently enquired of the wise men. {2:17} Then was fulfilled that which was spoken by Jeremy the prophet, saying, {2:18} In Rama was there a voice heard, lamentation, and weeping, and great mourning, Rachel weeping [for] her children, and would not be comforted, because they are not. {2:19} But when Herod was dead, behold, an angel of the Lord appeareth in a dream to Joseph in Egypt, {2:20} Saying, Arise, and take the **young child** and **His** mother, and go into the land of Israel: for they are dead which sought the **young child's** life. {2:21} And he arose, and took the **young child** and **His** mother, and came into the land of Israel. {2:22} But when he heard that Archelaus did reign in Judaea in the room of his Father Herod, he was afraid to go thither: notwithstanding, being warned of God in a dream, he turned aside into the parts of Galilee: {2:23} And he came and dwelt in a city called Nazareth: that it might be fulfilled which was spoken by the prophets, He shall be called a Nazarene.   {36}

{3:1} In those days came John the Baptist, preaching in the wilderness of Judaea, {3:2} And saying, Repent ye: for the kingdom of heaven is at hand. {3:3} For this is He that was spoken of by the prophet Esaias, saying, The voice of one crying in the wilderness, Prepare ye the way of the **Lord**, make **His** paths straight. {3:4} And the same John had his raiment of camel's hair, and a leathern girdle about his loins; and his meat was locusts and wild honey. {3:5} Then went out to him Jerusalem, and all Judaea, and all the region round about Jordan, {3:6} And were baptized of him in Jordan, confessing their sins. {3:7} But when he saw many of the Pharisees and Sadducees come to his baptism, he said unto them, O generation of vipers, who hath warned you to flee from the wrath to come? {3:8} Bring forth therefore fruits meet for repentance: {3:9} And think not to say within yourselves, We have Abraham to [our] Father: for I say unto you, that God is able of these stones to raise up children unto Abraham. {3:10} And now also the axe is laid unto the root of the trees: therefore every tree which bringeth not forth good fruit is hewn down, and cast into the fire. {3:11} I indeed baptize you with water unto repentance: but He that cometh after me is mightier than I, whose shoes I am not worthy to bear: He shall baptize you with the Holy Ghost, and [with] fire: {3:12} Whose fan [is] in His hand, and He will throughly purge His floor, and gather His wheat into the garner; but He will burn up the chaff with unquenchable fire.{3:13} Then cometh Jesus from Galilee to Jordan unto John, to be baptized of him. {3:14} But John forbad Him, saying, I have need to be baptized of thee, and comest thou to me? {3:15} And Jesus answering said unto him, Suffer [it to be so] now: for thus it becometh us to fulfil all righteousness. Then he suffered Him. {3:16} And Jesus, when He was baptized, went up straightway out of the water: and, lo, the heavens were opened unto Him, and he saw the Spirit of God descending like a dove, and lighting upon Him: {3:17} And lo a voice from heaven, saying, This is my beloved Son, in whom I am well pleased. {21}

{4:1} Then was Jesus led up of the Spirit into the wilderness to be tempted of the devil. {4:2} And when He had fasted forty days and forty nights, He was afterward an hungred. {4:3} And when the tempter came to Him, he said, If thou be the Son of God, command that these stones be made bread. {4:4} But He answered and said, It is written, Man shall not live by bread alone, but by every word that proceedeth out of the mouth of God. {4:5} Then the devil taketh Him up into the holy city, and setteth Him on a pinnacle of the temple, {4:6} And saith unto Him, If thou be the Son of God, cast thyself down: for it is written, He shall give His angels charge concerning thee: and in [their] hands they shall bear thee up, lest at any time thou dash thy foot against a stone. {4:7} Jesus said unto him, It is written again, Thou shalt not tempt the Lord thy God. {4:8} Again, the devil taketh Him up into an exceeding high mountain, and sheweth Him all the kingdoms of the world, and the glory of them; {4:9} And saith unto Him, All these things will I give thee, if thou wilt fall down and worship me. {4:10} Then saith Jesus unto him, Get thee hence, Satan: for it is written, Thou shalt worship the Lord thy God, and Him only shalt thou serve. {4:11} Then the devil leaveth Him, and, behold, angels came and ministered unto Him.{4:12} Now when Jesus had heard that John was cast into prison, He departed into Galilee; {4:13} And leaving Nazareth, He came and dwelt in Capernaum, which is upon the sea coast, in the borders of Zabulon and Nephthalim: {4:14} That it might be fulfilled which was spoken by Esaias the prophet, saying, {4:15} The land of Zabulon, and the land of Nephthalim, [by] the way of the sea, beyond Jordan, Galilee of the Gentiles; {4:16} The people which sat in darkness saw great light; and to them which sat in the region and shadow of death light is sprung up. {4:17} From that time Jesus began to preach, and to say, Repent: for the kingdom of heaven is at hand.{4:18} And Jesus, walking by the sea of Galilee, saw two brethren, Simon called Peter, and Andrew his brother, casting a net into the sea: for they were fishers. {4:19} And He saith unto them, Follow me, and I will make you fishers of men. {4:20} And they straightway left [their] nets, and followed Him. {4:21} And going on from thence, He saw other two brethren, James [the Son] of Zebedee, and John his brother, in a ship with Zebedee their Father, mending their nets; and

He called them. {4:22} And they immediately left the ship and their Father, and followed Him.{4:23} And Jesus went about all Galilee, teaching in their synagogues, and preaching the Gospel of the kingdom, and healing all manner of sickness and all manner of disease among the people. {4:24} And His fame went throughout all Syria: and they brought unto Him all sick people that were taken with divers diseases and torments, and those which were possessed with devils, and those which were lunatick, and those that had the palsy; and He healed them. {4:25} And there followed Him great multitudes of people from Galilee, and [from] Decapolis, and [from] Jerusalem, and [from] Judaea, and [from] beyond Jordan.   {48}

{5:1} And seeing the multitudes, He went up into a mountain: and when He was set, His disciples came unto Him: {5:2} And He opened His mouth, and taught them, saying, {5:3} Blessed [are] the poor in spirit: for theirs is the kingdom of heaven. {5:4} Blessed [are] they that mourn: for they shall be comforted. {5:5} Blessed [are] the meek: for they shall inherit the earth. {5:6} Blessed [are] they which do hunger and thirst after righteousness: for they shall be filled. {5:7} Blessed [are] the merciful: for they shall obtain mercy. {5:8} Blessed [are] the pure in heart: for they shall see God. {5:9} Blessed [are] the peacemakers: for they shall be called the children of God. {5:10} Blessed [are] they which are persecuted for righteousness sake: for theirs is the kingdom of heaven. {5:11} Blessed are ye, when [men] shall revile you, and persecute [you,] and shall say all manner of evil against you falsely, for my sake. {5:12} Rejoice, and be exceeding glad: for great [is] your reward in heaven: for so persecuted they the prophets which were before you.

{5:13} Ye are the salt of the earth: but if the salt have lost his savour, wherewith shall it be salted? it is thenceforth good for nothing, but to be cast out, and to be trodden under foot of men. {5:14} Ye are the light of the world. A city that is set on an hill cannot be hid. {5:15} Neither do men light a candle, and put it under a bushel, but on a candlestick; and it giveth light unto all that are in the house. {5:16} Let your light so shine before men, that they may see your good works, and glorify your Father which is in heaven.

{5:17} Think not that I am come to destroy the law, or the prophets: I am not come to destroy, but to fulfil. {5:18} For verily I say unto you, Till heaven and earth pass, one jot or one tittle shall in no wise pass from the law, till all be fulfilled. {5:19} Whosoever therefore shall break one of these least commandments, and shall teach men so, he shall be called the least in the kingdom of heaven: but whosoever shall do and teach [them,] the same shall be called great in the kingdom of heaven. {5:20} For I say unto you, That except your righteousness shall exceed [the righteousness] of the scribes and Pharisees, ye shall in no case enter into the kingdom of heaven.

{5:21} Ye have heard that it was said by them of old time, Thou shalt not kill; and whosoever shall kill shall be in danger of the judgment: {5:22} But I say unto you, That whosoever is angry with his brother without a cause shall be in danger of the judgment: and whosoever shall say to his brother, Raca, shall be in danger of the council: but whosoever shall say, Thou fool, shall be in danger of hell fire. {5:23} Therefore if thou bring thy gift to the altar, and there rememberest that thy brother hath ought against thee;

{5:24} Leave there thy gift before the altar, and go thy way; first be reconciled to thy brother, and then come and offer thy gift. {5:25} Agree with thine adversary quickly, whiles thou art in the way with him; lest at any time the adversary deliver thee to the judge, and the judge deliver thee to the officer, and thou be cast into prison. {5:26} Verily I say unto thee, Thou shalt by no means come out thence, till thou hast paid the uttermost farthing. {5:27} Ye have heard that it was said by them of old time, Thou shalt not commit adultery: {5:28} But I say unto you, That whosoever looketh on a woman to lust after her hath committed adultery with her already in his heart. {5:29} And if thy right eye offend thee, pluck it out, and cast [it] from thee: for it is profitable for thee that one of thy members should perish, and not [that] thy whole body should be cast into hell. {5:30} And if thy right hand offend thee, cut if off, and cast it from thee: for it is profitable for thee that one of thy members should perish, and not [that] thy whole body should be cast into hell. {5:31} It hath been said, Whosoever shall put away his wife, let him give her a writing of divorcement: {5:32} But I say unto you, That whosoever shall put away his wife, saving for the cause of fornication, causeth her to commit adultery: and whosoever shall marry her that is divorced committeth adultery. {5:33} Again, ye have heard that it hath been said by them of old time, Thou shalt not forswear thyself, but shalt perform unto the **Lord** thine oaths: {5:34} But I say unto you, Swear not at all; neither by heaven; for it is God's throne: {5:35} Nor by the earth; for it is His footstool: neither by Jerusalem; for it is the city of the great King. {5:36} Neither shalt thou swear by thy head, because thou canst not make one hair white or black. {5:37} But let your communication be, Yea, yea; Nay, nay: for whatsoever is more than these cometh of evil.

{5:38} Ye have heard that it hath been said, An eye for an eye, and a tooth for a tooth: {5:39} But I say unto you, That ye resist not evil: but whosoever shall smite thee on thy right cheek, turn to him the other also. {5:40} And if any man will sue thee at the law, and take away thy coat, let him have [thy] cloke also. {5:41} And whosoever shall compel thee to go a mile, go with him twain. {5:42} Give to him that asketh thee, and from him that would borrow of thee turn not thou away.

{5:43} Ye have heard that it hath been said, Thou shalt love thy neighbour, and hate thine enemy. {5:44} But I say unto you, Love your enemies, bless them that curse you, do good to them that hate you, and pray for them which despitefully use you, and persecute you; {5:45} That ye may be the children of your **Father** which is in heaven: for He maketh **His** sun to rise on the evil and on the good, and sendeth rain on the just and on the unjust. {5:46} For if ye love them which love you, what reward have ye? do not even the publicans the same? {5:47} And if ye salute your brethren only, what do ye more [than others?] do not even the publicans so? {5:48} Be ye therefore perfect, even as your **Father** which is in heaven is perfect. {22}

{6:1} Take heed that ye do not your alms before men, to be seen of them: otherwise ye have no reward of your **Father** which is in heaven. {6:2} Therefore when thou doest [thine] alms, do not sound a trumpet before thee, as the hypocrites do in the synagogues and in the streets, that they may have glory of men. Verily I say unto you, They have their reward. {6:3} But when thou doest alms, let not thy left hand know what thy right hand doeth: {6:4} That thine

alms may be in secret: and thy **Father** which seeth in secret himself shall reward thee openly.

{6:5} And when thou prayest, thou shalt not be as the hypocrites [are:] for they love to pray standing in the synagogues and in the corners of the streets, that they may be seen of men. Verily I say unto you, They have their reward. {6:6} But thou, when thou prayest, enter into thy closet, and when thou hast shut thy door, pray to thy **Father** which is in secret; and thy **Father** which seeth in secret shall reward thee openly. {6:7} But when ye pray, use not vain repetitions, as the heathen [do:] for they think that they shall be heard for their much speaking. {6:8} Be not ye therefore like unto them: for your **Father** knoweth what things ye have need of, before ye ask **Him**. {6:9} After this manner therefore pray ye: Our **Father** which art in heaven, Hallowed be thy name. {6:10} Thy kingdom come. Thy will be done in earth, as [it is] in heaven. {6:11} Give us this day our daily bread. {6:12} And forgive us our debts, as we forgive our debtors. {6:13} And lead us not into temptation, but deliver us from evil: For thine is the kingdom, and the power, and the glory, for ever. Amen. {6:14} For if ye forgive men their trespasses, your heavenly **Father** will also forgive you: {6:15} But if ye forgive not men their trespasses, neither will your **Father** forgive your trespasses.

{6:16} Moreover when ye fast, be not, as the hypocrites, of a sad countenance: for they disfigure their faces, that they may appear unto men to fast. Verily I say unto you, They have their reward. {6:17} But thou, when thou fastest, anoint thine head, and wash thy face; {6:18} That thou appear not unto men to fast, but unto thy **Father** which is in secret: and thy **Father**, which seeth in secret, shall reward thee openly.

{6:19} Lay not up for yourselves treasures upon earth, where moth and rust doth corrupt, and where thieves break through and steal: {6:20} But lay up for yourselves treasures in heaven, where neither moth nor rust doth corrupt, and where thieves do not break through nor steal: {6:21} For where your treasure is, there will your heart be also. {6:22} The light of the body is the eye: if therefore thine eye be single, thy whole body shall be full of light. {6:23} But if thine eye be evil, thy whole body shall be full of darkness. If therefore the light that is in thee be darkness, how great [is] that darkness!

{6:24} No man can serve two masters: for either he will hate the one, and love the other; or else he will hold to the one, and despise the other. Ye cannot serve **God** and mammon. {6:25} Therefore I say unto you, Take no thought for your life, what ye shall eat, or what ye shall drink; nor yet for your body, what ye shall put on. Is not the life more than meat, and the body than raiment? {6:26} Behold the fowls of the air: for they sow not, neither do they reap, nor gather into barns; yet your heavenly **Father** feedeth them. Are ye not much better than they? {6:27} Which of you by taking thought can add one cubit unto his stature? {6:28} And why take ye thought for raiment? Consider the lilies of the field, how they grow; they toil not, neither do they spin: {6:29} And yet I say unto you, That even Solomon in all his glory was not arrayed like one of these. {6:30} Wherefore, if **God** so clothe the grass of the field, which to day is, and to morrow is cast into the oven, [shall He] not much more [clothe] you, O ye of little faith? {6:31} Therefore take no thought, saying, What shall we eat? or, What shall we drink? or, Wherewithal shall we be clothed? {6:32} (For after all these things do the Gentiles seek:) for your heavenly **Father** knoweth that ye have need of all these things. {6:33} But seek ye first the kingdom of **God**, and **His** righteousness; and all these things shall be added unto you. {6:34} Take therefore no thought for the morrow: for the morrow shall take thought for the things of itself. Sufficient unto the day [is] the evil thereof. {5}

{7:1} Judge not, that ye be not judged. {7:2} For with what judgment ye judge, ye shall be judged: and with what measure ye mete, it shall be measured to you again. {7:3} And why beholdest thou the mote that is in thy brother's eye, but considerest not the beam that is in thine own eye? {7:4} Or how wilt thou say to thy brother, Let me pull out the mote out of thine eye; and, behold, a beam [is] in thine own eye? {7:5} Thou hypocrite, first cast out the beam out of thine own eye; and then shalt thou see clearly to cast out the mote out of thy brother's eye.{7:6} Give not that which is holy unto the dogs, neither cast ye your pearls before swine, lest they trample them under their feet, and turn again and rend you.{7:7} Ask, and it shall be given you; seek, and ye shall find; knock, and it shall be opened unto you: {7:8} For every one that asketh receiveth; and he that seeketh findeth; and to him that knocketh it shall be opened. {7:9} Or what man is there of you, whom if **his Son** ask bread, will He give **Him** a stone? {7:10} Or if **He** ask a fish, will He give **Him** a serpent? {7:11} If ye then, being evil, know how to give good gifts unto your children, how much more shall your **Father** which is in heaven give good things to them that ask **Him**? {7:12} Therefore all things whatsoever ye would that men should do to you, do ye even so to them: for this is the law and the prophets.{7:13} Enter ye in at the strait gate: for wide [is] the gate, and broad [is] the way, that leadeth to destruction, and many there be which go in thereat: {7:14} Because strait [is] the gate, and narrow [is] the way, which leadeth unto life, and few there be that find it.{7:15} Beware of false prophets, which come to you in sheep's clothing, but inwardly they are ravening wolves. {7:16} Ye shall know them by their fruits. Do men gather grapes of thorns, or figs of thistles? {7:17} Even so every good tree bringeth forth good fruit; but a corrupt tree bringeth forth evil fruit. {7:18} A good tree cannot bring forth evil fruit, neither [can] a corrupt tree bring forth good fruit. {7:19} Every tree that bringeth not forth good fruit is hewn down, and cast into the fire. {7:20} Wherefore by their fruits ye shall know them.{7:21} Not every one that saith unto **me**, **Lord**, **Lord**, shall enter into the kingdom of heaven; but he that doeth the will of **my Father** which is in heaven. {7:22} Many will say to **ME** in that day, **Lord**, **Lord**, have we not prophesied in **thy name**? and in **thy name** have cast out devils? and in **thy name** done many wonderful works? {7:23} And then will **I** profess unto them, **I** never knew you: depart from **ME**, ye that work iniquity.

{7:24} Therefore whosoever heareth these sayings of **mine**, and doeth them, **I** will liken him unto a wise man, which built his house upon a **rock**: {7:25} And the rain descended, and the floods came, and the winds blew, and beat upon that house; and it fell not: for it was founded upon a **rock**. {7:26} And every one that heareth these sayings of **mine**, and doeth them not, shall be likened unto a foolish man, which built his house upon the sand: {7:27} And the rain descended, and the floods came, and the winds blew, and beat upon that house; and it fell: and great was the fall of it. {7:28} And it came to pass, when **Jesus** had ended these sayings, the people were astonished at **His** doctrine: {7:29} For He taught them as [**one**] having authority, and not as the scribes. {30}

{8:1} When **He** was come down from the mountain, great multitudes followed **Him**. {8:2} And, behold, there came a leper and worshipped **Him**, saying, **Lord**, if **thou** wilt, **thou** canst make me clean. {8:3} And **Jesus** put forth [**His**] hand, and touched him, saying, **I** will; be thou clean. And immediately his leprosy was cleansed. {8:4} And **Jesus** saith unto him, See thou tell no man; but go thy way, shew thyself to the priest, and offer the gift that Moses commanded, for a testimony unto them.

{8:5} And when **Jesus** was entered into Capernaum, there came unto **Him** a centurion, beseeching **Him**, {8:6} And saying, **Lord**, my servant lieth at home sick of the palsy, grievously tormented. {8:7} And **Jesus** saith unto him, **I** will come and heal him. {8:8} The centurion answered and said, **Lord**, I am not worthy that **thou** shouldest come under my roof: but speak the word only, and my servant shall be healed. {8:9} For **I** am a man under authority, having soldiers under me: and I say to this [man,] Go, and he goeth; and to another, Come, and he cometh; and to my servant, Do this, and he doeth [it.]{8:10} When **Jesus** heard [it,] **He** marvelled, and said to them that followed, Verily **I** say unto you, **I** have not found so great faith, no, not in Israel. {8:11} And **I** say unto you, That many shall come from the east and west, and shall sit down with Abraham, and Isaac, and Jacob, in the kingdom of heaven. {8:12} But the children of the kingdom shall be cast out into outer darkness: there shall be weeping and gnashing of teeth. {8:13} And **Jesus** said unto the centurion, Go thy way; and as thou hast believed, so be it done unto thee. And his servant was healed in the selfsame hour.

{8:14} And when **Jesus** was come into Peter's house, **He** saw his wife's mother laid, and sick of a fever. {8:15} And **He** touched her hand, and the fever left her: and she arose, and ministered unto them.

{8:16} When the even was come, they brought unto **Him** many that were possessed with devils: and **He** cast out the spirits with [**His**] word, and healed all that were sick: {8:17} That it might be fulfilled which was spoken by Esaias the prophet, saying, **Himself** took our infirmities, and bare [our] sicknesses.

{8:18} Now when **Jesus** saw great multitudes about **Him, He** gave commandment to depart unto the other side. {8:19} And a certain scribe came, and said unto **Him**, **Master**, I will follow **thee** whithersoever thou goest. {8:20} And **Jesus** saith unto him, The foxes have holes, and the birds of the air [have] nests; but the **Son of man** hath not where to lay [**His**] head. {8:21} And another of his disciples said unto **Him**, **Lord**, suffer me first to go and bury my Father. {8:22} But **Jesus** said unto him, Follow **ME**; and let the dead bury their dead.

{8:23} And when **He** was entered into a ship, **His** disciples followed **Him**. {8:24} And, behold, there arose a great tempest in the sea, insomuch that the ship was covered with the waves: but **He** was asleep. {8:25} And **His** disciples came to [**Him**,] and awoke **Him**, saying, **Lord**, save us: we perish. {8:26} And **He** saith unto them, Why are ye fearful, O ye of little faith? Then **He** arose, and rebuked the winds and the sea; and there was a great calm. {8:27} But the men marvelled, saying, What manner of man is this, that even the winds and the sea obey Him! {8:28} And when He was come to the other side into the country of the Gergesenes, there met Him two possessed with devils, coming out of the tombs, exceeding fierce, so that no man might pass by that way. {8:29} And, behold, they cried out, saying, What have we to do with thee, Jesus, thou Son of God? art thou come hither to torment us before the time? {8:30} And there was a good way off from them an herd of many swine feeding. {8:31} So the devils besought Him, saying, If thou cast us out, suffer us to go away into the herd of swine. {8:32} And He said unto them, Go. And when they were come out, they went into the herd of swine: and, behold, the whole herd of swine ran violently down a steep place into the sea, and perished in the waters. {8:33} And they that kept them fled, and went their ways into the city, and told every thing, and what was befallen to the possessed of the devils. {8:34} And, behold, the whole city came out to meet Jesus: and when they saw Him, they besought [Him] that He would depart out of their coasts.   {68}

{9:1} And He entered into a ship, and passed over, and came into His own city. {9:2} And, behold, they brought to Him a man sick of the palsy, lying on a bed: and Jesus seeing their faith said unto the sick of the palsy; Son, be of good cheer; thy sins be forgiven thee. {9:3} And, behold, certain of the scribes said within themselves, This [man] blasphemeth. {9:4} And Jesus knowing their thoughts said, Wherefore think ye evil in your hearts? {9:5} For whether is easier, to say, [Thy] sins be forgiven thee; or to say, Arise, and walk? {9:6} But that ye may know that the Son of man hath power on earth to forgive sins, (then saith He to the sick of the palsy,) Arise, take up thy bed, and go unto thine house. {9:7} And he arose, and departed to his house. {9:8} But when the multitudes saw [it,] they marvelled, and glorified God, which had given such power unto men. {9:9} And as Jesus passed forth from thence, He saw a man, named Matthew, sitting at the receipt of custom: and He saith unto him, Follow ME. And he arose, and followed Him. {9:10} And it came to pass, as Jesus sat at meat in the house, behold, many publicans and sinners came and sat down with Him and His disciples. {9:11} And when the Pharisees saw [it,] they said unto His disciples, Why eateth your Master with publicans and sinners? {9:12} But when Jesus heard [that,] He said unto them, They that be whole need not a physician, but they that are sick. {9:13} But go ye and learn what [that] meaneth, I will have mercy, and not sacrifice: for I am not come to call the righteous, but sinners to repentance. {9:14} Then came to Him the disciples of John, saying, Why do we and the Pharisees fast oft, but thy disciples fast not? {9:15} And Jesus said unto them, Can the children of the bridechamber mourn, as long as the bridegroom is with them? but the days will come, when the bridegroom shall be taken from them, and then shall they fast. {9:16} No man putteth a piece of new cloth unto an old garment, for that which is put in to fill it up taketh from the garment, and the rent is made worse. {9:17} Neither do men put new wine into old bottles: else the bottles break, and the wine runneth out, and the bottles perish: but they put new wine into new bottles, and both are preserved.

{9:18} While He spake these things unto them, behold, there came a certain ruler, and worshipped Him, saying, my daughter is even now dead: but come and lay thy hand upon her, and she shall live. {9:19} And Jesus arose, and followed him, and [so did] His disciples.

{9:20} And, behold, a woman, which was diseased with an issue of blood twelve years, came behind [Him,] and touched the hem of His garment: {9:21} For she said within herself, If I may but touch His garment, I shall be whole. {9:22} But Jesus turned Him about, and when He saw her, He said, Daughter, be of good comfort; thy faith hath made thee whole. And the woman was made whole from that hour. {9:23} And when Jesus came into the ruler's house, and saw the minstrels and the people making a noise, {9:24} He said unto them, Give place: for the maid is not dead, but sleepeth. And they laughed Him to scorn. {9:25} But when the people were put forth, He went in, and took her by the hand, and the maid arose. {9:26} And the fame hereof went abroad into all that land. {9:27} And when Jesus departed thence, two blind men followed Him, crying, and saying, [Thou] Son of David, have mercy on us.

{9:28} And when He was come into the house, the blind men came to Him: and Jesus saith unto them, Believe ye that I am able to do this? They said unto Him, Yea, Lord. {9:29} Then touched He their eyes, saying, According to your faith be it unto you. {9:30} And their eyes were opened; and Jesus straitly charged them, saying, See [that] no man know [it.] {9:31} But they, when they were departed, spread abroad His fame in all that country. {9:32} As they went out, behold, they brought to Him a dumb man possessed with a devil. {9:33} And when the devil was cast out, the dumb spake: and the multitudes marvelled, saying, It was never so seen in Israel. {9:34} But the Pharisees said, He casteth out devils through the prince of the devils. {9:35} And Jesus went about all the cities and villages, teaching in their synagogues, and preaching the Gospel of the kingdom, and healing every sickness and every disease among the people.

{9:36} But when He saw the multitudes, He was moved with compassion on them, because they fainted, and were scattered abroad, as sheep having no Shepherd. {9:37} Then saith He unto His disciples, The harvest truly [is] plenteous, but the labourers [are] few; {9:38} Pray ye therefore the Lord of the harvest, that He will send forth labourers into His harvest.   {68}

{10:1} And when He had called unto [Him] His twelve disciples, He gave them power [against] unclean spirits, to cast them out, and to heal all manner of sickness and all manner of disease. {10:2} Now the names of the twelve apostles are these; The first, Simon, who is called Peter, and Andrew his brother; James [the Son] of Zebedee, and John his brother; {10:3} Philip, and Bartholomew; Thomas, and Matthew the publican; James [the Son] of Alphaeus, and Lebbaeus, whose surname was Thaddaeus; {10:4} Simon the Canaanite, and Judas Iscariot, who also betrayed Him. {10:5} These twelve Jesus sent forth, and commanded them, saying, Go not into the way of the Gentiles, and into [any] city of the Samaritans enter ye not: {10:6} But go rather to the lost sheep of the house of Israel. {10:7} And as ye go, preach, saying, The kingdom of heaven is at hand. {10:8} Heal the sick, cleanse the lepers, raise the dead, cast out devils: freely ye have received, freely give. {10:9} Provide neither gold, nor silver, nor brass in your purses, {10:10} Nor scrip for [your] journey, neither two coats, neither shoes, nor yet staves: for the workman is worthy of his meat. {10:11} And into whatsoever city or town ye shall enter, enquire who in it is worthy; and there abide till ye go thence. {10:12} And when ye come into an house, salute it. {10:13} And if the house be worthy, let your peace come upon it: but if it be not worthy, let your peace return to you. {10:14} And whosoever shall not receive you, nor hear your words, when ye depart out of that house or city, shake off the dust of your feet. {10:15} Verily I say unto you, It shall be more tolerable for the land of Sodom and Gomorrha in the day of judgment, than for that city.

{10:16} Behold, I send you forth as sheep in the midst of wolves: be ye therefore wise as serpents, and harmless as doves. {10:17} But beware of men: for they will deliver you up to the councils, and they will scourge you in their synagogues; {10:18} And ye shall be brought before governors and kings for my sake, for a testimony against them and the Gentiles. {10:19} But when they deliver you up, take no thought how or what ye shall speak: for it shall be given you in that same hour what ye shall speak. {10:20} For it is not ye that speak, but the Spirit of your Father which speaketh in you. {10:21} And the brother shall deliver up the brother to death, and the Father the child: and the children shall rise up against [their] parents, and cause them to be put to death. {10:22} And ye shall be hated of all [men] for my name's sake: but he that endureth to the end shall be saved. {10:23} But when they persecute you in this city, flee ye into another: for verily I say unto you, Ye shall not have gone over the cities of Israel, till the Son of man be come. {10:24} The disciple is not above [His] master, nor the servant above his Lord. {10:25} It is enough for the disciple that he be as his master, and the servant as his Lord. If they have called the master of the house Beelzebub, how much more [shall they call] them of His household? {10:26} Fear them not therefore: for there is nothing covered, that shall not be revealed; and hid, that shall not be known. {10:27} What I tell you in darkness, [that] speak ye in light: and what ye hear in the ear, [that] preach ye upon the housetops. {10:28} And fear not them which kill the body, but are not able to kill the soul: but rather fear Him which is able to destroy both soul and body in hell. {10:29} Are not two sparrows sold for a farthing? and one of them shall not fall on the ground without your Father. {10:30} But the very hairs of your head are all numbered. {10:31} Fear ye not therefore, ye are of more value than many sparrows. {10:32} Whosoever therefore shall confess ME before men, Him will I confess also before my Father which is in heaven. {10:33} But whosoever shall deny ME before men, Him will I also deny before my Father which is in heaven. {10:34} Think not that I am come to send peace on earth: I came not to send peace, but a sword. {10:35} For I am come to set a man at variance against his Father, and the daughter against her mother, and the daughter in law against her mother in law. {10:36} And a man's foes [shall be] they of his own household. {10:37} He that loveth Father or mother more than ME is not worthy of ME: and he that loveth Son or daughter more than ME is not worthy of ME. {10:38} And He that taketh not his cross, and followeth after ME, is not worthy of ME. {10:39} He that findeth his life shall lose it: and he that loseth his life for my sake shall find it.

{10:40} He that receiveth you receiveth ME, and he that receiveth ME receiveth Him that sent ME. {10:41} He that receiveth a prophet in the name of a prophet shall receive a prophet's reward; and he that receiveth a righteous man in the name of a righteous man shall receive a righteous man's reward. {10:42} And whosoever shall give to drink unto one of these little ones a cup of cold [water] only in the name of a disciple, verily I say unto you, he shall in no wise lose his reward.   {44}

{11:1} And it came to pass, when Jesus had made an end of commanding His twelve disciples, He departed thence to teach and to preach in their cities. {11:2} Now when John had heard in the prison the works of Christ, he sent two of his disciples, {11:3} And said unto Him, Art thou He that should come, or do we look for another? {11:4} Jesus answered and said unto them, Go and shew John again those things which ye do hear and see: {11:5} The blind receive their sight, and the lame walk, the lepers are cleansed, and the deaf hear, the dead are raised up, and the poor have the Gospel preached to them. {11:6} And blessed is [he,] whosoever shall not be offended in ME.

{11:7} And as they departed, Jesus began to say unto the multitudes concerning John, What went ye out into the wilderness to see? A reed shaken with the wind? {11:8} But what went ye out for to see? A man clothed in soft raiment? behold, they that wear soft [clothing] are in kings' houses. {11:9} But what went ye out for to see? A prophet? yea, I say unto you, and more than a prophet. {11:10} For this is [he,] of whom it is written, Behold, I send my messenger before thy face, which shall prepare thy way before thee. {11:11} Verily I say unto you, Among them that are born of women there hath not risen a greater than John the Baptist: notwithstanding he that is least in the kingdom of heaven is greater than he. {11:12} And from the days of John the Baptist until now the kingdom of heaven suffereth violence, and the violent take it by force. {11:13} For all the prophets and the law prophesied until John. {11:14} And if ye will receive [it,] this is Elias, which was for to come. {11:15} he that hath ears to hear, let him hear.

{11:16} But whereunto shall I liken this generation? It is like unto children sitting in the markets, and calling unto their fellows, {11:17} And saying, We have piped unto you, and ye have not danced; we have mourned unto you, and ye have not lamented. {11:18} For John came neither eating nor drinking, and they say, he hath a devil. {11:19} The Son of man came eating and drinking, and they say, Behold a man gluttonous, and a winebibber, a friend of publicans and sinners. But wisdom is justified of her children.

{11:20} Then began He to upbraid the cities wherein most of His mighty works were done, because they repented not: {11:21} Woe unto thee, Chorazin! woe unto thee, Bethsaida! for if the mighty works, which were done in you, had been done in Tyre and Sidon, they would have repented long ago in sackcloth and ashes. {11:22} But I say unto you, It shall be more tolerable for Tyre and Sidon at the day of judgment, than for you. {11:23} And thou, Capernaum, which art exalted unto heaven, shalt be brought down to hell: for if the mighty works, which have been done in thee, had been done in Sodom, it would have remained until this day. {11:24} But I say unto you, That it shall be more tolerable for the land of Sodom in the day of judgment, than for thee.

{11:25} At that time Jesus answered and said, I thank thee, O Father, Lord of heaven and earth, because thou hast hid these things from the wise and prudent, and hast revealed them unto babes. {11:26} Even so, Father: for so it seemed good in thy sight. {11:27} All things are delivered unto ME of my Father: and no man knoweth the Son, but the Father; neither knoweth any man the Father, save the Son, and [he] to whomsoever the Son will reveal [Him].

]{11:28} Come unto ME, all [ye] that labour and are heavy laden, and I will give you rest. {11:29} Take my yoke upon you, and learn of ME; for I am meek and lowly in heart: and ye shall find rest unto your souls. {11:30} For **my** yoke [is] easy, and **my** burden is light.　{38}

{12:1} At that time **Jesus** went on the sabbath day through the corn; and **His** disciples were an hungred, and began to pluck the ears of corn, and to eat. {12:2} But when the Pharisees saw [it,] they said unto **Him**, Behold, **thy** disciples do that which is not lawful to do upon the sabbath day. {12:3} But **He** said unto them, Have ye not read what David did, when he was an hungred, and they that were with him; {12:4} How he entered into the house of **God**, and did eat the shewbread, which was not lawful for him to eat, neither for them which were with him, but only for the priests? {12:5} Or have ye not read in the law, how that on the sabbath days the priests in the temple profane the sabbath, and are blameless? {12:6} But **I** say unto you, That in this place is [**one**] greater than the temple. {12:7} But if ye had known what [this] meaneth, **I** will have mercy, and not sacrifice, ye would not have condemned the guiltless. {12:8} For the **Son of man** is **Lord** even of the sabbath day. {12:9} And when **He** was departed thence, **He** went into their synagogue:{12:10} And, behold, there was a man which had [his] hand withered. And they asked **Him**, saying, Is it lawful to heal on the sabbath days? that they might accuse **Him**. {12:11} And **He** said unto them, What man shall there be among you, that shall have one sheep, and if it fall into a pit on the sabbath day, will he not lay hold on it, and lift [it] out? {12:12} How much then is a man better than a sheep? Wherefore it is lawful to do well on the sabbath days. {12:13} Then saith **He** to the man, Stretch forth thine hand. And he stretched [it] forth; and it was restored whole, like as the other.

{12:14} Then the Pharisees went out, and held a council against **Him**, how they might destroy **Him**. {12:15} But when **Jesus** knew [it,] **He** withdrew **himself** from thence: and great multitudes followed **Him**, and **He** healed them all; {12:16} And charged them that they should not make **Him** known: {12:17} That it might be fulfilled which was spoken by Esaias the prophet, saying, {12:18} Behold **my servant**, **whom I** have chosen; **my beloved**, in **whom my** soul is well pleased: **I** will put **my** spirit upon **Him**, and **He** shall shew judgment to the Gentiles. {12:19} **He** shall not strive, nor cry; neither shall any man hear **His** voice in the streets. {12:20} A bruised reed shall **He** not break, and smoking flax shall **He** not quench, till **He** send forth judgment unto victory. {12:21} And in **His name** shall the Gentiles trust.

{12:22} Then was brought unto **Him** one possessed with a devil, blind, and dumb: and **He** healed him, insomuch that the blind and dumb both spake and saw. {12:23} And all the people were amazed, and said, Is not this the **Son of David**? {12:24} But when the Pharisees heard [it,] they said, This [**fellow**] doth not cast out devils, but by Beelzebub the prince of the devils. {12:25} And **Jesus** knew their thoughts, and said unto them, Every kingdom divided against itself is brought to desolation; and every city or house divided against itself shall not stand: {12:26} And if Satan cast out Satan, he is divided against himself; how shall then his kingdom stand? {12:27} And if **I** by Beelzebub cast out devils, by whom do your children cast [them] out? therefore they shall be your judges. {12:28} But if **I** cast out devils by the Spirit of **God**, then the kingdom of **God** is come unto you. {12:29} Or else how can **one** enter into a strong man's house, and spoil his goods, except **He** first bind the strong man? and then **He** will spoil his house. {12:30} He that is not with **ME** is against **ME**; and he that

gathereth not with **ME** scattereth abroad.{12:31} Wherefore **I** say unto you, All manner of sin and blasphemy shall be forgiven unto men: but the blasphemy [against] the [Holy] Ghost shall not be forgiven unto men. {12:32} And whosoever speaketh a word against the **Son of man**, it shall be forgiven him: but whosoever speaketh against the **Holy Ghost**, it shall not be forgiven him, neither in this world, neither in the [world] to come. {12:33} Either make the tree good, and his fruit good; or else make the tree corrupt, and his fruit corrupt: for the tree is known by [his] fruit. {12:34} O generation of vipers, how can ye, being evil, speak good things? for out of the abundance of the heart the mouth speaketh. {12:35} A good man out of the good treasure of the heart bringeth forth good things: and an evil man out of the evil treasure bringeth forth evil things. {12:36} But **I** say unto you, That every idle word that men shall speak, they shall give account thereof in the day of judgment. {12:37} For by thy words thou shalt be justified, and by thy words thou shalt be condemned.{12:38}

Then certain of the scribes and of the Pharisees answered, saying, **Master**, we would see a sign from **thee**. {12:39} But **He** answered and said unto them, An evil and adulterous generation seeketh after a sign; and there shall no sign be given to it, but the sign of the prophet Jonas: {12:40} For as Jonas was three days and three nights in the whale's belly; so shall the **Son of man** be three days and three nights in the heart of the earth. {12:41} The men of Nineveh shall rise in judgment with this generation, and shall condemn it: because they repented at the preaching of Jonas; and, behold, a **greater** than Jonas [is] here. {12:42} The queen of the south shall rise up in the judgment with this generation, and shall condemn it: for she came from the uttermost parts of the earth to hear the wisdom of Solomon; and, behold, a **greater** than Solomon [is] here. {12:43} When the unclean spirit is gone out of a man, he walketh through dry places, seeking rest, and findeth none. {12:44} Then he saith, I will return into my house from whence I came out; and when he is come, he findeth [it] empty, swept, and garnished. {12:45} Then goeth he, and taketh with himself seven other spirits more wicked than himself, and they enter in and dwell there: and the last [state] of that man is worse than the first. Even so shall it be also unto this wicked generation.

{12:46} While **He** yet talked to the people, behold, [**His**] mother and **His** brethren stood without, desiring to speak with **Him**. {12:47} Then one said unto **Him**, Behold, **thy** mother and **thy** brethren stand without, desiring to speak with **thee**. {12:48} But **He** answered and said unto him that told **Him**, Who is **my** mother? and who are **my** brethren? {12:49} And **He** stretched forth **His** hand toward **His** disciples, and said, Behold **my** mother and **my** brethren! {12:50} For whosoever shall do the will of **my Father** which is in heaven, the same is **my** brother, and sister, and mother.　{80}

{13:1} The same day went **Jesus** out of the house, and sat by the sea side. {13:2} And great multitudes were gathered together unto **Him**, so that **He** went into a ship, and sat; and the whole multitude stood on the shore. {13:3} And **He** spake many things unto them in parables, saying, Behold, a **sower** went forth to sow; {13:4} And when **He** sowed, some [seeds] fell by the way side, and the fowls came and devoured them up: {13:5} Some fell upon stony places, where they had not much earth: and forthwith they sprung up, because they had no deepness of earth: {13:6} And when the sun was up, they were scorched; and because they had no root, they withered away. {13:7} And some fell among thorns; and the thorns sprung up, and choked them: {13:8} But other fell into good ground, and brought forth fruit, some an hundredfold, some sixtyfold, some thirtyfold. {13:9} Who hath ears to hear, let him hear. {13:10} And the disciples came, and said unto **Him**, Why speakest **thou** unto them in parables? {13:11} **He** answered and said unto them, Because it is given unto you to know the mysteries of the kingdom of heaven, but to them it is not given. {13:12} For whosoever hath, to him shall be given, and he shall have more abundance: but whosoever hath not, from him shall be taken away even that he hath. {13:13} Therefore speak **I** to them in parables: because they seeing see not; and hearing they hear not, neither do they understand. {13:14} And in them is fulfilled the prophecy of Esaias, which saith, By hearing ye shall hear, and shall not understand; and seeing ye shall see, and shall not perceive: {13:15} For this people's heart is waxed gross, and [their] ears are dull of hearing, and their eyes they have closed; lest at any time they should see with [their] eyes, and hear with [their] ears, and should understand with [their] heart, and should be converted, and **I** should heal them. {13:16} But blessed [are] your eyes, for they see: and your ears, for they hear. {13:17} For verily **I** say unto you, That many prophets and righteous [men] have desired to see [those things] which ye see, and have not seen [them;] and to hear [those things] which ye hear, and have not heard [them.

]{13:18} Hear ye therefore the parable of the **sower**. {13:19} When any one heareth the **word** of the kingdom, and understandeth [it] not, then cometh the wicked [one,] and catcheth away that which was sown in his heart. This is he which received seed by the way side. {13:20} But he that received the seed into stony places, the same is he that heareth the **word**, and anon with joy receiveth it; {13:21} Yet hath he not root in himself, but dureth for a while: for when tribulation or persecution ariseth because of the **word**, by and by he is offended. {13:22} He also that received seed among the thorns is he that heareth the **word**; and the care of this world, and the deceitfulness of riches, choke the **word**, and he becometh unfruitful. {13:23} But he that received seed into the good ground is he that heareth the **word**, and understandeth [it;] which also beareth fruit, and bringeth forth, some an hundredfold, some sixty, some thirty.

{13:24} Another parable put **He** forth unto them, saying, The kingdom of heaven is likened unto a **man** which sowed good seed in **His** field: {13:25} But while men slept, **His** enemy came and sowed tares among the wheat, and went his way. {13:26} But when the blade was sprung up, and brought forth fruit, then appeared the tares also. {13:27} So the servants of the **householder** came and said unto **Him**, **Sir**, didst not **thou** sow good seed in thy field? from whence then hath it tares? {13:28} **He** said unto them, An enemy hath done this. The servants said unto **Him**, Wilt **thou** then that we go and gather them up? {13:29} But **He** said, Nay; lest while ye gather up the tares, ye root up also the wheat with them. {13:30} Let both grow together until the harvest: and in the time of harvest **I** will say to the reapers, Gather ye together first the tares, and bind them in bundles to burn them: but gather the wheat into **my** barn.

{13:31} Another parable put **He** forth unto them, saying, The kingdom of heaven is like to a grain of mustard seed, which a **man** took, and sowed in **His** field: {13:32} Which indeed is the least of all seeds: but when it is grown, it is the greatest among herbs, and becometh a tree, so that the birds of the air come and lodge in the branches thereof.

{13:33} Another parable spake **He** unto them; The kingdom of heaven is like unto leaven, which a woman took, and hid in three measures of meal, till the whole was leavened. {13:34} All these things spake **Jesus** unto the multitude in parables; and without a parable spake **He** not unto them: {13:35} That it might be fulfilled which was spoken by the prophet, saying, **I** will open **my** mouth in parables; **I** will utter things which have been kept secret from the foundation of the world. {13:36} Then **Jesus** sent the multitude away, and went into the house: and **His** disciples came unto **Him**, saying, Declare unto us the parable of the tares of the field. {13:37} **He** answered and said unto them, **He** that soweth the good seed is the **Son of man**; {13:38} The field is the world; the good seed are the children of the kingdom; but the tares are the children of the wicked [one;]{13:39} The enemy that sowed them is the devil; the harvest is the end of the world; and the reapers are the angels. {13:40} As therefore the tares are gathered and burned in the fire; so shall it be in the end of this world. {13:41} The **Son of man** shall send forth **His** angels, and they shall gather out of **His** kingdom all things that offend, and them which do iniquity; {13:42} And shall cast them into a furnace of fire: there shall be wailing and gnashing of teeth. {13:43} Then shall the righteous shine forth as the sun in the kingdom of their **Father**. Who hath ears to hear, let him hear.

{13:44} Again, the kingdom of heaven is like unto treasure hid in a field; the which when a man hath found, he hideth, and for joy thereof goeth and selleth all that he hath, and buyeth that field.

{13:45} Again, the kingdom of heaven is like unto a merchant man, seeking goodly pearls: {13:46} Who, when he had found **one pearl** of great price, went and sold all that he had, and bought it.

{13:47} Again, the kingdom of heaven is like unto a net, that was cast into the sea, and gathered of every kind: {13:48} Which, when it was full, they drew to shore, and sat down, and gathered the good into vessels, but cast the bad away. {13:49} So shall it be at the end of the world: the angels shall come forth, and sever the wicked from among the just, {13:50} And shall cast them into the furnace of fire: there shall be wailing and gnashing of teeth. {13:51} **Jesus** saith unto them, Have ye understood all these things? They say unto **Him**, Yea, **Lord**. {13:52} Then said **He** unto them, Therefore every scribe [which is] instructed unto the kingdom of heaven is like unto a man [that is] an householder, which bringeth forth out of his treasure [things] new and old.{13:53} And it came to pass, [that] when **Jesus** had finished these parables, **He** departed thence. {13:54} And when **He** was come into **His** own country, **He** taught them in their synagogue, insomuch that they were astonished, and said, Whence hath this [**man**] this wisdom, and [these] mighty works? {13:55} Is not this the carpenter's **Son**? is not **His** mother called Mary? and **His** brethren, James, and Joses, and Simon, and Judas? {13:56} And **His** sisters, are they not all with us? Whence then hath this [**man**] all these things? {13:57} And they were offended in **Him**. But **Jesus** said unto them, A **prophet** is not without honour, save in **His** own country, and in **His** own house. {13:58} And **He** did not many mighty works there because of their unbelief.   {73}

{14:1} At that time Herod the tetrarch heard of the fame of **Jesus**, {14:2} And said unto his servants, This is John the Baptist; He is risen from the dead; and therefore mighty works do shew forth themselves in Him.

{14:3} For Herod had laid hold on John, and bound Him, and put [Him] in prison for Herodias' sake, his brother Philip's wife. {14:4} For John said unto him, It is not lawful for thee to have her. {14:5} And when he would have put Him to death, he feared the multitude, because they counted Him as a prophet. {14:6} But when Herod's birthday was kept, the daughter of Herodias danced before them, and pleased Herod. {14:7} Whereupon he promised with an oath to give her whatsoever she would ask. {14:8} And she, being before instructed of her mother, said, Give me here John Baptist's head in a charger. {14:9} And the king was sorry: nevertheless for the oath's sake, and them which sat with him at meat, he commanded [it] to be given [her.]{14:10} And he sent, and beheaded John in the prison. {14:11} And His head was brought in a charger, and given to the damsel: and she brought [it] to her mother. {14:12} And His disciples came, and took up the body, and buried it, and went and told Jesus.

{14:13} When Jesus heard [of it,] He departed thence by ship into a desert place apart: and when the people had heard [thereof,] they followed Him on foot out of the cities. {14:14} And Jesus went forth, and saw a great multitude, and was moved with compassion toward them, and He healed their sick.

{14:15} And when it was evening, His disciples came to Him, saying, This is a desert place, and the time is now past; send the multitude away, that they may go into the villages, and buy themselves victuals. {14:16} But Jesus said unto them, They need not depart; give ye them to eat. {14:17} And they say unto Him, We have here but five loaves, and two fishes. {14:18} He said, Bring them hither to ME. {14:19} And He commanded the multitude to sit down on the grass, and took the five loaves, and the two fishes, and looking up to heaven, He blessed, and brake, and gave the loaves to [His] disciples, and the disciples to the multitude. {14:20} And they did all eat, and were filled: and they took up of the fragments that remained twelve baskets full. {14:21} And they that had eaten were about five thousand men, beside women and children.

{14:22} And straightway Jesus constrained His disciples to get into a ship, and to go before Him unto the other side, while He sent the multitudes away. {14:23} And when He had sent the multitudes away, He went up into a mountain apart to pray: and when the evening was come, He was there alone. {14:24} But the ship was now in the midst of the sea, tossed with waves: for the wind was contrary. {14:25} And in the fourth watch of the night Jesus went unto them, walking on the sea. {14:26} And when the disciples saw Him walking on the sea, they were troubled, saying, It is a spirit; and they cried out for fear. {14:27} But straightway Jesus spake unto them, saying, Be of good cheer; it is I; be not afraid. {14:28} And Peter answered Him and said, Lord, if it be thou, bid me come unto thee on the water. {14:29} And He said, Come. And when Peter was come down out of the ship, he walked on the water, to go to Jesus. {14:30} But when he saw the wind boisterous, he was afraid; and beginning to sink, he cried, saying, Lord, save me. {14:31} And immediately Jesus stretched forth [His] hand, and caught him, and said unto him, O thou of little faith, wherefore didst thou doubt? {14:32} And when they were come into the ship, the wind ceased. {14:33} Then they that were in the ship came and worshipped Him, saying, Of a truth thou art the Son of God.

{14:34} And when they were gone over, they came into the land of Gennesaret. {14:35} And when the men of that place had knowledge of Him, they sent out into all that country round about, and brought unto Him all that were diseased; {14:36} And besought Him that they might only touch the hem of His garment: and as many as touched were made perfectly whole. {43}

{15:1} Then came to Jesus scribes and Pharisees, which were of Jerusalem, saying, {15:2} Why do thy disciples transgress the tradition of the elders? for they wash not their hands when they eat bread. {15:3} But He answered and said unto them, Why do ye also transgress the commandment of God by your tradition? {15:4} For God commanded, saying, Honour thy Father and mother: and, he that curseth Father or mother, let him die the death. {15:5} But ye say, Whosoever shall say to [his] Father or [his] mother, [It is] a gift, by whatsoever thou mightest be profited by me; {15:6} And honour not his Father or his mother, [he shall be free.] Thus have ye made the commandment of God of none effect by your tradition. {15:7} [Ye] hypocrites, well did Esaias prophesy of you, saying, {15:8} This people draweth nigh unto ME with their mouth, and honoureth ME with [their] lips; but their heart is far from ME. {15:9} But in vain they do worship ME, teaching [for] doctrines the commandments of men.{15:10} And He called the multitude, and said unto them, Hear, and understand: {15:11} Not that which goeth into the mouth defileth a man; but that which cometh out of the mouth, this defileth a man. {15:12} Then came His disciples, and said unto Him, Knowest thou that the Pharisees were offended, after they heard this saying? {15:13} But He answered and said, Every plant, which my heavenly Father hath not planted, shall be rooted up. {15:14} Let them alone: they be blind leaders of the blind. And if the blind lead the blind, both shall fall into the ditch. {15:15} Then answered Peter and said unto Him, Declare unto us this parable. {15:16} And Jesus said, Are ye also yet without understanding? {15:17} Do not ye yet understand, that whatsoever entereth in at the mouth goeth into the belly, and is cast out into the draught? {15:18} But those things which proceed out of the mouth come forth from the heart; and they defile the man. {15:19} For out of the heart proceed evil thoughts, murders, adulteries, fornications, thefts, false witness, blasphemies: {15:20} These are [the things] which defile a man: but to eat with unwashen hands defileth not a man.{15:21} Then Jesus went thence, and departed into the coasts of Tyre and Sidon. {15:22} And, behold, a woman of Canaan came out of the same coasts, and cried unto Him, saying, Have mercy on me, O Lord, [thou] Son of David; my daughter is grievously vexed with a devil. {15:23} But He answered her not a word. And His disciples came and besought Him, saying, Send her away; for she crieth after us. {15:24} But He answered and said, I am not sent but unto the lost sheep of the house of Israel. {15:25} Then came she and worshipped Him, saying, Lord, help me. {15:26} But He answered and said, It is not meet to take the children's bread, and to cast [it] to dogs. {15:27} And she said, Truth, Lord: yet the dogs eat of the crumbs which fall from their masters' table. {15:28} Then Jesus answered and said unto her, O woman, great [is] thy faith: be it unto thee even as thou wilt. And her daughter was made whole from that very hour. {15:29} And Jesus departed from thence, and came nigh unto the sea of Galilee; and went up into a mountain, and sat down there. {15:30} And great multitudes came unto Him, having with them [those that were] lame, blind, dumb, maimed, and many others, and cast them down at **Jesus**' feet; and **He** healed them: {15:31} Insomuch that the multitude wondered, when they saw the dumb to speak, the maimed to be whole, the lame to walk, and the blind to see: and they glorified the **God** of Israel.

{15:32} Then **Jesus** called **His** disciples [unto **Him**,] and said, **I** have compassion on the multitude, because they continue with **ME** now three days, and have nothing to eat: and **I** will not send them away fasting, lest they faint in the way. {15:33} And **His** disciples say unto **Him**, Whence should we have so much bread in the wilderness, as to fill so great a multitude? {15:34} And **Jesus** saith unto them, How many loaves have ye? And they said, Seven, and a few little fishes. {15:35} And **He** commanded the multitude to sit down on the ground. {15:36} And **He** took the seven loaves and the fishes, and gave thanks, and brake [them,] and gave to **His** disciples, and the disciples to the multitude. {15:37} And they did all eat, and were filled: and they took up of the broken [meat] that was left seven baskets full. {15:38} And they that did eat were four thousand men, beside women and children. {15:39} And **He** sent away the multitude, and took ship, and came into the coasts of Magdala,   {47}

{16:1} The Pharisees also with the Sadducees came, and tempting desired **Him** that **He** would shew them a sign from heaven. {16:2} **He** answered and said unto them, When it is evening, ye say, [It will be] fair weather: for the sky is red. {16:3} And in the morning, [It will be] foul weather to day: for the sky is red and lowring. O [ye] hypocrites, ye can discern the face of the sky; but can ye not [discern] the signs of the times? {16:4} A wicked and adulterous generation seeketh after a sign; and there shall no sign be given unto it, but the sign of the prophet Jonas. And **He** left them, and departed. {16:5} And when **His** disciples were come to the other side, they had forgotten to take bread.

{16:6} Then **Jesus** said unto them, Take heed and beware of the leaven of the Pharisees and of the Sadducees. {16:7} And they reasoned among themselves, saying, [It is] because we have taken no bread. {16:8} [Which] when **Jesus** perceived, **He** said unto them, O ye of little faith, why reason ye among yourselves, because ye have brought no bread? {16:9} Do ye not yet understand, neither remember the five loaves of the five thousand, and how many baskets ye took up? {16:10} Neither the seven loaves of the four thousand, and how many baskets ye took up? {16:11} How is it that ye do not understand that **I** spake [it] not to you concerning bread, that ye should beware of the leaven of the Pharisees and of the Sadducees? {16:12} Then understood they how that **He** bade [them] not beware of the leaven of bread, but of the doctrine of the Pharisees and of the Sadducees.

{16:13} When **Jesus** came into the coasts of Caesarea Philippi, **He** asked **His** disciples, saying, **Whom** do men say that **I** the **Son of man am**? {16:14} And they said, Some [say that thou art] John the Baptist: some, Elias; and others, Jeremias, or one of the prophets. {16:15} **He** saith unto them, But **whom** say ye that **I am**? {16:16} And Simon Peter answered and said, **Thou** art the **Christ**, the **Son of the living God**. {16:17} And **Jesus** answered and said unto **Him**, Blessed art thou, Simon Barjona: for flesh and blood hath not revealed [it] unto thee, but **my Father** which is in heaven. {16:18} And **I** say also unto thee, That thou art Peter, and upon this **Rock** **I** will build **my** church; and the gates of hell shall not prevail against it. {16:19} And **I** will give unto thee the keys of the kingdom of heaven: and

whatsoever thou shalt bind on earth shall be bound in heaven: and whatsoever thou shalt loose on earth shall be loosed in heaven. {16:20} Then charged **He His** disciples that they should tell no man that **He** was **Jesus** the **Christ**.{16:21} From that time forth began **Jesus** to shew unto **His** disciples, how that **He** must go unto Jerusalem, and suffer many things of the elders and chief priests and scribes, and be killed, and be raised again the third day. {16:22} Then Peter took **Him**, and began to rebuke **Him**, saying, Be it far from thee, **Lord**: this shall not be unto thee. {16:23} But **He** turned, and said unto Peter, Get thee behind **ME**, Satan: thou art an offence unto **ME**: for thou savourest not the things that be of **God**, but those that be of men.{16:24} Then said **Jesus** unto **His** disciples, If any [man] will come after **ME**, let him deny himself, and take up his cross, and follow **ME**. {16:25} For whosoever will save his life shall lose it: and whosoever will lose his life for **my** sake shall find it. {16:26} For what is a man profited, if he shall gain the whole world, and lose his own soul? or what shall a man give in exchange for his soul? {16:27} For the **Son of man** shall come in the glory of **His Father** with **His** angels; and then **He** shall reward every man according to his works. {16:28} Verily **I** say unto you, There be some standing here, which shall not taste of death, till they see the **Son of man** coming in **His** kingdom. {57}

{17:1} And after six days **Jesus** taketh Peter, James, and John his brother, and bringeth them up into an high mountain apart, {17:2} And was transfigured before them: and **His** face did shine as the sun, and **His** raiment was white as the light. {17:3} And, behold, there appeared unto them Moses and Elias talking with **Him**. {17:4} Then answered Peter, and said unto **Jesus**, **Lord**, it is good for us to be here: if thou wilt, let us make here three tabernacles; one for **thee**, and one for Moses, and one for Elias. {17:5} While he yet spake, behold, a bright cloud overshadowed them: and behold a voice out of the cloud, which said, This is **my beloved Son**, in **whom** **I am** well pleased; hear ye **Him**. {17:6} And when the disciples heard [it,] they fell on their face, and were sore afraid. {17:7} And **Jesus** came and touched them, and said, Arise, and be not afraid. {17:8} And when they had lifted up their eyes, they saw no man, save **Jesus** only. {17:9} And as they came down from the mountain, **Jesus** charged them, saying, Tell the vision to no man, until the **Son of man** be risen again from the dead. {17:10} And **His** disciples asked **Him**, saying, Why then say the scribes that Elias must first come? {17:11} And **Jesus** answered and said unto them, Elias truly shall first come, and restore all things. {17:12} But **I** say unto you, That Elias is come already, and they knew him not, but have done unto him whatsoever they listed. Likewise shall also the **Son of man** suffer of them. {17:13} Then the disciples understood that **He** spake unto them of John the Baptist.{17:14} And when they were come to the multitude, there came to **Him** a [certain] man, kneeling down to **Him**, and saying, {17:15} **Lord**, have mercy on my Son: for he is lunatick, and sore vexed: for ofttimes he falleth into the fire, and oft into the water. {17:16} And **I** brought him to **thy** disciples, and they could not cure him. {17:17} Then **Jesus** answered and said, O faithless and perverse generation, how long shall **I** be with you? how long shall **I** suffer you? bring him hither to **ME**. {17:18} And **Jesus** rebuked the devil; and he departed out of him: and the child was cured from that very hour. {17:19} Then came the disciples to **Jesus** apart, and said, Why could not we cast **Him** out? {17:20} And **Jesus** said unto them, Because of your unbelief: for verily **I** say unto you, If ye have faith as a grain of mustard seed, ye shall say unto this mountain, Remove hence to yonder place; and it shall remove; and nothing shall be impossible unto you. {17:21} Howbeit this kind goeth not out but by prayer and fasting.{17:22} And while they abode in Galilee, **Jesus** said unto them, The **Son of man** shall be betrayed into the hands of men: {17:23} And they shall kill **Him**, and the third day **He** shall be raised again. And they were exceeding sorry.{17:24} And when they were come to Capernaum, they that received tribute [money] came to Peter, and said, Doth not your **master** pay tribute? {17:25} He saith, Yes. And when he was come into the house, **Jesus** prevented him, saying, What thinkest thou, Simon? of whom do the kings of the earth take custom or tribute? of their own children, or of strangers? {17:26} Peter saith unto **Him**, Of strangers. **Jesus** saith unto him, Then are the children free. {17:27} Notwithstanding, lest **we** should offend them, go thou to the sea, and cast an hook, and take up the fish that first cometh up; and when thou hast opened his mouth, thou shalt find a piece of money: that take, and give unto them for **ME** and thee.   **{41}**

{18:1} At the same time came the disciples unto **Jesus**, saying, Who is the greatest in the kingdom of heaven? {18:2} And **Jesus** called a little child unto **Him**, and set him in the midst of them, {18:3} And said, Verily **I** say unto you, Except ye be converted, and become as little children, ye shall not enter into the kingdom of heaven. {18:4} Whosoever therefore shall humble himself as this little child, the same is greatest in the kingdom of heaven. {18:5} And whoso shall receive one such little child in **my name** receiveth **ME**. {18:6} But whoso shall offend one of these little ones which believe in **ME**, it were better for him that a millstone were hanged about his neck, and [that] he were drowned in the depth of the sea.

{18:7} Woe unto the world because of offences! for it must needs be that offences come; but woe to that man by **whom** the offence cometh! {18:8} Wherefore if thy hand or thy foot offend thee, cut them off, and cast [them] from thee: it is better for thee to enter into life halt or maimed, rather than having two hands or two feet to be cast into everlasting fire. {18:9} And if thine eye offend thee, pluck it out, and cast [it] from thee: it is better for thee to enter into life with one eye, rather than having two eyes to be cast into hell fire. {18:10} Take heed that ye despise not one of these little ones; for **I** say unto you, That in heaven their angels do always behold the face of **my Father** which is in heaven. {18:11} For the **Son of man** is come to save that which was lost. {18:12} How think ye? if a man have an hundred sheep, and one of them be gone astray, doth he not leave the ninety and nine, and goeth into the mountains, and seeketh that which is gone astray? {18:13} And if so be that he find it, verily **I** say unto you, he rejoiceth more of that [sheep,] than of the ninety and nine which went not astray. {18:14} Even so it is not the will of your **Father** which is in heaven, that one of these little ones should perish.

{18:15} Moreover if thy brother shall trespass against thee, go and tell him his fault between thee and him alone: if he shall hear thee, thou hast gained thy brother. {18:16} But if he will not hear [thee, then] take with thee one or two more, that in the mouth of two or three witnesses every word may be established. {18:17} And if he shall neglect to hear them, tell [it] unto the church: but if he neglect to hear the church, let him be unto thee as an heathen man and a

publican. {18:18} Verily **I** say unto you, Whatsoever ye shall bind on earth shall be bound in heaven: and whatsoever ye shall loose on earth shall be loosed in heaven. {18:19} Again **I** say unto you, That if two of you shall agree on earth as touching any thing that they shall ask, it shall be done for them of **my Father** which is in heaven. {18:20} For where two or three are gathered together in **my name**, there **am I** in the midst of them.{18:21} Then came Peter to **Him**, and said, **Lord**, how oft shall my brother sin against me, and I forgive him? till seven times? {18:22} **Jesus** saith unto him, **I** say not unto thee, Until seven times: but, Until seventy times seven.{18:23} Therefore is the kingdom of heaven likened unto a certain king, which would take account of **His** servants. {18:24} And when **He** had begun to reckon, one was brought unto **Him**, which owed **Him** ten thousand talents. {18:25} But forasmuch as he had not to pay, **His Lord** commanded him to be sold, and his wife, and children, and all that he had, and payment to be made. {18:26} The servant therefore fell down, and worshipped **Him**, saying, **Lord**, have patience with me, and I will pay thee all. {18:27} Then the **Lord** of that servant was moved with compassion, and loosed him, and forgave him the debt. {18:28} But the same servant went out, and found one of his fellowservants, which owed him an hundred pence: and he laid hands on him, and took [him] by the throat, saying, Pay me that thou owest. {18:29} And his fellowservant fell down at his feet, and besought him, saying, Have patience with me, and I will pay thee all. {18:30} And he would not: but went and cast him into prison, till he should pay the debt. {18:31} So when his fellowservants saw what was done, they were very sorry, and came and told unto their **Lord** all that was done. {18:32} Then **His Lord**, after that **He** had called him, said unto him, O thou wicked servant, **I** forgave thee all that debt, because thou desiredst **ME**: {18:33} Shouldest not thou also have had compassion on thy fellowservant, even as **I** had pity on thee? {18:34} And **His Lord** was wroth, and delivered him to the tormentors, till he should pay all that was due unto **Him**. {18:35} So likewise shall **my** heavenly **Father** do also unto you, if ye from your hearts forgive not every one his brother their trespasses. **{41}**

{19:1} And it came to pass, [that] when **Jesus** had finished these sayings, **He** departed from Galilee, and came into the coasts of Judaea beyond Jordan; {19:2} And great multitudes followed **Him**; and **He** healed them there.

{19:3} The Pharisees also came unto **Him**, tempting **Him**, and saying unto **Him**, Is it lawful for a man to put away his wife for every cause? {19:4} And **He** answered and said unto them, Have ye not read, that **He** which made [them] at the beginning made them male and female, {19:5} And said, For this cause shall a man leave **Father** and mother, and shall cleave to his wife: and they twain shall be one flesh? {19:6} Wherefore they are no more twain, but one flesh. What therefore **God** hath joined together, let not man put asunder. {19:7} They say unto **Him**, Why did Moses then command to give a writing of divorcement, and to put her away? {19:8} **He** saith unto them, Moses because of the hardness of your hearts suffered you to put away your wives: but from the beginning it was not so. {19:9} And **I** say unto you, Whosoever shall put away **His** wife, except [it be] for fornication, and shall marry another, committeth adultery: and whoso marrieth her which is put away doth commit adultery.

{19:10} **His** disciples say unto **Him**, If the case of the man be so with [his] wife, it is not good to marry. {19:11} But **He** said unto them, All [men] cannot receive this saying, save [they] to whom it is given. {19:12} For there are some eunuchs, which were so born from [their] mother's womb: and there are some eunuchs, which were made eunuchs of men: and there be eunuchs, which have made themselves eunuchs for the kingdom of heaven's sake. he that is able to receive [it,] let him receive [it.

]{19:13} Then were there brought unto **Him** little children, that **He** should put [**His**] hands on them, and pray: and the disciples rebuked them. {19:14} But **Jesus** said, Suffer little children, and forbid them not, to come unto **ME**: for of such is the kingdom of heaven. {19:15} And **He** laid [**His**] hands on them, and departed thence.

{19:16} And, behold, one came and said unto **Him**, **Good Master**, what good thing shall I do, that I may have eternal life? {19:17} And **He** said unto him, Why callest thou **ME** good? [there is] none good but one, [that is,] **God**: but if thou wilt enter into life, keep the commandments. {19:18} he saith unto **Him**, Which? **Jesus** said, Thou shalt do no murder, Thou shalt not commit adultery, Thou shalt not steal, Thou shalt not bear false witness, {19:19} Honour thy **Father** and [thy] mother: and, Thou shalt love thy neighbour as thyself. {19:20} The young man saith unto **Him**, All these things have I kept from my youth up: what lack I yet? {19:21} **Jesus** said unto him, If thou wilt be perfect, go [and] sell that thou hast, and give to the poor, and thou shalt have treasure in heaven: and come [and] follow **ME**. {19:22} But when the young man heard that saying, he went away sorrowful: for he had great possessions.

{19:23} Then said **Jesus** unto **His** disciples, Verily **I** say unto you, That a rich man shall hardly enter into the kingdom of heaven. {19:24} And again **I** say unto you, It is easier for a camel to go through the eye of a needle, than for a rich man to **enter into** the kingdom of **God**. {19:25} When **His** disciples heard [it,] they were exceedingly amazed, saying, Who then can be saved? {19:26} But **Jesus** beheld [them,] and said unto them, With men this is impossible; but with **God** all things are possible.{19:27} Then answered Peter and said unto **Him**, Behold, we have forsaken all, and followed **thee**; what shall we have therefore? {19:28} And **Jesus** said unto them, Verily **I** say unto you, That ye which have followed **ME**, in the regeneration when the **Son of man** shall sit in the throne of **His** glory, ye also shall sit upon twelve thrones, judging the twelve tribes of Israel. {19:29} And every one that hath forsaken houses, or brethren, or sisters, or **Father**, or mother, or wife, or children, or lands, for **my** name's sake, shall receive an hundredfold, and shall inherit everlasting life. {19:30} But many [that are] first shall be last; and the last [shall be] first. **{48}**

{20:1} For the kingdom of heaven is like unto a **man** [that is] an householder, which went out early in the morning to hire labourers into **His** vineyard. {20:2} And when **He** had agreed with the labourers for a penny a day, **He** sent them into **His** vineyard. {20:3} And **He** went out about the third hour, and saw others standing idle in the marketplace, {20:4} And said unto them; Go ye also into the vineyard, and whatsoever is right **I** will give you. And they went their way. {20:5} Again **He** went out about the sixth and ninth hour, and did likewise. {20:6} And about the eleventh hour **He** went out, and found others standing idle, and saith unto them, Why stand ye here all the day idle? {20:7} They say

unto **Him**, Because no man hath hired us. **He** saith unto them, Go ye also into the vineyard; and whatsoever is right, [that] shall ye receive. {20:8} So when even was come, the **Lord** of the vineyard saith unto **His** steward, Call the labourers, and give them [their] hire, beginning from the last unto the first. {20:9} And when they came that [were hired] about the eleventh hour, they received every man a penny. {20:10} But when the first came, they supposed that they should have received more; and they likewise received every man a penny. {20:11} And when they had received it, they murmured against the **goodman** of the house, {20:12} Saying, These last have wrought [but] one hour, and thou hast made them equal unto us, which have borne the burden and heat of the day. {20:13} But **He** answered one of them, and said, Friend, **I** do thee no wrong: didst not thou agree with **ME** for a penny? {20:14} Take [that] thine [is,] and go thy way: **I** will give unto this last, even as unto thee. {20:15} Is it not lawful for **ME** to do what **I** will with **mine own**? Is thine eye evil, because **I am** good? {20:16} So the last shall be first, and the first last: for many be called, but few chosen.

{20:17} And **Jesus** going up to Jerusalem took the twelve disciples apart in the way, and said unto them, {20:18} Behold, we go up to Jerusalem; and the **Son of man** shall be betrayed unto the chief priests and unto the scribes, and they shall condemn **Him** to death, {20:19} And shall deliver **Him** to the Gentiles to mock, and to scourge, and to crucify [**Him**:] and the third day **He** shall rise again.

{20:20} Then came to **Him** the mother of Zebedee's children with her sons, worshipping [**Him**,] and desiring a certain thing of **Him**. {20:21} And **He** said unto her, What wilt thou? She saith unto **Him**, Grant that these **my** two sons may sit, the one on **thy** right hand, and the other on the left, in **thy** kingdom. {20:22} But **Jesus** answered and said, Ye know not what ye ask. Are ye able to drink of the cup that **I** shall drink of, and to be baptized with the baptism that **I am** baptized with? They say unto **Him**, We are able. {20:23} And **He** saith unto them, Ye shall drink indeed of **my** cup, and be baptized with the baptism that **I am** baptized with: but to sit on **my** right hand, and on **my** left, is not **mine** to give, but [it shall be given to them] for **whom** it is prepared of **my Father**. {20:24} And when the ten heard [it,] they were moved with indignation against the two brethren. {20:25} But **Jesus** called them [unto **Him**,] and said, Ye know that the princes of the Gentiles exercise dominion over them, and they that are great exercise authority upon them. {20:26} But it shall not be so among you: but whosoever will be great among you, let him be your minister; {20:27} And whosoever will be chief among you, let him be your servant: {20:28} Even as the **Son of man** came not to be ministered unto, but to minister, and to give **His** life a ransom for many. {20:29} And as they departed from Jericho, a great multitude followed **Him**.

{20:30} And, behold, two blind men sitting by the way side, when they heard that **Jesus** passed by, cried out, saying, Have mercy on us, **O Lord**, [**thou**] **Son of David**. {20:31} And the multitude rebuked them, because they should hold their peace: but they cried the more, saying, Have mercy on us, **O Lord**, [**thou**] **Son of David**. {20:32} And **Jesus** stood still, and called them, and said, What will ye that **I** shall do unto you? {20:33} They say unto **Him**, **Lord**, that our eyes may be opened. {20:34} So **Jesus** had compassion [on them,] and touched their eyes: and immediately their eyes received sight, and they followed **Him**.
{69}

{21:1} And when they drew nigh unto Jerusalem, and were come to Bethphage, unto the mount of Olives, then sent **Jesus** two disciples, {21:2} Saying unto them, Go into the village over against you, and straightway ye shall find an ass tied, and a colt with her: loose [them,] and bring [them] unto **ME**. {21:3} And if any [man] say ought unto you, ye shall say, The **Lord** hath need of them; and straightway he will send them. {21:4} All this was done, that it might be fulfilled which was spoken by the prophet, saying, {21:5} Tell ye the daughter of Sion, Behold, thy **King** cometh unto thee, meek, and sitting upon an ass, and a colt the foal of an ass. {21:6} And the disciples went, and did as **Jesus** commanded them, {21:7} And brought the ass, and the colt, and put on them their clothes, and they set [**Him**] thereon. {21:8} And a very great multitude spread their garments in the way; others cut down branches from the trees, and strawed [them] in the way. {21:9} And the multitudes that went before, and that followed, cried, saying, Hosanna to the **Son of David**: Blessed [is] **He** that cometh in the name of the **Lord**; Hosanna in the highest. {21:10} And when **He** was come into Jerusalem, all the city was moved, saying, **Who** is this? {21:11} And the multitude said, This is **Jesus** the prophet of Nazareth of Galilee.

{21:12} And **Jesus** went into the temple of **God**, and cast out all them that sold and bought in the temple, and overthrew the tables of the moneychangers, and the seats of them that sold doves, {21:13} And said unto them, It is written, **my** house shall be called the house of prayer; but ye have made it a den of thieves. {21:14} And the blind and the lame came to **Him** in the temple; and **He** healed them. {21:15} And when the chief priests and scribes saw the wonderful things that **He** did, and the children crying in the temple, and saying, Hosanna to the **Son of David**; they were sore displeased, {21:16} And said unto **Him**, Hearest thou what these say? And **Jesus** saith unto them, Yea; have ye never read, Out of the mouth of babes and sucklings thou hast perfected praise?

{21:17} And **He** left them, and went out of the city into Bethany; and **He** lodged there. {21:18} Now in the morning as **He** returned into the city, **He** hungered. {21:19} And when **He** saw a fig tree in the way, **He** came to it, and found nothing thereon, but leaves only, and said unto it, Let no fruit grow on thee henceforward for ever. And presently the fig tree withered away. {21:20} And when the disciples saw [it,] they marvelled, saying, How soon is the fig tree withered away! {21:21} **Jesus** answered and said unto them, Verily **I** say unto you, If ye have faith, and doubt not, ye shall not only do this [which is done] to the fig tree, but also if ye shall say unto this mountain, Be thou removed, and be thou cast into the sea; it shall be done. {21:22} And all things, whatsoever ye shall ask in prayer, believing, ye shall receive.

{21:23} And when **He** was come into the temple, the chief priests and the elders of the people came unto **Him** as **He** was teaching, and said, By what authority doest **thou** these things? and who gave thee this authority? {21:24} And **Jesus** answered and said unto them, **I** also will ask you one thing, which if ye tell **ME**, **I** in like wise will tell you by what authority **I** do these things. {21:25} The baptism of John, whence was it? from heaven, or of men? And they reasoned with themselves, saying, If we shall say, From heaven; **He** will say unto us, Why did ye not then believe **Him**? {21:26} But if we shall say, Of men; we fear the people; for all hold John as a prophet. {21:27} And they answered **Jesus**, and said, We cannot tell. And **He** said unto them, Neither tell **I** you by what authority **I** do these things.

{21:28} But what think ye? A [certain] man had two sons; and **He** came to the first, and said, Son, go work to day in my vineyard. {21:29} **He** answered and said, I will not: but afterward **He** repented, and went. {21:30} And **He** came to the second, and said likewise. And **He** answered and said, I [go,] sir: and went not. {21:31} Whether of them twain did the will of [**His**] Father? They say unto **Him**, The first. **Jesus** saith unto them, Verily **I** say unto you, That the publicans and the harlots go into the kingdom of **God** before you. {21:32} For John came unto you in the way of righteousness, and ye believed **Him** not: but the publicans and the harlots believed **Him**: and ye, when ye had seen [it,] repented not afterward, that ye might believe **Him**.{21:33} Hear another parable: There was a certain householder, which planted a vineyard, and hedged it round about, and digged a winepress in it, and built a tower, and let it out to husbandmen, and went into a far country: {21:34} And when the time of the fruit drew near, **He** sent **His** servants to the husbandmen, that they might receive the fruits of it. {21:35} And the husbandmen took **His** servants, and beat one, and killed another, and stoned another. {21:36} Again, **He** sent other servants more than the first: and they did unto them likewise. {21:37} But last of all **He** sent unto them **His Son**, saying, They will reverence **my Son**. {21:38} But when the husbandmen saw the **Son**, they said among themselves, This is the **heir**; come, let us kill **Him**, and let us seize on **His** inheritance. {21:39} And they caught **Him**, and cast [**Him**] out of the vineyard, and slew [**Him**.]{21:40} When the **Lord** therefore of the vineyard cometh, what will **He** do unto those husbandmen? {21:41} They say unto **Him**, **He** will miserably destroy those wicked men, and will let out [**His**] vineyard unto other husbandmen, which shall render **Him** the fruits in their seasons. {21:42} **Jesus** saith unto them, Did ye never read in the scriptures, The **stone** which the builders rejected, the **same** is become the **head** of the corner: this is the **Lord**'s doing, and it is marvellous in our eyes? {21:43} Therefore say **I** unto you, The kingdom of **God** shall be taken from you, and given to a nation bringing forth the fruits thereof. {21:44} And whosoever shall fall on this **stone** shall be broken: but on whomsoever **it** shall fall, it will grind **him** to powder. {21:45} And when the chief priests and Pharisees had heard **His** parables, they perceived that **He** spake of them. {21:46} But when they sought to lay hands on **Him**, they feared the multitude, because they took **Him** for a prophet. {66}

{22:1} And **Jesus** answered and spake unto them again by parables, and said, {22:2} The kingdom of heaven is like unto a certain king, which made a marriage for **His Son**, {22:3} And sent forth **His** servants to call them that were bidden to the wedding: and they would not come. {22:4} Again, **He** sent forth other servants, saying, Tell them which are bidden, Behold, **I** have prepared **my** dinner: **my** oxen and [**my**] fatlings [are] killed, and all things [are] ready: come unto the **marriage**. {22:5} But they made light of [it,] and went their ways, one to **His** farm, another to **His** merchandise: {22:6} And the remnant took **His** servants, and entreated [them] spitefully, and slew [them.]{22:7} But when the king heard [thereof,] **He** was wroth: and **He** sent forth **His** armies, and destroyed those murderers, and burned up their city. {22:8} Then saith **He** to **His** servants, The **wedding** is ready, but they which were bidden were not worthy. {22:9} Go ye therefore into the highways, and as many as ye shall find, bid to the **marriage**. {22:10} So those servants went out into the highways, and gathered together all as many as they found, both bad and good: and the wedding was furnished with guests.

{22:11} And when the **king** came in to see the guests, **He** saw there a man which had not on a wedding garment: {22:12} And **He** saith unto him, Friend, how camest thou in hither not having a wedding garment? And he was speechless. {22:13} Then said the **king** to the servants, Bind him hand and foot, and take him away, and cast [him] into outer darkness; there shall be weeping and gnashing of teeth. {22:14} For many are called, but few [are] chosen.

{22:15} Then went the Pharisees, and took counsel how they might entangle **Him** in [**His**] talk. {22:16} And they sent out unto **Him** their disciples with the Herodians, saying, **Master**, we know that **thou** art true, and teachest the way of **God** in truth, neither carest **thou** for any [man:] for **thou** regardest not the person of men. {22:17} Tell us therefore, What thinkest **thou**? Is it lawful to give tribute unto Caesar, or not? {22:18} But **Jesus** perceived their wickedness, and said, Why tempt ye **ME**, [ye] hypocrites? {22:19} Shew **ME** the tribute money. And they brought unto **Him** a penny. {22:20} And **He** saith unto them, Whose [is] this image and superscription? {22:21} They say unto **Him**, Caesar's. Then saith **He** unto them, Render therefore unto Caesar the things which are Caesar's; and unto **God** the things that are **God**'s. {22:22} When they had heard [these words,] they marvelled, and left **Him**, and went their way.

{22:23} The same day came to **Him** the Sadducees, which say that there is no resurrection, and asked **Him**, {22:24} Saying, **Master**, Moses said, If a man die, having no children, his brother shall marry his wife, and raise up seed unto his brother. {22:25} Now there were with us seven brethren: and the first, when he had married a wife, deceased, and, having no issue, left his wife unto his brother: {22:26} Likewise the second also, and the third, unto the seventh. {22:27} And last of all the woman died also. {22:28} Therefore in the resurrection whose wife shall she be of the seven? for they all had her. {22:29} **Jesus** answered and said unto them, Ye do err, not knowing the scriptures, nor the power of **God**. {22:30} For in the resurrection they neither marry, nor are given in marriage, but are as the angels of **God** in heaven. {22:31} But as touching the resurrection of the dead, have ye not read that which was spoken unto you by **God**, saying, {22:32} **I am** the **God** of Abraham, and the **God** of Isaac, and the **God** of Jacob? **God** is not the **God** of the dead, but of the living. {22:33} And when the multitude heard [this,] they were astonished at **His** doctrine.

{22:34} But when the Pharisees had heard that **He** had put the Sadducees to silence, they were gathered together. {22:35} Then one of them, [which was] a lawyer, asked [**Him** a question,]tempting **Him**, and saying, {22:36} **Master**, which [is] the great commandment in the law? {22:37} **Jesus** said unto him, Thou shalt love the **Lord thy God** with all thy heart, and with all thy soul, and with all thy mind. {22:38} This is the first and great commandment. {22:39} And the second [is] like unto it, Thou shalt love thy neighbour as thyself. {22:40} On these two commandments hang all the law and the prophets.

{22:41} While the Pharisees were gathered together, **Jesus** asked them, {22:42} Saying, What think ye of **Christ**? whose **Son** is **He**? They say unto **Him**, [The **Son**] **of David**. {22:43} **He** saith unto them, How then doth David in spirit call **Him Lord**, saying, {22:44} The **LORD** said unto **my Lord**, Sit thou on **my** right hand, till **I** make **thine** enemies **thy** footstool? {22:45} If David then call **Him Lord**, how is **He His Son**? {22:46} And no man was able to answer **Him** a word, neither durst any [man] from that day forth ask **Him**

any more [questions]. **{61}**

{23:1} Then spake **Jesus** to the multitude, and to **His** disciples, {23:2} Saying, The scribes and the Pharisees sit in Moses' seat: {23:3} All therefore whatsoever they bid you observe, [that] observe and do; but do not ye after their works: for they say, and do not. {23:4} For they bind heavy burdens and grievous to be borne, and lay [them] on men's shoulders; but they [themselves] will not move them with one of their fingers. {23:5} But all their works they do for to be seen of men: they make broad their phylacteries, and enlarge the borders of their garments, {23:6} And love the uppermost rooms at feasts, and the chief seats in the synagogues, {23:7} And greetings in the markets, and to be called of men, Rabbi, Rabbi. {23:8} But be not ye called Rabbi: for one is your **Master**, [even] **Christ**; and all ye are brethren. {23:9} And call no [man] your **Father** upon the earth: for one is your **Father**, which is in heaven. {23:10} Neither be ye called masters: for one is your **Master**, [even] **Christ**. {23:11} But he that is greatest among you shall be your servant. {23:12} And whosoever shall exalt himself shall be abased; and he that shall humble himself shall be exalted.

{23:13} But woe unto you, scribes and Pharisees, hypocrites! for ye shut up the kingdom of heaven against men: for ye neither go in [yourselves,] neither suffer ye them that are entering to go in. {23:14} Woe unto you, scribes and Pharisees, hypocrites! for ye devour widows' houses, and for a pretence make long prayer: therefore ye shall receive the greater damnation. {23:15} Woe unto you, scribes and Pharisees, hypocrites! for ye compass sea and land to make one proselyte, and when he is made, ye make him twofold more the child of hell than yourselves. {23:16} Woe unto you, [ye] blind guides, which say, Whosoever shall swear by the temple, it is nothing; but whosoever shall swear by the gold of the temple, he is a debtor! {23:17} [Ye] fools and blind: for whether is greater, the gold, or the temple that sanctifieth the gold? {23:18} And, Whosoever shall swear by the altar, it is nothing; but whosoever sweareth by the gift that is upon it, he is guilty. {23:19} [Ye] fools and blind: for whether [is] greater, the gift, or the altar that sanctifieth the gift? {23:20} Whoso therefore shall swear by the altar, sweareth by it, and by all things thereon. {23:21} And whoso shall swear by the temple, sweareth by it, and by **Him** that dwelleth therein. {23:22} And he that shall swear by heaven, sweareth by the throne of **God**, and by **Him** that sitteth thereon. {23:23} Woe unto you, scribes and Pharisees, hypocrites! for ye pay tithe of mint and anise and cummin, and have omitted the weightier [matters] of the law, judgment, mercy, and faith: these ought ye to have done, and not to leave the other undone. {23:24} [Ye] blind guides, which strain at a gnat, and swallow a camel. {23:25} Woe unto you, scribes and Pharisees, hypocrites! for ye make clean the outside of the cup and of the platter, but within they are full of extortion and excess. {23:26} [Thou] blind Pharisee, cleanse first that [which is] within the cup and platter, that the outside of them may be clean also. {23:27} Woe unto you, scribes and Pharisees, hypocrites! for ye are like unto whited sepulchres, which indeed appear beautiful outward, but are within full of dead [men's] bones, and of all uncleanness. {23:28} Even so ye also outwardly appear righteous unto men, but within ye are full of hypocrisy and iniquity. {23:29} Woe unto you, scribes and Pharisees, hypocrites! because ye build the tombs of the prophets, and garnish the sepulchres of the righteous, {23:30} And say, If we had been in the days of our **Father**s, we would not have been partakers with them in the blood of the prophets. {23:31} Wherefore ye be witnesses unto yourselves, that ye are the children of them which killed the prophets. {23:32} Fill ye up then the measure of your **Father**s. {23:33} [Ye] serpents, [ye] generation of vipers, how can ye escape the damnation of hell?{23:34} Wherefore, behold, **I** send unto you prophets, and wise men, and scribes: and [some] of them ye shall kill and crucify; and [some] of them shall ye scourge in your synagogues, and persecute [them] from city to city: {23:35} That upon you may come all the righteous blood shed upon the earth, from the blood of righteous Abel unto the blood of Zacharias **Son** of Barachias, **whom** ye slew between the temple and the altar. {23:36} Verily **I** say unto you, All these things shall come upon this generation. {23:37} O Jerusalem, Jerusalem, [thou] that killest the prophets, and stonest them which are sent unto thee, how often would **I** have gathered thy children together, even as a **hen** gathereth her chickens under [her] wings, and ye would not! {23:38} Behold, your house is left unto you desolate. {23:39} For **I** say unto you, Ye shall not see **ME** henceforth, till ye shall say, Blessed [is] **He** that cometh in the name of the **Lord**. {15}

{24:1} And **Jesus** went out, and departed from the temple: and **His** disciples came to [**Him**] for to shew **Him** the buildings of the temple. {24:2} And **Jesus** said unto them, See ye not all these things? verily **I** say unto you, There shall not be left here one stone upon another, that shall not be thrown down.

{24:3} And as **He** sat upon the mount of Olives, the disciples came unto **Him** privately, saying, Tell us, when shall these things be? and what [shall be] the sign of **thy** coming, and of the end of the world? {24:4} And **Jesus** answered and said unto them, Take heed that no man deceive you. {24:5} For many shall come in **my** name, saying, **I am Christ**; and shall deceive many. {24:6} And ye shall hear of wars and rumours of wars: see that ye be not troubled: for all [these things] must come to pass, but the end is not yet. {24:7} For nation shall rise against nation, and kingdom against kingdom: and there shall be famines, and pestilences, and earthquakes, in divers places. {24:8} All these [are] the beginning of sorrows. {24:9} Then shall they deliver you up to be afflicted, and shall kill you: and ye shall be hated of all nations for **my name's** sake. {24:10} And then shall many be offended, and shall betray one another, and shall hate one another. {24:11} And many false prophets shall rise, and shall deceive many. {24:12} And because iniquity shall abound, the love of many shall wax cold. {24:13} But he that shall endure unto the end, the same shall be saved. {24:14} And this Gospel of the kingdom shall be preached in all the world for a witness unto all nations; and then shall the end come. {24:15} When ye therefore shall see the abomination of desolation, spoken of by Daniel the prophet, stand in the holy place, (whoso readeth, let him understand:) {24:16} Then let them which be in Judaea flee into the mountains: {24:17} Let him which is on the housetop not come down to take any thing out of his house: {24:18} Neither let him which is in the field return back to take his clothes. {24:19} And woe unto them that are with child, and to them that give suck in those days! {24:20} But pray ye that your flight be not in the winter, neither on the sabbath day: {24:21} For then shall be great tribulation, such as was not since the beginning of the world to this time, no, nor ever shall be. {24:22} And except those days should be shortened, there should no flesh be saved: but for the elect's sake those days shall be shortened. {24:23} Then if any man shall say unto you, Lo, here [is] **Christ**, or there; believe [it] not. {24:24} For there

shall arise false **Christs**, and false prophets, and shall shew great signs and wonders; insomuch that, if [it were] possible, they shall deceive the very elect. {24:25} Behold, **I** have told you before. {24:26} Wherefore if they shall say unto you, Behold, [**He** is] in the desert; go not forth: behold, **He** is in the secret chambers; believe [it] not. {24:27} For as the lightning cometh out of the east, and shineth even unto the west; so shall also the coming of the **Son of man** be. {24:28} For wheresoever the carcase is, there will the eagles be gathered together.

{24:29} Immediately after the tribulation of those days shall the sun be darkened, and the moon shall not give her light, and the stars shall fall from heaven, and the powers of the heavens shall be shaken: {24:30} And then shall appear the sign of the **Son of man** in heaven: and then shall all the tribes of the earth mourn, and they shall see the **Son of man** coming in the clouds of heaven with power and great glory. {24:31} And **He** shall send **His** angels with a great sound of a trumpet, and they shall gather together **His** elect from the four winds, from one end of heaven to the other. {24:32} Now learn a parable of the fig tree; When **His** branch is yet tender, and putteth forth leaves, ye know that summer is nigh: {24:33} So likewise ye, when ye shall see all these things, know that it is near, [even] at the doors. {24:34} Verily **I** say unto you, This generation shall not pass, till all these things be fulfilled. {24:35} Heaven and earth shall pass away, but **my** words shall not pass away.

{24:36} But of that day and hour knoweth no [man,] no, not the angels of heaven, but **my Father** only. {24:37} But as the days of Noe [were,] so shall also the coming of the **Son of man** be. {24:38} For as in the days that were before the flood they were eating and drinking, marrying and giving in marriage, until the day that Noe entered into the ark, {24:39} And knew not until the flood came, and took them all away; so shall also the coming of the **Son of man** be. {24:40} Then shall two be in the field; the one shall be taken, and the other left. {24:41} Two [women shall be] grinding at the mill; the one shall be taken, and the other left.{24:42} Watch therefore: for ye know not what hour your **Lord** doth come. {24:43} But know this, that if the goodman of the house had known in what watch the thief would come, he would have watched, and would not have suffered his house to be broken up. {24:44} Therefore be ye also ready: for in such an hour as ye think not the **Son of man** cometh. {24:45} Who then is a faithful and wise servant, **whom His Lord** hath made ruler over **His** household, to give them meat in due season? {24:46} Blessed [is] that servant, **whom His Lord** when **He** cometh shall find so doing. {24:47} Verily **I** say unto you, That **He** shall make him ruler over all **His** goods. {24:48} But and if that evil servant shall say in his heart, **my Lord** delayeth **His** coming; {24:49} And shall begin to smite [his] fellowservants, and to eat and drink with the drunken; {24:50} The **Lord** of that servant shall come in a day when he looketh not for [**Him**,] and in an hour that he is not aware of, {24:51} And shall cut him asunder, and appoint [him] his portion with the hypocrites: there shall be weeping and gnashing of teeth. {49}

{25:1} Then shall the kingdom of heaven be likened unto ten virgins, which took their lamps, and went forth to meet the **bridegroom**. {25:2} And five of them were wise, and five [were] foolish. {25:3} They that [were] foolish took their lamps, and took no oil with them: {25:4} But the wise took oil in their vessels with their lamps. {25:5} While the **bridegroom** tarried, they all slumbered and slept. {25:6} And at midnight there was a cry made, Behold, the

bridegroom cometh; go ye out to meet **Him**. {25:7} Then all those virgins arose, and trimmed their lamps. {25:8} And the foolish said unto the wise, Give us of your oil; for our lamps are gone out. {25:9} But the wise answered, saying, [Not so;] lest there be not enough for us and you: but go ye rather to them that sell, and buy for yourselves. {25:10} And while they went to buy, the **bridegroom** came; and they that were ready went in with **Him** to the **marriage**: and the door was shut. {25:11} Afterward came also the other virgins, saying, **Lord**, **Lord**, open to us. {25:12} But **He** answered and said, Verily **I** say unto you, **I** know you not. {25:13} Watch therefore, for ye know neither the day nor the hour wherein the **Son of man** cometh.

{25:14} For [the kingdom of heaven is] as a **man** travelling into a far country, [**who**] called **His own** servants, and delivered unto them **His** goods. {25:15} And unto one **He** gave five talents, to another two, and to another one; to every man according to his several ability; and straightway took **His** journey. {25:16} Then he that had received the five talents went and traded with the same, and made [them] other five talents. {25:17} And likewise he that [had received] two, he also gained other two. {25:18} But he that had received one went and digged in the earth, and hid his **Lord**'s money. {25:19} After a long time the **Lord** of those servants cometh, and reckoneth with them. {25:20} And so he that had received five talents came and brought other five talents, saying, **Lord**, **thou** deliveredst unto me five talents: behold, I have gained beside them five talents more. {25:21} his **Lord** said unto him, Well done, [thou] good and faithful servant: thou hast been faithful over a few things, **I** will make thee ruler over many things: enter thou into the joy of thy **Lord**. {25:22} He also that had received two talents came and said, **Lord**, **thou** deliveredst unto me two talents: behold, I have gained two other talents beside them. {25:23} His **Lord** said unto him, Well done, good and faithful servant; thou hast been faithful over a few things, **I** will make thee ruler over many things: enter thou into the joy of thy **Lord**. {25:24} Then he which had received the one talent came and said, **Lord**, I knew thee that **thou** art an hard man, reaping where **thou** hast not sown, and gathering where **thou** hast not strawed: {25:25} And I was afraid, and went and hid **thy** talent in the earth: lo, [there] **thou** hast [that is] **thine**. {25:26} **His Lord** answered and said unto **Him**, [Thou] wicked and slothful servant, thou knewest that **I** reap where **I** sowed not, and gather where **I** have not strawed: {25:27} Thou oughtest therefore to have put **my** money to the exchangers, and [then] at **my** coming **I** should have received **mine own** with usury. {25:28} Take therefore the talent from him, and give [it] unto him which hath ten talents. {25:29} For unto every one that hath shall be given, and **He** shall have abundance: but from him that hath not shall be taken away even that which he hath. {25:30} And cast ye the unprofitable servant into outer darkness: there shall be weeping and gnashing of teeth.

{25:31} When the **Son of man** shall come in **His** glory, and all the holy angels with **Him**, then shall **He** sit upon the throne of **His** glory: {25:32} And before **Him** shall be gathered all nations: and **He** shall separate them one from another, as a **Shepherd** divideth [**His**] sheep from the goats: {25:33} And **He** shall set the sheep on **His** right hand, but the goats on the left. {25:34} Then shall the **King** say unto them on **His** right hand, Come, ye blessed of **my Father**, inherit the kingdom prepared for you from the foundation of the world: {25:35} For **I** was an hungred, and ye gave **ME** meat: **I** was thirsty, and ye gave **ME** drink: **I** was a stranger, and ye took **ME** in: {25:36} Naked, and ye clothed **ME**: **I** was sick, and ye visited **ME**: **I** was in prison, and ye came unto **ME**.

{25:37} Then shall the righteous answer **Him**, saying, **Lord**, when saw we **thee** an hungred, and fed [**thee**?] or thirsty, and gave [**thee**] drink? {25:38} When saw we **thee** a stranger, and took [**thee**] in? or naked, and clothed [**thee**?]{25:39} Or when saw we **thee** sick, or in prison, and came unto **thee**? {25:40} And the **King** shall answer and say unto them, Verily **I** say unto you, Inasmuch as ye have done [it] unto one of the least of these **my** brethren, ye have done [it] unto **ME**. {25:41} Then shall **He** say also unto them on the left hand, Depart from **ME**, ye cursed, into everlasting fire, prepared for the devil and **His** angels: {25:42} For **I** was an hungred, and ye gave **ME** no meat: **I** was thirsty, and ye gave **ME** no drink: {25:43} **I** was a stranger, and ye took **ME** not in: naked, and ye clothed **ME** not: sick, and in prison, and ye visited **ME** not. {25:44} Then shall they also answer **Him**, saying, **Lord**, when saw we **thee** an hungred, or athirst, or a stranger, or naked, or sick, or in prison, and did not minister unto **thee**? {25:45} Then shall **He** answer them, saying, Verily **I** say unto you, Inasmuch as ye did [it] not to one of the least of these, ye did [it] not to **ME**. {25:46} And these shall go away into everlasting punishment: but the righteous into life eternal. {104}

{26:1} And it came to pass, when **Jesus** had finished all these sayings, **He** said unto **His** disciples, {26:2} Ye know that after two days is [the feast of] the passover, and the **Son of man** is betrayed to be crucified. {26:3} Then assembled together the chief priests, and the scribes, and the elders of the people, unto the palace of the high priest, who was called Caiaphas, {26:4} And consulted that they might take **Jesus** by subtilty, and kill [**Him**.]{26:5} But they said, Not on the feast [day,] lest there be an uproar among the people.

{26:6} Now when **Jesus** was in Bethany, in the house of Simon the leper, {26:7} There came unto **Him** a woman having an alabaster box of very precious ointment, and poured it on **His** head, as **He** sat [at meat.]{26:8} But when **His** disciples saw [it,] they had indignation, saying, To what purpose [is] this waste? {26:9} For this ointment might have been sold for much, and given to the poor. {26:10} When **Jesus** understood [it,] **He** said unto them, Why trouble ye the woman? for she hath wrought a good work upon **ME**. {26:11} For ye have the poor always with you; but **ME** ye have not always. {26:12} For in that she hath poured this ointment on **my** body, she did [it] for **my** burial. {26:13} Verily **I** say unto you, Wheresoever this Gospel shall be preached in the whole world, [there] shall also this, that this woman hath done, be told for a memorial of her.

{26:14} Then one of the twelve, called Judas Iscariot, went unto the chief priests, {26:15} And said [unto them,] What will ye give me, and **I** will deliver **Him** unto you? And they covenanted with him for thirty pieces of silver. {26:16} And from that time he sought opportunity to betray him.

{26:17} Now the first [day] of the [feast of] unleavened bread the disciples came to **Jesus**, saying unto **Him**, Where wilt **thou** that we prepare for **thee** to eat the passover? {26:18} And **He** said, Go into the city to such a man, and say unto him, The **Master** saith, **my** time is at hand; **I** will keep the passover at thy house with **my** disciples. {26:19} And the disciples did as **Jesus** had appointed them; and they made ready the passover. {26:20} Now when the even was come, **He** sat down with the twelve. {26:21} And as they did eat, **He** said, Verily **I** say unto you, that one of you shall betray **ME**. {26:22} And they were exceeding sorrowful, and began every one of them to say unto **Him**, **Lord**, is it I? {26:23} And **He** answered and said, he that dippeth [his] hand with **ME** in the dish, the same shall betray **ME**. {26:24} The **Son of man** goeth as it is written of **Him**: but woe unto that man by **whom** the **Son of man** is betrayed! it had been good for that man if he had not been born. {26:25} Then Judas, which betrayed **Him**, answered and said, **Master**, is it I? **He** said unto **Him**, Thou hast said.

{26:26} And as they were eating, **Jesus** took bread, and blessed [it,] and brake [it,] and gave [it] to the disciples, and said, Take, eat; this is **my body**. {26:27} And **He** took the cup, and gave thanks, and gave [it] to them, saying, Drink ye all of it; {26:28} For this is **my blood** of the new testament, which is shed for many for the remission of sins. {26:29} But **I** say unto you, **I** will not drink henceforth of this fruit of the vine, until that day when **I** drink it new with you in **my Father**'s kingdom. {26:30} And when they had sung an hymn, they went out into the mount of Olives. {26:31} Then saith **Jesus** unto them, All ye shall be offended because of **ME** this night: for it is written, **I** will smite the **Shepherd**, and the sheep of the flock shall be scattered abroad. {26:32} But after **I am** risen again, **I** will go before you into Galilee. {26:33} Peter answered and said unto **Him**, Though all [men] shall be offended because of **thee**, [yet] will **I** never be offended. {26:34} **Jesus** said unto **Him**, Verily **I** say unto thee, That this night, before the cock crow, thou shalt deny **ME** thrice. {26:35} Peter said unto **Him**, Though I should die with **thee**, yet will I not deny **thee**. Likewise also said all the disciples.

{26:36} Then cometh **Jesus** with them unto a place called Gethsemane, and saith unto the disciples, Sit ye here, while **I** go and pray yonder. {26:37} And **He** took with **Him** Peter and the two sons of Zebedee, and began to be sorrowful and very heavy. {26:38} Then saith **He** unto them, **my** soul is exceeding sorrowful, even unto death: tarry ye here, and watch with **ME**. {26:39} And **He** went a little farther, and fell on **His** face, and prayed, saying, O **my Father**, if it be possible, let this cup pass from **ME**: nevertheless not as **I** will, but as thou [wilt.]{26:40} And **He** cometh unto the disciples, and findeth them asleep, and saith unto Peter, What, could ye not watch with **ME** one hour? {26:41} Watch and pray, that ye enter not into temptation: the spirit indeed [is] willing, but the flesh [is] weak. {26:42} **He** went away again the second time, and prayed, saying, O **my Father**, if this cup may not pass away from **ME**, except **I** drink it, thy will be done. {26:43} And **He** came and found them asleep again: for their eyes were heavy. {26:44} And **He** left them, and went away again, and prayed the third time, saying the same words. {26:45} Then cometh **He** to **His** disciples, and saith unto them, Sleep on now, and take [your] rest: behold, the hour is at hand, and the **Son of man** is betrayed into the hands of sinners. {26:46} Rise, let us be going: behold, he is at hand that doth betray **ME**.

{26:47} And while **He** yet spake, lo, Judas, one of the twelve, came, and with him a great multitude with swords and staves, from the chief priests and elders of the people. {26:48} Now he that betrayed **Him** gave them a sign, saying, **Whom**soever I shall kiss, that same is **He**: hold **Him** fast. {26:49} And forthwith he came to **Jesus**, and said, Hail, **master**; and kissed **Him**. {26:50} And **Jesus** said unto him, Friend, wherefore art thou come? Then came they, and laid hands on **Jesus**, and took **Him**. {26:51} And, behold, one of them which were with **Jesus** stretched out [his] hand, and drew his sword, and struck a servant of the high priest's, and smote off his ear. {26:52} Then said **Jesus** unto **Him**, Put up again thy sword into his place: for all they that take the sword shall perish with the sword. {26:53} Thinkest thou that **I** cannot now pray to **my Father**, and **He**

shall presently give **ME** more than twelve legions of angels? {26:54} But how then shall the scriptures be fulfilled, that thus it must be? {26:55} In that same hour said **Jesus** to the multitudes, Are ye come out as against a thief with swords and staves for to take **ME**? **I** sat daily with you teaching in the temple, and ye laid no hold on **ME**. {26:56} But all this was done, that the scriptures of the prophets might be fulfilled. Then all the disciples forsook **Him**, and fled.

{26:57} And they that had laid hold on **Jesus** led [**Him**] away to Caiaphas the high priest, where the scribes and the elders were assembled. {26:58} But Peter followed **Him** afar off unto the high priest's palace, and went in, and sat with the servants, to see the end. {26:59} Now the chief priests, and elders, and all the council, sought false witness against **Jesus**, to put **Him** to death; {26:60} But found none: yea, though many false witnesses came, [yet] found they none. At the last came two false witnesses, {26:61} And said, This [**fellow**] said, **I am** able to destroy the **temple of God**, and to build it in three days. {26:62} And the high priest arose, and said unto **Him**, Answerest thou nothing? what [is it which] these witness against thee? {26:63} But **Jesus** held **His** peace. And the high priest answered and said unto **Him**, **I** adjure thee by the living **God**, that thou tell us whether **thou** be the **Christ**, the **Son of God**. {26:64} **Jesus** saith unto **Him**, Thou hast said: nevertheless **I** say unto you, Hereafter shall ye see the **Son of man** sitting on the right hand of power, and coming in the clouds of heaven. {26:65} Then the high priest rent **His** clothes, saying, **He** hath spoken blasphemy; what further need have we of witnesses? behold, now ye have heard **His** blasphemy. {26:66} What think ye? They answered and said, **He** is guilty of death. {26:67} Then did they spit in **His** face, and buffeted **Him**; and others smote [**Him**] with the palms of their hands, {26:68} Saying, Prophesy unto us, **thou Christ**, Who is he that smote thee?{26:69} Now Peter sat without in the palace: and a damsel came unto him, saying, Thou also wast with **Jesus** of Galilee. {26:70} But he denied before [them] all, saying, I know not what thou sayest. {26:71} And when he was gone out into the porch, another [maid] saw him, and said unto them that were there, This [fellow] was also with **Jesus of Nazareth**. {26:72} And again he denied with an oath, I do not know the **man**. {26:73} And after a while came unto [him] they that stood by, and said to Peter, Surely thou also art [one] of them; for thy speech bewrayeth thee. {26:74} Then began he to curse and to swear, [saying,] I know not the **man**. And immediately the cock crew. {26:75} And Peter remembered the word of **Jesus**, which said unto him, Before the cock crow, thou shalt deny **ME** thrice. And he went out, and wept bitterly. **{149}**

{27:1} When the morning was come, all the chief priests and elders of the people took counsel against **Jesus** to put **Him** to death: {27:2} And when they had bound **Him**, they led [**Him**] away, and delivered **Him** to Pontius Pilate the governor.

{27:3} Then Judas, which had betrayeth **Him**, when he saw that **He** was condemned, repented himself, and brought again the thirty pieces of silver to the chief priests and elders, {27:4} Saying, I have sinned in that I have betrayed the **innocent blood**. And they said, What [is that] to us? see thou [to that.]{27:5} And he cast down the pieces of silver in the temple, and departed, and went and hanged himself. {27:6} And the chief priests took the silver pieces, and said, It is not lawful for to put them into the treasury, because it is the price of **blood**. {27:7} And they took counsel, and bought with them the potter's field, to bury strangers in.

{27:8} Wherefore that field was called, The field of blood, unto this day. {27:9} Then was fulfilled that which was spoken by Jeremy the prophet, saying, And they took the thirty pieces of silver, the price of Him that was valued, whom they of the children of Israel did value; {27:10} And gave them for the potter's field, as the Lord appointed ME. {27:11} And Jesus stood before the governor: and the governor asked Him, saying, Art thou the King of the Jews? And Jesus said unto him, Thou sayest. {27:12} And when He was accused of the chief priests and elders, He answered nothing. {27:13} Then said Pilate unto Him, Hearest thou not how many things they witness against thee? {27:14} And He answered him to never a word; insomuch that the governor marvelled greatly. {27:15} Now at [that] feast the governor was wont to release unto the people a prisoner, whom they would. {27:16} And they had then a notable prisoner, called Barabbas. {27:17} Therefore when they were gathered together, Pilate said unto them, Whom will ye that I release unto you? Barabbas, or Jesus which is called Christ? {27:18} For he knew that for envy they had delivered Him.

{27:19} When he was set down on the judgment seat, his wife sent unto him, saying, Have thou nothing to do with that just man: for I have suffered many things this day in a dream because of Him. {27:20} But the chief priests and elders persuaded the multitude that they should ask Barabbas, and destroy Jesus. {27:21} The governor answered and said unto them, Whether of the twain will ye that I release unto you? They said, Barabbas. {27:22} Pilate saith unto them, What shall I do then with Jesus which is called Christ? [They] all say unto him, Let Him be crucified. {27:23} And the governor said, Why, what evil hath He done? But they cried out the more, saying, Let Him be crucified.

{27:24} When Pilate saw that he could prevail nothing, but [that] rather a tumult was made, he took water, and washed [his] hands before the multitude, saying, I am innocent of the blood of this just person: see ye [to it.]{27:25} Then answered all the people, and said, His blood [be] on us, and on our children.

{27:26} Then released he Barabbas unto them: and when he had scourged Jesus, he delivered [Him] to be crucified. {27:27} Then the soldiers of the governor took Jesus into the common hall, and gathered unto him the whole band [of soldiers.]{27:28} And they stripped Him, and put on Him a scarlet robe.

{27:29} And when they had platted a crown of thorns, they put [it] upon His head, and a reed in His right hand: and they bowed the knee before Him, and mocked Him, saying, Hail, King of the Jews! {27:30} And they spit upon Him, and took the reed, and smote Him on the head. {27:31} And after that they had mocked Him, they took the robe off from Him, and put His own raiment on Him, and led Him away to crucify [Him.]{27:32} And as they came out, they found a man of Cyrene, Simon by name: him they compelled to bear His cross. {27:33} And when they were come unto a place called Golgotha, that is to say, a place of a skull,

{27:34} They gave Him vinegar to drink mingled with gall: and when He had tasted [thereof,] He would not drink. {27:35} And they crucified Him, and parted His garments, casting lots: that it might be fulfilled which was spoken by the prophet, They parted my garments among them, and upon my vesture did they cast lots. {27:36} And sitting down they watched Him there; {27:37} And set up over His

head His accusation written, THIS IS JESUS THE KING OF THE JEWS. {27:38} Then were there two thieves crucified with Him, one on the right hand, and another on the left.{27:39} And they that passed by reviled Him, wagging their heads, {27:40} And saying, Thou that destroyest the temple, and buildest [it] in three days, save thyself. If thou be the Son of God, come down from the cross. {27:41} Likewise also the chief priests mocking [Him,] with the scribes and elders, said, {27:42} He saved others; himself He cannot save. If He be the King of Israel, let Him now come down from the cross, and we will believe Him. {27:43} He trusted in God; let Him deliver Him now, if He will have Him: for He said, I am the Son of God. {27:44} The thieves also, which were crucified with Him, cast the same in His teeth. {27:45} Now from the sixth hour there was darkness over all the land unto the ninth hour. {27:46} And about the ninth hour Jesus cried with a loud voice, saying, Eli, Eli, lama sabachthani? that is to say, my God, my God, why hast thou forsaken ME? {27:47} Some of them that stood there, when they heard [that,] said, This [man] calleth for Elias. {27:48} And straightway one of them ran, and took a spunge, and filled [it] with vinegar, and put [it] on a reed, and gave Him to drink. {27:49} The rest said, Let be, let us see whether Elias will come to save Him.

{27:50} Jesus, when He had cried again with a loud voice, yielded up the ghost. {27:51} And, behold, the veil of the temple was rent in twain from the top to the bottom; and the earth did quake, and the rocks rent; {27:52} And the graves were opened; and many bodies of the saints which slept arose, {27:53} And came out of the graves after His resurrection, and went into the holy city, and appeared unto many. {27:54} Now when the centurion, and they that were with Him, watching Jesus, saw the earthquake, and those things that were done, they feared greatly, saying, Truly this was the Son of God. {27:55} And many women were there beholding afar off, which followed Jesus from Galilee, ministering unto Him: {27:56} Among which was Mary Magdalene, and Mary the mother of James and Joses, and the mother of Zebedee's children. {27:57} When the even was come, there came a rich man of Arimathaea, named Joseph, who also himself was Jesus' disciple: {27:58} He went to Pilate, and begged the body of Jesus. Then Pilate commanded the body to be delivered. {27:59} And when Joseph had taken the body, he wrapped it in a clean linen cloth, {27:60} And laid it in his own new tomb, which he had hewn out in the rock: and he rolled a great stone to the door of the sepulchre, and departed. {27:61} And there was Mary Magdalene, and the other Mary, sitting over against the sepulchre.

{27:62} Now the next day, that followed the day of the preparation, the chief priests and Pharisees came together unto Pilate, {27:63} Saying, Sir, we remember that that deceiver said, while He was yet alive, After three days I will rise again. {27:64} Command therefore that the sepulchre be made sure until the third day, lest His disciples come by night, and steal Him away, and say unto the people, He is risen from the dead: so the last error shall be worse than the first. {27:65} Pilate said unto them, Ye have a watch: go your way, make [it] as sure as ye can. {27:66} So they went, and made the sepulchre sure, sealing the stone, and setting a watch. {116}

{28:1} In the end of the sabbath, as it began to dawn toward the first [day] of the week, came Mary Magdalene and the other Mary to see the sepulchre. {28:2} And, behold, there was a great earthquake: for the angel of the **Lord** descended from heaven, and came and rolled back the stone from the door, and sat upon it. {28:3} His countenance was like lightning, and His raiment white as snow: {28:4} And for fear of Him the keepers did shake, and became as dead [men.]{28:5} And the angel answered and said unto the women, Fear not ye: for I know that ye seek **Jesus**, which was crucified. {28:6} **He** is not here: for **He** is risen, as **He** said. Come, see the place where the **Lord** lay. {28:7} And go quickly, and tell **His** disciples that **He** is risen from the dead; and, behold, **He** goeth before you into Galilee; there shall ye see **Him**: lo, **I** have told you. {28:8} And they departed quickly from the sepulchre with fear and great joy; and did run to bring **His** disciples word.{28:9} And as they went to tell **His** disciples, behold, **Jesus** met them, saying, All hail. And they came and held **Him** by the feet, and worshipped **Him**. {28:10} Then said **Jesus** unto them, Be not afraid: go tell **my** brethren that they go into Galilee, and there shall they see **ME**.

{28:11} Now when they were going, behold, some of the watch came into the city, and shewed unto the chief priests all the things that were done. {28:12} And when they were assembled with the elders, and had taken counsel, they gave large money unto the soldiers, {28:13} Saying, Say ye, **His** disciples came by night, and stole **Him** [away] while we slept. {28:14} And if this come to the governor's ears, we will persuade him, and secure you. {28:15} So they took the money, and did as they were taught: and this saying is commonly reported among the Jews until this day.

{28:16} Then the eleven disciples went away into Galilee, into a mountain where **Jesus** had appointed them. {28:17} And when they saw **Him**, they worshipped **Him**: but some doubted. {28:18} And **Jesus** came and spake unto them, saying, All power is given unto **ME** in heaven and in earth. {28:19} Go ye therefore, and teach all nations, baptizing them in the name of the **Father**, and of the **Son**, and of the **Holy Ghost**: {28:20} Teaching them to observe all things whatsoever **I** have commanded you: and, lo, **I am** with you alway, [even] unto the end of the world. Amen.

{28}

The Gospel According to St. Mark   **TOTAL 1064**

{1:1} The beginning of the Gospel of **Jesus Christ**, the **Son of God**; {1:2} As it is written in the prophets, Behold, **I** send **my** messenger before **thy** face, which shall prepare **thy** way before **thee**. {1:3} The voice of one crying in the wilderness, Prepare ye the way of the **Lord**, make **His** paths straight. {1:4} John did baptize in the wilderness, and preach the baptism of repentance for the remission of sins. {1:5} And there went out unto him all the land of Judaea, and they of Jerusalem, and were all baptized of him in the river of Jordan, confessing their sins. {1:6} And John was clothed with camel's hair, and with a girdle of a skin about his loins; and he did eat locusts and wild honey; {1:7} And preached, saying, There cometh **one** mightier than **I** after me, the latchet of **whose** shoes **I** am not worthy to stoop down and unloose. {1:8} **I** indeed have baptized you with water: but **He** shall baptize you with the **Holy Ghost**. {1:9} And it came to pass in those days, that **Jesus** came from Nazareth of Galilee, and was baptized of John in Jordan. {1:10} And straightway coming up out of the water, he saw the heavens opened, and the Spirit like a dove descending upon **Him**: {1:11} And there came a voice from heaven, [saying,] **Thou** art **my beloved Son**, in **whom I am** well pleased. {1:12} And immediately the Spirit driveth **Him** into the wilderness. {1:13} And **He** was there in the wilderness forty days, tempted of Satan; and was with the wild beasts; and the angels ministered unto **Him**. {1:14} Now after that John was put in prison, **Jesus** came into Galilee, preaching the Gospel of the kingdom of **God**, {1:15} And saying, The time is fulfilled, and the kingdom of **God** is at hand: repent ye, and believe the Gospel. {1:16} Now as **He** walked by the sea of Galilee, **He** saw Simon and Andrew his brother casting a net into the sea: for they were fishers. {1:17} And **Jesus** said unto them, Come ye after **ME**, and **I** will make you to become fishers of men. {1:18} And straightway they forsook their nets, and followed **Him**. {1:19} And when **He** had gone a little farther thence, **He** saw James the [Son] of Zebedee, and John his brother, who also were in the ship mending their nets. {1:20} And straightway **He** called them: and they left their Father Zebedee in the ship with the hired servants, and went after **Him**. {1:21} And they went into Capernaum; and straightway on the sabbath day **He** entered into the synagogue, and taught. {1:22} And they were astonished at **His** doctrine: for **He** taught them as **one** that had authority, and not as the scribes. {1:23} And there was in their synagogue a man with an unclean spirit; and he cried out, {1:24} Saying, Let [us] alone; what have we to do with thee, **thou Jesus of Nazareth**? art **thou** come to destroy us? **I** know **thee** who **thou** art, the **Holy One of God**. {1:25} And **Jesus** rebuked him, saying, Hold thy peace, and come out of him. {1:26} And when the unclean spirit had torn Him, and cried with a loud voice, he came out of Him. {1:27} And they were all amazed, insomuch that they questioned among themselves, saying, What thing is this? what new doctrine [is] this? for with authority commandeth **He** even the unclean spirits, and they do obey **Him**. {1:28} And immediately **His** fame spread abroad throughout all the region round about Galilee. {1:29} And forthwith, when they were come out of the synagogue, **they** entered into the house of Simon and Andrew, with James and John. {1:30} But Simon's wife's mother lay sick of a fever, and anon they tell **Him** of her. {1:31} And **He** came and took her by the hand, and lifted her up; and immediately the fever left her, and she ministered unto them. {1:32} And at even, when the sun did set, they brought unto **Him** all that were diseased, and them that were possessed with devils. {1:33}

And all the city was gathered together at the door. {1:34} And **He** healed many that were sick of divers diseases, and cast out many devils; and suffered not the devils to speak, because they knew **Him**. {1:35} And in the morning, rising up a great while before day, **He** went out, and departed into a solitary place, and there prayed. {1:36} And Simon and they that were with **Him** followed after **Him**. {1:37} And when they had found **Him**, they said unto **Him**, All [men] seek for **thee**. {1:38} And **He** said unto them, Let us go into the next towns, that **I** may preach there also: for therefore came **I** forth. {1:39} And **He** preached in their synagogues throughout all Galilee, and cast out devils. {1:40} And there came a leper to **Him**, beseeching **Him**, and kneeling down to **Him**, and saying unto **Him**, If **thou** wilt, **thou** canst make **ME** clean. {1:41} And **Jesus**, moved with compassion, put forth [**His**] hand, and touched him, and saith unto him, **I** will; be thou clean. {1:42} And as soon as **He** had spoken, immediately the leprosy departed from him, and he was cleansed. {1:43} And **He** straitly charged him, and forthwith sent him away; {1:44} And saith unto him, See thou say nothing to any man: but go thy way, shew thyself to the priest, and offer for thy cleansing those things which Moses commanded, for a testimony unto them. {1:45} But he went out, and began to publish [it] much, and to blaze abroad the matter, insomuch that **Jesus** could no more openly enter into the city, but was without in desert places: and they came to **Him** from every quarter. **{77}**

_____{2:1} And again **He** entered into Capernaum, after [some] days; and it was noised that **He** was in the house. {2:2} And straightway many were gathered together, insomuch that there was no room to receive [them,] no, not so much as about the door: and **He** preached the word unto them. {2:3} And they come unto **Him**, bringing one sick of the palsy, which was borne of four. {2:4} And when they could not come nigh unto **Him** for the press, they uncovered the roof where **He** was: and when they had broken [it] up, they let down the bed wherein the sick of the palsy lay. {2:5} When **Jesus** saw their faith, **He** said unto the sick of the palsy, Son, thy sins be forgiven thee. {2:6} But there were certain of the scribes sitting there, and reasoning in their hearts, {2:7} Why doth this [**man**] thus speak blasphemies? who can forgive sins but **God** only? {2:8} And immediately when **Jesus** perceived in **His** spirit that they so reasoned within themselves, **He** said unto them, Why reason ye these things in your hearts? {2:9} Whether is it easier to say to the sick of the palsy, [Thy] sins be forgiven thee; or to say, Arise, and take up thy bed, and walk? {2:10} But that ye may know that the Son of man hath power on earth to forgive sins, (**He** saith to the sick of the palsy,) {2:11} **I** say unto thee, Arise, and take up thy bed, and go thy way into thine house. {2:12} And immediately he arose, took up the bed, and went forth before them all; insomuch that they were all amazed, and glorified **God**, saying, We never saw it on this fashion. {2:13} And **He** went forth again by the sea side; and all the multitude resorted unto **Him**, and **He** taught them. {2:14} And as **He** passed by, **He** saw Levi the [Son] of Alphaeus sitting at the receipt of custom, and said unto him, Follow **ME**. And **He** arose and followed **Him**. {2:15} And it came to pass, that, as **Jesus** sat at meat in his house, many publicans and sinners sat also together with **Jesus** and **His** disciples: for there were many, and they followed **Him**. {2:16} And when the scribes and Pharisees saw **Him** eat with publicans and sinners, they said unto **His** disciples, How is it that **He** eateth and drinketh with publicans and sinners? {2:17} When **Jesus** heard [it,] **He** saith unto them, They that are whole have no need of the **physician**, but they that are sick: **I** came not to call the righteous, but sinners to repentance. {2:18} And the disciples of John and of the

Pharisees used to fast: and they come and say unto **Him**, Why do the disciples of John and of the Pharisees fast, but **thy** disciples fast not? {2:19} And **Jesus** said unto them, Can the children of the bridechamber fast, while the **bridegroom** is with them? as long as they have the **bridegroom** with them, they cannot fast. {2:20} But the days will come, when the **bridegroom** shall be taken away from them, and then shall they fast in those days. {2:21} No man also seweth a piece of new cloth on an old garment: else the new piece that filled it up taketh away from the old, and the rent is made worse. {2:22} And no man putteth new wine into old bottles: else the new wine doth burst the bottles, and the wine is spilled, and the bottles will be marred: but new wine must be put into new bottles. {2:23} And it came to pass, that **He** went through the corn fields on the sabbath day; and **His** disciples began, as they went, to pluck the ears of corn. {2:24} And the Pharisees said unto **Him**, Behold, why do they on the sabbath day that which is not lawful? {2:25} And **He** said unto them, Have ye never read what David did, when he had need, and was an hungred, he, and they that were with him? {2:26} How he went into the house of **God** in the days of Abiathar the high priest, and did eat the shewbread, which is not lawful to eat but for the priests, and gave also to them which were with him? {2:27} And **He** said unto them, The sabbath was made for man, and not man for the sabbath: {2:28} Therefore the **Son of man** is **Lord** also of the sabbath.{47}

{3:1} And **He** entered again into the synagogue; and there was a man there which had a withered hand. {3:2} And they watched **Him**, whether **He** would heal him on the sabbath day; that they might accuse **Him**. {3:3} And **He** saith unto the man which had the withered hand, Stand forth. {3:4} And **He** saith unto them, Is it lawful to do good on the sabbath days, or to do evil? to save life, or to kill? But they held their peace. {3:5} And when **He** had looked round about on them with anger, being grieved for the hardness of their hearts, **He** saith unto the man, Stretch forth thine hand. And he stretched [it] out: and his hand was restored whole as the other. {3:6} And the Pharisees went forth, and straightway took counsel with the Herodians against **Him**, how they might destroy **Him**. {3:7} But **Jesus** withdrew **himself** with **His** disciples to the sea: and a great multitude from Galilee followed **Him**, and from Judaea, {3:8} And from Jerusalem, and from Idumaea, and [from] beyond Jordan; and they about Tyre and Sidon, a great multitude, when they had heard what great things **He** did, came unto **Him**. {3:9} And **He** spake to **His** disciples, that a small ship should wait on **Him** because of the multitude, lest they should throng **Him**. {3:10} For **He** had healed many; insomuch that they pressed upon **Him** for to touch **Him**, as many as had plagues. {3:11} And unclean spirits, when they saw **Him**, fell down before **Him**, and cried, saying, **Thou** art the **Son of God**. {3:12} And **He** straitly charged them that they should not make **Him** known. {3:13} And **He** goeth up into a mountain, and calleth [unto **Him**] **whom He** would: and they came unto **Him**. {3:14} And **He** ordained twelve, that they should be with **Him**, and that **He** might send them forth to preach, {3:15} And to have power to heal sicknesses, and to cast out devils: {3:16} And Simon **He** surnamed Peter; {3:17} And James the [Son] of Zebedee, and John the brother of James; and **He** surnamed them Boanerges, which is, The sons of thunder: {3:18} And Andrew, and Philip, and Bartholomew, and Matthew, and Thomas, and James the [Son] of Alphaeus, and Thaddaeus, and Simon the Canaanite, {3:19} And Judas Iscariot, which also betrayed **Him**: and they went into an house. {3:20} And the multitude cometh together again, so that they could not so much as eat bread. {3:21} And when **His** friends heard

[of it,] they went out to lay hold on **Him**: for they said, **He** is beside **himself**.

{3:22} And the scribes which came down from Jerusalem said, **He** hath Beelzebub, and by the prince of the devils casteth **He** out devils. {3:23} And **He** called them [unto **Him**,] and said unto them in parables, How can Satan cast out Satan? {3:24} And if a kingdom be divided against itself, that kingdom cannot stand. {3:25} And if a house be divided against itself, that house cannot stand. {3:26} And if Satan rise up against himself, and be divided, he cannot stand, but hath an end. {3:27} No **man** can enter into a strong man's house, and spoil **His** goods, except **He** will first bind the strong man; and then **He** will spoil his house. {3:28} Verily **I** say unto you, All sins shall be forgiven unto the sons of men, and blasphemies wherewith soever they shall blaspheme: {3:29} But he that shall blaspheme against the **Holy Ghost** hath never forgiveness, but is in danger of eternal damnation: {3:30} Because they said, **He** hath an unclean spirit.{3:31} There came then **His** brethren and **His** mother, and, standing without, sent unto **Him**, calling **Him**. {3:32} And the multitude sat about **Him**, and they said unto **Him**, Behold, **thy** mother and **thy** brethren without seek for **thee**. {3:33} And **He** answered them, saying, Who is **my** mother, or **my** brethren? {3:34} And **He** looked round about on them which sat about **Him**, and said, Behold **my** mother and **my** brethren! {3:35} For whosoever shall do the will of **God**, the same is **my** brother, and **my** sister, and mother. {71}

{4:1} And **He** began again to teach by the sea side: and there was gathered unto **Him** a great multitude, so that **He** entered into a ship, and sat in the sea; and the whole multitude was by the sea on the land. {4:2} And **He** taught them many things by parables, and said unto them in **His** doctrine, {4:3} Hearken; Behold, there went out a **sower** to sow: {4:4} And it came to pass, as **He** sowed, some fell by the way side, and the fowls of the air came and devoured it up. {4:5} And some fell on stony ground, where it had not much earth; and immediately it sprang up, because it had no depth of earth: {4:6} But when the sun was up, it was scorched; and because it had no root, it withered away. {4:7} And some fell among thorns, and the thorns grew up, and choked it, and it yielded no fruit. {4:8} And other fell on good ground, and did yield fruit that sprang up and increased; and brought forth, some thirty, and some sixty, and some an hundred. {4:9} And **He** said unto them, he that hath ears to hear, let him hear. {4:10} And when **He** was alone, they that were about **Him** with the twelve asked of **Him** the parable. {4:11} And **He** said unto them, Unto you it is given to know the mystery of the kingdom of **God**: but unto them that are without, all these [things] are done in parables: {4:12} That seeing they may see, and not perceive; and hearing they may hear, and not understand; lest at any time they should be converted, and [their] sins should be forgiven them. {4:13} And **He** said unto them, Know ye not this parable? and how then will ye know all parables?

{4:14} The **sower** soweth the word. {4:15} And these are they by the way side, where the word is sown; but when they have heard, Satan cometh immediately, and taketh away the word that was sown in their hearts. {4:16} And these are they likewise which are sown on stony ground; who, when they have heard the word, immediately receive it with gladness; {4:17} And have no root in themselves, and so endure but for a time: afterward, when affliction or persecution ariseth for the word's sake, immediately they are offended. {4:18} And these are they which are sown among thorns; such as hear the word, {4:19} And the cares of this world, and the deceitfulness of riches, and the lusts of other things entering in, choke the word, and it becometh unfruitful. {4:20} And these are they which are sown on good ground; such as hear the word, and receive [it,] and bring forth fruit, some thirtyfold, some sixty, and some an hundred.

{4:21} And He said unto them, Is a candle brought to be put under a bushel, or under a bed? and not to be set on a candlestick? {4:22} For there is nothing hid, which shall not be manifested; neither was any thing kept secret, but that it should come abroad. {4:23} If any man have ears to hear, let him hear. {4:24} And He said unto them, Take heed what ye hear: with what measure ye mete, it shall be measured to you: and unto you that hear shall more be given. {4:25} For he that hath, to him shall be given: and he that hath not, from him shall be taken even that which he hath. {4:26} And He said, So is the kingdom of God, as if a man should cast seed into the ground; {4:27} And should sleep, and rise night and day, and the seed should spring and grow up, he knoweth not how. {4:28} For the earth bringeth forth fruit of herself; first the blade, then the ear, after that the full corn in the ear. {4:29} But when the fruit is brought forth, immediately He putteth in the sickle, because the harvest is come.

{4:30} And He said, Whereunto shall we liken the kingdom of God? or with what comparison shall we compare it? {4:31} [It is] like a grain of mustard seed, which, when it is sown in the earth, is less than all the seeds that be in the earth: {4:32} But when it is sown, it groweth up, and becometh greater than all herbs, and shooteth out great branches; so that the fowls of the air may lodge under the shadow of it. {4:33} And with many such parables spake He the word unto them, as they were able to hear [it.]{4:34} But without a parable spake He not unto them: and when they were alone, He expounded all things to His disciples. {4:35} And the same day, when the even was come, He saith unto them, Let us pass over unto the other side. {4:36} And when they had sent away the multitude, they took Him even as He was in the ship. And there were also with Him other little ships. {4:37} And there arose a great storm of wind, and the waves beat into the ship, so that it was now full. {4:38} And He was in the hinder part of the ship, asleep on a pillow: and they awake Him, and say unto Him, Master, carest thou not that we perish? {4:39} And He arose, and rebuked the wind, and said unto the sea, Peace, be still. And the wind ceased, and there was a great calm. {4:40} And He said unto them, Why are ye so fearful? how is it that ye have no faith? {4:41} And they feared exceedingly, and said one to another, What manner of man is this, that even the wind and the sea obey Him?{37}

{5:1} And they came over unto the other side of the sea, into the country of the Gadarenes. {5:2} And when He was come out of the ship, immediately there met Him out of the tombs a man with an unclean spirit, {5:3} Who had [his] dwelling among the tombs; and no man could bind him, no, not with chains: {5:4} Because that he had been often bound with fetters and chains, and the chains had been plucked asunder by him, and the fetters broken in pieces: neither could any [man] tame him. {5:5} And always, night and day, he was in the mountains, and in the tombs, crying, and cutting himself with stones. {5:6} But when He saw Jesus afar off, he ran and worshipped Him, {5:7} And cried with a loud voice, and said, What have I to do with thee, Jesus, [thou] Son of the most high God? I adjure thee by

God, that thou torment me not. {5:8} For He said unto him, Come out of the man, [thou] unclean spirit. {5:9} And He asked him, What [is] thy name? And he answered, saying, my name [is] Legion: for we are many. {5:10} And he besought Him much that He would not send them away out of the country. {5:11} Now there was there nigh unto the mountains a great herd of swine feeding. {5:12} And all the devils besought Him, saying, Send us into the swine, that we may enter into them. {5:13} And forthwith Jesus gave them leave. And the unclean spirits went out, and entered into the swine: and the herd ran violently down a steep place into the sea, (they were about two thousand;) and were choked in the sea. {5:14} And they that fed the swine fled, and told [it] in the city, and in the country. And they went out to see what it was that was done. {5:15} And they come to Jesus, and see him that was possessed with the devil, and had the legion, sitting, and clothed, and in his right mind: and they were afraid. {5:16} And they that saw [it] told them how it befell to him that was possessed with the devil, and [also] concerning the swine. {5:17} And they began to pray Him to depart out of their coasts. {5:18} And when He was come into the ship, he that had been possessed with the devil prayed Him that he might be with Him. {5:19} Howbeit Jesus suffered him not, but saith unto him, Go home to thy friends, and tell them how great things the Lord hath done for thee, and hath had compassion on thee. {5:20} And he departed, and began to publish in Decapolis how great things Jesus had done for him: and all [men] did marvel. {5:21} And when Jesus was passed over again by ship unto the other side, much people gathered unto Him: and He was nigh unto the sea. {5:22} And, behold, there cometh one of the rulers of the synagogue, Jairus by name; and when he saw Him, he fell at His feet, {5:23} And besought Him greatly, saying, my little daughter lieth at the point of death: [I pray thee,] come and lay thy hands on her, that she may be healed; and she shall live. {5:24} And [Jesus] went with him; and much people followed Him, and thronged Him. {5:25} And a certain woman, which had an issue of blood twelve years, {5:26} And had suffered many things of many physicians, and had spent all that she had, and was nothing bettered, but rather grew worse, {5:27} When she had heard of Jesus, came in the press behind, and touched His garment. {5:28} For she said, If I may touch but His clothes, I shall be whole. {5:29} And straightway the fountain of her blood was dried up; and she felt in [her] body that she was healed of that plague. {5:30} And Jesus, immediately knowing in himself that virtue had gone out of Him, turned Him about in the press, and said, Who touched my clothes? {5:31} And His disciples said unto Him, Thou seest the multitude thronging thee, and sayest thou, Who touched ME? {5:32} And He looked round about to see her that had done this thing. {5:33} But the woman fearing and trembling, knowing what was done in her, came and fell down before Him, and told Him all the truth. {5:34} And He said unto her, Daughter, thy faith hath made thee whole; go in peace, and be whole of thy plague. {5:35} While He yet spake, there came from the ruler of the synagogue's [house certain] which said, Thy daughter is dead: why troublest thou the Master any further? {5:36} As soon as Jesus heard the word that was spoken, He saith unto the ruler of the synagogue, Be not afraid, only believe. {5:37} And He suffered no man to follow Him, save Peter, and James, and John the brother of James. {5:38} And He cometh to the house of the ruler of the synagogue, and seeth the tumult, and them that wept and wailed greatly. {5:39} And when He was come in, He saith unto them, Why make ye this ado, and weep? the damsel is not dead, but sleepeth. {5:40} And they laughed Him to scorn. But when He had put them all out, He taketh the Father and the mother of the damsel, and them that were with Him, and entereth in where the damsel was lying. {5:41} And **He** took the damsel by the hand, and said unto her, Talitha cumi; which is, being interpreted, Damsel, **I** say unto thee, arise. {5:42} And straightway the damsel arose, and walked; for she was [of the age] of twelve years. And they were astonished with a great astonishment. {5:43} And **He** charged them straitly that no man should know it; and commanded that something should be given her to eat. {68}

{6:1} And **He** went out from thence, and came into **His own** country; and **His** disciples follow **Him**. {6:2} And when the sabbath day was come, **He** began to teach in the synagogue: and many hearing [**Him**] were astonished, saying, From whence hath this [**man**] these things? and what wisdom [is] this which is given unto **Him**, that even such mighty works are wrought by **His** hands? {6:3} Is not this the **carpenter**, the **Son** of Mary, the **brother** of James, and Joses, and of Juda, and Simon? and are not **His** sisters here with us? And they were offended at **Him**. {6:4} But **Jesus** said unto them, A **prophet** is not without honour, but in **His own** country, and among **His own** kin, and in **His own** house. {6:5} And **He** could there do no mighty work, save that **He** laid **His** hands upon a few sick folk, and healed [them.]{6:6} And **He** marvelled because of their unbelief. And **He** went round about the villages, teaching.

{6:7} And **He** called [unto **Him**] the twelve, and began to send them forth by two and two; and gave them power over unclean spirits; {6:8} And commanded them that they should take nothing for [their] journey, save a staff only; no scrip, no bread, no money in [their] purse: {6:9} But [be] shod with sandals; and not put on two coats. {6:10} And **He** said unto them, In what place soever ye enter into an house, there abide till ye depart from that place. {6:11} And whosoever shall not receive you, nor hear you, when ye depart thence, shake off the dust under your feet for a testimony against them. Verily **I** say unto you, It shall be more tolerable for Sodom and Gomorrha in the day of judgment, than for that city. {6:12} And they went out, and preached that men should repent. {6:13} And they cast out many devils, and anointed with oil many that were sick, and healed [them.]{6:14} And king Herod heard [of **Him**;] (for **His** name was spread abroad:) and he said, That John the Baptist was risen from the dead, and therefore mighty works do shew forth themselves in **Him**. {6:15} Others said, That it is Elias. And others said, That it is a prophet, or as one of the prophets. {6:16} But when Herod heard [thereof,] he said, It is John, whom I beheaded: he is risen from the dead. {6:17} For Herod himself had sent forth and laid hold upon John, and bound him in prison for Herodias' sake, his brother Philip's wife: for he had married her. {6:18} For John had said unto Herod, It is not lawful for thee to have thy brother's wife. {6:19} Therefore Herodias had a quarrel against him, and would have killed him; but she could not: {6:20} For Herod feared John, knowing that he was a just man and an holy, and observed him; and when he heard him, he did many things, and heard him gladly. {6:21} And when a convenient day was come, that Herod on his birthday made a supper to his lords, high captains, and chief [estates] of Galilee; {6:22} And when the daughter of the said Herodias came in, and danced, and pleased Herod and them that sat with him, the king said unto the damsel, Ask of ME whatsoever thou wilt, and I will give [it] thee. {6:23} And he sware unto her, Whatsoever thou shalt ask of ME, I will give [it] thee, unto the half of my kingdom. {6:24} And she went forth, and said unto her mother, What shall I ask? And she said, The head of John the Baptist. {6:25} And she came in straightway with haste unto the king, and asked, saying, I will that thou give me by and by in a charger the

head of John the Baptist. {6:26} And the king was exceeding sorry; [yet] for his oath's sake, and for their sakes which sat with him, he would not reject her. {6:27} And immediately the king sent an executioner, and commanded his head to be brought: and he went and beheaded him in the prison, {6:28} And brought his head in a charger, and gave it to the damsel: and the damsel gave it to her mother. {6:29} And when his disciples heard [of it,] they came and took up his corpse, and laid it in a tomb. {6:30} And the apostles gathered themselves together unto **Jesus**, and told **Him** all things, both what they had done, and what they had taught. {6:31} And **He** said unto them, Come ye yourselves apart into a desert place, and rest a while: for there were many coming and going, and they had no leisure so much as to eat. {6:32} And they departed into a desert place by ship privately. {6:33} And the people saw them departing, and many knew **Him**, and ran afoot thither out of all cities, and outwent them, and came together unto **Him**. {6:34} And **Jesus**, when **He** came out, saw much people, and was moved with compassion toward them, because they were as sheep not having a **Shepherd**: and **He** began to teach them many things. {6:35} And when the day was now far spent, **His** disciples came unto **Him**, and said, This is a desert place, and now the time [is] far passed: {6:36} Send them away, that they may go into the country round about, and into the villages, and buy themselves bread: for they have nothing to eat. {6:37} **He** answered and said unto them, Give ye them to eat. And they say unto **Him**, Shall we go and buy two hundred pennyworth of bread, and give them to eat? {6:38} **He** saith unto them, How many loaves have ye? go and see. And when they knew, they say, Five, and two fishes. {6:39} And **He** commanded them to make all sit down by companies upon the green grass. {6:40} And they sat down in ranks, by hundreds, and by fifties. {6:41} And when **He** had taken the five loaves and the two fishes, **He** looked up to heaven, and blessed, and brake the loaves, and gave [them] to **His** disciples to set before them; and the two fishes divided **He** among them all. {6:42} And they did all eat, and were filled. {6:43} And they took up twelve baskets full of the fragments, and of the fishes. {6:44} And they that did eat of the loaves were about five thousand men. {6:45} And straightway **He** constrained **His** disciples to get into the ship, and to go to the other side before unto Bethsaida, while **He** sent away the people. {6:46} And when **He** had sent them away, **He** departed into a mountain to pray. {6:47} And when even was come, the ship was in the midst of the sea, and **He** alone on the land. {6:48} And **He** saw them toiling in rowing; for the wind was contrary unto them: and about the fourth watch of the night **He** cometh unto them, walking upon the sea, and would have passed by them. {6:49} But when they saw **Him** walking upon the sea, they supposed it had been a spirit, and cried out: {6:50} For they all saw **Him**, and were troubled. And immediately **He** talked with them, and saith unto them, Be of good cheer: it is **I**; be not afraid. {6:51} And **He** went up unto them into the ship; and the wind ceased: and they were sore amazed in themselves beyond measure, and wondered. {6:52} For they considered not [the miracle] of the loaves: for their heart was hardened. {6:53} And when they had passed over, they came into the land of Gennesaret, and drew to the shore. {6:54} And when they were come out of the ship, straightway they knew **Him**, {6:55} And ran through that whole region round about, and began to carry about in beds those that were sick, where they heard **He** was. {6:56} And whithersoever **He** entered, into villages, or cities, or country, they laid the sick in the streets, and besought **Him** that they might touch if it were but the border of **His** garment: and as many as touched **Him** were made whole.

{73}

{7:1} Then came together unto **Him** the Pharisees, and certain of the scribes, which came from Jerusalem. {7:2} And when they saw some of **His** disciples eat bread with defiled, that is to say, with unwashen, hands, they found fault. {7:3} For the Pharisees, and all the Jews, except they wash [their] hands oft, eat not, holding the tradition of the elders. {7:4} And [when they come] from the market, except they wash, they eat not. And many other things there be, which they have received to hold, [as] the washing of cups, and pots, brasen vessels, and of tables. {7:5} Then the Pharisees and scribes asked **Him**, Why walk not **thy** disciples according to the tradition of the elders, but eat bread with unwashen hands? {7:6} **He** answered and said unto them, Well hath Esaias prophesied of you hypocrites, as it is written, This people honoureth **ME** with [their] lips, but their heart is far from **ME**. {7:7} Howbeit in vain do they worship **ME**, teaching [for] doctrines the commandments of men. {7:8} For laying aside the commandment of **God**, ye hold the tradition of men, [as] the washing of pots and cups: and many other such like things ye do. {7:9} And **He** said unto them, Full well ye reject the commandment of **God**, that ye may keep your own tradition. {7:10} For Moses said, Honour thy Father and thy mother; and, Whoso curseth Father or mother, let him die the death: {7:11} But ye say, If a man shall say to his Father or mother, [It is] Corban, that is to say, a gift, by whatsoever thou mightest be profited by me; [he shall be free.]{7:12} And ye suffer him no more to do ought for his Father or his mother; {7:13} Making the word of **God** of none effect through your tradition, which ye have delivered: and many such like things do ye.

{7:14} And when **He** had called all the people [unto **Him**,] **He** said unto them, Hearken unto **ME** every one [of you,] and understand: {7:15} There is nothing from without a man, that entering into him can defile him: but the things which come out of him, those are they that defile the man. {7:16} If any man have ears to hear, let him hear. {7:17} And when **He** was entered into the house from the people, **His** disciples asked **Him** concerning the parable. {7:18} And **He** saith unto them, Are ye so without understanding also? Do ye not perceive, that whatsoever thing from without entereth into the man, [it] cannot defile him; {7:19} Because it entereth not into his heart, but into the belly, and goeth out into the draught, purging all meats? {7:20} And **He** said, That which cometh out of the man, that defileth the man. {7:21} For from within, out of the heart of men, proceed evil thoughts, adulteries, fornications, murders, {7:22} Thefts, covetousness, wickedness, deceit, lasciviousness, an evil eye, blasphemy, pride, foolishness: {7:23} All these evil things come from within, and defile the man.

{7:24} And from thence **He** arose, and went into the borders of Tyre and Sidon, and entered into an house, and would have no man know [it:] but **He** could not be hid. {7:25} For a [certain] woman, whose young daughter had an unclean spirit, heard of **Him**, and came and fell at **His** feet: {7:26} The woman was a Greek, a Syrophenician by nation; and she besought **Him** that **He** would cast forth the devil out of her daughter. {7:27} But **Jesus** said unto her, Let the children first be filled: for it is not meet to take the children's bread, and to cast [it] unto the dogs. {7:28} And she answered and said unto **Him**, Yes, **Lord**: yet the dogs under the table eat of the children's crumbs. {7:29} And **He** said unto her, For this saying go thy way; the devil is gone out of thy daughter. {7:30} And when she was come to her house, she found the devil gone out, and her daughter laid upon the bed.

{7:31} And again, departing from the coasts of Tyre and Sidon, **He** came unto the sea of Galilee, through the midst of the coasts of Decapolis. {7:32} And they bring unto **Him** one that was deaf, and had an impediment in his speech; and they beseech **Him** to put **His** hand upon him. {7:33} And **He** took him aside from the multitude, and put **His** fingers into his ears, and **He** spit, and touched his tongue; {7:34} And looking up to heaven, **He** sighed, and saith unto him, Ephphatha, that is, Be opened. {7:35} And straightway his ears were opened, and the string of his tongue was loosed, and he spake plain. {7:36} And **He** charged them that they should tell no man: but the more he charged them, so much the more a great deal they published [it;]{7:37} And were beyond measure astonished, saying, **He** hath done all things well: **He** maketh both the deaf to hear, and the dumb to speak. **{39}**

{8:1} In those days the multitude being very great, and having nothing to eat, **Jesus** called **His** disciples [unto **Him**,] and saith unto them, {8:2} **I** have compassion on the multitude, because they have now been with **ME** three days, and have nothing to eat: {8:3} And if **I** send them away fasting to their own houses, they will faint by the way: for divers of them came from far. {8:4} And **His** disciples answered **Him**, From whence can a man satisfy these [men] with bread here in the wilderness? {8:5} And **He** asked them, How many loaves have ye? And they said, Seven. {8:6} And **He** commanded the people to sit down on the ground: and **He** took the seven loaves, and gave thanks, and brake, and gave to **His** disciples to set before [them;] and they did set [them] before the people. {8:7} And they had a few small fishes: and **He** blessed, and commanded to set them also before [them.]{8:8} So they did eat, and were filled: and they took up of the broken [meat] that was left seven baskets. {8:9} And they that had eaten were about four thousand: and **He** sent them away. {8:10} And straightway **He** entered into a ship with **His** disciples, and came into the parts of Dalmanutha. {8:11} And the Pharisees came forth, and began to question with **Him**, seeking of **Him** a sign from heaven, tempting **Him**. {8:12} And **He** sighed deeply in **His** spirit, and saith, Why doth this generation seek after a sign? verily **I** say unto you, There shall no sign be given unto this generation. {8:13} And **He** left them, and entering into the ship again departed to the other side.

{8:14} Now [the disciples] had forgotten to take bread, neither had they in the ship with them more than one loaf. {8:15} And **He** charged them, saying, Take heed, beware of the leaven of the Pharisees, and [of] the leaven of Herod. {8:16} And they reasoned among themselves, saying, [It is] because we have no bread. {8:17} And when **Jesus** knew [it,] **He** saith unto them, Why reason ye, because ye have no bread? perceive ye not yet, neither understand? have ye your heart yet hardened? {8:18} Having eyes, see ye not? and having ears, hear ye not? and do ye not remember? {8:19} When **I** brake the five loaves among five thousand, how many baskets full of fragments took ye up? They say unto **Him**, Twelve. {8:20} And when the seven among four thousand, how many baskets full of fragments took ye up? And they said, Seven. {8:21} And **He** said unto them, How is it that ye do not understand?

{8:22} And **He** cometh to Bethsaida; and they bring a blind man unto **Him**, and besought **Him** to touch **Him**. {8:23} And **He** took the blind man by the hand, and led him out of the town; and when **He** had spit on his eyes, and put **His** hands upon him, **He** asked him if he saw ought. {8:24} And he looked up, and said, I see men as trees, walking. {8:25} After that **He** put [**His**] hands again upon his eyes, and made him look up: and he was restored, and saw every man clearly. {8:26} And **He** sent him away to his house, saying, Neither go into the town, nor tell [it] to any in the town.

{8:27} And **Jesus** went out, and **His** disciples, into the towns of Caesarea Philippi: and by the way **He** asked **His** disciples, saying unto them, **Whom** do men say that **I am**? {8:28} And they answered, John the Baptist: but some [say,] Elias; and others, One of the prophets. {8:29} And **He** saith unto them, But **whom** say ye that **I am**? And Peter answereth and saith unto **Him**, **Thou** art the **Christ**. {8:30} And **He** charged them that they should tell no man of **Him**. {8:31} And **He** began to teach them, that the **Son of man** must suffer many things, and be rejected of the elders, and [of] the chief priests, and scribes, and be killed, and after three days rise again. {8:32} And **He** spake that saying openly. And Peter took **Him**, and began to rebuke **Him**. {8:33} But when **He** had turned about and looked on **His** disciples, **He** rebuked Peter, saying, Get thee behind **ME**, Satan: for thou savourest not the things that be of **God**, but the things that be of men.

{8:34} And when **He** had called the people [unto **Him**] with **His** disciples also, **He** said unto them, Whosoever will come after **ME**, let him deny himself, and take up his cross, and follow **ME**. {8:35} For whosoever will save **His** life shall lose it; but whosoever shall lose his life for **my** sake and the Gospel's, the same shall save it. {8:36} For what shall it profit a man, if he shall gain the whole world, and lose his own soul? {8:37} Or what shall a man give in exchange for his soul? {8:38} Whosoever therefore shall be ashamed of **ME** and of **my** words in this adulterous and sinful generation; of **Him** also shall the **Son of man** be ashamed, when **He** cometh in the glory of **His Father** with the holy angels. {76}

{9:1} And **He** said unto them, Verily **I** say unto you, That there be some of them that stand here, which shall not taste of death, till they have seen the kingdom of **God** come with power.{9:2} And after six days **Jesus** taketh [with **Him**] Peter, and James, and John, and leadeth them up into an high mountain apart by themselves: and **He** was transfigured before them. {9:3} And **His** raiment became shining, exceeding white as snow; so as no fuller on earth can white them. {9:4} And there appeared unto **them** Elias with Moses: and they were talking with **Jesus**. {9:5} And Peter answered and said to **Jesus**, **Master**, it is good for us to be here: and let us make three tabernacles; one for **thee**, and one for Moses, and one for Elias. {9:6} For he wist not what to say; for they were sore afraid. {9:7} And there was a cloud that overshadowed **them**: and a voice came out of the cloud, saying, This is **my beloved Son**: hear **Him**. {9:8} And suddenly, when they had looked round about, they saw no man any more, save **Jesus** only with themselves. {9:9} And as **they** came down from the mountain, **He** charged them that they should tell no man what things they had seen, till the **Son of man** were risen from the dead. {9:10} And they kept that saying with themselves, questioning one with another what the rising from the dead should mean. {9:11} And they asked **Him**, saying, Why say the scribes that Elias must first come? {9:12} And **He** answered and told them, Elias verily cometh first, and restoreth all things; and how it is written of the **Son of man**, that **He** must suffer many things, and be set at nought. {9:13} But **I** say unto you, That Elias is indeed come, and they have done unto **Him** whatsoever they listed, as it is written of **Him**.
{9:14} And when **He** came to [**His**] disciples, **He** saw a great multitude about them, and the scribes questioning with them. {9:15} And straightway all the people, when

they beheld **Him**, were greatly amazed, and running to [**Him**] saluted **Him**. {9:16} And **He** asked the scribes, What question ye with them? {9:17} And one of the multitude answered and said, **Master**, I have brought unto **thee** my son, which hath a dumb spirit; {9:18} And wheresoever he taketh him, he teareth him: and he foameth, and gnasheth with his teeth, and pineth away: and I spake to **thy** disciples that they should cast him out; and they could not. {9:19} **He** answereth **Him**, and saith, O faithless generation, how long shall **I** be with you? how long shall **I** suffer you? bring him unto **ME**. {9:20} And they brought him unto **Him**: and when **He** saw **Him**, straightway the spirit tare him; and he fell on the ground, and wallowed foaming. {9:21} And **He** asked his Father, How long is it ago since this came unto him? And he said, Of a child. {9:22} And ofttimes it hath cast him into the fire, and into the waters, to destroy him: but if **thou** canst do any thing, have compassion on us, and help us. {9:23} **Jesus** said unto him, If thou canst believe, all things [are] possible to him that believeth. {9:24} And straightway the Father of the child cried out, and said with tears, **Lord**, I believe; help thou mine unbelief. {9:25} When **Jesus** saw that the people came running together, **He** rebuked the foul spirit, saying unto him, [Thou] dumb and deaf spirit, **I** charge thee, come out of him, and enter no more into him. {9:26} And [the spirit] cried, and rent him sore, and came out of him: and he was as one dead; insomuch that many said, he is dead. {9:27} But **Jesus** took him by the hand, and lifted him up; and he arose. {9:28} And when **He** was come into the house, **His** disciples asked **Him** privately, Why could not we cast him out? {9:29} And **He** said unto them, This kind can come forth by nothing, but by prayer and fasting.

{9:30} And they departed thence, and passed through Galilee; and **He** would not that any man should know [it.]{9:31} For **He** taught **His** disciples, and said unto them, The **Son of man** is delivered into the hands of men, and they shall kill **Him**; and after that **He** is killed, **He** shall rise the third day. {9:32} But they understood not that saying, and were afraid to ask **Him**. {9:33} And **He** came to Capernaum: and being in the house **He** asked them, What was it that ye disputed among yourselves by the way? {9:34} But they held their peace: for by the way they had disputed among themselves, who [should be] the greatest. {9:35} And **He** sat down, and called the twelve, and saith unto them, If any man desire to be first, [the same] shall be last of all, and servant of all. {9:36} And **He** took a child, and set him in the midst of them: and when **He** had taken him in **His** arms, **He** said unto them, {9:37} Whosoever shall receive one of such children in **my name**, receiveth **ME**: and whosoever shall receive **ME**, receiveth not **ME**, but **Him** that sent **ME**.

{9:38} And John answered **Him**, saying, **Master**, we saw one casting out devils in **thy name**, and he followeth not **us**: and we forbad him, because he followeth not **us**. {9:39} But **Jesus** said, Forbid him not: for there is no man which shall do a miracle in **my name**, that can lightly speak evil of **ME**. {9:40} For he that is not against **us** is on **our** part. {9:41} For whosoever shall give you a cup of water to drink in **my name**, because ye belong to **Christ**, verily **I** say unto you, he shall not lose his reward. {9:42} And whosoever shall offend one of [these] little ones that believe in **ME**, it is better for him that a millstone were hanged about his neck, and he were cast into the sea. {9:43} And if thy hand offend thee, cut it off: it is better for thee to enter into life maimed, than having two hands to go into hell, into the fire that never shall be quenched: {9:44} Where their worm dieth not, and the fire is not quenched. {9:45} And if thy foot offend thee, cut it off: it is better for thee to enter halt into life, than having two feet to be cast into hell, into the fire that never shall be quenched: {9:46} Where their worm dieth not, and the fire is not quenched. {9:47} And if thine eye offend thee, pluck it out: it is better for thee to enter into the kingdom of **God** with one eye, than having two eyes to be cast into hell fire: {9:48} Where their worm dieth not, and the fire is not quenched. {9:49} For every one shall be salted with fire, and every sacrifice shall be salted with salt. {9:50} Salt [is] good: but if the salt have lost his saltness, wherewith will ye season it? Have salt in yourselves, and have peace one with another. {93}

{10:1} And **He** arose from thence, and cometh into the coasts of Judaea by the farther side of Jordan: and the people resort unto **Him** again; and, as **He** was wont, **He** taught them again.

{10:2} And the Pharisees came to **Him**, and asked **Him**, Is it lawful for a man to put away [his] wife? tempting **Him**. {10:3} And **He** answered and said unto them, What did Moses command you? {10:4} And they said, Moses suffered to write a bill of divorcement, and to put [her] away. {10:5} And **Jesus** answered and said unto them, For the hardness of your heart he wrote you this precept. {10:6} But from the beginning of the creation **God** made them male and female. {10:7} For this cause shall a man leave his Father and mother, and cleave to his wife; {10:8} And they twain shall be one flesh: so then they are no more twain, but one flesh. {10:9} What therefore **God** hath joined together, let not man put asunder. {10:10} And in the house **His** disciples asked **Him** again of the same [matter.]{10:11} And **He** saith unto them, Whosoever shall put away his wife, and marry another, committeth adultery against her. {10:12} And if a woman shall put away her husband, and be married to another, she committeth adultery.{10:13} And they brought young children to **Him**, that **He** should touch them: and [**His**] disciples rebuked those that brought [them.]{10:14} But when **Jesus** saw [it,] **He** was much displeased, and said unto them, Suffer the little children to come unto **ME**, and forbid them not: for of such is the kingdom of **God**. {10:15} Verily **I** say unto you, Whosoever shall not receive the kingdom of **God** as a little child, he shall not enter therein. {10:16} And **He** took them up in **His** arms, put [**His**] hands upon them, and blessed them.

{10:17} And when **He** was gone forth into the way, there came one running, and kneeled to **Him**, and asked **Him**, **Good Master**, what shall **I** do that **I** may inherit eternal life? {10:18} And **Jesus** said unto him, Why callest thou **ME** good? [there is] none good but one, [that is,] **God**. {10:19} Thou knowest the commandments, Do not commit adultery, Do not kill, Do not steal, Do not bear false witness, Defraud not, Honour thy **Father** and mother. {10:20} And he answered and said unto **Him**, **Master**, all these have I observed from my youth. {10:21} Then **Jesus** beholding him loved **Him**, and said unto him, One thing thou lackest: go thy way, sell whatsoever thou hast, and give to the poor, and thou shalt have treasure in heaven: and come, take up the cross, and follow **ME**. {10:22} And he was sad at that saying, and went away grieved: for he had great possessions.

{10:23} And **Jesus** looked round about, and saith unto **His** disciples, How hardly shall they that have riches enter into the kingdom of **God**! {10:24} And the disciples were astonished at **His** words. But **Jesus** answereth again, and saith unto them, Children, how hard is it for them that trust in riches to enter into the kingdom of **God**! {10:25} It is easier for a camel to go through the eye of a needle, than for a rich man to enter into the kingdom of **God**. {10:26} And they were astonished out of measure, saying among themselves, Who then can be saved? {10:27} And **Jesus** looking upon them saith, With men [it is] impossible, but not with **God**: for with **God** all things are possible.

{10:28} Then Peter began to say unto **Him**, Lo, we have left all, and have followed **thee**. {10:29} And **Jesus** answered and said, Verily **I** say unto you, There is no man that hath left house, or brethren, or sisters, or Father, or mother, or wife, or children, or lands, for **my** sake, and the Gospel's, {10:30} But he shall receive an hundredfold now in this time, houses, and brethren, and sisters, and mothers, and children, and lands, with persecutions; and in the world to come eternal life. {10:31} But many [that are] first shall be last; and the last first.

{10:32} And they were in the way going up to Jerusalem; and **Jesus** went before them: and they were amazed; and as they followed, they were afraid. And **He** took again the twelve, and began to tell them what things should happen unto **Him**, {10:33} [Saying,] Behold, we go up to Jerusalem; and the **Son of man** shall be delivered unto the chief priests, and unto the scribes; and they shall condemn **Him** to death, and shall deliver **Him** to the Gentiles: {10:34} And they shall mock **Him**, and shall scourge **Him**, and shall spit upon **Him**, and shall kill **Him**: and the third day **He** shall rise again.

{10:35} And James and John, the sons of Zebedee, come unto **Him**, saying, **Master**, we would that **thou** shouldest do for us whatsoever we shall desire. {10:36} And **He** said unto them, What would ye that **I** should do for you? {10:37} They said unto **Him**, Grant unto us that we may sit, one on **thy** right hand, and the other on **thy** left hand, in **thy** glory. {10:38} But **Jesus** said unto them, Ye know not what ye ask: can ye drink of the cup that **I** drink of? and be baptized with the baptism that **I am** baptized with? {10:39} And they said unto **Him**, We can. And **Jesus** said unto them, Ye shall indeed drink of the cup that **I** drink of; and with the baptism that **I am** baptized withal shall ye be baptized: {10:40} But to sit on **my** right hand and on **my** left hand is not mine to give; but [it shall be given to them] for whom it is prepared. {10:41} And when the ten heard [it,] they began to be much displeased with James and John. {10:42} But **Jesus** called them [to **Him**,] and saith unto them, Ye know that they which are accounted to rule over the Gentiles exercise lordship over them; and their great ones exercise authority upon them. {10:43} But so shall it not be among you: but whosoever will be great among you, shall be your minister: {10:44} And whosoever of you will be the chiefest, shall be servant of all. {10:45} For even the **Son of man** came not to be ministered unto, but to minister, and to give **His** life a ransom for many.

{10:46} And they came to Jericho: and as **He** went out of Jericho with **His** disciples and a great number of people, blind Bartimaeus, the **Son** of Timaeus, sat by the highway side begging. {10:47} And when he heard that it was **Jesus of Nazareth**, he began to cry out, and say, **Jesus**, [thou] **Son of David**, have mercy on me. {10:48} And many charged him that he should hold his peace: but he cried the more a great deal, [**Thou**] **Son of David**, have mercy on me. {10:49} And **Jesus** stood still, and commanded him to be called. And they call the blind man, saying unto him, Be of good comfort, rise; **He** calleth thee. {10:50} And he, casting away his garment, rose, and came to **Jesus**. {10:51} And

Jesus answered and said unto him, What wilt thou that **I** should do unto thee? The blind man said unto **Him**, **Lord**, that I might receive my sight. {10:52} And **Jesus** said unto him, Go thy way; thy faith hath made thee whole. And immediately he received his sight, and followed **Jesus** in the way. {96}

{11:1} And when they came nigh to Jerusalem, unto Bethphage and Bethany, at the mount of Olives, **He** sendeth forth two of **His** disciples, {11:2} And saith unto them, Go your way into the village over against you: and as soon as ye be entered into it, ye shall find a colt tied, whereon never man sat; loose him, and bring [him.]{11:3} And if any man say unto you, Why do ye this? say ye that the **Lord** hath need of him; and straightway he will send him hither. {11:4} And they went their way, and found the colt tied by the door without in a place where two ways met; and they loose him. {11:5} And certain of them that stood there said unto them, What do ye, loosing the colt? {11:6} And they said unto them even as **Jesus** had commanded: and they let them go. {11:7} And they brought the colt to **Jesus**, and cast their garments on him; and **He** sat upon him. {11:8} And many spread their garments in the way: and others cut down branches off the trees, and strawed [them] in the way. {11:9} And they that went before, and they that followed, cried, saying, Hosanna; Blessed [is] **He** that cometh in the name of the **Lord**: {11:10} Blessed [be] the kingdom of our **Father** David, that cometh in the **name** of the **Lord**: Hosanna in the highest. {11:11} And **Jesus** entered into Jerusalem, and into the temple: and when **He** had looked round about upon all things, and now the eventide was come, **He** went out unto Bethany with the twelve.

{11:12} And on the morrow, when they were come from Bethany, **He** was hungry: {11:13} And seeing a fig tree afar off having leaves, **He** came, if haply **He** might find any thing thereon: and when **He** came to it, **He** found nothing but leaves; for the time of figs was not [yet.]{11:14} And **Jesus** answered and said unto it, No man eat fruit of thee hereafter for ever. And **His** disciples heard [it.

]{11:15} And they come to Jerusalem: and **Jesus** went into the temple, and began to cast out them that sold and bought in the temple, and overthrew the tables of the moneychangers, and the seats of them that sold doves; {11:16} And would not suffer that any man should carry [any] vessel through the temple. {11:17} And **He** taught, saying unto them, Is it not written, **my** house shall be called of all nations the house of prayer? but ye have made it a den of thieves. {11:18} And the scribes and chief priests heard [it,] and sought how they might destroy **Him**: for they feared **Him**, because all the people was astonished at **His** doctrine. {11:19} And when even was come, **He** went out of the city.

{11:20} And in the morning, as they passed by, they saw the fig tree dried up from the roots. {11:21} And Peter calling to remembrance saith unto **Him**, **Master**, behold, the fig tree which **thou** cursedst is withered away. {11:22} And **Jesus** answering saith unto them, Have faith in **God**. {11:23} For verily **I** say unto you, That whosoever shall say unto this mountain, Be thou removed, and be thou cast into the sea; and shall not doubt in his heart, but shall believe that those things which he saith shall come to pass; he shall have whatsoever he saith. {11:24} Therefore **I** say unto you, What things soever ye desire, when ye pray, believe that ye receive [them,] and ye shall have [them.]{11:25} And when ye stand praying, forgive, if ye have ought against any: that your **Father** also which is in heaven may forgive you your trespasses. {11:26} But if ye do not forgive,

neither will your **Father** which is in heaven forgive your trespasses.

{11:27} And they come again to Jerusalem: and as **He** was walking in the temple, there come to **Him** the chief priests, and the scribes, and the elders, {11:28} And say unto **Him**, By what authority doest **thou** these things? and who gave **thee** this authority to do these things? {11:29} And **Jesus** answered and said unto them, **I** will also ask of you one question, and answer **ME**, and **I** will tell you by what authority **I** do these things. {11:30} The baptism of John, was [it] from heaven, or of men? answer **ME**. {11:31} And they reasoned with themselves, saying, If we shall say, From heaven; **He** will say, Why then did ye not believe **Him**? {11:32} But if we shall say, Of men; they feared the people: for all [men] counted John, that **He** was a prophet indeed. {11:33} And they answered and said unto **Jesus**, We cannot tell. And **Jesus** answering saith unto them, Neither do **I** tell you by what authority **I** do these things. {49}

{12:1} And **He** began to speak unto them by parables. A [certain] man planted a vineyard, and set an hedge about [it,] and digged [a place for] the winefat, and built a tower, and let it out to husbandmen, and went into a far country. {12:2} And at the season **He** sent to the husbandmen a servant, that **He** might receive from the husbandmen of the fruit of the vineyard. {12:3} And they caught [him,] and beat him, and sent [him] away empty. {12:4} And again **He** sent unto them another servant; and at him they cast stones, and wounded [him] in the head, and sent [him] away shamefully handled. {12:5} And again **He** sent another; and him they killed, and many others; beating some, and killing some. {12:6} Having yet therefore one **Son**, **His** **wellbeloved**, **He** sent **Him** also last unto them, saying, They will reverence **my Son**. {12:7} But those husbandmen said among themselves, This is the **heir**; come, let us kill **Him**, and the inheritance shall be ours. {12:8} And they took **Him**, and killed [**Him**,] and cast [**Him**] out of the vineyard. {12:9} What shall therefore the **Lord** of the vineyard do? **He** will come and destroy the husbandmen, and will give the vineyard unto others. {12:10} And have ye not read this scripture; The **stone** which the builders rejected is become the **head of the corner**: {12:11} This was the **Lord**'s doing, and it is marvellous in our eyes? {12:12} And they sought to lay hold on **Him**, but feared the people: for they knew that **He** had spoken the parable against them: and they left **Him**, and went their way.

{12:13} And they send unto **Him** certain of the Pharisees and of the Herodians, to catch **Him** in [**His**] words. {12:14} And when they were come, they say unto **Him**, **Master**, we know that **thou** art true, and carest for no man: for **thou** regardest not the person of men, but teachest the way of **God** in truth: Is it lawful to give tribute to Caesar, or not? {12:15} Shall we give, or shall we not give? But **He**, knowing their hypocrisy, said unto them, Why tempt ye **ME**? bring **ME** a penny, that **I** may see [it.]{12:16} And they brought [it.] And **He** saith unto them, Whose [is] this image and superscription? And they said unto **Him**, Caesar's. {12:17} And **Jesus** answering said unto them, Render to Caesar the things that are Caesar's, and to **God** the things that are **God**'s. And they marvelled at **Him**.

{12:18} Then come unto **Him** the Sadducees, which say there is no resurrection; and they asked **Him**, saying, {12:19} **Master**, Moses wrote unto us, If a man's brother die, and leave [his] wife [behind him,] and leave no children, that his brother should take his wife, and raise up seed unto his brother. {12:20} Now there were seven brethren: and the first took a wife, and dying left no seed. {12:21} And the second took her, and died, neither left he any seed: and the third likewise. {12:22} And the seven had her, and left no seed: last of all the woman died also. {12:23} In the resurrection therefore, when they shall rise, whose wife shall she be of them? for the seven had her to wife. {12:24} And Jesus answering said unto them, Do ye not therefore err, because ye know not the scriptures, neither the power of God? {12:25} For when they shall rise from the dead, they neither marry, nor are given in marriage; but are as the angels which are in heaven. {12:26} And as touching the dead, that they rise: have ye not read in the book of Moses, how in the bush God spake unto Him, saying, I [am] the God of Abraham, and the God of Isaac, and the God of Jacob? {12:27} He is not the God of the dead, but the God of the living: ye therefore do greatly err.

{12:28} And one of the scribes came, and having heard them reasoning together, and perceiving that He had answered them well, asked Him, Which is the first commandment of all? {12:29} And Jesus answered him, The first of all the commandments [is,] Hear, O Israel; The Lord our God is one Lord: {12:30} And thou shalt love the Lord thy God with all thy heart, and with all thy soul, and with all thy mind, and with all thy strength: this is the first commandment. {12:31} And the second [is] like, [namely] this, Thou shalt love thy neighbour as thyself. There is none other commandment greater than these. {12:32} And the scribe said unto Him, Well, Master, thou hast said the truth: for there is one God; and there is none other but He: {12:33} And to love Him with all the heart, and with all the understanding, and with all the soul, and with all the strength, and to love [his] neighbour as himself, is more than all whole burnt offerings and sacrifices. {12:34} And when Jesus saw that he answered discreetly, He said unto him, Thou art not far from the kingdom of God. And no man after that durst ask Him [any question.

]{12:35} And Jesus answered and said, while He taught in the temple, How say the scribes that Christ is the Son of David? {12:36} For David himself said by the Holy Ghost, The Lord said to my Lord, Sit thou on my right hand, till I make thine enemies thy footstool. {12:37} David therefore himself calleth Him Lord; and whence is He [then] His Son? And the common people heard Him gladly.

{12:38} And He said unto them in His doctrine, Beware of the scribes, which love to go in long clothing, and [love] salutations in the marketplaces, {12:39} And the chief seats in the synagogues, and the uppermost rooms at feasts: {12:40} Which devour widows' houses, and for a pretence make long prayers: these shall receive greater damnation.

{12:41} And Jesus sat over against the treasury, and beheld how the people cast money into the treasury: and many that were rich cast in much. {12:42} And there came a certain poor widow, and she threw in two mites, which make a farthing. {12:43} And He called [unto Him] His disciples, and saith unto them, Verily I say unto you, That this poor widow hath cast more in, than all they which have cast into the treasury: {12:44} For all [they] did cast in of their abundance; but she of her want did cast in all that she had, [even] all her living. {73}

{13:1} And as He went out of the temple, one of His disciples saith unto Him, Master, see what manner of stones and what buildings [are here!]{13:2} And Jesus answering said unto him, Seest thou these great buildings? there shall not be left one stone upon another, that shall not be thrown

down. {13:3} And as He sat upon the mount of Olives over against the temple, Peter and James and John and Andrew asked Him privately, {13:4} Tell us, when shall these things be? and what [shall be] the sign when all these things shall be fulfilled? {13:5} And Jesus answering them began to say, Take heed lest any [man] deceive you: {13:6} For many shall come in my name, saying, I am [Christ;] and shall deceive many. {13:7} And when ye shall hear of wars and rumours of wars, be ye not troubled: for [such things] must needs be; but the end [shall] not [be] yet. {13:8} For nation shall rise against nation, and kingdom against kingdom: and there shall be earthquakes in divers places, and there shall be famines and troubles: these [are] the beginnings of sorrows.

{13:9} But take heed to yourselves: for they shall deliver you up to councils; and in the synagogues ye shall be beaten: and ye shall be brought before rulers and kings for my sake, for a testimony against them. {13:10} And the Gospel must first be published among all nations. {13:11} But when they shall lead [you,] and deliver you up, take no thought beforehand what ye shall speak, neither do ye premeditate: but whatsoever shall be given you in that hour, that speak ye: for it is not ye that speak, but the Holy Ghost. {13:12} Now the brother shall betray the brother to death, and the Father the Son; and children shall rise up against [their] parents, and shall cause them to be put to death. {13:13} And ye shall be hated of all [men] for my name's sake: but he that shall endure unto the end, the same shall be saved.

{13:14} But when ye shall see the abomination of desolation, spoken of by Daniel the prophet, standing where it ought not, (let him that readeth understand,) then let them that be in Judaea flee to the mountains: {13:15} And let him that is on the housetop not go down into the house, neither enter [therein,] to take any thing out of his house: {13:16} And let him that is in the field not turn back again for to take up his garment. {13:17} But woe to them that are with child, and to them that give suck in those days! {13:18} And pray ye that your flight be not in the winter. {13:19} For [in] those days shall be affliction, such as was not from the beginning of the creation which God created unto this time, neither shall be. {13:20} And except that the Lord had shortened those days, no flesh should be saved: but for the elect's sake, whom He hath chosen, He hath shortened the days. {13:21} And then if any man shall say to you, Lo, here [is] Christ; or, lo, [He is] there; believe [him] not: {13:22} For false Christs and false prophets shall rise, and shall shew signs and wonders, to seduce, if [it were] possible, even the elect. {13:23} But take ye heed: behold, I have foretold you all things.

{13:24} But in those days, after that tribulation, the sun shall be darkened, and the moon shall not give her light, {13:25} And the stars of heaven shall fall, and the powers that are in heaven shall be shaken. {13:26} And then shall they see the Son of man coming in the clouds with great power and glory. {13:27} And then shall He send His angels, and shall gather together His elect from the four winds, from the uttermost part of the earth to the uttermost part of heaven. {13:28} Now learn a parable of the fig tree; When her branch is yet tender, and putteth forth leaves, ye know that summer is near: {13:29} So ye in like manner, when ye shall see these things come to pass, know that it is nigh, [even] at the doors. {13:30} Verily I say unto you, that this generation shall not pass, till all these things be done. {13:31} Heaven and earth shall pass away: but my words shall not pass away.

{13:32} But of that day and [that] hour knoweth no man, no, not the angels which are in heaven, neither the **Son**, but the **Father**. {13:33} Take ye heed, watch and pray: for ye know not when the time is. {13:34} [For the **Son of man** is] as a man taking a far journey, who left **His** house, and gave authority to **His** servants, and to every man his work, and commanded the porter to watch. {13:35} Watch ye therefore: for ye know not when the **master** of the house cometh, at even, or at midnight, or at the cockcrowing, or in the morning: {13:36} Lest coming suddenly **He** find you sleeping. {13:37} And what **I** say unto you **I** say unto all, Watch. **{30}**

{14:1} After two days was [the feast of] the passover, and of unleavened bread: and the chief priests and the scribes sought how they might take **Him** by craft, and put [**Him**] to death. {14:2} But they said, Not on the feast [day,] lest there be an uproar of the people.

{14:3} And being in Bethany in the house of Simon the leper, as **He** sat at meat, there came a woman having an alabaster box of ointment of spikenard very precious; and she brake the box, and poured [it] on **His** head. {14:4} And there were some that had indignation within themselves, and said, Why was this waste of the ointment made? {14:5} For it might have been sold for more than three hundred pence, and have been given to the poor. And they murmured against her. {14:6} And **Jesus** said, Let her alone; why trouble ye her? she hath wrought a good work on **ME**. {14:7} For ye have the poor with you always, and whensoever ye will ye may do them good: but **ME** ye have not always. {14:8} She hath done what she could: she is come aforehand to anoint **my body** to the burying. {14:9} Verily **I** say unto you, Wheresoever this **Gospel** shall be preached throughout the whole world, [this] also that she hath done shall be spoken of for a memorial of her.

{14:10} And Judas Iscariot, one of the twelve, went unto the chief priests, to betray **Him** unto them. {14:11} And when they heard [it,] they were glad, and promised to give him money. And he sought how he might conveniently betray **Him**.

{14:12} And the first day of unleavened bread, when they killed the **passover**, **His** disciples said unto **Him**, Where wilt thou that we go and prepare that thou mayest eat the **passover**? {14:13} And **He** sendeth forth two of **His** disciples, and saith unto them, Go ye into the city, and there shall meet you a man bearing a pitcher of water: follow him. {14:14} And wheresoever he shall go in, say ye to the goodman of the house, The **Master** saith, Where is the guestchamber, where **I** shall eat the **passover** with **my** disciples? {14:15} And he will shew you a large upper room furnished [and] prepared: there make ready for **us**. {14:16} And **His** disciples went forth, and came into the city, and found as **He** had said unto them: and they made ready the **passover**. {14:17} And in the evening **He** cometh with the twelve. {14:18} And as they sat and did eat, **Jesus** said, Verily **I** say unto you, One of you which eateth with **ME** shall betray **ME**. {14:19} And they began to be sorrowful, and to say unto **Him** one by one, [Is] it **I**? and another [said, Is] it **I**? {14:20} And **He** answered and said unto them, [It is] one of the twelve, that dippeth with **ME** in the dish. {14:21} The **Son of man** indeed goeth, as it is written of **Him**: but woe to that man by **whom** the **Son of man** is betrayed! good were it for that man if he had never been born.

{14:22} And as they did eat, **Jesus** took bread, and

blessed, and brake [it,] and gave to them, and said, Take, eat: this is **my body**. {14:23} And **He** took the cup, and when **He** had given thanks, **He** gave [it] to them: and they all drank of it. {14:24} And **He** said unto them, This is **my blood** of the new testament, which is shed for many. {14:25} Verily **I** say unto you, **I** will drink no more of the fruit of the vine, until that day that **I** drink it new in the kingdom of **God**.

{14:26} And when they had sung an hymn, they went out into the mount of Olives. {14:27} And **Jesus** saith unto them, All ye shall be offended because of **ME** this night: for it is written, **I** will smite the **Shepherd**, and the sheep shall be scattered. {14:28} But after that **I am** risen, **I** will go before you into Galilee. {14:29} But Peter said unto **Him**, Although all shall be offended, yet [will] not **I**. {14:30} And **Jesus** saith unto him, Verily **I** say unto thee, That this day, [even] in this night, before the cock crow twice, thou shalt deny **ME** thrice. {14:31} But he spake the more vehemently, If **I** should die with thee, **I** will not deny thee in any wise. Likewise also said they all. {14:32} And they came to a place which was named Gethsemane: and **He** saith to **His** disciples, Sit ye here, while **I** shall pray. {14:33} And **He** taketh with **Him** Peter and James and John, and began to be sore amazed, and to be very heavy; {14:34} And saith unto them, **my soul** is exceeding sorrowful unto death: tarry ye here, and watch. {14:35} And **He** went forward a little, and fell on the ground, and prayed that, if it were possible, the hour might pass from **Him**. {14:36} And **He** said, Abba, **Father**, all things [are] possible unto thee; take away this cup from **ME**: nevertheless not what **I** will, but what thou wilt. {14:37} And **He** cometh, and findeth them sleeping, and saith unto Peter, Simon, sleepest thou? couldest not thou watch one hour? {14:38} Watch ye and pray, lest ye enter into temptation. The spirit truly [is] ready, but the flesh [is] weak. {14:39} And again **He** went away, and prayed, and spake the same words. {14:40} And when **He** returned, **He** found them asleep again, (for their eyes were heavy,) neither wist they what to answer **Him**. {14:41} And **He** cometh the third time, and saith unto them, Sleep on now, and take [your] rest: it is enough, the hour is come; behold, the **Son of man** is betrayed into the hands of sinners. {14:42} Rise up, let us go; lo, **He** that betrayeth **ME** is at hand.

{14:43} And immediately, while **He** yet spake, cometh Judas, one of the twelve, and with him a great multitude with swords and staves, from the chief priest and the scribes and the elders. {14:44} And he that betrayed **Him** had given them a token, saying, **Whomsoever** I shall kiss, that same is **He**; take **Him**, and lead [**Him**] away safely. {14:45} And as soon as he was come, he goeth straightway to **Him**, and saith, **Master**, **master**; and kissed **Him**. {14:46} And they laid their hands on **Him**, and took **Him**. {14:47} And one of them that stood by drew a sword, and smote a servant of the high priest, and cut off his ear. {14:48} And **Jesus** answered and said unto them, Are ye come out, as against a thief, with swords and [with] staves to take **ME**? {14:49} **I** was daily with you in the temple teaching, and ye took **ME** not: but the scriptures must be fulfilled. {14:50} And they all forsook **Him**, and fled. {14:51} And there followed **Him** a certain young man, having a linen cloth cast about [his] naked [body;] and the young men laid hold on him: {14:52} And he left the linen cloth, and fled from them naked.

{14:53} And they led Jesus away to the high priest: and with him were assembled all the chief priests and the elders and the scribes. {14:54} And Peter followed Him afar off, even into the palace of the high priest: and he sat with the servants, and warmed himself at the fire. {14:55} And the chief priests and all the council sought for witness against Jesus to put Him to death; and found none. {14:56} For many bare false witness against Him, but their witness agreed not together. {14:57} And there arose certain, and bare false witness against Him, saying, {14:58} We heard Him say, I will destroy this temple that is made with hands, and within three days I will build another made without hands. {14:59} But neither so did their witness agree together. {14:60} And the high priest stood up in the midst, and asked Jesus, saying, Answerest thou nothing? what [is it which] these witness against thee? {14:61} But He held His peace, and answered nothing. Again the high priest asked Him, and said unto Him, Art thou the Christ, the Son of the Blessed? {14:62} And Jesus said, I am: and ye shall see the Son of man sitting on the right hand of power, and coming in the clouds of heaven. {14:63} Then the high priest rent his clothes, and saith, What need we any further witnesses? {14:64} Ye have heard the blasphemy: what think ye? And they all condemned Him to be guilty of death. {14:65} And some began to spit on Him, and to cover His face, and to buffet Him, and to say unto Him, Prophesy: and the servants did strike Him with the palms of their hands.

{14:66} And as Peter was beneath in the palace, there cometh one of the maids of the high priest: {14:67} And when she saw Peter warming himself, she looked upon him, and said, And thou also wast with Jesus of Nazareth. {14:68} But he denied, saying, I know not, neither understand I what thou sayest. And he went out into the porch; and the cock crew. {14:69} And a maid saw him again, and began to say to them that stood by, This is [one] of them. {14:70} And he denied it again. And a little after, they that stood by said again to Peter, Surely thou art [one] of them: for thou art a Galilaean, and thy speech agreeth [thereto.]{14:71} But he began to curse and to swear, [saying,] I know not this man of whom ye speak. {14:72} And the second time the cock crew. And Peter called to mind the word that Jesus said unto him, Before the cock crow twice, thou shalt deny ME thrice. And when he thought thereon, he wept. {128}

{15:1} And straightway in the morning the chief priests held a consultation with the elders and scribes and the whole council, and bound Jesus, and carried [Him] away, and delivered [Him] to Pilate. {15:2} And Pilate asked Him, Art thou the King of the Jews? And He answering said unto him, Thou sayest [it.]{15:3} And the chief priests accused Him of many things: but He answered nothing. {15:4} And Pilate asked Him again, saying, Answerest thou nothing? behold how many things they witness against thee. {15:5} But Jesus yet answered nothing; so that Pilate marvelled. {15:6} Now at [that] feast he released unto them one prisoner, whomsoever they desired. {15:7} And there was [one] named Barabbas, [which lay] bound with them that had made insurrection with him, who had committed murder in the insurrection. {15:8} And the multitude crying aloud began to desire [him to do] as he had ever done unto them. {15:9} But Pilate answered them, saying, Will ye that I release unto you the King of the Jews? {15:10} For he knew that the chief priests had delivered Him for envy. {15:11} But the chief priests moved the people, that he should rather release Barabbas unto them. {15:12} And Pilate answered and said again unto them, What will ye then that I shall do [unto Him] whom ye call the King of the Jews? {15:13} And they cried out again, Crucify Him. {15:14} Then Pilate said unto them, Why, what evil hath He

done? And they cried out the more exceedingly, Crucify Him.

{15:15} And [so] Pilate, willing to content the people, released Barabbas unto them, and delivered Jesus, when he had scourged [Him,] to be crucified. {15:16} And the soldiers led Him away into the hall, called Praetorium; and they call together the whole band. {15:17} And they clothed Him with purple, and platted a crown of thorns, and put it about His [head,]{15:18} And began to salute Him, Hail, King of the Jews! {15:19} And they smote Him on the head with a reed, and did spit upon Him, and bowing [their] knees worshipped Him. {15:20} And when they had mocked Him, they took off the purple from Him, and put His own clothes on Him, and led Him out to crucify Him. {15:21} And they compel one Simon a Cyrenian, who passed by, coming out of the country, the Father of Alexander and Rufus, to bear His cross. {15:22} And they bring Him unto the place Golgotha, which is, being interpreted, The place of a skull. {15:23} And they gave Him to drink wine mingled with myrrh: but He received [it] not. {15:24} And when they had crucified Him, they parted His garments, casting lots upon them, what every man should take. {15:25} And it was the third hour, and they crucified Him. {15:26} And the superscription of His accusation was written over, THE KING OF THE JEWS. {15:27} And with Him they crucify two thieves; the one on His right hand, and the other on His left. {15:28} And the scripture was fulfilled, which saith, And He was numbered with the transgressors. {15:29} And they that passed by railed on Him, wagging their heads, and saying, Ah, thou that destroyest the temple, and buildest [it] in three days, {15:30} Save thyself, and come down from the cross. {15:31} Likewise also the chief priests mocking said among themselves with the scribes, He saved others; himself He cannot save. {15:32} Let Christ the King of Israel descend now from the cross, that we may see and believe. And they that were crucified with Him reviled Him. {15:33} And when the sixth hour was come, there was darkness over the whole land until the ninth hour. {15:34} And at the ninth hour Jesus cried with a loud voice, saying, Eloi, Eloi, lama sabachthani? which is, being interpreted, my God, my God, why hast thou forsaken ME? {15:35} And some of them that stood by, when they heard [it,] said, Behold, He calleth Elias. {15:36} And one ran and filled a spunge full of vinegar, and put [it] on a reed, and gave Him to drink, saying, Let alone; let us see whether Elias will come to take Him down. {15:37} And Jesus cried with a loud voice, and gave up the ghost. {15:38} And the veil of the temple was rent in twain from the top to the bottom.

{15:39} And when the centurion, which stood over against Him, saw that He so cried out, and gave up the ghost, he said, Truly this man was the Son of God. {15:40} There were also women looking on afar off: among whom was Mary Magdalene, and Mary the mother of James the less and of Joses, and Salome; {15:41} (Who also, when He was in Galilee, followed Him, and ministered unto Him;) and many other women which came up with Him unto Jerusalem.{15:42} And now when the even was come, because it was the preparation, that is, the day before the sabbath, {15:43} Joseph of Arimathaea, an honourable counsellor, which also waited for the kingdom of God, came, and went in boldly unto Pilate, and craved the body of Jesus. {15:44} And Pilate marvelled if He were already dead: and calling [unto him] the centurion, he asked him whether He had been any while dead. {15:45} And when he knew [it] of the centurion, he gave the body to Joseph. {15:46} And he bought fine linen, and took Him down, and wrapped Him in the linen, and laid **Him** in a sepulchre which was hewn out of a rock, and rolled a stone unto the door of the sepulchre. {15:47} And Mary Magdalene and Mary [the mother] of Joses beheld where **He** was laid. {83}

{16:1} And when the sabbath was past, Mary Magdalene, and Mary the [mother] of James, and Salome, had bought sweet spices, that they might come and anoint **Him**. {16:2} And very early in the morning the first [day] of the week, they came unto the sepulchre at the rising of the sun. {16:3} And they said among themselves, Who shall roll us away the stone from the door of the sepulchre? {16:4} And when they looked, they saw that the stone was rolled away: for it was very great. {16:5} And entering into the sepulchre, they saw a young man sitting on the right side, clothed in a long white garment; and they were affrighted. {16:6} And **He** saith unto them, Be not affrighted: Ye seek **Jesus of Nazareth,** which was crucified: **He** is risen; **He** is not here: behold the place where they laid **Him**. {16:7} But go your way, tell **His** disciples and Peter that **He** goeth before you into Galilee: there shall ye see **Him**, as **He** said unto you. {16:8} And they went out quickly, and fled from the sepulchre; for they trembled and were amazed: neither said they any thing to any [man;] for they were afraid.

{16:9} Now when [**Jesus**] was risen early the first [day] of the week, **He** appeared first to Mary Magdalene, out of whom **He** had cast seven devils. {16:10} [And] she went and told them that had been with **Him**, as they mourned and wept. {16:11} And they, when they had heard that **He** was alive, and had been seen of her, believed not.

{16:12} After that **He** appeared in another form unto two of them, as they walked, and went into the country. {16:13} And they went and told [it] unto the residue: neither believed they them.

{16:14} Afterward **He** appeared unto the eleven as they sat at meat, and upbraided them with their unbelief and hardness of heart, because they believed not them which had seen **Him** after **He** was risen. {16:15} And **He** said unto them, Go ye into all the world, and preach the Gospel to every creature. {16:16} he that believeth and is baptized shall be saved; but he that believeth not shall be damned. {16:17} And these signs shall follow them that believe; In **my** name shall they cast out devils; they shall speak with new tongues; {16:18} They shall take up serpents; and if they drink any deadly thing, it shall not hurt them; they shall lay hands on the sick, and they shall recover.

{16:19} So then after the **Lord** had spoken unto them, **He** was received up into heaven, and sat on the right hand of **God**. {16:20} And they went forth, and preached every where, the **Lord** working with [them,] and confirming the word with signs following. Amen.
{24}

The Gospel According to St. Luke **TOTAL 1496**

{1:1} Forasmuch as many have taken in hand to set forth in order a declaration of those things which are most surely believed among us, {1:2} Even as they delivered them unto us, which from the beginning were eyewitnesses, and ministers of the word; {1:3} It seemed good to me also, having had perfect understanding of all things from the very first, to write unto thee in order, most excellent Theophilus, {1:4} That thou mightest know the certainty of those things, wherein thou hast been instructed.

{1:5} There was in the days of Herod, the king of Judaea, a certain priest named Zacharias, of the course of Abia: and his wife [was] of the daughters of Aaron, and her name [was] Elisabeth. {1:6} And they were both righteous before **God**, walking in all the commandments and ordinances of the **Lord** blameless. {1:7} And they had no child, because that Elisabeth was barren, and they both were [now] well stricken in years. {1:8} And it came to pass, that while he executed the priest's office before **God** in the order of his course, {1:9} According to the custom of the priest's office, his lot was to burn incense when he went into the temple of the **Lord**. {1:10} And the whole multitude of the people were praying without at the time of incense. {1:11} And there appeared unto him an angel of the **Lord** standing on the right side of the altar of incense. {1:12} And when Zacharias saw [**Him**,] he was troubled, and fear fell upon him. {1:13} But the angel said unto him, Fear not, Zacharias: for thy prayer is heard; and thy wife Elisabeth shall bear thee a Son, and thou shalt call his name John. {1:14} And thou shalt have joy and gladness; and many shall rejoice at his birth. {1:15} For he shall be great in the sight of the **Lord**, and shall drink neither wine nor strong drink; and he shall be filled with the **Holy Ghost**, even from his mother's womb. {1:16} And many of the children of Israel shall he turn to the **Lord their God**. {1:17} And he shall go before **Him** in the spirit and power of Elias, to turn the hearts of the **Father**s to the children, and the disobedient to the wisdom of the just; to make ready a people prepared for the **Lord**. {1:18} And Zacharias said unto the angel, Whereby shall I know this? for I am an old man, and my wife well stricken in years. {1:19} And the angel answering said unto him, **I am** Gabriel, that stand in the presence of **God**; and **am** sent to speak unto thee, and to shew thee these glad tidings. {1:20} And, behold, thou shalt be dumb, and not able to speak, until the day that these things shall be performed, because thou believest not my words, which shall be fulfilled in their season. {1:21} And the people waited for Zacharias, and marvelled that he tarried so long in the temple. {1:22} And when he came out, he could not speak unto them: and they perceived that he had seen a vision in the temple: for He beckoned unto them, and remained speechless. {1:23} And it came to pass, that, as soon as the days of his ministration were accomplished, he departed to his own house. {1:24} And after those days his wife Elisabeth conceived, and hid herself five months, saying, {1:25} Thus hath the **Lord** dealt with me in the days wherein he looked on [me,] to take away my reproach among men. {1:26} And in the sixth month the angel Gabriel was sent from **God** unto a city of Galilee, named Nazareth, {1:27} To a virgin espoused to a man whose name was Joseph, of the house of David; and the virgin's name [was] Mary. {1:28} And the angel came in unto her, and said, Hail, [thou that art] highly favoured, the **Lord** [is] with thee: blessed [art] thou among women. {1:29} And when she saw [**Him**,] she was troubled at **His** saying, and

cast in her mind what manner of salutation this should be. {1:30} And the angel said unto her, Fear not, Mary: for thou hast found favour with **God**. {1:31} And, behold, thou shalt conceive in thy womb, and bring forth a **Son**, and shalt call **His name JESUS**. {1:32} **He** shall be great, and shall be called the **Son of the Highest**: and the **Lord God** shall give unto **Him** the throne of **His Father** David: {1:33} And **He** shall reign over the house of Jacob for ever; and of **His** kingdom there shall be no end. {1:34} Then said Mary unto the angel, How shall this be, seeing I know not a man? {1:35} And the angel answered and said unto her, The **Holy Ghost** shall come upon thee, and the power of the Highest shall overshadow thee: therefore also that holy thing which shall be born of thee shall be called the **Son of God**. {1:36} And, behold, thy cousin Elisabeth, she hath also conceived a Son in her old age: and this is the sixth month with her, who was called barren. {1:37} For with **God** nothing shall be impossible. {1:38} And Mary said, Behold the handmaid of the **Lord**; be it unto me according to thy word. And the angel departed from her. {1:39} And Mary arose in those days, and went into the hill country with haste, into a city of Juda; {1:40} And entered into the house of Zacharias, and saluted Elisabeth. {1:41} And it came to pass, that, when Elisabeth heard the salutation of Mary, the babe leaped in her womb; and Elisabeth was filled with the **Holy Ghost**: {1:42} And she spake out with a loud voice, and said, Blessed [art] thou among women, and blessed [is] the **fruit of thy womb**. {1:43} And whence [is] this to me, that the mother of my **Lord** should come to me? {1:44} For, lo, as soon as the voice of thy salutation sounded in mine ears, the babe leaped in my womb for joy. {1:45} And blessed [is] she that believed: for there shall be a performance of those things which were told her from the **Lord**. {1:46} And Mary said, my soul doth magnify the **Lord**, {1:47} And my spirit hath rejoiced in **God** my **Saviour**. {1:48} For **He** hath regarded the low estate of **His** handmaiden: for, behold, from henceforth all generations shall call me blessed. {1:49} For **He** that is mighty hath done to me great things; and holy [is] **His name**. {1:50} And **His** mercy [is] on them that fear **Him** from generation to generation. {1:51} **He** hath shewed strength with **His** arm; **He** hath scattered the proud in the imagination of their hearts. {1:52} **He** hath put down the mighty from [their] seats, and exalted them of low degree. {1:53} **He** hath filled the hungry with good things; and the rich **He** hath sent empty away. {1:54} **He** hath holpen **His** servant Israel, in remembrance of [**His**] mercy; {1:55} As **He** spake to our **Father**s, to Abraham, and to his seed for ever. {1:56} And Mary abode with her about three months, and returned to her own house. {1:57} Now Elisabeth's full time came that she should be delivered; and she brought forth a Son. {1:58} And her neighbours and her cousins heard how the **Lord** had shewed great mercy upon her; and they rejoiced with her. {1:59} And it came to pass, that on the eighth day they came to circumcise the child; and they called him Zacharias, after the name of his Father. {1:60} And his mother answered and said, Not [so;] but he shall be called John. {1:61} And they said unto her, There is none of thy kindred that is called by this name. {1:62} And they made signs to his Father, how he would have him called. {1:63} And he asked for a writing table, and wrote, saying, his name is John. And they marvelled all. {1:64} And his mouth was opened immediately, and his tongue [loosed,] and he spake, and praised **God**. {1:65} And fear came on all that dwelt round about them: and all these sayings were noised abroad throughout all the hill country of Judaea. {1:66} And all they that heard [them] laid [them] up in their hearts, saying, What manner of child shall this be! And the hand of the **Lord** was with him. {1:67} And his Father Zacharias was filled with the **Holy Ghost**, and prophesied, saying, {1:68} Blessed [be] the **Lord God** of Israel; for **He** hath visited and redeemed his people, {1:69} And hath raised up an horn of salvation for us in the house of his servant David; {1:70} As he spake by the mouth of his holy prophets, which have been since the world began: {1:71} That we should be saved from our enemies, and from the hand of all that hate us; {1:72} To perform the mercy [promised] to our Fathers, and to remember **His** holy covenant; {1:73} The oath which **He** sware to our Father Abraham, {1:74} That **He** would grant unto us, that we being delivered out of the hand of our enemies might serve **Him** without fear, {1:75} In holiness and righteousness before **Him**, all the days of our life. {1:76} And thou, child, shalt be called the prophet of the Highest: for thou shalt go before the face of the **Lord** to prepare **His** ways; {1:77} To give knowledge of salvation unto **His** people by the remission of their sins, {1:78} Through the tender mercy of our **God**; whereby the daspring from on high hath visited us, {1:79} To give light to them that sit in darkness and [in] the shadow of death, to guide our feet into the way of peace. {1:80} And the child grew, and waxed strong in spirit, and was in the deserts till the day of **His** shewing unto Israel. {40}

{2:1} And it came to pass in those days, that there went out a decree from Caesar Augustus, that all the world should be taxed. {2:2} ([And] this taxing was first made when Cyrenius was governor of Syria.) {2:3} And all went to be taxed, every one into his own city. {2:4} And Joseph also went up from Galilee, out of the city of Nazareth, into Judaea, unto the city of David, which is called Bethlehem; (because he was of the house and lineage of David:) {2:5} To be taxed with Mary his espoused wife, being great with child. {2:6} And so it was, that, while they were there, the days were accomplished that she should be delivered. {2:7} And she brought forth her firstborn Son, and wrapped **Him** in swaddling clothes, and laid **Him** in a manger; because there was no room for them in the inn. {2:8} And there were in the same country shepherds abiding in the field, keeping watch over their flock by night. {2:9} And, lo, the angel of the **Lord** came upon them, and the glory of the **Lord** shone round about them: and they were sore afraid. {2:10} And the angel said unto them, Fear not: for, behold, **I** bring you good tidings of great joy, which shall be to all people. {2:11} For unto you is born this day in the city of David a Saviour, which is **Christ** the **Lord**. {2:12} And this [shall be] a sign unto you; Ye shall find the babe wrapped in swaddling clothes, lying in a manger. {2:13} And suddenly there was with the angel a multitude of the heavenly host praising **God**, and saying, {2:14} Glory to **God** in the highest, and on earth peace, good will toward men. {2:15} And it came to pass, as the angels were gone away from them into heaven, the shepherds said one to another, Let us now go even unto Bethlehem, and see this thing which is come to pass, which the **Lord** hath made known unto us. {2:16} And they came with haste, and found Mary, and Joseph, and the babe lying in a manger. {2:17} And when they had seen [it,] they made known abroad the saying which was told them concerning this child. {2:18} And all they that heard [it] wondered at those things which were told them by the shepherds. {2:19} But Mary kept all these things, and pondered [them] in her heart. {2:20} And the shepherds returned, glorifying and praising **God** for all the things that they had heard and seen, as it was told unto them. {2:21} And when eight days were accomplished for the circumcising of the child, **His** name was called **JESUS**, which was so named of the angel before **He** was conceived in the womb. {2:22} And when the days of her purification according to the law of Moses were accomplished, they brought **Him** to Jerusalem, to present [**Him**] to the **Lord**;

{2:23} (As it is written in the law of the **Lord**, Every male that openeth the womb shall be called holy to the **Lord**;) {2:24} And to offer a sacrifice according to that which is said in the law of the **Lord**, A pair of turtledoves, or two young pigeons. {2:25} And, behold, there was a man in Jerusalem, whose name [was] Simeon; and the same man [was] just and devout, waiting for the consolation of Israel: and the **Holy Ghost** was upon him. {2:26} And it was revealed unto him by the **Holy Ghost**, that **He** should not see death, before he had seen the **Lord's Christ**. {2:27} And he came by the Spirit into the temple: and when the parents brought in the child Jesus, to do for **Him** after the custom of the law, {2:28} Then took he **Him** up in his arms, and blessed **God**, and said, {2:29} **Lord**, now lettest thou thy servant depart in peace, according to thy word: {2:30} For mine eyes have seen thy salvation, {2:31} Which thou hast prepared before the face of all people; {2:32} A light to lighten the Gentiles, and the glory of thy people Israel. {2:33} And Joseph and **His** mother marvelled at those things which were spoken of **Him**. {2:34} And Simeon blessed them, and said unto Mary **His** mother, Behold, this [child] is set for the fall and rising again of many in Israel; and for a sign which shall be spoken against; {2:35} (Yea, a sword shall pierce through thy own soul also,) that the thoughts of many hearts may be revealed. {2:36} And there was one Anna, a prophetess, the daughter of Phanuel, of the tribe of Aser: she was of a great age, and had lived with an husband seven years from her virginity; {2:37} And she [was] a widow of about fourscore and four years, which departed not from the temple, but served [**God**] with fastings and prayers night and day. {2:38} And she coming in that instant gave thanks likewise unto the **Lord**, and spake of **Him** to all them that looked for redemption in Jerusalem. {2:39} And when they had performed all things according to the law of the **Lord**, they returned into Galilee, to their own city Nazareth. {2:40} And the child grew, and waxed strong in spirit, filled with wisdom: and the grace of **God** was upon **Him**. {2:41} Now **His** parents went to Jerusalem every year at the feast of the passover. {2:42} And when **He** was twelve years old, they went up to Jerusalem after the custom of the feast. {2:43} And when they had fulfilled the days, as they returned, the child Jesus tarried behind in Jerusalem; and Joseph and **His** mother knew not [of it.]{2:44} But they, supposing **Him** to have been in the company, went a day's journey; and they sought **Him** among [their] kinsfolk and acquaintance. {2:45} And when they found **Him** not, they turned back again to Jerusalem, seeking **Him**. {2:46} And it came to pass, that after three days they found **Him** in the temple, sitting in the midst of the doctors, both hearing them, and asking them questions. {2:47} And all that heard **Him** were astonished at **His** understanding and answers. {2:48} And when they saw **Him**, they were amazed: and **His** mother said unto **Him**, **Son**, why hast **thou** thus dealt with us? behold, thy **Father** and **I** have sought **thee** sorrowing. {2:49} And **He** said unto them, How is it that ye sought **ME**? wist ye not that **I** must be about **my Father**'s business? {2:50} And they understood not the saying which **He** spake unto them. {2:51} And **He** went down with them, and came to Nazareth, and was subject unto them: but **His** mother kept all these sayings in her heart. {2:52} And **Jesus** increased in wisdom and stature, and in favour with **God** and man. {61}

{3:1} Now in the fifteenth year of the reign of Tiberius Caesar, Pontius Pilate being governor of Judaea, and Herod being tetrarch of Galilee, and his brother Philip tetrarch of Ituraea and of the region of Trachonitis, and Lysanias the tetrarch of Abilene, {3:2} Annas and Caiaphas being the high priests, the word of **God** came unto John the Son of

Zacharias in the wilderness. {3:3} And he came into all the country about Jordan, preaching the baptism of repentance for the remission of sins; {3:4} As it is written in the book of the words of Esaias the prophet, saying, The voice of one crying in the wilderness, Prepare ye the way of the **Lord**, make **His** paths straight. {3:5} Every valley shall be filled, and every mountain and hill shall be brought low; and the crooked shall be made straight, and the rough ways [shall be] made smooth; {3:6} And all flesh shall see the **salvation of God**. {3:7} Then said he to the multitude that came forth to be baptized of him, O generation of vipers, who hath warned you to flee from the wrath to come? {3:8} Bring forth therefore fruits worthy of repentance, and begin not to say within yourselves, We have Abraham to [our] Father: for I say unto you, That **God** is able of these stones to raise up children unto Abraham. {3:9} And now also the axe is laid unto the root of the trees: every tree therefore which bringeth not forth good fruit is hewn down, and cast into the fire. {3:10} And the people asked him, saying, What shall we do then? {3:11} He answereth and saith unto them, he that hath two coats, let him impart to him that hath none; and he that hath meat, let him do likewise. {3:12} Then came also publicans to be baptized, and said unto him, Master, what shall we do? {3:13} And he said unto them, Exact no more than that which is appointed you. {3:14} And the soldiers likewise demanded of him, saying, And what shall we do? And he said unto them, Do violence to no man, neither accuse [any] falsely; and be content with your wages. {3:15} And as the people were in expectation, and all men mused in their hearts of John, whether he were the **Christ**, or not; {3:16} John answered, saying unto [them] all, I indeed baptize you with water; but **one mightier** than I cometh, the latchet of **whose** shoes I am not worthy to unloose: **He** shall baptize you with the **Holy Ghost** and with fire: {3:17} **Whose** fan [is] in **His** hand, and **He** will throughly purge **His** floor, and will gather the wheat into **His** garner; but the chaff **He** will burn with fire unquenchable. {3:18} And many other things in his exhortation preached he unto the people. {3:19} But Herod the tetrarch, being reproved by him for Herodias his brother Philip's wife, and for all the evils which Herod had done, {3:20} Added yet this above all, that he shut up John in prison. {3:21} Now when all the people were baptized, it came to pass, that **Jesus** also being baptized, and praying, the heaven was opened, {3:22} And the **Holy Ghost** descended in a bodily shape like a dove upon **Him**, and a voice came from heaven, which said, **Thou art my beloved Son**; in **thee I am** well pleased. {3:23} And **Jesus himself** began to be about thirty years of age, being (as was supposed) the **Son** of Joseph, which was [the Son] of Heli, {3:24} Which was [the Son] of Matthat, which was [the Son] of Levi, which was [the Son] of Melchi, which was [the Son] of Janna, which was [the Son] of Joseph, {3:25} Which was [the Son] of Mattathias, which was [the Son] of Amos, which was [the Son] of Naum, which was [the Son] of Esli, which was [the Son] of Nagge, {3:26} Which was [the Son] of Maath, which was [the Son] of Mattathias, which was [the Son] of Semei, which was [the Son] of Joseph, which was [the Son] of Juda, {3:27} Which was [the Son] of Joanna, which was [the Son] of Rhesa, which was [the Son] of Zorobabel, which was [the Son] of Salathiel, which was [the Son] of Neri, {3:28} Which was [the Son] of Melchi, which was [the Son] of Addi, which was [the Son] of Cosam, which was [the Son] of Elmodam, which was [the Son] of Er, {3:29} Which was [the Son] of Jose, which was [the Son] of Eliezer, which was [the Son] of Jorim, which was [the Son] of Matthat, which was [the Son] of Levi, {3:30} Which was [the Son] of Simeon, which was [the Son] of Juda, which was [the Son] of Joseph, which was [the Son] of Jonan, which was [the

Son] of Eliakim, {3:31} Which was [the Son] of Melea, which was [the Son] of Menan, which was [the Son] of Mattatha, which was [the Son] of Nathan, which was [the Son] of David, {3:32} Which was [the Son] of Jesse, which was [the Son] of Obed, which was [the Son] of Booz, which was [the Son] of Salmon, which was [the Son] of Naasson, {3:33} Which was [the Son] of Aminadab, which was [the Son] of Aram, which was [the Son] of Esrom, which was [the Son] of Phares, which was [the Son] of Juda, {3:34} Which was [the Son] of Jacob, which was [the Son] of Isaac, which was [the Son] of Abraham, which was [the Son] of Thara, which was [the Son] of Nachor, {3:35} Which was [the Son] of Saruch, which was [the Son] of Ragau, which was [the Son] of Phalec, which was [the Son] of Heber, which was [the Son] of Sala, {3:36} Which was [the Son] of Cainan, which was [the Son] of Arphaxad, which was [the Son] of Sem, which was [the Son] of Noe, which was [the Son] of Lamech, {3:37} Which was [the Son] of Mathusala, which was [the Son] of Enoch, which was [the Son] of Jared, which was [the Son] of Maleleel, which was [the Son] of Cainan, {3:38} Which was [the Son] of Enos, which was [the Son] of Seth, which was [the Son] of Adam, which was [the Son] of **God**. {21}

{4:1} And **Jesus** being full of the **Holy Ghost** returned from Jordan, and was led by the Spirit into the wilderness, {4:2} Being forty days tempted of the devil. And in those days **He** did eat nothing: and when they were ended, **He** afterward hungered. {4:3} And the devil said unto **Him**, If thou be the **Son of God**, command this stone that it be made bread. {4:4} And **Jesus** answered him, saying, It is written, That man shall not live by bread alone, but by every word of **God**. {4:5} And the devil, taking **Him** up into an high mountain, shewed unto **Him** all the kingdoms of the world in a moment of time. {4:6} And the devil said unto **Him**, All this power will I give **thee**, and the glory of them: for that is delivered unto me; and to whomsoever I will I give it. {4:7} If **thou** therefore wilt worship me, all shall be **thine**. {4:8} And **Jesus** answered and said unto him, Get thee behind **ME**, Satan: for it is written, Thou shalt worship the **Lord** thy **God**, and **Him** only shalt thou serve. {4:9} And he brought **Him** to Jerusalem, and set **Him** on a pinnacle of the temple, and said unto **Him**, If **thou** be the **Son of God**, cast **thyself** down from hence: {4:10} For it is written, **He** shall give **His** angels charge over **thee**, to keep **thee**: {4:11} And in [their] hands they shall bear **thee** up, lest at any time thou dash **thy** foot against a stone. {4:12} And **Jesus** answering said unto him, It is said, Thou shalt not tempt the **Lord** thy **God**. {4:13} And when the devil had ended all the temptation, he departed from **Him** for a season.

{4:14} And **Jesus** returned in the power of the Spirit into Galilee: and there went out a fame of **Him** through all the region round about. {4:15} And **He** taught in their synagogues, being glorified of all.{4:16} And **He** came to Nazareth, where **He** had been brought up: and, as **His** custom was, **He** went into the synagogue on the sabbath day, and stood up for to read. {4:17} And there was delivered unto **Him** the book of the prophet Esaias. And when **He** had opened the book, **He** found the place where it was written, {4:18} The Spirit of the **Lord** is upon **ME**, because **He** hath anointed **ME** to preach the **Gospel** to the poor; **He** hath sent **ME** to heal the brokenhearted, to preach deliverance to the captives, and recovering of sight to the blind, to set at liberty them that are bruised, {4:19} To preach the **acceptable year** of the **Lord**. {4:20} And **He** closed the book, and **He** gave [it] again to the minister, and sat down. And the eyes of all them that were in the synagogue were fastened on **Him**. {4:21} And **He** began to say unto them, This day is this scripture fulfilled in your ears. {4:22} And all bare **Him** witness, and wondered at the gracious words which proceeded out of **His** mouth. And they said, Is not this **Joseph's Son**? {4:23} And **He** said unto them, Ye will surely say unto **ME** this proverb, **Physician**, heal **thyself**: whatsoever we have heard done in Capernaum, do also here in thy country. {4:24} And **He** said, Verily **I** say unto you, No **prophet** is accepted in **His own** country. {4:25} But **I** tell you of a truth, many widows were in Israel in the days of Elias, when the heaven was shut up three years and six months, when great famine was throughout all the land; {4:26} But unto none of them was Elias sent, save unto Sarepta, [a city] of Sidon, unto a woman [that was] a widow. {4:27} And many lepers were in Israel in the time of Eliseus the prophet; and none of them was cleansed, saving Naaman the Syrian. {4:28} And all they in the synagogue, when they heard these things, were filled with wrath, {4:29} And rose up, and thrust **Him** out of the city, and led **Him** unto the brow of the hill whereon their city was built, that they might cast **Him** down headlong. {4:30} But **He** passing through the midst of them went **His** way, {4:31} And came down to Capernaum, a city of Galilee, and taught them on the sabbath days. {4:32} And they were astonished at **His** doctrine: for **His** word was with power.

{4:33} And in the synagogue there was a man, which had a spirit of an unclean devil, and cried out with a loud voice, {4:34} Saying, Let [us] alone; what have we to do with thee, [thou] **Jesus of Nazareth**? art **thou** come to destroy us? **I** know **thee who thou** art; the **Holy One of God**. {4:35} And **Jesus** rebuked him, saying, Hold thy peace, and come out of him. And when the devil had thrown him in the midst, he came out of him, and hurt him not. {4:36} And they were all amazed, and spake among themselves, saying, What a word [is] this! for with authority and power **He** commandeth the unclean spirits, and they come out. {4:37} And the fame of **Him** went out into every place of the country round about.

{4:38} And **He** arose out of the synagogue, and entered into Simon's house. And Simon's wife's mother was taken with a great fever; and they besought **Him** for her. {4:39} And **He** stood over her, and rebuked the fever; and it left her: and immediately she arose and ministered unto them.

{4:40} Now when the sun was setting, all they that had any sick with divers diseases brought them unto **Him**; and **He** laid **His** hands on every one of them, and healed them. {4:41} And devils also came out of many, crying out, and saying, **Thou** art **Christ** the **Son of God**. And **He** rebuking [them] suffered them not to speak: for they knew that **He** was **Christ**. {4:42} And when it was day, **He** departed and went into a desert place: and the people sought **Him**, and came unto **Him**, and stayed **Him**, that **He** should not depart from them. {4:43} And **He** said unto them, **I** must preach the kingdom of **God** to other cities also: for therefore **am I** sent. {4:44} And **He** preached in the synagogues of Galilee. **{95}**

{5:1} And it came to pass, that, as the people pressed upon **Him** to hear the word of **God**, **He** stood by the lake of Gennesaret, {5:2} And saw two ships standing by the lake: but the fishermen were gone out of them, and were washing [their] nets. {5:3} And **He** entered into one of the ships, which was Simon's, and prayed him that he would thrust out a little from the land. And **He** sat down, and taught the people out of the ship. {5:4} Now when **He** had left speaking, **He** said unto Simon, Launch out into the deep, and let down your nets for a draught. {5:5} And Simon

answering said unto **Him**, **Master**, we have toiled all the night, and have taken nothing: nevertheless at **thy** word I will let down the net. {5:6} And when they had this done, they inclosed a great multitude of fishes: and their net brake. {5:7} And they beckoned unto [their] partners, which were in the other ship, that they should come and help them. And they came, and filled both the ships, so that they began to sink. {5:8} When Simon Peter saw [it,] he fell down at **Jesus'** knees, saying, Depart from me; for I am a sinful man, O **Lord**. {5:9} For he was astonished, and all that were with him, at the draught of the fishes which they had taken: {5:10} And so [was] also James, and John, the sons of Zebedee, which were partners with Simon. And **Jesus** said unto Simon, Fear not; from henceforth thou shalt catch men. {5:11} And when they had brought their ships to land, they forsook all, and followed **Him**.

{5:12} And it came to pass, when **He** was in a certain city, behold a man full of leprosy: who seeing **Jesus** fell on [his] face, and besought **Him**, saying, **Lord**, if **thou** wilt, **thou** canst make me clean. {5:13} And **He** put forth [**His**] hand, and touched him, saying, **I** will: be thou clean. And immediately the leprosy departed from him. {5:14} And **He** charged him to tell no man: but go, and shew thyself to the priest, and offer for thy cleansing, according as Moses commanded, for a testimony unto them. {5:15} But so much the more went there a fame abroad of **Him**: and great multitudes came together to hear, and to be healed by **Him** of their infirmities.

{5:16} And **He** withdrew **himself** into the wilderness, and prayed. {5:17} And it came to pass on a certain day, as **He** was teaching, that there were Pharisees and doctors of the law sitting by, which were come out of every town of Galilee, and Judaea, and Jerusalem: and the power of the **Lord** was [present] to heal them.

{5:18} And, behold, men brought in a bed a man which was taken with a palsy: and they sought [means] to bring him in, and to lay [him] before **Him**. {5:19} And when they could not find by what [way] they might bring him in because of the multitude, they went upon the housetop, and let Him down through the tiling with [his] couch into the midst before **Jesus**. {5:20} And when **He** saw their faith, **He** said unto him, Man, thy sins are forgiven thee. {5:21} And the scribes and the Pharisees began to reason, saying, **Who** is this which speaketh blasphemies? **Who** can forgive sins, but **God** alone? {5:22} But when **Jesus** perceived their thoughts, **He** answering said unto them, What reason ye in your hearts? {5:23} Whether is easier, to say, Thy sins be forgiven thee; or to say, Rise up and walk? {5:24} But that ye may know that the **Son of man** hath power upon earth to forgive sins, (**He** said unto the sick of the palsy,) **I** say unto thee, Arise, and take up thy couch, and go into thine house. {5:25} And immediately he rose up before them, and took up that whereon he lay, and departed to his own house, glorifying **God**. {5:26} And they were all amazed, and they glorified **God**, and were filled with fear, saying, We have seen strange things to day.

{5:27} And after these things **He** went forth, and saw a publican, named Levi, sitting at the receipt of custom: and **He** said unto him, Follow **ME**. {5:28} And he left all, rose up, and followed **Him**. {5:29} And Levi made him a great feast in his own house: and there was a great company of publicans and of others that sat down with them. {5:30} But their scribes and Pharisees murmured against **His** disciples, saying, Why do ye eat and drink with publicans and sinners? {5:31} And **Jesus** answering said unto them, They that are whole need not a physician; but they that are sick. {5:32} I came not to call the righteous, but sinners to repentance.

{5:33} And they said unto Him, Why do the disciples of John fast often, and make prayers, and likewise [the disciples] of the Pharisees; but thine eat and drink? {5:34} And He said unto them, Can ye make the children of the bridechamber fast, while the bridegroom is with them? {5:35} But the days will come, when the bridegroom shall be taken away from them, and then shall they fast in those days.

{5:36} And He spake also a parable unto them; No man putteth a piece of a new garment upon an old; if otherwise, then both the new maketh a rent, and the piece that was [taken] out of the new agreeth not with the old. {5:37} And no man putteth new wine into old bottles; else the new wine will burst the bottles, and be spilled, and the bottles shall perish. {5:38} But new wine must be put into new bottles; and both are preserved. {5:39} No man also having drunk old [wine] straightway desireth new: for He saith, The old is better.   {58}

{6:1} And it came to pass on the second sabbath after the first, that He went through the corn fields; and His disciples plucked the ears of corn, and did eat, rubbing [them] in [their] hands. {6:2} And certain of the Pharisees said unto them, Why do ye that which is not lawful to do on the sabbath days? {6:3} And Jesus answering them said, Have ye not read so much as this, what David did, when himself was an hungred, and they which were with him; {6:4} How he went into the house of God, and did take and eat the shewbread, and gave also to them that were with him; which it is not lawful to eat but for the priests alone? {6:5} And He said unto them, That the Son of man is Lord also of the sabbath. {6:6} And it came to pass also on another sabbath, that He entered into the synagogue and taught: and there was a man whose right hand was withered. {6:7} And the scribes and Pharisees watched Him, whether He would heal on the sabbath day; that they might find an accusation against Him. {6:8} But He knew their thoughts, and said to the man which had the withered hand, Rise up, and stand forth in the midst. And he arose and stood forth. {6:9} Then said Jesus unto them, I will ask you one thing; Is it lawful on the sabbath days to do good, or to do evil? to save life, or to destroy [it?]{6:10} And looking round about upon them all, He said unto the man, Stretch forth thy hand. And he did so: and his hand was restored whole as the other. {6:11} And they were filled with madness; and communed one with another what they might do to Jesus. {6:12} And it came to pass in those days, that He went out into a mountain to pray, and continued all night in prayer to God.

{6:13} And when it was day, He called [unto Him] His disciples: and of them He chose twelve, whom also He named apostles; {6:14} Simon, (whom He also named Peter,) and Andrew his brother, James and John, Philip and Bartholomew, {6:15} Matthew and Thomas, James the [Son] of Alphaeus, and Simon called Zelotes, {6:16} And Judas [the brother] of James, and Judas Iscariot, which also was the traitor.

{6:17} And He came down with them, and stood in the plain, and the company of His disciples, and a great multitude of people out of all Judaea and Jerusalem, and from the sea coast of Tyre and Sidon, which came to hear Him, and to be healed of their diseases; {6:18} And they that were vexed with unclean spirits: and they were healed.

{6:19} And the whole multitude sought to touch Him: for there went virtue out of Him, and healed [them] all.

{6:20} And He lifted up His eyes on His disciples, and said, Blessed [be ye] poor: for yours is the kingdom of God. {6:21} Blessed [are ye] that hunger now: for ye shall be filled. Blessed [are ye] that weep now: for ye shall laugh. {6:22} Blessed are ye, when men shall hate you, and when they shall separate you [from their company,] and shall reproach [you,] and cast out your name as evil, for the Son of man's sake. {6:23} Rejoice ye in that day, and leap for joy: for, behold, your reward [is] great in heaven: for in the like manner did their Fathers unto the prophets. {6:24} But woe unto you that are rich! for ye have received your consolation. {6:25} Woe unto you that are full! for ye shall hunger. Woe unto you that laugh now! for ye shall mourn and weep. {6:26} Woe unto you, when all men shall speak well of you! for so did their Fathers to the false prophets.

{6:27} But I say unto you which hear, Love your enemies, do good to them which hate you, {6:28} Bless them that curse you, and pray for them which despitefully use you. {6:29} And unto him that smiteth thee on the [one] cheek offer also the other; and him that taketh away thy cloke forbid not [to take thy] coat also. {6:30} Give to every man that asketh of thee; and of him that taketh away thy goods ask [them] not again. {6:31} And as ye would that men should do to you, do ye also to them likewise. {6:32} For if ye love them which love you, what thank have ye? for sinners also love those that love them. {6:33} And if ye do good to them which do good to you, what thank have ye? for sinners also do even the same. {6:34} And if ye lend [to them] of whom ye hope to receive, what thank have ye? for sinners also lend to sinners, to receive as much again. {6:35} But love ye your enemies, and do good, and lend, hoping for nothing again; and your reward shall be great, and ye shall be the children of the Highest: for he is kind unto the unthankful and [to] the evil. {6:36} Be ye therefore merciful, as your Father also is merciful. {6:37} Judge not, and ye shall not be judged: condemn not, and ye shall not be condemned: forgive, and ye shall be forgiven: {6:38} Give, and it shall be given unto you; good measure, pressed down, and shaken together, and running over, shall men give into your bosom. For with the same measure that ye mete withal it shall be measured to you again. {6:39} And He spake a parable unto them, Can the blind lead the blind? shall they not both fall into the ditch? {6:40} The disciple is not above His master: but every one that is perfect shall be as His master. {6:41} And why beholdest thou the mote that is in thy brother's eye, but perceivest not the beam that is in thine own eye? {6:42} Either how canst thou say to thy brother, Brother, let me pull out the mote that is in thine eye, when thou thyself beholdest not the beam that is in thine own eye? Thou hypocrite, cast out first the beam out of thine own eye, and then shalt thou see clearly to pull out the mote that is in thy brother's eye. {6:43} For a good tree bringeth not forth corrupt fruit; neither doth a corrupt tree bring forth good fruit. {6:44} For every tree is known by his own fruit. For of thorns men do not gather figs, nor of a bramble bush gather they grapes. {6:45} A good man out of the good treasure of his heart bringeth forth that which is good; and an evil man out of the evil treasure of his heart bringeth forth that which is evil: for of the abundance of the heart his mouth speaketh.

{6:46} And why call ye ME, Lord, Lord, and do not the things which I say? {6:47} Whosoever cometh to ME, and heareth my sayings, and doeth them, I will shew you to whom he is like: {6:48} He is like a man which built an house, and digged deep, and laid the foundation on a **rock**: and when the flood arose, the stream beat vehemently upon that house, and could not shake it: for it was founded upon a **rock**. {6:49} But he that heareth, and doeth not, is like a man that without a foundation built an house upon the earth; against which the stream did beat vehemently, and immediately it fell; and the ruin of that house was great. {48}

{7:1} Now when **He** had ended all **His** sayings in the audience of the people, **He** entered into Capernaum. {7:2} And a certain centurion's servant, who was dear unto him, was sick, and ready to die. {7:3} And when he heard of **Jesus**, he sent unto **Him** the elders of the Jews, beseeching **Him** that **He** would come and heal his servant. {7:4} And when they came to **Jesus**, they besought **Him** instantly, saying, That he was worthy for whom **He** should do this: {7:5} For he loveth our nation, and he hath built us a synagogue. {7:6} Then **Jesus** went with them. And when he was now not far from the house, the centurion sent friends to **Him**, saying unto **Him**, **Lord**, trouble not **thyself**: for I am not worthy that **thou** shouldest enter under my roof: {7:7} Wherefore neither thought I myself worthy to come unto **thee**: but say in a word, and my servant shall be healed. {7:8} For I also am a man set under authority, having under me soldiers, and I say unto one, Go, and he goeth; and to another, Come, and he cometh; and to my servant, Do this, and he doeth [it.]{7:9} When **Jesus** heard these things, **He** marvelled at him, and turned **Him** about, and said unto the people that followed **Him**, **I** say unto you, **I** have not found so great faith, no, not in Israel. {7:10} And they that were sent, returning to the house, found the servant whole that had been sick.

{7:11} And it came to pass the day after, that **He** went into a city called Nain; and many of **His** disciples went with **Him**, and much people. {7:12} Now when **He** came nigh to the gate of the city, behold, there was a dead man carried out, the only Son of his mother, and she was a widow: and much people of the city was with her. {7:13} And when the **Lord** saw her, **He** had compassion on her, and said unto her, Weep not. {7:14} And **He** came and touched the bier: and they that bare [him] stood still. And **He** said, Young man, I say unto thee, Arise. {7:15} And he that was dead sat up, and began to speak. And **He** delivered him to his mother. {7:16} And there came a fear on all: and they glorified **God**, saying, That a great prophet is risen up among us; and, That **God** hath visited his people. {7:17} And this rumour of **Him** went forth throughout all Judaea, and throughout all the region round about. {7:18} And the disciples of John shewed him of all these things.

{7:19} And John calling [unto him] two of his disciples sent [them] to **Jesus**, saying, Art **thou** **He** that should come? or look we for another? {7:20} When the men were come unto **Him**, they said, John Baptist hath sent us unto **thee**, saying, Art **thou** **He** that should come? or look we for another? {7:21} And in that same hour **He** cured many of [their] infirmities and plagues, and of evil spirits; and unto many [that were] blind **He** gave sight. {7:22} Then **Jesus** answering said unto them, Go your way, and tell John what things ye have seen and heard; how that the blind see, the lame walk, the lepers are cleansed, the deaf hear, the dead are raised, to the poor the **Gospel** is preached. {7:23} And blessed is [he,] whosoever shall not be offended in **ME**.

{7:24} And when the messengers of John were departed, **He** began to speak unto the people concerning John, What went ye out into the wilderness for to see? A reed shaken with the wind? {7:25} But what went ye out for to see? A

man clothed in soft raiment? Behold, they which are gorgeously apparelled, and live delicately, are in kings courts. {7:26} But what went ye out for to see? A prophet? Yea, I say unto you, and much more than a prophet. {7:27} This is [he,] of whom it is written, Behold, I send **my** messenger before **thy** face, which shall prepare **thy** way before **thee**. {7:28} For I say unto you, Among those that are born of women there is not a greater prophet than John the Baptist: but he that is least in the kingdom of **God** is greater than he. {7:29} And all the people that heard [**Him**,] and the publicans, justified **God**, being baptized with the baptism of John. {7:30} But the Pharisees and lawyers rejected the counsel of **God** against themselves, being not baptized of him.

{7:31} And the **Lord** said, Whereunto then shall I liken the men of this generation? and to what are they like? {7:32} They are like unto children sitting in the marketplace, and calling one to another, and saying, We have piped unto you, and ye have not danced; we have mourned to you, and ye have not wept. {7:33} For John the Baptist came neither eating bread nor drinking wine; and ye say, he hath a devil. {7:34} The **Son of man** is come eating and drinking; and ye say, Behold a gluttonous **man**, and a winebibber, a **friend** of publicans and sinners! {7:35} But wisdom is justified of all her children.

{7:36} And one of the Pharisees desired **Him** that **He** would eat with him. And **He** went into the Pharisee's house, and sat down to meat. {7:37} And, behold, a woman in the city, which was a sinner, when she knew that [**Jesus**] sat at meat in the Pharisee's house, brought an alabaster box of ointment, {7:38} And stood at **His** feet behind [**Him**] weeping, and began to wash **His** feet with tears, and did wipe [them] with the hairs of her head, and kissed **His** feet, and anointed [them] with the ointment. {7:39} Now when the Pharisee which had bidden him saw [it,] he spake within himself, saying, This **man**, if **He** were a **prophet**, would have known who and what manner of woman [this is] that toucheth **Him**: for she is a sinner. {7:40} And **Jesus** answering said unto him, Simon, I have somewhat to say unto thee. And he saith, **Master**, say on. {7:41} There was a certain **creditor** which had two debtors: the one owed five hundred pence, and the other fifty. {7:42} And when they had nothing to pay, **He** frankly forgave them both. Tell **ME** therefore, which of them will love **Him** most? {7:43} Simon answered and said, I suppose that [he,] to whom **He** forgave most. And **He** said unto him, Thou hast rightly judged. {7:44} And **He** turned to the woman, and said unto Simon, Seest thou this woman? I entered into thine house, thou gavest **ME** no water for **my** feet: but she hath washed **my** feet with tears, and wiped [them] with the hairs of her head. {7:45} Thou gavest **ME** no kiss: but this woman since the time I came in hath not ceased to kiss **my** feet. {7:46} **my** head with oil thou didst not anoint: but this woman hath anointed **my** feet with ointment. {7:47} Wherefore I say unto thee, Her sins, which are many, are forgiven; for she loved much: but to whom little is forgiven, [the same] loveth little. {7:48} And **He** said unto her, Thy sins are forgiven. {7:49} And they that sat at meat with **Him** began to say within themselves, Who is this that forgiveth sins also? {7:50} And **He** said to the woman, Thy faith hath saved thee; go in peace. {91}

{8:1} And it came to pass afterward, that **He** went throughout every city and village, preaching and shewing the glad tidings of the kingdom of **God**: and the twelve [were] with **Him**, {8:2} And certain women, which had been healed of evil spirits and infirmities, Mary called

Magdalene, out of whom went seven devils, {8:3} And Joanna the wife of Chuza Herod's steward, and Susanna, and many others, which ministered unto **Him** of their substance.

{8:4} And when much people were gathered together, and were come to **Him** out of every city, **He** spake by a parable: {8:5} A **sower** went out to sow **His** seed: and as **He** sowed, some fell by the way side; and it was trodden down, and the fowls of the air devoured it. {8:6} And some fell upon a rock; and as soon as it was sprung up, it withered away, because it lacked moisture. {8:7} And some fell among thorns; and the thorns sprang up with it, and choked it. {8:8} And other fell on good ground, and sprang up, and bare fruit an hundredfold. And when **He** had said these things, **He** cried, **He** that hath ears to hear, let him hear. {8:9} And **His** disciples asked **Him**, saying, What might this parable be? {8:10} And **He** said, Unto you it is given to know the mysteries of the kingdom of **God**: but to others in parables; that seeing they might not see, and hearing they might not understand. {8:11} Now the parable is this: The seed is the word of **God**. {8:12} Those by the way side are they that hear; then cometh the devil, and taketh away the word out of their hearts, lest they should believe and be saved. {8:13} They on the rock [are they,] which, when they hear, receive the word with joy; and these have no root, which for a while believe, and in time of temptation fall away. {8:14} And that which fell among thorns are they, which, when they have heard, go forth, and are choked with cares and riches and pleasures of [this] life, and bring no fruit to perfection. {8:15} But that on the good ground are they, which in an honest and good heart, having heard the word, keep [it,] and bring forth fruit with patience.

{8:16} No man, when he hath lighted a candle, covereth it with a vessel, or putteth [it] under a bed; but setteth [it] on a candlestick, that they which enter in may see the light. {8:17} For nothing is secret, that shall not be made manifest; neither [any thing] hid, that shall not be known and come abroad. {8:18} Take heed therefore how ye hear: for whosoever hath, to him shall be given; and whosoever hath not, from him shall be taken even that which he seemeth to have.

{8:19} Then came to **Him** [**His**] mother and **His** brethren, and could not come at **Him** for the press. {8:20} And it was told **Him** [by certain] which said, **Thy** mother and **thy** brethren stand without, desiring to see **thee**. {8:21} And **He** answered and said unto them, **my** mother and **my** brethren are these which hear the word of **God**, and do it.

{8:22} Now it came to pass on a certain day, that **He** went into a ship with **His** disciples: and **He** said unto them, Let us go over unto the other side of the lake. And they launched forth. {8:23} But as they sailed **He** fell asleep: and there came down a storm of wind on the lake; and they were filled [with water,] and were in jeopardy. {8:24} And they came to **Him**, and awoke **Him**, saying, **Master**, **master**, we perish. Then **He** arose, and rebuked the wind and the raging of the water: and they ceased, and there was a calm. {8:25} And **He** said unto them, Where is your faith? And they being afraid wondered, saying one to another, What manner of **man** is this! for **He** commandeth even the winds and water, and they obey **Him**.

{8:26} And they arrived at the country of the Gadarenes, which is over against Galilee. {8:27} And when **He** went forth to land, there met him out of the city a certain man, which had devils long time, and ware no clothes, neither

abode in [any] house, but in the tombs. {8:28} When he saw **Jesus**, he cried out, and fell down before **Him**, and with a loud voice said, What have I to do with thee, **Jesus**, [**thou**] **Son of God most high**? I beseech thee, torment me not. {8:29} (For **He** had commanded the unclean spirit to come out of the man. For oftentimes it had caught him: and he was kept bound with chains and in fetters; and he brake the bands, and was driven of the devil into the wilderness.) {8:30} And **Jesus** asked him, saying, What is thy name? And he said, Legion: because many devils were entered into him. {8:31} And they besought him that **He** would not command them to go out into the deep. {8:32} And there was there an herd of many swine feeding on the mountain: and they besought **Him** that **He** would suffer them to enter into them. And **He** suffered them. {8:33} Then went the devils out of the man, and entered into the swine: and the herd ran violently down a steep place into the lake, and were choked. {8:34} When they that fed [them] saw what was done, they fled, and went and told [it] in the city and in the country. {8:35} Then they went out to see what was done; and came to **Jesus**, and found the man, out of whom the devils were departed, sitting at the feet of **Jesus**, clothed, and in his right mind: and they were afraid. {8:36} They also which saw [it] told them by what means **He** that was possessed of the devils was healed.

{8:37} Then the whole multitude of the country of the Gadarenes round about besought **Him** to depart from them; for they were taken with great fear: and **He** went up into the ship, and returned back again. {8:38} Now the man out of whom the devils were departed besought **Him** that he might be with **Him**: but **Jesus** sent him away, saying, {8:39} Return to thine own house, and shew how great things **God** hath done unto thee. And he went his way, and published throughout the whole city how great things **Jesus** had done unto **Him**. {8:40} And it came to pass, that, when **Jesus** was returned, the people [gladly] received **Him**: for they were all waiting for **Him**.

{8:41} And, behold, there came a man named Jairus, and he was a ruler of the synagogue: and he fell down at **Jesus**' feet, and besought **Him** that **He** would come into his house: {8:42} For he had one only daughter, about twelve years of age, and she lay a dying. But as **He** went the people thronged **Him**.

{8:43} And a woman having an issue of blood twelve years, which had spent all her living upon physicians, neither could be healed of any, {8:44} Came behind [**Him**,] and touched the border of **His** garment: and immediately her issue of blood stanched. {8:45} And **Jesus** said, Who touched **ME**? When all denied, Peter and they that were with **Him** said, **Master**, the multitude throng **thee** and press [**thee**,] and sayest **thou**, Who touched **ME**? {8:46} And **Jesus** said, Somebody hath touched **ME**: for I perceive that virtue is gone out of **ME**. {8:47} And when the woman saw that she was not hid, she came trembling, and falling down before **Him**, she declared unto **Him** before all the people for what cause she had touched **Him** and how she was healed immediately. {8:48} And **He** said unto her, Daughter, be of good comfort: thy faith hath made thee whole; go in peace.

{8:49} While **He** yet spake, there cometh one from the ruler of the synagogue's [house,] saying to him, Thy daughter is dead; trouble not the **Master**. {8:50} But when **Jesus** heard [it,] **He** answered him, saying, Fear not: believe only, and she shall be made whole. {8:51} And when **He** came into the house, **He** suffered no man to go in, save Peter, and James, and John, and the Father and the mother of the maiden. {8:52} And all wept, and bewailed her: but **He** said, Weep not; she is not dead, but sleepeth. {8:53} And they laughed **Him** to scorn, knowing that she was dead. {8:54} And **He** put them all out, and took her by the hand, and called, saying, Maid, arise. {8:55} And her spirit came again, and she arose straightway: and **He** commanded to give her meat. {8:56} And her parents were astonished: but **He** charged them that they should tell no man what was done. {98}

{9:1} Then **He** called **His** twelve disciples together, and gave them power and authority over all devils, and to cure diseases. {9:2} And **He** sent them to preach the kingdom of **God**, and to heal the sick. {9:3} And **He** said unto them, Take nothing for [your] journey, neither staves, nor scrip, neither bread, neither money; neither have two coats apiece. {9:4} And whatsoever house ye enter into, there abide, and thence depart. {9:5} And whosoever will not receive you, when ye go out of that city, shake off the very dust from your feet for a testimony against them. {9:6} And they departed, and went through the towns, preaching the Gospel, and healing every where.

{9:7} Now Herod the tetrarch heard of all that was done by **Him**: and he was perplexed, because that it was said of some, that John was risen from the dead; {9:8} And of some, that Elias had appeared; and of others, that one of the old prophets was risen again. {9:9} And Herod said, John have **I** beheaded: but who is this, of whom **I** hear such things? And he desired to see **Him**.

{9:10} And the apostles, when they were returned, told **Him** all that they had done. And **He** took them, and went aside privately into a desert place belonging to the city called Bethsaida. {9:11} And the people, when they knew [it,] followed **Him**: and **He** received them, and spake unto them of the kingdom of **God**, and healed them that had need of healing. {9:12} And when the day began to wear away, then came the twelve, and said unto **Him**, Send the multitude away, that they may go into the towns and country round about, and lodge, and get victuals: for we are here in a desert place. {9:13} But **He** said unto them, Give ye them to eat. And they said, We have no more but five loaves and two fishes; except we should go and buy meat for all this people. {9:14} For they were about five thousand men. And **He** said to **His** disciples, Make them sit down by fifties in a company. {9:15} And they did so, and made them all sit down. {9:16} Then **He** took the five loaves and the two fishes, and looking up to heaven, **He** blessed them, and brake, and gave to the disciples to set before the multitude. {9:17} And they did eat, and were all filled: and there was taken up of fragments that remained to them twelve baskets.

{9:18} And it came to pass, as **He** was alone praying, **His** disciples were with **Him**: and **He** asked them, saying, Whom say the people that **I am**? {9:19} They answering said, John the Baptist; but some [say,] Elias; and others [say,] that one of the old prophets is risen again. {9:20} And **He** said unto them, But whom say ye that **I am**? Peter answering said, The **Christ of God**. {9:21} And **He** straitly charged them, and commanded [them] to tell no man that thing; {9:22} Saying, The **Son of man** must suffer many things, and be rejected of the elders and chief priests and scribes, and be slain, and be raised the third day.

{9:23} And **He** said to [them] all, If any [man] will come after **ME**, let him deny himself, and take up his cross daily, and follow **ME**. {9:24} For whosoever will save his life shall lose it: but whosoever will lose his life for **my** sake, the same shall save it. {9:25} For what is a man advantaged, if

he gain the whole world, and lose himself, or be cast away? {9:26} For whosoever shall be ashamed of **ME** and of **my** words, of **Him** shall the **Son of man** be ashamed, when **He** shall come in **His** own glory, and [in **His**] **Father**'s, and of the holy angels. {9:27} But **I** tell you of a truth, there be some standing here, which shall not taste of death, till they see the kingdom of **God**.

{9:28} And it came to pass about an eight days after these sayings, **He** took Peter and John and James, and went up into a mountain to pray. {9:29} And as **He** prayed, the fashion of **His** countenance was altered, and **His** raiment [was] white [and] glistering. {9:30} And, behold, there talked with **Him** two men, which were Moses and Elias: {9:31} Who appeared in glory, and spake of **His** decease which **He** should accomplish at Jerusalem. {9:32} But Peter and they that were with **Him** were heavy with sleep: and when they were awake, they saw **His** glory, and the two men that stood with **Him**. {9:33} And it came to pass, as they departed from **Him**, Peter said unto **Jesus**, **Master**, it is good for us to be here: and let us make three tabernacles; one for **thee**, and one for Moses, and one for Elias: not knowing what he said. {9:34} While he thus spake, there came a cloud, and overshadowed them: and they feared as they entered into the cloud. {9:35} And there came a voice out of the cloud, saying, This is **my** beloved **Son**: hear **Him**. {9:36} And when the voice was past, **Jesus** was found alone. And they kept [it] close, and told no man in those days any of those things which they had seen.

{9:37} And it came to pass, that on the next day, when they were come down from the hill, much people met **Him**. {9:38} And, behold, a man of the company cried out, saying, **Master**, **I** beseech thee, look upon my son: for he is mine only child. {9:39} And, lo, a spirit taketh him, and he suddenly crieth out; and it teareth him that he foameth again, and bruising him hardly departeth from him. {9:40} And **I** besought thy disciples to cast him out; and they could not. {9:41} And **Jesus** answering said, O faithless and perverse generation, how long shall **I** be with you, and suffer you? Bring thy Son hither. {9:42} And as he was yet a coming, the devil threw him down, and tare [him.] And **Jesus** rebuked the unclean spirit, and healed the child, and delivered him again to his Father.

{9:43} And they were all amazed at the mighty power of **God**. But while they wondered every one at all things which **Jesus** did, **He** said unto **His** disciples, {9:44} Let these sayings sink down into your ears: for the **Son of man** shall be delivered into the hands of men. {9:45} But they understood not this saying, and it was hid from them, that they perceived it not: and they feared to ask **Him** of that saying.

{9:46} Then there arose a reasoning among them, which of them should be greatest. {9:47} And **Jesus**, perceiving the thought of their heart, took a child, and set him by **Him**, {9:48} And said unto them, Whosoever shall receive this child in **my name** receiveth **ME**: and whosoever shall receive **ME** receiveth him that sent **ME**: for he that is least among you all, the same shall be great.

{9:49} And John answered and said, **Master**, we saw one casting out devils in thy name; and we forbad him, because he followeth not with **us**. {9:50} And **Jesus** said unto him, Forbid [him] not: for he that is not against **us** is for **us.**

{9:51} And it came to pass, when the time was come that **He** should be received up, **He** stedfastly set **His** face to go to

Jerusalem, {9:52} And sent messengers before **His** face: and they went, and entered into a village of the Samaritans, to make ready for **Him**. {9:53} And they did not receive **Him**, because **His** face was as though **He** would go to Jerusalem. {9:54} And when **His** disciples James and John saw [this,] they said, **Lord**, wilt thou that we command fire to come down from heaven, and consume them, even as Elias did? {9:55} But **He** turned, and rebuked them, and said, Ye know not what manner of spirit ye are of. {9:56} For the **Son of man** is not come to destroy men's lives, but to save [them.] And they went to another village.

{9:57} And it came to pass, that, as they went in the way, a certain [man] said unto **Him**, **Lord**, I will follow **thee** whithersoever **thou** goest. {9:58} And **Jesus** said unto him, Foxes have holes, and birds of the air [have] nests; but the **Son of man** hath not where to lay [**His**] head. {9:59} And **He** said unto another, Follow **ME**. But he said, **Lord**, suffer me first to go and bury my Father. {9:60} **Jesus** said unto **Him**, Let the dead bury their dead: but go thou and preach the kingdom of **God**. {9:61} And another also said, **Lord**, I will follow **thee**; but let me first go bid them farewell, which are at home at my house. {9:62} And **Jesus** said unto him, No man, having put his hand to the plough, and looking back, is fit for the kingdom of **God**. {111}

{10:1} After these things the **Lord** appointed other seventy also, and sent them two and two before **His** face into every city and place, whither **He himself** would come. {10:2} Therefore said **He** unto them, The harvest truly [is] great, but the labourers [are] few: pray ye therefore the **Lord of the harvest**, that **He** would send forth labourers into **His** harvest. {10:3} Go your ways: behold, I send you forth as lambs among wolves. {10:4} Carry neither purse, nor scrip, nor shoes: and salute no man by the way. {10:5} And into whatsoever house ye enter, first say, Peace [be] to this house. {10:6} And if the **Son of peace** be there, your peace shall rest upon it: if not, it shall turn to you again. {10:7} And in the same house remain, eating and drinking such things as they give: for the labourer is worthy of his hire. Go not from house to house. {10:8} And into whatsoever city ye enter, and they receive you, eat such things as are set before you: {10:9} And heal the sick that are therein, and say unto them, The kingdom of **God** is come nigh unto you. {10:10} But into whatsoever city ye enter, and they receive you not, go your ways out into the streets of the same, and say, {10:11} Even the very dust of your city, which cleaveth on us, we do wipe off against you: notwithstanding be ye sure of this, that the kingdom of **God** is come nigh unto you. {10:12} But I say unto you, that it shall be more tolerable in that day for Sodom, than for that city. {10:13} Woe unto thee, Chorazin! woe unto thee, Bethsaida! for if the mighty works had been done in Tyre and Sidon, which have been done in you, they had a great while ago repented, sitting in sackcloth and ashes. {10:14} But it shall be more tolerable for Tyre and Sidon at the judgment, than for you. {10:15} And thou, Capernaum, which art exalted to heaven, shalt be thrust down to hell. {10:16} He that heareth you heareth **ME**; and he that despiseth you despiseth **ME**; and he that despiseth **ME** despiseth **Him** that sent **ME**.

{10:17} And the seventy returned again with joy, saying, **Lord**, even the devils are subject unto us through **thy name**. {10:18} And **He** said unto them, I beheld Satan as lightning fall from heaven. {10:19} Behold, I give unto you power to tread on serpents and scorpions, and over all the power of the enemy: and nothing shall by any means hurt you. {10:20} Notwithstanding in this rejoice not, that the spirits are subject unto you; but rather rejoice, because your names

are written in heaven.

{10:21} In that hour **Jesus** rejoiced in spirit, and said, I thank thee, O **Father**, **Lord** of heaven and earth, that thou hast hid these things from the wise and prudent, and hast revealed them unto babes: even so, **Father**; for so it seemed good in thy sight. {10:22} All things are delivered to **ME** of **my** Father: and no man knoweth who the **Son** is, but the **Father**; and who the **Father** is, but the **Son**, and [he] to **whom** the **Son** will reveal [**Him**.]{10:23} And **He** turned **Him** unto [**His**] disciples, and said privately, Blessed [are] the eyes which see the things that ye see: {10:24} For I tell you, that many prophets and kings have desired to see those things which ye see, and have not seen [them;] and to hear those things which ye hear, and have not heard [them.

]{10:25} And, behold, a certain lawyer stood up, and tempted **Him**, saying, **Master**, what shall I do to inherit eternal life? {10:26} **He** said unto **Him**, What is written in the law? how readest thou? {10:27} And **He** answering said, Thou shalt love the **Lord** thy **God** with all thy heart, and with all thy soul, and with all thy strength, and with all thy mind; and thy neighbour as thyself. {10:28} And **He** said unto him, Thou hast answered right: this do, and thou shalt live. {10:29} But he, willing to justify himself, said unto **Jesus**, And who is my neighbour? {10:30} And **Jesus** answering said, A certain [man] went down from Jerusalem to Jericho, and fell among thieves, which stripped him of his raiment, and wounded [him,] and departed, leaving [him] half dead. {10:31} And by chance there came down a certain priest that way: and when he saw him, he passed by on the other side. {10:32} And likewise a Levite, when he was at the place, came and looked [on him,] and passed by on the other side. {10:33} But a certain Samaritan, as he journeyed, came where he was: and when he saw him, he had compassion [on him,]{10:34} And went to [him,] and bound up his wounds, pouring in oil and wine, and set him on his own beast, and brought him to an inn, and took care of him. {10:35} And on the morrow when he departed, he took out two pence, and gave [them] to the host, and said unto him, Take care of him; and whatsoever thou spendest more, when I come again, I will repay thee. {10:36} Which now of these three, thinkest thou, was neighbour unto him that fell among the thieves? {10:37} And he said, he that shewed mercy on him. Then said **Jesus** unto him, Go, and do thou likewise.

{10:38} Now it came to pass, as they went, that **He** entered into a certain village: and a certain woman named Martha received **Him** into her house. {10:39} And she had a sister called Mary, which also sat at **Jesus'** feet, and heard **His** word. {10:40} But Martha was cumbered about much serving, and came to **Him**, and said, **Lord**, dost **thou** not care that my sister hath left me to serve alone? bid her therefore that she help me. {10:41} And **Jesus** answered and said unto her, Martha, Martha, thou art careful and troubled about many things: {10:42} But one thing is **needful**: and Mary hath chosen that **good part**, which shall not be taken away from her. {49}

{11:1} And it came to pass, that, as **He** was praying in a certain place, when **He** ceased, one of **His** disciples said unto **Him**, **Lord**, teach us to pray, as John also taught his disciples. {11:2} And **He** said unto them, When ye pray, say, Our **Father** which art in heaven, Hallowed be thy name. Thy kingdom come. Thy will be done, as in heaven, so in earth. {11:3} Give us day by day our daily bread. {11:4}

And forgive us our sins; for we also forgive every one that is indebted to us. And lead us not into temptation; but deliver us from evil. {11:5} And **He** said unto them, Which of you shall have a friend, and shall go unto him at midnight, and say unto him, Friend, lend me three loaves; {11:6} For a friend of mine in his journey is come to me, and I have nothing to set before him? {11:7} And he from within shall answer and say, Trouble me not: the door is now shut, and my children are with ME in bed; I cannot rise and give thee. {11:8} I say unto you, Though he will not rise and give him, because he is his friend, yet because of his importunity he will rise and give him as many as he needeth. {11:9} And I say unto you, Ask, and it shall be given you; seek, and ye shall find; knock, and it shall be opened unto you. {11:10} For every one that asketh receiveth; and he that seeketh findeth; and to him that knocketh it shall be opened. {11:11} If a Son shall ask bread of any of you that is a Father, will he give him a stone? or if [he ask] a fish, will he for a fish give him a serpent? {11:12} Or if he shall ask an egg, will he offer him a scorpion? {11:13} If ye then, being evil, know how to give good gifts unto your children: how much more shall [your] heavenly **Father** give the Holy Spirit to them that ask him?

{11:14} And **He** was casting out a devil, and it was dumb. And it came to pass, when the devil was gone out, the dumb spake; and the people wondered. {11:15} But some of them said, **He** casteth out devils through Beelzebub the chief of the devils. {11:16} And others, tempting [**Him**,] sought of **Him** a sign from heaven. {11:17} But **He**, knowing their thoughts, said unto them, Every kingdom divided against itself is brought to desolation; and a house [divided] against a house falleth. {11:18} If Satan also be divided against himself, how shall **his** kingdom stand? because ye say that I cast out devils through Beelzebub. {11:19} And if I by Beelzebub cast out devils, by whom do your sons cast [them] out? therefore shall they be your judges. {11:20} But if I with the finger of **God** cast out devils, no doubt the kingdom of **God** is come upon you. {11:21} When a strong man armed keepeth his palace, his goods are in peace: {11:22} But when a **stronger** than he shall come upon him, and overcome him, **He** taketh from him all his armour wherein he trusted, and divideth his spoils. {11:23} **He** that is not with ME is against ME: and **He** that gathereth not with ME scattereth. {11:24} When the unclean spirit is gone out of a man, he walketh through dry places, seeking rest; and finding none, he saith, I will return unto my house whence I came out. {11:25} And when he cometh, he findeth [it] swept and garnished. {11:26} Then goeth he, and taketh [to him] seven other spirits more wicked than himself; and they enter in, and dwell there: and the last [state] of that man is worse than the first.

{11:27} And it came to pass, as **He** spake these things, a certain woman of the company lifted up her voice, and said unto **Him**, Blessed is the womb that bare **thee**, and the paps which **thou** hast sucked. {11:28} But **He** said, Yea rather, blessed [are] they that hear the **word of God**, and keep it.

{11:29} And when the people were gathered thick together, **He** began to say, This is an evil generation: they seek a sign; and there shall no sign be given it, but the sign of Jonas the prophet. {11:30} For as Jonas was a sign unto the Ninevites, so shall also the **Son of man** be to this generation. {11:31} The queen of the south shall rise up in the judgment with the men of this generation, and condemn them: for she came from the utmost parts of the earth to hear the wisdom of Solomon; and, behold, a **greater** than Solomon is here. {11:32} The men of Nineve shall rise up

in the judgment with this generation, and shall condemn it: for they repented at the preaching of Jonas; and, behold, a **greater** than Jonas [is] here. {11:33} No man, when he hath lighted a candle, putteth [it] in a secret place, neither under a bushel, but on a candlestick, that they which come in may see the **light**. {11:34} The **light** of the body is the eye: therefore when thine eye is single, thy whole body also is full of **light**; but when [thine eye] is evil, thy body also [is] full of darkness. {11:35} Take heed therefore that the light which is in thee be not darkness. {11:36} If thy whole body therefore [be] **full of light**, having no part dark, the whole shall be **full of light**, as when the bright shining of a candle doth give thee **light**.

{11:37} And as **He** spake, a certain Pharisee besought **Him** to dine with him: and **He** went in, and sat down to meat. {11:38} And when the Pharisee saw [it,] he marvelled that **He** had not first washed before dinner. {11:39} And the **Lord** said unto him, Now do ye Pharisees make clean the outside of the cup and the platter; but your inward part is full of ravening and wickedness. {11:40} [Ye] fools, did not **He** that made that which is without make that which is within also? {11:41} But rather give alms of such things as ye have; and, behold, all things are clean unto you. {11:42} But woe unto you, Pharisees! for ye tithe mint and rue and all manner of herbs, and pass over judgment and the love of **God**: these ought ye to have done, and not to leave the other undone. {11:43} Woe unto you, Pharisees! for ye love the uppermost seats in the synagogues, and greetings in the markets. {11:44} Woe unto you, scribes and Pharisees, hypocrites! for ye are as graves which appear not, and the men that walk over [them] are not aware [of them.

]{11:45} Then answered one of the lawyers, and said unto **Him**, **Master**, thus saying **thou** reproachest us also. {11:46} And **He** said, Woe unto you also, [ye] lawyers! for ye lade men with burdens grievous to be borne, and ye yourselves touch not the burdens with one of your fingers. {11:47} Woe unto you! for ye build the sepulchres of the prophets, and your Fathers killed them. {11:48} Truly ye bear witness that ye allow the deeds of your Fathers: for they indeed killed them, and ye build their sepulchres. {11:49} Therefore also said the wisdom of **God**, I will send them prophets and apostles, and [some] of them they shall slay and persecute: {11:50} That the blood of all the prophets, which was shed from the foundation of the world, may be required of this generation; {11:51} From the blood of Abel unto the blood of Zacharias, which perished between the altar and the temple: verily I say unto you, It shall be required of this generation. {11:52} Woe unto you, lawyers! for ye have taken away the key of knowledge: ye entered not in yourselves, and them that were entering in ye hindered. {11:53} And as **He** said these things unto them, the scribes and the Pharisees began to urge [**Him**] vehemently, and to provoke **Him** to speak of many things: {11:54} Laying wait for **Him**, and seeking to catch something out of **His** mouth, that they might accuse **Him**. {57}

{12:1} In the mean time, when there were gathered together an innumerable multitude of people, insomuch that they trode one upon another, **He** began to say unto **His** disciples first of all, Beware ye of the leaven of the Pharisees, which is hypocrisy. {12:2} For there is nothing covered, that shall not be revealed; neither hid, that shall not be known. {12:3} Therefore whatsoever ye have spoken in darkness shall be heard in the light; and that which ye have spoken in the ear in closets shall be proclaimed upon the housetops. {12:4} And I say unto you **my** friends, Be not afraid of them that kill the body, and after that have no more that they can do. {12:5} But **I** will forewarn you **whom** ye shall fear: Fear **Him**, which after **He** hath killed hath power to cast into hell; yea, **I** say unto you, Fear **Him**. {12:6} Are not five sparrows sold for two farthings, and not one of them is forgotten before **God**? {12:7} But even the very hairs of your head are all numbered. Fear not therefore: ye are of more value than many sparrows. {12:8} Also **I** say unto you, Whosoever shall confess **ME** before men, him shall the **Son of man** also confess before the angels of **God**: {12:9} But he that denieth **ME** before men shall be denied before the angels of **God**. {12:10} And whosoever shall speak a word against the **Son of man**, it shall be forgiven him: but unto him that blasphemeth against the **Holy Ghost** it shall not be forgiven. {12:11} And when they bring you unto the synagogues, and [unto] magistrates, and powers, take ye no thought how or what thing ye shall answer, or what ye shall say: {12:12} For the **Holy Ghost** shall teach you in the same hour what ye ought to say.

{12:13} And one of the company said unto **Him**, **Master**, speak to my brother, that me divide the inheritance with me. {12:14} And **He** said unto him, Man, who made **ME** a judge or a divider over you? {12:15} And **He** said unto them, Take heed, and beware of covetousness: for a man's life consisteth not in the abundance of the things which he possesseth. {12:16} And **He** spake a parable unto them, saying, The ground of a certain rich man brought forth plentifully: {12:17} And me thought within himself, saying, What shall I do, because I have no room where to bestow my fruits? {12:18} And me said, This will I do: I will pull down my barns, and build greater; and there will I bestow all my fruits and my goods. {12:19} And I will say to my soul, Soul, thou hast much goods laid up for many years; take thine ease, eat, drink, [and] be merry. {12:20} But God said unto him, [Thou] fool, this night thy soul shall be required of thee: then whose shall those things be, which thou hast provided? {12:21} So [is] me that layeth up treasure for himself, and is not rich toward **God**.

{12:22} And **He** said unto **His** disciples, Therefore **I** say unto you, Take no thought for your life, what ye shall eat; neither for the body, what ye shall put on. {12:23} The life is more than meat, and the body [is more] than raiment. {12:24} Consider the ravens: for they neither sow nor reap; which neither have storehouse nor barn; and **God** feedeth them: how much more are ye better than the fowls? {12:25} And which of you with taking thought can add to his stature one cubit? {12:26} If ye then be not able to do that thing which is least, why take ye thought for the rest? {12:27} Consider the lilies how they grow: they toil not, they spin not; and yet **I** say unto you, that Solomon in all his glory was not arrayed like one of these. {12:28} If then **God** so clothe the grass, which is to day in the field, and to morrow is cast into the oven; how much more [will **He** clothe] you, O ye of little faith? {12:29} And seek not ye what ye shall eat, or what ye shall drink, neither be ye of doubtful mind. {12:30} For all these things do the nations of the world seek after: and your **Father** knoweth that ye have need of these things.

{12:31} But rather seek ye the kingdom of **God**; and all these things shall be added unto you. {12:32} Fear not, little flock; for it is your **Father**'s good pleasure to give you the kingdom. {12:33} Sell that ye have, and give alms; provide yourselves bags which wax not old, a treasure in the heavens that faileth not, where no thief approacheth, neither moth corrupteth. {12:34} For where your treasure is, there will your heart be also. {12:35} Let your loins be girded about, and [your] lights burning; {12:36} And ye yourselves

like unto men that wait for their **Lord**, when **He** will return from the wedding; that when **He** cometh and knocketh, they may open unto **Him** immediately. {12:37} Blessed [are] those servants, **whom** the **Lord** when **He** cometh shall find watching: verily **I** say unto you, that **He** shall gird **himself**, and make them to sit down to meat, and will come forth and serve them. {12:38} And if **He** shall come in the second watch, or come in the third watch, and find [them] so, blessed are those servants. {12:39} And this know, that if the goodman of the house had known what hour the thief would come, he would have watched, and not have suffered his house to be broken through. {12:40} Be ye therefore ready also: for the **Son of man** cometh at an hour when ye think not.

{12:41} Then Peter said unto **Him**, **Lord**, speakest thou this parable unto us, or even to all? {12:42} And the **Lord** said, Who then is that faithful and wise steward, whom [**His**] **Lord** shall make ruler over **His** household, to give [them their] portion of meat in due season? {12:43} Blessed [is] that servant, whom **His Lord** when **He** cometh shall find so doing. {12:44} Of a truth **I** say unto you, that **He** will make him ruler over all that **He** hath. {12:45} But and if that servant say in his heart, **my Lord** delayeth **His** coming; and shall begin to beat the menservants and maidens, and to eat and drink, and to be drunken; {12:46} The **Lord** of that servant will come in a day when he looketh not for [**Him**,] and at an hour when he is not aware, and will cut him in sunder, and will appoint him his portion with the unbelievers. {12:47} And that servant, which knew **His Lord's** will, and prepared not [himself,] neither did according to **His** will, shall be beaten with many [stripes.]{12:48} But he that knew not, and did commit things worthy of stripes, shall be beaten with few [stripes.] For unto whomsoever much is given, of him shall be much required: and to whom men have committed much, of him they will ask the more.

{12:49} **I am** come to send fire on the earth; and what will **I** if it be already kindled? {12:50} But **I** have a baptism to be baptized with; and how am **I** straitened till it be accomplished! {12:51} Suppose ye that **I am** come to give peace on earth? **I** tell you, Nay; but rather division: {12:52} For from henceforth there shall be five in one house divided, three against two, and two against three. {12:53} The Father shall be divided against the Son, and the Son against the Father; the mother against the daughter, and the daughter against the mother; the mother in law against her daughter in law, and the daughter in law against her mother in law.

{12:54} And **He** said also to the people, When ye see a cloud rise out of the west, straightway ye say, There cometh a shower; and so it is. {12:55} And when [ye see] the south wind blow, ye say, There will be heat; and it cometh to pass. {12:56} [Ye] hypocrites, ye can discern the face of the sky and of the earth; but how is it that ye do not discern this time? {12:57} Yea, and why even of yourselves judge ye not what is right?{12:58} When thou goest with thine adversary to the magistrate, [as thou art] in the way, give diligence that thou mayest be delivered from him; lest he hale thee to the judge, and the judge deliver thee to the officer, and the officer cast thee into prison. {12:59} **I** tell thee, thou shalt not depart thence, till thou hast paid the very last mite.

{66}

{13:1} There were present at that season some that told **Him** of the Galilaeans, whose blood Pilate had mingled with their sacrifices. {13:2} And **Jesus** answering said unto them, Suppose ye that these Galilaeans were sinners above all the Galilaeans, because they suffered such things? {13:3} **I** tell you, Nay: but, except ye repent, ye shall all likewise perish. {13:4} Or those eighteen, upon **whom** the tower in Siloam fell, and slew them, think ye that they were sinners above all men that dwelt in Jerusalem? {13:5} **I** tell you, Nay: but, except ye repent, ye shall all likewise perish.

{13:6} **He** spake also this parable; A certain [man] had a fig tree planted in **His** vineyard; and **He** came and sought fruit thereon, and found none. {13:7} Then said **He** unto the **dresser** of **His** vineyard, Behold, these three years **I** come seeking fruit on this fig tree, and find none: cut it down; why cumbereth it the ground? {13:8} And **He** answering said unto **Him**, **Lord**, let it alone this year also, till **I** shall dig about it, and dung [it:]{13:9} And if it bear fruit, [well:] and if not, [then] after that thou shalt cut it down. {13:10} And **He** was teaching in one of the synagogues on the sabbath.

{13:11} And, behold, there was a woman which had a spirit of infirmity eighteen years, and was bowed together, and could in no wise lift up [herself.]{13:12} And when **Jesus** saw her, **He** called [her to **Him**,] and said unto her, Woman, thou art loosed from thine infirmity. {13:13} And **He** laid [**His**] hands on her: and immediately she was made straight, and glorified **God**. {13:14} And the ruler of the synagogue answered with indignation, because that **Jesus** had healed on the sabbath day, and said unto the people, There are six days in which men ought to work: in them therefore come and be healed, and not on the sabbath day. {13:15} The **Lord** then answered him, and said, [Thou] hypocrite, doth not each one of you on the sabbath loose his ox or [his] ass from the stall, and lead [him] away to watering? {13:16} And ought not this woman, being a daughter of Abraham, whom Satan hath bound, lo, these eighteen years, be loosed from this bond on the sabbath day? {13:17} And when **He** had said these things, all **His** adversaries were ashamed: and all the people rejoiced for all the glorious things that were done by **Him**.

{13:18} Then said **He**, Unto what is the kingdom of **God** like? and whereunto shall **I** resemble it? {13:19} It is like a **grain of mustard seed**, which a man took, and cast into **His** garden; and it grew, and waxed a great tree; and the fowls of the air lodged in the branches of it. {13:20} And again **He** said, Whereunto shall **I** liken the kingdom of **God**? {13:21} It is like **leaven**, which a woman took and hid in three measures of meal, till the whole was leavened. {13:22} And **He** went through the cities and villages, teaching, and journeying toward Jerusalem. {13:23} Then said one unto **Him**, **Lord**, are there few that be saved? And **He** said unto them,

{13:24} Strive to enter in at the strait gate: for many, **I** say unto you, will seek to enter in, and shall not be able. {13:25} When once the **master** of the house is risen up, and hath shut to the door, and ye begin to stand without, and to knock at the door, saying, **Lord**, **Lord**, open unto us; and **He** shall answer and say unto you, **I** know you not whence ye are: {13:26} Then shall ye begin to say, We have eaten and drunk in **thy** presence, and **thou** hast taught in our streets. {13:27} But **He** shall say, **I** tell you, **I** know you not whence ye are; depart from **ME**, all [ye] workers of iniquity. {13:28} There shall be weeping and gnashing of teeth, when ye shall see Abraham, and Isaac, and Jacob, and all the prophets, in the kingdom of **God**, and you [yourselves] thrust out. {13:29} And they shall come from the east, and [from] the

west, and from the north, and [from] the south, and shall sit down in the kingdom of **God**. {13:30} And, behold, there are last which shall be first, and there are first which shall be last.{13:31} The same day there came certain of the Pharisees, saying unto **Him**, Get **thee** out, and depart hence: for Herod will kill **thee**. {13:32} And **He** said unto them, Go ye, and tell that fox, Behold, **I** cast out devils, and **I** do cures to day and to morrow, and the third [day] **I** shall be perfected. {13:33} Nevertheless **I** must walk to day, and to morrow, and the [day] following: for it cannot be that a prophet perish out of Jerusalem. {13:34} O Jerusalem, Jerusalem, which killest the prophets, and stonest them that are sent unto thee; how often would **I** have gathered thy children together, as a **hen** [doth gather] **her** brood under [**her**] wings, and ye would not! {13:35} Behold, your house is left unto you desolate: and verily **I** say unto you, Ye shall not see **ME**, until [the time] come when ye shall say, Blessed [is] **He** that cometh in the name of the **Lord**. {56}

{14:1} And it came to pass, as **He** went into the house of one of the chief Pharisees to eat bread on the sabbath day, that they watched **Him**. {14:2} And, behold, there was a certain man before **Him** which had the dropsy. {14:3} And **Jesus** answering spake unto the lawyers and Pharisees, saying, Is it lawful to heal on the sabbath day? {14:4} And they held their peace. And **He** took [him,] and healed him, and let him go; {14:5} And answered them, saying, Which of you shall have an ass or an ox fallen into a pit, and will not straightway pull him out on the sabbath day? {14:6} And they could not answer **Him** again to these things.

{14:7} And **He** put forth a parable to those which were bidden, when **He** marked how they chose out the chief rooms; saying unto them, {14:8} When thou art bidden of any [man] to a wedding, sit not down in the highest room; lest a more honourable man than thou be bidden of him; {14:9} And he that bade thee and him come and say to thee, Give this man place; and thou begin with shame to take the lowest room. {14:10} But when thou art bidden, go and sit down in the lowest room; that when he that bade thee cometh, he may say unto thee, Friend, go up higher: then shalt thou have worship in the presence of them that sit at meat with thee. {14:11} For whosoever exalteth himself shall be abased; and he that humbleth himself shall be exalted.

{14:12} Then said **He** also to him that bade him, When thou makest a dinner or a supper, call not thy friends, nor thy brethren, neither thy kinsmen, nor [thy] rich neighbours; lest they also bid thee again, and a recompence be made thee. {14:13} But when thou makest a feast, call the poor, the maimed, the lame, the blind: {14:14} And thou shalt be blessed; for they cannot recompense thee: for thou shalt be recompensed at the resurrection of the just.

{14:15} And when one of them that sat at meat with **Him** heard these things, he said unto **Him**, Blessed [is] he that shall eat bread in the kingdom of **God**. {14:16} Then said **He** unto him, A **certain man** made a great supper, and bade many: {14:17} And sent **His** servant at supper time to say to them that were bidden, Come; for all things are now ready. {14:18} And they all with one [consent] began to make excuse. The first said unto **Him**, I have bought a piece of ground, and I must needs go and see it: I pray thee have me excused. {14:19} And another said, I have bought five yoke of oxen, and I go to prove them: I pray thee have me excused. {14:20} And another said, I have married a wife, and therefore I cannot come. {14:21} So that servant came, and shewed his **Lord** these things. Then the **master** of the house being angry said to **His** servant, Go out quickly into the streets and lanes of the city, and bring in hither the poor, and the maimed, and the halt, and the blind. {14:22} And the servant said, **Lord**, it is done as **thou** hast commanded, and yet there is room. {14:23} And the **Lord** said unto the servant, Go out into the highways and hedges, and compel [them] to come in, that **my** house may be filled. {14:24} For **I** say unto you, That none of those men which were bidden shall taste of **my** supper.

{14:25} And there went great multitudes with **Him**: and **He** turned, and said unto them, {14:26} If any [man] come to **ME**, and hate not his Father, and mother, and wife, and children, and brethren, and sisters, yea, and his own life also, **He** cannot be **my** disciple. {14:27} And whosoever doth not bear his cross, and come after **ME**, cannot be **my** disciple. {14:28} For which of you, intending to build a tower, sitteth not down first, and counteth the cost, whether he have [sufficient] to finish [it?]{14:29} Lest haply, after he hath laid the foundation, and is not able to finish [it,] all that behold [it] begin to mock him, {14:30} Saying, This man began to build, and was not able to finish. {14:31} Or what king, going to make war against another king, sitteth not down first, and consulteth whether he be able with ten thousand to meet him that cometh against him with twenty thousand? {14:32} Or else, while the other is yet a great way off, he sendeth an ambassage, and desireth conditions of peace. {14:33} So likewise, whosoever he be of you that forsaketh not all that he hath, he cannot be **my** disciple.

{14:34} Salt [is] good: but if the salt have lost his savour, wherewith shall it be seasoned? {14:35} It is neither fit for the land, nor yet for the dunghill; [but] men cast it out. He that hath ears to hear, let him hear. **{32}**

{15:1} Then drew near unto **Him** all the publicans and sinners for to hear **Him**. {15:2} And the Pharisees and scribes murmured, saying, This **man** receiveth sinners, and eateth with them.

{15:3} And **He** spake this parable unto them, saying, {15:4} What **man** of you, having an hundred sheep, if **He** lose one of them, doth not leave the ninety and nine in the wilderness, and go after that which is lost, until **He** find it? {15:5} And when **He** hath found [it,] **He** layeth [it] on **His** shoulders, rejoicing. {15:6} And when **He** cometh home, **He** calleth together [**His**] friends and neighbours, saying unto them, Rejoice with **ME**; for **I** have found **my** sheep which was lost. {15:7} **I** say unto you, that likewise joy shall be in heaven over one sinner that repenteth, more than over ninety and nine just persons, which need no repentance.

{15:8} Either what **woman** having ten pieces of silver, if **she** lose one piece, doth not light a candle, and sweep the house, and seek diligently till **she** find [it?]{15:9} And when **she** hath found [it,] **she** calleth [her] friends and [**her**] neighbours together, saying, Rejoice with **ME**; for **I** have found the piece which **I** had lost. {15:10} Likewise, **I** say unto you, there is joy in the presence of the angels of **God** over one sinner that repenteth.

{15:11} And **He** said, A certain man had two sons: {15:12} And the younger of them said to [his] Father, Father, give me the portion of goods that falleth [to m.] And he divided unto them [his] living. {15:13} And not many days after the younger Son gathered all together, and took his journey into a far country, and there wasted his

substance with riotous living. {15:14} And when He had spent all, there arose a mighty famine in that land; and He began to be in want. {15:15} And He went and joined himself to a citizen of that country; and He sent Him into His fields to feed swine. {15:16} And He would fain have filled His belly with the husks that the swine did eat: and no man gave unto Him. {15:17} And when He came to himself, He said, How many hired servants of my Father's have bread enough and to spare, and I perish with hunger! {15:18} I will arise and go to my Father, and will say unto Him, Father, I have sinned against heaven, and before thee, {15:19} And am no more worthy to be called thy Son: make ME as one of thy hired servants. {15:20} And He arose, and came to His Father. But when He was yet a great way off, His Father saw Him, and had compassion, and ran, and fell on His neck, and kissed Him. {15:21} And the Son said unto Him, Father, I have sinned against heaven, and in thy sight, and am no more worthy to be called thy Son. {15:22} But the Father said to His servants, Bring forth the best robe, and put [it] on Him; and put a ring on His hand, and shoes on [His] feet: {15:23} And bring hither the fatted calf, and kill [it;] and let us eat, and be merry: {15:24} For this my Son was dead, and is alive again; He was lost, and is found. And they began to be merry. {15:25} Now His elder Son was in the field: and as He came and drew nigh to the house, He heard musick and dancing. {15:26} And He called one of the servants, and asked what these things meant. {15:27} And He said unto Him, Thy brother is come; and thy Father hath killed the fatted calf, because He hath received Him safe and sound. {15:28} And He was angry, and would not go in: therefore came His Father out, and intreated Him. {15:29} And He answering said to [His] Father, Lo, these many years do I serve thee, neither transgressed I at any time thy commandment: and yet thou never gavest ME a kid, that I might make merry with my friends: {15:30} But as soon as this thy Son was come, which hath devoured thy living with harlots, thou hast killed for Him the fatted calf. {15:31} And He said unto Him, Son, thou art ever with ME, and all that I have is thine. {15:32} It was meet that we should make merry, and be glad: for this thy brother was dead, and is alive again; and was lost, and is found. **{28}**

{16:1} And **He** said also unto **His** disciples, There was a certain rich man, which had a steward; and the same was accused unto Him that He had wasted His goods. {16:2} And He called Him, and said unto Him, How is it that I hear this of thee? give an account of thy stewardship; for thou mayest be no longer steward. {16:3} Then the steward said within himself, What shall I do? for my Lord taketh away from ME the stewardship: I cannot dig; to beg I am ashamed. {16:4} I am resolved what to do, that, when I am put out of the stewardship, they may receive ME into their houses. {16:5} So He called every one of His Lord's debtors [unto Him,] and said unto the first, How much owest thou unto my Lord? {16:6} And He said, An hundred measures of oil. And He said unto Him, Take thy bill, and sit down quickly, and write fifty. {16:7} Then said He to another, And how much owest thou? And He said, An hundred measures of wheat. And He said unto Him, Take thy bill, and write fourscore. {16:8} And the Lord commended the unjust steward, because He had done wisely: for the children of this world are in their generation wiser than the children of light. {16:9} And **I** say unto you, Make to yourselves friends of the mammon of unrighteousness; that, when ye fail, they may receive you into everlasting habitations. {16:10} He that is faithful in that which is least is faithful also in much: and He that is unjust in the least is unjust also in much. {16:11} If therefore ye have not been faithful in the unrighteous mammon, who will commit to your trust the true [riches?

]{{16:12} And if ye have not been faithful in that which is another man's, who shall give you that which is your own?

{16:13} No servant can serve two masters: for either He will hate the one, and love the other; or else He will hold to the one, and despise the other. Ye cannot serve **God** and mammon. {16:14} And the Pharisees also, who were covetous, heard all these things: and they derided **Him**. {16:15} And **He** said unto them, Ye are they which justify yourselves before men; but **God** knoweth your hearts: for that which is highly esteemed among men is abomination in the sight of **God**. {16:16} The law and the prophets [were] until John: since that time the kingdom of **God** is preached, and every man presseth into it. {16:17} And it is easier for heaven and earth to pass, than one tittle of the law to fail. {16:18} Whosoever putteth away his wife, and marrieth another, committeth adultery: and whosoever marrieth her that is put away from [her] husband committeth adultery.

{16:19} There was a certain rich man, which was clothed in purple and fine linen, and fared sumptuously every day: {16:20} And there was a certain beggar named Lazarus, which was laid at his gate, full of sores, {16:21} And desiring to be fed with the crumbs which fell from the rich man's table: moreover the dogs came and licked his sores. {16:22} And it came to pass, that the beggar died, and was carried by the angels into Abraham's bosom: the rich man also died, and was buried; {16:23} And in hell he lift up his eyes, being in torments, and seeth Abraham afar off, and Lazarus in his bosom. {16:24} And he cried and said, Father Abraham, have mercy on me, and send Lazarus, that he may dip the tip of his finger in water, and cool my tongue; for I am tormented in this flame. {16:25} But Abraham said, son, remember that thou in thy lifetime receivedst thy good things, and likewise Lazarus evil things: but now he is comforted, and thou art tormented. {16:26} And beside all this, between us and you there is a great gulf fixed: so that they which would pass from hence to you cannot; neither can they pass to us, that [would come] from thence. {16:27} Then he said, I pray thee therefore, Father, that thou wouldest send him to my Father's house: {16:28} For I have five brethren; that he may testify unto them, lest they also come into this place of torment. {16:29} Abraham saith unto him, They have Moses and the prophets; let them hear them. {16:30} And he said, Nay, Father Abraham: but if one went unto them from the dead, they will repent. {16:31} And he said unto him, If they hear not Moses and the prophets, neither will they be persuaded, though one rose from the dead. **{5}**

{17:1} Then said **He** unto the disciples, It is impossible but that offences will come: but woe [unto Him,] through whom they come! {17:2} It were better for Him that a millstone were hanged about His neck, and He cast into the sea, than that He should offend one of these little ones.

{17:3} Take heed to yourselves: If thy brother trespass against thee, rebuke Him; and if He repent, forgive Him. {17:4} And if He trespass against thee seven times in a day, and seven times in a day turn again to thee, saying, I repent; thou shalt forgive Him. {17:5} And the apostles said unto the **Lord**, Increase our faith. {17:6} And the **Lord** said, If ye had faith as a grain of mustard seed, ye might say unto this sycamine tree, Be thou plucked up by the root, and be thou planted in the sea; and it should obey you. {17:7} But which of you, having a servant plowing or feeding cattle, will say unto Him by and by, when He is come from the field, Go and sit down to meat? {17:8} And will not rather say unto Him, Make ready wherewith I may sup, and gird

thyself, and serve **ME**, till **I** have eaten and drunken; and afterward thou shalt eat and drink? {17:9} Doth **He** thank that servant because he did the things that were commanded him? **I** trow not. {17:10} So likewise ye, when ye shall have done all those things which are commanded you, say, We are unprofitable servants: we have done that which was our duty to do.

{17:11} And it came to pass, as **He** went to Jerusalem, that **He** passed through the midst of Samaria and Galilee. {17:12} And as **He** entered into a certain village, there met **Him** ten men that were lepers, which stood afar off: {17:13} And they lifted up [their] voices, and said, **Jesus**, **Master**, have mercy on us. {17:14} And when **He** saw [them,] **He** said unto them, Go shew yourselves unto the priests. And it came to pass, that, as they went, they were cleansed. {17:15} And one of them, when he saw that he was healed, turned back, and with a loud voice glorified **God**, {17:16} And fell down on [his] face at **His** feet, giving **Him** thanks: and he was a Samaritan. {17:17} And **Jesus** answering said, Were there not ten cleansed? but where [are] the nine? {17:18} There are not found that returned to give glory to **God**, save this stranger. {17:19} And **He** said unto him, Arise, go thy way: thy faith hath made thee whole.

{17:20} And when **He** was demanded of the Pharisees, when the kingdom of **God** should come, **He** answered them and said, The kingdom of **God** cometh not with observation: {17:21} Neither shall they say, Lo here! or, lo there! for, behold, the kingdom of **God** is within you. {17:22} And **He** said unto the disciples, The days will come, when ye shall desire to see one of the days of the **Son of man**, and ye shall not see [it.]{17:23} And they shall say to you, See here; or, see there: go not after [them,] nor follow [them.]{17:24} For as the lightning, that lighteneth out of the one [part] under heaven, shineth unto the other [part] under heaven; so shall also the **Son of man** be in **His** day. {17:25} But first must **He** suffer many things, and be rejected of this generation. {17:26} And as it was in the days of Noe, so shall it be also in the days of the **Son of man**. {17:27} They did eat, they drank, they married wives, they were given in marriage, until the day that Noe entered into the ark, and the flood came, and destroyed them all. {17:28} Likewise also as it was in the days of Lot; they did eat, they drank, they bought, they sold, they planted, they builded; {17:29} But the same day that Lot went out of Sodom it rained fire and brimstone from heaven, and destroyed [them] all. {17:30} Even thus shall it be in the day when the **Son of man** is revealed. {17:31} In that day, he which shall be upon the housetop, and his stuff in the house, let him not come down to take it away: and he that is in the field, let him likewise not return back. {17:32} Remember Lot's wife. {17:33} Whosoever shall seek to save his life shall lose it; and whosoever shall lose his life shall preserve it. {17:34} **I** tell you, in that night there shall be two [men] in one bed; the one shall be taken, and the other shall be left. {17:35} Two [women] shall be grinding together; the one shall be taken, and the other left. {17:36} Two [men] shall be in the field; the one shall be taken, and the other left. {17:37} And they answered and said unto **Him**, Where, **Lord**? And **He** said unto them, Wheresoever the body is, thither will the eagles be gathered together. **{36}**

{18:1} And **He** spake a parable unto them [to this end,] that men ought always to pray, and not to faint; {18:2} Saying, There was in a city a judge, which feared not **God**, neither regarded man: {18:3} And there was a widow in that city; and she came unto him, saying, Avenge me of mine adversary. {18:4} And he would not for a while: but afterward he said within himself, Though I fear not God, nor regard man; {18:5} Yet because this widow troubleth me, I will avenge her, lest by her continual coming she weary me. {18:6} And the **Lord** said, Hear what the unjust judge saith. {18:7} And shall not God avenge **His** own elect, which cry day and night unto **Him**, though **He** bear long with them? {18:8} **I** tell you that **He** will avenge them speedily. Nevertheless when the Son of man cometh, shall **He** find faith on the earth? {18:9} And **He** spake this parable unto certain which trusted in themselves that they were righteous, and despised others: {18:10} Two men went up into the temple to pray; the one a Pharisee, and the other a publican. {18:11} The Pharisee stood and prayed thus with himself, **God**, I thank thee, that I am not as other men [are,] extortioners, unjust, adulterers, or even as this publican. {18:12} I fast twice in the week, I give tithes of all that I possess. {18:13} And the publican, standing afar off, would not lift up so much as [his] eyes unto heaven, but smote upon his breast, saying, **God** be merciful to me a sinner. {18:14} **I** tell you, this man went down to his house justified [rather] than the other: for every one that exalteth himself shall be abased; and he that humbleth himself shall be exalted. {18:15} And they brought unto **Him** also infants, that **He** would touch them: but when [His] disciples saw [it,] they rebuked them. {18:16} But **Jesus** called them [unto **Him**,] and said, Suffer little children to come unto **ME**, and forbid them not: for of such is the kingdom of **God**. {18:17} Verily I say unto you, Whosoever shall not receive the kingdom of **God** as a little child shall in no wise enter therein. {18:18} And a certain ruler asked **Him**, saying, **Good Master**, what shall **I** do to inherit eternal life? {18:19} And **Jesus** said unto him, Why callest thou **ME** good? none [is] good, save **one**, [that is,] **God**. {18:20} Thou knowest the commandments, Do not commit adultery, Do not kill, Do not steal, Do not bear false witness, Honour thy **Father** and thy mother. {18:21} And he said, All these have I kept from my youth up. {18:22} Now when **Jesus** heard these things, **He** said unto him, Yet lackest thou one thing: sell all that thou hast, and distribute unto the poor, and thou shalt have treasure in heaven: and come, follow **ME**. {18:23} And when he heard this, he was very sorrowful: for he was very rich. {18:24} And when **Jesus** saw that he was very sorrowful, **He** said, How hardly shall they that have riches enter into the kingdom of **God**! {18:25} For it is easier for a camel to go through a needle's eye, than for a rich man to enter into the kingdom of **God**. {18:26} And they that heard [it] said, Who then can be saved? {18:27} And **He** said, The things which are impossible with men are possible with **God**. {18:28} Then Peter said, Lo, we have left all, and followed **thee**. {18:29} And **He** said unto them, Verily **I** say unto you, There is no man that hath left house, or parents, or brethren, or wife, or children, for the kingdom of **God**'s sake, {18:30} Who shall not receive manifold more in this present time, and in the world to come life everlasting.

{18:31} Then **He** took [unto **Him**] the twelve, and said unto them, Behold, we go up to Jerusalem, and all things that are written by the prophets concerning the Son of man shall be accomplished. {18:32} For **He** shall be delivered unto the Gentiles, and shall be mocked, and spitefully entreated, and spitted on: {18:33} And they shall scourge [**Him**,] and put **Him** to death: and the third day **He** shall rise again. {18:34} And they understood none of these things: and this saying was hid from them, neither knew they the things which were spoken.

{18:35} And it came to pass, that as **He** was come nigh unto Jericho, a certain blind man sat by the way side begging: {18:36} And hearing the multitude pass by, he

asked what it meant. {18:37} And they told him, that **Jesus of Nazareth** passeth by. {18:38} And he cried, saying, **Jesus**, [thou] **Son of David**, have mercy on **me**. {18:39} And they which went before rebuked him, that he should hold his peace: but he cried so much the more, [**Thou**] **Son of David**, have mercy on me. {18:40} And **Jesus** stood, and commanded him to be brought unto **Him**: and when he was come near, **He** asked **him**, {18:41} Saying, What wilt thou that **I** shall do unto thee? And he said, **Lord**, that I may receive my sight. {18:42} And **Jesus** said unto him, Receive thy sight: thy faith hath saved thee. {18:43} And immediately he received his sight, and followed **Him**, glorifying **God**: and all the people, when they saw [it,] gave praise unto **God**. {50}

{19:1} And [**Jesus**] entered and passed through Jericho. {19:2} And, behold, [there was] a man named Zacchaeus, which was the chief among the publicans, and he was rich. {19:3} And he sought to see **Jesus who He** was; and could not for the press, because he was little of stature. {19:4} And he ran before, and climbed up into a sycomore tree to see **Him**: for **He** was to pass that [way.]{19:5} And when **Jesus** came to the place, **He** looked up, and saw him, and said unto him, Zacchaeus, make haste, and come down; for to day **I** must abide at thy house. {19:6} And he made haste, and came down, and received **Him** joyfully. {19:7} And when they saw [it,] they all murmured, saying, That **He** was gone to be guest with a man that is a sinner. {19:8} And Zacchaeus stood, and said unto the **Lord**; Behold, **Lord**, the half of my goods I give to the poor; and if I have taken any thing from any man by false accusation, I restore [him] fourfold. {19:9} And **Jesus** said unto him, This day is salvation come to this house, forsomuch as he also is a son of Abraham. {19:10} For the Son of man is come to seek and to save that which was lost. {19:11} And as they heard these things, **He** added and spake a parable, because **He** was nigh to Jerusalem, and because they thought that the kingdom of **God** should immediately appear. {19:12} **He** said therefore, A certain **nobleman** went into a far country to receive for **himself** a kingdom, and to return. {19:13} And **He** called **His** ten servants, and delivered them ten pounds, and said unto them, Occupy till **I** come. {19:14} But **His** citizens hated **Him**, and sent a message after **Him**, saying, We will not have this [**man**] to reign over us. {19:15} And it came to pass, that when **He** was returned, having received the kingdom, then **He** commanded these servants to be called unto **Him**, to **whom He** had given the money, that **He** might know how much every man had gained by trading. {19:16} Then came the first, saying, **Lord**, **thy** pound hath gained ten pounds. {19:17} And **He** said unto him, Well, thou good servant: because thou hast been faithful in a very little, have thou authority over ten cities. {19:18} And the second came, saying, **Lord**, **thy** pound hath gained five pounds. {19:19} And **He** said likewise to him, Be thou also over five cities. {19:20} And another came, saying, **Lord**, behold, [here is] **thy** pound, which I have kept laid up in a napkin: {19:21} For I feared **thee**, because **thou** art an austere man: **thou** takest up that **thou** layedst not down, and reapest that **thou** didst not sow. {19:22} And **He** saith unto him, Out of thine own mouth will **I** judge thee, [thou] wicked servant. Thou knewest that **I** was an austere man, taking up that **I** laid not down, and reaping that **I** did not sow: {19:23} Wherefore then gavest not thou **my** money into the bank, that at **my** coming **I** might have required **mine own** with usury? {19:24} And **He** said unto them that stood by, Take from him the pound, and give [it] to him that hath ten pounds. {19:25} (And they said unto **Him**, **Lord**, he hath ten pounds.) {19:26} For **I** say unto you, That unto every one which hath shall be given; and from him that hath not, even that he hath shall be taken away from him. {19:27} But those mine enemies, which would not that I should reign over them, bring hither, and slay [them] before ME.

{19:28} And when He had thus spoken, He went before, ascending up to Jerusalem. {19:29} And it came to pass, when He was come nigh to Bethphage and Bethany, at the mount called [the mount] of Olives, He sent two of His disciples, {19:30} Saying, Go ye into the village over against [you;] in the which at your entering ye shall find a colt tied, whereon yet never man sat: loose him, and bring [him hither.]{19:31} And if any man ask you, Why do ye loose [him?] thus shall ye say unto him, Because the Lord hath need of him. {19:32} And they that were sent went their way, and found even as He had said unto them. {19:33} And as they were loosing the colt, the owners thereof said unto them, Why loose ye the colt? {19:34} And they said, The Lord hath need of him. {19:35} And they brought him to Jesus: and they cast their garments upon the colt, and they set Jesus thereon. {19:36} And as He went, they spread their clothes in the way. {19:37} And when He was come nigh, even now at the descent of the mount of Olives, the whole multitude of the disciples began to rejoice and praise God with a loud voice for all the mighty works that they had seen; {19:38} Saying, Blessed [be] the King that cometh in the name of the Lord: peace in heaven, and glory in the highest. {19:39} And some of the Pharisees from among the multitude said unto Him, Master, rebuke thy disciples. {19:40} And He answered and said unto them, I tell you that, if these should hold their peace, the stones would immediately cry out.

{19:41} And when He was come near, He beheld the city, and wept over it, {19:42} Saying, If thou hadst known, even thou, at least in this thy day, the things [which belong] unto thy peace! but now they are hid from thine eyes. {19:43} For the days shall come upon thee, that thine enemies shall cast a trench about thee, and compass thee round, and keep thee in on every side, {19:44} And shall lay thee even with the ground, and thy children within thee; and they shall not leave in thee one stone upon another; because thou knewest not the time of thy visitation. {19:45} And He went into the temple, and began to cast out them that sold therein, and them that bought; {19:46} Saying unto them, It is written, my house is the house of prayer: but ye have made it a den of thieves. {19:47} And He taught daily in the temple. But the chief priests and the scribes and the chief of the people sought to destroy Him, {19:48} And could not find what they might do: for all the people were very attentive to hear Him. {87}

{20:1} And it came to pass, [that] on one of those days, as He taught the people in the temple, and preached the Gospel, the chief priests and the scribes came upon [Him] with the elders, {20:2} And spake unto Him, saying, Tell us, by what authority doest thou these things? or who is He that gave thee this authority? {20:3} And He answered and said unto them, I will also ask you one thing; and answer ME: {20:4} The baptism of John, was it from heaven, or of men? {20:5} And they reasoned with themselves, saying, If we shall say, From heaven; He will say, Why then believed ye him not? {20:6} But and if we say, Of men; all the people will stone us: for they be persuaded that John was a prophet. {20:7} And they answered, that they could not tell whence [it was.]{20:8} And Jesus said unto them, Neither tell I you by what authority I do these things. {20:9} Then began He to speak to the people this parable; A certain man planted a vineyard, and let it forth to husbandmen, and went into a far

country for a long time. {20:10} And at the season He sent a servant to the husbandmen, that they should give him of the fruit of the vineyard: but the husbandmen beat him, and sent [him] away empty. {20:11} And again He sent another servant: and they beat him also, and entreated [him] shamefully, and sent [him] away empty. {20:12} And again He sent a third: and they wounded him also, and cast [him] out. {20:13} Then said the Lord of the vineyard, What shall I do? I will send my beloved Son: it may be they will reverence [Him] when they see Him. {20:14} But when the husbandmen saw Him, they reasoned among themselves, saying, This is the heir: come, let us kill Him, that the inheritance may be ours. {20:15} So they cast Him out of the vineyard, and killed [Him.] What therefore shall the Lord of the vineyard do unto them? {20:16} He shall come and destroy these husbandmen, and shall give the vineyard to others. And when they heard [it,] they said, God forbid. {20:17} And He beheld them, and said, What is this then that is written, The stone which the builders rejected, the same is become the head of the corner? {20:18} Whosoever shall fall upon that stone shall be broken; but on whomsoever it shall fall, it will grind him to powder.

{20:19} And the chief priests and the scribes the same hour sought to lay hands on Him; and they feared the people: for they perceived that He had spoken this parable against them. {20:20} And they watched [Him,] and sent forth spies, which should feign themselves just men, that they might take hold of His words, that so they might deliver Him unto the power and authority of the governor. {20:21} And they asked Him, saying, Master, we know that thou sayest and teachest rightly, neither acceptest thou the person [of any,] but teachest the way of God truly: {20:22} Is it lawful for us to give tribute unto Caesar, or no? {20:23} But He perceived their craftiness, and said unto them, Why tempt ye ME? {20:24} Shew ME a penny. Whose image and superscription hath it? They answered and said, Caesar's. {20:25} And He said unto them, Render therefore unto Caesar the things which be Caesar's, and unto God the things which be God's. {20:26} And they could not take hold of His words before the people: and they marvelled at His answer, and held their peace.

{20:27} Then came to [Him] certain of the Sadducees, which deny that there is any resurrection; and they asked Him, {20:28} Saying, Master, Moses wrote unto us, If any man's brother die, having a wife, and he die without children, that his brother should take his wife, and raise up seed unto his brother. {20:29} There were therefore seven brethren: and the first took a wife, and died without children. {20:30} And the second took her to wife, and he died childless. {20:31} And the third took her; and in like manner the seven also: and they left no children, and died. {20:32} Last of all the woman died also. {20:33} Therefore in the resurrection whose wife of them is she? for seven had her to wife. {20:34} And Jesus answering said unto them, The children of this world marry, and are given in marriage: {20:35} But they which shall be accounted worthy to obtain that world, and the resurrection from the dead, neither marry, nor are given in marriage: {20:36} Neither can they die any more: for they are equal unto the angels; and are the children of God, being the children of the resurrection. {20:37} Now that the dead are raised, even Moses shewed at the bush, when he calleth the Lord the God of Abraham, and the God of Isaac, and the God of Jacob. {20:38} For He is not a God of the dead, but of the living: for all live unto Him.

{20:39} Then certain of the scribes answering said,

Master, thou hast well said. {20:40} And after that they durst not ask Him any [question at all.]{20:41} And He said unto them, How say they that Christ is David's Son? {20:42} And David himself saith in the book of Psalms, The LORD said unto my Lord, Sit thou on my right hand, {20:43} Till I make thine enemies thy footstool. {20:44} David therefore calleth Him Lord, how is He then His Son?

{20:45} Then in the audience of all the people He said unto His disciples, {20:46} Beware of the scribes, which desire to walk in long robes, and love greetings in the markets, and the highest seats in the synagogues, and the chief rooms at feasts; {20:47} Which devour widows' houses, and for a shew make long prayers: the same shall receive greater damnation. {69}

{21:1} And He looked up, and saw the rich men casting their gifts into the treasury. {21:2} And He saw also a certain poor widow casting in thither two mites. {21:3} And He said, Of a truth I say unto you, that this poor widow hath cast in more than they all: {21:4} For all these have of their abundance cast in unto the offerings of God: but she of her penury hath cast in all the living that she had.

{21:5} And as some spake of the temple, how it was adorned with goodly stones and gifts, He said, {21:6} [As for] these things which ye behold, the days will come, in the which there shall not be left one stone upon another, that shall not be thrown down. {21:7} And they asked Him, saying, Master, but when shall these things be? and what sign [will there be] when these things shall come to pass? {21:8} And He said, Take heed that ye be not deceived: for many shall come in my name, saying, I am [Christ;] and the time draweth near: go ye not therefore after them. {21:9} But when ye shall hear of wars and commotions, be not terrified: for these things must first come to pass; but the end [is] not by and by. {21:10} Then said He unto them, Nation shall rise against nation, and kingdom against kingdom: {21:11} And great earthquakes shall be in divers places, and famines, and pestilences; and fearful sights and great signs shall there be from heaven. {21:12} But before all these, they shall lay their hands on you, and persecute [you,] delivering [you] up to the synagogues, and into prisons, being brought before kings and rulers for my name's sake. {21:13} And it shall turn to you for a testimony. {21:14} Settle [it] therefore in your hearts, not to meditate before what ye shall answer: {21:15} For I will give you a mouth and wisdom, which all your adversaries shall not be able to gainsay nor resist. {21:16} And ye shall be betrayed both by parents, and brethren, and kinsfolks, and friends; and [some] of you shall they cause to be put to death. {21:17} And ye shall be hated of all [men] for my name's sake. {21:18} But there shall not an hair of your head perish. {21:19} In your patience possess ye your souls. {21:20} And when ye shall see Jerusalem compassed with armies, then know that the desolation thereof is nigh. {21:21} Then let them which are in Judaea flee to the mountains; and let them which are in the midst of it depart out; and let not them that are in the countries enter thereinto. {21:22} For these be the days of vengeance, that all things which are written may be fulfilled. {21:23} But woe unto them that are with child, and to them that give suck, in those days! for there shall be great distress in the land, and wrath upon this people. {21:24} And they shall fall by the edge of the sword, and shall be led away captive into all nations: and Jerusalem shall be trodden down of the Gentiles, until the times of the Gentiles be fulfilled.

{21:25} And there shall be signs in the sun, and in the moon, and in the stars; and upon the earth distress of nations, with perplexity; the sea and the waves roaring; {21:26} Men's hearts failing them for fear, and for looking after those things which are coming on the earth: for the powers of heaven shall be shaken. {21:27} And then shall they see the Son of man coming in a cloud with power and great glory. {21:28} And when these things begin to come to pass, then look up, and lift up your heads; for your redemption draweth nigh. {21:29} And He spake to them a parable; Behold the fig tree, and all the trees; {21:30} When they now shoot forth, ye see and know of your own selves that summer is now nigh at hand. {21:31} So likewise ye, when ye see these things come to pass, know ye that the kingdom of God is nigh at hand. {21:32} Verily I say unto you, This generation shall not pass away, till all be fulfilled. {21:33} Heaven and earth shall pass away: but my words shall not pass away.

{21:34} And take heed to yourselves, lest at any time your hearts be overcharged with surfeiting, and drunkenness, and cares of this life, and so that day come upon you unawares. {21:35} For as a snare shall it come on all them that dwell on the face of the whole earth. {21:36} Watch ye therefore, and pray always, that ye may be accounted worthy to escape all these things that shall come to pass, and to stand before the Son of man. {21:37} And in the day time He was teaching in the temple; and at night He went out, and abode in the mount that is called [the mount] of Olives. {21:38} And all the people came early in the morning to Him in the temple, for to hear Him. {27}

{22:1} Now the feast of unleavened bread drew nigh, which is called the Passover. {22:2} And the chief priests and scribes sought how they might kill Him; for they feared the people.

{22:3} Then entered Satan into Judas surnamed Iscariot, being of the number of the twelve. {22:4} And he went his way, and communed with the chief priests and captains, how he might betray Him unto them. {22:5} And they were glad, and covenanted to give him money. {22:6} And he promised, and sought opportunity to betray Him unto them in the absence of the multitude.

{22:7} Then came the day of unleavened bread, when the passover must be killed. {22:8} And He sent Peter and John, saying, Go and prepare us the passover, that we may eat. {22:9} And they said unto Him, Where wilt thou that we prepare? {22:10} And He said unto them, Behold, when ye are entered into the city, there shall a man meet you, bearing a pitcher of water; follow him into the house where he entereth in. {22:11} And ye shall say unto the goodman of the house, The Master saith unto thee, Where is the guestchamber, where I shall eat the passover with my disciples? {22:12} And he shall shew you a large upper room furnished: there make ready. {22:13} And they went, and found as He had said unto them: and they made ready the passover. {22:14} And when the hour was come, He sat down, and the twelve apostles with Him. {22:15} And He said unto them, With desire I have desired to eat this passover with you before I suffer: {22:16} For I say unto you, I will not any more eat thereof, until it be fulfilled in the kingdom of God. {22:17} And He took the cup, and gave thanks, and said, Take this, and divide [it] among yourselves: {22:18} For I say unto you, I will not drink of the fruit of the vine, until the kingdom of God shall come.

{22:19} And He took bread, and gave thanks, and brake [it,] and gave unto them, saying, This is my body which is given for you: this do in remembrance of **ME**. {22:20} Likewise also the cup after supper, saying, This cup [is] the new testament in **my blood**, which is shed for you.

{22:21} But, behold, the hand of him that betrayeth **ME** [is] with **ME** on the table. {22:22} And truly **the Son of man** goeth, as it was determined: but woe unto that man by **whom He** is betrayed! {22:23} And they began to enquire among themselves, which of them it was that should do this thing.

{22:24} And there was also a strife among them, which of them should be accounted the greatest. {22:25} And **He** said unto them, The kings of the Gentiles exercise lordship over them; and they that exercise authority upon them are called benefactors. {22:26} But ye [shall] not [be] so: but he that is greatest among you, let him be as the younger; and he that is chief, as he that doth serve. {22:27} For whether [is] greater, he that sitteth at meat, or he that serveth? [is] not he that sitteth at meat? but **I am** among you as **He** that serveth. {22:28} Ye are they which have continued with **ME** in **my** temptations. {22:29} And **I** appoint unto you a kingdom, as **my Father** hath appointed unto **ME**; {22:30} That ye may eat and drink at **my** table in **my** kingdom, and sit on thrones judging the twelve tribes of Israel.

{22:31} And the **Lord** said, Simon, Simon, behold, Satan hath desired [to have] you, that he may sift [you] as wheat: {22:32} But **I** have prayed for thee, that thy faith fail not: and when thou art converted, strengthen thy brethren. {22:33} And **He** said unto **Him**, **Lord**, I am ready to go with **thee**, both into prison, and to death. {22:34} And **He** said, **I** tell thee, Peter, the cock shall not crow this day, before that thou shalt thrice deny that thou knowest **ME**. {22:35} And **He** said unto them, When **I** sent you without purse, and scrip, and shoes, lacked ye any thing? And they said, Nothing. {22:36} Then said **He** unto them, But now, he that hath a purse, let him take [it,] and likewise [his] scrip: and he that hath no sword, let him sell his garment, and buy one. {22:37} For **I** say unto you, that this that is written must yet be accomplished in **ME**, And **He** was reckoned among the transgressors: for the things concerning **ME** have an end. {22:38} And they said, **Lord**, behold, here [are] two swords. And **He** said unto them, It is enough.

{22:39} And **He** came out, and went, as **He** was wont, to the mount of Olives; and **His** disciples also followed **Him**. {22:40} And when **He** was at the place, **He** said unto them, Pray that ye enter not into temptation. {22:41} And **He** was withdrawn from them about a stone's cast, and kneeled down, and prayed, {22:42} Saying, **Father**, if thou be willing, remove this cup from **ME**: nevertheless not **my** will, but thine, be done. {22:43} And there appeared an angel unto **Him** from heaven, strengthening **Him**. {22:44} And being in an agony **He** prayed more earnestly: and **His** sweat was as it were great drops of blood falling down to the ground. {22:45} And when **He** rose up from prayer, and was come to **His** disciples, **He** found them sleeping for sorrow, {22:46} And said unto them, Why sleep ye? rise and pray, lest ye enter into temptation.

{22:47} And while **He** yet spake, behold a multitude, and he that was called Judas, one of the twelve, went before them, and drew near unto **Jesus** to kiss **Him**. {22:48} But **Jesus** said unto him, Judas, betrayest thou the **Son of man** with a kiss? {22:49} When they which were about **Him** saw what would follow, they said unto **Him**, **Lord**, shall we smite with the sword?

{22:50} And one of them smote the servant of the high priest, and cut off his right ear. {22:51} And **Jesus** answered and said, Suffer ye thus far. And **He** touched his ear, and healed him. {22:52} Then **Jesus** said unto the chief priests, and captains of the temple, and the elders, which were come to **Him**, Be ye come out, as against a thief, with swords and staves? {22:53} When **I** was daily with you in the temple, ye stretched forth no hands against **ME**: but this is your hour, and the power of darkness.

{22:54} Then took they **Him**, and led [**Him**,] and brought **Him** into the high priest's house. And Peter followed afar off. {22:55} And when they had kindled a fire in the midst of the hall, and were set down together, Peter sat down among them. {22:56} But a certain maid beheld him as he sat by the fire, and earnestly looked upon him, and said, This man was also with **Him**. {22:57} And he denied **Him**, saying, Woman, I know **Him** not. {22:58} And after a little while another saw him, and said, Thou art also of them. And Peter said, Man, I am not. {22:59} And about the space of one hour after another confidently affirmed, saying, Of a truth this [fellow] also was with **Him**: for he is a Galilaean. {22:60} And Peter said, Man, I know not what thou sayest. And immediately, while he yet spake, the cock crew. {22:61} And the **Lord** turned, and looked upon Peter. And Peter remembered the word of the **Lord**, how **He** had said unto **Him**, Before the cock crow, thou shalt deny **ME** thrice. {22:62} And Peter went out, and wept bitterly.

{22:63} And the men that held **Jesus** mocked **Him**, and smote [**Him**.]{22:64} And when they had blindfolded **Him**, they struck **Him** on the face, and asked **Him**, saying, Prophesy, who is it that smote **thee**? {22:65} And many other things blasphemously spake they against **Him**.

{22:66} And as soon as it was day, the elders of the people and the chief priests and the scribes came together, and led **Him** into their council, saying, {22:67} Art **thou** the **Christ**? tell us. And **He** said unto them, If **I** tell you, ye will not believe: {22:68} And if **I** also ask [you,] ye will not answer **ME**, nor let [**ME**] go. {22:69} Hereafter shall the **Son of man** sit on the right hand of the power of **God**. {22:70} Then said they all, Art **thou** then the **Son of God**? And **He** said unto them, Ye say that **I am**. {22:71} And they said, What need we any further witness? for we ourselves have heard of **His own** mouth. {127}

{23:1} And the whole multitude of them arose, and led **Him** unto Pilate. {23:2} And they began to accuse **Him**, saying, We found this [**fellow**] perverting the nation, and forbidding to give tribute to Caesar, saying that **He himself** is **Christ** a King. {23:3} And Pilate asked **Him**, saying, Art **thou** the **King of the Jews**? And **He** answered **Him** and said, Thou sayest [it.]{23:4} Then said Pilate to the chief priests and [to] the people, I find no fault in this **man**. {23:5} And they were the more fierce, saying, **He** stirreth up the people, teaching throughout all Jewry, beginning from Galilee to this place. {23:6} When Pilate heard of Galilee, he asked whether the man were a Galilaean. {23:7} And as soon as he knew that he belonged unto Herod's jurisdiction, he sent **Him** to Herod, who himself also was at Jerusalem at that time.

{23:8} And when Herod saw **Jesus**, he was exceeding glad: for he was desirous to see **Him** of a long [season,] because he had heard many things of **Him**; and he hoped to have seen some miracle done by **Him**. {23:9} Then *he* questioned with **Him** in many words; but **He** answered **Him** nothing. {23:10} And the chief priests and scribes stood and vehemently accused **Him**. {23:11} And Herod with his men of war set **Him** at nought, and mocked [**Him**,] and arrayed **Him** in a gorgeous robe, and sent **Him** again to Pilate.

{23:12} And the same day Pilate and Herod were made friends together: for before they were at enmity between themselves.

{23:13} And Pilate, when he had called together the chief priests and the rulers and the people, {23:14} Said unto them, Ye have brought this man unto me, as one that perverteth the people: and, behold, I, having examined [**Him**] before you, have found no fault in this man touching those things whereof ye accuse **Him**: {23:15} No, nor yet Herod: for I sent you to him; and, lo, nothing worthy of death is done unto **Him**. {23:16} I will therefore chastise **Him**, and release [**Him**.]{23:17} (For of necessity he must release one unto them at the feast.) {23:18} And they cried out all at once, saying, Away with this [man,] and release unto us Barabbas: {23:19} (Who for a certain sedition made in the city, and for murder, was cast into prison.) {23:20} Pilate therefore, willing to release **Jesus**, spake again to them. {23:21} But they cried, saying, Crucify [**Him**,] crucify **Him**. {23:22} And he said unto them the third time, Why, what evil hath **He** done? I have found no cause of death in **Him**: I will therefore chastise **Him**, and let [**Him**] go. {23:23} And they were instant with loud voices, requiring that **He** might be crucified. And the voices of them and of the chief priests prevailed. {23:24} And Pilate gave sentence that it should be as they required. {23:25} And *he released unto them him that for sedition and murder was cast into prison, **whom** they had desired; but **he*** delivered **Jesus** to their will. {23:26} And as they led **Him** away, they laid hold upon one Simon, a Cyrenian, coming out of the country, and on him they laid the cross, that he might bear [it] after **Jesus**.

{23:27} And there followed **Him** a great company of people, and of women, which also bewailed and lamented **Him**. {23:28} But **Jesus** turning unto them said, Daughters of Jerusalem, weep not for **ME**, but weep for yourselves, and for your children. {23:29} For, behold, the days are coming, in the which they shall say, Blessed [are] the barren, and the wombs that never bare, and the paps which never gave suck. {23:30} Then shall they begin to say to the mountains, Fall on us; and to the hills, Cover us. {23:31} For if they do these things in a green tree, what shall be done in the dry? {23:32} And there were also two others, malefactors, led with **Him** to be put to death. {23:33} And when they were come to the place, which is called Calvary, there they crucified **Him**, and the malefactors, one on the right hand, and the other on the left.

{23:34} Then said **Jesus**, **Father**, forgive them; for they know not what they do. And they parted **His** raiment, and cast lots. {23:35} And the people stood beholding. And the rulers also with them derided [**Him**,] saying, **He** saved others; let **Him** save himself, if **He** be **Christ**, the **chosen of God**. {23:36} And the soldiers also mocked **Him**, coming to **Him**, and offering **Him** vinegar, {23:37} And saying, If **thou** be the **king of the Jews**, save **thyself**. {23:38} And a superscription also was written over **Him** in letters of Greek, and Latin, and Hebrew, **THIS IS THE KING OF THE JEWS**.

{23:39} And one of the malefactors which were hanged railed on **Him**, saying, If **thou** be **Christ**, save **thyself** and us. {23:40} But the other answering rebuked him, saying, Dost not thou fear **God**, seeing thou art in the same condemnation? {23:41} And we indeed justly; for we

receive the due reward of our deeds: but this **man** hath done nothing amiss. {23:42} And he said unto **Jesus**, **Lord**, remember me when thou comest into **thy** kingdom. {23:43} And **Jesus** said unto him, Verily **I** say unto **thee**, To day shalt thou be with **ME** in paradise. {23:44} And it was about the sixth hour, and there was a darkness over all the earth until the ninth hour. {23:45} And the sun was darkened, and the veil of the temple was rent in the midst.

{23:46} And when **Jesus** had cried with a loud voice, **He** said, **Father**, into thy hands **I** commend **my** spirit: and having said thus, **He** gave up the ghost. {23:47} Now when the centurion saw what was done, he glorified **God**, saying, Certainly this was a **righteous man**. {23:48} And all the people that came together to that sight, beholding the things which were done, smote their breasts, and returned. {23:49} And all **His** acquaintance, and the women that followed **Him** from Galilee, stood afar off, beholding these things.

{23:50} And, behold, [there was] a man named Joseph, a counsellor; [and he was] a good man, and a just: {23:51} (The same had not consented to the counsel and deed of them;) [he was] of Arimathaea, a city of the Jews: who also himself waited for the kingdom of **God**. {23:52} This [man] went unto Pilate, and begged the body of **Jesus**. {23:53} And he took **it** down, and wrapped **it** in linen, and laid **it** in a sepulchre that was hewn in stone, wherein never man before was laid. {23:54} And that day was the preparation, and the sabbath drew on. {23:55} And the women also, which came with **Him** from Galilee, followed after, and beheld the sepulchre, and how **His** body was laid. {23:56} And they returned, and prepared spices and ointments; and rested the sabbath day according to the commandment. **{73}**

{24:1} Now upon the first [day] of the week, very early in the morning, they came unto the sepulchre, bringing the spices which they had prepared, and certain [others] with them. {24:2} And they found the stone rolled away from the sepulchre. {24:3} And they entered in, and found not the **body** of the **Lord Jesus**. {24:4} And it came to pass, as they were much perplexed thereabout, behold, two men stood by them in shining garments: {24:5} And as they were afraid, and bowed down [their] faces to the earth, they said unto them, Why seek ye the **living** among the dead? {24:6} **He** is not here, but is risen: remember how **He** spake unto you when **He** was yet in Galilee, {24:7} Saying, The **Son of man** must be delivered into the hands of sinful men, and be crucified, and the third day rise again. {24:8} And they remembered **His** words, {24:9} And returned from the sepulchre, and told all these things unto the eleven, and to all the rest. {24:10} It was Mary Magdalene, and Joanna, and Mary [the mother] of James, and other [women that were] with them, which told these things unto the apostles. {24:11} And their words seemed to them as idle tales, and they believed them not. {24:12} Then arose Peter, and ran unto the sepulchre; and stooping down, he beheld the linen clothes laid by themselves, and departed, wondering in himself at that which was come to pass.

{24:13} And, behold, two of them went that same day to a village called Emmaus, which was from Jerusalem [about] threescore furlongs. {24:14} And they talked together of all these things which had happened. {24:15} And it came to pass, that, while they communed [together] and reasoned, **Jesus himself** drew near, and went with them. {24:16} But their eyes were holden that they should not know **Him**. {24:17} And **He** said unto them, What manner of communications [are] these that ye have one to another, as ye walk, and are sad? {24:18} And the one of them, whose name was Cleopas, answering said unto **Him**, Art **thou** only a stranger in Jerusalem, and hast not known the things which are come to pass there in these days? {24:19} And **He** said unto them, What things? And they said unto **Him**, Concerning **Jesus of Nazareth**, which was a **prophet** mighty in deed and word before **God** and all the people: {24:20} And how the chief priests and our rulers delivered **Him** to be condemned to death, and have crucified **Him**. {24:21} But we trusted that it had been **He** which should have redeemed Israel: and beside all this, to day is the third day since these things were done. {24:22} Yea, and certain women also of our company made us astonished, which were early at the sepulchre; {24:23} And when they found not **His body**, they came, saying, that they had also seen a vision of angels, which said that **He** was **alive**. {24:24} And certain of them which were with us went to the sepulchre, and found [it] even so as the women had said: but **Him** they saw not. {24:25} Then **He** said unto them, O fools, and slow of heart to believe all that the prophets have spoken: {24:26} Ought not **Christ** to have suffered these things, and to enter into **His** glory? {24:27} And beginning at Moses and all the prophets, **He** expounded unto them in all the scriptures the things concerning **himself**. {24:28} And they drew nigh unto the village, whither they went: and **He** made as though **He** would have gone further. {24:29} But they constrained **Him**, saying, Abide with us: for it is toward evening, and the day is far spent. And **He** went in to tarry with them. {24:30} And it came to pass, as **He** sat at meat with them, **He** took bread, and blessed [it,] and brake, and gave to them. {24:31} And their eyes were opened, and they knew **Him**; and **He** vanished out of their sight. {24:32} And they said one to another, Did not our heart burn within us, while **He** talked with us by the way, and while **He** opened to us the scriptures? {24:33} And they rose up the same hour, and returned to Jerusalem, and found the eleven gathered together, and them that were with them, {24:34} Saying, The **Lord** is risen indeed, and hath appeared to Simon. {24:35} And they told what things [were done] in the way, and how **He** was known of them in breaking of bread.

{24:36} And as they thus spake, **Jesus himself** stood in the midst of them, and saith unto them, Peace [be] unto you. {24:37} But they were terrified and affrighted, and supposed that they had seen a spirit. {24:38} And **He** said unto them, Why are ye troubled? and why do thoughts arise in your hearts? {24:39} Behold **my** hands and **my** feet, that it is **I myself**: handle **ME**, and see; for a spirit hath not flesh and bones, as ye see **ME** have. {24:40} And when **He** had thus spoken, **He** shewed them [**His**] hands and [**His**] feet. {24:41} And while they yet believed not for joy, and wondered, **He** said unto them, Have ye here any meat? {24:42} And they gave **Him** a piece of a broiled fish, and of an honeycomb. {24:43} And **He** took [it,] and did eat before them. {24:44} And **He** said unto them, These [are] the words which **I** spake unto you, while **I** was yet with you, that all things must be fulfilled, which were written in the law of Moses, and [in] the prophets, and [in] the psalms, concerning **ME**. {24:45} Then opened **He** their understanding, that they might understand the scriptures, {24:46} And said unto them, Thus it is written, and thus it behoved **Christ** to suffer, and to rise from the dead the third day: {24:47} And that repentance and remission of sins should be preached in **His name** among all nations, beginning at Jerusalem. {24:48} And ye are witnesses of these things.

{24:49} And, behold, **I** send the promise of **my Father** upon you: but tarry ye in the city of Jerusalem, until ye be endued with power from on high.

{24:50} And **He** led them out as far as to Bethany, and **He** lifted up **His** hands, and blessed them. {24:51} And it came to pass, while **He** blessed them, **He** was parted from them, and carried up into heaven. {24:52} And they worshipped **Him**, and returned to Jerusalem with great joy: {24:53} And were continually in the temple, praising and blessing **God**. Amen.

{75}

The Gospel According to St. John **TOTAL 2152**

{1:1} In the beginning was the **Word**, and the **Word** was with **God**, and the **Word** was **God**. {1:2} The same was in the beginning with **God**. {1:3} All things were made by **Him**; and without **Him** was not any thing made that was made. {1:4} In **Him** was life; and the life was the **light** of men. {1:5} And the **light** shineth in darkness; and the darkness comprehended it not.

{1:6} There was a man sent from **God**, whose name [was] John. {1:7} The same came for a witness, to bear witness of the **Light**, that all [men] through **Him** might believe. {1:8} He was not that **Light**, but [was sent] to bear witness of that **Light**. {1:9} [That] was the true **Light**, which lighteth every man that cometh into the world. {1:10} **He** was in the world, and the world was made by **Him**, and the world knew **Him** not. {1:11} **He** came unto **His** own, and **His** own received **Him** not. {1:12} But as many as received **Him**, to them gave **He** power to become the sons of **God**, [even] to them that believe on **His** **name**: {1:13} Which were born, not of blood, nor of the will of the flesh, nor of the will of man, but of **God**. {1:14} And the **Word** was made **flesh**, and dwelt among us, (and we beheld **His** glory, the glory as of the only begotten of the **Father**,) full of grace and truth.

{1:15} John bare witness of **Him**, and cried, saying, This was **He** of whom I spake, **He** that cometh after me is preferred before me: for **He** was before me. {1:16} And of **His** fulness have all we received, and grace for grace. {1:17} For the law was given by Moses, [but] grace and truth came by **Jesus Christ**. {1:18} No man hath seen **God** at any time; the only begotten **Son**, which is in the bosom of the **Father**, **He** hath declared [**Him**.

]{1:19} And this is the record of John, when the Jews sent priests and Levites from Jerusalem to ask him, Who art thou? {1:20} And he confessed, and denied not; but confessed, I am not the **Christ**. {1:21} And they asked him, What then? Art thou Elias? And he saith, I am not. Art thou that prophet? And he answered, No. {1:22} Then said they unto him, Who art thou? that we may give an answer to them that sent us. What sayest thou of thyself? {1:23} he said, I [am] the voice of one crying in the wilderness, Make straight the way of the **Lord**, as said the prophet Esaias. {1:24} And they which were sent were of the Pharisees. {1:25} And they asked him, and said unto him, Why baptizest thou then, if thou be not that **Christ**, nor Elias, neither that prophet? {1:26} John answered them, saying, I baptize with water: but there standeth one among you, whom ye know not; {1:27} **He** it is, who coming after me is preferred before me, **whose** shoe's latchet I am not worthy to unloose. {1:28} These things were done in Bethabara beyond Jordan, where John was baptizing.

{1:29} The next day John seeth **Jesus** coming unto him, and saith, Behold the **Lamb of God**, which taketh away the sin of the world. {1:30} This is **He** of **whom** I said, After me cometh a **man** which is preferred before me: for **He** was before me. {1:31} And I knew **Him** not: but that **He** should be made manifest to Israel, therefore am I come baptizing with water. {1:32} And John bare record, saying, I saw the Spirit descending from heaven like a dove, and it abode upon **Him**. {1:33} And I knew **Him** not: but **He** that sent me to baptize with water, the same said unto me, Upon **whom** thou shalt see the Spirit descending, and remaining on **Him**, the same is **He** which baptizeth with the **Holy Ghost**. {1:34}

And I saw, and bare record that this is the **Son of God**.

{1:35} Again the next day after John stood, and two of his disciples; {1:36} And looking upon **Jesus** as **He** walked, he saith, Behold the **Lamb of God**! {1:37} And the two disciples heard him speak, and they followed **Jesus**. {1:38} Then **Jesus** turned, and saw them following, and saith unto them, What seek ye? They said unto **Him**, **Rabbi**, (which is to say, being interpreted, **Master**,) where dwellest **thou**? {1:39} **He** saith unto them, Come and see. They came and saw where **He** dwelt, and abode with **Him** that day: for it was about the tenth hour. {1:40} One of the two which heard John [speak,] and followed **Him**, was Andrew, Simon Peter's brother. {1:41} **He** first findeth his own brother Simon, and saith unto him, We have found the **Messias**, which is, being interpreted, the **Christ**. {1:42} And he brought him to **Jesus**. And when **Jesus** beheld him, **He** said, Thou art Simon the son of Jona: thou shalt be called Cephas, which is by interpretation, A stone.

{1:43} The day following **Jesus** would go forth into Galilee, and findeth Philip, and saith unto him, Follow **ME**. {1:44} Now Philip was of Bethsaida, the city of Andrew and Peter. {1:45} Philip findeth Nathanael, and saith unto him, We have found **Him**, of **whom** Moses in the law, and the prophets, did write, **Jesus of Nazareth**, the **Son** of Joseph. {1:46} And Nathanael said unto him, Can there any good thing come out of Nazareth? Philip saith unto him, Come and see. {1:47} **Jesus** saw Nathanael coming to **Him**, and saith of him, Behold an Israelite indeed, in whom is no guile! {1:48} Nathanael saith unto **Him**, Whence knowest **thou** me? **Jesus** answered and said unto him, Before that Philip called thee, when thou wast under the fig tree, **I** saw thee. {1:49} Nathanael answered and saith unto **Him**, **Rabbi**, **thou** art the **Son of God**; **thou** art the **King of Israel**. {1:50} **Jesus** answered and said unto him, Because **I** said unto thee, **I** saw thee under the fig tree, believest thou? thou shalt see greater things than these. {1:51} And **He** saith unto him, Verily, verily, **I** say unto you, Hereafter ye shall see heaven open, and the angels of **God** ascending and descending upon the **Son of man**.   **{89}**

{2:1} And the third day there was a marriage in Cana of Galilee; and the mother of **Jesus** was there: {2:2} And both **Jesus** was called, and **His** disciples, to the marriage. {2:3} And when they wanted wine, the mother of **Jesus** saith unto **Him**, They have no wine. {2:4} **Jesus** saith unto her, Woman, what have **I** to do with thee? mine hour is not yet come. {2:5} **His** mother saith unto the servants, Whatsoever **He** saith unto you, do [it.]{2:6} And there were set there six waterpots of stone, after the manner of the purifying of the Jews, containing two or three firkins apiece. {2:7} **Jesus** saith unto them, Fill the waterpots with water. And they filled them up to the brim. {2:8} And **He** saith unto them, Draw out now, and bear unto the governor of the feast. And they bare [it.]{2:9} When the ruler of the feast had tasted the water that was made wine, and knew not whence it was: (but the servants which drew the water knew;) the governor of the feast called the bridegroom, {2:10} And saith unto him, Every man at the beginning doth set forth good wine; and when men have well drunk, then that which is worse: [but] thou hast kept the good wine until now. {2:11} This beginning of miracles did **Jesus** in Cana of Galilee, and manifested forth **His** glory; and **His** disciples believed on **Him**.

{2:12} After this **He** went down to Capernaum, **He**, and **His** mother, and **His** brethren, and **His** disciples: and they continued there not many days.

{2:13} And the Jews' passover was at hand, and **Jesus** went up to Jerusalem, {2:14} And found in the temple those that sold oxen and sheep and doves, and the changers of money sitting: {2:15} And when **He** had made a scourge of small cords, **He** drove them all out of the temple, and the sheep, and the oxen; and poured out the changers' money, and overthrew the tables; {2:16} And said unto them that sold doves, Take these things hence; make not **my Father**'s house an house of merchandise. {2:17} And **His** disciples remembered that it was written, The zeal of thine house hath eaten **ME** up.

{2:18} Then answered the Jews and said unto **Him**, What sign shewest **thou** unto us, seeing that **thou** doest these things? {2:19} **Jesus** answered and said unto them, Destroy **this temple**, and in three days **I** will raise **it** up. {2:20} Then said the Jews, Forty and six years was this temple in building, and wilt thou rear it up in three days? {2:21} But **He** spake of the **temple** of **His body**. {2:22} When therefore **He** was risen from the dead, **His** disciples remembered that **He** had said this unto them; and they believed the scripture, and the word which **Jesus** had said.

{2:23} Now when **He** was in Jerusalem at the passover, in the feast [day,] many believed in **His name**, when they saw the miracles which **He** did. {2:24} But **Jesus** did not commit **himself** unto them, because **He** knew all [men,]{2:25} And needed not that any should testify of man: for **He** knew what was in man. {49}

{3:1} There was a man of the Pharisees, named Nicodemus, a ruler of the Jews: {3:2} The same came to **Jesus** by night, and said unto **Him**, **Rabbi**, we know that **thou** art a teacher come from **God**: for no man can do these miracles that **thou** doest, except **God** be with **Him**. {3:3} **Jesus** answered and said unto **Him**, Verily, verily, **I** say unto thee, Except a man be born again, he cannot see the kingdom of **God**. {3:4} Nicodemus saith unto **Him**, How can a man be born when he is old? can he enter the second time into his mother's womb, and be born? {3:5} **Jesus** answered, Verily, verily, **I** say unto thee, Except a man be born of water and [of] the Spirit, he cannot enter into the kingdom of **God**. {3:6} That which is born of the flesh is flesh; and that which is born of the Spirit is spirit. {3:7} Marvel not that **I** said unto thee, Ye must be born again. {3:8} The wind bloweth where it listeth, and thou hearest the sound thereof, but canst not tell whence it cometh, and whither it goeth: so is every one that is born of the Spirit. {3:9} Nicodemus answered and said unto **Him**, How can these things be? {3:10} **Jesus** answered and said unto him, Art thou a master of Israel, and knowest not these things? {3:11} Verily, verily, **I** say unto thee, **We** speak that **we** do know, and testify that **we** have seen; and ye receive not our witness. {3:12} If **I** have told you earthly things, and ye believe not, how shall ye believe, if **I** tell you [of] heavenly things? {3:13} And no man hath ascended up to heaven, but **He** that came down from heaven, [even] the **Son of man** which is in heaven.

{3:14} And as Moses lifted up the **serpent** in the wilderness, even so must the **Son of man** be lifted up: {3:15} That whosoever believeth in **Him** should not perish, but have eternal life.

{3:16} For **God** so loved the world, that **He** gave **His only begotten Son**, that whosoever believeth in **Him** should not perish, but have everlasting life. {3:17} For **God** sent not **His Son** into the world to condemn the world; but that the world through **Him** might be saved.

{3:18} **He** that believeth on **Him** is not condemned: but **He** that believeth not is condemned already, because **He** hath not believed in the **name** of the **only begotten Son of God**. {3:19} And this is the condemnation, that **light** is come into the world, and men loved darkness rather than **light**, because their deeds were evil. {3:20} For every one that doeth evil hateth the **light**, neither cometh to the **light**, lest his deeds should be reproved. {3:21} But he that doeth truth cometh to the **light**, that his deeds may be made manifest, that they are wrought in **God**.

{3:22} After these things came **Jesus** and **His** disciples into the land of Judaea; and there **He** tarried with them, and baptized.

{3:23} And John also was baptizing in Aenon near to Salim, because there was much water there: and they came, and were baptized. {3:24} For John was not yet cast into prison.

{3:25} Then there arose a question between [some] of John's disciples and the Jews about purifying. {3:26} And they came unto John, and said unto him, Rabbi, **He** that was with thee beyond Jordan, to **whom** thou barest witness, behold, the same baptizeth, and all [men] come to **Him**. {3:27} John answered and said, A **man** can receive nothing, except it be given **Him** from heaven. {3:28} Ye yourselves bear me witness, that I said, I am not the **Christ**, but that I am sent before **Him**. {3:29} **He** that hath the bride is the **bridegroom**: but the friend of the **bridegroom**, which standeth and heareth **Him**, rejoiceth greatly because of the **bridegroom's** voice: this my joy therefore is fulfilled. {3:30} **He** must increase, but I [must] decrease. {3:31} **He** that cometh from above is above all: He that is of the earth is earthly, and speaketh of the earth: **He** that cometh from heaven is above all. {3:32} And what **He** hath seen and heard, that **He** testifieth; and no man receiveth **His** testimony. {3:33} He that hath received **His** testimony hath set to **His** seal that **God** is true. {3:34} For **He whom God** hath sent speaketh the words of **God**: for **God** giveth not the Spirit by measure [unto **Him**.]{3:35} The **Father** loveth the **Son**, and hath given all things into **His** hand. {3:36} He that believeth on the **Son** hath everlasting life: and He that believeth not the **Son** shall not see life; but the wrath of **God** abideth on him. {71}

{4:1} When therefore the **Lord** knew how the Pharisees had heard that **Jesus** made and baptized more disciples than John, {4:2} (Though **Jesus** himself baptized not, but **His** disciples,) {4:3} **He** left Judaea, and departed again into Galilee. {4:4} And **He** must needs go through Samaria. {4:5} Then cometh **He** to a city of Samaria, which is called Sychar, near to the parcel of ground that Jacob gave to his **Son** Joseph. {4:6} Now Jacob's well was there. **Jesus** therefore, being wearied with [**His**] journey, sat thus on the well: [and] it was about the sixth hour. {4:7} There cometh a woman of Samaria to draw water: **Jesus** saith unto her, Give **ME** to drink. {4:8} (For **His** disciples were gone away unto the city to buy meat.) {4:9} Then saith the woman of Samaria unto **Him**, How is it that **thou**, being a Jew, askest drink of me, which am a woman of Samaria? for the Jews have no dealings with the Samaritans. {4:10} **Jesus** answered and said unto her, If thou knewest the **gift of God**, and **who** it is that saith to thee, Give **ME** to drink; thou wouldest have asked of **Him**, and **He** would have given thee **living water**. {4:11} The woman saith unto **Him**, **Sir**, **thou** hast nothing to draw with, and the well is deep: from whence then hast **thou** that **living water**? {4:12} Art **thou** greater than our **Father** Jacob, which gave us the well, and drank thereof himself, and his children, and his cattle? {4:13} **Jesus** answered and said unto her, Whosoever drinketh of this water shall thirst again: {4:14} But whosoever drinketh of the water that **I** shall give him shall never thirst; but the water that **I** shall give him shall be in him a well of water springing up into everlasting life. {4:15} The woman saith unto **Him**, Sir, give me this water, that I thirst not, neither come hither to draw. {4:16} **Jesus** saith unto her, Go, call thy husband, and come hither. {4:17} The woman answered and said, I have no husband. **Jesus** said unto her, Thou hast well said, I have no husband: {4:18} For thou hast had five husbands; and he whom thou now hast is not thy husband: in that saidst thou truly. {4:19} The woman saith unto **Him**, **Sir**, I perceive that **thou** art a prophet. {4:20} Our **Father**s worshipped in this mountain; and ye say, that in Jerusalem is the place where men ought to worship. {4:21} **Jesus** saith unto her, Woman, believe **ME**, the hour cometh, when ye shall neither in this mountain, nor yet at Jerusalem, worship the **Father**. {4:22} Ye worship ye know not what: we know what we worship: for salvation is of the Jews. {4:23} But the hour cometh, and now is, when the true worshippers shall worship the **Father** in spirit and in truth: for the **Father** seeketh such to worship **Him**. {4:24} **God** [is] a Spirit: and they that worship **Him** must worship [**Him**] in spirit and in truth. {4:25} The woman saith unto **Him**, I know that Messias cometh, which is called **Christ**: when **He** is come, **He** will tell us all things. {4:26} **Jesus** saith unto her, **I** that speak unto thee **am** [**He**.

]{4:27} And upon this came **His** disciples, and marvelled that **He** talked with the woman: yet no man said, What seekest **thou**? or, Why talkest **thou** with her? {4:28} The woman then left her waterpot, and went her way into the city, and saith to the men, {4:29} Come, see a **man**, which told me all things that ever I did: is not this the **Christ**? {4:30} Then they went out of the city, and came unto **Him**.

{4:31} In the mean while **His** disciples prayed **Him**, saying, Master, eat. {4:32} But **He** said unto them, **I** have meat to eat that ye know not of. {4:33} Therefore said the disciples one to another, Hath any man brought **Him** [ought] to eat? {4:34} **Jesus** saith unto them, **my** meat is to do the will of **Him** that sent **ME**, and to finish **His** work. {4:35} Say not ye, There are yet four months, and [then] cometh harvest? behold, **I** say unto you, Lift up your eyes, and look on the fields; for they are white already to harvest. {4:36} And he that reapeth receiveth wages, and gathereth fruit unto life eternal: that both he that soweth and he that reapeth may rejoice together. {4:37} And herein is that saying true, One soweth, and another reapeth. {4:38} **I** sent you to reap that whereon ye bestowed no labour: other men laboured, and ye are entered into their labours.

{4:39} And many of the Samaritans of that city believed on **Him** for the saying of the woman, which testified, **He** told me all that ever I did. {4:40} So when the Samaritans were come unto **Him**, they besought **Him** that **He** would tarry with them: and **He** abode there two days. {4:41} And many more believed because of **His** own word; {4:42} And said unto the woman, Now we believe, not because of thy saying: for we have heard [**Him**] ourselves, and know that this is indeed the **Christ**, the **Saviour of the world**.

{4:43} Now after two days **He** departed thence, and went into Galilee. {4:44} For **Jesus himself** testified, that a **prophet** hath no honour in **His own** country. {4:45} Then when **He** was come into Galilee, the Galilaeans received **Him**, having seen all the things that **He** did at Jerusalem at the feast: for they also went unto the feast. {4:46} So **Jesus**

came again into Cana of Galilee, where **He** made the water wine. And there was a certain nobleman, whose Son was sick at Capernaum. {4:47} When he heard that **Jesus** was come out of Judaea into Galilee, he went unto **Him**, and besought **Him** that **He** would come down, and heal his Son: for he was at the point of death. {4:48} Then said **Jesus** unto him, Except ye see signs and wonders, ye will not believe. {4:49} The nobleman saith unto **Him**, **Sir**, come down ere my child die. {4:50} **Jesus** saith unto him, Go thy way; thy Son liveth. And the man believed the word that **Jesus** had spoken unto him, and he went his way. {4:51} And as he was now going down, his servants met him, and told [him,] saying, Thy Son liveth. {4:52} Then enquired he of them the hour when he began to amend. And they said unto him, Yesterday at the seventh hour the fever left him. {4:53} So the Father knew that [it was] at the same hour, in the which **Jesus** said unto him, Thy Son liveth: and himself believed, and his whole house. {4:54} This [is] again the second miracle [that] **Jesus** did, when **He** was come out of Judaea into Galilee. {100}

{5:1} After this there was a feast of the Jews; and **Jesus** went up to Jerusalem. {5:2} Now there is at Jerusalem by the sheep [market] a pool, which is called in the Hebrew tongue Bethesda, having five porches. {5:3} In these lay a great multitude of impotent folk, of blind, halt, withered, waiting for the moving of the water. {5:4} For an angel went down at a certain season into the pool, and troubled the water: whosoever then first after the troubling of the water stepped in was made whole of whatsoever disease he had. {5:5} And a certain man was there, which had an infirmity thirty and eight years. {5:6} When **Jesus** saw him lie, and knew that **He** had been now a long time [in that case,] **He** saith unto him, Wilt thou be made whole? {5:7} The impotent man answered **Him**, **Sir**, I have no man, when the water is troubled, to put me into the pool: but while I am coming, another steppeth down before me. {5:8} **Jesus** saith unto him, Rise, take up thy bed, and walk. {5:9} And immediately the man was made whole, and took up his bed, and walked: and on the same day was the sabbath.

{5:10} The Jews therefore said unto him that was cured, It is the sabbath day: it is not lawful for thee to carry [thy] bed. {5:11} he answered them, **He** that made me whole, the same said unto me, Take up thy bed, and walk. {5:12} Then asked they him, What **man** is that which said unto thee, Take up thy bed, and walk? {5:13} And he that was healed wist not who it was: for **Jesus** had conveyed **himself** away, a multitude being in [that] place. {5:14} Afterward **Jesus** findeth him in the temple, and said unto him, Behold, thou art made whole: sin no more, lest a worse thing come unto thee. {5:15} The man departed, and told the Jews that it was **Jesus**, which had made him whole. {5:16} And therefore did the Jews persecute **Jesus**, and sought to slay **Him**, because **He** had done these things on the sabbath day.{5:17} But **Jesus** answered them, **my** Father worketh hitherto, and **I** work. {5:18} Therefore the Jews sought the more to kill **Him**, because **He** not only had broken the sabbath, but said also that **God** was **His Father**, making **himself** equal with **God**. {5:19} Then answered **Jesus** and said unto them, Verily, verily, **I** say unto you, The **Son** can do nothing of **himself**, but what **He** seeth the **Father** do: for what things soever **He** doeth, these also doeth the **Son** likewise. {5:20} For the **Father** loveth the **Son**, and sheweth **Him** all things that himself doeth: and **He** will shew **Him** greater works than these, that ye may marvel. {5:21} For as the **Father** raiseth up the dead, and quickeneth [them;] even so the **Son** quickeneth whom **He** will. {5:22} For the **Father** judgeth no man, but hath committed all judgment unto the **Son**: {5:23} That all [men] should honour the **Son**, even as they honour the **Father**. He that honoureth not the **Son** honoureth not the **Father** which hath sent **Him**. {5:24} Verily, verily, **I** say unto you, he that heareth **my** word, and believeth on **Him** that sent **ME**, hath everlasting life, and shall not come into condemnation; but is passed from death unto life. {5:25} Verily, verily, **I** say unto you, The hour is coming, and now is, when the dead shall hear the voice of the **Son of God**: and they that hear shall live. {5:26} For as the **Father** hath life in himself; so hath **He** given to the **Son** to have life in **himself**; {5:27} And hath given **Him** authority to execute judgment also, because **He** is the **Son of man**. {5:28} Marvel not at this: for the hour is coming, in the which all that are in the graves shall hear **His** voice, {5:29} And shall come forth; they that have done good, unto the resurrection of life; and they that have done evil, unto the resurrection of damnation. {5:30} **I** can of **mine own self** do nothing: as **I** hear, **I** judge: and **my** judgment is just; because **I** seek not **mine own** will, but the will of the **Father** which hath sent **ME**. {5:31} If **I** bear witness of myself, **my** witness is not true.

{5:32} There is another that beareth witness of **ME**; and **I** know that the witness which **He** witnesseth of **ME** is true. {5:33} Ye sent unto John, and he bare witness unto the **truth**. {5:34} But **I** receive not testimony from man: but these things **I** say, that ye might be saved. {5:35} He was a burning and a shining light: and ye were willing for a season to rejoice in his light.

{5:36} But **I** have greater witness than [that] of John: for the works which the **Father** hath given **ME** to finish, the same works that **I** do, bear witness of **ME**, that the **Father** hath sent **ME**. {5:37} And the **Father** himself, which hath sent **ME**, hath borne witness of **ME**. Ye have neither heard **His** voice at any time, nor seen **His** shape. {5:38} And ye have not **His** word abiding in you: for **whom He** hath sent, **Him** ye believe not.

{5:39} Search the scriptures; for in them ye think ye have eternal life: and they are they which testify of **ME**. {5:40} And ye will not come to **ME**, that ye might have life. {5:41} **I** receive not honour from men. {5:42} But **I** know you, that ye have not the love of **God** in you. {5:43} **I am** come in **my** **Father**'s name, and ye receive **ME** not: if another shall come in his own name, him ye will receive. {5:44} How can ye believe, which receive honour one of another, and seek not the honour that [cometh] from **God** only? {5:45} Do not think that **I** will accuse you to the **Father**: there is [one] that accuseth you, [even] Moses, in whom ye trust. {5:46} For had ye believed Moses, ye would have believed **ME**: for He wrote of **ME**. {5:47} But if ye believe not his writings, how shall ye believe **my** words? {84}

{6:1} After these things **Jesus** went over the sea of Galilee, which is [the sea] of Tiberias. {6:2} And a great multitude followed **Him**, because they saw **His** miracles which **He** did on them that were diseased. {6:3} And **Jesus** went up into a mountain, and there **He** sat with **His** disciples. {6:4} And the **passover**, a feast of the Jews, was nigh.

{6:5} When **Jesus** then lifted up [**His**] eyes, and saw a great company come unto **Him**, **He** saith unto Philip, Whence shall **we** buy bread, that these may eat? {6:6} And this **He** said to prove him: for **He** himself knew what **He** would do. {6:7} Philip answered **Him**, Two hundred pennyworth of bread is not sufficient for them, that every one of them may take a little. {6:8} One of **His** disciples, Andrew, Simon

Peter's brother, saith unto **Him**, {6:9} There is a lad here, which hath five barley loaves, and two small fishes: but what are they among so many? {6:10} And **Jesus** said, Make the men sit down. Now there was much grass in the place. So the men sat down, in number about five thousand. {6:11} And **Jesus** took the loaves; and when **He** had given thanks, **He** distributed to the disciples, and the disciples to them that were set down; and likewise of the fishes as much as they would. {6:12} When they were filled, **He** said unto **His** disciples, Gather up the fragments that remain, that nothing be lost. {6:13} Therefore they gathered [them] together, and filled twelve baskets with the fragments of the five barley loaves, which remained over and above unto them that had eaten. {6:14} Then those men, when they had seen the miracle that **Jesus** did, said, This is of a truth that **prophet** that should come into the world.

{6:15} When **Jesus** therefore perceived that they would come and take **Him** by force, to make **Him** a **king**, **He** departed again into a mountain **himself** alone. {6:16} And when even was [now] come, **His** disciples went down unto the sea, {6:17} And entered into a ship, and went over the sea toward Capernaum. And it was now dark, and **Jesus** was not come to them. {6:18} And the sea arose by reason of a great wind that blew. {6:19} So when they had rowed about five and twenty or thirty furlongs, they see **Jesus** walking on the sea, and drawing nigh unto the ship: and they were afraid. {6:20} But **He** saith unto them, It is **I**; be not afraid. {6:21} Then they willingly received **Him** into the ship: and immediately the ship was at the land whither they went.

{6:22} The day following, when the people which stood on the other side of the sea saw that there was none other boat there, save that one whereinto **His** disciples were entered, and that **Jesus** went not with **His** disciples into the boat, but [that] **His** disciples were gone away alone; {6:23} (Howbeit there came other boats from Tiberias nigh unto the place where they did eat bread, after that the **Lord** had given thanks:) {6:24} When the people therefore saw that **Jesus** was not there, neither **His** disciples, they also took shipping, and came to Capernaum, seeking for **Jesus**. {6:25} And when they had found **Him** on the other side of the sea, they said unto **Him**, **Rabbi**, when camest thou hither? {6:26} **Jesus** answered them and said, Verily, verily, **I** say unto you, Ye seek **ME**, not because ye saw the miracles, but because ye did eat of the loaves, and were filled. {6:27} Labour not for the meat which perisheth, but for that meat which endureth unto everlasting life, which the **Son of man** shall give unto you: for **Him** hath **God** the **Father** sealed. {6:28} Then said they unto **Him**, What shall we do, that we might work the works of **God**? {6:29} **Jesus** answered and said unto them, This is the work of **God**, that ye believe on **Him whom He** hath sent. {6:30} They said therefore unto **Him**, What sign shewest thou then, that we may see, and believe thee? what dost thou work? {6:31} Our **Father**s did eat manna in the desert; as it is written, he gave them bread from heaven to eat. {6:32} Then **Jesus** said unto them, Verily, verily, **I** say unto you, Moses gave you not that bread from heaven; but **my** **Father** giveth you the **true bread** from heaven. {6:33} For the **bread** of **God** is **He** which cometh down from heaven, and giveth life unto the world. {6:34} Then said they unto **Him**, **Lord**, evermore give us this **bread**. {6:35} And **Jesus** said unto them, **I am** the **bread of life**: He that cometh to **ME** shall never hunger; and he that believeth on **ME** shall never thirst. {6:36} But **I** said unto you, That ye also have seen **ME**, and believe not. {6:37} All that the **Father** giveth **ME** shall come to **ME**; and him that cometh to **ME** **I** will in no wise cast out. {6:38} For **I** came down from heaven, not to do mine own will, but the will of

Him that sent **ME**. {6:39} And this is the **Father**'s will which hath sent **ME**, that of all which **He** hath given **ME I** should lose nothing, but should raise it up again at the last day. {6:40} And this is the will of **Him** that sent **ME**, that every one which seeth the **Son**, and believeth on **Him**, may have everlasting life: and **I** will raise him up at the last day. {6:41} The Jews then murmured at **Him**, because **He** said, **I am** the **bread** which came down from heaven. {6:42} And they said, Is not this **Jesus**, the **Son** of Joseph, whose **Father** and mother we know? how is it then that **He** saith, **I** came down from heaven? {6:43} **Jesus** therefore answered and said unto them, Murmur not among yourselves. {6:44} No man can come to **ME**, except the **Father** which hath sent **ME** draw him: and **I** will raise him up at the last day. {6:45} It is written in the prophets, And they shall be all taught of **God**. Every man therefore that hath heard, and hath learned of the **Father**, cometh unto **ME**. {6:46} Not that any man hath seen the **Father**, save **He** which is of **God**, **He** hath seen the **Father**. {6:47} Verily, verily, **I** say unto you, he that believeth on **ME** hath everlasting life. {6:48} **I am** that **bread of life**. {6:49} Your **Father**s did eat manna in the wilderness, and are dead. {6:50} This is the **bread** which cometh down from heaven, that a man may eat thereof, and not die. {6:51} **I am** the **living bread** which came down from heaven: if any man eat of this **bread**, he shall live for ever: and the **bread** that **I** will give is **my flesh**, which **I** will give for the life of the world. {6:52} The Jews therefore strove among themselves, saying, How can this **man** give us [**His**] **flesh** to eat? {6:53} Then **Jesus** said unto them, Verily, verily, **I** say unto you, Except ye eat the **flesh** of the **Son of man**, and drink **His blood**, ye have no life in you. {6:54} Whoso eateth **my flesh**, and drinketh **my blood**, hath eternal life; and **I** will raise **Him** up at the last day. {6:55} For **my flesh** is meat indeed, and **my blood** is drink indeed. {6:56} **He** that eateth **my flesh**, and **drinketh my blood**, dwelleth in **ME**, and **I** in **Him**. {6:57} As the living **Father** hath sent **ME**, and **I** live by the **Father**: so he that eateth **ME**, even he shall live by **ME**. {6:58} This is that **bread** which came down from heaven: not as your **Father**s did eat manna, and are dead: He that eateth of this **bread** shall live for ever. {6:59} These things said **He** in the synagogue, as **He** taught in Capernaum. {6:60} Many therefore of **His** disciples, when they had heard [this,] said, This is an hard saying; who can hear it? {6:61} When **Jesus** knew in **himself** that **His** disciples murmured at it, **He** said unto them, Doth this offend you? {6:62} [What] and if ye shall see the **Son of man** ascend up where **He** was before? {6:63} It is the spirit that quickeneth; the flesh profiteth nothing: the words that **I** speak unto you, [they] are spirit, and [they] are life. {6:64} But there are some of you that believe not. For **Jesus** knew from the beginning who they were that believed not, and who should betray **Him**. {6:65} And **He** said, Therefore said **I** unto you, that no man can come unto **ME**, except it were given unto him of **my Father**.

{6:66} From that [time] many of **His** disciples went back, and walked no more with **Him**. {6:67} Then said **Jesus** unto the twelve, Will ye also go away? {6:68} Then Simon Peter answered **Him**, **Lord**, to **whom** shall we go? **thou** hast the words of eternal life. {6:69} And we believe and are sure that thou art that **Christ**, the **Son of the living God**. {6:70} **Jesus** answered them, Have not **I** chosen you twelve, and one of you is a devil? {6:71} **He** spake of Judas Iscariot [the Son] of Simon: for he it was that should betray **Him**, being one of the twelve. {181}

{7:1} After these things **Jesus** walked in Galilee: for **He** would not walk in Jewry, because the Jews sought to kill **Him**. {7:2} Now the Jews' feast of tabernacles was at hand.

{7:3} **His** brethren therefore said unto **Him**, Depart hence, and go into Judaea, that **thy** disciples also may see the works that **thou** doest. {7:4} For [there is] no man [that] doeth any thing in secret, and **He himself** seeketh to be known openly. If **thou** do these things, shew **thyself** to the world. {7:5} For neither did **His** brethren believe in **Him**. {7:6} Then **Jesus** said unto them, **my** time is not yet come: but your time is alway ready. {7:7} The world cannot hate you; but **ME** it hateth, because **I** testify of it, that the works thereof are evil. {7:8} Go ye up unto this feast: **I** go not up yet unto this feast; for **my** time is not yet full come. {7:9} When **He** had said these words unto them, **He** abode [still] in Galilee.

{7:10} But when **His** brethren were gone up, then went **He** also up unto the feast, not openly, but as it were in secret. {7:11} Then the Jews sought **Him** at the feast, and said, Where is **He**? {7:12} And there was much murmuring among the people concerning **Him**: for some said, **He** is a good man: others said, Nay; but **He** deceiveth the people. {7:13} Howbeit no man spake openly of **Him** for fear of the Jews.

{7:14} Now about the midst of the feast **Jesus** went up into the temple, and taught. {7:15} And the Jews marvelled, saying, How knoweth this **man** letters, having never learned? {7:16} **Jesus** answered them, and said, **my** doctrine is not **mine**, but **His** that sent **ME**. {7:17} If any man will do **His** will, he shall know of the doctrine, whether it be of **God**, or [whether] **I** speak of **myself**. {7:18} He that speaketh of himself seeketh his own glory: but **He** that seeketh **His** glory that sent **Him**, the same is true, and no unrighteousness is in **Him**. {7:19} Did not Moses give you the law, and [yet] none of you keepeth the law? Why go ye about to kill **ME**? {7:20} The people answered and said, **Thou** hast a devil: who goeth about to kill **thee**? {7:21} **Jesus** answered and said unto them, **I** have done one work, and ye all marvel. {7:22} Moses therefore gave unto you circumcision; (not because it is of Moses, but of the **Father**s;) and ye on the sabbath day circumcise a man. {7:23} If a man on the sabbath day receive circumcision, that the law of Moses should not be broken; are ye angry at **ME**, because **I** have made a man every whit whole on the sabbath day? {7:24} Judge not according to the appearance, but judge righteous judgment. {7:25} Then said some of them of Jerusalem, Is not this **He**, **whom** they seek to kill? {7:26} But, lo, **He** speaketh boldly, and they say nothing unto **Him**. Do the rulers know indeed that this is the very **Christ**? {7:27} Howbeit we know this **man** whence **He** is: but when **Christ** cometh, no man knoweth whence **He** is. {7:28} Then cried **Jesus** in the temple as **He** taught, saying, Ye both know **ME**, and ye know whence **I am**: and **I am** not come of **myself**, but **He** that sent **ME** is true, **whom** ye know not. {7:29} But **I** know **Him**: for **I am** from **Him**, and **He** hath sent **ME**. {7:30} Then they sought to take **Him**: but no man laid hands on **Him**, because **His** hour was not yet come. {7:31} And many of the people believed on **Him**, and said, When **Christ** cometh, will **He** do more miracles than these which this [**man**] hath done?

{7:32} The Pharisees heard that the people murmured such things concerning **Him**; and the Pharisees and the chief priests sent officers to take **Him**. {7:33} Then said **Jesus** unto them, Yet a little while **am I** with you, and [then] **I** go unto **Him** that sent **ME**. {7:34} Ye shall seek **ME**, and shall not find [**ME**:] and where **I am**, [thither] ye cannot come. {7:35} Then said the Jews among themselves, Whither will **He** go, that we shall not find **Him**? will **He** go unto the dispersed among the Gentiles, and teach the Gentiles?

{7:36} What [manner of] saying is this that **He** said, Ye shall seek **ME**, and shall not find [**ME:**] and where **I am**, [thither] ye cannot come? {7:37} In the last day, that great [day] of the feast, **Jesus** stood and cried, saying, If any man thirst, let **Him** come unto **ME**, and drink. {7:38} **He** that believeth on **ME**, as the scripture hath said, out of his belly shall flow rivers of **living water**. {7:39} (But this spake **He** of the Spirit, which they that believe on **Him** should receive: for the **Holy Ghost** was not yet [given;] because that **Jesus** was not yet glorified.)

{7:40} Many of the people therefore, when they heard this saying, said, Of a truth this is the **Prophet**. {7:41} Others said, This is the **Christ**. But some said, Shall **Christ** come out of Galilee? {7:42} Hath not the scripture said, That **Christ** cometh of the seed of David, and out of the town of Bethlehem, where David was? {7:43} So there was a division among the people because of **Him**. {7:44} And some of them would have taken **Him**; but no man laid hands on **Him**.{7:45} Then came the officers to the chief priests and Pharisees; and they said unto them, Why have ye not brought **Him**? {7:46} The officers answered, Never **man** spake like this **man**. {7:47} Then answered them the Pharisees, Are ye also deceived? {7:48} Have any of the rulers or of the Pharisees believed on **Him**? {7:49} But this people who knoweth not the law are cursed. {7:50} Nicodemus saith unto them, (he that came to **Jesus** by night, being one of them,) {7:51} Doth our law judge [any] **man**, before it hear **Him**, and know what **He** doeth? {7:52} They answered and said unto him, Art thou also of Galilee? Search, and look: for out of Galilee ariseth no **prophet**. {7:53} And every man went unto his own house. **{113}**

{8:1} **Jesus** went unto the mount of Olives. {8:2} And early in the morning **He** came again into the temple, and all the people came unto **Him**; and **He** sat down, and taught them. {8:3} And the scribes and Pharisees brought unto **Him** a woman taken in adultery; and when they had set her in the midst, {8:4} They say unto **Him**, **Master**, this woman was taken in adultery, in the very act. {8:5} Now Moses in the law commanded us, that such should be stoned: but what sayest thou? {8:6} This they said, tempting **Him**, that they might have to accuse **Him**. But **Jesus** stooped down, and with [**His**] finger wrote on the ground, [as though **He** heard them not.]{8:7} So when they continued asking **Him**, **He** lifted up **himself**, and said unto them, he that is without sin among you, let him first cast a stone at her. {8:8} And again **He** stooped down, and wrote on the ground. {8:9} And they which heard [it,] being convicted by [their own] conscience, went out one by one, beginning at the eldest, [even] unto the last: and **Jesus** was left alone, and the woman standing in the midst. {8:10} When **Jesus** had lifted up **himself**, and saw none but the woman, **He** said unto her, Woman, where are those thine accusers? hath no man condemned thee? {8:11} She said, No man, **Lord**. And **Jesus** said unto her, Neither do **I** condemn thee: go, and sin no more.

{8:12} Then spake **Jesus** again unto them, saying, **I am** the **light** of the world: he that followeth **ME** shall not walk in darkness, but shall have the **light** of life. {8:13} The Pharisees therefore said unto **Him**, **Thou** bearest record of **thyself**; **thy** record is not true. {8:14} **Jesus** answered and said unto them, Though **I** bear record of **myself**, [yet] **my** record is true: for **I** know whence **I** came, and whither **I** go; but ye cannot tell whence **I** come, and whither **I** go. {8:15} Ye judge after the flesh; **I** judge no man. {8:16} And yet if **I** judge, **my** judgment is true: for **I am** not alone, but **I** and the

Father that sent **ME**. {8:17} It is also written in your law, that the testimony of two men is true. {8:18} **I am** one that bear witness of **myself**, and the **Father** that sent **ME** beareth witness of **ME**. {8:19} Then said they unto **Him**, Where is thy **Father**? **Jesus** answered, Ye neither know **ME**, nor **my Father**: if ye had known **ME**, ye should have known **my Father** also. {8:20} These words spake **Jesus** in the treasury, as **He** taught in the temple: and no man laid hands on **Him**; for **His** hour was not yet come. {8:21} Then said **Jesus** again unto them, **I** go **my** way, and ye shall seek **ME**, and shall die in your sins: whither **I** go, ye cannot come. {8:22} Then said the Jews, Will **He** kill **himself**? because **He** saith, Whither **I** go, ye cannot come. {8:23} And **He** said unto them, Ye are from beneath; **I am** from above: ye are of this world; **I am** not of this world. {8:24} **I** said therefore unto you, that ye shall die in your sins: for if ye believe not that **I am** [**He**,] ye shall die in your sins. {8:25} Then said they unto **Him**, Who art **thou**? And **Jesus** saith unto them, Even [the same] that **I** said unto you from the beginning. {8:26} **I** have many things to say and to judge of you: but **He** that sent **ME** is true; and **I** speak to the world those things which **I** have heard of **Him**. {8:27} They understood not that **He** spake to them of the **Father**. {8:28} Then said **Jesus** unto them, When ye have lifted up the **Son of man**, then shall ye know that **I am** [**He**,] and [that] **I** do nothing of **myself**; but as **my Father** hath taught **ME**, **I** speak these things. {8:29} And **He** that sent **ME** is with **ME**: the **Father** hath not left **ME** alone; for **I** do always those things that please **Him**. {8:30} As **He** spake these words, many believed on **Him**. {8:31} Then said **Jesus** to those Jews which believed on **Him**, If ye continue in **my** word, [then] are ye **my** disciples indeed; {8:32} And ye shall know the **truth**, and the **truth** shall make you free.

{8:33} They answered **Him**, We be Abraham's seed, and were never in bondage to any man: how sayest **thou**, Ye shall be made free? {8:34} **Jesus** answered them, Verily, verily, **I** say unto you, Whosoever committeth sin is the servant of sin. {8:35} And the servant abideth not in the house for ever: [but] the **Son** abideth ever. {8:36} If the **Son** therefore shall make you free, ye shall be free indeed. {8:37} **I** know that ye are Abraham's seed; but ye seek to kill **ME**, because **my** word hath no place in you. {8:38} **I** speak that which **I** have seen with **my Father**: and ye do that which ye have seen with your **Father**. {8:39} They answered and said unto **Him**, Abraham is our Father. **Jesus** saith unto them, If ye were Abraham's children, ye would do the works of Abraham. {8:40} But now ye seek to kill **ME**, a man that hath told you the **truth**, which **I** have heard of **God**: this did not Abraham. {8:41} Ye do the deeds of your Father. Then said they to **Him**, We be not born of fornication; we have one **Father**, [even] **God**. {8:42} **Jesus** said unto them, If **God** were your **Father**, ye would love **ME**: for **I** proceeded forth and came from **God**; neither came **I** of **myself**, but **He** sent **ME**. {8:43} Why do ye not understand **my** speech? [even] because ye cannot hear **my** word. {8:44} Ye are of your Father the devil, and the lusts of [your] Father ye will do. He was a murderer from the beginning, and abode not in the truth, because there is no truth in him. When he speaketh a lie, he speaketh of his own: for he is a liar, and the Father of it. {8:45} And because **I** tell [you] the **truth**, ye believe **ME** not. {8:46} Which of you convinceth **ME** of sin? And if **I** say the **truth**, why do ye not believe **ME**? {8:47} He that is of **God** heareth **God**'s words: ye therefore hear [them] not, because ye are not of **God**. {8:48} Then answered the Jews, and said unto **Him**, Say we not well that thou art a Samaritan, and hast a devil? {8:49} **Jesus** answered, **I** have not a devil; but **I** honour **my Father**, and ye do dishonour **ME**. {8:50} And **I** seek not **mine own** glory:

there is one that seeketh and judgeth. {8:51} Verily, verily, I say unto you, If a man keep my saying, he shall never see death. {8:52} Then said the Jews unto Him, Now we know that thou hast a devil. Abraham is dead, and the prophets; and thou sayest, If a man keep my saying, he shall never taste of death. {8:53} Art thou greater than our Father Abraham, which is dead? and the prophets are dead: whom makest thou thyself? {8:54} Jesus answered, If I honour myself, my honour is nothing: it is my Father that honoureth ME; of whom ye say, that He is your God: {8:55} Yet ye have not known Him; but I know Him: and if I should say, I know Him not, I shall be a liar like unto you: but I know Him, and keep His saying. {8:56} Your Father Abraham rejoiced to see my day: and He saw [it,] and was glad. {8:57} Then said the Jews unto Him, Thou art not yet fifty years old, and hast thou seen Abraham? {8:58} Jesus said unto them, Verily, verily, I say unto you, Before Abraham was, I am. {8:59} Then took they up stones to cast at Him: but Jesus hid himself, and went out of the temple, going through the midst of them, and so passed by. {178}

{9:1} And as [Jesus] passed by, He saw a man which was blind from [his] birth. {9:2} And His disciples asked Him, saying, Master, who did sin, this man, or his parents, that he was born blind? {9:3} Jesus answered, Neither hath this man sinned, nor his parents: but that the works of God should be made manifest in him. {9:4} I must work the works of him that sent ME, while it is day: the night cometh, when no man can work. {9:5} As long as I am in the world, I am the light of the world. {9:6} When He had thus spoken, He spat on the ground, and made clay of the spittle, and He anointed the eyes of the blind man with the clay, {9:7} And said unto him, Go, wash in the pool of Siloam, (which is by interpretation, Sent.) He went his way therefore, and washed, and came seeing.

{9:8} The neighbours therefore, and they which before had seen him that he was blind, said, Is not this he that sat and begged? {9:9} Some said, This is he: others [said,] he is like him: [but] he said, I am [he.]{9:10} Therefore said they unto him, how were thine eyes opened? {9:11} he answered and said, A man that is called Jesus made clay, and anointed mine eyes, and said unto ME, Go to the pool of Siloam, and wash: and I went and washed, and I received sight. {9:12} Then said they unto him, Where is He? He said, I know not.

{9:13} They brought to the Pharisees him that aforetime was blind. {9:14} And it was the sabbath day when Jesus made the clay, and opened his eyes. {9:15} Then again the Pharisees also asked him how he had received his sight. He said unto them, He put clay upon mine eyes, and I washed, and do see. {9:16} Therefore said some of the Pharisees, This man is not of God, because He keepeth not the sabbath day. Others said, How can a man that is a sinner do such miracles? And there was a division among them. {9:17} They say unto the blind man again, What sayest thou of Him, that He hath opened thine eyes? He said, He is a prophet. {9:18} But the Jews did not believe concerning Him, that he had been blind, and received his sight, until they called the parents of him that had received his sight. {9:19} And they asked them, saying, Is this your Son, who ye say was born blind? how then doth he now see? {9:20} His parents answered them and said, We know that this is our Son, and that he was born blind: {9:21} But by what means he now seeth, we know not; or who hath opened his eyes, we know not: He is of age; ask him: He shall speak for himself. {9:22} These [words] spake his parents, because they feared the Jews: for the Jews had agreed already, that if

any man did confess that He was Christ, He should be put out of the synagogue. {9:23} Therefore said His parents, he is of age; ask him. {9:24} Then again called they the man that was blind, and said unto him, Give God the praise: we know that this man is a sinner. {9:25} He answered and said, Whether He be a sinner [or no,] I know not: one thing I know, that, whereas I was blind, now I see. {9:26} Then said they to him again, What did He to thee? how opened He thine eyes? {9:27} He answered them, I have told you already, and ye did not hear: wherefore would ye hear [it] again? will ye also be His disciples? {9:28} Then they reviled him, and said, Thou art His disciple; but we are Moses' disciples. {9:29} We know that God spake unto Moses: [as for] this [fellow,] we know not from whence He is. {9:30} The man answered and said unto them, Why herein is a marvellous thing, that ye know not from whence He is, and [yet] He hath opened mine eyes. {9:31} Now we know that God heareth not sinners: but if any man be a worshipper of God, and doeth His will, Him He heareth. {9:32} Since the world began was it not heard that any man opened the eyes of one that was born blind. {9:33} If this man were not of God, He could do nothing. {9:34} They answered and said unto him, Thou wast altogether born in sins, and dost thou teach us? And they cast him out. {9:35} Jesus heard that they had cast him out; and when He had found him, He said unto him, Dost thou believe on the Son of God? {9:36} He answered and said, Who is He, Lord, that I might believe on Him? {9:37} And Jesus said unto him, Thou hast both seen Him, and it is He that talketh with thee. {9:38} And He said, Lord, I believe. And he worshipped Him.

{9:39} And Jesus said, For judgment I am come into this world, that they which see not might see; and that they which see might be made blind. {9:40} And [some] of the Pharisees which were with Him heard these words, and said unto Him, Are we blind also? {9:41} Jesus said unto them, If ye were blind, ye should have no sin: but now ye say, We see; therefore your sin remaineth. {64}

{10:1} Verily, verily, I say unto you, he that entereth not by the door into the sheepfold, but climbeth up some other way, the same is a thief and a robber. {10:2} But He that entereth in by the door is the Shepherd of the sheep. {10:3} To Him the porter openeth; and the sheep hear His voice: and He calleth His own sheep by name, and leadeth them out. {10:4} And when He putteth forth His own sheep, He goeth before them, and the sheep follow Him: for they know His voice. {10:5} And a stranger will they not follow, but will flee from Him: for they know not the voice of strangers. {10:6} This parable spake Jesus unto them: but they understood not what things they were which He spake unto them. {10:7} Then said Jesus unto them again, Verily, verily, I say unto you, I am the door of the sheep. {10:8} All that ever came before ME are thieves and robbers: but the sheep did not hear them. {10:9} I am the door: by ME if any man enter in, he shall be saved, and shall go in and out, and find pasture. {10:10} The thief cometh not, but for to steal, and to kill, and to destroy: I am come that they might have life, and that they might have [it] more abundantly. {10:11} I am the good Shepherd: the good Shepherd giveth His life for the sheep. {10:12} But he that is an hireling, and not the Shepherd, whose own the sheep are not, seeth the wolf coming, and leaveth the sheep, and fleeth: and the wolf catcheth them, and scattereth the sheep. {10:13} The hireling fleeth, because he is an hireling, and careth not for the sheep. {10:14} I am the good Shepherd, and know my [sheep,] and am known of mine. {10:15} As the Father knoweth ME, even so know I the Father: and I lay down my life for the sheep. {10:16} And other sheep I have, which are not of this fold: them also I must bring, and they shall hear my voice; and there shall be one fold, [and] one Shepherd. {10:17} Therefore doth my Father love ME, because I lay down my life, that I might take it again. {10:18} No man taketh it from ME, but I lay it down of myself. I have power to lay it down, and I have power to take it again. This commandment have I received of my Father.

{10:19} There was a division therefore again among the Jews for these sayings. {10:20} And many of them said, He hath a devil, and is mad; why hear ye Him? {10:21} Others said, These are not the words of Him that hath a devil. Can a devil open the eyes of the blind?

{10:22} And it was at Jerusalem the feast of the dedication, and it was winter. {10:23} And Jesus walked in the temple in Solomon's porch. {10:24} Then came the Jews round about Him, and said unto Him, How long dost thou make us to doubt? If thou be the Christ, tell us plainly. {10:25} Jesus answered them, I told you, and ye believed not: the works that I do in my Father's name, they bear witness of ME. {10:26} But ye believe not, because ye are not of my sheep, as I said unto you. {10:27} my sheep hear my voice, and I know them, and they follow ME: {10:28} And I give unto them eternal life; and they shall never perish, neither shall any [man] pluck them out of my hand. {10:29} my Father, which gave [them] ME, is greater than all; and no [man] is able to pluck [them] out of my Father's hand. {10:30} I and [my] Father are one. {10:31} Then the Jews took up stones again to stone Him. {10:32} Jesus answered them, Many good works have I shewed you from my Father; for which of those works do ye stone ME? {10:33} The Jews answered Him, saying, For a good work we stone thee not; but for blasphemy; and because that thou, being a man, makest thyself God. {10:34} Jesus answered them, Is it not written in your law, I said, Ye are Gods? {10:35} If He called them Gods, unto whom the word of God came, and the scripture cannot be broken; {10:36} Say ye of Him, whom the Father hath sanctified, and sent into the world, Thou blasphemest; because I said, I am the Son of God? {10:37} If I do not the works of my Father, believe ME not. {10:38} But if I do, though ye believe not ME, believe the works: that ye may know, and believe, that the Father is in ME, and I in Him. {10:39} Therefore they sought again to take Him: but He escaped out of their hand, {10:40} And went away again beyond Jordan into the place where John at first baptized; and there He abode. {10:41} And many resorted unto Him, and said, John did no miracle: but all things that John spake of this man were true. {10:42} And many believed on Him there. {115}

{11:1} Now a certain [man] was sick, [named] Lazarus, of Bethany, the town of Mary and her sister Martha. {11:2} (It was [that] Mary which anointed the Lord with ointment, and wiped His feet with her hair, whose brother Lazarus was sick.) {11:3} Therefore his sisters sent unto Him, saying, Lord, behold, He whom thou lovest is sick. {11:4} When Jesus heard [that,] He said, This sickness is not unto death, but for the glory of God, that the Son of God might be glorified thereby. {11:5} Now Jesus loved Martha, and her sister, and Lazarus. {11:6} When He had heard therefore that He was sick, He abode two days still in the same place where He was. {11:7} Then after that saith He to [His] disciples, Let us go into Judaea again. {11:8} [His] disciples say unto Him, Master, the Jews of late sought to stone thee; and goest thou thither again? {11:9} Jesus answered, Are there not twelve hours in the day? If any man walk in the

day, He stumbleth not, because He seeth the light of this world. {11:10} But if a man walk in the night, he stumbleth, because there is no light in him. {11:11} These things said He: and after that He saith unto them, Our friend Lazarus sleepeth; but I go, that I may awake him out of sleep. {11:12} Then said His disciples, Lord, if he sleep, he shall do well. {11:13} Howbeit Jesus spake of his death: but they thought that He had spoken of taking of rest in sleep. {11:14} Then said Jesus unto them plainly, Lazarus is dead. {11:15} And I am glad for your sakes that I was not there, to the intent ye may believe; nevertheless let us go unto him. {11:16} Then said Thomas, which is called Didymus, unto his fellowdisciples, Let us also go, that we may die with Him. {11:17} Then when Jesus came, He found that he had [lain] in the grave four days already. {11:18} Now Bethany was nigh unto Jerusalem, about fifteen furlongs off: {11:19} And many of the Jews came to Martha and Mary, to comfort them concerning their brother. {11:20} Then Martha, as soon as she heard that Jesus was coming, went and met Him: but Mary sat [still] in the house. {11:21} Then said Martha unto Jesus, Lord, if thou hadst been here, my brother had not died. {11:22} But I know, that even now, whatsoever thou wilt ask of God, God will give [it] thee. {11:23} Jesus saith unto her, Thy brother shall rise again. {11:24} Martha saith unto Him, I know that me shall rise again in the resurrection at the last day. {11:25} Jesus said unto her, I am the resurrection, and the life: He that believeth in ME, though me were dead, yet shall me live: {11:26} And whosoever liveth and believeth in ME shall never die. Believest thou this? {11:27} She saith unto Him, Yea, Lord: I believe that thou art the Christ, the Son of God, which should come into the world. {11:28} And when she had so said, she went her way, and called Mary her sister secretly, saying, The Master is come, and calleth for thee. {11:29} As soon as she heard [that,] she arose quickly, and came unto Him. {11:30} Now Jesus was not yet come into the town, but was in that place where Martha met Him. {11:31} The Jews then which were with her in the house, and comforted her, when they saw Mary, that she rose up hastily and went out, followed her, saying, She goeth unto the grave to weep there. {11:32} Then when Mary was come where Jesus was, and saw Him, she fell down at His feet, saying unto Him, Lord, if thou hadst been here, my brother had not died. {11:33} When Jesus therefore saw her weeping, and the Jews also weeping which came with her, He groaned in the spirit, and was troubled, {11:34} And said, Where have ye laid Him? They said unto Him, Lord, come and see. {11:35} Jesus wept. {11:36} Then said the Jews, Behold how He loved Him! {11:37} And some of them said, Could not this man, which opened the eyes of the blind, have caused that even this man should not have died? {11:38} Jesus therefore again groaning in himself cometh to the grave. It was a cave, and a stone lay upon it. {11:39} Jesus said, Take ye away the stone. Martha, the sister of him that was dead, saith unto Him, Lord, by this time he stinketh: for he hath been [dead] four days. {11:40} Jesus saith unto her, Said I not unto thee, that, if thou wouldest believe, thou shouldest see the glory of God? {11:41} Then they took away the stone [from the place] where the dead was laid. And Jesus lifted up [His] eyes, and said, Father, I thank thee that thou hast heard ME. {11:42} And I knew that thou hearest ME always: but because of the people which stand by I said [it,] that they may believe that thou hast sent ME. {11:43} And when He thus had spoken, He cried with a loud voice, Lazarus, come forth. {11:44} And he that was dead came forth, bound hand and foot with graveclothes: and his face was bound about with a napkin. Jesus saith unto them, Loose him, and let him go. {11:45} Then many of the Jews which came to Mary, and had seen the things which Jesus did, believed on **Him**. {11:46} But some of them went their ways to the Pharisees, and told them what things **Jesus** had done.

{11:47} Then gathered the chief priests and the Pharisees a council, and said, What do we? for this **man** doeth many miracles. {11:48} If we let **Him** thus alone, all [men] will believe on **Him**: and the Romans shall come and take away both our place and nation. {11:49} And one of them, [named] Caiaphas, being the high priest that same year, said unto them, Ye know nothing at all, {11:50} Nor consider that it is expedient for us, that one **man** should die for the people, and that the whole nation perish not. {11:51} And this spake he not of himself: but being high priest that year, he prophesied that **Jesus** should die for that nation; {11:52} And not for that nation only, but that also **He** should gather together in one the children of **God** that were scattered abroad. {11:53} Then from that day forth they took counsel together for to put **Him** to death. {11:54} **Jesus** therefore walked no more openly among the Jews; but went thence unto a country near to the wilderness, into a city called Ephraim, and there continued with **His** disciples.

{11:55} And the Jews' **passover** was nigh at hand: and many went out of the country up to Jerusalem before the **passover**, to purify themselves. {11:56} Then sought they for **Jesus**, and spake among themselves, as they stood in the temple, What think ye, that **He** will not come to the feast? {11:57} Now both the chief priests and the Pharisees had given a commandment, that, if any man knew where **He** were, **He** should shew [it,] that they might take **Him**.{116}

{12:1} Then **Jesus** six days before the **passover** came to Bethany, where Lazarus was which had been dead, **whom He** raised from the dead. {12:2} There they made **Him** a supper; and Martha served: but Lazarus was one of them that sat at the table with **Him**. {12:3} Then took Mary a pound of ointment of spikenard, very costly, and anointed the feet of **Jesus**, and wiped **His** feet with her hair: and the house was filled with the odour of the ointment. {12:4} Then saith one of **His** disciples, Judas Iscariot, Simon's [son,] which should betray **Him**, {12:5} Why was not this ointment sold for three hundred pence, and given to the poor? {12:6} This he said, not that he cared for the poor; but because he was a thief, and had the bag, and bare what was put therein. {12:7} Then said **Jesus**, Let her alone: against the day of **my** burying hath she kept this. {12:8} For the poor always ye have with you; but **ME** ye have not always. {12:9} Much people of the Jews therefore knew that **He** was there: and they came not for **Jesus**' sake only, but that they might see Lazarus also, **whom He** had raised from the dead.

{12:10} But the chief priests consulted that they might put Lazarus also to death; {12:11} Because that by reason of him many of the Jews went away, and believed on **Jesus**.

{12:12} On the next day much people that were come to the feast, when they heard that **Jesus** was coming to Jerusalem, {12:13} Took branches of palm trees, and went forth to meet **Him**, and cried, Hosanna: Blessed [is] the **King of Israel** that cometh in the name of the **Lord**. {12:14} And **Jesus**, when **He** had found a young ass, sat thereon; as it is written, {12:15} Fear not, daughter of Sion: behold, thy **King** cometh, sitting on an ass's colt. {12:16} These things understood not **His** disciples at the first: but when **Jesus** was glorified, then remembered they that these things were written of **Him**, and [that] they had done these things unto **Him**. {12:17} The people therefore that was with **Him** when

He called Lazarus out of his grave, and raised him from the dead, bare record. {12:18} For this cause the people also met **Him**, for that they heard that **He** had done this miracle. {12:19} The Pharisees therefore said among themselves, Perceive ye how ye prevail nothing? behold, the world is gone after **Him**.

{12:20} And there were certain Greeks among them that came up to worship at the feast: {12:21} The same came therefore to Philip, which was of Bethsaida of Galilee, and desired **Him**, saying, Sir, we would see **Jesus**. {12:22} Philip cometh and telleth Andrew: and again Andrew and Philip tell **Jesus**.

{12:23} And **Jesus** answered them, saying, The hour is come, that the **Son of man** should be glorified. {12:24} Verily, verily, **I** say unto you, Except a **corn of wheat** fall into the ground and die, it abideth alone: but if **it** die, **it** bringeth forth much fruit. {12:25} He that loveth his life shall lose it; and he that hateth his life in this world shall keep it unto life eternal. {12:26} If any man serve **ME**, let him follow **ME**; and where **I am**, there shall also **my** servant be: if any man serve **ME**, him will [**my**] **Father** honour. {12:27} Now is **my** soul troubled; and what shall **I** say? **Father**, save **ME** from this hour: but for this cause came **I** unto this hour. {12:28} **Father**, glorify thy name. Then came there a voice from heaven, [saying,] **I** have both glorified [it,] and will glorify [it] again. {12:29} The people therefore, that stood by, and heard [it,] said that it thundered: others said, An angel spake to **Him**. {12:30} **Jesus** answered and said, This voice came not because of **ME**, but for your sakes. {12:31} Now is the judgment of this world: now shall the prince of this world be cast out. {12:32} And **I**, if **I** be lifted up from the earth, will draw all [men] unto **ME**. {12:33} This **He** said, signifying what death **He** should die. {12:34} The people answered **Him**, We have heard out of the law that **Christ** abideth for ever: and how sayest **thou**, The **Son of man** must be lifted up? who is this **Son of man**? {12:35} Then **Jesus** said unto them, Yet a little while is the **light** with you. Walk while ye have the **light**, lest darkness come upon you: for he that walketh in darkness knoweth not whither he goeth. {12:36} While ye have **light**, believe in the **light**, that ye may be the children of **light**. These things spake **Jesus**, and departed, and did hide **himself** from them.

{12:37} But though **He** had done so many miracles before them, yet they believed not on **Him**: {12:38} That the saying of Esaias the prophet might be fulfilled, which he spake, **Lord**, who hath believed our report? and to **whom** hath the **arm** of the **Lord** been revealed? {12:39} Therefore they could not believe, because that Esaias said again, {12:40} **He** hath blinded their eyes, and hardened their heart; that they should not see with [their] eyes, nor understand with [their] heart, and be converted, and **I** should heal them. {12:41} These things said Esaias, when he saw **His** glory, and spake of **Him**.

{12:42} Nevertheless among the chief rulers also many believed on **Him**; but because of the Pharisees they did not confess [**Him**,] lest they should be put out of the synagogue: {12:43} For they loved the praise of men more than the praise of **God**.

{12:44} **Jesus** cried and said, he that believeth on **ME**, believeth not on **ME**, but on **Him** that sent **ME**. {12:45} And he that seeth **ME** seeth **Him** that sent **ME**. {12:46} **I am** come a **light** into the world, that whosoever believeth on **ME** should not abide in darkness. {12:47} And if any man hear my words, and believe not, I judge him not: for I came not to judge the world, but to save the world. {12:48} He that rejecteth ME, and receiveth not my words, hath one that judgeth him: the word that I have spoken, the same shall judge him in the last day. {12:49} For I have not spoken of myself; but the Father which sent ME, He gave ME a commandment, what I should say, and what I should speak. {12:50} And I know that His commandment is life everlasting: whatsoever I speak therefore, even as the Father said unto ME, so I speak. {108}

{13:1} Now before the feast of the passover, when Jesus knew that His hour was come that He should depart out of this world unto the Father, having loved His own which were in the world, He loved them unto the end. {13:2} And supper being ended, the devil having now put into the heart of Judas Iscariot, Simon's [Son,] to betray Him; {13:3} Jesus knowing that the Father had given all things into His hands, and that He was come from God, and went to God; {13:4} He riseth from supper, and laid aside His garments; and took a towel, and girded himself. {13:5} After that He poureth water into a bason, and began to wash the disciples' feet, and to wipe [them] with the towel wherewith He was girded. {13:6} Then cometh He to Simon Peter: and Peter saith unto Him, Lord, dost thou wash my feet? {13:7} Jesus answered and said unto him, What I do thou knowest not now; but thou shalt know hereafter. {13:8} Peter saith unto Him, Thou shalt never wash my feet. Jesus answered him, If I wash thee not, thou hast no part with ME. {13:9} Simon Peter saith unto Him, Lord, not my feet only, but also [my] hands and [my] head. {13:10} Jesus saith to him, He that is washed needeth not save to wash [his] feet, but is clean every whit: and ye are clean, but not all. {13:11} For He knew who should betray Him; therefore said He, Ye are not all clean. {13:12} So after He had washed their feet, and had taken His garments, and was set down again, He said unto them, Know ye what I have done to you? {13:13} Ye call ME Master and Lord: and ye say well; for so I am. {13:14} If I then, [your] Lord and Master, have washed your feet; ye also ought to wash one another's feet. {13:15} For I have given you an example, that ye should do as I have done to you. {13:16} Verily, verily, I say unto you, The servant is not greater than His Lord; neither He that is sent greater than He that sent Him. {13:17} If ye know these things, happy are ye if ye do them.

{13:18} I speak not of you all: I know whom I have chosen: but that the scripture may be fulfilled, He that eateth bread with ME hath lifted up his heel against ME. {13:19} Now I tell you before it come, that, when it is come to pass, ye may believe that I am [He.]{13:20} Verily, verily, I say unto you, he that receiveth whomsoever I send receiveth ME; and he that receiveth ME receiveth Him that sent ME. {13:21} When Jesus had thus said, He was troubled in spirit, and testified, and said, Verily, verily, I say unto you, that one of you shall betray ME. {13:22} Then the disciples looked one on another, doubting of whom He spake. {13:23} Now there was leaning on Jesus' bosom one of His disciples, whom Jesus loved. {13:24} Simon Peter therefore beckoned to him, that he should ask who it should be of whom He spake. {13:25} He then lying on Jesus' breast saith unto Him, Lord, who is it? {13:26} Jesus answered, He it is, to whom I shall give a sop, when I have dipped [it.] And when He had dipped the sop, He gave [it] to Judas Iscariot, [the Son] of Simon. {13:27} And after the sop Satan entered into him. Then said Jesus unto him, That thou doest, do quickly. {13:28} Now no man at the table knew for what intent He spake this unto him. {13:29} For some [of them] thought, because Judas had the bag, that

Jesus had said unto him, Buy [those things] that we have need of against the feast; or, that he should give something to the poor. {13:30} he then having received the sop went immediately out: and it was night.

{13:31} Therefore, when he was gone out, Jesus said, Now is the Son of man glorified, and God is glorified in Him. {13:32} If God be glorified in Him, God shall also glorify Him in himself, and shall straightway glorify Him. {13:33} Little children, yet a little while I am with you. Ye shall seek ME: and as I said unto the Jews, Whither I go, ye cannot come; so now I say to you. {13:34} A new commandment I give unto you, That ye love one another; as I have loved you, that ye also love one another. {13:35} By this shall all [men] know that ye are my disciples, if ye have love one to another.

{13:36} Simon Peter said unto Him, Lord, whither goest thou? Jesus answered him, Whither I go, thou canst not follow ME now; but thou shalt follow ME afterwards. {13:37} Peter said unto Him, Lord, why cannot I follow thee now? I will lay down my life for thy sake. {13:38} Jesus answered him, Wilt thou lay down thy life for my sake? Verily, verily, I say unto thee, The cock shall not crow, till thou hast denied ME thrice. {110}

{14:1} Let not your heart be troubled: ye believe in God, believe also in ME. {14:2} In my Father's house are many mansions: if [it were] not so, I would have told you. I go to prepare a place for you. {14:3} And if I go and prepare a place for you, I will come again, and receive you unto myself; that where I am, [there] ye may be also. {14:4} And whither I go ye know, and the way ye know. {14:5} Thomas saith unto Him, Lord, we know not whither thou goest; and how can we know the way? {14:6} Jesus saith unto him, I am the way, the truth, and the life: no man cometh unto the Father, but by ME. {14:7} If ye had known ME, ye should have known my Father also: and from henceforth ye know Him, and have seen Him. {14:8} Philip saith unto Him, Lord, shew us the Father, and it sufficeth us. {14:9} Jesus saith unto him, Have I been so long time with you, and yet hast thou not known ME, Philip? He that hath seen ME hath seen the Father; and how sayest thou [then,] Shew us the Father? {14:10} Believest thou not that I am in the Father, and the Father in ME? the words that I speak unto you I speak not of myself: but the Father that dwelleth in ME, He doeth the works. {14:11} Believe ME that I [am] in the Father, and the Father in ME: or else believe ME for the very works' sake. {14:12} Verily, verily, I say unto you, He that believeth on ME, the works that I do shall He do also; and greater [works] than these shall He do; because I go unto my Father. {14:13} And whatsoever ye shall ask in my name, that will I do, that the Father may be glorified in the Son. {14:14} If ye shall ask any thing in my name, I will do [it.

]{14:15} If ye love ME, keep my commandments. {14:16} And I will pray the Father, and He shall give you another Comforter, that He may abide with you for ever; {14:17} [Even] the Spirit of truth; whom the world cannot receive, because it seeth Him not, neither knoweth Him: but ye know Him; for He dwelleth with you, and shall be in you. {14:18} I will not leave you comfortless: I will come to you. {14:19} Yet a little while, and the world seeth ME no more; but ye see ME: because I live, ye shall live also. {14:20} At that day ye shall know that I [am] in my Father, and ye in ME, and I in you. {14:21} He that hath my commandments, and keepeth them, He it is that loveth ME: and He that loveth ME shall be loved of my Father, and I will love him, and will manifest **myself** to him. {14:22} Judas saith unto **Him**, not Iscariot, **Lord**, how is it that **thou** wilt manifest **thyself** unto us, and not unto the world? {14:23} **Jesus** answered and said unto him, If a man love **ME**, **He** will keep **my** words: and **my** Father will love him, and **we** will come unto him, and make **our** abode with him. {14:24} **He** that loveth **ME** not keepeth not **my** sayings: and the word which ye hear is not **mine**, but the **Father**'s which sent **ME**. {14:25} These things have **I** spoken unto you, being [yet] present with you. {14:26} But the Comforter, [which is] the **Holy Ghost**, **whom** the **Father** will send in **my** name, **He** shall teach you all things, and bring all things to your remembrance, whatsoever **I** have said unto you. {14:27} Peace **I** leave with you, **my** peace **I** give unto you: not as the world giveth, give **I** unto you. Let not your heart be troubled, neither let it be afraid. {14:28} Ye have heard how **I** said unto you, **I** go away, and come [again] unto you. If ye loved **ME**, ye would rejoice, because **I** said, **I** go unto the **Father**: for **my Father** is greater than **I**. {14:29} And now **I** have told you before it come to pass, that, when it is come to pass, ye might believe. {14:30} Hereafter **I** will not talk much with you: for the prince of this world cometh, and hath nothing in **ME**. {14:31} But that the world may know that **I** love the **Father**; and as the **Father** gave **ME** commandment, even so **I** do. Arise, let **us** go hence. **{106}**

{15:1} **I am** the **true vine**, and **my Father** is the husbandman. {15:2} Every branch in **ME** that beareth not fruit **He** taketh away: and every [branch] that beareth fruit, **He** purgeth it, that it may bring forth more fruit. {15:3} Now ye are clean through the word which **I** have spoken unto you. {15:4} Abide in **ME**, and **I** in you. As the branch cannot bear fruit of itself, except it abide in the **vine**; no more can ye, except ye abide in **ME**. {15:5} **I am** the **vine**, ye [are] the branches: he that abideth in **ME**, and **I** in him, the same bringeth forth much fruit: for without **ME** ye can do nothing. {15:6} If a man abide not in **ME**, he is cast forth as a branch, and is withered; and men gather them, and cast [them] into the fire, and they are burned. {15:7} If ye abide in **ME**, and **my** words abide in you, ye shall ask what ye will, and it shall be done unto you. {15:8} Herein is **my Father** glorified, that ye bear much fruit; so shall ye be **my** disciples. {15:9} As the **Father** hath loved **ME**, so have **I** loved you: continue ye in **my** love. {15:10} If ye keep **my** commandments, ye shall abide in **my** love; even as **I** have kept **my Father**'s commandments, and abide in **His** love. {15:11} These things have **I** spoken unto you, that **my** joy might remain in you, and [that] your joy might be full. {15:12} This is **my** commandment, That ye love one another, as **I** have loved you. {15:13} Greater love hath no man than this, that a man lay down **His** life for **His** friends. {15:14} Ye are **my** friends, if ye do whatsoever **I** command you. {15:15} Henceforth **I** call you not servants; for the servant knoweth not what **His Lord** doeth: but **I** have called you friends; for all things that **I** have heard of **my Father I** have made known unto you. {15:16} Ye have not chosen **ME**, but **I** have chosen you, and ordained you, that ye should go and bring forth fruit, and [that] your fruit should remain: that whatsoever ye shall ask of the **Father** in **my** name, **He** may give it you. {15:17} These things **I** command you, that ye love one another. {15:18} If the world hate you, ye know that [it hated] **ME** before it hated you. {15:19} If ye were of the world, the world would love his own: but because ye are not of the world, but **I** have chosen you out of the world, therefore the world hateth you. {15:20} Remember the word that **I** said unto you, The servant is not greater than **His Lord**. If they have persecuted **ME**, they will also persecute you; if they have kept **my** saying, they will keep yours also. {15:21} But all these things will they do unto you for **my**

name's sake, because they know not **Him** that sent **ME**. {15:22} If **I** had not come and spoken unto them, they had not had sin: but now they have no cloke for their sin. {15:23} He that hateth **ME** hateth **my** Father also. {15:24} If **I** had not done among them the works which none other man did, they had not had sin: but now have they both seen and hated both **ME** and **my** Father. {15:25} But [this cometh to pass,] that the word might be fulfilled that is written in their law, They hated **ME** without a cause. {15:26} But when the Comforter is come, **whom I** will send unto you from the **Father**, [even] the Spirit of truth, which proceedeth from the **Father**, **He** shall testify of **ME**: {15:27} And ye also shall bear witness, because ye have been with **ME** from the beginning. **{66}**

{16:1} These things have **I** spoken unto you, that ye should not be offended. {16:2} They shall put you out of the synagogues: yea, the time cometh, that whosoever killeth you will think that he doeth **God** service. {16:3} And these things will they do unto you, because they have not known the **Father**, nor **ME**. {16:4} But these things have **I** told you, that when the time shall come, ye may remember that **I** told you of them. And these things **I** said not unto you at the beginning, because **I** was with you. {16:5} But now **I** go **my** way to **Him** that sent **ME**; and none of you asketh **ME**, Whither goest thou? {16:6} But because **I** have said these things unto you, sorrow hath filled your heart. {16:7} Nevertheless **I** tell you the truth; It is expedient for you that **I** go away: for if **I** go not away, the Comforter will not come unto you; but if **I** depart, **I** will send **Him** unto you. {16:8} And when **He** is come, **He** will reprove the world of sin, and of righteousness, and of judgment: {16:9} Of sin, because they believe not on **ME**; {16:10} Of righteousness, because **I** go to **my** Father, and ye see **ME** no more; {16:11} Of judgment, because the prince of this world is judged. {16:12} **I** have yet many things to say unto you, but ye cannot bear them now. {16:13} Howbeit when **He**, the Spirit of truth, is come, **He** will guide you into all **truth**: for **He** shall not speak of himself; but whatsoever **He** shall hear, [that] shall **He** speak: and **He** will shew you things to come. {16:14} **He** shall glorify **ME**: for **He** shall receive of **mine**, and shall shew [it] unto you. {16:15} All things that the **Father** hath are **mine**: therefore said **I**, that **He** shall take of **mine**, and shall shew [it] unto you. {16:16} A little while, and ye shall not see **ME**: and again, a little while, and ye shall see **ME**, because **I** go to the **Father**. {16:17} Then said [some] of **His** disciples among themselves, What is this that **He** saith unto us, A little while, and ye shall not see **ME**: and again, a little while, and ye shall see **ME**: and, Because **I** go to the **Father**? {16:18} They said therefore, What is this that **He** saith, A little while? we cannot tell what **He** saith. {16:19} Now **Jesus** knew that they were desirous to ask **Him**, and said unto them, Do ye enquire among yourselves of that **I** said, A little while, and ye shall not see **ME**: and again, a little while, and ye shall see **ME**? {16:20} Verily, verily, **I** say unto you, That ye shall weep and lament, but the world shall rejoice: and ye shall be sorrowful, but your sorrow shall be turned into joy. {16:21} A woman when she is in travail hath sorrow, because her hour is come: but as soon as she is delivered of the child, she remembereth no more the anguish, for joy that a man is born into the world. {16:22} And ye now therefore have sorrow: but **I** will see you again, and your heart shall rejoice, and your joy no man taketh from you. {16:23} And in that day ye shall ask **ME** nothing. Verily, verily, **I** say unto you, Whatsoever ye shall ask the **Father** in **my name**, **He** will give [it] you. {16:24} Hitherto have ye asked nothing in **my name**: ask, and ye shall receive, that your joy may be full. {16:25} These things have **I** spoken unto you in proverbs: but the time cometh, when I shall no more speak unto you in proverbs, but I shall shew you plainly of the **Father**. {16:26} At that day ye shall ask in **my name**: and I say not unto you, that I will pray the **Father** for you: {16:27} For the **Father** himself loveth you, because ye have loved **ME**, and have believed that I came out from **God**. {16:28} I came forth from the **Father**, and **am** come into the world: again, I leave the world, and go to the **Father**. {16:29} **His** disciples said unto **Him**, Lo, now speakest **thou** plainly, and speakest no proverb. {16:30} Now are we sure that **thou** knowest all things, and needest not that any man should ask **thee**: by this we believe that **thou** camest forth from **God**. {16:31} **Jesus** answered them, Do ye now believe? {16:32} Behold, the hour cometh, yea, is now come, that ye shall be scattered, every man to his own, and shall leave **ME** alone: and yet I **am** not alone, because the **Father** is with **ME**. {16:33} These things I have spoken unto you, that in **ME** ye might have peace. In the world ye shall have tribulation: but be of good cheer; I have overcome the world. {76}

{17:1} These words spake **Jesus**, and lifted up **His** eyes to heaven, and said, **Father**, the hour is come; glorify thy **Son**, that thy **Son** also may glorify thee: {17:2} As thou hast given **Him** power over all flesh, that **He** should give eternal life to as many as thou hast given **Him**. {17:3} And this is life eternal, that they might know thee the only true **God**, and **Jesus Christ**, **whom** thou hast sent. {17:4} I have glorified thee on the earth: I have finished the work which thou gavest **ME** to do. {17:5} And now, O **Father**, glorify thou **ME** with thine own self with the glory which I had with thee before the world was. {17:6} I have manifested thy name unto the men which thou gavest **ME** out of the world: thine they were, and thou gavest them **ME**; and they have kept thy word. {17:7} Now they have known that all things whatsoever thou hast given **ME** are of thee. {17:8} For I have given unto them the words which thou gavest **ME**; and they have received [them,] and have known surely that I came out from thee, and they have believed that thou didst send **ME**. {17:9} I pray for them: I pray not for the world, but for them which thou hast given **ME**; for they are thine. {17:10} And all **mine** are thine, and thine are **mine**; and I **am** glorified in them. {17:11} And now I **am** no more in the world, but these are in the world, and I come to thee. Holy **Father**, keep through thine own name those **whom** thou hast given **ME**, that they may be one, as **we** [are.] {17:12} While I was with them in the world, I kept them in thy name: those that thou gavest **ME** I have kept, and none of them is lost, but the son of perdition; that the scripture might be fulfilled. {17:13} And now come I to thee; and these things I speak in the world, that they might have **my** joy fulfilled in themselves. {17:14} I have given them thy word; and the world hath hated them, because they are not of the world, even as I **am** not of the world. {17:15} I pray not that thou shouldest take them out of the world, but that thou shouldest keep them from the evil. {17:16} They are not of the world, even as I **am** not of the world. {17:17} Sanctify them through thy truth: thy word is truth. {17:18} As thou hast sent **ME** into the world, even so have I also sent them into the world. {17:19} And for their sakes I sanctify **myself**, that they also might be sanctified through the truth. {17:20} Neither pray I for these alone, but for them also which shall believe on **ME** through their word; {17:21} That they all may be one; as thou, **Father**, [art] in **ME**, and I in thee, that they also may be one in **us**: that the world may believe that thou hast sent **ME**. {17:22} And the glory which thou gavest **ME** I have given them; that they may be one, even as **we** are one: {17:23} I in them, and thou in **ME**, that they may be made perfect in one; and that the world may know that thou hast sent **ME**, and hast loved them, as thou hast loved **ME**.

{17:24} **Father**, I will that they also, **whom** thou hast given **ME**, be with **ME** where I **am**; that they may behold **my** glory, which thou hast given **ME**: for thou lovedst **ME** before the foundation of the world. {17:25} O righteous **Father**, the world hath not known thee: but I have known thee, and these have known that thou hast sent **ME**. {17:26} And I have declared unto them thy name, and will declare [it:] that the love wherewith thou hast loved **ME** may be in them, and I in them. {78}

{18:1} When **Jesus** had spoken these words, **He** went forth with **His** disciples over the brook Cedron, where was a garden, into the which **He** entered, and **His** disciples. {18:2} And Judas also, which betrayed **Him**, knew the place: for **Jesus** ofttimes resorted thither with **His** disciples. {18:3} Judas then, having received a band [of men] and officers from the chief priests and Pharisees, cometh thither with lanterns and torches and weapons. {18:4} **Jesus** therefore, knowing all things that should come upon **Him**, went forth, and said unto them, **Whom** seek ye? {18:5} They answered **Him**, **Jesus of Nazareth**. **Jesus** saith unto them, I **am** [**He**.] And Judas also, which betrayed **Him**, stood with them. {18:6} As soon then as **He** had said unto them, I **am** [**He**,] they went backward, and fell to the ground. {18:7} Then asked **He** them again, **Whom** seek ye? And they said, **Jesus of Nazareth**. {18:8} **Jesus** answered, I have told you that I **am** [**He**:] if therefore ye seek **ME**, let these go their way: {18:9} That the saying might be fulfilled, which **He** spake, Of them which **thou** gavest **ME** have I lost none. {18:10} Then Simon Peter having a sword drew it, and smote the high priest's servant, and cut off his right ear. The servant's name was Malchus. {18:11} Then said **Jesus** unto Peter, Put up thy sword into the sheath: the cup which **my Father** hath given **ME**, shall I not drink it? {18:12} Then the band and the captain and officers of the Jews took **Jesus**, and bound **Him**, {18:13} And led **Him** away to Annas first; for he was Father in law to Caiaphas, which was the high priest that same year. {18:14} Now Caiaphas was he, which gave counsel to the Jews, that it was expedient that **one man** should die for the people.{18:15} And Simon Peter followed **Jesus**, and [so did] another disciple: that disciple was known unto the high priest, and went in with **Jesus** into the palace of the high priest. {18:16} But Peter stood at the door without. Then went out that other disciple, which was known unto the high priest, and spake unto her that kept the door, and brought in Peter. {18:17} Then saith the damsel that kept the door unto Peter, Art not thou also [one] of this **man's** disciples? He saith, I am not. {18:18} And the servants and officers stood there, who had made a fire of coals; for it was cold: and they warmed themselves: and Peter stood with them, and warmed himself.

{18:19} The high priest then asked **Jesus** of **His** disciples, and of **His** doctrine. {18:20} **Jesus** answered him, I spake openly to the world; I ever taught in the synagogue, and in the temple, whither the Jews always resort; and in secret have I said nothing. {18:21} Why askest thou **ME**? ask them which heard **ME**, what I have said unto them: behold, they know what I said. {18:22} And when **He** had thus spoken, one of the officers which stood by struck **Jesus** with the palm of his hand, saying, Answerest thou the high priest so? {18:23} **Jesus** answered him, If I have spoken evil, bear witness of the evil: but if well, why smitest thou **ME**? {18:24} Now Annas had sent **Him** bound unto Caiaphas the high priest. {18:25} And Simon Peter stood and warmed himself. They said therefore unto him, Art not thou also [one] of **His** disciples? He denied [it,] and said, I am not.

{18:26} One of the servants of the high priest, being [his] kinsman whose ear Peter cut off, saith, Did not I see thee in the garden with Him? {18:27} Peter then denied again: and immediately the cock crew.

{18:28} Then led they Jesus from Caiaphas unto the hall of judgment: and it was early; and they themselves went not into the judgment hall, lest they should be defiled; but that they might eat the passover. {18:29} Pilate then went out unto them, and said, What accusation bring ye against this man? {18:30} They answered and said unto him, If He were not a malefactor, we would not have delivered Him up unto thee. {18:31} Then said Pilate unto them, Take ye Him, and judge Him according to your law. The Jews therefore said unto him, It is not lawful for us to put any man to death: {18:32} That the saying of Jesus might be fulfilled, which He spake, signifying what death He should die. {18:33} Then Pilate entered into the judgment hall again, and called Jesus, and said unto Him, Art thou the King of the Jews? {18:34} Jesus answered him, Sayest thou this thing of thyself, or did others tell it thee of ME? {18:35} Pilate answered, am I a Jew? Thine own nation and the chief priests have delivered thee unto me: what hast thou done? {18:36} Jesus answered, my kingdom is not of this world: if my kingdom were of this world, then would my servants fight, that I should not be delivered to the Jews: but now is my kingdom not from hence. {18:37} Pilate therefore said unto Him, Art thou a king then? Jesus answered, Thou sayest that I am a king. To this end was I born, and for this cause came I into the world, that I should bear witness unto the truth. Every one that is of the truth heareth my voice. {18:38} Pilate saith unto Him, What is truth? And when he had said this, He went out again unto the Jews, and saith unto them, I find in Him no fault [at all.]{18:39} But ye have a custom, that I should release unto you one at the passover: will ye therefore that I release unto you the King of the Jews? {18:40} Then cried they all again, saying, Not this man, but Barabbas. Now Barabbas was a robber. {108}

{19:1} Then Pilate therefore took Jesus, and scourged [Him.]{19:2} And the soldiers platted a crown of thorns, and put [it] on His head, and they put on Him a purple robe, {19:3} And said, Hail, King of the Jews! and they smote Him with their hands. {19:4} Pilate therefore went forth again, and saith unto them, Behold, I bring Him forth to you, that ye may know that I find no fault in Him. {19:5} Then came Jesus forth, wearing the crown of thorns, and the purple robe. And [Pilate] saith unto them, Behold the man! {19:6} When the chief priests therefore and officers saw Him, they cried out, saying, Crucify [Him,] crucify [Him.] Pilate saith unto them, Take ye Him, and crucify [Him:] for I find no fault in Him. {19:7} The Jews answered him, We have a law, and by our law He ought to die, because He made himself the Son of God.

{19:8} When Pilate therefore heard that saying, He was the more afraid; {19:9} And went again into the judgment hall, and saith unto Jesus, Whence art thou? But Jesus gave him no answer. {19:10} Then saith Pilate unto Him, Speakest thou not unto me? knowest thou not that I have power to crucify thee, and have power to release thee? {19:11} Jesus answered, Thou couldest have no power [at all] against ME, except it were given thee from above: therefore He that delivered ME unto thee hath the greater sin. {19:12} And from thenceforth Pilate sought to release Him: but the Jews cried out, saying, If thou let this man go, thou art not Caesar's friend: whosoever maketh himself a king speaketh against Caesar.

{19:13} When Pilate therefore heard that saying, He brought Jesus forth, and sat down in the judgment seat in a place that is called the Pavement, but in the Hebrew, Gabbatha. {19:14} And it was the preparation of the passover, and about the sixth hour: and he saith unto the Jews, Behold your King! {19:15} But they cried out, Away with [Him,] away with [Him,] crucify Him. Pilate saith unto them, Shall I crucify your King? The chief priests answered, We have no king but Caesar. {19:16} Then deliveredhe Him therefore unto them to be crucified. And they took Jesus, and led [Him] away. {19:17} And He bearing His cross went forth into a place called [the place] of a skull, which is called in the Hebrew Golgotha: {19:18} Where they crucified Him, and two others with Him, on either side one, and Jesus in the midst.

{19:19} And Pilate wrote a title, and put [it] on the cross. And the writing was, JESUS OF NAZARETH THE KING OF THE JEWS. {19:20} This title then read many of the Jews: for the place where Jesus was crucified was nigh to the city: and it was written in Hebrew, [and] Greek, [and] Latin. {19:21} Then said the chief priests of the Jews to Pilate, Write not, The King of the Jews; but that He said, I am King of the Jews. {19:22} Pilate answered, What I have written I have written.

{19:23} Then the soldiers, when they had crucified Jesus, took His garments, and made four parts, to every soldier a part; and also [His] coat: now the coat was without seam, woven from the top throughout. {19:24} They said therefore among themselves, Let us not rend it, but cast lots for it, whose it shall be: that the scripture might be fulfilled, which saith, They parted my raiment among them, and for my vesture they did cast lots. These things therefore the soldiers did.

{19:25} Now there stood by the cross of Jesus His mother, and His mother's sister, Mary the [wife] of Cleophas, and Mary Magdalene. {19:26} When Jesus therefore saw His mother, and the disciple standing by, whom He loved, He saith unto His mother, Woman, behold thy Son! {19:27} Then saith He to the disciple, Behold thy mother! And from that hour that disciple took her unto His own [home.

]{19:28} After this, Jesus knowing that all things were now accomplished, that the scripture might be fulfilled, saith, I thirst. {19:29} Now there was set a vessel full of vinegar: and they filled a spunge with vinegar, and put [it] upon hyssop, and put [it] to His mouth. {19:30} When Jesus therefore had received the vinegar, He said, It is finished: and He bowed His head, and gave up the ghost. {19:31} The Jews therefore, because it was the preparation, that the bodies should not remain upon the cross on the sabbath day, (for that sabbath day was an high day,) besought Pilate that their legs might be broken, and [that] they might be taken away. {19:32} Then came the soldiers, and brake the legs of the first, and of the other which was crucified with Him. {19:33} But when they came to Jesus, and saw that He was dead already, they brake not His legs: {19:34} But one of the soldiers with a spear pierced His side, and forthwith came there out blood and water. {19:35} And He that saw [it] bare record, and His record is true: and He knoweth that He saith true, that ye might believe. {19:36} For these things were done, that the scripture should be fulfilled, A bone of Him shall not be broken. {19:37} And again another scripture saith, They shall look on Him whom they pierced.

{19:38} And after this Joseph of Arimathaea, being a disciple of Jesus, but secretly for fear of the Jews, besought

Pilate that **He** might take away the **body** of **Jesus**: and Pilate gave [him] leave. He came therefore, and took the **body** of **Jesus**. {19:39} And there came also Nicodemus, which at the first came to **Jesus** by night, and brought a mixture of myrrh and aloes, about an hundred pound [weight.]{19:40} Then took they the **body** of **Jesus**, and wound it in linen clothes with the spices, as the manner of the Jews is to bury. {19:41} Now in the place where **He** was crucified there was a garden; and in the garden a new sepulchre, wherein was never man yet laid. {19:42} There laid they **Jesus** therefore because of the Jews' preparation [day;] for the sepulchre was nigh at hand. **{101}**

{20:1} The first [day] of the week cometh Mary Magdalene early, when it was yet dark, unto the sepulchre, and seeth the stone taken away from the sepulchre. {20:2} Then she runneth, and cometh to Simon Peter, and to the other disciple, **whom** **Jesus** loved, and saith unto them, They have taken away the **Lord** out of the sepulchre, and we know not where they have laid **Him**. {20:3} Peter therefore went forth, and that other disciple, and came to the sepulchre. {20:4} So they ran both together: and the other disciple did outrun Peter, and came first to the sepulchre. {20:5} And he stooping down, [and looking in,] saw the linen clothes lying; yet went he not in. {20:6} Then cometh Simon Peter following him, and went into the sepulchre, and seeth the linen clothes lie, {20:7} And the napkin, that was about **His** head, not lying with the linen clothes, but wrapped together in a place by itself. {20:8} Then went in also that other disciple, which came first to the sepulchre, and he saw, and believed. {20:9} For as yet they knew not the scripture, that **He** must rise again from the dead. {20:10} Then the disciples went away again unto their own home.

{20:11} But Mary stood without at the sepulchre weeping: and as she wept, she stooped down, [and looked] into the sepulchre, {20:12} And seeth two angels in white sitting, the one at the head, and the other at the feet, where the **body** of **Jesus** had lain. {20:13} And they say unto her, Woman, why weepest thou? She saith unto them, Because they have taken away **my Lord**, and I know not where they have laid **Him**. {20:14} And when she had thus said, she turned herself back, and saw **Jesus** standing, and knew not that it was **Jesus**. {20:15} **Jesus** saith unto her, Woman, why weepest thou? **whom** seekest thou? She, supposing **Him** to be the gardener, saith unto **Him**, **Sir**, if thou have borne **Him** hence, tell me where **thou** hast laid **Him**, and I will take **Him** away. {20:16} **Jesus** saith unto her, Mary. She turned herself, and saith unto **Him**, **Rabboni**; which is to say, **Master**. {20:17} **Jesus** saith unto her, Touch **ME** not; for **I am** not yet ascended to **my Father**: but go to **my** brethren, and say unto them, **I** ascend unto **my Father**, and your **Father**; and [to] **my God**, and your **God**. {20:18} Mary Magdalene came and told the disciples that she had seen the **Lord**, and [that] **He** had spoken these things unto her.

{20:19} Then the same day at evening, being the first [day] of the week, when the doors were shut where the disciples were assembled for fear of the Jews, came **Jesus** and stood in the midst, and saith unto them, Peace [be] unto you. {20:20} And when **He** had so said, **He** shewed unto them [**His**] hands and **His** side. Then were the disciples glad, when they saw the **Lord**. {20:21} Then said **Jesus** to them again, Peace [be] unto you: as [**my**] **Father** hath sent **ME**, even so send **I** you. {20:22} And when **He** had said this, **He** breathed on [them,] and saith unto them, Receive ye the **Holy Ghost**: {20:23} Whose soever sins ye remit, they are remitted unto them; [and] whose soever [sins] ye retain, they are retained.

{20:24} But Thomas, one of the twelve, called Didymus, was not with them when **Jesus** came. {20:25} The other disciples therefore said unto him, We have seen the **Lord**. But he said unto them, Except I shall see in **His** hands the print of the nails, and put my finger into the print of the nails, and thrust my hand into **His** side, I will not believe.

{20:26} And after eight days again **His** disciples were within, and Thomas with them: [then] came **Jesus**, the doors being shut, and stood in the midst, and said, Peace [be] unto you. {20:27} Then saith **He** to Thomas, reach hither thy finger, and behold **my** hands; and reach hither thy hand, and thrust [it] into **my** side: and be not faithless, but believing. {20:28} And Thomas answered and said unto **Him**, **my Lord** and **my God**. {20:29} **Jesus** saith unto him, Thomas, because thou hast seen **ME**, thou hast believed: blessed [are] they that have not seen, and [yet] have believed.

{20:30} And many other signs truly did **Jesus** in the presence of **His** disciples, which are not written in this book: {20:31} But these are written, that ye might believe that **Jesus** is **the Christ**, the **Son of God**; and that believing ye might have life through **His name**. **{70}**

{21:1} After these things **Jesus** shewed **himself** again to the disciples at the sea of Tiberias; and on this wise shewed **He** [**himself**.]{21:2} There were together Simon Peter, and Thomas called Didymus, and Nathanael of Cana in Galilee, and the [sons] of Zebedee, and two other of **His** disciples. {21:3} Simon Peter saith unto them, I go a fishing. They say unto him, We also go with thee. They went forth, and entered into a ship immediately; and that night they caught nothing. {21:4} But when the morning was now come, **Jesus** stood on the shore: but the disciples knew not that it was **Jesus**. {21:5} Then **Jesus** saith unto them, Children, have ye any meat? They answered **Him**, No. {21:6} And **He** said unto them, Cast the net on the right side of the ship, and ye shall find. They cast therefore, and now they were not able to draw it for the multitude of fishes. {21:7} Therefore that disciple **whom Jesus** loved saith unto Peter, It is the **Lord**. Now when Simon Peter heard that it was the **Lord**, He girt [**His**] fisher's coat [unto him,] (for he was naked,) and did cast himself into the sea. {21:8} And the other disciples came in a little ship; (for they were not far from land, but as it were two hundred cubits,) dragging the net with fishes. {21:9} As soon then as they were come to land, they saw a fire of coals there, and fish laid thereon, and bread. {21:10} **Jesus** saith unto them, Bring of the fish which ye have now caught. {21:11} Simon Peter went up, and drew the net to land full of great fishes, and hundred and fifty and three: and for all there were so many, yet was not the net broken. {21:12} **Jesus** saith unto them, Come [and] dine. And none of the disciples durst ask **Him**, **Who art thou**? knowing that it was the **Lord**. {21:13} **Jesus** then cometh, and taketh bread, and giveth them, and fish likewise. {21:14} This is now the third time that **Jesus** shewed **himself** to **His** disciples, after that **He** was risen from the dead.

{21:15} So when they had dined, **Jesus** saith to Simon Peter, Simon, [Son] of Jonas, lovest **thou ME** more than these? He saith unto **Him**, Yea, **Lord**; thou knowest that I love **thee**. **He** saith unto him, Feed **my** lambs. {21:16} **He** saith to him again the second time, Simon, [Son] of Jonas, lovest thou **ME**? He saith unto **Him**, Yea, **Lord**; thou knowest that I love **thee**. **He** saith unto him, Feed **my** sheep. {21:17} **He** saith unto him the third time, Simon, [Son] of Jonas, lovest thou **ME**? Peter was grieved because **He** said unto him the third time, Lovest thou **ME**? And he said unto **Him**, **Lord**, thou knowest all things; thou knowest that I love thee. Jesus saith unto him, Feed my sheep. {21:18} Verily, verily, I say unto thee, When thou wast young, thou girdedst thyself, and walkedst whither thou wouldest: but when thou shalt be old, thou shalt stretch forth thy hands, and another shall gird thee, and carry [thee] whither thou wouldest not. {21:19} This spake He, signifying by what death he should glorify God. And when He had spoken this, He saith unto him, Follow ME. {21:20} Then Peter, turning about, seeth the disciple whom Jesus loved following; which also leaned on His breast at supper, and said, Lord, which is he that betrayeth thee? {21:21} Peter seeing him saith to Jesus, Lord, and what [shall] this man [do?]{21:22} Jesus saith unto him, If I will that he tarry till I come, what [is that] to thee? follow thou ME. {21:23} Then went this saying abroad among the brethren, that that disciple should not die: yet Jesus said not unto him, He shall not die; but, If I will that he tarry till I come, what [is that] to thee? {21:24} This is the disciple which testifieth of these things, and wrote these things: and we know that His testimony is true. {21:25} And there are also many other things which Jesus did, the which, if they should be written every one, I suppose that even the world itself could not contain the books that should be written. Amen.{69}

The Acts of the Apostles **TOTAL 500**

{1:1} The former treatise have I made, O Theophilus, of all that **Jesus** began both to do and teach, {1:2} Until the day in which **He** was taken up, after that **He** through the **Holy Ghost** had given commandments unto the apostles whom **He** had chosen: {1:3} To whom also **He** shewed **himself** alive after **His** passion by many infallible proofs, being seen of them forty days, and speaking of the things pertaining to the kingdom of **God**: {1:4} And, being assembled together with [them,] commanded them that they should not depart from Jerusalem, but wait for the promise of the **Father**, which, [saith **He**,] ye have heard of **ME**. {1:5} For John truly baptized with water; but ye shall be baptized with the **Holy Ghost** not many days hence. {1:6} When they therefore were come together, they asked of **Him**, saying, **Lord**, wilt thou at this time restore again the kingdom to Israel? {1:7} And **He** said unto them, It is not for you to know the times or the seasons, which the **Father** hath put in **His** own power. {1:8} But ye shall receive power, after that the **Holy Ghost** is come upon you: and ye shall be witnesses unto **ME** both in Jerusalem, and in all Judaea, and in Samaria, and unto the uttermost part of the earth. {1:9} And when **He** had spoken these things, while they beheld, **He** was taken up; and a cloud received **Him** out of their sight. {1:10} And while they looked stedfastly toward heaven as **He** went up, behold, two men stood by them in white apparel; {1:11} Which also said, Ye men of Galilee, why stand ye gazing up into heaven? this same **Jesus**, which is taken up from you into heaven, shall so come in like manner as ye have seen **Him** go into heaven. {1:12} Then returned they unto Jerusalem from the mount called Olivet, which is from Jerusalem a sabbath day's journey. {1:13} And when they were come in, they went up into an upper room, where abode both Peter, and James, and John, and Andrew, Philip, and Thomas, Bartholomew, and Matthew, James [the Son] of Alphaeus, and Simon Zelotes, and Judas [the brother] of James. {1:14} These all continued with one accord in prayer and supplication, with the women, and Mary the mother of **Jesus**, and with **His** brethren.

{1:15} And in those days Peter stood up in the midst of the disciples, and said, (the number of names together were about an hundred and twenty,) {1:16} Men [and] brethren, this scripture must needs have been fulfilled, which the **Holy Ghost** by the mouth of David spake before concerning Judas, which was guide to them that took **Jesus**. {1:17} For he was numbered with us, and had obtained part of this ministry. {1:18} Now this man purchased a field with the reward of iniquity; and falling headlong, he burst asunder in the midst, and all his bowels gushed out. {1:19} And it was known unto all the dwellers at Jerusalem; insomuch as that field is called in their proper tongue, Aceldama, that is to say, The field of blood. {1:20} For it is written in the book of Psalms, Let his habitation be desolate, and let no man dwell therein: and his bishoprick let another take. {1:21} Wherefore of these men which have companied with us all the time that the **Lord Jesus** went in and out among us, {1:22} Beginning from the baptism of John, unto that same day that **He** was taken up from us, must one be ordained to be a witness with us of **His** resurrection. {1:23} And they appointed two, Joseph called Barsabas, who was surnamed Justus, and Matthias. {1:24} And they prayed, and said, Thou, **Lord**, which knowest the hearts of all [men,] shew whether of these two thou hast chosen, {1:25} That he may take part of this ministry and apostleship, from which Judas by transgression fell, that he might go to his own place.

{1:26} And they gave forth their lots; and the lot fell upon Matthias; and he was numbered with the eleven apostles. **{28}**

{2:1} And when the day of Pentecost was fully come, they were all with one accord in one place. {2:2} And suddenly there came a sound from heaven as of a rushing mighty wind, and it filled all the house where they were sitting. {2:3} And there appeared unto them cloven tongues like as of fire, and it sat upon each of them. {2:4} And they were all filled with the **Holy Ghost**, and began to speak with other tongues, as the Spirit gave them utterance. {2:5} And there were dwelling at Jerusalem Jews, devout men, out of every nation under heaven. {2:6} Now when this was noised abroad, the multitude came together, and were confounded, because that every man heard them speak in his own language. {2:7} And they were all amazed and marvelled, saying one to another, Behold, are not all these which speak Galilaeans? {2:8} And how hear we every man in our own tongue, wherein we were born? {2:9} Parthians, and Medes, and Elamites, and the dwellers in Mesopotamia, and in Judaea, and Cappadocia, in Pontus, and Asia, {2:10} Phrygia, and Pamphylia, in Egypt, and in the parts of Libya about Cyrene, and strangers of Rome, Jews and proselytes, {2:11} Cretes and Arabians, we do hear them speak in our tongues the wonderful works of **God**. {2:12} And they were all amazed, and were in doubt, saying one to another, What meaneth this? {2:13} Others mocking said, These men are full of new wine.{2:14} But Peter, standing up with the eleven, lifted up his voice, and said unto them, Ye men of Judaea, and all [ye] that dwell at Jerusalem, be this known unto you, and hearken to my words: {2:15} For these are not drunken, as ye suppose, seeing it is [but] the third hour of the day. {2:16} But this is that which was spoken by the prophet Joel; {2:17} And it shall come to pass in the last days, saith **God**, **I** will pour out of **my** Spirit upon all flesh: and your sons and your daughters shall prophesy, and your young men shall see visions, and your old men shall dream dreams: {2:18} And on **my** servants and on **my** handmaidens **I** will pour out in those days of **my** Spirit; and they shall prophesy: {2:19} And **I** will shew wonders in heaven above, and signs in the earth beneath; blood, and fire, and vapour of smoke: {2:20} The sun shall be turned into darkness, and the moon into blood, before that great and notable day of the **Lord** come: {2:21} And it shall come to pass, [that] whosoever shall call on the **name** of the **Lord** shall be saved. {2:22} Ye men of Israel, hear these words; **Jesus of Nazareth**, a **man** approved of **God** among you by miracles and wonders and signs, which **God** did by **Him** in the midst of you, as ye yourselves also know: {2:23} **Him**, being delivered by the determinate counsel and foreknowledge of **God**, ye have taken, and by wicked hands have crucified and slain: {2:24} **Whom God** hath raised up, having loosed the pains of death: because it was not possible that **He** should be holden of it. {2:25} For David speaketh concerning **Him**, I foresaw the **Lord** always before my face, for **He** is on my right hand, that I should not be moved: {2:26} Therefore did **my** heart rejoice, and **my** tongue was glad; moreover also **my** flesh shall rest in hope: {2:27} Because thou wilt not leave **my** soul in hell, neither wilt thou suffer thine **Holy One** to see corruption. {2:28} Thou hast made known to me the ways of life; thou shalt make me full of joy with thy countenance. {2:29} Men [and] brethren, let me freely speak unto you of the patriarch David, that he is both dead and buried, and his sepulchre is with us unto this day. {2:30} Therefore being a prophet, and knowing that God had sworn with an oath to him, that of the fruit of his loins, according to the flesh, he would raise up

Christ to sit on his throne; {2:31} He seeing this before spake of the resurrection of Christ, that His soul was not left in hell, neither His flesh did see corruption. {2:32} This Jesus hath God raised up, whereof we all are witnesses. {2:33} Therefore being by the right hand of God exalted, and having received of the Father the promise of the Holy Ghost, He hath shed forth this, which ye now see and hear. {2:34} For David is not ascended into the heavens: but he saith himself, The LORD said unto my Lord, Sit thou on my right hand, {2:35} Until I make thy foes thy footstool. {2:36} Therefore let all the house of Israel know assuredly, that God hath made that same Jesus, whom ye have crucified, both Lord and Christ.

{2:37} Now when they heard [this,] they were pricked in their heart, and said unto Peter and to the rest of the apostles, Men [and] brethren, what shall we do? {2:38} Then Peter said unto them, Repent, and be baptized every one of you in the name of Jesus Christ for the remission of sins, and ye shall receive the gift of the Holy Ghost. {2:39} For the promise is unto you, and to your children, and to all that are afar off, [even] as many as the Lord our God shall call. {2:40} And with many other words did he testify and exhort, saying, Save yourselves from this untoward generation. {2:41} Then they that gladly received his word were baptized: and the same day there were added [unto them] about three thousand souls. {2:42} And they continued stedfastly in the apostles' doctrine and fellowship, and in breaking of bread, and in prayers. {2:43} And fear came upon every soul: and many wonders and signs were done by the apostles. {2:44} And all that believed were together, and had all things common; {2:45} And sold their possessions and goods, and parted them to all [men,] as every man had need. {2:46} And they, continuing daily with one accord in the temple, and breaking bread from house to house, did eat their meat with gladness and singleness of heart, {2:47} Praising God, and having favour with all the people. And the Lord added to the church daily such as should be saved. {44}

{3:1} Now Peter and John went up together into the temple at the hour of prayer, [being] the ninth [hour.]{3:2} And a certain man lame from His mother's womb was carried, whom they laid daily at the gate of the temple which is called Beautiful, to ask alms of them that entered into the temple; {3:3} Who seeing Peter and John about to go into the temple asked an alms. {3:4} And Peter, fastening His eyes upon Him with John, said, Look on us. {3:5} And He gave heed unto them, expecting to receive something of them. {3:6} Then Peter said, Silver and gold have I none; but such as I have give I thee: In the name of Jesus Christ of Nazareth rise up and walk. {3:7} And He took Him by the right hand, and lifted [Him] up: and immediately His feet and ancle bones received strength. {3:8} And He leaping up stood, and walked, and entered with them into the temple, walking, and leaping, and praising God. {3:9} And all the people saw Him walking and praising God: {3:10} And they knew that it was He which sat for alms at the Beautiful gate of the temple: and they were filled with wonder and amazement at that which had happened unto Him. {3:11} And as the lame man which was healed held Peter and John, all the people ran together unto them in the porch that is called Solomon's, greatly wondering.

{3:12} And when Peter saw [it,] He answered unto the people, Ye men of Israel, why marvel ye at this? or why look ye so earnestly on us, as though by our own power or

holiness we had made this man to walk? {3:13} The God of Abraham, and of Isaac, and of Jacob, the God of our Fathers, hath glorified His Son Jesus; whom ye delivered up, and denied Him in the presence of Pilate, when he was determined to let [Him] go. {3:14} But ye denied the Holy One and the Just, and desired a murderer to be granted unto you; {3:15} And killed the Prince of life, whom God hath raised from the dead; whereof we are witnesses. {3:16} And His name through faith in His name hath made this man strong, whom ye see and know: yea, the faith which is by Him hath given Him this perfect soundness in the presence of you all. {3:17} And now, brethren, I wot that through ignorance ye did [it,] as [did] also your rulers. {3:18} But those things, which God before had shewed by the mouth of all His prophets, that Christ should suffer, He hath so fulfilled.

{3:19} Repent ye therefore, and be converted, that your sins may be blotted out, when the times of refreshing shall come from the presence of the Lord; {3:20} And He shall send Jesus Christ, which before was preached unto you: {3:21} Whom the heaven must receive until the times of restitution of all things, which God hath spoken by the mouth of all His holy prophets since the world began. {3:22} For Moses truly said unto the Fathers, A prophet shall the Lord your God raise up unto you of your brethren, like unto me; Him shall ye hear in all things whatsoever He shall say unto you. {3:23} And it shall come to pass, [that] every soul, which will not hear that prophet, shall be destroyed from among the people. {3:24} Yea, and all the prophets from Samuel and those that follow after, as many as have spoken, have likewise foretold of these days. {3:25} Ye are the children of the prophets, and of the covenant which God made with our Fathers, saying unto Abraham, And in thy seed shall all the kindreds of the earth be blessed. {3:26} Unto you first God, having raised up His Son Jesus, sent Him to bless you, in turning away every one of you from his iniquities. {31}

{4:1} And as they spake unto the people, the priests, and the captain of the temple, and the Sadducees, came upon them, {4:2} Being grieved that they taught the people, and preached through Jesus the resurrection from the dead. {4:3} And they laid hands on them, and put [them] in hold unto the next day: for it was now eventide. {4:4} Howbeit many of them which heard the word believed; and the number of the men was about five thousand.

{4:5} And it came to pass on the morrow, that their rulers, and elders, and scribes, {4:6} And Annas the high priest, and Caiaphas, and John, and Alexander, and as many as were of the kindred of the high priest, were gathered together at Jerusalem. {4:7} And when they had set them in the midst, they asked, By what power, or by what name, have ye done this? {4:8} Then Peter, filled with the Holy Ghost, said unto them, Ye rulers of the people, and elders of Israel, {4:9} If we this day be examined of the good deed done to the impotent man, by what means he is made whole; {4:10} Be it known unto you all, and to all the people of Israel, that by the name of Jesus Christ of Nazareth, whom ye crucified, whom God raised from the dead, [even] by Him doth this man stand here before you whole. {4:11} This is the stone which was set at nought of you builders, which is become the head of the corner. {4:12} Neither is there salvation in any other: for there is none other name under heaven given among men, whereby we must be saved.

{4:13} Now when they saw the boldness of Peter and John, and perceived that they were unlearned and ignorant men, they marvelled; and they took knowledge of them, that they had been with **Jesus**. {4:14} And beholding the man which was healed standing with them, they could say nothing against it. {4:15} But when they had commanded them to go aside out of the council, they conferred among themselves, {4:16} Saying, What shall we do to these men? for that indeed a notable miracle hath been done by them [is] manifest to all them that dwell in Jerusalem; and we cannot deny [it.]{4:17} But that it spread no further among the people, let us straitly threaten them, that they speak henceforth to no man in this **name**. {4:18} And they called them, and commanded them not to speak at all nor teach in the **name** of **Jesus**. {4:19} But Peter and John answered and said unto them, Whether it be right in the sight of **God** to hearken unto you more than unto **God**, judge ye. {4:20} For we cannot but speak the things which we have seen and heard. {4:21} So when they had further threatened them, they let them go, finding nothing how they might punish them, because of the people: for all [men] glorified **God** for that which was done. {4:22} For the man was above forty years old, on **whom** this miracle of healing was shewed.

{4:23} And being let go, they went to their own company, and reported all that the chief priests and elders had said unto them. {4:24} And when they heard that, they lifted up their voice to **God** with one accord, and said, **Lord**, thou [art] **God**, which hast made heaven, and earth, and the sea, and all that in them is: {4:25} Who by the mouth of thy servant David hast said, Why did the heathen rage, and the people imagine vain things? {4:26} The kings of the earth stood up, and the rulers were gathered together against the **Lord**, and against **His Christ**. {4:27} For of a truth against thy **holy child Jesus**, **whom** thou hast anointed, both Herod, and Pontius Pilate, with the Gentiles, and the people of Israel, were gathered together, {4:28} For to do whatsoever thy hand and thy counsel determined before to be done. {4:29} And now, **Lord**, behold their threatenings: and grant unto thy servants, that with all boldness they may speak thy word, {4:30} By stretching forth thine hand to heal; and that signs and wonders may be done by the name of thy **holy child Jesus**.{4:31} And when they had prayed, the place was shaken where they were assembled together; and they were all filled with the **Holy Ghost**, and they spake the word of **God** with boldness. {4:32} And the multitude of them that believed were of one heart and of one soul: neither said any [of them] that ought of the things which he possessed was his own; but they had all things common. {4:33} And with great power gave the apostles witness of the resurrection of the **Lord Jesus**: and great grace was upon them all. {4:34} Neither was there any among them that lacked: for as many as were possessors of lands or houses sold them, and brought the prices of the things that were sold, {4:35} And laid [them] down at the apostles' feet: and distribution was made unto every man according as He had need. {4:36} And Joses, who by the apostles was surnamed Barnabas, (which is, being interpreted, The Son of consolation,) a Levite, [and] of the country of Cyprus, {4:37} Having land, sold [it,] and brought the money, and laid [it] at the apostles' feet. {27}

{5:1} But a certain man named Ananias, with Sapphira His wife, sold a possession, {5:2} And kept back [part] of the price, His wife also being privy [to it,] and brought a certain part, and laid [it] at the apostles' feet. {5:3} But Peter said, Ananias, why hath Satan filled thine heart to lie to the **Holy Ghost**, and to keep back [part] of the price of the land? {5:4} Whiles it remained, was it not thine own? and after it was sold, was it not in thine own power? why hast

thou conceived this thing in thine heart? thou hast not lied unto men, but unto **God**. {5:5} And Ananias hearing these words fell down, and gave up the ghost: and great fear came on all them that heard these things. {5:6} And the young men arose, wound him up, and carried [him] out, and buried [him.]{5:7} And it was about the space of three hours after, when his wife, not knowing what was done, came in. {5:8} And Peter answered unto her, Tell me whether ye sold the land for so much? And she said, Yea, for so much. {5:9} Then Peter said unto her, How is it that ye have agreed together to tempt the Spirit of the **Lord**? behold, the feet of them which have buried thy husband [are] at the door, and shall carry thee out. {5:10} Then fell she down straightway at his feet, and yielded up the ghost: and the young men came in, and found her dead, and, carrying [her] forth, buried [her] by her husband. {5:11} And great fear came upon all the church, and upon as many as heard these things.

{5:12} And by the hands of the apostles were many signs and wonders wrought among the people; (and they were all with one accord in Solomon's porch. {5:13} And of the rest durst no man join himself to them: but the people magnified them. {5:14} And believers were the more added to the **Lord**, multitudes both of men and women.) {5:15} Insomuch that they brought forth the sick into the streets, and laid [them] on beds and couches, that at the least the shadow of Peter passing by might overshadow some of them. {5:16} There came also a multitude [out] of the cities round about unto Jerusalem, bringing sick folks, and them which were vexed with unclean spirits: and they were healed every one.

{5:17} Then the high priest rose up, and all they that were with him, (which is the sect of the Sadducees,) and were filled with indignation, {5:18} And laid their hands on the apostles, and put them in the common prison. {5:19} But the angel of the **Lord** by night opened the prison doors, and brought them forth, and said, {5:20} Go, stand and speak in the temple to the people all the words of this life. {5:21} And when they heard [that,] they entered into the temple early in the morning, and taught. But the high priest came, and they that were with him, and called the council together, and all the senate of the children of Israel and sent to the prison to have them brought. {5:22} But when the officers came, and found them not in the prison, they returned, and told, {5:23} Saying, The prison truly found we shut with all safety, and the keepers standing without before the doors: but when we had opened, we found no man within. {5:24} Now when the high priest and the captain of the temple and the chief priests heard these things, they doubted of them whereunto this would grow. {5:25} Then came one and told them, saying, Behold, the men whom ye put in prison are standing in the temple, and teaching the people. {5:26} Then went the captain with the officers, and brought them without violence: for they feared the people, lest they should have been stoned. {5:27} And when they had brought them, they set [them] before the council: and the high priest asked them, {5:28} Saying, Did not we straitly command you that ye should not teach in this **name**? and, behold, ye have filled Jerusalem with your doctrine, and intend to bring this **man's blood** upon us.

{5:29} Then Peter and the [other] apostles answered and said, We ought to obey **God** rather than men. {5:30} The **God** of our **Father**s raised up **Jesus**, **whom** ye slew and hanged on a tree. {5:31} **Him** hath **God** exalted with **His** right hand [to be] a **Prince** and a **Saviour**, for to give repentance to Israel, and forgiveness of sins. {5:32} And we are **His** witnesses of these things; and [so is] also the Holy

Ghost, **whom God** hath given to them that obey His.

{5:33} When they heard [that,] they were cut [to the heart,] and took counsel to slay them. {5:34} Then stood there up one in the council, a Pharisee, named Gamaliel, a doctor of the law, had in reputation among all the people, and commanded to put the apostles forth a little space; {5:35} And said unto them, Ye men of Israel, take heed to yourselves what ye intend to do as touching these men. {5:36} For before these days rose up Theudas, boasting himself to be somebody; to whom a number of men, about four hundred, joined themselves: who was slain; and all, as many as obeyed him, were scattered, and brought to nought. {5:37} After this man rose up Judas of Galilee in the days of the taxing, and drew away much people after him: He also perished; and all, [even] as many as obeyed him, were dispersed. {5:38} And now I say unto you, Refrain from these men, and let them alone: for if this counsel or this work be of men, it will come to nought: {5:39} But if it be of God, ye cannot overthrow it; lest haply ye be found even to fight against God. {5:40} And to him they agreed: and when they had called the apostles, and beaten [them,] they commanded that they should not speak in the name of Jesus, and let them go.{5:41} And they departed from the presence of the council, rejoicing that they were counted worthy to suffer shame for His name. {5:42} And daily in the temple, and in every house, they ceased not to teach and preach Jesus Christ.{18}

{6:1} And in those days, when the number of the disciples was multiplied, there arose a murmuring of the Grecians against the Hebrews, because their widows were neglected in the daily ministration. {6:2} Then the twelve called the multitude of the disciples [unto them,] and said, It is not reason that we should leave the word of God, and serve tables. {6:3} Wherefore, brethren, look ye out among you seven men of honest report, full of the **Holy Ghost** and wisdom, **whom** we may appoint over this business. {6:4} But we will give ourselves continually to prayer, and to the ministry of the word.

{6:5} And the saying pleased the whole multitude: and they chose Stephen, a man full of faith and of the **Holy Ghost**, and Philip, and Prochorus, and Nicanor, and Timon, and Parmenas, and Nicolas a proselyte of Antioch: {6:6} **Whom** they set before the apostles: and when they had prayed, they laid [their] hands on them. {6:7} And the word of **God** increased; and the number of the disciples multiplied in Jerusalem greatly; and a great company of the priests were obedient to the faith. {6:8} And Stephen, full of faith and power, did great wonders and miracles among the people.

{6:9} Then there arose certain of [the synagogue,] which is called the synagogue of the Libertines, and Cyrenians, and Alexandrians, and of them of Cilicia and of Asia, disputing with Stephen. {6:10} And they were not able to resist the wisdom and the spirit by which He spake. {6:11} Then they suborned men, which said, We have heard Him speak blasphemous words against Moses, and [against] God. {6:12} And they stirred up the people, and the elders, and the scribes, and came upon [Him,] and caught Him, and brought [Him] to the council, {6:13} And set up false witnesses, which said, This man ceaseth not to speak blasphemous words against this holy place, and the law: {6:14} For we have heard Him say, that this **Jesus of Nazareth** shall destroy this place, and shall change the

customs which Moses delivered us. {6:15} And all that sat in the council, looking stedfastly on Him, saw His face as it had been the face of an angel. {1}

{7:1} Then said the high priest, Are these things so? {7:2} And He said, Men, brethren, and Fathers, hearken; The **God** of glory appeared unto our Father Abraham, when He was in Mesopotamia, before He dwelt in Charran, {7:3} And said unto Him, Get thee out of thy country, and from thy kindred, and come into the land which I shall shew thee. {7:4} Then came He out of the land of the Chaldaeans, and dwelt in Charran: and from thence, when His Father was dead, He removed Him into this land, wherein ye now dwell. {7:5} And He gave Him none inheritance in it, no, not [so much as] to set His foot on: yet He promised that He would give it to Him for a possession, and to His **seed** after Him, when [as yet] He had no child. {7:6} And God spake on this wise, That His seed should sojourn in a strange land; and that they should bring them into bondage, and entreat [them] evil four hundred years. {7:7} And the nation to whom they shall be in bondage will I judge, said **God**: and after that shall they come forth, and serve ME in this place. {7:8} And He gave Him the covenant of circumcision: and so [Abraham] begat Isaac, and circumcised Him the eighth day; and Isaac [begat] Jacob; and Jacob [begat] the twelve patriarchs. {7:9} And the patriarchs, moved with envy, sold Joseph into Egypt: but God was with Him, {7:10} And delivered Him out of all His afflictions, and gave Him favour and wisdom in the sight of Pharaoh king of Egypt; and He made Him governor over Egypt and all His house. {7:11} Now there came a dearth over all the land of Egypt and Chanaan, and great affliction: and our Fathers found no sustenance. {7:12} But when Jacob heard that there was corn in Egypt, He sent out our Fathers first. {7:13} And at the second [time] Joseph was made known to His brethren; and Joseph's kindred was made known unto Pharaoh. {7:14} Then sent Joseph, and called His Father Jacob to [Him,] and all His kindred, threescore and fifteen souls. {7:15} So Jacob went down into Egypt, and died, He, and our Fathers, {7:16} And were carried over into Sychem, and laid in the sepulchre that Abraham bought for a sum of money of the sons of Emmor [the Father] of Sychem. {7:17} But when the time of the promise drew nigh, which **God** had sworn to Abraham, the people grew and multiplied in Egypt, {7:18} Till another king arose, which knew not Joseph. {7:19} The same dealt subtilly with our kindred, and evil entreated our **Father**s, so that they cast out their young children, to the end they might not live. {7:20} In which time Moses was born, and was exceeding fair, and nourished up in His Father's house three months: {7:21} And when He was cast out, Pharaoh's daughter took Him up, and nourished Him for her own Son. {7:22} And Moses was learned in all the wisdom of the Egyptians, and was mighty in words and in deeds. {7:23} And when He was full forty years old, it came into His heart to visit His brethren the children of Israel. {7:24} And seeing one [of them] suffer wrong, He defended [Him,] and avenged Him that was oppressed, and smote the Egyptian: {7:25} For He supposed His brethren would have understood how that God by His hand would deliver them: but they understood not. {7:26} And the next day He shewed himself unto them as they strove, and would have set them at one again, saying, Sirs, ye are brethren; why do ye wrong one to another? {7:27} But He that did His neighbour wrong thrust Him away, saying, Who made thee a ruler and a judge over us? {7:28} Wilt thou kill ME, as thou diddest the Egyptian yesterday? {7:29} Then fled Moses at this saying, and was a stranger in the land of Madian, where He begat two sons. {7:30} And when forty years were expired, there appeared to Him in the wilderness of mount Sina an angel of the Lord in a flame of fire in a bush. {7:31} When Moses saw [it,] He wondered at the sight: and as He drew near to behold [it,] the voice of the **Lord** came unto Him, {7:32} [Saying,] **I** [**am**] the **God** of thy **Father**s, the **God** of Abraham, and the **God** of Isaac, and the **God** of Jacob. Then Moses trembled, and durst not behold. {7:33} Then said the **Lord** to Him, Put off thy shoes from thy feet: for the place where thou standest is holy ground. {7:34} **I** have seen, **I** have seen the affliction of **my** people which is in Egypt, and **I** have heard their groaning, and **am** come down to deliver them. And now come, **I** will send thee into Egypt. {7:35} This Moses whom they refused, saying, Who made thee a ruler and a judge? the same did **God** send [to be] a ruler and a deliverer by the hand of the angel which appeared to Him in the bush. {7:36} **He** brought them out, after that **He** had shewed wonders and signs in the land of Egypt, and in the Red sea, and in the wilderness forty years.

{7:37} This is that Moses, which said unto the children of Israel, A **prophet** shall the **Lord** your **God** raise up unto you of your brethren, like unto me; **Him** shall ye hear. {7:38} This is **He**, that was in the church in the wilderness with the angel which spake to him in the mount Sina, and [with] our **Father**s: who received the lively oracles to give unto us: {7:39} To **whom** our **Father**s would not obey, but thrust [**Him**] from them, and in their hearts turned back again into Egypt, {7:40} Saying unto Aaron, Make us **God**s to go before us: for [as for] this Moses, which brought us out of the land of Egypt, we wot not what is become of Him. {7:41} And they made a calf in those days, and offered sacrifice unto the idol, and rejoiced in the works of their own hands. {7:42} Then **God** turned, and gave them up to worship the host of heaven; as it is written in the book of the prophets, O ye house of Israel, have ye offered to **ME** slain beasts and sacrifices [by the space of] forty years in the wilderness? {7:43} Yea, ye took up the tabernacle of Moloch, and the star of your **God** Remphan, figures which ye made to worship them: and **I** will carry you away beyond Babylon. {7:44} Our **Father**s had the tabernacle of witness in the wilderness, as **He** had appointed, speaking unto Moses, that **He** should make it according to the fashion that He had seen. {7:45} Which also our **Father**s that came after brought in with **Jesus** into the possession of the Gentiles, **whom God** drave out before the face of our **Father**s, unto the days of David; {7:46} Who found favour before **God**, and desired to find a tabernacle for the **God** of Jacob. {7:47} But Solomon built **Him** an house. {7:48} Howbeit the **most High** dwelleth not in temples made with hands; as saith the prophet, {7:49} Heaven [is] **my** throne, and earth [is] **my** footstool: what house will ye build **ME**? saith the **Lord**: or what [is] the place of **my** rest? {7:50} Hath not **my** hand made all these things?

{7:51} Ye stiffnecked and uncircumcised in heart and ears, ye do always resist the **Holy Ghost**: as your **Father**s [did,] so [do] ye. {7:52} Which of the prophets have not your **Father**s persecuted? and they have slain them which shewed before of the coming of the Just One; of **whom** ye have been now the betrayers and murderers: {7:53} Who have received the law by the disposition of angels, and have not kept [it.

]{7:54} When they heard these things, they were cut to the heart, and they gnashed on Him with [their] teeth. {7:55} But He, being full of the **Holy Ghost**, looked up stedfastly into heaven, and saw the glory of **God**, and **Jesus** standing on the right hand of God, {7:56} And said, Behold, **I** see the heavens opened, and the **Son of man** standing on the right hand of **God**. {7:57} Then they cried out with a loud voice,

and stopped their ears, and ran upon Him with one accord, {7:58} And cast [Him] out of the city, and stoned [Him:] and the witnesses laid down their clothes at a young man's feet, whose name was Saul. {7:59} And they stoned Stephen, calling upon [**God**,] and saying, **Lord Jesus**, receive my spirit. {7:60} And he kneeled down, and cried with a loud voice, **Lord**, lay not this sin to their charge. And when he had said this, he fell asleep. {**42**}

{8:1} And Saul was consenting unto **His** death. And at that time there was a great persecution against the church which was at Jerusalem; and they were all scattered abroad throughout the regions of Judaea and Samaria, except the apostles. {8:2} And devout men carried Stephen [to **His** burial,] and made great lamentation over Him. {8:3} As for Saul, He made havock of the church, entering into every house, and haling men and women committed [them] to prison. {8:4} Therefore they that were scattered abroad went every where preaching the word. {8:5} Then Philip went down to the city of Samaria, and preached **Christ** unto them. {8:6} And the people with one accord gave heed unto those things which Philip spake, hearing and seeing the miracles which He did. {8:7} For unclean spirits, crying with loud voice, came out of many that were possessed [with them:] and many taken with palsies, and that were lame, were healed. {8:8} And there was great joy in that city. {8:9} But there was a certain man, called Simon, which beforetime in the same city used sorcery, and bewitched the people of Samaria, giving out that himself was some great one: {8:10} To **whom** they all gave heed, from the least to the greatest, saying, This man is the great power of **God**. {8:11} And to Him they had regard, because that of long time He had bewitched them with sorceries. {8:12} But when they believed Philip preaching the things concerning the kingdom of **God**, and the **name** of **Jesus Christ**, they were baptized, both men and women. {8:13} Then Simon himself believed also: and when He was baptized, He continued with Philip, and wondered, beholding the miracles and signs which were done. {8:14} Now when the apostles which were at Jerusalem heard that Samaria had received the word of **God**, they sent unto them Peter and John: {8:15} Who, when they were come down, prayed for them, that they might receive the **Holy Ghost**: {8:16} (For as yet **He** was fallen upon none of them: only they were baptized in the **name** of the **Lord Jesus**.) {8:17} Then laid they [their] hands on them, and they received the **Holy Ghost**. {8:18} And when Simon saw that through laying on of the apostles' hands the **Holy Ghost** was given, He offered them money, {8:19} Saying, Give ME also this power, that on whomsoever I lay hands, He may receive the **Holy Ghost**. {8:20} But Peter said unto Him, Thy money perish with thee, because thou hast thought that the gift of God may be purchased with money. {8:21} Thou hast neither part nor lot in this matter: for thy heart is not right in the sight of God. {8:22} Repent therefore of this thy wickedness, and pray God, if perhaps the thought of thine heart may be forgiven thee. {8:23} For I perceive that thou art in the gall of bitterness, and [in] the bond of iniquity. {8:24} Then answered Simon, and said, Pray ye to the **Lord** for me, that none of these things which ye have spoken come upon me. {8:25} And they, when they had testified and preached the word of the **Lord**, returned to Jerusalem, and preached the Gospel in many villages of the Samaritans. {8:26} And the angel of the Lord spake unto Philip, saying, Arise, and go toward the south unto the way that goeth down from Jerusalem unto Gaza, which is desert. {8:27} And He arose and went: and, behold, a man of Ethiopia, an eunuch of great authority under Candace queen of the Ethiopians, who had the charge of all her treasure, and had come to Jerusalem for to worship, {8:28} Was returning, and sitting in His chariot read Esaias the prophet. {8:29} Then the Spirit said unto Philip, Go near, and join thyself to this chariot. {8:30} And Philip ran thither to [Him,] and heard Him read the prophet Esaias, and said, Understandest thou what thou readest? {8:31} And He said, How can I, except some man should guide me? And He desired Philip that He would come up and sit with Him. {8:32} The place of the scripture which He read was this, He was led as a sheep to the slaughter; and like a lamb dumb before His shearer, so opened He not His mouth: {8:33} In His humiliation His judgment was taken away: and who shall declare His generation? for His life is taken from the earth. {8:34} And the eunuch answered Philip, and said, I pray thee, of whom speaketh the prophet this? of himself, or of some other man? {8:35} Then Philip opened His mouth, and began at the same scripture, and preached unto Him Jesus. {8:36} And as they went on [their] way, they came unto a certain water: and the eunuch said, See, [here is] water; what doth hinder me to be baptized? {8:37} And Philip said, If thou believest with all thine heart, thou mayest. And He answered and said, I believe that Jesus Christ is the Son of God. {8:38} And He commanded the chariot to stand still: and they went down both into the water, both Philip and the eunuch; and He baptized Him. {8:39} And when they were come up out of the water, the Spirit of the Lord caught away Philip, that the eunuch saw Him no more: and He went on His way rejoicing. {8:40} But Philip was found at Azotus: and passing through He preached in all the cities, till He came to Caesarea. {29}

{9:1} And Saul, yet breathing out threatenings and slaughter against the disciples of the Lord, went unto the high priest, {9:2} And desired of Him letters to Damascus to the synagogues, that if He found any of this way, whether they were men or women, He might bring them bound unto Jerusalem. {9:3} And as He journeyed, He came near Damascus: and suddenly there shined round about Him a light from heaven: {9:4} And He fell to the earth, and heard a voice saying unto Him, Saul, Saul, why persecutest thou ME? {9:5} And He said, Who art thou, Lord? And the Lord said, I am Jesus whom thou persecutest: [it is] hard for thee to kick against the pricks. {9:6} And He trembling and astonished said, Lord, what wilt thou have me to do? And the Lord [said] unto Him, Arise, and go into the city, and it shall be told thee what thou must do. {9:7} And the men which journeyed with Him stood speechless, hearing a voice, but seeing no man. {9:8} And Saul arose from the earth; and when His eyes were opened, He saw no man: but they led Him by the hand, and brought [Him] into Damascus. {9:9} And He was three days without sight, and neither did eat nor drink.

{9:10} And there was a certain disciple at Damascus, named Ananias; and to Him said the Lord in a vision, Ananias. And He said, Behold, I [am here,] Lord. {9:11} And the Lord [said] unto Him, Arise, and go into the street which is called Straight, and enquire in the house of Judas for [one] called Saul, of Tarsus: for, behold, He prayeth, {9:12} And hath seen in a vision a man named Ananias coming in, and putting [His] hand on Him, that He might receive His sight. {9:13} Then Ananias answered, Lord, I have heard by many of this man, how much evil He hath done to thy saints at Jerusalem: {9:14} And here He hath authority from the chief priests to bind all that call on thy name. {9:15} But the Lord said unto Him, Go thy way: for He is a chosen vessel unto ME, to bear my name before the Gentiles, and kings, and the children of Israel: {9:16} For I will shew Him how great things He must suffer for my

name's sake. {9:17} And Ananias went His way, and entered into the house; and putting His hands on Him said, Brother Saul, the Lord, [even] Jesus, that appeared unto thee in the way as thou camest, hath sent me, that thou mightest receive thy sight, and be filled with the Holy Ghost. {9:18} And immediately there fell from His eyes as it had been scales: and He received sight forthwith, and arose, and was baptized. {9:19} And when He had received meat, He was strengthened. Then was Saul certain days with the disciples which were at Damascus. {9:20} And straightway He preached Christ in the synagogues, that He is the Son of God. {9:21} But all that heard [Him] were amazed, and said; Is not this He that destroyed them which called on this name in Jerusalem, and came hither for that intent, that He might bring them bound unto the chief priests? {9:22} But Saul increased the more in strength, and confounded the Jews which dwelt at Damascus, proving that this is very Christ.

{9:23} And after that many days were fulfilled, the Jews took counsel to kill Him: {9:24} But their laying await was known of Saul. And they watched the gates day and night to kill Him. {9:25} Then the disciples took Him by night, and let [Him] down by the wall in a basket. {9:26} And when Saul was come to Jerusalem, He assayed to join himself to the disciples: but they were all afraid of Him, and believed not that He was a disciple. {9:27} But Barnabas took Him, and brought [Him] to the apostles, and declared unto them how He had seen the Lord in the way, and that He had spoken to Him, and how He had preached boldly at Damascus in the name of Jesus. {9:28} And He was with them coming in and going out at Jerusalem. {9:29} And He spake boldly in the name of the Lord Jesus, and disputed against the Grecians: but they went about to slay Him. {9:30} [Which] when the brethren knew, they brought Him down to Caesarea, and sent Him forth to Tarsus. {9:31} Then had the churches rest throughout all Judaea and Galilee and Samaria, and were edified; and walking in the fear of the Lord, and in the comfort of the Holy Ghost, were multiplied.

{9:32} And it came to pass, as Peter passed throughout all [quarters,] He came down also to the saints which dwelt at Lydda. {9:33} And there He found a certain man named Aeneas, which had kept His bed eight years, and was sick of the palsy. {9:34} And Peter said unto Him, Aeneas, Jesus Christ maketh thee whole: arise, and make thy bed. And He arose immediately. {9:35} And all that dwelt at Lydda and Saron saw Him, and turned to the Lord. {9:36} Now there was at Joppa a certain disciple named Tabitha, which by interpretation is called Dorcas: this woman was full of good works and almsdeeds which she did. {9:37} And it came to pass in those days, that she was sick, and died: whom when they had washed, they laid [her] in an upper chamber. {9:38} And forasmuch as Lydda was nigh to Joppa, and the disciples had heard that Peter was there, they sent unto Him two men, desiring [Him] that He would not delay to come to them. {9:39} Then Peter arose and went with them. When He was come, they brought Him into the upper chamber: and all the widows stood by Him weeping, and shewing the coats and garments which Dorcas made, while she was with them. {9:40} But Peter put them all forth, and kneeled down, and prayed; and turning [Him] to the body said, Tabitha, arise. And she opened her eyes: and when she saw Peter, she sat up. {9:41} And He gave her [His] hand, and lifted her up, and when He had called the saints and widows, presented her alive. {9:42} And it was known throughout all Joppa; and many believed in the Lord. {9:43} And it came to pass, that He tarried many days in Joppa with one Simon a tanner. {38}

{10:1} There was a certain man in Caesarea called Cornelius, a centurion of the band called the Italian [band,] {10:2} A devout [man,] and one that feared **God** with all His house, which gave much alms to the people, and prayed to God alway. {10:3} He saw in a vision evidently about the ninth hour of the day an angel of **God** coming in to Him, and saying unto Him, Cornelius. {10:4} And when He looked on Him, He was afraid, and said, What is it, Lord? And He said unto Him, Thy prayers and thine alms are come up for a memorial before **God**. {10:5} And now send men to Joppa, and call for [one] Simon, whose surname is Peter: {10:6} He lodgeth with one Simon a tanner, whose house is by the sea side: He shall tell thee what thou oughtest to do. {10:7} And when the angel which spake unto Cornelius was departed, He called two of His household servants, and a devout soldier of them that waited on Him continually; {10:8} And when He had declared all [these] things unto them, He sent them to Joppa.

{10:9} On the morrow, as they went on their journey, and drew nigh unto the city, Peter went up upon the housetop to pray about the sixth hour: {10:10} And He became very hungry, and would have eaten: but while they made ready, He fell into a trance, {10:11} And saw heaven opened, and a certain vessel descending unto Him, as it had been a great sheet knit at the four corners, and let down to the earth: {10:12} Wherein were all manner of fourfooted beasts of the earth, and wild beasts, and creeping things, and fowls of the air. {10:13} And there came a voice to Him, Rise, Peter; kill, and eat. {10:14} But Peter said, Not so, **Lord**; for I have never eaten any thing that is common or unclean. {10:15} And the **voice** [spake] unto Him again the second time, What God hath cleansed, [that] call not thou common. {10:16} This was done thrice: and the vessel was received up again into heaven. {10:17} Now while Peter doubted in himself what this vision which He had seen should mean, behold, the men which were sent from Cornelius had made enquiry for Simon's house, and stood before the gate, {10:18} And called, and asked whether Simon, which was surnamed Peter, were lodged there.

{10:19} While Peter thought on the vision, the Spirit said unto Him, Behold, three men seek thee. {10:20} Arise therefore, and get thee down, and go with them, doubting nothing: for I have sent them. {10:21} Then Peter went down to the men which were sent unto Him from Cornelius; and said, Behold, I am He whom ye seek: what [is] the cause wherefore ye are come? {10:22} And they said, Cornelius the centurion, a just man, and one that feareth **God**, and of good report among all the nation of the Jews, was warned from **God** by an holy angel to send for thee into His house, and to hear words of thee. {10:23} Then called He them in, and lodged [them.] And on the morrow Peter went away with them, and certain brethren from Joppa accompanied Him. {10:24} And the morrow after they entered into Caesarea. And Cornelius waited for them, and had called together His kinsmen and near friends. {10:25} And as Peter was coming in, Cornelius met Him, and fell down at His feet, and worshipped [Him.]{10:26} But Peter took Him up, saying, Stand up; I myself also am a man. {10:27} And as He talked with Him, He went in, and found many that were come together. {10:28} And He said unto them, Ye know how that it is an unlawful thing for a man that is a Jew to keep company, or come unto one of another nation; but God hath shewed ME that I should not call any man common or unclean. {10:29} Therefore came I [unto you] without gainsaying, as soon as I was sent for: I ask therefore for what intent ye have sent for ME? {10:30} And Cornelius said, Four days ago I was fasting until this hour; and at the

ninth hour I prayed in my house, and, behold, a man stood before ME in bright clothing, {10:31} And said, Cornelius, thy prayer is heard, and thine alms are had in remembrance in the sight of **God**. {10:32} Send therefore to Joppa, and call hither Simon, whose surname is Peter; He is lodged in the house of [one] Simon a tanner by the sea side: who, when He cometh, shall speak unto thee. {10:33} Immediately therefore I sent to thee; and thou hast well done that thou art come. Now therefore are we all here present before **God**, to hear all things that are commanded thee of **God**.

{10:34} Then Peter opened [His] mouth, and said, Of a truth I perceive that **God** is no respecter of persons: {10:35} But in every nation He that feareth **Him**, and worketh righteousness, is accepted with **Him**. {10:36} The **word** which [**God**] sent unto the children of Israel, preaching peace by **Jesus Christ**: (**He is Lord** of all:) {10:37} That **word**, [I say,] ye know, which was published throughout all Judaea, and began from Galilee, after the baptism which John preached; {10:38} How **God** anointed **Jesus of Nazareth** with the **Holy Ghost** and with power: **who** went about doing good, and healing all that were oppressed of the devil; for **God** was with **Him**. {10:39} And we are witnesses of all things which **He** did both in the land of the Jews, and in Jerusalem; **whom** they slew and hanged on a tree: {10:40} **Him God** raised up the third day, and shewed **Him** openly; {10:41} Not to all the people, but unto witnesses chosen before of **God**, [even] to us, who did eat and drink with **Him** after **He** rose from the dead. {10:42} And **He** commanded us to preach unto the people, and to testify that it is **He** which was ordained of **God** [to be] the **Judge** of quick and dead. {10:43} To **Him** give all the prophets witness, that through **His name** whosoever believeth in **Him** shall receive remission of sins.

{10:44} While Peter yet spake these words, the **Holy Ghost** fell on all them which heard the **word**. {10:45} And they of the circumcision which believed were astonished, as many as came with Peter, because that on the Gentiles also was poured out the gift of the **Holy Ghost**. {10:46} For they heard them speak with tongues, and magnify **God**. Then answered Peter, {10:47} Can any man forbid water, that these should not be baptized, which have received the **Holy Ghost** as well as we? {10:48} And **He** commanded them to be baptized in the **name** of the **Lord**. Then prayed they Him to tarry certain days. **{26}**

{11:1} And the apostles and brethren that were in Judaea heard that the Gentiles had also received the **word of God**. {11:2} And when Peter was come up to Jerusalem, they that were of the circumcision contended with Him, {11:3} Saying, Thou wentest in to men uncircumcised, and didst eat with them. {11:4} But Peter rehearsed [the matter] from the beginning, and expounded [it] by order unto them, saying, {11:5} I was in the city of Joppa praying: and in a trance I saw a vision, A certain vessel descend, as it had been a great sheet, let down from heaven by four corners; and it came even to ME: {11:6} Upon the which when I had fastened mine eyes, I considered, and saw fourfooted beasts of the earth, and wild beasts, and creeping things, and fowls of the air. {11:7} And I heard a **voice** saying unto ME, Arise, Peter; slay and eat. {11:8} But I said, Not so, **Lord**: for nothing common or unclean hath at any time entered into my mouth. {11:9} But the **voice** answered me again from heaven, What **God** hath cleansed, [that] call not thou common. {11:10} And this was done three times: and all were drawn up again into heaven. {11:11} And, behold, immediately there were three men already come unto the house where I was, sent from Caesarea unto me. {11:12} And the spirit bade me go with them, nothing doubting. Moreover these six brethren accompanied me, and we entered into the man's house: {11:13} And He shewed us how He had seen an angel in His house, which stood and said unto Him, Send men to Joppa, and call for Simon, whose surname is Peter; {11:14} Who shall tell thee words, whereby thou and all thy house shall be saved. {11:15} And as I began to speak, the **Holy Ghost** fell on them, as on us at the beginning. {11:16} Then remembered I the word of the **Lord**, how that **He** said, John indeed baptized with water; but ye shall be baptized with the **Holy Ghost**. {11:17} Forasmuch then as **God** gave them the like gift as [**He** did] unto us, who believed on the **Lord Jesus Christ**; what was I, that I could withstand **God**? {11:18} When they heard these things, they held their peace, and glorified **God**, saying, Then hath **God** also to the Gentiles granted repentance unto life.

{11:19} Now they which were scattered abroad upon the persecution that arose about Stephen travelled as far as Phenice, and Cyprus, and Antioch, preaching the word to none but unto the Jews only. {11:20} And some of them were men of Cyprus and Cyrene, which, when they were come to Antioch, spake unto the Grecians, preaching the **Lord Jesus**. {11:21} And the hand of the **Lord** was with them: and a great number believed, and turned unto the **Lord**.

{11:22} Then tidings of these things came unto the ears of the church which was in Jerusalem: and they sent forth Barnabas, that He should go as far as Antioch. {11:23} Who, when He came, and had seen the grace of **God**, was glad, and exhorted them all, that with purpose of heart they would cleave unto the **Lord**. {11:24} For He was a good man, and full of the **Holy Ghost** and of faith: and much people was added unto the **Lord**. {11:25} Then departed Barnabas to Tarsus, for to seek Saul: {11:26} And when He had found Him, He brought Him unto Antioch. And it came to pass, that a whole year they assembled themselves with the church, and taught much people. And the disciples were called Christians first in Antioch.

{11:27} And in these days came prophets from Jerusalem unto Antioch. {11:28} And there stood up one of them named Agabus, and signified by the spirit that there should be great dearth throughout all the world: which came to pass in the days of Claudius Caesar. {11:29} Then the disciples, every man according to His ability, determined to send relief unto the brethren which dwelt in Judaea: {11:30} Which also they did, and sent it to the elders by the hands of Barnabas and Saul. **{16}**

{12:1} Now about that time Herod the king stretched forth [His] hands to vex certain of the church. {12:2} And He killed James the brother of John with the sword. {12:3} And because He saw it pleased the Jews, He proceeded further to take Peter also. (Then were the days of unleavened bread.) {12:4} And when He had apprehended Him, He put [Him] in prison, and delivered [Him] to four quaternions of soldiers to keep Him; intending after Easter to bring Him forth to the people. {12:5} Peter therefore was kept in prison: but prayer was made without ceasing of the church unto **God** for Him. {12:6} And when Herod would have brought Him forth, the same night Peter was sleeping between two soldiers, bound with two chains: and the keepers before the door kept the prison. {12:7} And, behold, the angel of the **Lord** came upon [Him,] and a light shined in the prison: and He smote Peter on the side, and

raised Him up, saying, Arise up quickly. And His chains fell off from [His] hands. {12:8} And the angel said unto Him, Gird thyself, and bind on thy sandals. And so He did. And He saith unto Him, Cast thy garment about thee, and follow ME. {12:9} And He went out, and followed Him; and wist not that it was true which was done by the angel; but thought He saw a vision. {12:10} When they were past the first and the second ward, they came unto the iron gate that leadeth unto the city; which opened to them of His own accord: and they went out, and passed on through one street; and forthwith the angel departed from Him. {12:11} And when Peter was come to himself, He said, Now I know of a surety, that the **Lord** hath sent **His** angel, and hath delivered ME out of the hand of Herod, and [from] all the expectation of the people of the Jews. {12:12} And when He had considered [the thing,] He came to the house of Mary the mother of John, whose surname was Mark; where many were gathered together praying. {12:13} And as Peter knocked at the door of the gate, a damsel came to hearken, named Rhoda. {12:14} And when she knew Peter's voice, she opened not the gate for gladness, but ran in, and told how Peter stood before the gate. {12:15} And they said unto her, Thou art mad. But she constantly affirmed that it was even so. Then said they, It is His angel. {12:16} But Peter continued knocking: and when they had opened [the door,] and saw Him, they were astonished. {12:17} But He, beckoning unto them with the hand to hold their peace, declared unto them how the **Lord** had brought Him out of the prison. And He said, Go shew these things unto James, and to the brethren. And He departed, and went into another place. {12:18} Now as soon as it was day, there was no small stir among the soldiers, what was become of Peter. {12:19} And when Herod had sought for Him, and found Him not, He examined the keepers, and commanded that [they] should be put to death. And He went down from Judaea to Caesarea, and [there] abode.

{12:20} And Herod was highly displeased with them of Tyre and Sidon: but they came with one accord to Him, and, having made Blastus the king's chamberlain their friend, desired peace; because their country was nourished by the king's [country.]{12:21} And upon a set day Herod, arrayed in royal apparel, sat upon His throne, and made an oration unto them. {12:22} And the people gave a shout, [saying, It is] the voice of a God, and not of a man. {12:23} And immediately the angel of the **Lord** smote Him, because He gave not **God** the glory: and He was eaten of worms, and gave up the ghost.

{12:24} But the **word of God** grew and multiplied. {12:25} And Barnabas and Saul returned from Jerusalem, when they had fulfilled [their] ministry, and took with them John, whose surname was Mark. **{6}**

{13:1} Now there were in the church that was at Antioch certain prophets and teachers; as Barnabas, and Simeon that was called Niger, and Lucius of Cyrene, and Manaen, which had been brought up with Herod the tetrarch, and Saul. {13:2} As they ministered to the **Lord**, and fasted, the **Holy Ghost** said, Separate **ME** Barnabas and Saul for the work whereunto I have called them. {13:3} And when they had fasted and prayed, and laid [their] hands on them, they sent [them] away.

{13:4} So they, being sent forth by the **Holy Ghost**, departed unto Seleucia; and from thence they sailed to Cyprus. {13:5} And when they were at Salamis, they preached the word of **God** in the synagogues of the Jews: and they had also John to [their] minister. {13:6} And when they had gone through the isle unto Paphos, they found a certain sorcerer, a false prophet, a Jew, whose name [was] Bar-Jesus: {13:7} Which was with the deputy of the country, Sergius Paulus, a prudent man; who called for Barnabas and Saul, and desired to hear the word of God. {13:8} But Elymas the sorcerer (for so is his name by interpretation) withstood them, seeking to turn away the deputy from the faith. {13:9} Then Saul, (who also [is called] Paul,) filled with the Holy Ghost, set His eyes on Him, {13:10} And said, O full of all subtilty and all mischief, [thou] child of the devil, [thou] enemy of all righteousness, wilt thou not cease to pervert the right ways of the Lord? {13:11} And now, behold, the hand of the Lord [is] upon thee, and thou shalt be blind, not seeing the sun for a season. And immediately there fell on Him a mist and a darkness; and He went about seeking some to lead Him by the hand. {13:12} Then the deputy, when He saw what was done, believed, being astonished at the doctrine of the Lord. {13:13} Now when Paul and His company loosed from Paphos, they came to Perga in Pamphylia: and John departing from them returned to Jerusalem.

{13:14} But when they departed from Perga, they came to Antioch in Pisidia, and went into the synagogue on the sabbath day, and sat down. {13:15} And after the reading of the law and the prophets the rulers of the synagogue sent unto them, saying, [Ye] men [and] brethren, if ye have any word of exhortation for the people, say on. {13:16} Then Paul stood up, and beckoning with [His] hand said, Men of Israel, and ye that fear God, give audience. {13:17} The God of this people of Israel chose our Fathers, and exalted the people when they dwelt as strangers in the land of Egypt, and with an high arm brought He them out of it. {13:18} And about the time of forty years suffered He their manners in the wilderness. {13:19} And when He had destroyed seven nations in the land of Chanaan, He divided their land to them by lot. {13:20} And after that He gave [unto them] judges about the space of four hundred and fifty years, until Samuel the prophet. {13:21} And afterward they desired a king: and God gave unto them Saul the Son of Cis, a man of the tribe of Benjamin, by the space of forty years. {13:22} And when He had removed Him, He raised up unto them David to be their king; to whom also He gave testimony, and said, I have found David the [Son] of Jesse, a man after mine own heart, which shall fulfil all my will. {13:23} Of this man's seed hath God according to [His] promise raised unto Israel a Saviour, Jesus: {13:24} When John had first preached before His coming the baptism of repentance to all the people of Israel. {13:25} And as John fulfilled His course, He said, Whom think ye that I am? I am not [He.] But, behold, there cometh one after ME, whose shoes of [His] feet I am not worthy to loose. {13:26} Men [and] brethren, children of the stock of Abraham, and whosoever among you feareth God, to you is the word of this salvation sent. {13:27} For they that dwell at Jerusalem, and their rulers, because they knew Him not, nor yet the voices of the prophets which are read every sabbath day, they have fulfilled [them] in condemning [Him.]{13:28} And though they found no cause of death [in Him,] yet desired they Pilate that He should be slain. {13:29} And when they had fulfilled all that was written of Him, they took [Him] down from the tree, and laid [Him] in a sepulchre. {13:30} But God raised Him from the dead: {13:31} And He was seen many days of them which came up with Him from Galilee to Jerusalem, who are His witnesses unto the people. {13:32} And we declare unto you glad tidings, how that the promise which was made unto the Fathers, {13:33} God hath fulfilled the same unto us their children, in that He hath raised up Jesus again; as it

is also written in the second psalm, Thou art my Son, this day have I begotten thee. {13:34} And as concerning that He raised Him up from the dead, [now] no more to return to corruption, He said on this wise, I will give you the sure mercies of David. {13:35} Wherefore He saith also in another [psalm,] Thou shalt not suffer thine Holy One to see corruption. {13:36} For David, after He had served His own generation by the will of God, fell on sleep, and was laid unto His Fathers, and saw corruption: {13:37} But He, whom God raised again, saw no corruption.

{13:38} Be it known unto you therefore, men [and] brethren, that through this man is preached unto you the forgiveness of sins: {13:39} And by Him all that believe are justified from all things, from which ye could not be justified by the law of Moses. {13:40} Beware therefore, lest that come upon you, which is spoken of in the prophets; {13:41} Behold, ye despisers, and wonder, and perish: for I work a work in your days, a work which ye shall in no wise believe, though a man declare it unto you. {13:42} And when the Jews were gone out of the synagogue, the Gentiles besought that these words might be preached to them the next sabbath. {13:43} Now when the congregation was broken up, many of the Jews and religious proselytes followed Paul and Barnabas: who, speaking to them, persuaded them to continue in the grace of God.

{13:44} And the next sabbath day came almost the whole city together to hear the word of God. {13:45} But when the Jews saw the multitudes, they were filled with envy, and spake against those things which were spoken by Paul, contradicting and blaspheming. {13:46} Then Paul and Barnabas waxed bold, and said, It was necessary that the word of God should first have been spoken to you: but seeing ye put it from you, and judge yourselves unworthy of everlasting life, lo, we turn to the Gentiles. {13:47} For so hath the Lord commanded us, [saying,] I have set thee to be a light of the Gentiles, that thou shouldest be for salvation unto the ends of the earth. {13:48} And when the Gentiles heard this, they were glad, and glorified the word of the Lord: and as many as were ordained to eternal life believed. {13:49} And the word of the Lord was published throughout all the region. {13:50} But the Jews stirred up the devout and honourable women, and the chief men of the city, and raised persecution against Paul and Barnabas, and expelled them out of their coasts. {13:51} But they shook off the dust of their feet against them, and came unto Iconium. {13:52} And the disciples were filled with joy, and with the Holy Ghost. {41}

{14:1} And it came to pass in Iconium, that they went both together into the synagogue of the Jews, and so spake, that a great multitude both of the Jews and also of the Greeks believed. {14:2} But the unbelieving Jews stirred up the Gentiles, and made their minds evil affected against the brethren. {14:3} Long time therefore abode they speaking boldly in the Lord, which gave testimony unto the word of His grace, and granted signs and wonders to be done by their hands. {14:4} But the multitude of the city was divided: and part held with the Jews, and part with the apostles. {14:5} And when there was an assault made both of the Gentiles, and also of the Jews with their rulers, to use [them] despitefully, and to stone them, {14:6} They were ware of [it,] and fled unto Lystra and Derbe, cities of Lycaonia, and unto the region that lieth round about: {14:7} And there they preached the Gospel.

{14:8} And there sat a certain man at Lystra, impotent in His feet, being a cripple from His mother's womb, who never had walked: {14:9} The same heard Paul speak: who stedfastly beholding Him, and perceiving that He had faith to be healed, {14:10} Said with a loud voice, Stand upright on thy feet. And He leaped and walked. {14:11} And when the people saw what Paul had done, they lifted up their voices, saying in the speech of Lycaonia, The **God**s are come down to us in the likeness of men. {14:12} And they called Barnabas, Jupiter; and Paul, Mercurius, because He was the chief speaker. {14:13} Then the priest of Jupiter, which was before their city, brought oxen and garlands unto the gates, and would have done sacrifice with the people. {14:14} [Which] when the apostles, Barnabas and Paul, heard [of,] they rent their clothes, and ran in among the people, crying out, {14:15} And saying, Sirs, why do ye these things? We also are men of like passions with you, and preach unto you that ye should turn from these vanities unto the living **God**, which made heaven, and earth, and the sea, and all things that are therein: {14:16} Who in times past suffered all nations to walk in their own ways. {14:17} Nevertheless He left not himself without witness, in that He did good, and gave us rain from heaven, and fruitful seasons, filling our hearts with food and gladness. {14:18} And with these sayings scarce restrained they the people, that they had not done sacrifice unto them.

{14:19} And there came thither [certain] Jews from Antioch and Iconium, who persuaded the people, and, having stoned Paul, drew [Him] out of the city, supposing He had been dead. {14:20} Howbeit, as the disciples stood round about Him, He rose up, and came into the city: and the next day He departed with Barnabas to Derbe. {14:21} And when they had preached the Gospel to that city, and had taught many, they returned again to Lystra, and [to] Iconium, and Antioch, {14:22} Confirming the souls of the disciples, [and] exhorting them to continue in the faith, and that we must through much tribulation enter into the kingdom of **God**. {14:23} And when they had ordained them elders in every church, and had prayed with fasting, they commended them to the **Lord**, on **whom** they believed. {14:24} And after they had passed throughout Pisidia, they came to Pamphylia. {14:25} And when they had preached the word in Perga, they went down into Attalia: {14:26} And thence sailed to Antioch, from whence they had been recommended to the grace of **God** for the work which they fulfilled. {14:27} And when they were come, and had gathered the church together, they rehearsed all that **God** had done with them, and how **He** had opened the door of faith unto the Gentiles. {14:28} And there they abode long time with the disciples.

{15:1} And certain men which came down from Judaea taught the brethren, [and said,] Except ye be circumcised after the manner of Moses, ye cannot be saved. {15:2} When therefore Paul and Barnabas had no small dissension and disputation with them, they determined that Paul and Barnabas, and certain other of them, should go up to Jerusalem unto the apostles and elders about this question. {15:3} And being brought on their way by the church, they passed through Phenice and Samaria, declaring the conversion of the Gentiles: and they caused great joy unto all the brethren. {15:4} And when they were come to Jerusalem, they were received of the church, and [of] the apostles and elders, and they declared all things that **God** had done with them. {15:5} But there rose up certain of the sect of the Pharisees which believed, saying, That it was needful to circumcise them, and to command [them] to keep the law of Moses.

{15:6} And the apostles and elders came together for to consider of this matter. {15:7} And when there had been much disputing, Peter rose up, and said unto them, Men [and] brethren, ye know how that a good while ago **God** made choice among us, that the Gentiles by my mouth should hear the **word of the** Gospel, and believe. {15:8} And **God**, which knoweth the hearts, bare them witness, giving them the **Holy Ghost**, even as [**He** did] unto us; {15:9} And put no difference between us and them, purifying their hearts by faith. {15:10} Now therefore why tempt ye **God**, to put a yoke upon the neck of the disciples, which neither our **Father**s nor we were able to bear? {15:11} But we believe that through the grace of the **Lord Jesus Christ** we shall be saved, even as they.

{15:12} Then all the multitude kept silence, and gave audience to Barnabas and Paul, declaring what miracles and wonders **God** had wrought among the Gentiles by them.

{15:13} And after they had held their peace, James answered, saying, Men [and] brethren, hearken unto me: {15:14} Simeon hath declared how **God** at the first did visit the Gentiles, to take out of them a people for **His name**. {15:15} And to this agree the words of the prophets; as it is written, {15:16} After this I will return, and will build again the tabernacle of David, which is fallen down; and I will build again the ruins thereof, and I will set it up: {15:17} That the residue of men might seek after the **Lord**, and all the Gentiles, upon **whom my name** is called, saith the **Lord,** who doeth all these things. {15:18} Known unto **God** are all **His** works from the beginning of the world. {15:19} Wherefore my sentence is, that we trouble not them, which from among the Gentiles are turned to **God**: {15:20} But that we write unto them, that they abstain from pollutions of idols, and [from] fornication, and [from] things strangled, and [from] blood. {15:21} For Moses of old time hath in every city them that preach **Him**, being read in the synagogues every sabbath day. {15:22} Then pleased it the apostles and elders, with the whole church, to send chosen men of their own company to Antioch with Paul and Barnabas; [namely,] Judas surnamed Barsabas, and Silas, chief men among the brethren: {15:23} And they wrote [letters] by them after this manner; The apostles and elders and brethren [send] greeting unto the brethren which are of the Gentiles in Antioch and Syria and Cilicia: {15:24} Forasmuch as we have heard, that certain which went out from us have troubled you with words, subverting your souls, saying, [Ye must] be circumcised, and keep the law: to whom we gave no [such] commandment: {15:25} It seemed good unto us, being assembled with one accord, to send chosen men unto you with our beloved Barnabas and Paul, {15:26} Men that have hazarded their lives for the **name** of our **Lord Jesus Christ**. {15:27} We have sent therefore Judas and Silas, who shall also tell [you] the same things by mouth. {15:28} For it seemed good to the **Holy Ghost**, and to us, to lay upon you no greater burden than these necessary things; {15:29} That ye abstain from meats offered to idols, and from blood, and from things strangled, and from fornication: from which if ye keep yourselves, ye shall do well. Fare ye well. {15:30} So when they were dismissed, they came to Antioch: and when they had gathered the multitude together, they delivered the epistle: {15:31} [Which] when they had read, they rejoiced for the consolation. {15:32} And Judas and Silas, being prophets also themselves, exhorted the brethren with many words, and confirmed [them.]{15:33} And after they had tarried [there] a space, they were let go in peace from the brethren unto the apostles. {15:34} Notwithstanding it pleased Silas to abide there still. {15:35} Paul also and Barnabas continued in Antioch, teaching and preaching the word of the **Lord**, with many others also.

{15:36} And some days after Paul said unto Barnabas, Let us go again and visit our brethren in every city where we have preached the **word of the Lord**, [and see] how they do. {15:37} And Barnabas determined to take with them John, whose surname was Mark. {15:38} But Paul thought not good to take him with them, who departed from them from Pamphylia, and went not with them to the work. {15:39} And the contention was so sharp between them, that they departed asunder one from the other: and so Barnabas took Mark, and sailed unto Cyprus; {15:40} And Paul chose Silas, and departed, being recommended by the brethren unto the grace of **God**. {15:41} And He went through Syria and Cilicia, confirming the churches. **{22}**

{16:1} Then came He to Derbe and Lystra: and, behold, a certain disciple was there, named Timotheus, the Son of a certain woman, which was a Jewess, and believed; but His Father [was] a Greek: {16:2} Which was well reported of by the brethren that were at Lystra and Iconium. {16:3} Him would Paul have to go forth with Him; and took and circumcised Him because of the Jews which were in those quarters: for they knew all that His Father was a Greek. {16:4} And as they went through the cities, they delivered them the decrees for to keep, that were ordained of the apostles and elders which were at Jerusalem. {16:5} And so were the churches established in the faith, and increased in number daily. {16:6} Now when they had gone throughout Phrygia and the region of Galatia, and were forbidden of the **Holy Ghost** to preach **the word** in Asia, {16:7} After they were come to Mysia, they assayed to go into Bithynia: but the Spirit suffered them not. {16:8} And they passing by Mysia came down to Troas. {16:9} And a vision appeared to Paul in the night; There stood a man of Macedonia, and prayed Him, saying, Come over into Macedonia, and help us. {16:10} And after He had seen the vision, immediately we endeavoured to go into Macedonia, assuredly gathering that the **Lord** had called us for to preach the **Gospel** unto them. {16:11} Therefore loosing from Troas, we came with a straight course to Samothracia, and the next day to Neapolis; {16:12} And from thence to Philippi, which is the chief city of that part of Macedonia, [and] a colony: and we were in that city abiding certain days. {16:13} And on the sabbath we went out of the city by a river side, where prayer was wont to be made; and we sat down, and spake unto the women which resorted [thither.

]{16:14} And a certain woman named Lydia, a seller of purple, of the city of Thyatira, which worshipped **God**, heard [us:] whose heart the **Lord** opened, that she attended unto the things which were spoken of Paul. {16:15} And when she was baptized, and her household, she besought [us,] saying, If ye have judged me to be faithful to the **Lord**, come into my house, and abide [there.] And she constrained us.

{16:16} And it came to pass, as we went to prayer, a certain damsel possessed with a spirit of divination met us, which brought her masters much gain by soothsaying: {16:17} The same followed Paul and us, and cried, saying, These men are the servants of the most high **God**, which shew unto us the way of salvation. {16:18} And this did she many days. But Paul, being grieved, turned and said to the spirit, I command thee in the **name** of **Jesus Christ** to come out of her. And he came out the same hour.

{16:19} And when her masters saw that the hope of their gains was gone, they caught Paul and Silas, and drew [them] into the marketplace unto the rulers, {16:20} And brought them to the magistrates, saying, These men, being Jews, do exceedingly trouble our city, {16:21} And teach customs, which are not lawful for us to receive, neither to observe, being Romans. {16:22} And the multitude rose up together against them: and the magistrates rent off their clothes, and commanded to beat [them.]{16:23} And when they had laid many stripes upon them, they cast [them] into prison, charging the jailer to keep them safely: {16:24} Who, having received such a charge, thrust them into the inner prison, and made their feet fast in the stocks.

{16:25} And at midnight Paul and Silas prayed, and sang praises unto **God**: and the prisoners heard them. {16:26} And suddenly there was a great earthquake, so that the foundations of the prison were shaken: and immediately all the doors were opened, and every one's bands were loosed. {16:27} And the keeper of the prison awaking out of His sleep, and seeing the prison doors open, He drew out His sword, and would have killed himself, supposing that the prisoners had been fled. {16:28} But Paul cried with a loud voice, saying, Do thyself no harm: for we are all here. {16:29} Then He called for a light, and sprang in, and came trembling, and fell down before Paul and Silas, {16:30} And brought them out, and said, Sirs, what must I do to be saved? {16:31} And they said, Believe on the **Lord Jesus Christ**, and thou shalt be saved, and thy house. {16:32} And they spake unto Him the **word of the Lord**, and to all that were in His house. {16:33} And He took them the same hour of the night, and washed [their] stripes; and was baptized, He and all His, straightway. {16:34} And when He had brought them into His house, He set meat before them, and rejoiced, believing in God with all His house. {16:35} And when it was day, the magistrates sent the serjeants, saying, Let those men go. {16:36} And the keeper of the prison told this saying to Paul, The magistrates have sent to let you go: now therefore depart, and go in peace. {16:37} But Paul said unto them, They have beaten us openly uncondemned, being Romans, and have cast [us] into prison; and now do they thrust us out privily? nay verily; but let them come themselves and fetch us out. {16:38} And the serjeants told these words unto the magistrates: and they feared, when they heard that they were Romans. {16:39} And they came and besought them, and brought [them] out, and desired [them] to depart out of the city. {16:40} And they went out of the prison, and entered into [the house of] Lydia and when they had seen the brethren, they comforted them, and departed. **{11}**

{17:1} Now when they had passed through Amphipolis and Apollonia, they came to Thessalonica, where was a synagogue of the Jews: {17:2} And Paul, as His manner was, went in unto them, and three sabbath days reasoned with them out of the scriptures, {17:3} Opening and alleging, that **Christ** must needs have suffered, and risen again from the dead; and that this **Jesus**, **whom** I preach unto you, is **Christ**. {17:4} And some of them believed, and consorted with Paul and Silas; and of the devout Greeks a great multitude, and of the chief women not a few.

{17:5} But the Jews which believed not, moved with envy, took unto them certain lewd fellows of the baser sort, and gathered a company, and set all the city on an uproar, and assaulted the house of Jason, and sought to bring them out to the people. {17:6} And when they found them not, they drew Jason and certain brethren unto the rulers of the city, crying, These that have turned the world upside down are come hither also; {17:7} **Whom** Jason hath received: and these all do contrary to the decrees of Caesar, saying that there is another king, [one] Jesus. {17:8} And they troubled the people and the rulers of the city, when they heard these things. {17:9} And when they had taken security of Jason, and of the other, they let them go.

{17:10} And the brethren immediately sent away Paul and Silas by night unto Berea: who coming [thither] went into the synagogue of the Jews. {17:11} These were more noble than those in Thessalonica, in that they received the word with all readiness of mind, and searched the scriptures daily, whether those things were so. {17:12} Therefore many of them believed; also of honourable women which were Greeks, and of men, not a few. {17:13} But when the Jews of Thessalonica had knowledge that the word of God was preached of Paul at Berea, they came thither also, and stirred up the people. {17:14} And then immediately the brethren sent away Paul to go as it were to the sea: but Silas and Timotheus abode there still. {17:15} And they that conducted Paul brought Him unto Athens: and receiving a commandment unto Silas and Timotheus for to come to Him with all speed, they departed.

{17:16} Now while Paul waited for them at Athens, His spirit was stirred in Him, when He saw the city wholly given to idolatry. {17:17} Therefore disputed He in the synagogue with the Jews, and with the devout persons, and in the market daily with them that met with Him. {17:18} Then certain philosophers of the Epicureans, and of the Stoicks, encountered Him. And some said, What will this babbler say? other some, He seemeth to be a setter forth of strange Gods: because He preached unto them Jesus, and the resurrection. {17:19} And they took Him, and brought Him unto Areopagus, saying, May we know what this new doctrine, whereof thou speakest, [is?]{17:20} For thou bringest certain strange things to our ears: we would know therefore what these things mean. {17:21} (For all the Athenians and strangers which were there spent their time in nothing else, but either to tell, or to hear some new thing.)

{17:22} Then Paul stood in the midst of Mars' hill, and said, [Ye] men of Athens, I perceive that in all things ye are too superstitious. {17:23} For as I passed by, and beheld your devotions, I found an altar with this inscription, TO THE UNKNOWN GOD. Whom therefore ye ignorantly worship, Him declare I unto you. {17:24} God that made the world and all things therein, seeing that He is Lord of heaven and earth, dwelleth not in temples made with hands; {17:25} Neither is worshipped with men's hands, as though He needed any thing, seeing He giveth to all life, and breath, and all things; {17:26} And hath made of one blood all nations of men for to dwell on all the face of the earth, and hath determined the times before appointed, and the bounds of their habitation; {17:27} That they should seek the Lord, if haply they might feel after Him, and find Him, though He be not far from every one of us: {17:28} For in Him we live, and move, and have our being; as certain also of your own poets have said, For we are also His offspring. {17:29} Forasmuch then as we are the offspring of God, we ought not to think that the Godhead is like unto gold, or silver, or stone, graven by art and man's device. {17:30} And the times of this ignorance God winked at; but now commandeth all men every where to repent: {17:31} Because He hath appointed a day, in the which He will judge the world in righteousness by [that] man whom He hath ordained; [whereof] He hath given assurance unto all [men,] in that He hath raised Him from the dead.

{17:32} And when they heard of the resurrection of the dead, some mocked: and others said, We will hear thee

again of this [matter.]{17:33} So Paul departed from among them. {17:34} Howbeit certain men clave unto Him, and believed: among the which [was] Dionysius the Areopagite, and a woman named Damaris, and others with them. {21}

{18:1} After these things Paul departed from Athens, and came to Corinth; {18:2} And found a certain Jew named Aquila, born in Pontus, lately come from Italy, with His wife Priscilla; (because that Claudius had commanded all Jews to depart from Rome:) and came unto them. {18:3} And because He was of the same craft, He abode with them, and wrought: for by their occupation they were tentmakers. {18:4} And He reasoned in the synagogue every sabbath, and persuaded the Jews and the Greeks. {18:5} And when Silas and Timotheus were come from Macedonia, Paul was pressed in the spirit, and testified to the Jews [that] Jesus [was] Christ. {18:6} And when they opposed themselves, and blasphemed, He shook [His] raiment, and said unto them, Your blood [be] upon your own heads; I [am] clean: from henceforth I will go unto the Gentiles.

{18:7} And He departed thence, and entered into a certain [man's] house, named Justus, [one] that worshipped God, whose house joined hard to the synagogue. {18:8} And Crispus, the chief ruler of the synagogue, believed on the Lord with all His house; and many of the Corinthians hearing believed, and were baptized. {18:9} Then spake the Lord to Paul in the night by a vision, Be not afraid, but speak, and hold not thy peace: {18:10} For I am with thee, and no man shall set on thee to hurt thee: for I have much people in this city. {18:11} And He continued [there] a year and six months, teaching the word of God among them.

{18:12} And when Gallio was the deputy of Achaia, the Jews made insurrection with one accord against Paul, and brought Him to the judgment seat, {18:13} Saying, This [fellow] persuadeth men to worship God contrary to the law. {18:14} And when Paul was now about to open [His] mouth, Gallio said unto the Jews, If it were a matter of wrong or wicked lewdness, O [ye] Jews, reason would that I should bear with you: {18:15} But if it be a question of words and names, and [of] your law, look ye [to it;] for I will be no judge of such [matters.]{18:16} And He drave them from the judgment seat. {18:17} Then all the Greeks took Sosthenes, the chief ruler of the synagogue, and beat [Him] before the judgment seat. And Gallio cared for none of those things.

{18:18} And Paul [after this] tarried [there] yet a good while, and then took His leave of the brethren, and sailed thence into Syria, and with Him Priscilla and Aquila; having shorn [His] head in Cenchrea: for He had a vow. {18:19} And He came to Ephesus, and left them there: but He himself entered into the synagogue, and reasoned with the Jews. {18:20} When they desired [Him] to tarry longer time with them, He consented not; {18:21} But bade them farewell, saying, I must by all means keep this feast that cometh in Jerusalem: but I will return again unto you, if God will. And He sailed from Ephesus. {18:22} And when He had landed at Caesarea, and gone up, and saluted the church, He went down to Antioch. {18:23} And after He had spent some time [there,] He departed, and went over [all] the country of Galatia and Phrygia in order, strengthening all the disciples.

{18:24} And a certain Jew named Apollos, born at Alexandria, an eloquent man, [and] mighty in the scriptures, came to Ephesus. {18:25} This man was instructed in the way of the Lord; and being fervent in the spirit, He spake and taught diligently the things of the **Lord**, knowing only the baptism of John. {18:26} And He began to speak boldly in the synagogue: whom when Aquila and Priscilla had heard, they took him unto [them,] and expounded unto him the **way of God** more perfectly. {18:27} And when He was disposed to pass into Achaia, the brethren wrote, exhorting the disciples to receive Him: who, when He was come, helped them much which had believed through grace: {18:28} For He mightily convinced the Jews, [and that] publickly, shewing by the scriptures that **Jesus** was **Christ**. {11}

{19:1} And it came to pass, that, while Apollos was at Corinth, Paul having passed through the upper coasts came to Ephesus: and finding certain disciples, {19:2} He said unto them, Have ye received the **Holy Ghost** since ye believed? And they said unto Him, We have not so much as heard whether there be any **Holy Ghost**. {19:3} And He said unto them, Unto what then were ye baptized? And they said, Unto John's baptism. {19:4} Then said Paul, John verily baptized with the baptism of repentance, saying unto the people, that they should believe on **Him** which should come after **Him**, that is, on **Christ Jesus**. {19:5} When they heard [this,] they were baptized in the **name** of the **Lord Jesus**. {19:6} And when Paul had laid [**His**] hands upon them, the **Holy Ghost** came on them; and they spake with tongues, and prophesied. {19:7} And all the men were about twelve. {19:8} And He went into the synagogue, and spake boldly for the space of three months, disputing and persuading the things concerning the **kingdom of God**. {19:9} But when divers were hardened, and believed not, but spake evil of **that way** before the multitude, He departed from them, and separated the disciples, disputing daily in the school of one Tyrannus. {19:10} And this continued by the space of two years; so that all they which dwelt in Asia heard the **word of the Lord Jesus**, both Jews and Greeks. {19:11} And **God** wrought special miracles by the hands of Paul: {19:12} So that from His body were brought unto the sick handkerchiefs or aprons, and the diseases departed from them, and the evil spirits went out of them.

{19:13} Then certain of the vagabond Jews, exorcists, took upon them to call over them which had evil spirits the **name** of the **Lord Jesus**, saying, We adjure you by **Jesus whom** Paul preacheth. {19:14} And there were seven sons of [one] Sceva, a Jew, [and] chief of the priests, which did so. {19:15} And the evil spirit answered and said, **Jesus** I know, and Paul I know; but who are ye? {19:16} And the man in whom the evil spirit was leaped on them, and overcame them, and prevailed against them, so that they fled out of that house naked and wounded. {19:17} And this was known to all the Jews and Greeks also dwelling at Ephesus; and fear fell on them all, and the **name** of the **Lord Jesus** was magnified. {19:18} And many that believed came, and confessed, and shewed their deeds. {19:19} Many of them also which used curious arts brought their books together, and burned them before all [men:] and they counted the price of them, and found it fifty thousand [pieces] of silver. {19:20} So mightily grew the **word of God** and prevailed.

{19:21} After these things were ended, Paul purposed in the spirit, when He had passed through Macedonia and Achaia, to go to Jerusalem, saying, After I have been there, I must also see Rome. {19:22} So He sent into Macedonia two of them that ministered unto Him, Timotheus and Erastus; but He himself stayed in Asia for a season. {19:23} And the same time there arose no small stir about that way. {19:24} For a certain [man] named Demetrius, a silversmith, which made silver shrines for Diana, brought

no small gain unto the craftsmen; {19:25} Whom He called together with the workmen of like occupation, and said, Sirs, ye know that by this craft we have our wealth. {19:26} Moreover ye see and hear, that not alone at Ephesus, but almost throughout all Asia, this Paul hath persuaded and turned away much people, saying that they be no **Gods**, which are made with hands: {19:27} So that not only this our craft is in danger to be set at nought; but also that the temple of the great Goddess Diana should be despised, and her magnificence should be destroyed, whom all Asia and the world worshippeth. {19:28} And when they heard [these sayings,] they were full of wrath, and cried out, saying, Great [is] Diana of the Ephesians. {19:29} And the whole city was filled with confusion: and having caught Gaius and Aristarchus, men of Macedonia, Paul's companions in travel, they rushed with one accord into the theatre. {19:30} And when Paul would have entered in unto the people, the disciples suffered Him not. {19:31} And certain of the chief of Asia, which were His friends, sent unto Him, desiring [Him] that He would not adventure himself into the theatre. {19:32} Some therefore cried one thing, and some another: for the assembly was confused; and the more part knew not wherefore they were come together. {19:33} And they drew Alexander out of the multitude, the Jews putting Him forward. And Alexander beckoned with the hand, and would have made His defence unto the people. {19:34} But when they knew that He was a Jew, all with one voice about the space of two hours cried out, Great [is] Diana of the Ephesians. {19:35} And when the townclerk had appeased the people, He said, [Ye] men of Ephesus, what man is there that knoweth not how that the city of the Ephesians is a worshipper of the great Goddess Diana, and of the [image] which fell down from Jupiter? {19:36} Seeing then that these things cannot be spoken against, ye ought to be quiet, and to do nothing rashly. {19:37} For ye have brought hither these men, which are neither robbers of churches, nor yet blasphemers of your Goddess. {19:38} Wherefore if Demetrius, and the craftsmen which are with Him, have a matter against any man, the law is open, and there are deputies: let them implead one another. {19:39} But if ye enquire any thing concerning other matters, it shall be determined in a lawful assembly. {19:40} For we are in danger to be called in question for this day's uproar, there being no cause whereby we may give an account of this concourse. {19:41} And when He had thus spoken, **He** dismissed the assembly. {20}

{20:1} And after the uproar was ceased, Paul called unto [Him] the disciples, and embraced [them,] and departed for to go into Macedonia. {20:2} And when He had gone over those parts, and had given them much exhortation, He came into Greece, {20:3} And [there] abode three months. And when the Jews laid wait for Him, as He was about to sail into Syria, He purposed to return through Macedonia. {20:4} And there accompanied Him into Asia Sopater of Berea; and of the Thessalonians, Aristarchus and Secundus; and Gaius of Derbe, and Timotheus; and of Asia, Tychicus and Trophimus. {20:5} These going before tarried for us at Troas. {20:6} And we sailed away from Philippi after the days of unleavened bread, and came unto them to Troas in five days; where we abode seven days. {20:7} And upon the first [day] of the week, when the disciples came together to break bread, Paul preached unto them, ready to depart on the morrow; and continued His speech until midnight. {20:8} And there were many lights in the upper chamber, where they were gathered together. {20:9} And there sat in a window a certain young man named Eutychus, being fallen into a deep sleep: and as Paul was long preaching, He sunk down with sleep, and fell down from the third loft, and was taken up dead. {20:10} And Paul went down, and fell on Him, and embracing [Him] said, Trouble not yourselves; for His life is in Him. {20:11} When He therefore was come up again, and had broken bread, and eaten, and talked a long while, even till break of day, so He departed. {20:12} And they brought the young man alive, and were not a little comforted.

{20:13} And we went before to ship, and sailed unto Assos, there intending to take in Paul: for so had He appointed, minding himself to go afoot. {20:14} And when He met with us at Assos, we took Him in, and came to Mitylene. {20:15} And we sailed thence, and came the next [day] over against Chios; and the next [day] we arrived at Samos, and tarried at Trogyllium; and the next [day] we came to Miletus. {20:16} For Paul had determined to sail by Ephesus, because He would not spend the time in Asia: for He hasted, if it were possible for Him, to be at Jerusalem the day of Pentecost.

{20:17} And from Miletus He sent to Ephesus, and called the elders of the church. {20:18} And when they were come to Him, He said unto them, Ye know, from the first day that I came into Asia, after what manner I have been with you at all seasons, {20:19} Serving the **Lord** with all humility of mind, and with many tears, and temptations, which befell me by the lying in wait of the Jews: {20:20} [And] how I kept back nothing that was profitable [unto you,] but have shewed you, and have taught you publickly, and from house to house, {20:21} Testifying both to the Jews, and also to the Greeks, repentance toward **God**, and faith toward our **Lord Jesus Christ**. {20:22} And now, behold, I go bound in the spirit unto Jerusalem, not knowing the things that shall befall me there: {20:23} Save that the **Holy Ghost** witnesseth in every city, saying that bonds and afflictions abide me. {20:24} But none of these things move me, neither count I my life dear unto myself, so that I might finish my course with joy, and the ministry, which I have received of the **Lord Jesus**, to testify the Gospel of the grace of **God**. {20:25} And now, behold, I know that ye all, among whom I have gone preaching the kingdom of God, shall see my face no more. {20:26} Wherefore I take you to record this day, that I [am] pure from the blood of all [men.] {20:27} For I have not shunned to declare unto you all the counsel of **God**.

{20:28} Take heed therefore unto yourselves, and to all the flock, over the which the **Holy Ghost** hath made you overseers, to feed the church of **God**, which **He** hath purchased with **His own blood**. {20:29} For I know this, that after my departing shall grievous wolves enter in among you, not sparing the flock. {20:30} Also of your own selves shall men arise, speaking perverse things, to draw away disciples after them. {20:31} Therefore watch, and remember, that by the space of three years I ceased not to warn every one night and day with tears. {20:32} And now, brethren, I commend you to **God**, and to the **word of His grace**, which is able to build you up, and to give you an inheritance among all them which are sanctified. {20:33} I have coveted no man's silver, or gold, or apparel. {20:34} Yea, ye yourselves know, that these hands have ministered unto my necessities, and to them that were with me. {20:35} I have shewed you all things, how that so labouring ye ought to support the weak, and to remember the words of the **Lord Jesus**, how **He** said, It is more blessed to give than to receive.

{20:36} And when He had thus spoken, He kneeled down, and prayed with them all. {20:37} And they all wept sore,

and fell on Paul's neck, and kissed Him, {20:38} Sorrowing most of all for the words which He spake, that they should see His face no more. And they accompanied Him unto the ship. **{13}**

{21:1} And it came to pass, that after we were gotten from them, and had launched, we came with a straight course unto Coos, and the [day] following unto Rhodes, and from thence unto Patara: {21:2} And finding a ship sailing over unto Phenicia, we went aboard, and set forth. {21:3} Now when we had discovered Cyprus, we left it on the left hand, and sailed into Syria, and landed at Tyre: for there the ship was to unlade her burden. {21:4} And finding disciples, we tarried there seven days: who said to Paul through the Spirit, that He should not go up to Jerusalem. {21:5} And when we had accomplished those days, we departed and went our way; and they all brought us on our way, with wives and children, till [we were] out of the city: and we kneeled down on the shore, and prayed. {21:6} And when we had taken our leave one of another, we took ship; and they returned home again. {21:7} And when we had finished [our] course from Tyre, we came to Ptolemais, and saluted the brethren, and abode with them one day. {21:8} And the next [day] we that were of Paul's company departed, and came unto Caesarea: and we entered into the house of Philip the evangelist, which was [one] of the seven; and abode with Him. {21:9} And the same man had four daughters, virgins, which did prophesy. {21:10} And as we tarried [there] many days, there came down from Judaea a certain prophet, named Agabus. {21:11} And when He was come unto us, He took Paul's girdle, and bound His own hands and feet, and said, Thus saith the **Holy Ghost**, So shall the Jews at Jerusalem bind the man that owneth this girdle, and shall deliver [Him] into the hands of the Gentiles. {21:12} And when we heard these things, both we, and they of that place, besought Him not to go up to Jerusalem. {21:13} Then Paul answered, What mean ye to weep and to break mine heart? for I am ready not to be bound only, but also to die at Jerusalem for the **name** of the **Lord Jesus.** {21:14} And when He would not be persuaded, we ceased, saying, The will of the **Lord** be done.

{21:15} And after those days we took up our carriages, and went up to Jerusalem. {21:16} There went with us also [certain] of the disciples of Caesarea, and brought with them one Mnason of Cyprus, an old disciple, with whom we should lodge. {21:17} And when we were come to Jerusalem, the brethren received us gladly. {21:18} And the [day] following Paul went in with us unto James; and all the elders were present. {21:19} And when He had saluted them, He declared particularly what things **God** had wrought among the Gentiles by His ministry. {21:20} And when they heard [it,] they glorified the **Lord**, and said unto Him, Thou seest, brother, how many thousands of Jews there are which believe; and they are all zealous of the law: {21:21} And they are informed of thee, that thou teachest all the Jews which are among the Gentiles to forsake Moses, saying that they ought not to circumcise [their] children, neither to walk after the customs. {21:22} What is it therefore? the multitude must needs come together: for they will hear that thou art come. {21:23} Do therefore this that we say to thee: We have four men which have a vow on them; {21:24} Them take, and purify thyself with them, and be at charges with them, that they may shave [their] heads: and all may know that those things, whereof they were informed concerning thee, are nothing; but [that] thou thyself also walkest orderly, and keepest the law. {21:25} As touching the Gentiles which believe, we have written [and] concluded that they observe no such thing, save only that they keep themselves from [things] offered to idols, and from blood, and from strangled, and from fornication. {21:26} Then Paul took the men, and the next day purifying himself with them entered into the temple, to signify the accomplishment of the days of purification, until that an offering should be offered for every one of them.{21:27} And when the seven days were almost ended, the Jews which were of Asia, when they saw Him in the temple, stirred up all the people, and laid hands on Him, {21:28} Crying out, Men of Israel, help: This is the man, that teacheth all [men] every where against the people, and the law, and this place: and further brought Greeks also into the temple, and hath polluted this holy place. {21:29} (For they had seen before with Him in the city Trophimus an Ephesian, whom they supposed that Paul had brought into the temple.) {21:30} And all the city was moved, and the people ran together: and they took Paul, and drew Him out of the temple: and forthwith the doors were shut. {21:31} And as they went about to kill Him, tidings came unto the chief captain of the band, that all Jerusalem was in an uproar. {21:32} Who immediately took soldiers and centurions, and ran down unto them: and when they saw the chief captain and the soldiers, they left beating of Paul. {21:33} Then the chief captain came near, and took Him, and commanded [Him] to be bound with two chains; and demanded who He was, and what He had done. {21:34} And some cried one thing, some another, among the multitude: and when He could not know the certainty for the tumult, He commanded Him to be carried into the castle. {21:35} And when He came upon the stairs, so it was, that He was borne of the soldiers for the violence of the people. {21:36} For the multitude of the people followed after, crying, Away with Him. {21:37} And as Paul was to be led into the castle, He said unto the chief captain, May I speak unto thee? Who said, Canst thou speak Greek? {21:38} Art not thou that Egyptian, which before these days madest an uproar, and leddest out into the wilderness four thousand men that were murderers? {21:39} But Paul said, I am a man [which am] a Jew of Tarsus, [a city] in Cilicia, a citizen of no mean city: and, I beseech thee, suffer ME to speak unto the people. {21:40} And when He had given Him licence, Paul stood on the stairs, and beckoned with the hand unto the people. And when there was made a great silence, He spake unto [them] in the Hebrew tongue, saying:

{1}

{22:1} Men, brethren, and Fathers, hear ye my defence [which I make] now unto you. {22:2} (And when they heard that He spake in the Hebrew tongue to them, they kept the more silence: and He saith,) {22:3} I am verily a man [which am] a Jew, born in Tarsus, a city in Cilicia, yet brought up in this city at the feet of Gamaliel, [and] taught according to the perfect manner of the law of the Fathers, and was zealous toward **God**, as ye all are this day. {22:4} And I persecuted this **way** unto the death, binding and delivering into prisons both men and women. {22:5} As also the high priest doth bear me witness, and all the estate of the elders: from whom also I received letters unto the brethren, and went to Damascus, to bring them which were there bound unto Jerusalem, for to be punished. {22:6} And it came to pass, that, as I made my journey, and was come nigh unto Damascus about noon, suddenly there shone from heaven a great light round about me. {22:7} And I fell unto the ground, and heard a **voice** saying unto me, Saul, Saul, why persecutest thou **ME**? {22:8} And I answered, **Who art thou, Lord**? And **He** said unto me, **I am Jesus of Nazareth, whom** thou persecutest. {22:9} And they that were with me saw indeed the light, and were afraid; but they heard not the voice of **Him** that spake to me. {22:10} And I said, What

shall I do, **Lord**? And the **Lord** said unto me, Arise, and go into Damascus; and there it shall be told thee of all things which are appointed for thee to do. {22:11} And when I could not see for the glory of that light, being led by the hand of them that were with me, I came into Damascus. {22:12} And one Ananias, a devout man according to the law, having a good report of all the Jews which dwelt [there,]{22:13} Came unto me, and stood, and said unto me, Brother Saul, receive thy sight. And the same hour I looked up upon Him. {22:14} And He said, The **God** of our **Father**s hath chosen thee, that thou shouldest know **His** will, and see that **Just One**, and shouldest hear the **voice of His mouth**. {22:15} For thou shalt be **His** witness unto all men of what thou hast seen and heard. {22:16} And now why tarriest thou? arise, and be baptized, and wash away thy sins, calling on the **name** of the **Lord**. {22:17} And it came to pass, that, when I was come again to Jerusalem, even while I prayed in the temple, I was in a trance; {22:18} And saw **Him** saying unto me, Make haste, and get thee quickly out of Jerusalem: for they will not receive thy testimony concerning me. {22:19} And I said, **Lord**, they know that I imprisoned and beat in every synagogue them that believed on thee: {22:20} And when the blood of thy martyr Stephen was shed, I also was standing by, and consenting unto His death, and kept the raiment of them that slew Him. {22:21} And **He** said unto me, Depart: for **I** will send thee far hence unto the Gentiles. {22:22} And they gave Him audience unto this word, and [then] lifted up their voices, and said, Away with such a [fellow] from the earth: for it is not fit that He should live. {22:23} And as they cried out, and cast off [their] clothes, and threw dust into the air, {22:24} The chief captain commanded Him to be brought into the castle, and bade that He should be examined by scourging; that He might know wherefore they cried so against Him. {22:25} And as they bound Him with thongs, Paul said unto the centurion that stood by, Is it lawful for you to scourge a man that is a Roman, and uncondemned? {22:26} When the centurion heard [that,] He went and told the chief captain, saying, Take heed what thou doest: for this man is a Roman. {22:27} Then the chief captain came, and said unto Him, Tell ME, art thou a Roman? He said, Yea. {22:28} And the chief captain answered, With a great sum obtained **I** this freedom. And Paul said, But I was [free] born. {22:29} Then straightway they departed from Him which should have examined Him: and the chief captain also was afraid, after He knew that He was a Roman, and because He had bound Him. {22:30} On the morrow, because He would have known the certainty wherefore He was accused of the Jews, He loosed Him from [His] bands, and commanded the chief priests and all their council to appear, and brought Paul down, and set Him before them. **{23}**

{23:1} And Paul, earnestly beholding the council, said, Men [and] brethren, I have lived in all good conscience before **God** until this day. {23:2} And the high priest Ananias commanded them that stood by Him to smite Him on the mouth. {23:3} Then said Paul unto Him, **God** shall smite thee, [thou] whited wall: for sittest thou to judge ME after the law, and commandest ME to be smitten contrary to the law? {23:4} And they that stood by said, Revilest thou **God**'s high priest? {23:5} Then said Paul, I wist not, brethren, that He was the high priest: for it is written, Thou shalt not speak evil of the ruler of thy people. {23:6} But when Paul perceived that the one part were Sadducees, and the other Pharisees, He cried out in the council, Men [and] brethren, I am a Pharisee, the Son of a Pharisee: of the hope and resurrection of the dead I am called in question. {23:7} And when He had so said, there arose a dissension between the Pharisees and the Sadducees: and the multitude was divided. {23:8} For the Sadducees say that there is no resurrection, neither angel, nor spirit: but the Pharisees confess both. {23:9} And there arose a great cry: and the scribes [that were] of the Pharisees' part arose, and strove, saying, We find no evil in this man: but if a spirit or an angel hath spoken to Him, let us not fight against God. {23:10} And when there arose a great dissension, the chief captain, fearing lest Paul should have been pulled in pieces of them, commanded the soldiers to go down, and to take Him by force from among them, and to bring [Him] into the castle. {23:11} And the night following the **Lord** stood by Him, and said, Be of good cheer, Paul: for as thou hast testified of **ME** in Jerusalem, so must thou bear witness also at Rome. {23:12} And when it was day, certain of the Jews banded together, and bound themselves under a curse, saying that they would neither eat nor drink till they had killed Paul. {23:13} And they were more than forty which had made this conspiracy. {23:14} And they came to the chief priests and elders, and said, We have bound ourselves under a great curse, that we will eat nothing until we have slain Paul. {23:15} Now therefore ye with the council signify to the chief captain that He bring Him down unto you to morrow, as though ye would enquire something more perfectly concerning Him: and we, or ever He come near, are ready to kill Him. {23:16} And when Paul's sister's Son heard of their lying in wait, He went and entered into the castle, and told Paul. {23:17} Then Paul called one of the centurions unto [Him,] and said, Bring this young man unto the chief captain: for He hath a certain thing to tell Him. {23:18} So He took Him, and brought [Him] to the chief captain, and said, Paul the prisoner called ME unto [Him,] and prayed ME to bring this young man unto thee, who hath something to say unto thee. {23:19} Then the chief captain took Him by the hand, and went [with Him] aside privately, and asked [Him,] What is that thou hast to tell ME? {23:20} And He said, The Jews have agreed to desire thee that thou wouldest bring down Paul to morrow into the council, as though they would enquire somewhat of Him more perfectly. {23:21} But do not thou yield unto them: for there lie in wait for Him of them more than forty men, which have bound themselves with an oath, that they will neither eat nor drink till they have killed Him: and now are they ready, looking for a promise from thee. {23:22} So the chief captain [then] let the young man depart, and charged [Him, See thou] tell no man that thou hast shewed these things to me. {23:23} And He called unto [Him] two centurions, saying, Make ready two hundred soldiers to go to Caesarea, and horsemen threescore and ten, and spearmen two hundred, at the third hour of the night; {23:24} And provide [them] beasts, that they may set Paul on, and bring [Him] safe unto Felix the governor. {23:25} And He wrote a letter after this manner: {23:26} Claudius Lysias unto the most excellent governor Felix [sendeth] greeting. {23:27} This man was taken of the Jews, and should have been killed of them: then came I with an army, and rescued Him, having understood that He was a Roman. {23:28} And when I would have known the cause wherefore they accused Him, I brought Him forth into their council: {23:29} Whom I perceived to be accused of questions of their law, but to have nothing laid to His charge worthy of death or of bonds. {23:30} And when it was told me how that the Jews laid wait for the man, I sent straightway to thee, and gave commandment to His accusers also to say before thee what [they had] against Him. Farewell. {23:31} Then the soldiers, as it was commanded them, took Paul, and brought [Him] by night to Antipatris. {23:32} On the morrow they left the horsemen to go with Him, and returned to the castle: {23:33} Who, when they came to Caesarea, and delivered the epistle to the governor,

presented Paul also before Him. {23:34} And when the governor had read [the letter,] He asked of what province He was. And when He understood that [He was] of Cilicia; {23:35} I will hear thee, said He, when thine accusers are also come. And He commanded Him to be kept in Herod's judgment hall. {2}

{24:1} And after five days Ananias the high priest descended with the elders, and [with] a certain orator [named] Tertullus, who informed the governor against Paul. {24:2} And when He was called forth, Tertullus began to accuse [Him,] saying, Seeing that by thee we enjoy great quietness, and that very worthy deeds are done unto this nation by thy providence, {24:3} We accept [it] always, and in all places, most noble Felix, with all thankfulness. {24:4} Notwithstanding, that I be not further tedious unto thee, I pray thee that thou wouldest hear us of thy clemency a few words. {24:5} For we have found this man [a] pestilent [fellow,] and a mover of sedition among all the Jews throughout the world, and a ringleader of the sect of the Nazarenes: {24:6} Who also hath gone about to profane the temple: whom we took, and would have judged according to our law. {24:7} But the chief captain Lysias came [upon us,] and with great violence took [Him] away out of our hands, {24:8} Commanding His accusers to come unto thee: by examining of whom thyself mayest take knowledge of all these things, whereof we accuse Him. {24:9} And the Jews also assented, saying that these things were so. {24:10} Then Paul, after that the governor had beckoned unto Him to speak, answered, Forasmuch as I know that thou hast been of many years a judge unto this nation, I do the more cheerfully answer for myself: {24:11} Because that thou mayest understand, that there are yet but twelve days since I went up to Jerusalem for to worship. {24:12} And they neither found me in the temple disputing with any man, neither raising up the people, neither in the synagogues, nor in the city: {24:13} Neither can they prove the things whereof they now accuse me. {24:14} But this I confess unto thee, that after the way which they call heresy, so worship I the **God** of my Fathers, believing all things which are written in the law and in the prophets: {24:15} And have hope toward **God**, which they themselves also allow, that there shall be a resurrection of the dead, both of the just and unjust. {24:16} And herein do I exercise myself, to have always a conscience void of offence toward **God**, and [toward] men. {24:17} Now after many years I came to bring alms to my nation, and offerings. {24:18} Whereupon certain Jews from Asia found me purified in the temple, neither with multitude, nor with tumult. {24:19} Who ought to have been here before thee, and object, if they had ought against me. {24:20} Or else let these same [here] say, if they have found any evil doing in me, while I stood before the council, {24:21} Except it be for this one voice, that I cried standing among them, Touching the resurrection of the dead I am called in question by you this day.

{24:22} And when Felix heard these things, having more perfect knowledge of [that] way, He deferred them, and said, When Lysias the chief captain shall come down, I will know the uttermost of your matter. {24:23} And He commanded a centurion to keep Paul, and to let [Him] have liberty, and that He should forbid none of His acquaintance to minister or come unto Him.

{24:24} And after certain days, when Felix came with His wife Drusilla, which was a Jewess, He sent for Paul, and heard Him concerning the faith in **Christ**. {24:25} And as He reasoned of righteousness, temperance, and judgment to come Felix trembled, and answered, Go thy way for this time; when I have a convenient season, I will call for thee. {24:26} He hoped also that money should have been given Him of Paul, that He might loose Him: wherefore He sent for Him the oftener, and communed with Him. {24:27} But after two years Porcius Festus came into Felix' room: and Felix, willing to shew the Jews a pleasure, left Paul bound.{1}

{25:1} Now when Festus was come into the province, after three days He ascended from Caesarea to Jerusalem. {25:2} Then the high priest and the chief of the Jews informed Him against Paul, and besought Him, {25:3} And desired favour against Him, that He would send for Him to Jerusalem, laying wait in the way to kill Him. {25:4} But Festus answered, that Paul should be kept at Caesarea, and that He himself would depart shortly [thither.]{25:5} Let them therefore, said He, which among you are able, go down with [me,] and accuse this man, if there be any wickedness in Him. {25:6} And when He had tarried among them more than ten days, He went down unto Caesarea; and the next day sitting on the judgment seat commanded Paul to be brought. {25:7} And when He was come, the Jews which came down from Jerusalem stood round about, and laid many and grievous complaints against Paul, which they could not prove. {25:8} While He answered for himself, Neither against the law of the Jews, neither against the temple, nor yet against Caesar, have I offended any thing at all. {25:9} But Festus, willing to do the Jews a pleasure, answered Paul, and said, Wilt thou go up to Jerusalem, and there be judged of these things before me? {25:10} Then said Paul, I stand at Caesar's judgment seat, where I ought to be judged: to the Jews have I done no wrong, as thou very well knowest. {25:11} For if I be an offender, or have committed any thing worthy of death, I refuse not to die: but if there be none of these things whereof these accuse me no man may deliver me unto them. I appeal unto Caesar. {25:12} Then Festus, when He had conferred with the council, answered, Hast thou appealed unto Caesar? unto Caesar shalt thou go.

{25:13} And after certain days king Agrippa and Bernice came unto Caesarea to salute Festus. {25:14} And when they had been there many days, Festus declared Paul's cause unto the king, saying, There is a certain man left in bonds by Felix: {25:15} About whom, when I was at Jerusalem, the chief priests and the elders of the Jews informed [ME,] desiring [to have] judgment against Him. {25:16} To whom I answered, It is not the manner of the Romans to deliver any man to die, before that He which is accused have the accusers face to face, and have licence to answer for himself concerning the crime laid against Him. {25:17} Therefore, when they were come hither, without any delay on the morrow I sat on the judgment seat, and commanded the man to be brought forth. {25:18} Against whom when the accusers stood up, they brought none accusation of such things as I supposed: {25:19} But had certain questions against Him of their own superstition, and of one **Jesus**, which was dead, **whom** Paul affirmed to be alive. {25:20} And because I doubted of such manner of questions, I asked [Him] whether He would go to Jerusalem, and there be judged of these matters. {25:21} But when Paul had appealed to be reserved unto the hearing of Augustus, I commanded Him to be kept till I might send Him to Caesar. {25:22} Then Agrippa said unto Festus, I would also hear the man myself. To morrow, said He, thou shalt hear Him.

{25:23} And on the morrow, when Agrippa was come, and Bernice, with great pomp, and was entered into the place of hearing, with the chief captains, and principal men

of the city, at Festus' commandment Paul was brought forth. {25:24} And Festus said, King Agrippa, and all men which are here present with us, ye see this man, about whom all the multitude of the Jews have dealt with me, both at Jerusalem, and [also] here, crying that He ought not to live any longer. {25:25} But when I found that He had committed nothing worthy of death, and that He himself hath appealed to Augustus, I have determined to send Him. {25:26} Of whom I have no certain thing to write unto my Lord. Wherefore I have brought Him forth before you, and specially before thee, O king Agrippa, that, after examination had, I might have somewhat to write. {25:27} For it seemeth to me unreasonable to send a prisoner, and not withal to signify the crimes [laid] against Him.{0}

{26:1} Then Agrippa said unto Paul, Thou art permitted to speak for thyself. Then Paul stretched forth the hand, and answered for himself: {26:2} I think myself happy, king Agrippa, because I shall answer for myself this day before thee touching all the things whereof I am accused of the Jews: {26:3} Especially [because I know] thee to be expert in all customs and questions which are among the Jews: wherefore I beseech thee to hear me patiently. {26:4} my manner of life from my youth, which was at the first among mine own nation at Jerusalem, know all the Jews; {26:5} Which knew me from the beginning, if they would testify, that after the most straitest sect of our religion I lived a Pharisee. {26:6} And now I stand and am judged for the hope of the promise made of **God** unto our Fathers: {26:7} Unto which [promise] our twelve tribes, instantly serving [**God**] day and night, hope to come. For which hope's sake, king Agrippa, I am accused of the Jews. {26:8} Why should it be thought a thing incredible with you, that **God** should raise the dead? {26:9} I verily thought with myself, that I ought to do many things contrary to the **name** of **Jesus of Nazareth**. {26:10} Which thing I also did in Jerusalem: and many of the saints did I shut up in prison, having received authority from the chief priests; and when they were put to death, I gave my voice against [them.]{26:11} And I punished them oft in every synagogue, and compelled [them] to blaspheme; and being exceedingly mad against them, I persecuted [them] even unto strange cities. {26:12} Whereupon as I went to Damascus with authority and commission from the chief priests, {26:13} At midday, O king, I saw in the way a **light** from heaven, above the brightness of the sun, shining round about me and them which journeyed with me. {26:14} And when we were all fallen to the earth, I heard a **voice** speaking unto me, and saying in the Hebrew tongue, Saul, Saul, why persecutest thou **ME**? [it is] hard for thee to kick against the pricks. {26:15} And I said, **Who** art **thou, Lord**? And **He** said, **I am Jesus whom** thou persecutest. {26:16} But rise, and stand upon thy feet: for I have appeared unto thee for this purpose, to make thee a minister and a witness both of these things which thou hast seen, and of those things in the which I will appear unto thee; {26:17} Delivering thee from the people, and [from] the Gentiles, unto **whom** now I send thee, {26:18} To open their eyes, [and] to turn [them] from darkness to light, and [from] the power of Satan unto **God**, that they may receive forgiveness of sins, and inheritance among them which are sanctified by faith that is in **ME**. {26:19} Whereupon, O king Agrippa, I was not disobedient unto the heavenly vision: {26:20} But shewed first unto them of Damascus, and at Jerusalem, and throughout all the coasts of Judaea, and [then] to the Gentiles, that they should repent and turn to **God**, and do works meet for repentance. {26:21} For these causes the Jews caught me in the temple, and went about to kill [me.]{26:22} Having therefore obtained help of **God**, I continue unto this day, witnessing both to small and great, saying none other things than those which the prophets and Moses did say should come: {26:23} That **Christ** should suffer, [and] that **He** should be the first that should rise from the dead, and should shew light unto the people, and to the Gentiles.

{26:24} And as He thus spake for himself, Festus said with a loud voice, Paul, thou art beside thyself; much learning doth make thee mad. {26:25} But He said, I am not mad, most noble Festus; but speak forth the words of truth and soberness. {26:26} For the king knoweth of these things, before whom also I speak freely: for I am persuaded that none of these things are hidden from Him; for this thing was not done in a corner. {26:27} King Agrippa, believest thou the prophets? I know that thou believest. {26:28} Then Agrippa said unto Paul, Almost thou persuadest me to be a Christian. {26:29} And Paul said, I would to **God**, that not only thou, but also all that hear me this day, were both almost, and altogether such as I am, except these bonds. {26:30} And when He had thus spoken, the king rose up, and the governor, and Bernice, and they that sat with them: {26:31} And when they were gone aside, they talked between themselves, saying, This man doeth nothing worthy of death or of bonds. {26:32} Then said Agrippa unto Festus, This man might have been set at liberty, if He had not appealed unto Caesar. **{20}**

{27:1} And when it was determined that we should sail into Italy, they delivered Paul and certain other prisoners unto [one] named Julius, a centurion of Augustus' band. {27:2} And entering into a ship of Adramyttium, we launched, meaning to sail by the coasts of Asia; [one] Aristarchus, a Macedonian of Thessalonica, being with us. {27:3} And the next [day] we touched at Sidon. And Julius courteously entreated Paul, and gave [Him] liberty to go unto His friends to refresh himself. {27:4} And when we had launched from thence, we sailed under Cyprus, because the winds were contrary. {27:5} And when we had sailed over the sea of Cilicia and Pamphylia, we came to Myra, [a city] of Lycia. {27:6} And there the centurion found a ship of Alexandria sailing into Italy; and He put us therein. {27:7} And when we had sailed slowly many days, and scarce were come over against Cnidus, the wind not suffering us, we sailed under Crete, over against Salmone; {27:8} And, hardly passing it, came unto a place which is called The fair havens; nigh whereunto was the city [of] Lasea.

{27:9} Now when much time was spent, and when sailing was now dangerous, because the fast was now already past, Paul admonished [them,]{27:10} And said unto them, Sirs, I perceive that this voyage will be with hurt and much damage, not only of the lading and ship, but also of our lives. {27:11} Nevertheless the centurion believed the master and the owner of the ship, more than those things which were spoken by Paul. {27:12} And because the haven was not commodious to winter in, the more part advised to depart thence also, if by any means they might attain to Phenice, [and there] to winter; [which is] an haven of Crete, and lieth toward the south west and north west. {27:13} And when the south wind blew softly, supposing that they had obtained [their] purpose, loosing [thence,] they sailed close by Crete. {27:14} But not long after there arose against it a tempestuous wind, called Euroclydon. {27:15} And when the ship was caught, and could not bear up into the wind, we let [her] drive. {27:16} And running under a certain island which is called Clauda, we had much work to come by the boat: {27:17} Which when they had taken up, they used helps, undergirding the ship; and, fearing lest they

should fall into the quicksands, strake sail, and so were driven. {27:18} And we being exceedingly tossed with a tempest, the next [day] they lightened the ship; {27:19} And the third [day] we cast out with our own hands the tackling of the ship. {27:20} And when neither sun nor stars in many days appeared, and no small tempest lay on [us,] all hope that we should be saved was then taken away. {27:21} But after long abstinence Paul stood forth in the midst of them, and said, Sirs, ye should have hearkened unto me, and not have loosed from Crete, and to have gained this harm and loss. {27:22} And now I exhort you to be of good cheer: for there shall be no loss of [any man's] life among you, but of the ship. {27:23} For there stood by me this night the angel of **God**, whose I am, and **whom** I serve, {27:24} Saying, Fear not, Paul; thou must be brought before Caesar: and, lo, **God** hath given thee all them that sail with thee. {27:25} Wherefore, sirs, be of good cheer: for I believe **God**, that it shall be even as it was told me. {27:26} Howbeit we must be cast upon a certain island. {27:27} But when the fourteenth night was come, as we were driven up and down in Adria, about midnight the shipmen deemed that they drew near to some country; {27:28} And sounded, and found [it] twenty fathoms: and when they had gone a little further, they sounded again, and found [it] fifteen fathoms. {27:29} Then fearing lest we should have fallen upon rocks, they cast four anchors out of the stern, and wished for the day. {27:30} And as the shipmen were about to flee out of the ship, when they had let down the boat into the sea, under colour as though they would have cast anchors out of the foreship, {27:31} Paul said to the centurion and to the soldiers, Except these abide in the ship, ye cannot be saved. {27:32} Then the soldiers cut off the ropes of the boat, and let her fall off. {27:33} And while the day was coming on, Paul besought [them] all to take meat, saying, This day is the fourteenth day that ye have tarried and continued fasting, having taken nothing. {27:34} Wherefore I pray you to take [some] meat: for this is for your health: for there shall not an hair fall from the head of any of you. {27:35} And when He had thus spoken, He took bread, and gave thanks to **God** in presence of them all: and when He had broken [it,] He began to eat. {27:36} Then were they all of good cheer, and they also took [some] meat. {27:37} And we were in all in the ship two hundred threescore and sixteen souls. {27:38} And when they had eaten enough, they lightened the ship, and cast out the wheat into the sea. {27:39} And when it was day, they knew not the land: but they discovered a certain creek with a shore, into the which they were minded, if it were possible, to thrust in the ship. {27:40} And when they had taken up the anchors, they committed [themselves] unto the sea, and loosed the rudder bands, and hoised up the mainsail to the wind, and made toward shore. {27:41} And falling into a place where two seas met, they ran the ship aground; and the forepart stuck fast, and remained unmoveable, but the hinder part was broken with the violence of the waves. {27:42} And the soldiers' counsel was to kill the prisoners, lest any of them should swim out, and escape. {27:43} But the centurion, willing to save Paul, kept them from [their] purpose; and commanded that they which could swim should cast [themselves] first [into the sea,] and get to land: {27:44} And the rest, some on boards, and some on [broken pieces] of the ship. And so it came to pass, that they escaped all safe to land. **{4}**

{28:1} And when they were escaped, then they knew that the island was called Melita. {28:2} And the barbarous people shewed us no little kindness: for they kindled a fire, and received us every one, because of the present rain, and because of the cold. {28:3} And when Paul had gathered a bundle of sticks, and laid [them] on the fire, there came a viper out of the heat, and fastened on His hand. {28:4} And when the barbarians saw the [venomous] beast hang on His hand, they said among themselves, No doubt this man is a murderer, whom, though He hath escaped the sea, yet vengeance suffereth not to live. {28:5} And He shook off the beast into the fire, and felt no harm. {28:6} Howbeit they looked when He should have swollen, or fallen down dead suddenly: but after they had looked a great while, and saw no harm come to Him, they changed their minds, and said that He was a God.

{28:7} In the same quarters were possessions of the chief man of the island, whose name was Publius; who received us, and lodged us three days courteously. {28:8} And it came to pass, that the Father of Publius lay sick of a fever and of a bloody flux: to whom Paul entered in, and prayed, and laid His hands on Him, and healed Him. {28:9} So when this was done, others also, which had diseases in the island, came, and were healed: {28:10} Who also honoured us with many honours; and when we departed, they laded [us] with such things as were necessary.

{28:11} And after three months we departed in a ship of Alexandria, which had wintered in the isle, whose sign was Castor and Pollux. {28:12} And landing at Syracuse, we tarried [there] three days. {28:13} And from thence we fetched a compass, and came to Rhegium: and after one day the south wind blew, and we came the next day to Puteoli: {28:14} Where we found brethren, and were desired to tarry with them seven days: and so we went toward Rome. {28:15} And from thence, when the brethren heard of us, they came to meet us as far as Appii Forum, and The three taverns: whom when Paul saw, He thanked **God**, and took courage. {28:16} And when we came to Rome, the centurion delivered the prisoners to the captain of the guard: but Paul was suffered to dwell by himself with a soldier that kept Him.

{28:17} And it came to pass, that after three days Paul called the chief of the Jews together: and when they were come together, He said unto them, Men [and] brethren, though I have committed nothing against the people, or customs of our Fathers, yet was I delivered prisoner from Jerusalem into the hands of the Romans. {28:18} Who, when they had examined me, would have let [me] go, because there was no cause of death in ME. {28:19} But when the Jews spake against [it,] I was constrained to appeal unto Caesar; not that I had ought to accuse my nation of. {28:20} For this cause therefore have I called for you, to see [you,] and to speak with [you:] because that for the hope of Israel I am bound with this chain. {28:21} And they said unto Him, We neither received letters out of Judaea concerning thee, neither any of the brethren that came shewed or spake any harm of thee. {28:22} But we desire to hear of thee what thou thinkest: for as concerning this sect, we know that every where it is spoken against. {28:23} And when they had appointed Him a day, there came many to Him into [His] lodging; to whom He expounded and testified the kingdom of **God**, persuading them concerning **Jesus**, both out of the law of Moses, and [out of] the prophets, from morning till evening. {28:24} And some believed the things which were spoken, and some believed not. {28:25} And when they agreed not among themselves, they departed, after that Paul had spoken one word, Well spake the **Holy Ghost** by Esaias the prophet unto our Fathers, {28:26} Saying, Go unto this people, and say, Hearing ye shall hear, and shall not understand; and seeing ye shall see, and not perceive: {28:27} For the heart of this people is

waxed gross, and their ears are dull of hearing, and their eyes have they closed; lest they should see with [their] eyes, and hear with [their] ears, and understand with [their] heart, and should be converted, and I should heal them. {28:28} Be it known therefore unto you, that the salvation of **God** is sent unto the Gentiles, and [that] they will hear it. {28:29} And when He had said these words, the Jews departed, and had great reasoning among themselves.

{28:30} And Paul dwelt two whole years in His own hired house, and received all that came in unto Him, {28:31} Preaching the kingdom of **God**, and teaching those things which concern the **Lord Jesus Christ**, with all confidence, no man forbidding Him. {4}

The Epistle of Paul the Apostle to the Romans **TOTAL 253**

{1:1} Paul, a servant of **Jesus Christ**, called [to be] an apostle, separated unto the Gospel of God, {1:2} (Which **He** had promised afore by **His** prophets in the holy scriptures,) {1:3} Concerning **His Son Jesus Christ** our **Lord**, which was made of the seed of David according to the flesh; {1:4} And declared [to be] the **Son of God** with power, according to the spirit of holiness, by the resurrection from the dead: {1:5} By **whom** we have received grace and apostleship, for obedience to the faith among all nations, for **His name**: {1:6} Among **whom** are ye also the called of **Jesus Christ**: {1:7} To all that be in Rome, beloved of God, called [to be] saints: Grace to you and peace from **God** our **Father**, and the **Lord Jesus Christ**.

{1:8} First, I thank my **God** through **Jesus Christ** for you all, that your faith is spoken of throughout the whole world. {1:9} For **God** is my witness, whom I serve with my spirit in the Gospel of **His Son**, that without ceasing I make mention of you always in my prayers; {1:10} Making request, if by any means now at length I might have a prosperous journey by the will of God to come unto you. {1:11} For I long to see you, that I may impart unto you some spiritual gift, to the end ye may be established; {1:12} That is, that I may be comforted together with you by the mutual faith both of you and me. {1:13} Now I would not have you ignorant, brethren, that oftentimes I purposed to come unto you, (but was let hitherto,) that I might have some fruit among you also, even as among other Gentiles. {1:14} I am debtor both to the Greeks, and to the Barbarians; both to the wise, and to the unwise. {1:15} So, as much as in me is, I am ready to preach the Gospel to you that are at Rome also. {1:16} For I am not ashamed of the Gospel of **Christ**: for it is the **power** of God unto salvation to every one that believeth; to the Jew first, and also to the Greek. {1:17} For therein is the righteousness of God revealed from faith to faith: as it is written, The just shall live by faith.

{1:18} For the wrath of **God** is revealed from heaven against all unGodliness and unrighteousness of men, who hold the truth in unrighteousness; {1:19} Because that which may be known of **God** is manifest in them; for **God** hath shewed [it] unto them. {1:20} For the invisible things of **Him** from the creation of the world are clearly seen, being understood by the things that are made, [even] **His** eternal power and Godhead; so that they are without excuse: {1:21} Because that, when they knew **God**, they glorified [**Him**] not as **God**, neither were thankful; but became vain in their imaginations, and their foolish heart was darkened. {1:22} Professing themselves to be wise, they became fools, {1:23} And changed the glory of the uncorruptible **God** into an image made like to corruptible man, and to birds, and fourfooted beasts, and creeping things.

{1:24} Wherefore **God** also gave them up to uncleanness through the lusts of their own hearts, to dishonour their own bodies between themselves: {1:25} Who changed the truth of **God** into a lie, and worshipped and served the creature more than the Creator, who is blessed for ever. Amen. {1:26} For this cause **God** gave them up unto vile affections: for even their women did change the natural use into that which is against nature: {1:27} And likewise also the men, leaving the natural use of the woman, burned in their lust one toward another; men with men working that which is unseemly, and receiving in themselves that

recompence of their error which was meet. {1:28} And even as they did not like to retain **God** in [their] knowledge, **God** gave them over to a reprobate mind, to do those things which are not convenient; {1:29} Being filled with all unrighteousness, fornication, wickedness, covetousness, maliciousness; full of envy, murder, debate, deceit, malignity; whisperers, {1:30} Backbiters, haters of **God**, despiteful, proud, boasters, inventors of evil things, disobedient to parents, {1:31} Without understanding, covenantbreakers, without natural affection, implacable, unmerciful: {1:32} Who knowing the judgment of **God**, that they which commit such things are worthy of death, not only do the same, but have pleasure in them that do them.**{24}**

{2:1} Therefore thou art inexcusable, O man, whosoever thou art that judgest: for wherein thou judgest another, thou condemnest thyself; for thou that judgest doest the same things. {2:2} But we are sure that the judgment of **God** is according to truth against them which commit such things. {2:3} And thinkest thou this, O man, that judgest them which do such things, and doest the same, that thou shalt escape the judgment of **God**? {2:4} Or despisest thou the riches of **His** goodness and forbearance and longsuffering; not knowing that the goodness of **God** leadeth thee to repentance? {2:5} But after thy hardness and impenitent heart treasurest up unto thyself wrath against the day of wrath and revelation of the righteous judgment of **God**; {2:6} Who will render to every man according to **His** deeds: {2:7} To them who by patient continuance in well doing seek for glory and honour and immortality, eternal life: {2:8} But unto them that are contentious, and do not obey the truth, but obey unrighteousness, indignation and wrath, {2:9} Tribulation and anguish, upon every soul of man that doeth evil, of the Jew first, and also of the Gentile; {2:10} But glory, honour, and peace, to every man that worketh good, to the Jew first, and also to the Gentile: {2:11} For there is no respect of persons with **God**. {2:12} For as many as have sinned without law shall also perish without law: and as many as have sinned in the law shall be judged by the law; {2:13} (For not the hearers of the law [are] just before **God**, but the doers of the law shall be justified. {2:14} For when the Gentiles, which have not the law, do by nature the things contained in the law, these, having not the law, are a law unto themselves: {2:15} Which shew the work of the law written in their hearts, their conscience also bearing witness, and [their] thoughts the mean while accusing or else excusing one another;) {2:16} In the day when **God** shall judge the secrets of men by **Jesus Christ** according to my Gospel.

{2:17} Behold, thou art called a Jew, and restest in the law, and makest thy boast of **God**, {2:18} And knowest [**His**] will, and approvest the things that are more excellent, being instructed out of the law; {2:19} And art confident that thou thyself art a guide of the blind, a light of them which are in darkness, {2:20} An instructor of the foolish, a teacher of babes, which hast the form of knowledge and of the truth in the law. {2:21} Thou therefore which teachest another, teachest thou not thyself? thou that preachest a man should not steal, dost thou steal? {2:22} Thou that sayest a man should not commit adultery, dost thou commit adultery? thou that abhorrest idols, dost thou commit sacrilege? {2:23} Thou that makest thy boast of the law, through breaking the law dishonourest thou **God**? {2:24} For the name of **God** is blasphemed among the Gentiles through you, as it is written. {2:25} For circumcision verily profiteth, if thou keep the law: but if thou be a breaker of the law, thy circumcision is made uncircumcision. {2:26} Therefore if the uncircumcision keep the righteousness of the law, shall not his uncircumcision be counted for circumcision? {2:27} And shall not uncircumcision which is by nature, if it fulfil the law, judge thee, who by the letter and circumcision dost transgress the law? {2:28} For he is not a Jew, which is one outwardly; neither [is that] circumcision, which is outward in the flesh: {2:29} But he [is] a Jew, which is one inwardly; and circumcision [is that] of the heart, in the spirit, [and] not in the letter; whose praise [is] not of men, but of **God**. {0}

{3:1} What advantage then hath the Jew? or what profit [is there] of circumcision? {3:2} Much every way: chiefly, because that unto them were committed the oracles of **God**. {3:3} For what if some did not believe? shall their unbelief make the faith of **God** without effect? {3:4} **God** forbid: yea, let **God** be true, but every man a liar; as it is written, That thou mightest be justified in thy sayings, and mightest overcome when thou art judged. {3:5} But if our unrighteousness commend the righteousness of **God**, what shall we say? [Is] **God** unrighteous who taketh vengeance? (I speak as a man) {3:6} **God** forbid: for then how shall **God** judge the world? {3:7} For if the truth of **God** hath more abounded through my lie unto **His** glory; why yet am I also judged as a sinner? {3:8} And not [rather,] (as we be slanderously reported, and as some affirm that we say,) Let us do evil, that good may come? whose damnation is just.

{3:9} What then? are we better [than they?] No, in no wise: for we have before proved both Jews and Gentiles, that they are all under sin; {3:10} As it is written, There is none righteous, no, not one: {3:11} There is none that understandeth, there is none that seeketh after **God**. {3:12} They are all gone out of the way, they are together become unprofitable; there is none that doeth good, no, not one. {3:13} Their throat [is] an open sepulchre; with their tongues they have used deceit; the poison of asps [is] under their lips: {3:14} Whose mouth [is] full of cursing and bitterness: {3:15} Their feet [are] swift to shed blood: {3:16} Destruction and misery [are] in their ways: {3:17} And the way of peace have they not known: {3:18} There is no fear of **God** before their eyes.

{3:19} Now we know that what things soever the law saith, it saith to them who are under the law: that every mouth may be stopped, and all the world may become guilty before **God**. {3:20} Therefore by the deeds of the law there shall no flesh be justified in **His** sight: for by the law [is] the knowledge of sin.

{3:21} But now the righteousness of **God** without the law is manifested, being witnessed by the law and the prophets; {3:22} Even the righteousness of **God** [which is] by faith of **Jesus Christ** unto all and upon all them that believe: for there is no difference: {3:23} For all have sinned, and come short of the glory of **God**; {3:24} Being justified freely by **His** grace through the redemption that is in **Christ Jesus**: {3:25} **Whom God** hath set forth [to be] a propitiation through faith in **His blood**, to declare **His** righteousness for the remission of sins that are past, through the forbearance of **God**; {3:26} To declare, [I say,] at this time **His** righteousness: that **He** might be just, and the **justifier** of **Him** which believeth in **Jesus**. {3:27} Where [is] boasting then? It is excluded. By what law? of works? Nay: but by the law of faith. {3:28} Therefore we conclude that a man is justified by faith without the deeds of the law. {3:29} [Is **He**] the **God** of the Jews only? [is **He**] not also of the Gentiles? Yes, of the Gentiles also: {3:30} Seeing [it is] one **God**, which shall justify the circumcision by faith, and uncircumcision through faith. {3:31} Do we then make void

the law through faith? **God** forbid: yea, we establish the law. {12} {4:1} What shall we say then that Abraham our **Father**, as pertaining to the flesh, hath found? {4:2} For if Abraham were justified by works, **He** hath [whereof] to glory; but not before **God**. {4:3} For what saith the scripture? Abraham believed **God**, and it was counted unto Him for righteousness. {4:4} Now to Him that worketh is the reward not reckoned of grace, but of debt. {4:5} But to Him that worketh not, but believeth on Him that justifieth the un**God**ly, **His** faith is counted for righteousness. {4:6} Even as David also describeth the blessedness of the man, unto whom **God** imputeth righteousness without works, {4:7} [Saying,] Blessed [are] they whose iniquities are forgiven, and whose sins are covered. {4:8} Blessed [is] the man to whom the **Lord** will not impute sin. {4:9} [Cometh] this blessedness then upon the circumcision [only,] or upon the uncircumcision also? for we say that faith was reckoned to Abraham for righteousness. {4:10} How was it then reckoned? when He was in circumcision, or in uncircumcision? Not in circumcision, but in uncircumcision. {4:11} And He received the sign of circumcision, a seal of the righteousness of the faith which [He had yet] being uncircumcised: that He might be the Father of all them that believe, though they be not circumcised; that righteousness might be imputed unto them also: {4:12} And the Father of circumcision to them who are not of the circumcision only, but who also walk in the steps of that faith of our Father Abraham, which [He had] being [yet] uncircumcised. {4:13} For the promise, that He should be the heir of the world, [was] not to Abraham, or to His **seed**, through the law, but through the righteousness of faith. {4:14} For if they which are of the law [be] heirs, faith is made void, and the promise made of none effect: {4:15} Because the law worketh wrath: for where no law is, [there is] no transgression. {4:16} Therefore [it is] of faith, that [it might be] by grace; to the end the promise might be sure to all the seed; not to that only which is of the law, but to that also which is of the faith of Abraham; who is the Father of us all, {4:17} (As it is written, I have made thee a Father of many nations,) before **Him whom** He believed, [even] **God**, who quickeneth the dead, and calleth those things which be not as though they were. {4:18} Who against hope believed in hope, that He might become the Father of many nations; according to that which was spoken, So shall thy **seed** be. {4:19} And being not weak in faith, He considered not His own body now dead, when He was about an hundred years old, neither yet the deadness of Sarah's womb: {4:20} He staggered not at the promise of **God** through unbelief; but was strong in faith, giving glory to **God**; {4:21} And being fully persuaded that, what **He** had promised, **He** was able also to perform. {4:22} And therefore it was imputed to Him for righteousness. {4:23} Now it was not written for His sake alone, that it was imputed to Him; {4:24} But for us also, to whom it shall be imputed, if we believe on Him that raised up **Jesus** our **Lord** from the dead; {4:25} Who was delivered for our offences, and was raised again for our justification. {8}

{5:1} Therefore being justified by faith, we have peace with **God** through our **Lord Jesus Christ**: {5:2} By **whom** also we have access by faith into this grace wherein we stand, and rejoice in hope of the glory of **God**. {5:3} And not only [so,] but we glory in tribulations also: knowing that tribulation worketh patience; {5:4} And patience, experience; and experience, hope: {5:5} And hope maketh not ashamed; because the love of **God** is shed abroad in our hearts by the **Holy Ghost** which is given unto us. {5:6} For when we were yet without strength, in due time **Christ** died for the unGodly. {5:7} For scarcely for a righteous man will one die: yet peradventure for a good man some would even dare to die. {5:8} But **God** commendeth **His** love toward us, in that, while we were yet sinners, **Christ** died for us. {5:9} Much more then, being now justified by **His blood**, we shall be saved from wrath through **Him**. {5:10} For if, when we were enemies, we were reconciled to **God** by the death of **His Son**, much more, being reconciled, we shall be saved by **His** life. {5:11} And not only [so,] but we also joy in **God** through our **Lord Jesus Christ**, by **whom** we have now received the atonement.

{5:12} Wherefore, as by one man sin entered into the world, and death by sin; and so death passed upon all men, for that all have sinned: {5:13} (For until the law sin was in the world: but sin is not imputed when there is no law. {5:14} Nevertheless death reigned from Adam to Moses, even over them that had not sinned after the similitude of Adam's transgression, who is the figure of **Him** that was to come. {5:15} But not as the offence, so also [is] the free gift. For if through the offence of one many be dead, much more the grace of **God**, and the gift by grace, [which is] by one **man**, **Jesus Christ**, hath abounded unto many. {5:16} And not as [it was] by one that sinned, [so is] the gift: for the judgment [was] by one to condemnation, but the free gift [is] of many offences unto justification. {5:17} For if by one man's offence death reigned by one; much more they which receive abundance of grace and of the gift of righteousness shall reign in life by one, **Jesus Christ**.) {5:18} Therefore as by the offence of one [judgment came] upon all men to condemnation; even so by the righteousness of **one** [the free gift came] upon all men unto justification of life. {5:19} For as by one man's disobedience many were made sinners, so by the obedience of **one** shall many be made righteous. {5:20} Moreover the law entered, that the offence might abound. But where sin abounded, grace did much more abound: {5:21} That as sin hath reigned unto death, even so might grace reign through righteousness unto eternal life by **Jesus Christ** our **Lord**. {26}

{6:1} What shall we say then? Shall we continue in sin, that grace may abound? {6:2} **God** forbid. How shall we, that are dead to sin, live any longer therein? {6:3} Know ye not, that so many of us as were baptized into **Jesus Christ** were baptized into **His** death? {6:4} Therefore we are buried with **Him** by baptism into death: that like as **Christ** was raised up from the dead by the glory of the **Father**, even so we also should walk in newness of life. {6:5} For if we have been planted together in the likeness of **His** death, we shall be also [in the likeness of **His**] resurrection: {6:6} Knowing this, that our old man is crucified with [**Him**,] that the body of sin might be destroyed, that henceforth we should not serve sin. {6:7} For **He** that is dead is freed from sin. {6:8} Now if we be dead with **Christ**, we believe that we shall also live with **Him**: {6:9} Knowing that **Christ** being raised from the dead dieth no more; death hath no more dominion over **Him**. {6:10} For in that **He** died, **He** died unto sin once: but in that **He** liveth, **He** liveth unto **God**. {6:11} Likewise reckon ye also yourselves to be dead indeed unto sin, but alive unto **God** through **Jesus Christ** our **Lord**. {6:12} Let not sin therefore reign in your mortal body, that ye should obey it in the lusts thereof. {6:13} Neither yield ye your members [as] instruments of unrighteousness unto sin: but yield yourselves unto **God**, as those that are alive from the dead, and your members [as] instruments of righteousness unto **God**. {6:14} For sin shall not have dominion over you: for ye are not under the law, but under grace. {6:15} What then? shall we sin, because we are not under the law, but under grace? **God** forbid.

{6:16} Know ye not, that to whom ye yield yourselves servants to obey, **His** servants ye are to whom ye obey; whether of sin unto death, or of obedience unto righteousness? {6:17} But **God** be thanked, that ye were the servants of sin, but ye have obeyed from the heart that form of doctrine which was delivered you. {6:18} Being then made free from sin, ye became the servants of righteousness. {6:19} I speak after the manner of men because of the infirmity of your flesh: for as ye have yielded your members servants to uncleanness and to iniquity unto iniquity; even so now yield your members servants to righteousness unto holiness. {6:20} For when ye were the servants of sin, ye were free from righteousness. {6:21} What fruit had ye then in those things whereof ye are now ashamed? for the end of those things [is] death. {6:22} But now being made free from sin, and become servants to **God**, ye have your fruit unto holiness, and the end everlasting life. {6:23} For the wages of sin [is] death; but the gift of **God** [is] eternal life through **Jesus Christ** our **Lord**. {22}

{7:1} Know ye not, brethren, (for I speak to them that know the law,) how that the law hath dominion over a man as long as He liveth? {7:2} For the woman which hath an husband is bound by the law to [her] husband so long as He liveth; but if the husband be dead, she is loosed from the law of [her] husband. {7:3} So then if, while [her] husband liveth, she be married to another man, she shall be called an adulteress: but if her husband be dead, she is free from that law; so that she is no adulteress, though she be married to another **man**. {7:4} Wherefore, my brethren, ye also are become dead to the law by the **body** of **Christ**; that ye should be married to another, [even] to **Him** who is raised from the dead, that we should bring forth fruit unto **God**. {7:5} For when we were in the flesh, the motions of sins, which were by the law, did work in our members to bring forth fruit unto death. {7:6} But now we are delivered from the law, that being dead wherein we were held; that we should serve in newness of spirit, and not [in] the oldness of the letter.

{7:7} What shall we say then? [Is] the law sin? **God** forbid. Nay, I had not known sin, but by the law: for I had not known lust, except the law had said, Thou shalt not covet. {7:8} But sin, taking occasion by the commandment, wrought in me all manner of concupiscence. For without the law sin [was] dead. {7:9} For I was alive without the law once: but when the commandment came, sin revived, and I died. {7:10} And the commandment, which [was ordained] to life, I found [to be] unto death. {7:11} For sin, taking occasion by the commandment, deceived me, and by it slew [me.]{7:12} Wherefore the law [is] holy, and the commandment holy, and just, and good. {7:13} Was then that which is good made death unto me? **God** forbid. But sin, that it might appear sin, working death in me by that which is good; that sin by the commandment might become exceeding sinful. {7:14} For we know that the law is spiritual: but I am carnal, sold under sin. {7:15} For that which I do I allow not: for what I would, that do I not; but what I hate, that do I. {7:16} If then I do that which I would not, I consent unto the law that [it is] good. {7:17} Now then it is no more I that do it, but sin that dwelleth in me. {7:18} For I know that in me (that is, in my flesh,) dwelleth no good thing: for to will is present with me; but [how] to perform that which is good I find not. {7:19} For the good that I would I do not: but the evil which I would not, that I do. {7:20} Now if I do that I would not, it is no more I that do it, but sin that dwelleth in me. {7:21} I find then a law, that, when I would do good, evil is present with me. {7:22} For I delight in the law of **God** after the inward man: {7:23}

But I see another law in my members, warring against the law of my mind, and bringing me into captivity to the law of sin which is in my members. {7:24} O wretched man that I am! who shall deliver me from the body of this death? {7:25} I thank God through Jesus Christ our Lord. So then with the mind I myself serve the law of God; but with the flesh the law of sin. {7}

{8:1} [There is] therefore now no condemnation to them which are in Christ Jesus, who walk not after the flesh, but after the Spirit. {8:2} For the law of the Spirit of life in Christ Jesus hath made me free from the law of sin and death. {8:3} For what the law could not do, in that it was weak through the flesh, God sending His own Son in the likeness of sinful flesh, and for sin, condemned sin in the flesh: {8:4} That the righteousness of the law might be fulfilled in us, who walk not after the flesh, but after the Spirit. {8:5} For they that are after the flesh do mind the things of the flesh; but they that are after the Spirit the things of the Spirit. {8:6} For to be carnally minded [is] death; but to be spiritually minded [is] life and peace. {8:7} Because the carnal mind [is] enmity against God: for it is not subject to the law of God, neither indeed can be. {8:8} So then they that are in the flesh cannot please God. {8:9} But ye are not in the flesh, but in the Spirit, if so be that the Spirit of God dwell in you. Now if any man have not the Spirit of Christ, He is none of His. {8:10} And if Christ [be] in you, the body [is] dead because of sin; but the Spirit [is] life because of righteousness. {8:11} But if the Spirit of Him that raised up Jesus from the dead dwell in you, He that raised up Christ from the dead shall also quicken your mortal bodies by His Spirit that dwelleth in you.

{8:12} Therefore, brethren, we are debtors, not to the flesh, to live after the flesh. {8:13} For if ye live after the flesh, ye shall die: but if ye through the Spirit do mortify the deeds of the body, ye shall live. {8:14} For as many as are led by the Spirit of God, they are the sons of God. {8:15} For ye have not received the spirit of bondage again to fear; but ye have received the Spirit of adoption, whereby we cry, Abba, Father. {8:16} The Spirit itself beareth witness with our spirit, that we are the children of God: {8:17} And if children, then heirs; heirs of God, and joint-heirs with Christ; if so be that we suffer with [Him,] that we may be also glorified together.

{8:18} For I reckon that the sufferings of this present time [are] not worthy [to be compared] with the glory which shall be revealed in us. {8:19} For the earnest expectation of the creature waiteth for the manifestation of the sons of God. {8:20} For the creature was made subject to vanity, not willingly, but by reason of Him who hath subjected [the same] in hope, {8:21} Because the creature itself also shall be delivered from the bondage of corruption into the glorious liberty of the children of God. {8:22} For we know that the whole creation groaneth and travaileth in pain together until now. {8:23} And not only [they,] but ourselves also, which have the firstfruits of the Spirit, even we ourselves groan within ourselves, waiting for the adoption, [to wit,] the redemption of our body. {8:24} For we are saved by hope: but hope that is seen is not hope: for what a man seeth, why doth He yet hope for? {8:25} But if we hope for that we see not, [then] do we with patience wait for [it.]{8:26} Likewise the Spirit also helpeth our infirmities: for we know not what we should pray for as we ought: but the Spirit itself maketh intercession for us with groanings which cannot be uttered. {8:27} And He that searcheth the hearts knoweth what [is] the mind of the Spirit, because He maketh intercession for the saints

according to [the will of] God. {8:28} And we know that all things work together for good to them that love God, to them who are the called according to [His] purpose. {8:29} For whom He did foreknow, He also did predestinate [to be] conformed to the image of His Son, that He might be the firstborn among many brethren. {8:30} Moreover whom He did predestinate, them He also called: and whom He called, them He also justified: and whom He justified, them He also glorified. {8:31} What shall we then say to these things? If God [be] for us, who [can be] against us? {8:32} He that spared not His own Son, but delivered Him up for us all, how shall He not with Him also freely give us all things? {8:33} Who shall lay any thing to the charge of God's elect? [It is] God that justifieth. {8:34} Who [is] He that condemneth? [It is] Christ that died, yea rather, that is risen again, who is even at the right hand of God, who also maketh intercession for us. {8:35} Who shall separate us from the love of Christ? [shall] tribulation, or distress, or persecution, or famine, or nakedness, or peril, or sword? {8:36} As it is written, For thy sake we are killed all the day long; we are accounted as sheep for the slaughter. {8:37} Nay, in all these things we are more than conquerors through Him that loved us. {8:38} For I am persuaded, that neither death, nor life, nor angels, nor principalities, nor powers, nor things present, nor things to come, {8:39} Nor height, nor depth, nor any other creature, shall be able to separate us from the love of God, which is in Christ Jesus our Lord. {22}

{9:1} I say the truth in Christ, I lie not, my conscience also bearing me witness in the Holy Ghost, {9:2} That I have great heaviness and continual sorrow in my heart. {9:3} For I could wish that myself were accursed from Christ for my brethren, my kinsmen according to the flesh: {9:4} Who are Israelites; to whom [pertaineth] the adoption, and the glory, and the covenants, and the giving of the law, and the service [of God,] and the promises; {9:5} Whose [are] the Fathers, and of whom as concerning the flesh Christ [came,] who is over all, God blessed for ever. Amen.{9:6} Not as though the word of God hath taken none effect. For they [are] not all Israel, which are of Israel: {9:7} Neither, because they are the seed of Abraham, [are they] all children: but, In Isaac shall thy seed be called. {9:8} That is, They which are the children of the flesh, these [are] not the children of God: but the children of the promise are counted for the seed. {9:9} For this [is] the word of promise, At this time will I come, and Sarah shall have a Son. {9:10} And not only [this;] but when Rebecca also had conceived by one, [even] by our Father Isaac; {9:11} (For [the children] being not yet born, neither having done any good or evil, that the purpose of God according to election might stand, not of works, but of Him that calleth;) {9:12} It was said unto her, The elder shall serve the younger. {9:13} As it is written, Jacob have I loved, but Esau have I hated.

{9:14} What shall we say then? [Is there] unrighteousness with God? God forbid. {9:15} For He saith to Moses, I will have mercy on whom I will have mercy, and I will have compassion on whom I will have compassion. {9:16} So then [it is] not of him that willeth, nor of him that runneth, but of God that sheweth mercy. {9:17} For the scripture saith unto Pharaoh, Even for this same purpose have I raised thee up, that I might shew my power in thee, and that my name might be declared throughout all the earth. {9:18} Therefore hath He mercy on *whom* He will [have mercy,] and whom He will He hardeneth. {9:19} Thou wilt say then unto me, Why doth He yet find fault? For who hath resisted His will? {9:20} Nay but, O man, who art thou that repliest against **God**? Shall the thing formed say to **Him** that formed [it,] Why hast thou made me thus? {9:21} Hath not the potter power over the clay, of the same lump to make one vessel unto honour, and another unto dishonour? {9:22} [What] if **God**, willing to shew [**His**] wrath, and to make **His** power known, endured with much longsuffering the vessels of wrath fitted to destruction: {9:23} And that **He** might make known the riches of **His** glory on the vessels of mercy, which **He** had afore prepared unto glory, {9:24} Even us, whom **He** hath called, not of the Jews only, but also of the Gentiles? {9:25} As **He** saith also in Osee, I will call them **my** people, which were not **my** people; and her beloved, which was not beloved. {9:26} And it shall come to pass, [that] in the place where it was said unto them, Ye [are] not **my** people; there shall they be called the children of the living **God**. {9:27} Esaias also crieth concerning Israel, Though the number of the children of Israel be as the sand of the sea, a remnant shall be saved: {9:28} For **He** will finish the work, and cut [it] short in righteousness: because a short work will the **Lord** make upon the earth. {9:29} And as Esaias said before, Except the **Lord of Sabaoth** had left us a **seed**, we had been as Sodoma, and been made like unto Gomorrha. {9:30} What shall we say then? That the Gentiles, which followed not after righteousness, have attained to righteousness, even the righteousness which is of faith. {9:31} But Israel, which followed after the law of righteousness, hath not attained to the law of righteousness. {9:32} Wherefore? Because [they sought it] not by faith, but as it were by the works of the law. For they stumbled at that stumblingstone; {9:33} As it is written, Behold, I lay in Sion a **stumblingstone** and **rock of offence**: and whosoever believeth on **Him** shall not be ashamed. **{13}**

{10:1} Brethren, my heart's desire and prayer to **God** for Israel is, that they might be saved. {10:2} For I bear them record that they have a zeal of **God**, but not according to knowledge. {10:3} For they being ignorant of **God**'s righteousness, and going about to establish their own righteousness, have not submitted themselves unto the righteousness of **God**. {10:4} For **Christ** [is] the end of the law for righteousness to every one that believeth. {10:5} For Moses describeth the righteousness which is of the law, That the man which doeth those things shall live by them. {10:6} But the righteousness which is of faith speaketh on this wise, Say not in thine heart, Who shall ascend into heaven? (that is, to bring **Christ** down [from above:]) {10:7} Or, Who shall descend into the deep? (that is, to bring up **Christ** again from the dead.) {10:8} But what saith it? The word is nigh thee, [even] in thy mouth, and in thy heart: that is, the word of faith, which we preach; {10:9} That if thou shalt confess with thy mouth the **Lord Jesus**, and shalt believe in thine heart that **God** hath raised **Him** from the dead, thou shalt be saved. {10:10} For with the heart man believeth unto righteousness; and with the mouth confession is made unto salvation. {10:11} For the scripture saith, Whosoever believeth on **Him** shall not be ashamed. {10:12} For there is no difference between the Jew and the Greek: for the same **Lord** over all is rich unto all that call upon **Him**. {10:13} For whosoever shall call upon the **name** of the **Lord** shall be saved. {10:14} How then shall they call on **Him** in **whom** they have not believed? and how shall they believe in **Him** of **whom** they have not heard? and how shall they hear without a preacher? {10:15} And how shall they preach, except they be sent? as it is written, How beautiful are the feet of them that preach the **Gospel** of peace, and bring glad tidings of good things! {10:16} But they have not all obeyed the **Gospel**. For Esaias saith, **Lord**, who hath believed our report? {10:17} So then faith [cometh] by hearing, and hearing by the **word of God**. {10:18} But I say,

Have they not heard? Yes verily, their sound went into all the earth, and their words unto the ends of the world. {10:19} But I say, Did not Israel know? First Moses saith, I will provoke you to jealousy by [them that are] no people, [and] by a foolish nation I will anger you. {10:20} But Esaias is very bold, and saith, I was found of them that sought **me** not; I was made manifest unto them that asked not after **me**. {10:21} But to Israel **He** saith, All day long I have stretched forth **my** hands unto a disobedient and gainsaying people. **{17}**

{11:1} I say then, Hath **God** cast away his people? **God** forbid. For I also am an Israelite, of the seed of Abraham, [of] the tribe of Benjamin. {11:2} **God** hath not cast away **His** people which **He** foreknew. Wot ye not what the scripture saith of Elias? how **He** maketh intercession to **God** against Israel, saying, {11:3} **Lord**, they have killed thy prophets, and digged down thine altars; and I am left alone, and they seek my life. {11:4} But what saith the answer of **God** unto him? I have reserved to myself seven thousand men, who have not bowed the knee to [the image of] Baal. {11:5} Even so then at this present time also there is a remnant according to the election of grace. {11:6} And if by grace, then [is it] no more of works: otherwise grace is no more grace. But if [it be] of works, then is it no more grace: otherwise work is no more work.

{11:7} What then? Israel hath not obtained that which He seeketh for; but the election hath obtained it, and the rest were blinded {11:8} (According as it is written, **God** hath given them the spirit of slumber, eyes that they should not see, and ears that they should not hear;) unto this day. {11:9} And David saith, Let their table be made a snare, and a trap, and a stumblingblock, and a recompence unto them: {11:10} Let their eyes be darkened, that they may not see, and bow down their back alway. {11:11} I say then, Have they stumbled that they should fall? **God** forbid: but [rather] through their fall salvation [is come] unto the Gentiles, for to provoke them to jealousy. {11:12} Now if the fall of them [be] the riches of the world, and the diminishing of them the riches of the Gentiles; how much more their fulness?

{11:13} For I speak to you Gentiles, inasmuch as I am the apostle of the Gentiles, I magnify mine office: {11:14} If by any means I may provoke to emulation [them which are] my flesh, and might save some of them. {11:15} For if the casting away of them [be] the reconciling of the world, what [shall] the receiving [of them be,] but life from the dead? {11:16} For if the firstfruit [be] holy, the lump [is] also [holy:] and if the root [be] holy, so [are] the branches. {11:17} And if some of the branches be broken off, and thou, being a wild olive tree, wert graffed in among them, and with them partakest of the root and fatness of the olive tree; {11:18} Boast not against the branches. But if thou boast, thou bearest not the root, but the root thee. {11:19} Thou wilt say then, The branches were broken off, that I might be graffed in. {11:20} Well; because of unbelief they were broken off, and thou standest by faith. Be not highminded, but fear: {11:21} For if **God** spared not the natural branches, [take heed] lest **He** also spare not thee. {11:22} Behold therefore the goodness and severity of **God**: on them which fell, severity; but toward thee, goodness, if thou continue in [**His**] goodness: otherwise thou also shalt be cut off. {11:23} And they also, if they abide not still in unbelief, shall be graffed in: for **God** is able to graff them in again. {11:24} For if thou wert cut out of the olive tree which is wild by nature, and wert graffed contrary to nature into a good olive tree: how much more shall these, which be the natural [branches,] be graffed into their own olive tree?

{11:25} For I would not, brethren, that ye should be ignorant of this mystery, lest ye should be wise in your own conceits; that blindness in part is happened to Israel, until the fulness of the Gentiles be come in. {11:26} And so all Israel shall be saved: as it is written, There shall come out of Sion the **Deliverer**, and shall turn away un**God**liness from Jacob: {11:27} For this [is] **my** covenant unto them, when I shall take away their sins. {11:28} As concerning the **Gospel**, [they are] enemies for your sakes: but as touching the election, [they are] beloved for the **Father**s' sakes. {11:29} For the gifts and calling of **God** [are] without repentance. {11:30} For as ye in times past have not believed **God**, yet have now obtained mercy through their unbelief: {11:31} Even so have these also now not believed, that through your mercy they also may obtain mercy. {11:32} For **God** hath concluded them all in unbelief, that **He** might have mercy upon all.

{11:33} O the depth of the riches both of the wisdom and knowledge of **God**! how unsearchable [are] **His** judgments, and **His** ways past finding out! {11:34} For who hath known the mind of the **Lord**? or who hath been **His** counsellor? {11:35} Or who hath first given to **Him**, and it shall be recompensed unto **Him** again? {11:36} For of **Him**, and through **Him**, and to **Him**, [are] all things: to **whom** [be] glory for ever. Amen. {9}

{12:1} I beseech you therefore, brethren, by the mercies of **God**, that ye present your bodies a living sacrifice, holy, acceptable unto **God**, [which is] your reasonable service. {12:2} And be not conformed to this world: but be ye transformed by the renewing of your mind, that ye may prove what is that good, and acceptable, and perfect, will of **God**.

{12:3} For I say, through the grace given unto me, to every man that is among you, not to think [of himself] more highly than **He** ought to think; but to think soberly, according as **God** hath dealt to every man the measure of faith. {12:4} For as we have many members in one body, and all members have not the same office: {12:5} So we, [being] many, are one body in **Christ**, and every one members one of another. {12:6} Having then gifts differing according to the grace that is given to us, whether prophecy, [let us prophesy] according to the proportion of faith; {12:7} Or ministry, [let us wait] on [our] ministering: or he that teacheth, on teaching; {12:8} Or he that exhorteth, on exhortation: he that giveth, [let him do it] with simplicity; he that ruleth, with diligence; he that sheweth mercy, with cheerfulness.

{12:9} [Let] love be without dissimulation. Abhor that which is evil; cleave to that which is good. {12:10} [Be] kindly affectioned one to another with brotherly love; in honour preferring one another; {12:11} Not slothful in business; fervent in spirit; serving the **Lord**; {12:12} Rejoicing in hope; patient in tribulation; continuing instant in prayer; {12:13} Distributing to the necessity of saints; given to hospitality. {12:14} Bless them which persecute you: bless, and curse not. {12:15} Rejoice with them that do rejoice, and weep with them that weep. {12:16} [Be] of the same mind one toward another. Mind not high things, but condescend to men of low estate. Be not wise in your own conceits. {12:17} Recompense to no man evil for evil. Provide things honest in the sight of all men. {12:18} If it be possible, as much as lieth in you, live peaceably with all men. {12:19} Dearly beloved, avenge not yourselves, but

[rather] give place unto wrath: for it is written, Vengeance [is] mine; I will repay, saith the **Lord**. {12:20} Therefore if thine enemy hunger, feed him; if he thirst, give him drink: for in so doing thou shalt heap coals of fire on his head. {12:21} Be not overcome of evil, but overcome evil with good. {6}

{13:1} Let every soul be subject unto the higher powers. For there is no power but of **God**: the powers that be are ordained of **God**. {13:2} Whosoever therefore resisteth the power, resisteth the ordinance of **God**: and they that resist shall receive to themselves damnation. {13:3} For rulers are not a terror to good works, but to the evil. Wilt thou then not be afraid of the power? do that which is good, and thou shalt have praise of the same: {13:4} For He is the minister of God to thee for good. But if thou do that which is evil, be afraid; for He beareth not the sword in vain: for He is the minister of **God**, a revenger to [execute] wrath upon Him that doeth evil. {13:5} Wherefore [ye] must needs be subject, not only for wrath, but also for conscience sake. {13:6} For for this cause pay ye tribute also: for they are **God**'s ministers, attending continually upon this very thing. {13:7} Render therefore to all their dues: tribute to whom tribute [is due;] custom to whom custom; fear to whom fear; honour to whom honour. {13:8} Owe no man any thing, but to love one another: for He that loveth another hath fulfilled the law. {13:9} For this, Thou shalt not commit adultery, Thou shalt not kill, Thou shalt not steal, Thou shalt not bear false witness, Thou shalt not covet; and if [there be] any other commandment, it is briefly comprehended in this saying, namely, Thou shalt love thy neighbour as thyself. {13:10} Love worketh no ill to His neighbour: therefore love [is] the fulfilling of the law. {13:11} And that, knowing the time, that now [it is] high time to awake out of sleep: for now [is] our salvation nearer than when we believed. {13:12} The night is far spent, the day is at hand: let us therefore cast off the works of darkness, and let us put on the armour of light. {13:13} Let us walk honestly, as in the day; not in rioting and drunkenness, not in chambering and wantonness, not in strife and envying. {13:14} But put ye on the **Lord Jesus Christ**, and make not provision for the flesh, to [fulfil] the lusts [thereof]. {3}

]{14:1} Him that is weak in the faith receive ye, [but] not to doubtful disputations. {14:2} For one believeth that he may eat all things: another, who is weak, eateth herbs. {14:3} Let not him that eateth despise him that eateth not; and let not him which eateth not judge him that eateth: for **God** hath received him. {14:4} Who art thou that judgest another man's servant? to his own **master** he standeth or falleth. Yea, he shall be holden up: for **God** is able to make him stand. {14:5} One man esteemeth one day above another: another esteemeth every day [alike.] Let every man be fully persuaded in his own mind. {14:6} He that regardeth the day, regardeth [it] unto the **Lord**; and He that regardeth not the day, to the **Lord** He doth not regard [it.] He that eateth, eateth to the **Lord**, for He giveth **God** thanks; and He that eateth not, to the **Lord** He eateth not, and giveth **God** thanks. {14:7} For none of us liveth to himself, and no man dieth to himself. {14:8} For whether we live, we live unto the **Lord**; and whether we die, we die unto the **Lord**: whether we live therefore, or die, we are the **Lord**'s. {14:9} For to this end **Christ** both died, and rose, and revived, that **He** might be **Lord** both of the dead and living. {14:10} But why dost thou judge thy brother? or why dost thou set at nought thy brother? for we shall all stand before the judgment seat of **Christ**. {14:11} For it is written, [As] I live, saith the **Lord**, every knee shall bow to **ME**, and every tongue shall confess to **God**. {14:12} So then every one of us shall give account of himself to **God**. {14:13} Let us not therefore judge one another any more: but judge this rather, that no man put a stumblingblock or an occasion to fall in [his] brother's way. {14:14} I know, and am persuaded by the **Lord Jesus**, that [there is] nothing unclean of itself: but to him that esteemeth any thing to be unclean, to him [it is] unclean. {14:15} But if thy brother be grieved with [thy] meat, now walkest thou not charitably. Destroy not him with thy meat, for whom **Christ** died. {14:16} Let not then your good be evil spoken of: {14:17} For the kingdom of **God** is not meat and drink; but righteousness, and peace, and joy in the **Holy Ghost**. {14:18} For he that in these things serveth **Christ** [is] acceptable to **God**, and approved of men. {14:19} Let us therefore follow after the things which make for peace, and things wherewith one may edify another. {14:20} For meat destroy not the work of **God**. All things indeed [are] pure; but [it is] evil for that man who eateth with offence. {14:21} [It is] good neither to eat flesh, nor to drink wine, nor [any thing] whereby thy brother stumbleth, or is offended, or is made weak. {14:22} Hast thou faith? have [it] to thyself before **God**. Happy [is] he that condemneth not himself in that thing which he alloweth. {14:23} And he that doubteth is damned if he eat, because [he eateth] not of faith: for whatsoever [is] not of faith is sin. {19}

{15:1} We then that are strong ought to bear the infirmities of the weak, and not to please ourselves. {15:2} Let every one of us please [his] neighbour for [his] good to edification. {15:3} For even **Christ** pleased not **himself**; but, as it is written, The reproaches of them that reproached thee fell on **ME**. {15:4} For whatsoever things were written aforetime were written for our learning, that we through patience and comfort of the scriptures might have hope. {15:5} Now the **God** of patience and consolation grant you to be likeminded one toward another according to **Christ Jesus**: {15:6} That ye may with one mind [and] one mouth glorify **God**, even the **Father** of our **Lord Jesus Christ**.

{15:7} Wherefore receive ye one another, as **Christ** also received us to the glory of **God**. {15:8} Now I say that **Jesus Christ** was a **minister** of the circumcision for the truth of **God**, to confirm the promises [made] unto the **Father**s: {15:9} And that the Gentiles might glorify **God** for [**His**] mercy; as it is written, For this cause I will confess to **thee** among the Gentiles, and sing unto **thy name**. {15:10} And again **He** saith, Rejoice, ye Gentiles, with **His** people. {15:11} And again, Praise the **Lord**, all ye Gentiles; and laud **Him**, all ye people. {15:12} And again, Esaias saith, There shall be a **root of Jesse**, and **He** that shall rise to reign over the Gentiles; in **Him** shall the Gentiles trust. {15:13} Now the **God** of hope fill you with all joy and peace in believing, that ye may abound in hope, through the power of the **Holy Ghost**. {15:14} And I myself also am persuaded of you, my brethren, that ye also are full of goodness, filled with all knowledge, able also to admonish one another. {15:15} Nevertheless, brethren, I have written the more boldly unto you in some sort, as putting you in mind, because of the grace that is given to me of **God**, {15:16} That I should be the minister of **Jesus Christ** to the Gentiles, ministering the **Gospel** of **God**, that the offering up of the Gentiles might be acceptable, being sanctified by the **Holy Ghost**. {15:17} I have therefore whereof I may glory through **Jesus Christ** in those things which pertain to **God**. {15:18} For I will not dare to speak of any of those things which **Christ** hath not wrought by me, to make the Gentiles obedient, by word and deed, {15:19} Through mighty signs and wonders, by the power of the Spirit of **God**; so that from Jerusalem, and round about unto Illyricum, I have

fully preached the **Gospel** of **Christ**. {15:20} Yea, so have I strived to preach the Gospel, not where **Christ** was named, lest I should build upon another man's foundation: {15:21} But as it is written, To **whom He** was not spoken of, they shall see: and they that have not heard shall understand. {15:22} For which cause also I have been much hindered from coming to you. {15:23} But now having no more place in these parts, and having a great desire these many years to come unto you; {15:24} Whensoever I take my journey into Spain, I will come to you: for I trust to see you in my journey, and to be brought on my way thitherward by you, if first I be somewhat filled with your [company.]{15:25} But now I go unto Jerusalem to minister unto the saints. {15:26} For it hath pleased them of Macedonia and Achaia to make a certain contribution for the poor saints which are at Jerusalem. {15:27} It hath pleased them verily; and their debtors they are. For if the Gentiles have been made partakers of their spiritual things, their duty is also to minister unto them in carnal things. {15:28} When therefore I have performed this, and have sealed to them this fruit, I will come by you into Spain. {15:29} And I am sure that, when I come unto you, I shall come in the fulness of the blessing of the **Gospel** of **Christ**.

{15:30} Now I beseech you, brethren, for the **Lord Jesus Christ**'s sake, and for the love of the Spirit, that ye strive together with me in [your] prayers to **God** for me; {15:31} That I may be delivered from them that do not believe in Judaea; and that my service which [I have] for Jerusalem may be accepted of the saints; {15:32} That I may come unto you with joy by the will of **God**, and may with you be refreshed. {15:33} Now the **God** of peace [be] with you all. Amen. {35}

{16:1} I commend unto you Phebe our sister, which is a servant of the church which is at Cenchrea: {16:2} That ye receive her in the **Lord**, as becometh saints, and that ye assist her in whatsoever business she hath need of you: for she hath been a succourer of many, and of myself also. {16:3} Greet Priscilla and Aquila my helpers in **Christ Jesus**: {16:4} Who have for my life laid down their own necks: unto whom not only I give thanks, but also all the churches of the Gentiles. {16:5} Likewise [greet] the church that is in their house. Salute my wellbeloved Epaenetus, who is the firstfruits of Achaia unto **Christ**. {16:6} Greet Mary, who bestowed much labour on us. {16:7} Salute Andronicus and Junia, my kinsmen, and my fellowprisoners, who are of note among the apostles, who also were in **Christ** before me. {16:8} Greet Amplias my beloved in the **Lord**. {16:9} Salute Urbane, our helper in **Christ**, and Stachys my beloved. {16:10} Salute Apelles approved in **Christ**. Salute them which are of Aristobulus' [household.]{16:11} Salute Herodion my kinsman. Greet them that be of the [household] of Narcissus, which are in the **Lord**. {16:12} Salute Tryphena and Tryphosa, who labour in the **Lord**. Salute the beloved Persis, which laboured much in the **Lord**. {16:13} Salute Rufus chosen in the **Lord**, and his mother and mine. {16:14} Salute Asyncritus, Phlegon, Hermas, Patrobas, Hermes, and the brethren which are with them. {16:15} Salute Philologus, and Julia, Nereus, and his sister, and Olympas, and all the saints which are with them. {16:16} Salute one another with an holy kiss. The churches of **Christ** salute you.

{16:17} Now I beseech you, brethren, mark them which cause divisions and offences contrary to the doctrine which ye have learned; and avoid them. {16:18} For they that are such serve not our **Lord Jesus Christ**, but their own belly; and by good words and fair speeches deceive the hearts of the simple. {16:19} For your obedience is come abroad unto all [men.] I am glad therefore on your behalf: but yet I would have you wise unto that which is good, and simple concerning evil. {16:20} And the **God of peace** shall bruise Satan under your feet shortly. The grace of our **Lord Jesus Christ** [be] with you. Amen.

{16:21} Timotheus my workfellow, and Lucius, and Jason, and Sosipater, my kinsmen, salute you. {16:22} I Tertius, who wrote [this] epistle, salute you in the **Lord**. {16:23} Gaius mine host, and of the whole church, saluteth you. Erastus the chamberlain of the city saluteth you, and Quartus a brother. {16:24} The grace of our **Lord Jesus Christ** [be] with you all. Amen.

{16:25} Now to **Him** that is of power to stablish you according to my Gospel, and the preaching of **Jesus Christ**, according to the revelation of the **mystery**, which was kept secret since the world began, {16:26} But now is made manifest, and by the scriptures of the prophets, according to the commandment of the everlasting **God**, made known to all nations for the obedience of faith: {16:27} To **God** only wise, [be] glory through **Jesus Christ** for ever. Amen. **{30}**

The First Epistle of Paul the Apostle to the Corinthians
TOTAL 243

{1:1} Paul, called [to be] an apostle of **Jesus Christ** through the will of **God**, and Sosthenes [our] brother, {1:2} Unto the church of **God** which is at Corinth, to them that are sanctified in **Christ Jesus**, called [to be] saints, with all that in every place call upon the **name** of **Jesus Christ** our **Lord**, both theirs and ours: {1:3} Grace [be] unto you, and peace, from **God** our **Father**, and [from] the **Lord Jesus Christ**.

{1:4} I thank my **God** always on your behalf, for the grace of **God** which is given you by **Jesus Christ**; {1:5} That in every thing ye are enriched by **Him**, in all utterance, and [in] all knowledge; {1:6} Even as the testimony of **Christ** was confirmed in you: {1:7} So that ye come behind in no gift; waiting for the coming of our **Lord Jesus Christ**: {1:8} **Who** shall also confirm you unto the end, [that ye may be] blameless in the day of our **Lord Jesus Christ**. {1:9} **God** [is] faithful, by **whom** ye were called unto the fellowship of **His Son Jesus Christ** our **Lord**.

{1:10} Now I beseech you, brethren, by the **name** of our **Lord Jesus Christ**, that ye all speak the same thing, and [that] there be no divisions among you; but [that] ye be perfectly joined together in the same mind and in the same judgment. {1:11} For it hath been declared unto me of you, my brethren, by them [which are of the house] of Chloe, that there are contentions among you. {1:12} Now this I say, that every one of you saith, I am of Paul; and I of Apollos; and I of Cephas; and I of **Christ**. {1:13} Is **Christ** divided? was Paul crucified for you? or were ye baptized in the name of Paul? {1:14} I thank **God** that I baptized none of you, but Crispus and Gaius; {1:15} Lest any should say that I had baptized in mine own name. {1:16} And I baptized also the household of Stephanas: besides, I know not whether I baptized any other. {1:17} For **Christ** sent me not to baptize, but to preach the Gospel: not with wisdom of words, lest the cross of **Christ** should be made of none effect.

{1:18} For the preaching of the cross is to them that perish foolishness; but unto us which are saved it is the power of **God**. {1:19} For it is written, I will destroy the wisdom of the wise, and will bring to nothing the understanding of the prudent. {1:20} Where [is] the wise? where [is] the scribe? where [is] the disputer of this world? hath not **God** made foolish the wisdom of this world? {1:21} For after that in the wisdom of **God** the world by wisdom knew not **God**, it pleased **God** by the foolishness of preaching to save them that believe. {1:22} For the Jews require a sign, and the Greeks seek after wisdom: {1:23} But we preach **Christ** crucified, unto the Jews a stumblingblock, and unto the Greeks foolishness; {1:24} But unto them which are called, both Jews and Greeks, **Christ** the **power of God**, and the **wisdom of God**. {1:25} Because the foolishness of **God** is wiser than men; and the weakness of **God** is stronger than men. {1:26} For ye see your calling, brethren, how that not many wise men after the flesh, not many mighty, not many noble, [are called:]{1:27} But **God** hath chosen the foolish things of the world to confound the wise; and **God** hath chosen the weak things of the world to confound the things which are mighty; {1:28} And base things of the world, and things which are despised, hath **God** chosen, [yea,] and things which are not, to bring to nought things that are: {1:29} That no flesh should glory in **His** presence. {1:30} But of **Him** are ye in **Christ Jesus**, **who** of God is made unto us **wisdom**, and **righteousness**, and **sanctification**, and **redemption**: {1:31}

That, according as it is written, he that glorieth, let him glory in the **Lord**. **{49}**

{2:1} And I, brethren, when I came to you, came not with excellency of speech or of wisdom, declaring unto you the testimony of **God**. {2:2} For I determined not to know any thing among you, save **Jesus Christ**, and **Him** crucified. {2:3} And I was with you in weakness, and in fear, and in much trembling. {2:4} And my speech and my preaching [was] not with enticing words of man's wisdom, but in demonstration of the Spirit and of power: {2:5} That your faith should not stand in the wisdom of men, but in the **power of God**. {2:6} Howbeit we speak **wisdom** among them that are perfect: yet not the **wisdom** of this world, nor of the princes of this world, that come to nought: {2:7} But we speak the **wisdom of God** in a mystery, [even] the hidden [**wisdom**,] which **God** ordained before the world unto our glory: {2:8} Which none of the princes of this world knew: for had they known [it,] they would not have crucified the **Lord of glory**. {2:9} But as it is written, Eye hath not seen, nor ear heard, neither have entered into the heart of man, the things which **God** hath prepared for them that love **Him**. {2:10} But **God** hath revealed [them] unto us by **His** Spirit: for the Spirit searcheth all things, yea, the deep things of **God**. {2:11} For what man knoweth the things of a man, save the spirit of man which is in him? even so the things of **God** knoweth no man, but the Spirit of **God**. {2:12} Now we have received, not the spirit of the world, but the spirit which is of **God**; that we might know the things that are freely given to us of **God**. {2:13} Which things also we speak, not in the words which man's wisdom teacheth, but which the **Holy Ghost** teacheth; comparing spiritual things with spiritual. {2:14} But the natural man receiveth not the things of the Spirit of **God**: for they are foolishness unto him: neither can he know [them,] because they are spiritually discerned. {2:15} But he that is spiritual judgeth all things, yet he himself is judged of no man. {2:16} For who hath known the mind of the **Lord**, that he may instruct **Him**? But we have the mind of **Christ**. **{13}**

{3:1} And I, brethren, could not speak unto you as unto spiritual, but as unto carnal, [even] as unto babes in **Christ**. {3:2} I have fed you with milk, and not with meat: for hitherto ye were not able [to bear it,] neither yet now are ye able.

{3:3} For ye are yet carnal: for whereas [there is] among you envying, and strife, and divisions, are ye not carnal, and walk as men? {3:4} For while one saith, I am of Paul; and another, I [am] of Apollos; are ye not carnal? {3:5} Who then is Paul, and who [is] Apollos, but ministers by whom ye believed, even as the **Lord** gave to every man? {3:6} I have planted, Apollos watered; but God gave the increase. {3:7} So then neither is He that planteth any thing, neither He that watereth; but God that giveth the increase. {3:8} Now He that planteth and He that watereth are one: and every man shall receive His own reward according to His own labour. {3:9} For we are labourers together with **God**: ye are **God**'s husbandry, [ye are] **God**'s building. {3:10} According to the grace of **God** which is given unto me, as a wise masterbuilder, I have laid the foundation, and another buildeth thereon. But let every man take heed how He buildeth thereupon. {3:11} For other **foundation** can no man lay than that is laid, which is **Jesus Christ**. {3:12} Now if any man build upon this **foundation** gold, silver, precious stones, wood, hay, stubble; {3:13} Every man's work shall be made manifest: for the day shall declare it, because it shall be revealed by fire; and the fire shall try every man's work of what sort it is. {3:14} If any man's work abide which He hath built thereupon, He shall receive a reward. {3:15} If any man's work shall be burned, He shall suffer loss: but He himself shall be saved; yet so as by fire. {3:16} Know ye not that ye are the temple of **God**, and [that] the Spirit of **God** dwelleth in you? {3:17} If any man defile the temple of **God**, Him shall **God** destroy; for the temple of **God** is holy, which [temple] ye are.

{3:18} Let no man deceive himself. If any man among you seemeth to be wise in this world, let Him become a fool, that He may be wise. {3:19} For the wisdom of this world is foolishness with God. For it is written, He taketh the wise in their own craftiness. {3:20} And again, The **Lord** knoweth the thoughts of the wise, that they are vain. {3:21} Therefore let no man glory in men. For all things are yours; {3:22} Whether Paul, or Apollos, or Cephas, or the world, or life, or death, or things present, or things to come; all are yours; {3:23} And ye are **Christ**'s; and **Christ** [is] God's.{9}

{4:1} Let a man so account of us, as of the ministers of **Christ**, and stewards of the mysteries of **God**. {4:2} Moreover it is required in stewards, that a man be found faithful. {4:3} But with me it is a very small thing that I should be judged of you, or of man's judgment: yea, I judge not mine own self. {4:4} For I know nothing by myself; yet am I not hereby justified: but He that judgeth me is the **Lord**. {4:5} Therefore judge nothing before the time, until the **Lord** come, **who** both will bring to light the hidden things of darkness, and will make manifest the counsels of the hearts: and then shall every man have praise of **God**. {4:6} And these things, brethren, I have in a figure transferred to myself and [to] Apollos for your sakes; that ye might learn in us not to think [of men] above that which is written, that no one of you be puffed up for one against another. {4:7} For who maketh thee to differ [from another?] and what hast thou that thou didst not receive? now if thou didst receive [it,] why dost thou glory, as if thou hadst not received [it?]{4:8} Now ye are full, now ye are rich, ye have reigned as kings without us: and I would to **God** ye did reign, that we also might reign with you. {4:9} For I think that **God** hath set forth us the apostles last, as it were appointed to death: for we are made a spectacle unto the world, and to angels, and to men. {4:10} We [are] fools for **Christ**'s sake, but ye [are] wise in **Christ**; we [are] weak, but ye [are] strong; ye [are] honourable, but we [are] despised. {4:11} Even unto this present hour we both hunger, and thirst, and are naked, and are buffeted, and have no certain dwellingplace; {4:12} And labour, working with our own hands: being reviled, we bless; being persecuted, we suffer it: {4:13} Being defamed, we intreat: we are made as the filth of the world, [and are] the offscouring of all things unto this day. {4:14} I write not these things to shame you, but as my beloved sons I warn [you.]{4:15} For though ye have ten thousand instructers in **Christ**, yet [have ye] not many **Fathers**: for in **Christ Jesus** I have begotten you through the Gospel. {4:16} Wherefore I beseech you, be ye followers of me. {4:17} For this cause have I sent unto you Timotheus, who is my beloved Son, and faithful in the **Lord**, who shall bring you into remembrance of my ways which be in **Christ**, as I teach every where in every church. {4:18} Now some are puffed up, as though I would not come to you. {4:19} But I will come to you shortly, if the **Lord** will, and will know, not the speech of them which are puffed up, but the power. {4:20} For the kingdom of **God** [is] not in word, but in power. {4:21} What will ye? shall I come unto you with a rod, or in love, and [in] the spirit of meekness? {13}

{5:1} It is reported commonly [that there is] fornication among you, and such fornication as is not so much as

named among the Gentiles, that one should have his Father's wife. {5:2} And ye are puffed up, and have not rather mourned, that he that hath done this deed might be taken away from among you. {5:3} For I verily, as absent in body, but present in spirit, have judged already, as though I were present, [concerning] him that hath so done this deed, {5:4} In the **name** of our **Lord Jesus Christ**, when ye are gathered together, and my spirit, with the power of our **Lord Jesus Christ**, {5:5} To deliver such an one unto Satan for the destruction of the flesh, that the spirit may be saved in the day of the **Lord Jesus**. {5:6} Your glorying [is] not good. Know ye not that a little leaven leaveneth the whole lump? {5:7} Purge out therefore the old leaven, that ye may be a new lump, as ye are unleavened. For even **Christ** our **passover** is sacrificed for us: {5:8} Therefore let us keep the feast, not with old leaven, neither with the leaven of malice and wickedness; but with the unleavened [bread] of sincerity and truth. {5:9} I wrote unto you in an epistle not to company with fornicators: {5:10} Yet not altogether with the fornicators of this world, or with the covetous, or extortioners, or with idolaters; for then must ye needs go out of the world. {5:11} But now I have written unto you not to keep company, if any man that is called a brother be a fornicator, or covetous, or an idolater, or a railer, or a drunkard, or an extortioner; with such an one no not to eat. {5:12} For what have I to do to judge them also that are without? do not ye judge them that are within? {5:13} But them that are without **God** judgeth. Therefore put away from among yourselves that wicked person. {11}

{6:1} Dare any of you, having a matter against another, go to law before the unjust, and not before the saints? {6:2} Do ye not know that the saints shall judge the world? and if the world shall be judged by you, are ye unworthy to judge the smallest matters? {6:3} Know ye not that we shall judge angels? how much more things that pertain to this life? {6:4} If then ye have judgments of things pertaining to this life, set them to judge who are least esteemed in the church. {6:5} I speak to your shame. Is it so, that there is not a wise man among you? no, not one that shall be able to judge between His brethren? {6:6} But brother goeth to law with brother, and that before the unbelievers. {6:7} Now therefore there is utterly a fault among you, because ye go to law one with another. Why do ye not rather take wrong? why do ye not rather [suffer yourselves to] be defrauded? {6:8} Nay, ye do wrong, and defraud, and that [your] brethren. {6:9} Know ye not that the unrighteous shall not inherit the kingdom of **God**? Be not deceived: neither fornicators, nor idolaters, nor adulterers, nor effeminate, nor abusers of themselves with mankind, {6:10} Nor thieves, nor covetous, nor drunkards, nor revilers, nor extortioners, shall inherit the kingdom of **God**. {6:11} And such were some of you: but ye are washed, but ye are sanctified, but ye are justified in the **name** of the **Lord Jesus**, and by the Spirit of our **God**.

{6:12} All things are lawful unto me, but all things are not expedient: all things are lawful for me, but I will not be brought under the power of any. {6:13} Meats for the belly, and the belly for meats: but **God** shall destroy both it and them. Now the body [is] not for fornication, but for the **Lord**; and the **Lord** for the body. {6:14} And **God** hath both raised up the **Lord**, and will also raise up us by **His own** power. {6:15} Know ye not that your bodies are the members of **Christ**? shall I then take the members of **Christ**, and make [them] the members of an harlot? **God** forbid. {6:16} What? know ye not that He which is joined to an harlot is one body? for two, saith He, shall be one flesh. {6:17} But He that is joined unto the **Lord** is one spirit.

{6:18} Flee fornication. Every sin that a man doeth is without the body; but He that committeth fornication sinneth against His own body. {6:19} What? know ye not that your body is the temple of the **Holy Ghost** [which is] in you, which ye have of **God**, and ye are not your own? {6:20} For ye are bought with a price: therefore glorify **God** in your body, and in your spirit, which are **God**'s. {11}

{7:1} Now concerning the things whereof ye wrote unto me: [It is] good for a man not to touch a woman. {7:2} Nevertheless, [to avoid] fornication, let every man have his own wife, and let every woman have her own husband. {7:3} Let the husband render unto the wife due benevolence: and likewise also the wife unto the husband. {7:4} The wife hath not power of her own body, but the husband: and likewise also the husband hath not power of his own body, but the wife. {7:5} Defraud ye not one the other, except [it be] with consent for a time, that ye may give yourselves to fasting and prayer; and come together again, that Satan tempt you not for your incontinency. {7:6} But I speak this by permission, [and] not of commandment. {7:7} For I would that all men were even as I myself. But every man hath his proper gift of **God**, one after this manner, and another after that.

{7:8} I say therefore to the unmarried and widows, It is good for them if they abide even as I. {7:9} But if they cannot contain, let them marry: for it is better to marry than to burn. {7:10} And unto the married I command, [yet] not I, but the **Lord**, Let not the wife depart from [her] husband: {7:11} But and if she depart, let her remain unmarried, or be reconciled to [her] husband: and let not the husband put away [his] wife. {7:12} But to the rest speak I, not the **Lord**: If any brother hath a wife that believeth not, and she be pleased to dwell with him, let him not put her away. {7:13} And the woman which hath an husband that believeth not, and if he be pleased to dwell with her, let her not leave him. {7:14} For the unbelieving husband is sanctified by the wife, and the unbelieving wife is sanctified by the husband: else were your children unclean; but now are they holy. {7:15} But if the unbelieving depart, let him depart. A brother or a sister is not under bondage in such [cases:] but **God** hath called us to peace. {7:16} For what knowest thou, O wife, whether thou shalt save [thy] husband? or how knowest thou, O man, whether thou shalt save [thy] wife? {7:17} But as **God** hath distributed to every man, as the **Lord** hath called every one, so let him walk. And so ordain I in all churches. {7:18} Is any man called being circumcised? let him not become uncircumcised. Is any called in uncircumcision? let him not be circumcised. {7:19} Circumcision is nothing, and uncircumcision is nothing, but the keeping of the commandments of **God**. {7:20} Let every man abide in the same calling wherein he was called. {7:21} Art thou called [being] a servant? care not for it: but if thou mayest be made free, use [it] rather. {7:22} For he that is called in the **Lord**, [being] a servant, is the **Lord**'s freeman: likewise also he that is called, [being] free, is **Christ**'s servant. {7:23} Ye are bought with a **price**; be not ye the servants of men. {7:24} Brethren, let every man, wherein he is called, therein abide with **God**.

{7:25} Now concerning virgins I have no commandment of the **Lord**: yet I give my judgment, as one that hath obtained mercy of the **Lord** to be faithful. {7:26} I suppose therefore that this is good for the present distress, [I say,] that [it is] good for a man so to be. {7:27} Art thou bound unto a wife? seek not to be loosed. Art thou loosed from a wife? seek not a wife. {7:28} But and if thou marry, thou hast not sinned; and if a virgin marry, she hath not sinned.

Nevertheless such shall have trouble in the flesh: but I spare you. {7:29} But this I say, brethren, the time [is] short: it remaineth, that both they that have wives be as though they had none; {7:30} And they that weep, as though they wept not; and they that rejoice, as though they rejoiced not; and they that buy, as though they possessed not; {7:31} And they that use this world, as not abusing [it:] for the fashion of this world passeth away. {7:32} But I would have you without carefulness. He that is unmarried careth for the things that belong to the **Lord**, how he may please the **Lord**: {7:33} But he that is married careth for the things that are of the world, how he may please [his] wife. {7:34} There is difference [also] between a wife and a virgin. The unmarried woman careth for the things of the **Lord**, that she may be holy both in body and in spirit: but she that is married careth for the things of the world, how she may please [her] husband. {7:35} And this I speak for your own profit; not that I may cast a snare upon you, but for that which is comely, and that ye may attend upon the **Lord** without distraction. {7:36} But if any man think that he behaveth himself uncomely toward his virgin, if she pass the flower of [her] age, and need so require, let him do what he will, he sinneth not: let them marry. {7:37} Nevertheless he that standeth stedfast in his heart, having no necessity, but hath power over his own will, and hath so decreed in his heart that he will keep his virgin, doeth well. {7:38} So then he that giveth [her] in marriage doeth well; but he that giveth [her] not in marriage doeth better. {7:39} The wife is bound by the law as long as her husband liveth; but if her husband be dead, she is at liberty to be married to whom she will; only in the **Lord**. {7:40} But she is happier if she so abide, after my judgment: and I think also that I have the Spirit of **God**. {14}

{8:1} Now as touching things offered unto idols, we know that we all have knowledge. Knowledge puffeth up, but charity edifieth. {8:2} And if any man think that he knoweth any thing, he knoweth nothing yet as he ought to know. {8:3} But if any man love **God**, the same is known of **Him**. {8:4} As concerning therefore the eating of those things that are offered in sacrifice unto idols, we know that an idol [is] nothing in the world, and that [there is] none other **God** but one. {8:5} For though there be that are called **God**s, whether in heaven or in earth, (as there be **God**s many, and lords many,) {8:6} But to us [there is but] one **God**, the **Father**, of **whom** [are] all things, and we in **Him**; and one **Lord Jesus Christ**, by **whom** [are] all things, and we by **Him**. {8:7} Howbeit [there is] not in every man that knowledge: for some with conscience of the idol unto this hour eat [it] as a thing offered unto an idol; and their conscience being weak is defiled. {8:8} But meat commendeth us not to **God**: for neither, if we eat, are we the better; neither, if we eat not, are we the worse. {8:9} But take heed lest by any means this liberty of yours become a stumblingblock to them that are weak. {8:10} For if any man see thee which hast knowledge sit at meat in the idol's temple, shall not the conscience of him which is weak be emboldened to eat those things which are offered to idols; {8:11} And through thy knowledge shall the weak brother perish, for **whom Christ** died? {8:12} But when ye sin so against the brethren, and wound their weak conscience, ye sin against **Christ**. {8:13} Wherefore, if meat make my brother to offend, I will eat no flesh while the world standeth, lest I make my brother to offend. {8}

{9:1} Am I not an apostle? am I not free? have I not seen **Jesus Christ** our **Lord**? are not ye my work in the **Lord**? {9:2} If I be not an apostle unto others, yet doubtless I am to you: for the seal of mine apostleship are ye in the **Lord**.

{9:3} Mine answer to them that do examine me is this, {9:4} Have we not power to eat and to drink? {9:5} Have we not power to lead about a sister, a wife, as well as other apostles, and [as] the brethren of the **Lord**, and Cephas? {9:6} Or I only and Barnabas, have not we power to forbear working? {9:7} Who goeth a warfare any time at his own charges? who planteth a vineyard, and eateth not of the fruit thereof? or who feedeth a flock, and eateth not of the milk of the flock? {9:8} Say I these things as a man? or saith not the law the same also? {9:9} For it is written in the law of Moses, Thou shalt not muzzle the mouth of the ox that treadeth out the corn. Doth God take care for oxen? {9:10} Or saith he [it] altogether for our sakes? For our sakes, no doubt, [this] is written: that he that ploweth should plow in hope; and that he that thresheth in hope should be partaker of his hope. {9:11} If we have sown unto you spiritual things, [is it] a great thing if we shall reap your carnal things? {9:12} If others be partakers of [this] power over you, [are] not we rather? Nevertheless we have not used this power; but suffer all things, lest we should hinder the Gospel of **Christ**. {9:13} Do ye not know that they which minister about holy things live [of the things] of the temple? and they which wait at the altar are partakers with the altar? {9:14} Even so hath the **Lord** ordained that they which preach the Gospel should live of the Gospel. {9:15} But I have used none of these things: neither have I written these things, that it should be so done unto me: for [it were] better for me to die, than that any man should make my glorying void. {9:16} For though I preach the Gospel, I have nothing to glory of: for necessity is laid upon me; yea, woe is unto me, if I preach not the Gospel! {9:17} For if I do this thing willingly, I have a reward: but if against my will, a dispensation [of the Gospel] is committed unto me. {9:18} What is my reward then? [Verily] that, when I preach the Gospel, I may make the Gospel of **Christ** without charge, that I abuse not my power in the Gospel. {9:19} For though I be free from all [men,] yet have I made myself servant unto all, that I might gain the more. {9:20} And unto the Jews I became as a Jew, that I might gain the Jews; to them that are under the law, as under the law, that I might gain them that are under the law; {9:21} To them that are without law, as without law, (being not without law to **God**, but under the law to **Christ**,) that I might gain them that are without law. {9:22} To the weak became I as weak, that I might gain the weak: I am made all things to all [men,] that I might by all means save some. {9:23} And this I do for the Gospel's sake, that I might be partaker thereof with [you.]{9:24} Know ye not that they which run in a race run all, but one receiveth the prize? So run, that ye may obtain. {9:25} And every man that striveth for the mastery is temperate in all things. Now they [do it] to obtain a corruptible crown; but we an incorruptible. {9:26} I therefore so run, not as uncertainly; so fight I, not as one that beateth the air: {9:27} But I keep under my body, and bring [it] into subjection: lest that by any means, when I have preached to others, I myself should be a castaway.{10}

{10:1} Moreover, brethren, I would not that ye should be ignorant, how that all our Fathers were under the cloud, and all passed through the sea; {10:2} And were all baptized unto Moses in the cloud and in the sea; {10:3} And did all eat the same spiritual meat; {10:4} And did all drink the same spiritual drink: for they drank of that spiritual Rock that followed them: and that Rock was **Christ**. {10:5} But with many of them **God** was not well pleased: for they were overthrown in the wilderness. {10:6} Now these things were our examples, to the intent we should not lust after evil things, as they also lusted. {10:7} Neither be ye idolaters, as [were] some of them; as it is written, The people sat down

to eat and drink, and rose up to play. {10:8} Neither let us commit fornication, as some of them committed, and fell in one day three and twenty thousand. {10:9} Neither let us tempt **Christ**, as some of them also tempted, and were destroyed of serpents. {10:10} Neither murmur ye, as some of them also murmured, and were destroyed of the destroyer. {10:11} Now all these things happened unto them for ensamples: and they are written for our admonition, upon whom the ends of the world are come. {10:12} Wherefore let him that thinketh he standeth take heed lest he fall. {10:13} There hath no temptation taken you but such as is common to man: but **God** [is] faithful, who will not suffer you to be tempted above that ye are able; but will with the temptation also make a way to escape, that ye may be able to bear [it.

]{10:14} Wherefore, my dearly beloved, flee from idolatry. {10:15} I speak as to wise men; judge ye what I say. {10:16} The cup of blessing which we bless, is it not the communion of the blood of **Christ**? The bread which we break, is it not the communion of the body of **Christ**? {10:17} For we [being] many are one bread, [and] one body: for we are all partakers of that one bread. {10:18} Behold Israel after the flesh: are not they which eat of the sacrifices partakers of the altar? {10:19} What say I then? that the idol is any thing, or that which is offered in sacrifice to idols is any thing? {10:20} But [I say,] that the things which the Gentiles sacrifice, they sacrifice to devils, and not to God: and I would not that ye should have fellowship with devils. {10:21} Ye cannot drink the cup of the **Lord**, and the cup of devils: ye cannot be partakers of the **Lord**'s table, and of the table of devils. {10:22} Do we provoke the **Lord** to jealousy? are we stronger than **He**? {10:23} All things are lawful for me, but all things are not expedient: all things are lawful for me, but all things edify not. {10:24} Let no man seek his own, but every man another's [wealth.]{10:25} Whatsoever is sold in the shambles, [that] eat, asking no question for conscience sake: {10:26} For the earth [is] the **Lord**'s, and the fulness thereof. {10:27} If any of them that believe not bid you [to a feast,] and ye be disposed to go; whatsoever is set before you, eat, asking no question for conscience sake. {10:28} But if any man say unto you, This is offered in sacrifice unto idols, eat not for his sake that shewed it, and for conscience sake: for the earth [is] the **Lord**'s, and the fulness thereof: {10:29} Conscience, I say, not thine own, but of the other: for why is my liberty judged of another [man's] conscience? {10:30} For if I by grace be a partaker, why am I evil spoken of for that for which I give thanks? {10:31} Whether therefore ye eat, or drink, or whatsoever ye do, do all to the glory of **God**. {10:32} Give none offence, neither to the Jews, nor to the Gentiles, nor to the church of **God**: {10:33} Even as I please all [men] in all [things,] not seeking mine own profit, but the [profit] of many, that they may be saved. {19}

{11:1} Be ye followers of me, even as I also [am] of **Christ**.

{11:2} Now I praise you, brethren, that ye remember me in all things, and keep the ordinances, as I delivered [them] to you. {11:3} But I would have you know, that the head of every man is **Christ**; and the head of the woman [is] the man; and the head of **Christ** [is] **God**. {11:4} Every man praying or prophesying, having [his] head covered, dishonoureth his head. {11:5} But every woman that prayeth or prophesieth with [her] head uncovered dishonoureth her head: for that is even all one as if she were shaven. {11:6} For if the woman be not covered, let her also be shorn: but if it be a shame for a woman to be shorn or shaven, let her be covered. {11:7} For a man indeed ought not to cover [his] head, forasmuch as he is the image and glory of **God**: but the woman is the glory of the man. {11:8} For the man is not of the woman; but the woman of the man. {11:9} Neither was the man created for the woman; but the woman for the man. {11:10} For this cause ought the woman to have power on [her] head because of the angels. {11:11} Nevertheless neither is the man without the woman, neither the woman without the man, in the **Lord**. {11:12} For as the woman [is] of the man, even so [is] the man also by the woman; but all things of **God**. {11:13} Judge in yourselves: is it comely that a woman pray unto **God** uncovered? {11:14} Doth not even nature itself teach you, that, if a man have long hair, it is a shame unto him? {11:15} But if a woman have long hair, it is a glory to her: for [her] hair is given her for a covering. {11:16} But if any man seem to be contentious, we have no such custom, neither the churches of **God**.

{11:17} Now in this that I declare [unto you] I praise [you] not, that ye come together not for the better, but for the worse. {11:18} For first of all, when ye come together in the church, I hear that there be divisions among you; and I partly believe it. {11:19} For there must be also heresies among you, that they which are approved may be made manifest among you. {11:20} When ye come together therefore into one place, [this] is not to eat the **Lord**'s supper. {11:21} For in eating every one taketh before [other] His own supper: and one is hungry, and another is drunken. {11:22} What? have ye not houses to eat and to drink in? or despise ye the church of **God**, and shame them that have not? What shall I say to you? shall I praise you in this? I praise [you] not. {11:23} For I have received of the **Lord** that which also I delivered unto you, That the **Lord Jesus** the [same] night in which **He** was betrayed took **bread**: {11:24} And when **He** had given thanks, **He** brake [it,] and said, Take, eat: this is **my body**, which is broken for you: this do in remembrance of **ME**. {11:25} After the same manner also [**He** took] the cup, when **He** had supped, saying, This cup is the new testament in **my blood**: this do ye, as oft as ye drink [it,] in remembrance of **ME**. {11:26} For as often as ye eat this **bread**, and drink [this] **cup**, ye do shew the **Lord's** death till **He** come. {11:27} Wherefore whosoever shall eat this **bread**, and drink this **cup** of the **Lord**, unworthily, shall be guilty of the **body** and **blood** of the **Lord**. {11:28} But let a man examine himself, and so let him eat of [that] **bread**, and drink of [that] **cup**. {11:29} For he that eateth and drinketh unworthily, eateth and drinketh damnation to himself, not discerning the **Lord**'s **body**. {11:30} For this cause many [are] weak and sickly among you, and many sleep. {11:31} For if we would judge ourselves, we should not be judged. {11:32} But when we are judged, we are chastened of the **Lord**, that we should not be condemned with the world. {11:33} Wherefore, my brethren, when ye come together to eat, tarry one for another. {11:34} And if any man hunger, let him eat at home; that ye come not together unto condemnation. And the rest will I set in order when I come.

{32}

{12:1} Now concerning spiritual [gifts,] brethren, I would not have you ignorant. {12:2} Ye know that ye were Gentiles, carried away unto these dumb idols, even as ye were led. {12:3} Wherefore I give you to understand, that no man speaking by the Spirit of **God** calleth **Jesus** accursed: and [that] no man can say that **Jesus** is the **Lord**, but by the **Holy Ghost**. {12:4} Now there are diversities of gifts, but the same Spirit. {12:5} And there are differences of administrations, but the same **Lord**. {12:6} And there are diversities of operations, but it is the same **God** which

worketh all in all. {12:7} But the manifestation of the Spirit is given to every man to profit withal. {12:8} For to one is given by the Spirit the word of wisdom; to another the word of knowledge by the same Spirit; {12:9} To another faith by the same Spirit; to another the gifts of healing by the same Spirit; {12:10} To another the working of miracles; to another prophecy; to another discerning of spirits; to another [divers] kinds of tongues; to another the interpretation of tongues: {12:11} But all these worketh that one and the selfsame Spirit, dividing to every man severally as **He** will. {12:12} For as the body is one, and hath many members, and all the members of that one body, being many, are one body: so also [is] **Christ**. {12:13} For by one Spirit are we all baptized into one body, whether [we be] Jews or Gentiles, whether [we be] bond or free; and have been all made to drink into one Spirit. {12:14} For the body is not one member, but many. {12:15} If the foot shall say, Because I am not the hand, I am not of the body; is it therefore not of the body? {12:16} And if the ear shall say, Because I am not the eye, I am not of the body; is it therefore not of the body? {12:17} If the whole body [were] an eye, where [were] the hearing? If the whole [were] hearing, where [were] the smelling? {12:18} But now hath **God** set the members every one of them in the body, as it hath pleased **Him**. {12:19} And if they were all one member, where [were] the body? {12:20} But now [are they] many members, yet but one body. {12:21} And the eye cannot say unto the hand, I have no need of thee: nor again the head to the feet, I have no need of you. {12:22} Nay, much more those members of the body, which seem to be more feeble, are necessary: {12:23} And those [members] of the body, which we think to be less honourable, upon these we bestow more abundant honour; and our uncomely [parts] have more abundant comeliness. {12:24} For our comely [parts] have no need: but **God** hath tempered the body together, having given more abundant honour to that [part] which lacked: {12:25} That there should be no schism in the body; but [that] the members should have the same care one for another. {12:26} And whether one member suffer, all the members suffer with it; or one member be honoured, all the members rejoice with it. {12:27} Now ye are the body of **Christ**, and members in particular. {12:28} And **God** hath set some in the church, first apostles, secondarily prophets, thirdly teachers, after that miracles, then gifts of healings, helps, governments, diversities of tongues. {12:29} [Are] all apostles? [are] all prophets? [are] all teachers? [are] all workers of miracles? {12:30} Have all the gifts of healing? do all speak with tongues? do all interpret? {12:31} But covet earnestly the best gifts: and yet shew I unto you a more excellent way. **{7}**

{13:1} Though I speak with the tongues of men and of angels, and have not charity, I am become [as]sounding brass, or a tinkling cymbal. {13:2} And though I have [the gift of] prophecy, and understand all mysteries, and all knowledge; and though I have all faith, so that I could remove mountains, and have not charity, I am nothing. {13:3} And though I bestow all my goods to feed [the poor,] and though I give my body to be burned, and have not charity, it profiteth me nothing. {13:4} Charity suffereth long, [and] is kind; charity envieth not; charity vaunteth not itself, is not puffed up, {13:5} Doth not behave itself unseemly, seeketh not her own, is not easily provoked, thinketh no evil; {13:6} Rejoiceth not in iniquity, but rejoiceth in the truth; {13:7} Beareth all things, believeth all things, hopeth all things, endureth all things. {13:8} Charity never faileth: but whether [there be] prophecies, they shall fail; whether [there be] tongues, they shall cease; whether [there be] knowledge, it shall vanish away. {13:9} For we know in part, and we prophesy in part. {13:10} But when that which is perfect is come, then that which is in part shall be done away. {13:11} When I was a child, I spake as a child, I understood as a child, I thought as a child: but when I became a man, I put away childish things. {13:12} For now we see through a glass, darkly; but then face to face: now I know in part; but then shall I know even as also I am known. {13:13} And now abideth faith, hope, charity, these three; but the greatest of these [is] charity.

{14:1} Follow after charity, and desire spiritual [gifts,] but rather that ye may prophesy. {14:2} For he that speaketh in an [unknown] tongue speaketh not unto men, but unto God: for no man understandeth [him;] howbeit in the spirit he speaketh mysteries. {14:3} But he that prophesieth speaketh unto men [to] edification, and exhortation, and comfort. {14:4} he that speaketh in an [unknown] tongue edifieth himself; but he that prophesieth edifieth the church. {14:5} I would that ye all spake with tongues, but rather that ye prophesied: for greater [is] he that prophesieth than he that speaketh with tongues, except he interpret, that the church may receive edifying. {14:6} Now, brethren, if I come unto you speaking with tongues, what shall I profit you, except I shall speak to you either by revelation, or by knowledge, or by prophesying, or by doctrine? {14:7} And even things without life giving sound, whether pipe or harp, except they give a distinction in the sounds, how shall it be known what is piped or harped? {14:8} For if the trumpet give an uncertain sound, who shall prepare himself to the battle? {14:9} So likewise ye, except ye utter by the tongue words easy to be understood, how shall it be known what is spoken? for ye shall speak into the air. {14:10} There are, it may be, so many kinds of voices in the world, and none of them [is] without signification. {14:11} Therefore if I know not the meaning of the voice, I shall be unto him that speaketh a barbarian, and he that speaketh [shall be] a barbarian unto me. {14:12} Even so ye, forasmuch as ye are zealous of spiritual [gifts,] seek that ye may excel to the edifying of the church. {14:13} Wherefore let him that speaketh in an [unknown] tongue pray that he may interpret. {14:14} For if I pray in an [unknown] tongue, my spirit prayeth, but my understanding is unfruitful. {14:15} What is it then? I will pray with the spirit, and I will pray with the understanding also: I will sing with the spirit, and I will sing with the understanding also. {14:16} Else when thou shalt bless with the spirit, how shall he that occupieth the room of the unlearned say Amen at thy giving of thanks, seeing he understandeth not what thou sayest? {14:17} For thou verily givest thanks well, but the other is not edified. {14:18} I thank my God, I speak with tongues more than ye all: {14:19} Yet in the church I had rather speak five words with my understanding, that [by my voice] I might teach others also, than ten thousand words in an [unknown] tongue. {14:20} Brethren, be not children in understanding: howbeit in malice be ye children, but in understanding be men. {14:21} In the law it is written, With [men of] other tongues and other lips will I speak unto this people; and yet for all that will they not hear me, saith the Lord. {14:22} Wherefore tongues are for a sign, not to them that believe, but to them that believe not: but prophesying [serveth] not for them that believe not, but for them which believe. {14:23} If therefore the whole church be come together into one place, and all speak with tongues, and there come in [those that are] unlearned, or unbelievers, will they not say that ye are mad? {14:24} But if all prophesy, and there come in one that believeth not, or [one] unlearned, he is convinced of all, he is judged of all: {14:25} And thus are the secrets of his heart made manifest; and so falling down on [his] face he will worship God, and

report that God is in you of a truth. {14:26} How is it then, brethren? when ye come together, every one of you hath a psalm, hath a doctrine, hath a tongue, hath a revelation, hath an interpretation. Let all things be done unto edifying. {14:27} If any man speak in an [unknown] tongue, [let it be] by two, or at the most [by] three, and [that] by course; and let one interpret. {14:28} But if there be no interpreter, let him keep silence in the church; and let him speak to himself, and to God. {14:29} Let the prophets speak two or three, and let the other judge. {14:30} If [any thing] be revealed to another that sitteth by, let the first hold his peace. {14:31} For ye may all prophesy one by one, that all may learn, and all may be comforted. {14:32} And the spirits of the prophets are subject to the prophets. {14:33} For God is not [the author] of confusion, but of peace, as in all churches of the saints. {14:34} Let your women keep silence in the churches: for it is not permitted unto them to speak; but [they are commanded] to be under obedience, as also saith the law. {14:35} And if they will learn any thing, let them ask their husbands at home: for it is a shame for women to speak in the church. {14:36} What? came the word of God out from you? or came it unto you only? {14:37} If any man think himself to be a prophet, or spiritual, let him acknowledge that the things that I write unto you are the commandments of the Lord. {14:38} But if any man be ignorant, let him be ignorant. {14:39} Wherefore, brethren, covet to prophesy, and forbid not to speak with tongues. {14:40} Let all things be done decently and in order. {1}

{15:1} Moreover, brethren, I declare unto you the Gospel which I preached unto you, which also ye have received, and wherein ye stand; {15:2} By which also ye are saved, if ye keep in memory what I preached unto you, unless ye have believed in vain. {15:3} For I delivered unto you first of all that which I also received, how that Christ died for our sins according to the scriptures; {15:4} And that He was buried, and that He rose again the third day according to the scriptures: {15:5} And that He was seen of Cephas, then of the twelve: {15:6} After that, He was seen of above five hundred brethren at once; of whom the greater part remain unto this present, but some are fallen asleep. {15:7} After that, He was seen of James; then of all the apostles. {15:8} And last of all He was seen of me also, as of one born out of due time. {15:9} For I am the least of the apostles, that am not meet to be called an apostle, because I persecuted the church of God. {15:10} But by the grace of God I am what I am: and His grace [which was bestowed] upon me was not in vain; but I laboured more abundantly than they all: yet not I, but the grace of God which was with me. {15:11} Therefore whether [it were] I or they, so we preach, and so ye believed. {15:12} Now if Christ be preached that He rose from the dead, how say some among you that there is no resurrection of the dead? {15:13} But if there be no resurrection of the dead, then is Christ not risen: {15:14} And if Christ be not risen, then [is] our preaching vain, and your faith [is] also vain. {15:15} Yea, and we are found false witnesses of God; because we have testified of God that He raised up Christ: whom He raised not up, if so be that the dead rise not. {15:16} For if the dead rise not, then is not Christ raised: {15:17} And if Christ be not raised, your faith [is] vain; ye are yet in your sins. {15:18} Then they also which are fallen asleep in Christ are perished. {15:19} If in this life only we have hope in Christ, we are of all men most miserable. {15:20} But now is Christ risen from the dead, [and] become the firstfruits of them that slept. {15:21} For since by man [came] death, by man [came] also the resurrection of the dead. {15:22} For as in Adam all die, even so in Christ shall all be made alive. {15:23} But every man in his own order: **Christ** the firstfruits; afterward they that are **Christ**'s at **His** coming. {15:24} Then [cometh] the end, when **He** shall have delivered up the kingdom to **God**, even the **Father**; when **He** shall have put down all rule and all authority and power. {15:25} For **He** must reign, till **He** hath put all enemies under **His** feet. {15:26} The last enemy [that] shall be destroyed [is] death. {15:27} For **He** hath put all things under **His** feet. But when **He** saith, all things are put under [**Him**, it is] manifest that **He** is excepted, which did put all things under **Him**. {15:28} And when all things shall be subdued unto **Him**, then shall the **Son** also **himself** be subject unto **Him** that put all things under **Him**, that **God** may be all in all. {15:29} Else what shall they do which are baptized for the dead, if the dead rise not at all? why are they then baptized for the dead? {15:30} And why stand we in jeopardy every hour? {15:31} I protest by your rejoicing which I have in **Christ Jesus** our **Lord**, I die daily. {15:32} If after the manner of men I have fought with beasts at Ephesus, what advantageth it me, if the dead rise not? let us eat and drink; for to morrow we die. {15:33} Be not deceived: evil communications corrupt good manners. {15:34} Awake to righteousness, and sin not; for some have not the knowledge of **God**: I speak [this] to your shame.

{15:35} But some [man] will say, How are the dead raised up? and with what body do they come? {15:36} [Thou] fool, that which thou sowest is not quickened, except it die: {15:37} And that which thou sowest, thou sowest not that body that shall be, but bare grain, it may chance of wheat, or of some other [grain:]{15:38} But **God** giveth it a body as it hath pleased **Him**, and to every seed His own body. {15:39} All flesh [is] not the same flesh: but [there is] one [kind of] flesh of men, another flesh of beasts, another of fishes, [and] another of birds. {15:40} [There are] also celestial bodies, and bodies terrestrial: but the glory of the celestial [is] one, and the [glory] of the terrestrial [is] another. {15:41} [There is] one glory of the sun, and another glory of the moon, and another glory of the stars: for [one] star differeth from [another] star in glory. {15:42} So also [is] the resurrection of the dead. It is sown in corruption; it is raised in incorruption: {15:43} It is sown in dishonour; it is raised in glory: it is sown in weakness; it is raised in power: {15:44} It is sown a natural body; it is raised a spiritual body. There is a natural body, and there is a spiritual body. {15:45} And so it is written, The first man Adam was made a living soul; the last **Adam** [was made] a quickening spirit. {15:46} Howbeit that [was] not first which is spiritual, but that which is natural; and afterward that which is spiritual. {15:47} The first man [is] of the earth, earthy: the **second man** [is] the **Lord** from heaven. {15:48} As [is] the earthy, such [are] they also that are earthy: and as [is] the heavenly, such [are] they also that are heavenly. {15:49} And as we have borne the image of the earthy, we shall also bear the image of the heavenly. {15:50} Now this I say, brethren, that flesh and blood cannot inherit the kingdom of **God**; neither doth corruption inherit incorruption. {15:51} Behold, I shew you a mystery; We shall not all sleep, but we shall all be changed, {15:52} In a moment, in the twinkling of an eye, at the last trump: for the trumpet shall sound, and the dead shall be raised incorruptible, and we shall be changed. {15:53} For this corruptible must put on incorruption, and this mortal [must] put on immortality. {15:54} So when this corruptible shall have put on incorruption, and this mortal shall have put on immortality, then shall be brought to pass the saying that is written, Death is swallowed up in victory. {15:55} O death, where [is] thy sting? O grave, where [is] thy victory? {15:56} The sting of death [is] sin; and the strength of sin [is] the law. {15:57} But thanks [be] to **God**, which giveth

us the victory through our **Lord Jesus Christ**. {15:58} Therefore, my beloved brethren, be ye stedfast, unmovable, always abounding in the work of the **Lord**, forasmuch as ye know that your labour is not in vain in the **Lord**. {46}

{16:1} Now concerning the collection for the saints, as I have given order to the churches of Galatia, even so do ye. {16:2} Upon the first [day] of the week let every one of you lay by him in store, as [God] hath prospered him, that there be no gatherings when I come. {16:3} And when I come, whomsoever ye shall approve by [your] letters, them will I send to bring your liberality unto Jerusalem. {16:4} And if it be meet that I go also, they shall go with me. {16:5} Now I will come unto you, when I shall pass through Macedonia: for I do pass through Macedonia. {16:6} And it may be that I will abide, yea, and winter with you, that ye may bring me on my journey whithersoever I go. {16:7} For I will not see you now by the way; but I trust to tarry a while with you, if the **Lord** permit. {16:8} But I will tarry at Ephesus until Pentecost. {16:9} For a great door and effectual is opened unto me, and [there are] many adversaries. {16:10} Now if Timotheus come, see that he may be with you without fear: for he worketh the work of the **Lord**, as I also [do.]{16:11} Let no man therefore despise him: but conduct him forth in peace, that he may come unto me: for I look for him with the brethren. {16:12} As touching [our] brother Apollos, I greatly desired him to come unto you with the brethren: but his will was not at all to come at this time; but he will come when he shall have convenient time. {16:13} Watch ye, stand fast in the faith, quit you like men, be strong. {16:14} Let all your things be done with charity. {16:15} I beseech you, brethren, (ye know the house of Stephanas, that it is the firstfruits of Achaia, and [that] they have addicted themselves to the ministry of the saints,) {16:16} That ye submit yourselves unto such, and to every one that helpeth with [us,] and laboureth. {16:17} I am glad of the coming of Stephanas and Fortunatus and Achaicus: for that which was lacking on your part they have supplied. {16:18} For they have refreshed my spirit and yours: therefore acknowledge ye them that are such.

{16:19} The churches of Asia salute you. Aquila and Priscilla salute you much in the **Lord**, with the church that is in their house. {16:20} All the brethren greet you. Greet ye one another with an holy kiss. {16:21} The salutation of [me] Paul with mine own hand. {16:22} If any man love not the **Lord Jesus Christ**, let Him be Anathema Maranatha. {16:23} The grace of our **Lord Jesus Christ** [be] with you. {16:24} my love [be] with you all in **Christ Jesus**. Amen. {11}

The Second Epistle of Paul the Apostle to the Corinthians
TOTAL 140

{1:1} Paul, an apostle of **Jesus Christ** by the will of **God**, and Timothy [our] brother, unto the church of **God** which is at Corinth, with all the saints which are in all Achaia: {1:2} Grace be to you and peace from **God** our **Father**, and [from] the **Lord Jesus Christ**. {1:3} Blessed [be] **God**, even the **Father** of our **Lord Jesus Christ**, the **Father** of mercies, and the **God** of all comfort; {1:4} Who comforteth us in all our tribulation, that we may be able to comfort them which are in any trouble, by the comfort wherewith we ourselves are comforted of **God**. {1:5} For as the sufferings of **Christ** abound in us, so our consolation also aboundeth by **Christ**. {1:6} And whether we be afflicted, [it is] for your consolation and salvation, which is effectual in the enduring of the same sufferings which we also suffer: or whether we be comforted, [it is] for your consolation and salvation. {1:7} And our hope of you [is] stedfast, knowing, that as ye are partakers of the sufferings, so [shall ye be] also of the consolation. {1:8} For we would not, brethren, have you ignorant of our trouble which came to us in Asia, that we were pressed out of measure, above strength, insomuch that we despaired even of life: {1:9} But we had the sentence of death in ourselves, that we should not trust in ourselves, but in **God** which raiseth the dead: {1:10} Who delivered us from so great a death, and doth deliver: in **whom** we trust that **He** will yet deliver [us;]{1:11} Ye also helping together by prayer for us, that for the gift [bestowed] upon us by the means of many persons thanks may be given by many on our behalf.

{1:12} For our rejoicing is this, the testimony of our conscience, that in simplicity and **God**ly sincerity, not with fleshly wisdom, but by the grace of **God**, we have had our conversation in the world, and more abundantly to you-ward. {1:13} For we write none other things unto you, than what ye read or acknowledge; and I trust ye shall acknowledge even to the end; {1:14} As also ye have acknowledged us in part, that we are your rejoicing, even as ye also [are] ours in the day of the **Lord Jesus**.

{1:15} And in this confidence I was minded to come unto you before, that ye might have a second benefit; {1:16} And to pass by you into Macedonia, and to come again out of Macedonia unto you, and of you to be brought on my way toward Judaea. {1:17} When I therefore was thus minded, did I use lightness? or the things that I purpose, do I purpose according to the flesh, that with me there should be yea yea, and nay nay? {1:18} But [as] **God** [is] true, our word toward you was not yea and nay. {1:19} For the **Son of God**, **Jesus Christ**, **who** was preached among you by us, [even] by **me** and Silvanus and Timotheus, was not yea and nay, but in **Him** was yea. {1:20} For all the promises of **God** in **Him** [are] yea, and in **Him** Amen, unto the glory of **God** by us. {1:21} Now **He** which stablisheth us with you in **Christ**, and hath anointed us, [is] **God**; {1:22} Who hath also sealed us, and given the earnest of the Spirit in our hearts. {1:23} Moreover I call God for a record upon my soul, that to spare you I came not as yet unto Corinth. {1:24} Not for that we have dominion over your faith, but are helpers of your joy: for by faith ye stand. **{22}**

{2:1} But I determined this with myself, that I would not come again to you in heaviness. {2:2} For if I make you sorry, who is He then that maketh me glad, but the same which is made sorry by me? {2:3} And I wrote this same unto you, lest, when I came, I should have sorrow from them of whom I ought to rejoice; having confidence in you all, that my joy is [the joy] of you all. {2:4} For out of much affliction and anguish of heart I wrote unto you with many tears; not that ye should be grieved, but that ye might know the love which I have more abundantly unto you. {2:5} But if any have caused grief, he hath not grieved me, but in part: that I may not overcharge you all. {2:6} Sufficient to such a man is this punishment, which [was inflicted] of many. {2:7} So that contrariwise ye [ought] rather to forgive [him,] and comfort [him,] lest perhaps such a one should be swallowed up with overmuch sorrow. {2:8} Wherefore I beseech you that ye would confirm [your] love toward him. {2:9} For to this end also did I write, that I might know the proof of you, whether ye be obedient in all things. {2:10} To whom ye forgive any thing, I [forgive] also: for if I forgave any thing, to whom I forgave [it,] for your sakes [forgave I it] in the **person** of **Christ**; {2:11} Lest Satan should get an advantage of us: for we are not ignorant of his devices. {2:12} Furthermore, when I came to Troas to [preach] **Christ's** Gospel, and a door was opened unto **me** of the **Lord**, {2:13} I had no rest in my spirit, because I found not Titus my brother: but taking my leave of them, I went from thence into Macedonia. {2:14} Now thanks [be] unto **God**, which always causeth us to triumph in **Christ,** and maketh manifest the savour of **His** knowledge by us in every place. {2:15} For we are unto **God** a sweet savour of **Christ**, in them that are saved, and in them that perish: {2:16} To the one [we are] the savour of death unto death; and to the other the savour of life unto life. And who [is] sufficient for these things? {2:17} For we are not as many, which corrupt the word of **God**: but as of sincerity, but as of **God**, in the sight of **God** speak we in **Christ**. **{8}**

{3:1} Do we begin again to commend ourselves? or need we, as some [others,] epistles of commendation to you, or [letters] of commendation from you? {3:2} Ye are our epistle written in our hearts, known and read of all men: {3:3} [Forasmuch as ye are] manifestly declared to be the epistle of **Christ** ministered by us, written not with ink, but with the Spirit of the living **God**; not in tables of stone, but in fleshy tables of the heart.

{3:4} And such trust have we through **Christ** to God-ward: {3:5} Not that we are sufficient of ourselves to think any thing as of ourselves; but our sufficiency [is] of **God**; {3:6} Who also hath made us able ministers of the new testament; not of the letter, but of the **spirit**: for the letter killeth, but the **spirit** giveth life. {3:7} But if the ministration of death, written [and] engraven in stones, was glorious, so that the children of Israel could not stedfastly behold the face of Moses for the glory of **His** countenance; which [glory] was to be done away: {3:8} How shall not the ministration of the **spirit** be rather glorious? {3:9} For if the ministration of condemnation [be] glory, much more doth the ministration of righteousness exceed in glory. {3:10} For even that which was made glorious had no glory in this respect, by reason of the glory that excelleth. {3:11} For if that which is done away [was] glorious, much more that which remaineth [is] glorious. {3:12} Seeing then that we have such hope, we use great plainness of speech: {3:13} And not as Moses, [which] put a vail over **His** face, that the children of Israel could not stedfastly look to the end of that which is abolished: {3:14} But their minds were blinded: for until this day remaineth the same vail untaken away in the reading of the old testament; which [vail] is done away in **Christ**. {3:15} But even unto this day, when Moses is read, the vail is upon their heart. {3:16} Nevertheless when it shall turn to the **Lord**, the vail shall be taken away. {3:17} Now the **Lord** is that **Spirit**: and where the **Spirit of the Lord** [is,] there [is] liberty. {3:18} But we all, with open face beholding as in a glass the glory of the **Lord**, are changed into the same image from glory to glory, [even] as by the **Spirit of the Lord**. {12}

{4:1} Therefore seeing we have this ministry, as we have received mercy, we faint not; {4:2} But have renounced the hidden things of dishonesty, not walking in craftiness, nor handling the word of **God** deceitfully; but by manifestation of the truth commending ourselves to every man's conscience in the sight of **God**. {4:3} But if our Gospel be hid, it is hid to them that are lost: {4:4} In **whom** the **God** of this world hath blinded the minds of them which believe not, lest the light of the glorious Gospel of **Christ**, **who** is the image of **God**, should shine unto them. {4:5} For we preach not ourselves, but **Christ Jesus** the **Lord**; and ourselves your servants for **Jesus**' sake. {4:6} For **God**, who commanded the **light** to shine out of darkness, hath shined in our hearts, to [give] the **light** of the knowledge of the glory of **God** in the face of **Jesus Christ**.

{4:7} But we have this treasure in earthen vessels, that the excellency of the power may be of **God**, and not of us. {4:8} [We are] troubled on every side, yet not distressed; [we are] perplexed, but not in despair; {4:9} Persecuted, but not forsaken; cast down, but not destroyed; {4:10} Always bearing about in the body the dying of the **Lord Jesus**, that the **life** also of **Jesus** might be made manifest in our body. {4:11} For we which live are alway delivered unto death for **Jesus**' sake, that the **life** also of **Jesus** might be made manifest in our mortal flesh. {4:12} So then death worketh in us, but **life** in you. {4:13} We having the same spirit of faith, according as it is written, I believed, and therefore have I spoken; we also believe, and therefore speak; {4:14} Knowing that **He** which raised up the **Lord Jesus** shall raise up us also by **Jesus**, and shall present [us] with you. {4:15} For all things [are] for your sakes, that the abundant grace might through the thanksgiving of many redound to the glory of **God**. {4:16} For which cause we faint not; but though our outward man perish, yet the inward [man] is renewed day by day. {4:17} For our light affliction, which is but for a moment, worketh for us a far more exceeding [and] eternal weight of glory; {4:18} While we look not at the things which are seen, but at the things which are not seen: for the things which are seen [are] temporal; but the things which are not seen [are] eternal. {21}

{5:1} For we know that if our earthly house of [this] tabernacle were dissolved, we have a building of **God**, an house not made with hands, eternal in the heavens. {5:2} For in this we groan, earnestly desiring to be clothed upon with our house which is from heaven: {5:3} If so be that being clothed we shall not be found naked. {5:4} For we that are in [this] tabernacle do groan, being burdened: not for that we would be unclothed, but clothed upon, that mortality might be swallowed up of life. {5:5} Now **He** that hath wrought us for the selfsame thing [is] **God**, who also hath given unto us the earnest of the Spirit. {5:6} Therefore [we are] always confident, knowing that, whilst we are at home in the body, we are absent from the **Lord**: {5:7} (For we walk by faith, not by sight:) {5:8} We are confident, [I say,] and willing rather to be absent from the body, and to be present with the **Lord**. {5:9} Wherefore we labour, that, whether present or absent, we may be accepted of **Him**. {5:10} For we must all appear before the judgment seat of **Christ**; that every one may receive the things [done] in [**His**] body, according to that He hath done, whether [it be] good or bad.

{5:11} Knowing therefore the terror of the **Lord**, we persuade men; but we are made manifest unto **God**; and I trust also are made manifest in your consciences. {5:12} For we commend not ourselves again unto you, but give you occasion to glory on our behalf, that ye may have somewhat to [answer] them which glory in appearance, and not in heart. {5:13} For whether we be beside ourselves, [it is] to **God**: or whether we be sober, [it is] for your cause. {5:14} For the love of **Christ** constraineth us; because we thus judge, that if **one** died for all, then were all dead: {5:15} And [that] **He** died for all, that they which live should not henceforth live unto themselves, but unto **Him** which died for them, and rose again. {5:16} Wherefore henceforth know we no man after the flesh: yea, though we have known **Christ** after the flesh, yet now henceforth know we [**Him**] no more. {5:17} Therefore if any man [be] in **Christ**, [**He** is] a new creature: old things are passed away; behold, all things are become new. {5:18} And all things [are] of **God**, who hath reconciled us to himself by **Jesus Christ**, and hath given to us the ministry of reconciliation; {5:19} To wit, that **God** was in **Christ**, reconciling the world unto **himself**, not imputing their trespasses unto them; and hath committed unto us the word of reconciliation. {5:20} Now then we are ambassadors for **Christ**, as though **God** did beseech [you] by us: we pray [you] in **Christ**'s stead, be ye reconciled to **God**. {5:21} For **He** hath made **Him** [to be] sin for us, who knew no sin; that we might be made the righteousness of **God** in **Him**. {19} {6:1} We then, [as] workers together [with **Him**,] beseech [you] also that ye receive not the grace of **God** in vain. {6:2} (For **He** saith, **I** have heard thee in a time accepted, and in the day of salvation have **I** succoured thee: behold, now [is] the accepted time; behold, now [is] the day of salvation.) {6:3} Giving no offence in any thing, that the ministry be not blamed: {6:4} But in all [things] approving ourselves as the ministers of **God**, in much patience, in afflictions, in necessities, in distresses, {6:5} In stripes, in imprisonments, in tumults, in labours, in watchings, in fastings; {6:6} By pureness, by knowledge, by longsuffering, by kindness, by the **Holy Ghost**, by love unfeigned, {6:7} By the **word of truth**, by the power of **God**, by the armour of righteousness on the right hand and on the left, {6:8} By honour and dishonour, by evil report and good report: as deceivers, and [yet] true; {6:9} As unknown, and [yet] well known; as dying, and, behold, we live; as chastened, and not killed; {6:10} As sorrowful, yet alway rejoicing; as poor, yet making many rich; as having nothing, and [yet] possessing all things. {6:11} O [ye] Corinthians, our mouth is open unto you, our heart is enlarged. {6:12} Ye are not straitened in us, but ye are straitened in your own bowels. {6:13} Now for a recompence in the same, (**I** speak as unto [**my**] children,) be ye also enlarged. {6:14} Be ye not unequally yoked together with unbelievers: for what fellowship hath righteousness with unrighteousness? and what communion hath **light** with darkness? {6:15} And what concord hath **Christ** with Belial? or what part hath **He** that believeth with an infidel? {6:16} And what agreement hath the temple of **God** with idols? for ye are the temple of the living **God**; as **God** hath said, **I** will dwell in them, and walk in [them;] and **I** will be their **God**, and they shall be **my** people. {6:17} Wherefore come out from among them, and be ye separate, saith the **Lord**, and touch not the unclean [thing;] and **I** will receive you, {6:18} And will be a **Father** unto you, and ye shall be **my** sons and daughters, saith the **Lord Almighty.**{8}
{7:1} Having therefore these promises, dearly beloved, let

us cleanse ourselves from all filthiness of the flesh and spirit, perfecting holiness in the fear of **God**.

{7:2} Receive us; we have wronged no man, we have corrupted no man, we have defrauded no man. {7:3} I speak not [this] to condemn [you:] for I have said before, that ye are in our hearts to die and live with [you.]{7:4} Great [is] my boldness of speech toward you, great [is] my glorying of you: I am filled with comfort, I am exceeding joyful in all our tribulation. {7:5} For, when we were come into Macedonia, our flesh had no rest, but we were troubled on every side; without [were] fightings, within [were] fears. {7:6} Nevertheless God, that comforteth those that are cast down, comforted us by the coming of Titus; {7:7} And not by His coming only, but by the consolation wherewith He was comforted in you, when He told us your earnest desire, your mourning, your fervent mind toward me; so that I rejoiced the more. {7:8} For though I made you sorry with a letter, I do not repent, though I did repent: for I perceive that the same epistle hath made you sorry, though [it were] but for a season. {7:9} Now I rejoice, not that ye were made sorry, but that ye sorrowed to repentance: for ye were made sorry after a **God**ly manner, that ye might receive damage by us in nothing. {7:10} For **God**ly sorrow worketh repentance to salvation not to be repented of: but the sorrow of the world worketh death. {7:11} For behold this selfsame thing, that ye sorrowed after a **God**ly sort, what carefulness it wrought in you, yea, [what] clearing of yourselves, yea, [what] indignation, yea, [what] fear, yea, [what] vehement desire, yea, [what] zeal, yea, [what] revenge! In all [things] ye have approved yourselves to be clear in this matter. {7:12} Wherefore, though I wrote unto you, [I did it] not for his cause that had done the wrong, nor for his cause that suffered wrong, but that our care for you in the sight of **God** might appear unto you. {7:13} Therefore we were comforted in your comfort: yea, and exceedingly the more joyed we for the joy of Titus, because his spirit was refreshed by you all. {7:14} For if I have boasted any thing to him of you, I am not ashamed; but as we spake all things to you in truth, even so our boasting, which [I made] before Titus, is found a truth. {7:15} And his inward affection is more abundant toward you, whilst He remembereth the obedience of you all, how with fear and trembling ye received Him. {7:16} I rejoice therefore that I have confidence in you in all [things].

{8:1} Moreover, brethren, we do you to wit of the grace of **God** bestowed on the churches of Macedonia; {8:2} How that in a great trial of affliction the abundance of their joy and their deep poverty abounded unto the riches of their liberality. {8:3} For to [their] power, I bear record, yea, and beyond [their] power [they were] willing of themselves; {8:4} Praying us with much intreaty that we would receive the gift, and [take upon us] the fellowship of the ministering to the saints. {8:5} And [this they did,] not as we hoped, but first gave their own selves to the **Lord**, and unto us by the will of **God**. {8:6} Insomuch that we desired Titus, that as he had begun, so he would also finish in you the same grace also. {8:7} Therefore, as ye abound in every [thing, in] faith, and utterance, and knowledge, and [in] all diligence, and [in] your love to us, [see] that ye abound in this grace also. {8:8} I speak not by commandment, but by occasion of the forwardness of others, and to prove the sincerity of your love. {8:9} For ye know the grace of our **Lord Jesus Christ**, that, though **He** was rich, yet for your sakes **He** became poor, that ye through **His** poverty might be rich. {8:10} And herein I give [my] advice: for this is expedient for you, who have begun before, not only to do, but also to be forward a year ago. {8:11} Now therefore perform the

doing [of it;] that as [there was] a readiness to will, so [there may be] a performance also out of that which ye have. {8:12} For if there be first a willing mind, [it is] accepted according to that a man hath, [and] not according to that he hath not. {8:13} For [I mean] not that other men be eased, and ye burdened: {8:14} But by an equality, [that] now at this time your abundance [may be a supply] for their want, that their abundance also may be [a supply] for your want: that there may be equality: {8:15} As it is written, he that [had gathered] much had nothing over; and He that [had gathered] little had no lack. {8:16} But thanks [be] to God, which put the same earnest care into the heart of Titus for you. {8:17} For indeed he accepted the exhortation; but being more forward, of his own accord he went unto you. {8:18} And we have sent with him the brother, whose praise is in the Gospel throughout all the churches; {8:19} And not [that] only, but who was also chosen of the churches to travel with us with this grace, which is administered by us to the glory of the same **Lord**, and [declaration of] your ready mind: {8:20} Avoiding this, that no man should blame us in this abundance which is administered by us: {8:21} Providing for honest things, not only in the sight of the **Lord**, but also in the sight of men. {8:22} And we have sent with them our brother, whom we have oftentimes proved diligent in many things, but now much more diligent, upon the great confidence which [I have] in you. {8:23} Whether [any do enquire] of Titus, [he is] my partner and fellowhelper concerning you: or our brethren [be enquired of, they are] the messengers of the churches, [and] the glory of **Christ**. {8:24} Wherefore shew ye to them, and before the churches, the proof of your love, and of our boasting on your behalf. **{10}**

{9:1} For as touching the ministering to the saints, it is superfluous for me to write to you: {9:2} For I know the forwardness of your mind, for which I boast of you to them of Macedonia, that Achaia was ready a year ago; and your zeal hath provoked very many. {9:3} Yet have I sent the brethren, lest our boasting of you should be in vain in this behalf; that, as I said, ye may be ready: {9:4} Lest haply if they of Macedonia come with me, and find you unprepared, we (that we say not, ye) should be ashamed in this same confident boasting. {9:5} Therefore I thought it necessary to exhort the brethren, that they would go before unto you, and make up beforehand your bounty, whereof ye had notice before, that the same might be ready, as [a matter of] bounty, and not as [of] covetousness. {9:6} But this [I say,] he which soweth sparingly shall reap also sparingly; and he which soweth bountifully shall reap also bountifully. {9:7} Every man according as he purposeth in his heart, [so let him give;] not grudgingly, or of necessity: for **God** loveth a cheerful giver. {9:8} And **God** [is] able to make all grace abound toward you; that ye, always having all sufficiency in all [things,] may abound to every good work: {9:9} (As it is written, **He** hath dispersed abroad; **He** hath given to the poor: **His** righteousness remaineth for ever. {9:10} Now **He** that ministereth seed to the sower both minister bread for [your] food, and multiply your seed sown, and increase the fruits of your righteousness;) {9:11} Being enriched in every thing to all bountifulness, which causeth through us thanksgiving to **God**. {9:12} For the administration of this service not only supplieth the want of the saints, but is abundant also by many thanksgivings unto **God**; {9:13} Whiles by the experiment of this ministration they glorify **God** for your professed subjection into the Gospel of **Christ**, and for [your] liberal distribution unto them, and unto all [men;]{9:14} And by their prayer for you, which long after you for the exceeding grace of **God** in you. {9:15} Thanks [be] unto **God** for **His** unspeakable gift.

{6}

{10:1} Now I Paul myself beseech you by the meekness and gentleness of **Christ**, who in presence [am] base among you, but being absent am bold toward you: {10:2} But I beseech [you,] that I may not be bold when I am present with that confidence, wherewith I think to be bold against some, which think of us as if we walked according to the flesh. {10:3} For though we walk in the flesh, we do not war after the flesh: {10:4} (For the weapons of our warfare [are] not carnal, but mighty through **God** to the pulling down of strong holds;) {10:5} Casting down imaginations, and every high thing that exalteth itself against the knowledge of **God**, and bringing into captivity every thought to the obedience of **Christ**; {10:6} And having in a readiness to revenge all disobedience, when your obedience is fulfilled. {10:7} Do ye look on things after the outward appearance? If any man trust to himself that he is **Christ**'s, let him of himself think this again, that, as he [is] **Christ**'s, even so [are] we **Christ**'s. {10:8} For though I should boast somewhat more of our authority, which the **Lord** hath given us for edification, and not for your destruction, I should not be ashamed: {10:9} That I may not seem as if I would terrify you by letters. {10:10} For [his] letters, say they, [are] weighty and powerful; but [his] bodily presence [is] weak, and [his] speech contemptible. {10:11} Let such an one think this, that, such as we are in word by letters when we are absent, such [will we be] also in deed when we are present. {10:12} For we dare not make ourselves of the number, or compare ourselves with some that commend themselves: but they measuring themselves by themselves, and comparing themselves among themselves, are not wise. {10:13} But we will not boast of things without [our] measure, but according to the measure of the rule which **God** hath distributed to us, a measure to reach even unto you. {10:14} For we stretch not ourselves beyond [our measure,] as though we reached not unto you: for we are come as far as to you also in [preaching] the Gospel of **Christ**: {10:15} Not boasting of things without [our] measure, [that is,] of other men's labours; but having hope, when your faith is increased, that we shall be enlarged by you according to our rule abundantly, {10:16} To preach the Gospel in the [regions] beyond you, [and] not to boast in another man's line of things made ready to our hand. {10:17} But he that glorieth, let him glory in the **Lord**. {10:18} For not he that commendeth himself is approved, but whom the **Lord** commendeth. {10}

{11:1} Would to **God** ye could bear with me a little in [my] folly: and indeed bear with me. {11:2} For I am jealous over you with **God**ly jealousy: for I have espoused you to one husband, that I may present [you as] a chaste virgin to **Christ**. {11:3} But I fear, lest by any means, as the serpent beguiled Eve through his subtilty, so your minds should be corrupted from the simplicity that is in **Christ**. {11:4} For if he that cometh preacheth another **Jesus**, whom we have not preached, or [if] ye receive another spirit, which ye have not received, or another Gospel, which ye have not accepted, ye might well bear with [him.]{11:5} For I suppose I was not a whit behind the very chiefest apostles. {11:6} But though [I be] rude in speech, yet not in knowledge; but we have been throughly made manifest among you in all things. {11:7} Have I committed an offence in abasing myself that ye might be exalted, because I have preached to you the Gospel of **God** freely? {11:8} I robbed other churches, taking wages [of them,] to do you service. {11:9} And when I was present with you, and wanted, I was chargeable to no man: for that which was lacking to me the brethren which came from Macedonia supplied: and in all [things] I have kept myself from being burdensome unto you, and so will I keep [myself.]{11:10}

As the truth of **Christ** is in me, no man shall stop me of this boasting in the regions of Achaia. {11:11} Wherefore? because I love you not? God knoweth. {11:12} But what I do, that I will do, that I may cut off occasion from them which desire occasion; that wherein they glory, they may be found even as we. {11:13} For such [are] false apostles, deceitful workers, transforming themselves into the apostles of **Christ**. {11:14} And no marvel; for Satan himself is transformed into an angel of light. {11:15} Therefore [it is] no great thing if his ministers also be transformed as the ministers of righteousness; whose end shall be according to their works.

{11:16} I say again, Let no man think me a fool; if otherwise, yet as a fool receive me, that I may boast myself a little. {11:17} That which I speak, I speak [it] not after the **Lord**, but as it were foolishly, in this confidence of boasting. {11:18} Seeing that many glory after the flesh, I will glory also. {11:19} For ye suffer fools gladly, seeing ye [yourselves] are wise. {11:20} For ye suffer, if a man bring you into bondage, if a man devour [you,] if a man take [of you,] if a man exalt himself, if a man smite you on the face. {11:21} I speak as concerning reproach, as though we had been weak. Howbeit whereinsoever any is bold, (I speak foolishly,) I am bold also. {11:22} Are they Hebrews? so [am] I. Are they Israelites? so [am] I. Are they the seed of Abraham? so [am] I. {11:23} Are they ministers of **Christ**? (I speak as a fool) I [am] more; in labours more abundant, in stripes above measure, in prisons more frequent, in deaths oft. {11:24} Of the Jews five times received I forty [stripes] save one. {11:25} Thrice was I beaten with rods, once was I stoned, thrice I suffered shipwreck, a night and a day I have been in the deep; {11:26} [In] journeyings often, [in] perils of waters, [in] perils of robbers, [in] perils by [mine own] countrymen, [in] perils by the heathen, [in] perils in the city, [in] perils in the wilderness, [in] perils in the sea, [in] perils among false brethren; {11:27} In weariness and painfulness, in watchings often, in hunger and thirst, in fastings often, in cold and nakedness. {11:28} Beside those things that are without, that which cometh upon me daily, the care of all the churches. {11:29} Who is weak, and I am not weak? who is offended, and I burn not? {11:30} If I must needs glory, I will glory of the things which concern mine infirmities. {11:31} The **God** and **Father** of our **Lord Jesus Christ**, which is blessed for evermore, knoweth that I lie not. {11:32} In Damascus the governor under Aretas the king kept the city of the Damascenes with a garrison, desirous to apprehend me: {11:33} And through a window in a basket was I let down by the wall, and escaped his hands.

{13}

{12:1} It is not expedient for me doubtless to glory. I will come to visions and revelations of the **Lord**. {12:2} I knew a man in **Christ** above fourteen years ago, (whether in the body, I cannot tell; or whether out of the body, I cannot tell: God knoweth;) such an one caught up to the third heaven. {12:3} And I knew such a man, (whether in the body, or out of the body, I cannot tell: God knoweth;) {12:4} How that he was caught up into paradise, and heard unspeakable words, which it is not lawful for a man to utter. {12:5} Of such an one will I glory: yet of myself I will not glory, but in mine infirmities. {12:6} For though I would desire to glory, I shall not be a fool; for I will say the truth: but [now] I forbear, lest any man should think of me above that which he seeth me [to be,] or [that] He heareth of me. {12:7} And lest I should be exalted above measure through the abundance of the revelations, there was given to me a thorn in the flesh, the messenger of Satan to buffet me, lest I should be exalted above measure. {12:8} For this thing I besought the **Lord** thrice, that it might depart from **me**. {12:9} And **He** said unto **me**, **my** grace is sufficient for thee: for **my** strength is made perfect in weakness. Most gladly therefore will I rather glory in my infirmities, that the power of **Christ** may rest upon me. {12:10} Therefore I take pleasure in infirmities, in reproaches, in necessities, in persecutions, in distresses for **Christ**'s sake: for when I am weak, then am I strong.

{12:11} I am become a fool in glorying; ye have compelled me: for I ought to have been commended of you: for in nothing am I behind the very chiefest apostles, though I be nothing. {12:12} Truly the signs of an apostle were wrought among you in all patience, in signs, and wonders, and mighty deeds. {12:13} For what is it wherein ye were inferior to other churches, except [it be] that I myself was not burdensome to you? forgive me this wrong. {12:14} Behold, the third time I am ready to come to you; and I will not be burdensome to you: for I seek not yours, but you: for the children ought not to lay up for the parents, but the parents for the children. {12:15} And I will very gladly spend and be spent for you; though the more abundantly I love you, the less I be loved. {12:16} But be it so, I did not burden you: nevertheless, being crafty, I caught you with guile. {12:17} Did I make a gain of you by any of them whom I sent unto you? {12:18} I desired Titus, and with [him] I sent a brother. Did Titus make a gain of you? walked we not in the same spirit? [walked we] not in the same steps? {12:19} Again, think ye that we excuse ourselves unto you? we speak before **God** in **Christ**: but [we do] all things, dearly beloved, for your edifying. {12:20} For I fear, lest, when I come, I shall not find you such as I would, and [that] I shall be found unto you such as ye would not: lest [there be] debates, envyings, wraths, strifes, backbitings, whisperings, swellings, tumults: {12:21} [And] lest, when I come again, my God will humble me among you, and [that] I shall bewail many which have sinned already, and have not repented of the uncleanness and fornication and lasciviousness which they have committed. **{1}**

{13:1} This [is] the third [time] I am coming to you. In the mouth of two or three witnesses shall every word be established. {13:2} I told you before, and foretell you, as if I were present, the second time; and being absent now I write to them which heretofore have sinned, and to all other, that, if I come again, I will not spare: {13:3} Since ye seek a proof of **Christ** speaking in me, which to you-ward is not weak, but is mighty in you. {13:4} For though **He** was crucified through weakness, yet **He** **liveth** by the power of **God**. For we also are weak in him, but we shall live with **Him** by the power of **God** toward you. {13:5} Examine yourselves, whether ye be in the faith; prove your own selves. Know ye not your own selves, how that **Jesus Christ** is in you, except ye be reprobates? {13:6} But I trust that ye shall know that we are not reprobates. {13:7} Now I pray to God that ye do no evil; not that we should appear approved, but that ye should do that which is honest, though we be as reprobates. {13:8} For we can do nothing against the truth, but for the truth. {13:9} For we are glad, when we are weak, and ye are strong: and this also we wish, [even] your perfection. {13:10} Therefore I write these things being absent, lest being present I should use sharpness, according to the power which the Lord hath given **me** to edification, and not to destruction.

{13:11} Finally, brethren, farewell. Be perfect, be of good comfort, be of one mind, live in peace; and the **God** of love and peace shall be with you. {13:12} Greet one another with an holy kiss.

{13:13} All the saints salute you. {13:14} The grace of the **Lord** **Jesus** **Christ**, and the love of **God**, and the communion of the **Holy Ghost**, [be] with you all. Amen.

{10}

The Epistle of Paul the Apostle to the Galatians **TOTAL 116**

{1:1} Paul, an apostle, (not of men, neither by man, but by **Jesus Christ**, and **God** the **Father**, who raised **Him** from the dead;) {1:2} And all the brethren which are with me, unto the churches of Galatia: {1:3} Grace [be] to you and peace from **God** the **Father**, and [from] our **Lord Jesus Christ**, {1:4} Who gave **himself** for our sins, that **He** might deliver us from this present evil world, according to the will of **God** and our **Father**: {1:5} To **whom** [be] glory for ever and ever. Amen.

{1:6} I marvel that ye are so soon removed from **Him** that called you into the grace of **Christ** unto another Gospel: {1:7} Which is not another; but there be some that trouble you, and would pervert the Gospel of **Christ**. {1:8} But though we, or an angel from heaven, preach any other Gospel unto you than that which we have preached unto you, let **Him** be accursed. {1:9} As we said before, so say I now again, If any [man] preach any other Gospel unto you than that ye have received, let **Him** be accursed.

{1:10} For do I now persuade men, or God? or do I seek to please men? for if I yet pleased men, I should not be the servant of **Christ**. {1:11} But I certify you, brethren, that the Gospel which was preached of me is not after man. {1:12} For I neither received it of man, neither was I taught [it,] but by the revelation of **Jesus Christ**. {1:13} For ye have heard of my conversation in time past in the Jews' religion, how that beyond measure I persecuted the church of God, and wasted it: {1:14} And profited in the Jews' religion above many my equals in mine own nation, being more exceedingly zealous of the traditions of my Fathers. {1:15} But when it pleased **God**, who separated me from my mother's womb, and called [me] by **His** grace, {1:16} To reveal **His Son** in me, that I might preach **Him** among the heathen; immediately I conferred not with flesh and blood: {1:17} Neither went I up to Jerusalem to them which were apostles before me; but I went into Arabia, and returned again unto Damascus. {1:18} Then after three years I went up to Jerusalem to see Peter, and abode with **Him** fifteen days. {1:19} But other of the apostles saw I none, save James the **Lord's** brother. {1:20} Now the things which I write unto you, behold, before God, I lie not. {1:21} Afterwards I came into the regions of Syria and Cilicia; {1:22} And was unknown by face unto the churches of Judaea which were in **Christ**: {1:23} But they had heard only, That he which persecuted us in times past now preacheth the faith which once he destroyed. {1:24} And they glorified God in me. **{20}**

{2:1} Then fourteen years after I went up again to Jerusalem with Barnabas, and took Titus with [me] also. {2:2} And I went up by revelation, and communicated unto them that Gospel which I preach among the Gentiles, but privately to them which were of reputation, lest by any means I should run, or had run, in vain. {2:3} But neither Titus, who was with me, being a Greek, was compelled to be circumcised: {2:4} And that because of false brethren unawares brought in, who came in privily to spy out our liberty which we have in **Christ Jesus**, that they might bring us into bondage: {2:5} To whom we gave place by subjection, no, not for an hour; that the truth of the Gospel might continue with you. {2:6} But of these who seemed to be somewhat, (whatsoever they were, it maketh no matter to me: God accepteth no man's person:) for they who seemed [to be somewhat] in conference added nothing to me: {2:7}

But contrariwise, when they saw that the Gospel of the uncircumcision was committed unto me, as [the Gospel] of the circumcision [was] unto Peter; {2:8} (For **He** that wrought effectually in Peter to the apostleship of the circumcision, the same was mighty in me toward the Gentiles:) {2:9} And when James, Cephas, and John, who seemed to be pillars, perceived the grace that was given unto me, they gave to me and Barnabas the right hands of fellowship; that we [should go] unto the heathen, and they unto the circumcision. {2:10} Only [they would] that we should remember the poor; the same which I also was forward to do. {2:11} But when Peter was come to Antioch, I withstood him to the face, because he was to be blamed. {2:12} For before that certain came from James, he did eat with the Gentiles: but when they were come, he withdrew and separated himself, fearing them which were of the circumcision. {2:13} And the other Jews dissembled likewise with him; insomuch that Barnabas also was carried away with their dissimulation. {2:14} But when I saw that they walked not uprightly according to the truth of the Gospel, I said unto Peter before [them] all, If thou, being a Jew, livest after the manner of Gentiles, and not as do the Jews, why compellest thou the Gentiles to live as do the Jews? {2:15} We [who are] Jews by nature, and not sinners of the Gentiles, {2:16} Knowing that a man is not justified by the works of the law, but by the faith of **Jesus Christ**, even we have believed in **Jesus Christ**, that we might be justified by the faith of **Christ**, and not by the works of the law: for by the works of the law shall no flesh be justified. {2:17} But if, while we seek to be justified by **Christ**, we ourselves also are found sinners, [is] therefore **Christ** the minister of sin? **God** forbid. {2:18} For if I build again the things which I destroyed, I make myself a transgressor. {2:19} For I through the law am dead to the law, that I might live unto God. {2:20} I am crucified with **Christ**: nevertheless **I** live; yet not **I**, but **Christ** liveth in **me**: and the life which **I** now live in the flesh **I** live by the faith of the **Son of God**, who loved **me**, and gave **himself** for **me**. {2:21} I do not frustrate the grace of **God**: for if righteousness [come] by the law, then **Christ** is dead in vain. **{20}**

{3:1} O foolish Galatians, who hath bewitched you, that ye should not obey the truth, before whose eyes **Jesus Christ** hath been evidently set forth, crucified among you? {3:2} This only would I learn of you, Received ye the Spirit by the works of the law, or by the hearing of faith? {3:3} Are ye so foolish? having begun in the Spirit, are ye now made perfect by the flesh? {3:4} Have ye suffered so many things in vain? if [it be] yet in vain. {3:5} he therefore that ministereth to you the Spirit, and worketh miracles among you, [doeth he it] by the works of the law, or by the hearing of faith? {3:6} Even as Abraham believed God, and it was accounted to him for righteousness. {3:7} Know ye therefore that they which are of faith, the same are the children of Abraham. {3:8} And the scripture, foreseeing that God would justify the heathen through faith, preached before the Gospel unto Abraham, [saying,] In thee shall all nations be blessed. {3:9} So then they which be of faith are blessed with faithful Abraham. {3:10} For as many as are of the works of the law are under the curse: for it is written, Cursed [is] every one that continueth not in all things which are written in the book of the law to do them. {3:11} But that no man is justified by the law in the sight of **God**, [it is] evident: for, The just shall live by faith. {3:12} And the law is not of faith: but, The man that doeth them shall live in them. {3:13} **Christ** hath redeemed us from the curse of the law, being made a curse for us: for it is written, Cursed [is] every one that hangeth on a tree: {3:14} That the blessing of Abraham might come on the Gentiles through **Jesus Christ**; that we might receive the promise of the Spirit through faith. {3:15} Brethren, I speak after the manner of men; Though [it be] but a man's covenant, yet [if it be] confirmed, no man disannulleth, or addeth thereto. {3:16} Now to Abraham and **His** seed were the promises made. **He** saith not, And to seeds, as of many; but as of **one**, And to **thy seed**, which is **Christ**. {3:17} And this I say, [that] the covenant, that was confirmed before of **God** in **Christ**, the law, which was four hundred and thirty years after, cannot disannul, that it should make the **promise** of none effect. {3:18} For if the inheritance [be] of the law, [it is] no more of **promise**: but **God** gave [it] to Abraham by **promise**. {3:19} Wherefore then [serveth] the law? It was added because of transgressions, till the **seed** should come to **whom** the promise was made; [and it was] ordained by angels in the hand of a mediator. {3:20} Now a mediator is not [a mediator] of one, but **God** is one. {3:21} [Is] the law then against the promises of **God**? **God** forbid: for if there had been a law given which could have given life, verily righteousness should have been by the law. {3:22} But the scripture hath concluded all under sin, that the **promise** by faith of **Jesus Christ** might be given to them that believe.

{3:23} But before faith came, we were kept under the law, shut up unto the faith which should afterwards be revealed. {3:24} Wherefore the law was our schoolmaster [to bring us] unto **Christ**, that we might be justified by faith. {3:25} But after that faith is come, we are no longer under a schoolmaster. {3:26} For ye are all the children of **God** by faith in **Christ Jesus**. {3:27} For as many of you as have been baptized into **Christ** have put on **Christ**. {3:28} There is neither Jew nor Greek, there is neither bond nor free, there is neither male nor female: for ye are all one in **Christ Jesus**. {3:29} And if ye [be] **Christ**'s, then are ye Abraham's **seed**, and heirs according to the **promise**. {29}

{4:1} Now I say, [That] the heir, as long as he is a child, differeth nothing from a servant, though he be Lord of all; {4:2} But is under tutors and governors until the time appointed of the **Father**. {4:3} Even so we, when we were children, were in bondage under the elements of the world: {4:4} But when the fulness of the time was come, **God** sent forth **His Son**, made of a woman, made under the law, {4:5} To redeem them that were under the law, that we might receive the adoption of sons. {4:6} And because ye are sons, **God** hath sent forth the **Spirit** of **His Son** into your hearts, crying, Abba, **Father**. {4:7} Wherefore thou art no more a servant, but a Son; and if a Son, then an heir of **God** through **Christ**.{4:8} Howbeit then, when ye knew not God, ye did service unto them which by nature are no Gods. {4:9} But now, after that ye have known God, or rather are known of God, how turn ye again to the weak and beggarly elements, whereunto ye desire again to be in bondage? {4:10} Ye observe days, and months, and times, and years. {4:11} I am afraid of you, lest I have bestowed upon you labour in vain.

{4:12} Brethren, I beseech you, be as I [am;] for I [am] as ye [are:] ye have not injured me at all. {4:13} Ye know how through infirmity of the flesh I preached the Gospel unto you at the first. {4:14} And my temptation which was in my flesh ye despised not, nor rejected; but received me as an angel of **God**, [even] as **Christ Jesus**. {4:15} Where is then the blessedness ye spake of? for I bear you record, that, if [it had been] possible, ye would have plucked out your own eyes, and have given them to me. {4:16} am I therefore

become your enemy, because I tell you the truth? {4:17} They zealously affect you, [but] not well; yea, they would exclude you, that ye might affect them. {4:18} But [it is] good to be zealously affected always in [a] good [thing,] and not only when I am present with you. {4:19} my little children, of whom I travail in birth again until **Christ** be formed in you, {4:20} I desire to be present with you now, and to change my voice; for I stand in doubt of you.

{4:21} Tell me, ye that desire to be under the law, do ye not hear the law? {4:22} For it is written, that Abraham had two sons, the one by a bondmaid, the other by a freewoman. {4:23} But he [who was] of the bondwoman was born after the flesh; but **He** of the freewoman [was] by **promise**. {4:24} Which things are an allegory: for these are the two covenants; the one from the mount Sinai, which gendereth to bondage, which is Agar. {4:25} For this Agar is mount Sinai in Arabia, and answereth to Jerusalem which now is, and is in bondage with her children. {4:26} But Jerusalem which is above is free, which is the mother of us all. {4:27} But it is written, Rejoice, [thou] barren that bearest not; break forth and cry, thou that travailest not: for the desolate hath many more children than she which hath an husband. {4:28} Now we, brethren, as Isaac was, are the children of **promise**. {4:29} But as then He that was born after the flesh persecuted **Him** [that was born] after the **Spirit**, even so [it is] now. {4:30} Nevertheless what saith the scripture? Cast out the bondwoman and her Son: for the Son of the bondwoman shall not be heir with the **Son** of the free woman. {4:31} So then, brethren, we are not children of the bondwoman, but of the free. {13}

{5:1} Stand fast therefore in the liberty wherewith **Christ** hath made us free, and be not entangled again with the yoke of bondage.{5:2} Behold, I Paul say unto you, that if ye be circumcised, **Christ** shall profit you nothing. {5:3} For I testify again to every man that is circumcised, that he is a debtor to do the whole law. {5:4} **Christ** is become of no effect unto you, whosoever of you are justified by the law; ye are fallen from grace. {5:5} For we through the **Spirit** wait for the hope of righteousness by faith. {5:6} For in **Jesus Christ** neither circumcision availeth any thing, nor uncircumcision; but faith which worketh by love. {5:7} Ye did run well; who did hinder you that ye should not obey the truth? {5:8} This persuasion [cometh] not of **Him** that calleth you. {5:9} A little leaven leaveneth the whole lump. {5:10} I have confidence in you through the **Lord**, that ye will be none otherwise minded: but he that troubleth you shall bear his judgment, whosoever he be. {5:11} And I, brethren, if I yet preach circumcision, why do I yet suffer persecution? then is the offence of the cross ceased. {5:12} I would they were even cut off which trouble you. {5:13} For, brethren, ye have been called unto liberty; only [use] not liberty for an occasion to the flesh, but by love serve one another. {5:14} For all the law is fulfilled in one word, [even] in this; Thou shalt love thy neighbour as thyself. {5:15} But if ye bite and devour one another, take heed that ye be not consumed one of another. {5:16} [This] I say then, Walk in the **Spirit**, and ye shall not fulfil the lust of the flesh. {5:17} For the flesh lusteth against the **Spirit**, and the **Spirit** against the flesh: and these are contrary the one to the other: so that ye cannot do the things that ye would. {5:18} But if ye be led of the **Spirit,** ye are not under the law. {5:19} Now the works of the flesh are manifest, which are [these;] Adultery, fornication, uncleanness, lasciviousness, {5:20} Idolatry, witchcraft, hatred, variance, emulations, wrath, strife, seditions, heresies, {5:21} Envyings, murders, drunkenness, revellings, and such like: of the which I tell you before, as I have also told [you] in time past, that they which do such things shall not inherit the kingdom of God. {5:22} But the fruit of the Spirit is love, joy, peace, longsuffering, gentleness, goodness, faith, {5:23} Meekness, temperance: against such there is no law. {5:24} And they that are Christ's have crucified the flesh with the affections and lusts. {5:25} If we live in the Spirit, let us also walk in the Spirit. {5:26} Let us not be desirous of vain glory, provoking one another, envying one another.

{6:1} Brethren, if a man be overtaken in a fault, ye which are spiritual, restore such an one in the spirit of meekness; considering thyself, lest thou also be tempted. {6:2} Bear ye one another's burdens, and so fulfil the law of Christ. {6:3} For if a man think himself to be something, when he is nothing, he deceiveth himself. {6:4} But let every man prove his own work, and then shall he have rejoicing in himself alone, and not in another. {6:5} For every man shall bear his own burden. {6:6} Let him that is taught in the word communicate unto him that teacheth in all good things. {6:7} Be not deceived; God is not mocked: for whatsoever a man soweth, that shall he also reap. {6:8} For he that soweth to his flesh shall of the flesh reap corruption; but he that soweth to the Spirit shall of the Spirit reap life everlasting. {6:9} And let us not be weary in well doing: for in due season we shall reap, if we faint not. {6:10} As we have therefore opportunity, let us do good unto all [men,] especially unto them who are of the household of faith. {6:11} Ye see how large a letter I have written unto you with mine own hand. {6:12} As many as desire to make a fair shew in the flesh, they constrain you to be circumcised; only lest they should suffer persecution for the cross of Christ. {6:13} For neither they themselves who are circumcised keep the law; but desire to have you circumcised, that they may glory in your flesh. {6:14} But God forbid that I should glory, save in the cross of our Lord Jesus Christ, by whom the world is crucified unto me, and I unto the world. {6:15} For in Christ Jesus neither circumcision availeth any thing, nor uncircumcision, but a new creature. {6:16} And as many as walk according to this rule, peace [be] on them, and mercy, and upon the Israel of God. {6:17} From henceforth let no man trouble me: for I bear in my body the marks of the Lord Jesus. {6:18} Brethren, the grace of our Lord Jesus Christ [be] with your spirit. Amen.
{3}

The Epistle of Paul the Apostle to the Ephesians **TOTAL 181**

{1:1} Paul, an apostle of **Jesus Christ** by the will of **God**, to the saints which are at Ephesus, and to the faithful in **Christ Jesus**: {1:2} Grace [be] to you, and peace, from **God** our **Father**, and [from] the **Lord Jesus Christ**.

{1:3} Blessed [be] the **God** and **Father** of our **Lord Jesus Christ**, who hath blessed us with all spiritual blessings in heavenly [places] in **Christ**: {1:4} According as **He** hath chosen us in **Him** before the foundation of the world, that we should be holy and without blame before **Him** in love: {1:5} Having predestinated us unto the adoption of children by **Jesus Christ** to himself, according to the good pleasure of **His** will, {1:6} To the praise of the glory of **His** grace, wherein **He** hath made us accepted in the **beloved**. {1:7} In **whom** we have redemption through **His** blood, the forgiveness of sins, according to the riches of **His** grace; {1:8} Wherein **He** hath abounded toward us in all wisdom and prudence; {1:9} Having made known unto us the mystery of **His** will, according to **His** good pleasure which **He** hath purposed in himself: {1:10} That in the dispensation of the fulness of times **He** might gather together in one all things in **Christ**, both which are in heaven, and which are on earth; [even] in **Him**: {1:11} In **whom** also we have obtained an inheritance, being predestinated according to the purpose of **Him** who worketh all things after the counsel of **His** own will: {1:12} That we should be to the praise of **His** glory, who first trusted in **Christ**. {1:13} In **whom** ye also [trusted,] after that ye heard the word of truth, the **Gospel** of your salvation: in **whom** also after that ye believed, ye were sealed with that holy Spirit of promise, {1:14} Which is the earnest of our inheritance until the redemption of the purchased possession, unto the praise of **His** glory. {1:15} Wherefore I also, after I heard of your faith in the **Lord Jesus**, and love unto all the saints, {1:16} Cease not to give thanks for you, making mention of you in **my** prayers; {1:17} That the **God** of our **Lord Jesus Christ**, the **Father** of glory, may give unto you the spirit of wisdom and revelation in the knowledge of **Him**: {1:18} The eyes of your understanding being enlightened; that ye may know what is the hope of **His** calling, and what the riches of the glory of **His** inheritance in the saints, {1:19} And what [is] the exceeding greatness of **His** power to us-ward who believe, according to the working of **His** mighty power, {1:20} Which **He** wrought in **Christ**, when **He** raised **Him** from the dead, and set [**Him**] at **His** own right hand in the heavenly [places,]{1:21} Far above all principality, and power, and might, and dominion, and every name that is named, not only in this world, but also in that which is to come: {1:22} And hath put all [things] under **His** feet, and gave **Him** [to be] the **head** over all [things] to the church, {1:23} Which is **His** body, the fulness of **Him** that filleth all in all.{41}

{2:1} And you [hath **He** quickened,] who were dead in trespasses and sins; {2:2} Wherein in time past ye walked according to the course of this world, according to the prince of the power of the air, the spirit that now worketh in the children of disobedience: {2:3} Among **whom** also we all had our conversation in times past in the lusts of our flesh, fulfilling the desires of the flesh and of the mind; and were by nature the children of wrath, even as others. {2:4} But **God**, who is rich in mercy, for **His** great love wherewith **He** loved us, {2:5} Even when we were dead in sins, hath quickened us together with **Christ**, (by grace ye are saved;)

{2:6} And hath raised [us] up together, and made [us] sit together in heavenly [places] in **Christ Jesus**: {2:7} That in the ages to come **He** might shew the exceeding riches of **His** grace in [**His**] kindness toward us through **Christ Jesus**. {2:8} For by grace are ye saved through faith; and that not of yourselves: [it is] the **gift** of **God**: {2:9} Not of works, lest any man should boast. {2:10} For we are **His** workmanship, created in **Christ Jesus** unto good works, which **God** hath before ordained that we should walk in them.{2:11} Wherefore remember, that ye [being] in time past Gentiles in the flesh, who are called Uncircumcision by that which is called the Circumcision in the flesh made by hands; {2:12} That at that time ye were without **Christ**, being aliens from the commonwealth of Israel, and strangers from the covenants of promise, having no hope, and without **God** in the world: {2:13} But now in **Christ Jesus** ye who sometimes were far off are made nigh by the **blood** of **Christ**. {2:14} For **He** is our peace, who hath made both one, and hath broken down the middle wall of partition [between us;]{2:15} Having abolished in **His flesh** the enmity, [even] the law of commandments [contained] in ordinances; for to make in **himself** of twain one new man, [so] making peace; {2:16} And that **He** might reconcile both unto **God** in one **body** by the cross, having slain the enmity thereby: {2:17} And came and preached peace to you which were afar off, and to them that were nigh. {2:18} For through **Him** we both have access by **one Spirit** unto the **Father**. {2:19} Now therefore ye are no more strangers and foreigners, but fellowcitizens with the saints, and of the household of **God**; {2:20} And are built upon the foundation of the apostles and prophets, **Jesus Christ himself** being the **chief corner** [**stone**;]{2:21} In **whom** all the building fitly framed together groweth unto an holy temple in the **Lord**: {2:22} In **whom** ye also are builded together for an habitation of **God** through the **Spirit**. {33}

{3:1} For this cause I Paul, the prisoner of **Jesus Christ** for you Gentiles, {3:2} If ye have heard of the dispensation of the grace of **God** which is given me to youward: {3:3} How that by revelation **He** made known unto me the mystery; (as I wrote afore in few words, {3:4} Whereby, when ye read, ye may understand my knowledge in the mystery of **Christ**) {3:5} Which in other ages was not made known unto the sons of men, as it is now revealed unto **His** holy apostles and prophets by the Spirit; {3:6} That the Gentiles should be fellowheirs, and of the same **body**, and partakers of **His promise** in **Christ** by the **Gospel**: {3:7} Whereof I was made a minister, according to the gift of the grace of **God** given unto me by the effectual working of **His** power. {3:8} Unto me, who am less than the least of all saints, is this grace given, that I should preach among the Gentiles the unsearchable riches of **Christ**; {3:9} And to make all [men] see what [is] the fellowship of the mystery, which from the beginning of the world hath been hid in **God**, who created all things by **Jesus Christ**: {3:10} To the intent that now unto the principalities and powers in heavenly [places] might be known by the church the **manifold wisdom** of **God**, {3:11} According to the eternal purpose which **He** purposed in **Christ Jesus** our **Lord**: {3:12} In **whom** we have boldness and access with confidence by the faith of **Him**. {3:13} Wherefore I desire that ye faint not at my tribulations for you, which is your glory. {3:14} For this cause I bow my knees unto the **Father** of our **Lord Jesus Christ**, {3:15} Of **whom** the whole family in heaven and earth is named, {3:16} That **He** would grant you, according to the riches of **His** glory, to be strengthened with might by **His Spirit** in the inner man; {3:17} That **Christ** may dwell in your hearts by faith; that ye, being rooted and grounded in love, {3:18} May be able to comprehend with all saints what [is] the breadth, and length, and depth, and height; {3:19} And to know the love of **Christ**, which passeth knowledge, that ye might be filled with all the fulness of **God**.{3:20} Now unto **Him** that is able to do exceeding abundantly above all that we ask or think, according to the power that worketh in us, {3:21} Unto **Him** [be] glory in the church by **Christ Jesus** throughout all ages, world without end. Amen. {25}

{4:1} I therefore, the prisoner of the **Lord**, beseech you that ye walk worthy of the vocation wherewith ye are called, {4:2} With all lowliness and meekness, with longsuffering, forbearing one another in love; {4:3} Endeavouring to keep the unity of the Spirit in the bond of peace. {4:4} [There is] one **body**, and one **Spirit**, even as ye are called in one hope of your calling; {4:5} One **Lord**, one faith, one baptism, {4:6} One **God** and **Father** of all, who [is] above all, and through all, and in you all. {4:7} But unto every one of us is given grace according to the measure of the **gift** of **Christ**. {4:8} Wherefore **He** saith, When **He** ascended up on high, **He** led captivity captive, and gave gifts unto men. {4:9} (Now that **He** ascended, what is it but that **He** also descended first into the lower parts of the earth? {4:10} **He** that descended is the same also that ascended up far above all heavens, that **He** might fill all things.) {4:11} And **He** gave some, apostles; and some, prophets; and some, evangelists; and some, pastors and teachers; {4:12} For the perfecting of the saints, for the work of the ministry, for the edifying of the **body** of **Christ**: {4:13} Till we all come in the unity of the faith, and of the knowledge of the **Son of God,** unto a perfect man, unto the measure of the stature of the fulness of **Christ**: {4:14} That we [henceforth] be no more children, tossed to and fro, and carried about with every wind of doctrine, by the sleight of men, [and] cunning craftiness, whereby they lie in wait to deceive; {4:15} But speaking the truth in love, may grow up into **Him** in all things, which is the **head**, [even] **Christ**: {4:16} From **whom** the whole body fitly joined together and compacted by that which every joint supplieth, according to the effectual working in the measure of every part, maketh increase of the **body** unto the edifying of itself in love.

{4:17} This I say therefore, and testify in the **Lord**, that ye henceforth walk not as other Gentiles walk, in the vanity of their mind, {4:18} Having the understanding darkened, being alienated from the **life** of **God** through the ignorance that is in them, because of the blindness of their heart: {4:19} Who being past feeling have given themselves over unto lasciviousness, to work all uncleanness with greediness. {4:20} But ye have not so learned **Christ**; {4:21} If so be that ye have heard **Him**, and have been taught by **Him**, as the truth is in **Jesus**: {4:22} That ye put off concerning the former conversation the old man, which is corrupt according to the deceitful lusts; {4:23} And be renewed in the spirit of your mind; {4:24} And that ye put on the **new man**, which after **God** is created in righteousness and true holiness.

{4:25} Wherefore putting away lying, speak every man truth with his neighbour: for we are members one of another. {4:26} Be ye angry, and sin not: let not the sun go down upon your wrath: {4:27} Neither give place to the devil. {4:28} Let him that stole steal no more: but rather let him labour, working with [his] hands the thing which is good, that he may have to give to him that needeth. {4:29}

Let no corrupt communication proceed out of your mouth, but that which is good to the use of edifying, that it may minister grace unto the hearers. {4:30} And grieve not the holy Spirit of **God**, whereby ye are sealed unto the day of redemption. {4:31} Let all bitterness, and wrath, and anger, and clamour, and evil speaking, be put away from you, with all malice: {4:32} And be ye kind one to another, tenderhearted, forgiving one another, even as **God** for **Christ's** sake hath forgiven you. {31}

{5:1} Be ye therefore followers of **God**, as dear children; {5:2} And walk in love, as **Christ** also hath loved us, and hath given **himself** for us an **offering** and a **sacrifice** to **God** for a sweetsmelling savour. {5:3} But fornication, and all uncleanness, or covetousness, let it not be once named among you, as becometh saints; {5:4} Neither filthiness, nor foolish talking, nor jesting, which are not convenient: but rather giving of thanks. {5:5} For this ye know, that no whoremonger, nor unclean person, nor covetous man, who is an idolater, hath any inheritance in the kingdom of **Christ** and of **God**. {5:6} Let no man deceive you with vain words: for because of these things cometh the wrath of **God** upon the children of disobedience. {5:7} Be not ye therefore partakers with them. {5:8} For ye were sometimes darkness, but now [are ye] light in the **Lord**: walk as children of light; {5:9} (For the fruit of the Spirit is in all goodness and righteousness and truth;) {5:10} Proving what is acceptable unto the **Lord**. {5:11} And have no fellowship with the unfruitful works of darkness, but rather reprove [them.]{5:12} For it is a shame even to speak of those things which are done of them in secret. {5:13} But all things that are reproved are made manifest by the light: for whatsoever doth make manifest is light. {5:14} Wherefore **He** saith, Awake thou that sleepest, and arise from the dead, and **Christ** shall give thee light. {5:15} See then that ye walk circumspectly, not as fools, but as wise, {5:16} Redeeming the time, because the days are evil. {5:17} Wherefore be ye not unwise, but understanding what the will of the **Lord** [is.]{5:18} And be not drunk with wine, wherein is excess; but be filled with the Spirit; {5:19} Speaking to yourselves in psalms and hymns and spiritual songs, singing and making melody in your heart to the **Lord**; {5:20} Giving thanks always for all things unto **God** and the **Father** in the **name** of our **Lord Jesus Christ**; {5:21} Submitting yourselves one to another in the fear of **God**. {5:22} Wives, submit yourselves unto your own husbands, as unto the **Lord**. {5:23} For the husband is the head of the wife, even as **Christ** is the **head** of the church: and **He** is the **Saviour** of the **body**. {5:24} Therefore as the church is subject unto **Christ**, so [let] the wives [be] to their own husbands in every thing. {5:25} Husbands, love your wives, even as **Christ** also loved the church, and gave **himself** for it; {5:26} That **He** might sanctify and cleanse it with the washing of water by the word, {5:27} That **He** might present it to **himself** a glorious church, not having spot, or wrinkle, or any such thing; but that it should be holy and without blemish. {5:28} So ought men to love their wives as their own bodies. He that loveth his wife loveth himself. {5:29} For no man ever yet hated his own flesh; but nourisheth and cherisheth it, even as the **Lord** the church: {5:30} For we are members of **His body**, of **His flesh**, and of **His bones**. {5:31} For this cause shall a man leave his Father and mother, and shall be joined unto his wife, and they two shall be one flesh. {5:32} This is a great mystery: but I speak concerning **Christ** and the church. {5:33} Nevertheless let every one of you in particular so love his wife even as himself; and the wife [see] that she reverence [her] husband. {34}   {6:1} Children, obey your parents in the **Lord**: for this is right. {6:2} Honour thy **Father** and mother; (which is the first commandment with promise;) {6:3} That it may be well with thee, and thou mayest live long on the earth. {6:4} And, ye **Father**s, provoke not your children to wrath: but bring them up in the nurture and admonition of the **Lord**. {6:5} Servants, be obedient to them that are [your] masters according to the flesh, with fear and trembling, in singleness of your heart, as unto **Christ**; {6:6} Not with eyeservice, as menpleasers; but as the servants of **Christ**, doing the will of **God** from the heart; {6:7} With good will doing service, as to the **Lord**, and not to men: {6:8} Knowing that whatsoever good thing any man doeth, the same shall he receive of the **Lord**, whether [he be] bond or free. {6:9} And, ye masters, do the same things unto them, forbearing threatening: knowing that your Master also is in heaven; neither is there respect of persons with **Him**.

{6:10} Finally, my brethren, be strong in the **Lord**, and in the power of **His** might. {6:11} Put on the whole armour of **God**, that ye may be able to stand against the wiles of the devil. {6:12} For we wrestle not against flesh and blood, but against principalities, against powers, against the rulers of the darkness of this world, against spiritual wickedness in high [places.]{6:13} Wherefore take unto you the whole armour of **God**, that ye may be able to withstand in the evil day, and having done all, to stand. {6:14} Stand therefore, having your loins girt about with truth, and having on the breastplate of righteousness; {6:15} And your feet shod with the preparation of the Gospel of peace; {6:16} Above all, taking the shield of faith, wherewith ye shall be able to quench all the fiery darts of the wicked. {6:17} And take the helmet of salvation, and the sword of the Spirit, which is the word of **God**: {6:18} Praying always with all prayer and supplication in the Spirit, and watching thereunto with all perseverance and supplication for all saints; {6:19} And for me, that utterance may be given unto me, that I may open my mouth boldly, to make known the mystery of the Gospel, {6:20} For which I am an ambassador in bonds: that therein I may speak boldly, as I ought to speak.

{6:21} But that ye also may know my affairs, [and] how I do, Tychicus, a beloved brother and faithful minister in the **Lord**, shall make known to you all things: {6:22} Whom I have sent unto you for the same purpose, that ye might know our affairs, and [that] He might comfort your hearts.

{6:23} Peace [be] to the brethren, and love with faith, from **God** the **Father** and the **Lord Jesus Christ**. {6:24} Grace [be] with all them that love our **Lord Jesus Christ** in sincerity. Amen.
{17}

The Epistle of Paul the Apostle to the Philippians
TOTAL 110

{1:1} Paul and Timotheus, the servants of **Jesus Christ**, to all the saints in **Christ Jesus** which are at Philippi, with the bishops and deacons: {1:2} Grace [be] unto you, and peace, from **God** our **Father**, and [from] the **Lord Christ**. {1:3} I thank my **God** upon every remembrance of you, {1:4} Always in every prayer of mine for you all making request with joy, {1:5} For your fellowship in the Gospel from the first day until now; {1:6} Being confident of this very thing, that **He** which hath begun a good work in you will perform [it] until the day of **Jesus Christ**: {1:7} Even as it is meet for **me** to think this of you all, because I have you in my heart; inasmuch as both in my bonds, and in the defence and confirmation of the Gospel, ye all are partakers of my grace. {1:8} For **God** is my record, how greatly I long after you all in the bowels of **Jesus Christ**. {1:9} And this I pray, that your love may abound yet more and more in knowledge and [in] all judgment; {1:10} That ye may approve things that are excellent; that ye may be sincere and without offence till the day of **Christ**; {1:11} Being filled with the fruits of righteousness, which are by **Jesus Christ**, unto the glory and praise of **God**.{1:12} But I would ye should understand, brethren, that the things [which happened] unto me have fallen out rather unto the furtherance of the Gospel; {1:13} So that my bonds in **Christ** are manifest in all the palace, and in all other [places;]{1:14} And many of the brethren in the **Lord**, waxing confident by my bonds, are much more bold to speak the word without fear. {1:15} Some indeed preach **Christ** even of envy and strife; and some also of good will: {1:16} The one preach **Christ** of contention, not sincerely, supposing to add affliction to my bonds: {1:17} But the other of love, knowing that I am set for the defence of the Gospel. {1:18} What then? notwithstanding, every way, whether in pretence, or in truth, **Christ** is preached; and I therein do rejoice, yea, and will rejoice. {1:19} For I know that this shall turn to my salvation through your prayer, and the supply of the **Spirit** of **Jesus Christ**, {1:20} According to my earnest expectation and [my] hope, that in nothing I shall be ashamed, but [that] with all boldness, as always, [so] now also **Christ** shall be magnified in my body, whether [it be] by life, or by death. {1:21} For to me to live [is] **Christ**, and to die [is] gain. {1:22} But if I live in the flesh, this [is] the fruit of my labour: yet what I shall choose I wot not. {1:23} For I am in a strait betwixt two, having a desire to depart, and to be with **Christ**; which is far better: {1:24} Nevertheless to abide in the flesh [is] more needful for you. {1:25} And having this confidence, I know that I shall abide and continue with you all for your furtherance and joy of faith; {1:26} That your rejoicing may be more abundant in **Jesus Christ** for me by my coming to you again. {1:27} Only let your conversation be as it becometh the Gospel of **Christ**: that whether I come and see you, or else be absent, I may hear of your affairs, that ye stand fast in one spirit, with one mind striving together for the faith of the Gospel; {1:28} And in nothing terrified by your adversaries: which is to them an evident token of perdition, but to you of salvation, and that of **God**. {1:29} For unto you it is given in the behalf of **Christ**, not only to believe on **Him**, but also to suffer for **His** sake; {1:30} Having the same conflict which ye saw in me, and now hear [to be] in me. {31}

{2:1} If [there be] therefore any consolation in **Christ**, if any comfort of love, if any fellowship of the **Spirit**, if any bowels and mercies, {2:2} Fulfil ye my joy, that ye be likeminded, having the same love, [being] of one accord, of one mind. {2:3} [Let] nothing [be done] through strife or vainglory; but in lowliness of mind let each esteem other better than themselves. {2:4} Look not every man on **His** own things, but every man also on the things of others. {2:5} Let this **mind** be in you, which was also in **Christ Jesus**: {2:6} Who, being in the form of **God**, thought it not robbery to be equal with **God**: {2:7} But made **himself** of no reputation, and took upon **Him** the form of a **servant**, and was made in the likeness of men: {2:8} And being found in fashion as a **man**, **He** humbled **himself**, and became obedient unto death, even the death of the cross. {2:9} Wherefore **God** also hath highly exalted **Him**, and given **Him** a **name** which is above every **name**: {2:10} That at the **name** of **Jesus** every knee should bow, of [things] in heaven, and [things] in earth, and [things] under the earth; {2:11} And [that] every tongue should confess that **Jesus Christ** [is] **Lord**, to the glory of **God** the **Father**.

{2:12} Wherefore, my beloved, as ye have always obeyed, not as in my presence only, but now much more in my absence, work out your own salvation with fear and trembling. {2:13} For it is God which worketh in you both to will and to do of [His] good pleasure. {2:14} Do all things without murmurings and disputings: {2:15} That ye may be blameless and harmless, the sons of God, without rebuke, in the midst of a crooked and perverse nation, among whom ye shine as lights in the world; {2:16} Holding forth the **word of life**; that I may rejoice in the day of **Christ**, that I have not run in vain, neither laboured in vain. {2:17} Yea, and if I be offered upon the sacrifice and service of your faith, I joy, and rejoice with you all. {2:18} For the same cause also do ye joy, and rejoice with me.

{2:19} But I trust in the **Lord Jesus** to send Timotheus shortly unto you, that I also may be of good comfort, when I know your state. {2:20} For I have no man likeminded, who will naturally care for your state. {2:21} For all seek their own, not the things which are **Jesus Christ's**. {2:22} But ye know the proof of him, that, as a **Son** with the Father, he hath served with me in the Gospel. {2:23} Him therefore I hope to send presently, so soon as I shall see how it will go with me. {2:24} But I trust in the **Lord** that I also myself shall come shortly. {2:25} Yet I supposed it necessary to send to you Epaphroditus, my brother, and companion in labour, and fellow soldier, but your messenger, and he that ministered to my wants. {2:26} For he longed after you all, and was full of heaviness, because that ye had heard that he had been sick. {2:27} For indeed he was sick nigh unto death: but God had mercy on him; and not on him only, but on me also, lest I should have sorrow upon sorrow. {2:28} I sent him therefore the more carefully, that, when ye see him again, ye may rejoice, and that I may be the less sorrowful. {2:29} Receive him therefore in the **Lord** with all gladness; and hold such in reputation: {2:30} Because for the work of **Christ he** was nigh unto death, not regarding his life, to supply your lack of service toward **me**. {30}

{3:1} Finally, my brethren, rejoice in the **Lord**. To write the same things to you, to me indeed [is] not grievous, but for you [it is] safe.{3:2} Beware of dogs, beware of evil workers, beware of the concision. {3:3} For we are the circumcision, which worship **God** in the spirit, and rejoice in **Christ Jesus**, and have no confidence in the flesh. {3:4} Though I might also have confidence in the flesh. If any other man thinketh that he hath whereof he might trust in the flesh, I more: {3:5} Circumcised the eighth day, of the stock of Israel, [of] the tribe of Benjamin, an Hebrew of the Hebrews; as touching the law, a Pharisee; {3:6} Concerning zeal, persecuting the church; touching the righteousness which is in the law, blameless. {3:7} But what things were gain to me, those I counted loss for **Christ**. {3:8} Yea doubtless, and I count all things [but] loss for the excellency of the knowledge of **Christ Jesus my Lord**: for whom I have suffered the loss of all things, and do count them [but] dung, that I may win **Christ**, {3:9} And be found in **Him**, not having mine own righteousness, which is of the law, but that which is through the faith of **Christ**, the righteousness which is of **God** by faith: {3:10} That I may know **Him**, and the power of **His resurrection**, and the fellowship of **His** sufferings, being made conformable unto **His** death; {3:11} If by any means I might attain unto the **resurrection** of the dead. {3:12} Not as though I had already attained, either were already perfect: but I follow after, if that I may apprehend that for which also I am apprehended of **Christ Jesus**. {3:13} Brethren, I count not myself to have apprehended: but [this] one thing [I do,] forgetting those things which are behind, and reaching forth unto those things which are before, {3:14} I press toward the mark for the prize of the high calling of **God** in **Christ Jesus**. {3:15} Let us therefore, as many as be perfect, be thus minded: and if in any thing ye be otherwise minded, **God** shall reveal even this unto you. {3:16} Nevertheless, whereto we have already attained, let us walk by the same rule, let us mind the same thing. {3:17} Brethren, be followers together of me, and mark them which walk so as ye have us for an ensample. {3:18} (For many walk, of whom I have told you often, and now tell you even weeping, [that they are] the enemies of the cross of **Christ**: {3:19} Whose end [is] destruction, whose **God** [is their] belly, and [whose] glory [is] in their shame, who mind earthly things.) {3:20} For our conversation is in heaven; from whence also we look for the **Saviour**, the **Lord Jesus Christ**: {3:21} **Who** shall change our vile body, that it may be fashioned like unto **His** glorious body, according to the working whereby **He** is able even to subdue all things unto **himself**. {29}

{4:1} Therefore, my brethren dearly beloved and longed for, my joy and crown, so stand fast in the **Lord**, [my] dearly beloved. {4:2} I beseech Euodias, and beseech Syntyche, that they be of the same mind in the **Lord**. {4:3} And I intreat thee also, true yokefellow, help those women which laboured with me in the Gospel, with Clement also, and [with] other my fellowlabourers, whose names [are] in the book of life. {4:4} Rejoice in the **Lord** alway: [and] again I say, Rejoice. {4:5} Let your moderation be known unto all men. The **Lord** [is] at hand. {4:6} Be careful for nothing; but in every thing by prayer and supplication with thanksgiving let your requests be made known unto **God**. {4:7} And the peace of **God**, which passeth all understanding, shall keep your hearts and minds through **Christ Jesus**. {4:8} Finally, brethren, **whatsoever** things are true, **whatsoever** things [are] honest, **whatsoever** things [are] just, **whatsoever** things [are] pure, **whatsoever** things [are] lovely, **whatsoever** things [are] of good report; if [there be] any **virtue**, and if [there be] any **praise**, think on these things. {4:9} Those things, which ye have both learned, and received, and heard, and seen in me, do: and the God of peace shall be with you.{4:10} But I rejoiced in the **Lord** greatly, that now at the last your care of me hath flourished again; wherein ye were also careful, but ye lacked opportunity. {4:11} Not that I speak in respect of want: for I have learned, in whatsoever state I am, [therewith] to be content. {4:12} I know both how to be abased, and I know how to abound: every where

and in all things I am instructed both to be full and to be hungry, both to abound and to suffer need. {4:13} I can do all things through **Christ** which strengtheneth me. {4:14} Notwithstanding ye have well done, that ye did communicate with my affliction. {4:15} Now ye Philippians know also, that in the beginning of the Gospel, when I departed from Macedonia, no church communicated with me as concerning giving and receiving, but ye only. {4:16} For even in Thessalonica ye sent once and again unto my necessity. {4:17} Not because I desire a gift: but I desire fruit that may abound to your account. {4:18} But I have all, and abound: I am full, having received of Epaphroditus the things [which were sent] from you, an odour of a sweet smell, a sacrifice acceptable, wellpleasing to God. {4:19} But my **God** shall supply all your need according to **His** riches in glory by **Christ Jesus.** {4:20} Now unto **God** and our **Father** [be] glory for ever and ever. Amen.

{4:21} Salute every saint in **Christ Jesus**. The brethren which are with me greet you. {4:22} All the saints salute you, chiefly they that are of Caesar's household. {20}

The Epistle of Paul the Apostle to the Colossians
TOTAL 111

{1:1} Paul, an apostle of **Jesus Christ** by the will of **God**, and Timotheus [our] brother, {1:2} To the saints and faithful brethren in **Christ** which are at Colosse: Grace [be] unto you, and peace, from **God** our **Father** and the **Lord Jesus Christ**. {1:3} We give thanks to **God** and the **Father** of our **Lord Jesus Christ**, praying always for you, {1:4} Since we heard of your faith in **Christ Jesus**, and of the love [which ye have] to all the saints, {1:5} For the hope which is laid up for you in heaven, whereof ye heard before in the **word of the truth** of the Gospel; {1:6} Which is come unto you, as [it is] in all the world; and bringeth forth fruit, as [it doth] also in you, since the day ye heard [of it,] and knew the grace of **God** in truth: {1:7} As ye also learned of Epaphras our dear fellowservant, who is for you a faithful minister of **Christ**; {1:8} Who also declared unto us your love in the Spirit. {1:9} For this cause we also, since the day we heard [it,] do not cease to pray for you, and to desire that ye might be filled with the knowledge of **His** will in all wisdom and spiritual understanding; {1:10} That ye might walk worthy of the **Lord** unto all pleasing, being fruitful in every good work, and increasing in the knowledge of **God**; {1:11} Strengthened with all might, according to **His** glorious power, unto all patience and longsuffering with joyfulness; {1:12} Giving thanks unto the **Father**, which hath made us meet to be partakers of the inheritance of the saints in light: {1:13} Who hath delivered us from the power of darkness, and hath translated [us] into the kingdom of **His dear Son**: {1:14} In **whom** we have redemption through **His blood**, [even] the forgiveness of sins: {1:15} **Who** is the **image** of the invisible **God**, the **firstborn** of every creature: {1:16} For by **Him** were all things created, that are in heaven, and that are in earth, visible and invisible, whether [they be] thrones, or dominions, or principalities, or powers: all things were created by **Him**, and for **Him**: {1:17} And **He** is before all things, and by **Him** all things consist. {1:18} And **He** is the head of the **body**, the church: **who** is the **beginning**, the **firstborn** from the dead; that in all [things] **He** might have the preeminence. {1:19} For it pleased [the **Father**] that in **Him** should all fulness dwell; {1:20} And, having made peace through the **blood of His** cross, by **Him** to reconcile all things unto **himself**; by **Him**, [I say,] whether [they be] things in earth, or things in heaven. {1:21} And you, that were sometime alienated and enemies in [your] mind by wicked works, yet now hath **He** reconciled {1:22} In the **body** of **His flesh** through death, to present you holy and unblameable and unreproveable in **His** sight: {1:23} If ye continue in the faith grounded and settled, and [be] not moved away from the **hope** of the Gospel, which ye have heard, [and] which was preached to every creature which is under heaven; whereof I Paul am made a minister; {1:24} Who now rejoice in my sufferings for you, and fill up that which is behind of the afflictions of **Christ** in my flesh for **His body's** sake, which is the church: {1:25} Whereof I am made a minister, according to the dispensation of **God** which is given to **me** for you, to fulfil the word of **God**; {1:26} [Even] the **mystery** which hath been hid from ages and from generations, but now is made manifest to **His** saints: {1:27} To **whom God** would make known what [is] the riches of the glory of this **mystery** among the Gentiles; which is **Christ** in you, the hope of glory: {1:28} **Whom** we preach, warning every man, and teaching every man in all wisdom; that we may present every man perfect in **Christ Jesus**: {1:29} Whereunto I also labour, striving according to **His** working, which worketh in me mightily. {56}

{2:1} For I would that ye knew what great conflict I have for you, and [for] them at Laodicea, and [for] as many as have not seen my face in the flesh; {2:2} That their hearts might be comforted, being knit together in love, and unto all riches of the full assurance of understanding, to the acknowledgement of the **mystery** of **God**, and of the **Father**, and of **Christ**; {2:3} In **whom** are hid all the treasures of wisdom and knowledge. {2:4} And this I say, lest any man should beguile you with enticing words. {2:5} For though I be absent in the flesh, yet am I with you in the spirit, joying and beholding your order, and the stedfastness of your faith in **Christ**.

{2:6} As ye have therefore received **Christ Jesus** the **Lord**, [so] walk ye in **Him**: {2:7} Rooted and built up in **Him**, and stablished in the faith, as ye have been taught, abounding therein with thanksgiving. {2:8} Beware lest any man spoil you through philosophy and vain deceit, after the tradition of men, after the rudiments of the world, and not after **Christ**. {2:9} For in **Him** dwelleth all the fulness of the **God**head bodily. {2:10} And ye are complete in **Him**, which is the **head** of all principality and power: {2:11} In **whom** also ye are circumcised with the circumcision made without hands, in putting off the body of the sins of the flesh by the circumcision of **Christ**: {2:12} Buried with **Him** in baptism, wherein also ye are risen with [**Him**] through the faith of the operation of **God**, who hath raised **Him** from the dead. {2:13} And you, being dead in your sins and the uncircumcision of your flesh, hath **He** quickened together with **Him**, having forgiven you all trespasses; {2:14} Blotting out the handwriting of ordinances that was against us, which was contrary to us, and took it out of the way, nailing it to **His** cross; {2:15} [And] having spoiled principalities and powers, **He** made a shew of them openly, triumphing over them in it. {2:16} Let no man therefore judge you in meat, or in drink, or in respect of an holyday, or of the new moon, or of the sabbath [days:]{2:17} Which are a shadow of things to come; but the body [is] of **Christ**. {2:18} Let no man beguile you of your reward in a voluntary humility and worshipping of angels, intruding into those things which he hath not seen, vainly puffed up by his fleshly mind, {2:19} And not holding the **Head**, from which all the body by joints and bands having nourishment ministered, and knit together, increaseth with the increase of **God**.{2:20} Wherefore if ye be dead with **Christ** from the rudiments of the world, why, as though living in the world, are ye subject to ordinances, {2:21} (Touch not; taste not; handle not; {2:22} Which all are to perish with the using;) after the commandments and doctrines of men? {2:23} Which things have indeed a shew of wisdom in will worship, and humility, and neglecting of the body; not in any honour to the satisfying of the flesh. {24}

{3:1} If ye then be risen with **Christ**, seek those things which are above, where **Christ** sitteth on the right hand of God. {3:2} Set your affection on things above, not on things on the earth. {3:3} For ye are dead, and your life is hid with **Christ** in God. {3:4} When **Christ**, [**who** is] our life, shall appear, then shall ye also appear with **Him** in glory.

{3:5} Mortify therefore your members which are upon the earth; fornication, uncleanness, inordinate affection, evil concupiscence, and covetousness, which is idolatry: {3:6} For which things' sake the wrath of **God** cometh on the children of disobedience: {3:7} In the which ye also walked some time, when ye lived in them. {3:8} But now ye also put off all these; anger, wrath, malice, blasphemy, filthy communication out of your mouth. {3:9} Lie not one to another, seeing that ye have put off the old man with his deeds; {3:10} And have put on the new [man,] which is renewed in knowledge after the image of Him that created him: {3:11} Where there is neither Greek nor Jew, circumcision nor uncircumcision, Barbarian, Scythian, bond [nor] free: but Christ [is] all, and in all. {3:12} Put on therefore, as the elect of God, holy and beloved, bowels of mercies, kindness, humbleness of mind, meekness, longsuffering; {3:13} Forbearing one another, and forgiving one another, if any man have a quarrel against any: even as Christ forgave you, so also [do] ye. {3:14} And above all these things [put on] charity, which is the bond of perfectness. {3:15} And let the peace of God rule in your hearts, to the which also ye are called in one body; and be ye thankful. {3:16} Let the word of Christ dwell in you richly in all wisdom; teaching and admonishing one another in psalms and hymns and spiritual songs, singing with grace in your hearts to the Lord. {3:17} And whatsoever ye do in word or deed, [do] all in the name of the Lord Jesus, giving thanks to God and the Father by Him.

{3:18} Wives, submit yourselves unto your own husbands, as it is fit in the Lord. {3:19} Husbands, love [your] wives, and be not bitter against them. {3:20} Children, obey [your] parents in all things: for this is well pleasing unto the Lord. {3:21} Fathers, provoke not your children [to anger,] lest they be discouraged. {3:22} Servants, obey in all things [your] masters according to the flesh; not with eyeservice, as menpleasers; but in singleness of heart, fearing God: {3:23} And whatsoever ye do, do [it] heartily, as to the Lord, and not unto men; {3:24} Knowing that of the Lord ye shall receive the reward of the inheritance: for ye serve the Lord Christ. {3:25} But He that doeth wrong shall receive for the wrong which He hath done: and there is no respect of persons. {25}

{4:1} Masters, give unto [your] servants that which is just and equal; knowing that ye also have a Master in heaven. {4:2} Continue in prayer, and watch in the same with thanksgiving; {4:3} Withal praying also for us, that God would open unto us a door of utterance, to speak the mystery of Christ, for which I am also in bonds: {4:4} That I may make it manifest, as I ought to speak. {4:5} Walk in wisdom toward them that are without, redeeming the time. {4:6} Let your speech [be] alway with grace, seasoned with salt, that ye may know how ye ought to answer every man.

{4:7} All my state shall Tychicus declare unto you, [who is] a beloved brother, and a faithful minister and fellowservant in the Lord: {4:8} Whom I have sent unto you for the same purpose, that he might know your estate, and comfort your hearts; {4:9} With Onesimus, a faithful and beloved brother, who is [one] of you. They shall make known unto you all things which [are done] here.

{4:10} Aristarchus my fellowprisoner saluteth you, and Marcus, sister's son to Barnabas, (touching whom ye received commandments: if he come unto you, receive him;) {4:11} And Jesus, which is called Justus, who are of the circumcision. These only [are my] fellow workers unto the kingdom of God, which have been a comfort unto me. {4:12} Epaphras, who is [one] of you, a servant of Christ, saluteth you, always labouring fervently for you in prayers, that ye may stand perfect and complete in all the will of God. {4:13} For I bear him record, that he hath a great zeal for you, and them [that are] in Laodicea, and them in Hierapolis. {4:14} Luke, the beloved physician, and Demas,

greet you. {4:15} Salute the brethren which are in Laodicea, and Nymphas, and the church which is in his house. {4:16} And when this epistle is read among you, cause that it be read also in the church of the Laodiceans; and that ye likewise read the [epistle] from Laodicea. {4:17} And say to Archippus, Take heed to the ministry which thou hast received in the Lord, that thou fulfil it.

{4:18} The salutation by the hand of me Paul. Remember my bonds. Grace [be] with you. Amen.
{6}

The First Epistle of Paul to the Thessalonians **TOTAL 102**

{1:1} Paul, and Silvanus, and Timotheus, unto the church of the Thessalonians [which is] in **God** the **Father** and [in] the **Lord Jesus Christ**: Grace [be] unto you, and peace, from **God** our **Father**, and the **Lord Jesus Christ**. {1:2} We give thanks to **God** always for you all, making mention of you in our prayers; {1:3} Remembering without ceasing your work of faith, and labour of love, and patience of hope in our **Lord Jesus Christ**, in the sight of **God** and our **Father**; {1:4} Knowing, brethren beloved, your election of **God**. {1:5} For our Gospel came not unto you in word only, but also in power, and in the **Holy Ghost**, and in much assurance; as ye know what manner of men we were among you for your sake. {1:6} And ye became followers of us, and of the **Lord**, having received the word in much affliction, with joy of the **Holy Ghost**: {1:7} So that ye were ensamples to all that believe in Macedonia and Achaia. {1:8} For from you sounded out the word of the **Lord** not only in Macedonia and Achaia, but also in every place your faith to **God**-ward is spread abroad; so that we need not to speak any thing. {1:9} For they themselves shew of us what manner of entering in we had unto you, and how ye turned to **God** from idols to serve the living and true **God**; {1:10} And to wait for **His Son** from heaven, whom **He** raised from the dead, [even] **Jesus**, which delivered us from the wrath to come. {14}

{2:1} For yourselves, brethren, know our entrance in unto you, that it was not in vain: {2:2} But even after that we had suffered before, and were shamefully entreated, as ye know, at Philippi, we were bold in our **God** to speak unto you the Gospel of **God** with much contention. {2:3} For our exhortation [was] not of deceit, nor of uncleanness, nor in guile: {2:4} But as we were allowed of **God** to be put in trust with the Gospel, even so we speak; not as pleasing men, but **God**, which trieth our hearts. {2:5} For neither at any time used we flattering words, as ye know, nor a cloke of covetousness; **God** [is] witness: {2:6} Nor of men sought we glory, neither of you, nor [yet] of others, when we might have been burdensome, as the apostles of **Christ**. {2:7} But we were gentle among you, even as a nurse cherisheth her children: {2:8} So being affectionately desirous of you, we were willing to have imparted unto you, not the Gospel of **God** only, but also our own souls, because ye were dear unto us. {2:9} For ye remember, brethren, our labour and travail: for labouring night and day, because we would not be chargeable unto any of you, we preached unto you the Gospel of **God**. {2:10} Ye [are] witnesses, and **God** [also,] how holily and justly and unblameably we behaved ourselves among you that believe: {2:11} As ye know how we exhorted and comforted and charged every one of you, as a **Father** [doth] **His** children, {2:12} That ye would walk worthy of **God**, who hath called you unto **His** kingdom and glory.

{2:13} For this cause also thank we **God** without ceasing, because, when ye received the word of **God** which ye heard of us, ye received [it] not [as] the word of men, but as it is in truth, the word of **God**, which effectually worketh also in you that believe. {2:14} For ye, brethren, became followers of the churches of **God** which in Judaea are in **Christ Jesus**: for ye also have suffered like things of your own countrymen, even as they [have] of the Jews: {2:15} Who both killed the **Lord Jesus**, and their own prophets, and have persecuted us; and they please not **God**, and are contrary to all men: {2:16} Forbidding us to speak to the Gentiles that

they might be saved, to fill up their sins alway: for the wrath is come upon them to the uttermost.

{2:17} But we, brethren, being taken from you for a short time in presence, not in heart, endeavoured the more abundantly to see your face with great desire. {2:18} Wherefore we would have come unto you, even **I** Paul, once and again; but Satan hindered us. {2:19} For what [is] our hope, or joy, or crown of rejoicing? [Are] not even ye in the presence of our **Lord Jesus Christ** at **His** coming? {2:20} For ye are our glory and joy. {10}

{3:1} Wherefore when we could no longer forbear, we thought it good to be left at Athens alone; {3:2} And sent Timotheus, our brother, and minister of **God**, and our fellowlabourer in the Gospel of **Christ**, to establish you, and to comfort you concerning your faith: {3:3} That no man should be moved by these afflictions: for yourselves know that we are appointed thereunto. {3:4} For verily, when we were with you, we told you before that we should suffer tribulation; even as it came to pass, and ye know. {3:5} For this cause, when **I** could no longer forbear, **I** sent to know your faith, lest by some means the tempter have tempted you, and our labour be in vain. {3:6} But now when Timotheus came from you unto us, and brought us good tidings of your faith and charity, and that ye have good remembrance of us always, desiring greatly to see us, as we also [to see] you: {3:7} Therefore, brethren, we were comforted over you in all our affliction and distress by your faith: {3:8} For now we live, if ye stand fast in the **Lord**. {3:9} For what thanks can we render to **God** again for you, for all the joy wherewith we joy for your sakes before our **God**; {3:10} Night and day praying exceedingly that we might see your face, and might perfect that which is lacking in your faith? {3:11} Now **God** himself and our **Father**, and our **Lord Jesus Christ**, direct our way unto you. {3:12} And the **Lord** make you to increase and abound in love one toward another, and toward all [men,] even as we [do] toward you: {3:13} To the end he may stablish your hearts unblameable in holiness before **God**, even our **Father**, at the coming of our **Lord Jesus Christ** with all **His** saints.

{10}

{4:1} Furthermore then we beseech you, brethren, and exhort [you] by the **Lord Jesus**, that as ye have received of us how ye ought to walk and to please **God**, [so] ye would abound more and more. {4:2} For ye know what commandments we gave you by the **Lord Jesus**. {4:3} For this is the will of **God**, [even] your sanctification, that ye should abstain from fornication: {4:4} That every one of you should know how to possess his vessel in sanctification and honour; {4:5} Not in the lust of concupiscence, even as the Gentiles which know not **God**: {4:6} That no [man] go beyond and defraud his brother in [any] matter: because that the **Lord** [is] the avenger of all such, as we also have forewarned you and testified. {4:7} For **God** hath not called us unto uncleanness, but unto holiness. {4:8} **He** therefore that despiseth, despiseth not man, but **God**, who hath also given unto us **His** holy Spirit. {4:9} But as touching brotherly love ye need not that **I** write unto you: for ye yourselves are taught of **God** to love one another. {4:10} And indeed ye do it toward all the brethren which are in all Macedonia: but we beseech you, brethren, that ye increase more and more; {4:11} And that ye study to be quiet, and to do your own business, and to work with your own hands, as we commanded you; {4:12} That ye may walk honestly toward them that are without, and [that] ye may have lack of nothing.

{4:13} But **I** would not have you to be ignorant, brethren, concerning them which are asleep, that ye sorrow not, even as others which have no hope. {4:14} For if we believe that **Jesus** died and rose again, even so them also which sleep in **Jesus** will **God** bring with **Him**. {4:15} For this we say unto you by the word of the **Lord**, that we which are alive [and] remain unto the coming of the **Lord** shall not prevent them which are asleep. {4:16} For the **Lord** himself shall descend from heaven with a shout, with the voice of the archangel, and with the trump of **God**: and the dead in **Christ** shall rise first: {4:17} Then we which are alive [and] remain shall be caught up together with them in the clouds, to meet the **Lord** in the air: and so shall we ever be with the **Lord**. {4:18} Wherefore comfort one another with these words. **{14}**

{5:1} But of the times and the seasons, brethren, ye have no need that I write unto you. {5:2} For yourselves know perfectly that the day of the **Lord** so cometh as a thief in the night. {5:3} For when they shall say, Peace and safety; then sudden destruction cometh upon them, as travail upon a woman with child; and they shall not escape. {5:4} But ye, brethren, are not in darkness, that that day should overtake you as a thief. {5:5} Ye are all the children of light, and the children of the day: we are not of the night, nor of darkness. {5:6} Therefore let us not sleep, as [do] others; but let us watch and be sober. {5:7} For they that sleep sleep in the night; and they that be drunken are drunken in the night. {5:8} But let us, who are of the day, be sober, putting on the breastplate of faith and love; and for an helmet, the hope of salvation. {5:9} For **God** hath not appointed us to wrath, but to obtain salvation by our **Lord Jesus Christ**, {5:10} Who died for us, that, whether we wake or sleep, we should live together with **Him**. {5:11} Wherefore comfort yourselves together, and edify one another, even as also ye do.

{5:12} And we beseech you, brethren, to know them which labour among you, and are over you in the **Lord**, and admonish you; {5:13} And to esteem them very highly in love for their work's sake. [And] be at peace among yourselves. {5:14} Now we exhort you, brethren, warn them that are unruly, comfort the feebleminded, support the weak, be patient toward all [men.]{5:15} See that none render evil for evil unto any [man;] but ever follow that which is good, both among yourselves, and to all [men.]{5:16} Rejoice evermore. {5:17} Pray without ceasing. {5:18} In every thing give thanks: for this is the will of **God** in **Christ Jesus** concerning you. {5:19} Quench not the Spirit. {5:20} Despise not prophesyings. {5:21} Prove all things; hold fast that which is good. {5:22} Abstain from all appearance of evil. {5:23} And the very **God** of peace sanctify you wholly; and [**I** pray **God**] your whole spirit and soul and body be preserved blameless unto the coming of our **Lord Jesus Christ**. {5:24} Faithful [is] **He** that calleth you, **who** also will do [it].{5:25} Brethren, pray for us.{5:26} Greet all the brethren with an holy kiss. {5:27} **I** charge you by the **Lord** that this epistle be read unto all the holy brethren.

{14}

The Second Epistle of Paul the Apostle to the Thessalonians
TOTAL 51

{1:1} Paul, and Silvanus, and Timotheus, unto the church of the Thessalonians in **God** our **Father** and the **Lord Jesus Christ**: {1:2} Grace unto you, and peace, from **God** our **Father** and the **Lord Jesus Christ**.

{1:3} We are bound to thank **God** always for you, brethren, as it is meet, because that your faith groweth exceedingly, and the charity of every one of you all toward each other aboundeth; {1:4} So that we ourselves glory in you in the churches of **God** for your patience and faith in all your persecutions and tribulations that ye endure: {1:5} [Which is] a manifest token of the righteous judgment of **God**, that ye may be counted worthy of the kingdom of **God**, for which ye also suffer: {1:6} Seeing [it is] a righteous thing with **God** to recompense tribulation to them that trouble you; {1:7} And to you who are troubled rest with us, when the **Lord Jesus** shall be revealed from heaven with **His** mighty angels, {1:8} In flaming fire taking vengeance on them that know not **God**, and that obey not the Gospel of our **Lord Jesus Christ**: {1:9} Who shall be punished with everlasting destruction from the presence of the **Lord**, and from the glory of **His** power; {1:10} When **He** shall come to be glorified in **His** saints, and to be admired in all them that believe (because our testimony among you was believed) in that day. {1:11} Wherefore also we pray always for you, that our **God** would count you worthy of [this] calling, and fulfil all the good pleasure of [**His**] goodness, and the work of faith with power: {1:12} That the **name** of our **Lord Jesus Christ** may be glorified in you, and ye in **Him**, according to the grace of our **God** and the **Lord Jesus Christ**. {25}

{2:1} Now we beseech you, brethren, by the coming of our **Lord Jesus Christ**, and [by] our gathering together unto **Him**, {2:2} That ye be not soon shaken in mind, or be troubled, neither by spirit, nor by word, nor by letter as from us, as that the day of **Christ** is at hand. {2:3} Let no man deceive you by any means: for [that day shall not come,] except there come a falling away first, and that man of sin be revealed, the Son of perdition; {2:4} Who opposeth and exalteth himself above all that is called God, or that is worshipped; so that he as God sitteth in the temple of God, shewing himself that he is God. {2:5} Remember ye not, that, when I was yet with you, I told you these things? {2:6} And now ye know what withholdeth that he might be revealed in his time. {2:7} For the mystery of iniquity doth already work: only He who now letteth [will let,] until he be taken out of the way. {2:8} And then shall that Wicked be revealed, whom the **Lord** shall consume with the spirit of **His** mouth, and shall destroy with the brightness of **His** coming: {2:9} [Even him,] whose coming is after the working of Satan with all power and signs and lying wonders, {2:10} And with all deceivableness of unrighteousness in them that perish; because they received not the love of the truth, that they might be saved. {2:11} And for this cause **God** shall send them strong delusion, that they should believe a lie: {2:12} That they all might be damned who believed not the truth, but had pleasure in unrighteousness.

{2:13} But we are bound to give thanks alway to **God** for you, brethren beloved of the **Lord**, because **God** hath from the beginning chosen you to salvation through sanctification of the Spirit and belief of the truth: {2:14} Whereunto **He** called you by our Gospel, to the obtaining of the glory of our **Lord Jesus Christ**. {2:15} Therefore, brethren, stand fast, and hold the traditions which ye have been taught, whether by word, or our epistle. {2:16} Now our **Lord Jesus Christ himself**, and **God**, even our **Father**, which hath loved us, and hath given [us] everlasting consolation and good hope through grace, {2:17} Comfort your hearts, and stablish you in every good word and work. {17}

{3:1} Finally, brethren, pray for us, that the word of the **Lord** may have [free] course, and be glorified, even as [it is] with you: {3:2} And that we may be delivered from unreasonable and wicked men: for all [men] have not faith. {3:3} But the **Lord** is faithful, **who** shall stablish you, and keep [you] from evil. {3:4} And we have confidence in the **Lord** touching you, that ye both do and will do the things which we command you. {3:5} And the **Lord** direct your hearts into the love of **God**, and into the patient waiting for **Christ**.

{3:6} Now we command you, brethren, in the **name** of our **Lord Jesus Christ**, that ye withdraw yourselves from every brother that walketh disorderly, and not after the tradition which he received of us. {3:7} For yourselves know how ye ought to follow us: for we behaved not ourselves disorderly among you; {3:8} Neither did we eat any man's bread for nought; but wrought with labour and travail night and day, that we might not be chargeable to any of you: {3:9} Not because we have not power, but to make ourselves an ensample unto you to follow us. {3:10} For even when we were with you, this we commanded you, that if any would not work, neither should he eat. {3:11} For we hear that there are some which walk among you disorderly, working not at all, but are busybodies. {3:12} Now them that are such we command and exhort by our **Lord Jesus Christ**, that with quietness they work, and eat their own bread. {3:13} But ye, brethren, be not weary in well doing. {3:14} And if any man obey not our word by this epistle, note that man, and have no company with him, that he may be ashamed. {3:15} Yet count [him] not as an enemy, but admonish [him] as a brother. {3:16} Now the **Lord** of peace **himself** give you peace always by all means. The **Lord** [be] with you all.

{3:17} The salutation of Paul with mine own hand, which is the token in every epistle: so I write. {3:18} The grace of our **Lord Jesus Christ** [be] with you all. Amen. {19}

First Epistle of Paul the Apostle to Timothy **TOTAL 62**

{1:1} Paul, an apostle of **Jesus Christ** by the commandment of **God** our **Saviour**, and **Lord Jesus Christ**, [which is] our **hope**; {1:2} Unto Timothy, [my] own Son in the faith: Grace, mercy, [and] peace, from **God** our **Father** and **Jesus Christ** our **Lord**.

{1:3} As I besought thee to abide still at Ephesus, when I went into Macedonia, that thou mightest charge some that they teach no other doctrine, {1:4} Neither give heed to fables and endless genealogies, which minister questions, rather than **God**ly edifying which is in faith: [so do.]{1:5} Now the end of the commandment is charity out of a pure heart, and [of] a good conscience, and [of] faith unfeigned: {1:6} From which some having swerved have turned aside unto vain jangling; {1:7} Desiring to be teachers of the law; understanding neither what they say, nor whereof they affirm. {1:8} But we know that the law [is] good, if a man use it lawfully; {1:9} Knowing this, that the law is not made for a righteous man, but for the lawless and disobedient, for the un**God**ly and for sinners, for unholy and profane, for murderers of **Father**s and murderers of mothers, for manslayers, {1:10} For whoremongers, for them that defile themselves with mankind, for mensteelers, for liars, for perjured persons, and if there be any other thing that is contrary to sound doctrine; {1:11} According to the glorious Gospel of the blessed **God**, which was committed to my trust. {1:12} And I thank **Christ Jesus** our **Lord**, **who** hath enabled me, for that **He** counted me faithful, putting me into the ministry; {1:13} Who was before a blasphemer, and a persecutor, and injurious: but I obtained mercy, because I did [it] ignorantly in unbelief. {1:14} And the grace of our **Lord** was exceeding abundant with faith and love which is in **Christ Jesus**. {1:15} This [is] a faithful saying, and worthy of all acceptation, that **Christ Jesus** came into the world to save sinners; of whom I am chief. {1:16} Howbeit for this cause I obtained mercy, that in me first **Jesus Christ** might shew forth all longsuffering, for a pattern to them which should hereafter believe on **Him** to life everlasting. {1:17} Now unto the **King eternal**, immortal, invisible, the only **wise God**, [be] honour and glory for ever and ever. Amen. {1:18} This charge I commit unto thee, Son Timothy, according to the prophecies which went before on thee, that thou by them mightest war a good warfare; {1:19} Holding faith, and a good conscience; which some having put away concerning faith have made shipwreck: {1:20} Of whom is Hymenaeus and Alexander; whom I have delivered unto Satan, that they may learn not to blaspheme. **{25}**

{2:1} I exhort therefore, that, first of all, supplications, prayers, intercessions, [and] giving of thanks, be made for all men; {2:2} For kings, and [for] all that are in authority; that we may lead a quiet and peaceable life in all **God**liness and honesty. {2:3} For this [is] good and acceptable in the sight of **God** our **Saviour**; {2:4} Who will have all men to be saved, and to come unto the knowledge of the truth. {2:5} For [there is] one **God**, and one mediator between **God** and men, the **man Christ Jesus**; {2:6} Who gave **himself** a ransom for all, to be testified in due time. {2:7} Whereunto I am ordained a preacher, and an apostle, (I speak the truth in **Christ**, [and] lie not;) a teacher of the Gentiles in faith and verity. {2:8} I will therefore that men pray every where, lifting up holy hands, without wrath and doubting. {2:9} In like manner also, that women adorn themselves in modest apparel, with shamefacedness and sobriety; not with broided hair, or gold, or pearls, or costly

array; {2:10} But (which becometh women professing **God**liness) with good works. {2:11} Let the woman learn in silence with all subjection. {2:12} But I suffer not a woman to teach, nor to usurp authority over the man, but to be in silence. {2:13} For Adam was first formed, then Eve. {2:14} And Adam was not deceived, but the woman being deceived was in the transgression. {2:15} Notwithstanding she shall be saved in childbearing, if they continue in faith and charity and holiness with sobriety. **{6}**

{3:1} This [is] a true saying, If a man desire the office of a bishop, he desireth a good work. {3:2} A bishop then must be blameless, the husband of one wife, vigilant, sober, of good behaviour, given to hospitality, apt to teach; {3:3} Not given to wine, no striker, not greedy of filthy lucre; but patient, not a brawler, not covetous; {3:4} One that ruleth well his own house, having his children in subjection with all gravity; {3:5} (For if a man know not how to rule his own house, how shall he take care of the church of God?) {3:6} Not a novice, lest being lifted up with pride he fall into the condemnation of the devil. {3:7} Moreover he must have a good report of them which are without; lest he fall into reproach and the snare of the devil. {3:8} Likewise [must] the deacons [be] grave, not doubletongued, not given to much wine, not greedy of filthy lucre; {3:9} Holding the mystery of the faith in a pure conscience. {3:10} And let these also first be proved; then let them use the office of a deacon, being [found] blameless. {3:11} Even so [must their] wives be grave, not slanderers, sober, faithful in all things. {3:12} Let the deacons be the husbands of one wife, ruling their children and their own houses well. {3:13} For they that have used the office of a deacon well purchase to themselves a good degree, and great boldness in the faith which is in **Christ Jesus**. {3:14} These things write I unto thee, hoping to come unto thee shortly: {3:15} But if I tarry long, that thou mayest know how thou oughtest to behave thyself in the house of **God**, which is the church of the living **God**, the pillar and ground of the truth. {3:16} And without controversy great is the mystery of **God**liness: **God** was manifest in the flesh, justified in the Spirit, seen of angels, preached unto the Gentiles, believed on in the world, received up into glory. **{2}**

{4:1} Now the Spirit speaketh expressly, that in the latter times some shall depart from the faith, giving heed to seducing spirits, and doctrines of devils; {4:2} Speaking lies in hypocrisy; having their conscience seared with a hot iron; {4:3} Forbidding to marry, [and commanding] to abstain from meats, which **God** hath created to be received with thanksgiving of them which believe and know the truth. {4:4} For every creature of **God** [is] good, and nothing to be refused, if it be received with thanksgiving: {4:5} For it is sanctified by the word of **God** and prayer. {4:6} If thou put the brethren in remembrance of these things, thou shalt be a good minister of **Jesus Christ,** nourished up in the words of faith and of good doctrine, whereunto thou hast attained. {4:7} But refuse profane and old wives' fables, and exercise thyself [rather] unto **God**liness. {4:8} For bodily exercise profiteth little: but **God**liness is profitable unto all things, having promise of the life that now is, and of that which is to come. {4:9} This [is] a faithful saying and worthy of all acceptation. {4:10} For therefore we both labour and suffer reproach, because we trust in the living **God**, who is the **Saviour** of all men, specially of those that believe.

{4:11} These things command and teach. {4:12} Let no man despise thy youth; but be thou an example of the believers, in word, in conversation, in charity, in spirit, in faith, in purity. {4:13} Till I come, give attendance to reading, to exhortation, to doctrine. {4:14} Neglect not the gift that is in thee, which was given thee by prophecy, with the laying on of the hands of the presbytery. {4:15} Meditate upon these things; give thyself wholly to them; that thy profiting may appear to all. {4:16} Take heed unto thyself, and unto the doctrine; continue in them: for in doing this thou shalt both save thyself, and them that hear thee. {3}

{5:1} Rebuke not an elder, but intreat [him] as a Father; [and] the younger men as brethren; {5:2} The elder women as mothers; the younger as sisters, with all purity. {5:3} Honour widows that are widows indeed. {5:4} But if any widow have children or nephews, let them learn first to shew piety at home, and to requite their parents: for that is good and acceptable before God. {5:5} Now she that is a widow indeed, and desolate, trusteth in God, and continueth in supplications and prayers night and day. {5:6} But she that liveth in pleasure is dead while she liveth. {5:7} And these things give in charge, that they may be blameless. {5:8} But if any provide not for his own, and specially for those of his own house, he hath denied the faith, and is worse than an infidel. {5:9} Let not a widow be taken into the number under threescore years old, having been the wife of one man, {5:10} Well reported of for good works; if she have brought up children, if she have lodged strangers, if she have washed the saints' feet, if she have relieved the afflicted, if she have diligently followed every good work. {5:11} But the younger widows refuse: for when they have begun to wax wanton against Christ, they will marry; {5:12} Having damnation, because they have cast off their first faith. {5:13} And withal they learn [to be] idle, wandering about from house to house; and not only idle, but tattlers also and busybodies, speaking things which they ought not. {5:14} I will therefore that the younger women marry, bear children, guide the house, give none occasion to the adversary to speak reproachfully. {5:15} For some are already turned aside after Satan. {5:16} If any man or woman that believeth have widows, let them relieve them, and let not the church be charged; that it may relieve them that are widows indeed. {5:17} Let the elders that rule well be counted worthy of double honour, especially they who labour in the word and doctrine. {5:18} For the scripture saith, Thou shalt not muzzle the ox that treadeth out the corn. And, The labourer [is] worthy of his reward. {5:19} Against an elder receive not an accusation, but before two or three witnesses. {5:20} Them that sin rebuke before all, that others also may fear. {5:21} I charge [thee] before God, and the Lord Jesus Christ, and the elect angels, that thou observe these things without preferring one before another, doing nothing by partiality. {5:22} Lay hands suddenly on no man, neither be partaker of other men's sins: keep thyself pure. {5:23} Drink no longer water, but use a little wine for thy stomach's sake and thine often infirmities. {5:24} Some men's sins are open beforehand, going before to judgment; and some [men] they follow after. {5:25} Likewise also the good works [of some] are manifest beforehand; and they that are otherwise cannot be hid. {4}

{6:1} Let as many servants as are under the yoke count their own masters worthy of all honour, that the name of God and [His] doctrine be not blasphemed. {6:2} And they that have believing masters, let them not despise [them,] because they are brethren; but rather do [them] service, because they are faithful and beloved, partakers of the benefit. These things teach and exhort.

{6:3} If any man teach otherwise, and consent not to wholesome words, [even] the words of our Lord Jesus Christ, and to the doctrine which is according to Godliness;

{6:4} He is proud, knowing nothing, but doting about questions and strifes of words, whereof cometh envy, strife, railings, evil surmisings, {6:5} Perverse disputings of men of corrupt minds, and destitute of the truth, supposing that gain is Godliness: from such withdraw thyself. {6:6} But Godliness with contentment is great gain. {6:7} For we brought nothing into [this] world, [and it is] certain we can carry nothing out. {6:8} And having food and raiment let us be therewith content. {6:9} But they that will be rich fall into temptation and a snare, and [into] many foolish and hurtful lusts, which drown men in destruction and perdition. {6:10} For the love of money is the root of all evil: which while some coveted after, they have erred from the faith, and pierced themselves through with many sorrows. {6:11} But thou, O man of God, flee these things; and follow after righteousness, Godliness, faith, love, patience, meekness. {6:12} Fight the good fight of faith, lay hold on eternal life, whereunto thou art also called, and hast professed a good profession before many witnesses. {6:13} I give thee charge in the sight of God, who quickeneth all things, and [before] Christ Jesus, who before Pontius Pilate witnessed a good confession; {6:14} That thou keep [this] commandment without spot, unrebukeable, until the appearing of our Lord Jesus Christ: {6:15} Which in His times He shall shew, [who is] the blessed and only Potentate, the King of kings, and Lord of lords; {6:16} Who only hath immortality, dwelling in the light which no man can approach unto; whom no man hath seen, nor can see: to whom [be] honour and power everlasting. Amen. {6:17} Charge them that are rich in this world, that they be not highminded, nor trust in uncertain riches, but in the living God, who giveth us richly all things to enjoy; {6:18} That they do good, that they be rich in good works, ready to distribute, willing to communicate; {6:19} Laying up in store for themselves a good foundation against the time to come, that they may lay hold on eternal life. {6:20} O Timothy, keep that which is committed to thy trust, avoiding profane [and] vain babblings, and oppositions of science falsely so called: {6:21} Which some professing have erred concerning the faith. Grace [be] with thee. Amen. {22}

Second Epistle of Paul the Apostle to Timothy **TOTAL 72**

{1:1} Paul, an apostle of **Jesus Christ** by the will of **God**, according to the promise of life which is in **Christ Jesus**, {1:2} To Timothy, [my] dearly beloved Son: Grace, mercy, [and] peace, from **God** the **Father** and **Christ Jesus** our **Lord**. {1:3} I thank **God**, **whom** I serve from [my] foreFathers with pure conscience, that without ceasing I have remembrance of thee in my prayers night and day; {1:4} Greatly desiring to see thee, being mindful of thy tears, that I may be filled with joy; {1:5} When I call to remembrance the unfeigned faith that is in thee, which dwelt first in thy grandmother Lois, and thy mother Eunice; and I am persuaded that in thee also. {1:6} Wherefore I put thee in remembrance that thou stir up the gift of **God**, which is in thee by the putting on of my hands. {1:7} For **God** hath not given us the spirit of fear; but of power, and of love, and of a sound mind. {1:8} Be not thou therefore ashamed of the testimony of our **Lord**, nor of me **His** prisoner: but be thou partaker of the afflictions of the Gospel according to the power of **God**; {1:9} Who hath saved us, and called [us] with an holy calling, not according to our works, but according to **His** own purpose and grace, which was given us in **Christ Jesus** before the world began, {1:10} But is now made manifest by the appearing of our **Saviour Jesus Christ**, who hath abolished death, and hath brought life and immortality to light through the Gospel: {1:11} Whereunto I am appointed a preacher, and an apostle, and a teacher of the Gentiles. {1:12} For the which cause I also suffer these things: nevertheless I am not ashamed: for I know **whom** I have believed, and am persuaded that **He** is able to keep that which I have committed unto **Him** against that day. {1:13} Hold fast the form of sound words, which thou hast heard of me, in faith and love which is in **Christ Jesus**. {1:14} That good thing which was committed unto thee keep by the **Holy Ghost** which dwelleth in us. {1:15} This thou knowest, that all they which are in Asia be turned away from me; of **whom** are Phygellus and Hermogenes. {1:16} The **Lord** give mercy unto the house of Onesiphorus; for he oft refreshed me, and was not ashamed of my chain: {1:17} But, when he was in Rome, he sought me out very diligently, and found [me.]{1:18} The **Lord** grant unto him that he may find mercy of the **Lord** in that day: and in how many things he ministered unto me at Ephesus, thou knowest very well. {22}

{2:1} Thou therefore, my Son, be strong in the grace that is in **Christ Jesus**. {2:2} And the things that thou hast heard of **me** among many witnesses, the same commit thou to faithful men, who shall be able to teach others also. {2:3} Thou therefore endure hardness, as a good soldier of **Jesus Christ**. {2:4} No man that warreth entangleth himself with the affairs of [this] life; that he may please **Him who** hath chosen him to be a soldier. {2:5} And if a man also strive for masteries, [yet] is he not crowned, except he strive lawfully. {2:6} The husbandman that laboureth must be first partaker of the fruits. {2:7} Consider what I say; and the **Lord** give thee understanding in all things. {2:8} Remember that **Jesus Christ** of the **seed** of David was raised from the dead according to my Gospel: {2:9} Wherein I suffer trouble, as an evil doer, [even] unto bonds; but the word of God is not bound. {2:10} Therefore I endure all things for the elect's sakes, that they may also obtain the salvation which is in **Christ Jesus** with eternal glory. {2:11} [It is] a faithful saying: For if we be dead with [**Him**,] we shall also live with [**Him**:]{2:12} If we suffer, we shall also reign with [**Him**:] if we deny [**Him**,] **He** also will deny us: {2:13} If we

believe not, [yet] **He** abideth faithful: **He** cannot deny **himself**. {2:14} Of these things put [them] in remembrance, charging [them] before the **Lord** that they strive not about words to no profit, [but] to the subverting of the hearers. {2:15} Study to shew thyself approved unto **God**, a workman that needeth not to be ashamed, rightly dividing the word of truth. {2:16} But shun profane [and] vain babblings: for they will increase unto more un**God**liness. {2:17} And their word will eat as doth a canker: of **whom** is Hymenaeus and Philetus; {2:18} Who concerning the truth have erred, saying that the resurrection is past already; and overthrow the faith of some. {2:19} Nevertheless the **foundation** of **God** standeth sure, having this seal, The **Lord** knoweth them that are **His**. And, Let every one that nameth the **name** of **Christ** depart from iniquity. {2:20} But in a great house there are not only vessels of gold and of silver, but also of wood and of earth; and some to honour, and some to dishonour. {2:21} If a man therefore purge himself from these, he shall be a vessel unto honour, sanctified, and meet for the **master's** use, [and] prepared unto every good work. {2:22} Flee also youthful lusts: but follow righteousness, faith, charity, peace, with them that call on the **Lord** out of a pure heart. {2:23} But foolish and unlearned questions avoid, knowing that they do gender strifes. {2:24} And the servant of the **Lord** must not strive; but be gentle unto all [men,] apt to teach, patient, {2:25} In meekness instructing those that oppose themselves; if **God** peradventure will give them repentance to the acknowledging of the truth; {2:26} And [that] they may recover themselves out of the snare of the devil, who are taken captive by him at his will. {29}

{3:1} This know also, that in the last days perilous times shall come. {3:2} For men shall be lovers of their own selves, covetous, boasters, proud, blasphemers, disobedient to parents, unthankful, unholy, {3:3} Without natural affection, trucebreakers, false accusers, incontinent, fierce, despisers of those that are good, {3:4} Traitors, heady, highminded, lovers of pleasures more than lovers of **God**; {3:5} Having a form of **God**liness, but denying the power thereof: from such turn away. {3:6} For of this sort are they which creep into houses, and lead captive silly women laden with sins, led away with divers lusts, {3:7} Ever learning, and never able to come to the knowledge of the truth. {3:8} Now as Jannes and Jambres withstood Moses, so do these also resist the truth: men of corrupt minds, reprobate concerning the faith. {3:9} But they shall proceed no further: for their folly shall be manifest unto all [men,] as theirs also was. {3:10} But thou hast fully known my doctrine, manner of life, purpose, faith, longsuffering, charity, patience, {3:11} Persecutions, afflictions, which came unto me at Antioch, at Iconium, at Lystra; what persecutions I endured: but out of [them] all the **Lord** delivered **me**. {3:12} Yea, and all that will live **God**ly in **Christ Jesus** shall suffer persecution. {3:13} But evil men and seducers shall wax worse and worse, deceiving, and being deceived. {3:14} But continue thou in the things which thou hast learned and hast been assured of, knowing of **whom** thou hast learned [them;]{3:15} And that from a child thou hast known the holy scriptures, which are able to make thee wise unto salvation through faith which is in **Christ Jesus**. {3:16} All scripture [is] given by inspiration of **God**, and [is] profitable for doctrine, for reproof, for correction, for instruction in righteousness: {3:17} That the man of **God** may be perfect, throughly furnished unto all good works. {4}

{4:1} I charge [thee] therefore before **God**, and the **Lord Jesus Christ**, **who** shall judge the quick and the dead at **His** appearing and **His** kingdom; {4:2} Preach the word; be instant in season, out of season; reprove, rebuke, exhort with all longsuffering and doctrine. {4:3} For the time will come when they will not endure sound doctrine; but after their own lusts shall they heap to themselves teachers, having itching ears; {4:4} And they shall turn away [their] ears from the truth, and shall be turned unto fables. {4:5} But watch thou in all things, endure afflictions, do the work of an evangelist, make full proof of thy ministry. {4:6} For I am now ready to be offered, and the time of my departure is at hand. {4:7} I have fought a good fight, I have finished [my] course, I have kept the faith: {4:8} Henceforth there is laid up for me a crown of righteousness, which the **Lord**, the righteous **judge**, shall give me at that day: and not to **me** only, but unto all them also that love **His** appearing.

{4:9} Do thy diligence to come shortly unto me: {4:10} For Demas hath forsaken me, having loved this present world, and is departed unto Thessalonica; Crescens to Galatia, Titus unto Dalmatia. {4:11} Only Luke is with me. Take Mark, and bring him with thee: for He is profitable to me for the ministry. {4:12} And Tychicus have I sent to Ephesus. {4:13} The cloke that I left at Troas with Carpus, when thou comest, bring [with thee,] and the books, [but] especially the parchments. {4:14} Alexander the coppersmith did me much evil: the **Lord** reward him according to His works: {4:15} Of whom be thou ware also; for he hath greatly withstood our words. {4:16} At my first answer no man stood with me, but all [men] forsook me: [I pray **God**] that it may not be laid to their charge. {4:17} Notwithstanding the **Lord** stood with me, and strengthened me; that by me the preaching might be fully known, and [that] all the Gentiles might hear: and I was delivered out of the mouth of the lion. {4:18} And the **Lord** shall deliver me from every evil work, and will preserve [me] unto **His** heavenly kingdom: to **whom** [be] glory for ever and ever. Amen.

{4:19} Salute Prisca and Aquila, and the household of Onesiphorus. {4:20} Erastus abode at Corinth: but Trophimus have I left at Miletum sick. {4:21} Do thy diligence to come before winter. Eubulus greeteth thee, and Pudens, and Linus, and Claudia, and all the brethren.

{4:22} The **Lord Jesus Christ** [be] with thy spirit. Grace [be] with you. Amen.
{17}

The Epistle of Paul to Titus   TOTAL 24

{1:1} Paul, a servant of **God**, and an apostle of **Jesus Christ**, according to the faith of **God**'s elect, and the acknowledging of the truth which is after **God**liness; {1:2} In hope of eternal life, which **God**, that cannot lie, promised before the world began; {1:3} But hath in due times manifested **His** word through preaching, which is committed unto me according to the commandment of **God** our **Saviour**; {1:4} To Titus, [mine] own Son after the common faith: Grace, mercy, [and] peace, from **God** the **Father** and the **Lord Jesus Christ** our **Saviour**.

{1:5} For this cause left I thee in Crete, that thou shouldest set in order the things that are wanting, and ordain elders in every city, as I had appointed thee: {1:6} If any be blameless, the husband of one wife, having faithful children not accused of riot or unruly. {1:7} For a bishop must be blameless, as the steward of **God**; not selfwilled, not soon angry, not given to wine, no striker, not given to filthy lucre; {1:8} But a lover of hospitality, a lover of good men, sober, just, holy, temperate; {1:9} Holding fast the faithful word as He hath been taught, that He may be able by sound doctrine both to exhort and to convince the gainsayers. {1:10} For there are many unruly and vain talkers and deceivers, specially they of the circumcision: {1:11} Whose mouths must be stopped, who subvert whole houses, teaching things which they ought not, for filthy lucre's sake. {1:12} One of themselves, [even] a prophet of their own, said, The Cretians [are] alway liars, evil beasts, slow bellies. {1:13} This witness is true. Wherefore rebuke them sharply, that they may be sound in the faith; {1:14} Not giving heed to Jewish fables, and commandments of men, that turn from the truth. {1:15} Unto the pure all things [are] pure: but unto them that are defiled and unbelieving [is] nothing pure; but even their mind and conscience is defiled. {1:16} They profess that they know **God**; but in works they deny [**Him**,] being abominable, and disobedient, and unto every good work reprobate. {9}

{2:1} But speak thou the things which become sound doctrine: {2:2} That the aged men be sober, grave, temperate, sound in faith, in charity, in patience. {2:3} The aged women likewise, that [they be] in behaviour as becometh holiness, not false accusers, not given to much wine, teachers of good things; {2:4} That they may teach the young women to be sober, to love their husbands, to love their children, {2:5} [To be] discreet, chaste, keepers at home, good, obedient to their own husbands, that the word of **God** be not blasphemed. {2:6} Young men likewise exhort to be sober minded. {2:7} In all things shewing thyself a pattern of good works: in doctrine [shewing] uncorruptness, gravity, sincerity, {2:8} Sound speech, that cannot be condemned; that he that is of the contrary part may be ashamed, having no evil thing to say of you. {2:9} [Exhort] servants to be obedient unto their own masters, [and] to please [them] well in all [things;] not answering again; {2:10} Not purloining, but shewing all good fidelity; that they may adorn the doctrine of **God** our **Saviour** in all things. {2:11} For the grace of **God** that bringeth salvation hath appeared to all men, {2:12} Teaching us that, denying un**God**liness and worldly lusts, we should live soberly, righteously, and **God**ly, in this present world; {2:13} Looking for that blessed hope, and the glorious appearing of the **great God** and our **Saviour Jesus Christ**; {2:14} **Who** gave **himself** for us, that **He** might redeem us from all iniquity, and purify unto himself a peculiar people, zealous

of good works. {2:15} These things speak, and exhort, and rebuke with all authority. Let no man despise thee. {8}

{3:1} Put them in mind to be subject to principalities and powers, to obey magistrates, to be ready to every good work, {3:2} To speak evil of no man, to be no brawlers, [but] gentle, shewing all meekness unto all men. {3:3} For we ourselves also were sometimes foolish, disobedient, deceived, serving divers lusts and pleasures, living in malice and envy, hateful, [and] hating one another. {3:4} But after that the kindness and love of **God** our **Saviour** toward man appeared, {3:5} Not by works of righteousness which we have done, but according to **His** mercy **He** saved us, by the washing of regeneration, and renewing of the **Holy Ghost**; {3:6} Which **He** shed on us abundantly through **Jesus Christ** our **Saviour**; {3:7} That being justified by **His** grace, we should be made heirs according to the hope of eternal life. {3:8} [This is] a faithful saying, and these things I will that thou affirm constantly, that they which have believed in **God** might be careful to maintain good works. These things are good and profitable unto men. {3:9} But avoid foolish questions, and genealogies, and contentions, and strivings about the law; for they are unprofitable and vain. {3:10} A man that is an heretick after the first and second admonition reject; {3:11} Knowing that he that is such is subverted, and sinneth, being condemned of himself.

{3:12} When I shall send Artemas unto thee, or Tychicus, be diligent to come unto me to Nicopolis: for I have determined there to winter. {3:13} Bring Zenas the lawyer and Apollos on their journey diligently, that nothing be wanting unto them. {3:14} And let ours also learn to maintain good works for necessary uses, that they be not unfruitful.

{3:15} All that are with me salute thee. Greet them that love us in the faith. Grace [be] with you all. Amen. {7}

Epistle of Paul to Philemon **TOTAL 20**

{1:1} Paul, a prisoner of **Jesus Christ**, and Timothy our brother, unto Philemon our dearly beloved, and fellowlabourer, {1:2} And to [our] beloved Apphia, and Archippus our fellowsoldier, and to the church in thy house: {1:3} Grace to you, and peace, from **God** our **Father** and the **Lord Jesus Christ**.

{1:4} I thank my **God**, making mention of thee always in my prayers, {1:5} Hearing of thy love and faith, which thou hast toward the **Lord Jesus**, and toward all saints; {1:6} That the communication of thy faith may become effectual by the acknowledging of every good thing which is in you in **Christ Jesus**. {1:7} For we have great joy and consolation in thy love, because the bowels of the saints are refreshed by thee, brother. {1:8} Wherefore, though I might be much bold in **Christ** to enjoin thee that which is convenient, {1:9} Yet for love's sake I rather beseech [thee,] being such an one as Paul the aged, and now also a prisoner of **Jesus Christ**. {1:10} I beseech thee for my Son Onesimus, whom I have begotten in my bonds: {1:11} Which in time past was to thee unprofitable, but now profitable to thee and to me: {1:12} Whom I have sent again: thou therefore receive him, that is, mine own bowels: {1:13} Whom I would have retained with me, that in thy stead he might have ministered unto me in the bonds of the Gospel: {1:14} But without thy mind would I do nothing; that thy benefit should not be as it were of necessity, but willingly. {1:15} For perhaps he therefore departed for a season, that thou shouldest receive him for ever; {1:16} Not now as a servant, but above a servant, a brother beloved, specially to me, but how much more unto thee, both in the flesh, and in the **Lord**? {1:17} If thou count me therefore a partner, receive Him as myself. {1:18} If he hath wronged thee, or oweth [thee] ought, put that on mine account; {1:19} I Paul have written [it] with mine own hand, I will repay [it:] albeit I do not say to thee how thou owest unto me even thine own self besides. {1:20} Yea, brother, let me have joy of thee in the **Lord**: refresh my bowels in the **Lord**.

{1:21} Having confidence in thy obedience I wrote unto thee, knowing that thou wilt also do more than I say. {1:22} But withal prepare me also a lodging: for I trust that through your prayers I shall be given unto you.

{1:23} There salute thee Epaphras, my fellowprisoner in **Christ Jesus**; {1:24} Marcus, Aristarchus, Demas, Lucas, fellowlabourers.

{1:25} The grace of our **Lord Jesus Christ** [be] with your spirit. Amen.
{20}

The Epistle to the Hebrews   TOTAL 428

{1:1} **God**, who at sundry times and in divers manners spake in time past unto the **Father**s by the prophets, {1:2} Hath in these last days spoken unto us by [**His**] **Son**, whom **He** hath appointed **heir** of all things, by **whom** also **He** made the worlds; {1:3} **Who** being the brightness of [**His**] glory, and the **express image** of **His** person, and upholding all things by the word of **His** power, when **He** had by **himself** purged our sins, sat down on the right hand of the Majesty on high; {1:4} Being made so much better than the angels, as **He** hath by inheritance obtained a more excellent **name** than they. {1:5} For unto which of the angels said **He** at any time, **Thou** art **my Son**, this day have **I** begotten **thee**? And again, **I** will be to **Him** a **Father**, and **He** shall be to **me** a **Son**? {1:6} And again, when **He** bringeth in the **firstbegotten** into the world, **He** saith, And let all the angels of **God** worship **Him**. {1:7} And of the angels **He** saith, Who maketh **His** angels spirits, and **His** ministers a flame of fire. {1:8} But unto the **Son** [**He** saith,] **Thy** throne, **O God**, [is] for ever and ever: a sceptre of righteousness [is] the sceptre of thy kingdom. {1:9} **Thou** hast loved righteousness, and hated iniquity; therefore **God**, [even] **thy God**, hath anointed **thee** with the oil of gladness above **thy** fellows. {1:10} And, **Thou, Lord**, in the beginning hast laid the foundation of the earth; and the heavens are the works of **thine** hands: {1:11} They shall perish; but **thou** remainest; and they all shall wax old as doth a garment; {1:12} And as a vesture shalt **thou** fold them up, and they shall be changed: but **thou** art the same, and **thy** years shall not fail. {1:13} But to which of the angels said **He** at any times, Sit on **my** right hand, until **I** make **thine** enemies **thy** footstool? {1:14} Are they not all ministering spirits, sent forth to minister for them who shall be heirs of salvation? **{40}**

{2:1} Therefore we ought to give the more earnest heed to the things which we have heard, lest at any time we should let [them] slip. {2:2} For if the word spoken by angels was stedfast, and every transgression and disobedience received a just recompence of reward; {2:3} How shall we escape, if we neglect so great **salvation**; which at the first began to be spoken by the **Lord**, and was confirmed unto us by them that heard [**Him**;]{2:4} **God** also bearing [them] witness, both with signs and wonders, and with divers miracles, and gifts of the **Holy Ghost**, according to **His** own will?

{2:5} For unto the angels hath **He** not put in subjection the world to come, whereof we speak. {2:6} But one in a certain place testified, saying, What is **man**, that thou art mindful of **Him**? or the **Son of man**, that thou visitest **Him**? {2:7} Thou madest **Him** a little lower than the angels; thou crownedst **Him** with glory and honour, and didst set **Him** over the works of thy hands: {2:8} Thou hast put all things in subjection under **His** feet. For in that **He** put all in subjection under **Him**, **He** left nothing [that is] not put under **Him**. But now we see not yet all things put under **Him**. {2:9} But we see **Jesus**, **who** was made a little lower than the angels for the suffering of death, crowned with glory and honour; that **He** by the grace of **God** should taste death for every man. {2:10} For it became **Him**, for **whom** [are] all things, and by **whom** [are] all things, in bringing many sons unto glory, to make the **captain** of their **salvation** perfect through sufferings. {2:11} For both **He** that sanctifieth and they who are sanctified [are] all of one: for which cause **He** is not ashamed to call them brethren, {2:12} Saying, **I** will declare thy **name** unto **my** brethren, in the midst of the church will **I** sing praise unto **thee**. {2:13} And again, **I** will

put **my** trust in **Him**. And again, Behold **I** and the children which **God** hath given **me**. {2:14} Forasmuch then as the children are partakers of flesh and blood, **He** also **himself** likewise took part of the same; that through death **He** might destroy him that had the power of death, that is, the devil; {2:15} And deliver them who through fear of death were all their lifetime subject to bondage. {2:16} For verily **He** took not on [**Him** the nature of] angels; but **He** took on [**Him**] the **seed** of Abraham. {2:17} Wherefore in all things it behoved **Him** to be made like unto [**His**] brethren, that **He** might be a merciful and faithful **high priest** in things [pertaining] to **God**, to make reconciliation for the sins of the people. {2:18} For in that **He** himself hath suffered being tempted, **He** is able to succour them that are tempted. **{46}**

{3:1} Wherefore, holy brethren, partakers of the heavenly calling, consider the **Apostle** and **High Priest** of our profession, **Christ Jesus**; {3:2} **Who** was faithful to **Him** that appointed **Him**, as also Moses [was faithful] in all **His** house. {3:3} For this [**man**] was counted worthy of more glory than Moses, inasmuch as **He** who hath builded the house hath more honour than the house. {3:4} For every house is builded by some [**man**;] but **He** that built all things [is] **God**. {3:5} And Moses verily [was] faithful in all **His** house, as a servant, for a testimony of those things which were to be spoken after; {3:6} But **Christ** as a **Son** over **His** own house; whose house are we, if we hold fast the confidence and the rejoicing of the hope firm unto the end. {3:7} Wherefore (as the **Holy Ghost** saith, To day if ye will hear **His voice**, {3:8} Harden not your hearts, as in the provocation, in the day of temptation in the wilderness: {3:9} When your **Father**s tempted **me**, proved **me**, and saw **my** works forty years. {3:10} Wherefore **I** was grieved with that generation, and said, They do alway err in [their] heart; and they have not known **my** ways. {3:11} So **I** sware in **my** wrath, They shall not enter into **my** rest.) {3:12} Take heed, brethren, lest there be in any of you an evil heart of unbelief, in departing from the **living God**. {3:13} But exhort one another daily, while it is called To day; lest any of you be hardened through the deceitfulness of sin. {3:14} For we are made partakers of **Christ**, if we hold the beginning of our confidence stedfast unto the end; {3:15} While it is said, To day if ye will hear **His voice**, harden not your hearts, as in the provocation. {3:16} For some, when they had heard, did provoke: howbeit not all that came out of Egypt by Moses. {3:17} But with **whom** was **He** grieved forty years? [was it] not with them that had sinned, whose carcases fell in the wilderness? {3:18} And to **whom** sware **He** that they should not enter into **His** rest, but to them that believed not? {3:19} So we see that they could not enter in because of unbelief.

{31}

{4:1} Let us therefore fear, lest, a promise being left [us] of entering into **His** rest, any of you should seem to come short of it. {4:2} For unto us was the Gospel preached, as well as unto them: but the **word** preached did not profit them, not being mixed with faith in them that heard [it.]{4:3} For we which have believed do enter into rest, as **He** said, As **I** have sworn in **my** wrath, if they shall enter into **my** rest: although the works were finished from the foundation of the world. {4:4} For **He** spake in a certain place of the seventh [day] on this wise, And **God** did rest the seventh day from all **His** works. {4:5} And in this [place] again, If they shall enter into **my** rest. {4:6} Seeing therefore it remaineth that some must enter therein, and they to **whom** it was first preached entered not in because of unbelief: {4:7} Again, **He** limiteth a certain day, saying in David, To day, after so long a time; as it is said, To day if ye will hear **His voice**, harden not your hearts. {4:8} For if **Jesus** had given them rest, then would **He** not afterward have spoken of another day. {4:9} There remaineth therefore a rest to the people of God. {4:10} For He that is entered into His rest, He also hath ceased from His own works, as God [did] from His. {4:11} Let us labour therefore to enter into that rest, lest any man fall after the same example of unbelief. {4:12} For the word of God [is] quick, and powerful, and sharper than any twoedged sword, piercing even to the dividing asunder of soul and spirit, and of the joints and marrow, and [is] a discerner of the thoughts and intents of the heart. {4:13} Neither is there any creature that is not manifest in His sight: but all things [are] naked and opened unto the eyes of Him with whom we have to do. {4:14} Seeing then that we have a great high priest, that is passed into the heavens, Jesus the Son of God, let us hold fast [our] profession. {4:15} For we have not an high priest which cannot be touched with the feeling of our infirmities; but was in all points tempted like as [we are, yet] without sin. {4:16} Let us therefore come boldly unto the throne of grace, that we may obtain mercy, and find grace to help in time of need. {26}

{5:1} For every high priest taken from among men is ordained for men in things [pertaining] to God, that He may offer both gifts and sacrifices for sins: {5:2} Who can have compassion on the ignorant, and on them that are out of the way; for that He himself also is compassed with infirmity. {5:3} And by reason hereof He ought, as for the people, so also for himself, to offer for sins. {5:4} And no man taketh this honour unto himself, but He that is called of God, as [was] Aaron. {5:5} So also Christ glorified not himself to be made an high priest; but He that said unto Him, Thou art my Son, to day have I begotten thee. {5:6} As He saith also in another [place,] Thou [art] a priest for ever after the order of Melchisedec. {5:7} Who in the days of His flesh, when He had offered up prayers and supplications with strong crying and tears unto Him that was able to save Him from death, and was heard in that He feared; {5:8} Though He were a Son, yet learned He obedience by the things which He suffered; {5:9} And being made perfect, He became the author of eternal salvation unto all them that obey Him; {5:10} Called of God an high priest after the order of Melchisedec.

{5:11} Of whom we have many things to say, and hard to be uttered, seeing ye are dull of hearing. {5:12} For when for the time ye ought to be teachers, ye have need that one teach you again which [be] the first principles of the oracles of God; and are become such as have need of milk, and not of strong meat. {5:13} For every one that useth milk [is] unskilful in the word of righteousness: for He is a babe. {5:14} But strong meat belongeth to them that are of full age, [even] those who by reason of use have their senses exercised to discern both good and evil. {31}

{6:1} Therefore leaving the principles of the doctrine of Christ, let us go on unto perfection; not laying again the foundation of repentance from dead works, and of faith toward God, {6:2} Of the doctrine of baptisms, and of laying on of hands, and of resurrection of the dead, and of eternal judgment. {6:3} And this will we do, if God permit. {6:4} For [it is] impossible for those who were once enlightened, and have tasted of the heavenly gift, and were made partakers of the Holy Ghost, {6:5} And have tasted the good word of God, and the powers of the world to come, {6:6} If they shall fall away, to renew them again unto repentance; seeing they crucify to themselves the Son of God afresh, and put [Him] to an open shame. {6:7} For the earth which drinketh in the rain that cometh oft upon it, and bringeth forth herbs meet for them by whom it is dressed,

receiveth blessing from God: {6:8} But that which beareth thorns and briers [is] rejected, and [is] nigh unto cursing; whose end [is] to be burned. {6:9} But, beloved, we are persuaded better things of you, and things that accompany salvation, though we thus speak. {6:10} For God [is] not unrighteous to forget your work and labour of love, which ye have shewed toward His name, in that ye have ministered to the saints, and do minister. {6:11} And we desire that every one of you do shew the same diligence to the full assurance of hope unto the end: {6:12} That ye be not slothful, but followers of them who through faith and patience inherit the promises. {6:13} For when God made promise to Abraham, because He could swear by no greater, He sware by himself, {6:14} Saying, Surely blessing I will bless thee, and multiplying I will multiply thee. {6:15} And so, after He had patiently endured, He obtained the promise. {6:16} For men verily swear by the greater: and an oath for confirmation [is] to them an end of all strife. {6:17} Wherein God, willing more abundantly to shew unto the heirs of promise the immutability of His counsel, confirmed [it] by an oath: {6:18} That by two immutable things, in which [it was] impossible for God to lie, we might have a strong consolation, who have fled for refuge to lay hold upon the hope set before us: {6:19} Which [hope] we have as an anchor of the soul, both sure and stedfast, and which entereth into that within the veil; {6:20} Whither the forerunner is for us entered, [even] Jesus, made an high priest for ever after the order of Melchisedec. {24}

{7:1} For this Melchisedec, king of Salem, priest of the most high God, who met Abraham returning from the slaughter of the kings, and blessed Him; {7:2} To whom also Abraham gave a tenth part of all; first being by interpretation King of righteousness, and after that also King of Salem, which is, King of peace; {7:3} Without Father, without mother, without descent, having neither beginning of days, nor end of life; but made like unto the Son of God; abideth a priest continually. {7:4} Now consider how great this man [was,] unto whom even the patriarch Abraham gave the tenth of the spoils. {7:5} And verily they that are of the sons of Levi, who receive the office of the priesthood, have a commandment to take tithes of the people according to the law, that is, of their brethren, though they come out of the loins of Abraham: {7:6} But He whose descent is not counted from them received tithes of Abraham, and blessed Him that had the promises. {7:7} And without all contradiction the less is blessed of the better. {7:8} And here men that die receive tithes; but there He [receiveth them,] of whom it is witnessed that He liveth. {7:9} And as I may so say, Levi also, who receiveth tithes, payed tithes in Abraham. {7:10} For He was yet in the loins of His Father, when Melchisedec met Him. {7:11} If therefore perfection were by the Levitical priesthood, (for under it the people received the law,) what further need [was there] that another priest should rise after the order of Melchisedec, and not be called after the order of Aaron? {7:12} For the priesthood being changed, there is made of necessity a change also of the law. {7:13} For He of whom these things are spoken pertaineth to another tribe, of which no man gave attendance at the altar. {7:14} For [it is] evident that our Lord sprang out of Juda; of which tribe Moses spake nothing concerning priesthood. {7:15} And it is yet far more evident: for that after the similitude of Melchisedec there ariseth another priest, {7:16} Who is made, not after the law of a carnal commandment, but after the power of an endless life. {7:17} For He testifieth, Thou [art] a priest for ever after the order of Melchisedec. {7:18} For there is verily a disannulling of the commandment going before for the weakness and unprofitableness thereof.

{7:19} For the law made nothing perfect, but the bringing in of a better hope [did;] by the which we draw nigh unto **God**. {7:20} And inasmuch as not without an oath [**He** was made **priest**:]{7:21} (For those priests were made without an oath; but this with an oath by **Him** that said unto **Him**, The **Lord** sware and will not repent, **Thou** [art] a **priest** for ever after the order of **Melchisedec**:) {7:22} By so much was **Jesus** made a surety of a better testament. {7:23} And they truly were many priests, because they were not suffered to continue by reason of death: {7:24} But this [**man**,] because **He** continueth ever, hath an unchangeable priesthood. {7:25} Wherefore **He** is able also to save them to the uttermost that come unto **God** by **Him**, seeing **He** ever liveth to make intercession for them. {7:26} For such an **high priest** became us, [**who** is] **holy**, **harmless**, **undefiled**, **separate** from sinners, and made higher than the heavens; {7:27} **Who** needeth not daily, as those high priests, to offer up sacrifice, first for **His own** sins, and then for the people's: for this **He** did once, when **He** offered up **himself**. {7:28} For the law maketh men high priests which have infirmity; but the word of the oath, which was since the law, [maketh] the **Son**, who is consecrated for evermore. {57}

{8:1} Now of the things which we have spoken [this is] the sum: We have such an **high priest**, **who** is set on the right hand of the throne of the Majesty in the heavens; {8:2} A **minister** of the sanctuary, and of the true tabernacle, which the **Lord** pitched, and not man. {8:3} For every **high priest** is ordained to offer gifts and sacrifices: wherefore [it is] of necessity that this **man** have somewhat also to offer. {8:4} For if **He** were on earth, **He** should not be a **priest**, seeing that there are **priests** that offer gifts according to the law: {8:5} **Who** serve unto the example and shadow of heavenly things, as Moses was admonished of **God** when **He** was about to make the tabernacle: for, See, saith **He**, [that] thou make all things according to the pattern shewed to thee in the mount. {8:6} But now hath **He** obtained a more excellent ministry, by how much also **He** is the **mediator** of a better covenant, which was established upon better promises. {8:7} For if that first [covenant] had been faultless, then should no place have been sought for the second. {8:8} For finding fault with them, **He** saith, Behold, the days come, saith the **Lord**, when **I** will make a new covenant with the house of Israel and with the house of Judah: {8:9} Not according to the covenant that **I** made with their **Father**s in the day when **I** took them by the hand to lead them out of the land of Egypt; because they continued not in **my** covenant, and **I** regarded them not, saith the **Lord**. {8:10} For this [is] the covenant that **I** will make with the house of Israel after those days, saith the **Lord**; **I** will put **my** laws into their mind, and write them in their hearts: and **I** will be to them a **God**, and they shall be to **me** a people: {8:11} And they shall not teach every man **His** neighbour, and every man **His** brother, saying, Know the **Lord**: for all shall know **me**, from the least to the greatest. {8:12} For **I** will be merciful to their unrighteousness, and their sins and their iniquities will **I** remember no more. {8:13} In that **He** saith, A new [covenant,] **He** hath made the first old. Now that which decayeth and waxeth old [is] ready to vanish away. {38}

{9:1} Then verily the first [covenant] had also ordinances of divine service, and a worldly sanctuary. {9:2} For there was a tabernacle made; the first, wherein [was] the candlestick, and the table, and the shewbread; which is called the sanctuary. {9:3} And after the second veil, the tabernacle which is called the Holiest of all; {9:4} Which had the golden censer, and the ark of the covenant overlaid round about with gold, wherein [was] the golden pot that

had manna, and Aaron's rod that budded, and the tables of the covenant; {9:5} And over it the cherubims of glory shadowing the mercyseat; of which we cannot now speak particularly. {9:6} Now when these things were thus ordained, the priests went always into the first tabernacle, accomplishing the service [of **God**.]{9:7} But into the second [went] the **high priest** alone once every year, not without **blood**, which **He** offered for **himself**, and [for] the errors of the people: {9:8} The **Holy Ghost** this signifying, that the way into the holiest of all was not yet made manifest, while as the first tabernacle was yet standing: {9:9} Which [was] a figure for the time then present, in which were offered both gifts and sacrifices, that could not make **Him** that did the service perfect, as pertaining to the conscience; {9:10} [Which stood] only in meats and drinks, and divers washings, and carnal ordinances, imposed [on them] until the time of reformation. {9:11} But **Christ** being come an **high priest** of good things to come, by a greater and more perfect tabernacle, not made with hands, that is to say, not of this building; {9:12} Neither by the blood of goats and calves, but by **His** own **blood He** entered in once into the holy place, having obtained eternal redemption [for us.]{9:13} For if the blood of bulls and of goats, and the ashes of an heifer sprinkling the unclean, sanctifieth to the purifying of the flesh: {9:14} How much more shall the **blood** of **Christ**, **who** through the eternal Spirit offered **himself** without spot to **God**, purge your conscience from dead works to serve the living **God**? {9:15} And for this cause **He** is the **mediator** of the new testament, that by means of death, for the redemption of the transgressions [that were] under the first testament, they which are called might receive the promise of eternal inheritance. {9:16} For where a testament [is,] there must also of necessity be the death of the **testator**. {9:17} For a testament [is] of force after men are dead: otherwise it is of no strength at all while the **testator** liveth. {9:18} Whereupon neither the first [testament] was dedicated without blood. {9:19} For when Moses had spoken every precept to all the people according to the law, **He** took the blood of calves and of goats, with water, and scarlet wool, and hyssop, and sprinkled both the book, and all the people, {9:20} Saying, This [is] the blood of the testament which **God** hath enjoined unto you. {9:21} Moreover He sprinkled with blood both the tabernacle, and all the vessels of the ministry. {9:22} And almost all things are by the law purged with blood; and without shedding of blood is no remission. {9:23} [It was] therefore necessary that the patterns of things in the heavens should be purified with these; but the heavenly things themselves with better sacrifices than these. {9:24} For **Christ** is not entered into the holy places made with hands, [which are] the figures of the true; but into heaven itself, now to appear in the presence of **God** for us: {9:25} Nor yet that **He** should offer **himself** often, as the **high priest** entereth into the holy place every year with blood of others; {9:26} For then must **He** often have suffered since the foundation of the world: but now once in the end of the world hath **He** appeared to put away sin by the sacrifice of **himself**. {9:27} And as it is appointed unto men once to die, but after this the judgment: {9:28} So **Christ** was once offered to bear the sins of many; and unto them that look for **Him** shall **He** appear the second time without sin unto salvation. {30}

{10:1} For the law having a shadow of good things to come, [and] not the very image of the things, can never with those sacrifices which they offered year by year continually make the comers thereunto perfect. {10:2} For then would they not have ceased to be offered? because that the worshippers once purged should have had no more conscience of sins. {10:3} But in those [sacrifices there is] a remembrance again [made] of sins every year. {10:4} For [it is] not possible that the blood of bulls and of goats should take away sins. {10:5} Wherefore when **He** cometh into the world, **He** saith, Sacrifice and offering thou wouldest not, but a body hast thou prepared **me**: {10:6} In burnt offerings and [sacrifices] for sin thou hast had no pleasure. {10:7} Then said **I**, Lo, **I** come (in the volume of the book it is written of **me**,) to do thy will, O **God**. {10:8} Above when **He** said, Sacrifice and offering and burnt offerings and [offering] for sin thou wouldest not, neither hadst pleasure [therein;] which are offered by the law; {10:9} Then said **He**, Lo, **I** come to do thy will, O **God**. **He** taketh away the first, that **He** may establish the second. {10:10} By the which will we are sanctified through the offering of the **body** of **Jesus Christ** once [for all.]{10:11} And every **priest** standeth daily ministering and offering oftentimes the same sacrifices, which can never take away sins: {10:12} But this **man**, after **He** had offered one sacrifice for sins for ever, sat down on the right hand of **God**; {10:13} From henceforth expecting till **His** enemies be made **His** footstool. {10:14} For by one offering **He** hath perfected for ever them that are sanctified. {10:15} [Whereof] the **Holy Ghost** also is a witness to us: for after that **He** had said before, {10:16} This [is] the covenant that **I** will make with them after those days, saith the **Lord**, **I** will put **my** laws into their hearts, and in their minds will **I** write them; {10:17} And their sins and iniquities will **I** remember no more. {10:18} Now where remission of these [is, there is] no more offering for sin.

{10:19} Having therefore, brethren, boldness to enter into the holiest by the **blood** of **Jesus**, {10:20} By a **new and living way**, which **He** hath consecrated for us, through the veil, that is to say, **His** flesh; {10:21} And [having] an **high priest** over the house of **God**; {10:22} Let us draw near with a true heart in full assurance of faith, having our hearts sprinkled from an evil conscience, and our bodies washed with pure water. {10:23} Let us hold fast the profession of [our] faith without wavering; (for **He** is faithful that promised;) {10:24} And let us consider one another to provoke unto love and to good works: {10:25} Not forsaking the assembling of ourselves together, as the manner of some [is;] but exhorting [one another:] and so much the more, as ye see the day approaching. {10:26} For if we sin wilfully after that we have received the knowledge of the **truth**, there remaineth no more sacrifice for sins, {10:27} But a certain fearful looking for of judgment and fiery indignation, which shall devour the adversaries. {10:28} He that despised Moses' law died without mercy under two or three witnesses: {10:29} Of how much sorer punishment, suppose ye, shall He be thought worthy, who hath trodden under foot the **Son of God**, and hath counted the **blood** of the covenant, wherewith He was sanctified, an unholy thing, and hath done despite unto the Spirit of grace? {10:30} For we know **Him** that hath said, Vengeance [belongeth] unto **me**, **I** will recompense, saith the **Lord**. And again, The **Lord** shall judge **His** people. {10:31} [It is] a fearful thing to fall into the hands of the **living God**. {10:32} But call to remembrance the former days, in which, after ye were illuminated, ye endured a great fight of afflictions; {10:33} Partly, whilst ye were made a gazingstock both by reproaches and afflictions; and partly, whilst ye became companions of them that were so used. {10:34} For ye had compassion of me in **my** bonds, and took joyfully the spoiling of your goods, knowing in yourselves that ye have in heaven a better and an enduring substance. {10:35} Cast not away therefore your confidence, which hath great recompence of reward. {10:36} For ye have need of patience, that, after ye have {20}

done the will of **God**, ye might receive the promise. {10:37} For yet a little while, and **He** that shall come will come, and will not tarry. {10:38} Now the just shall live by faith: but if [any man] draw back, **my** soul shall have no pleasure in Him. {10:39} But we are not of them who draw back unto perdition; but of them that believe to the saving of the soul.

{11:1} Now faith is the substance of things hoped for, the evidence of things not seen. {11:2} For by it the elders obtained a good report. {11:3} Through faith we understand that the worlds were framed by the **word of God**, so that things which are seen were not made of things which do appear. {11:4} By faith Abel offered unto **God** a more excellent sacrifice than Cain, by which He obtained witness that He was righteous, **God** testifying of His gifts: and by it He being dead yet speaketh. {11:5} By faith Enoch was translated that He should not see death; and was not found, because **God** had translated Him: for before His translation He had this testimony, that He pleased **God**. {11:6} But without faith [it is] impossible to please [**Him**:] for **He** that cometh to **God** must believe that **He** is, and [that] **He** is a rewarder of them that diligently seek Him. {11:7} By faith Noah, being warned of **God** of things not seen as yet, moved with fear, prepared an ark to the saving of His house; by the which He condemned the world, and became heir of the righteousness which is by faith. {11:8} By faith Abraham, when He was called to go out into a place which He should after receive for an inheritance, obeyed; and He went out, not knowing whither He went. {11:9} By faith He sojourned in the land of promise, as [in] a strange country, dwelling in tabernacles with Isaac and Jacob, the heirs with Him of the same promise: {11:10} For He looked for a city which hath foundations, whose **builder** and **maker** [is] **God**. {11:11} Through faith also Sara herself received strength to conceive seed, and was delivered of a child when she was past age, because she judged **Him** faithful **who** had promised. {11:12} Therefore sprang there even of one, and Him as good as dead, [so many] as the stars of the sky in multitude, and as the sand which is by the sea shore innumerable. {11:13} These all died in faith, not having received the promises, but having seen them afar off, and were persuaded of [them,] and embraced [them,] and confessed that they were strangers and pilgrims on the earth. {11:14} For they that say such things declare plainly that they seek a country. {11:15} And truly, if they had been mindful of that [country] from whence they came out, they might have had opportunity to have returned. {11:16} But now they desire a better [country,] that is, an heavenly: wherefore **God** is not ashamed to be called their **God**: for **He** hath prepared for them a city. {11:17} By faith Abraham, when He was tried, offered up Isaac: and He that had received the promises offered up His only begotten [Son,]{11:18} Of whom it was said, That in Isaac shall thy seed be called: {11:19} Accounting that **God** [was] able to raise [Him] up, even from the dead; from whence also He received Him in a figure. {11:20} By faith Isaac blessed Jacob and Esau concerning things to come. {11:21} By faith Jacob, when He was a dying, blessed both the sons of Joseph; and worshipped, [leaning] upon the top of His staff. {11:22} By faith Joseph, when He died, made mention of the departing of the children of Israel; and gave commandment concerning His bones. {11:23} By faith Moses, when He was born, was hid three months of His parents, because they saw [He was] a proper child; and they were not afraid of the king's commandment. {11:24} By faith Moses, when He was come to years, refused to be called the Son of Pharaoh's daughter; {11:25} Choosing rather to suffer affliction with the people of **God**, than to enjoy the pleasures of sin for a season; {11:26} Esteeming the reproach of **Christ** greater riches than the treasures in Egypt: for He had respect unto the recompence of the reward. {11:27} By faith He forsook Egypt, not fearing the wrath of the king: for He endured, as seeing Him who is invisible. {11:28} Through faith He kept the passover, and the sprinkling of blood, lest He that destroyed the firstborn should touch them. {11:29} By faith they passed through the Red sea as by dry [land:] which the Egyptians assaying to do were drowned. {11:30} By faith the walls of Jericho fell down, after they were compassed about seven days. {11:31} By faith the harlot Rahab perished not with them that believed not, when she had received the spies with peace. {11:32} And what shall I more say? for the time would fail me to tell of Gedeon, and [of] Barak, and [of] Samson, and [of] Jephthae; [of] David also, and Samuel, and [of] the prophets: {11:33} Who through faith subdued kingdoms, wrought righteousness, obtained promises, stopped the mouths of lions, {11:34} Quenched the violence of fire, escaped the edge of the sword, out of weakness were made strong, waxed valiant in fight, turned to flight the armies of the aliens. {11:35} Women received their dead raised to life again: and others were tortured, not accepting deliverance; that they might obtain a better resurrection: {11:36} And others had trial of [cruel] mockings and scourgings, yea, moreover of bonds and imprisonment: {11:37} They were stoned, they were sawn asunder, were tempted, were slain with the sword: they wandered about in sheepskins and goatskins; being destitute, afflicted, tormented; {11:38} (Of whom the world was not worthy:) they wandered in deserts, and [in] mountains, and [in] dens and caves of the earth. {11:39} And these all, having obtained a good report through faith, received not the promise: {11:40} God having provided some better thing for us, that they without us should not be made perfect. {24}

{12:1} Wherefore seeing we also are compassed about with so great a cloud of witnesses, let us lay aside every weight, and the sin which doth so easily beset us, and let us run with patience the race that is set before us, {12:2} Looking unto Jesus the author and finisher of [our] faith; who for the joy that was set before Him endured the cross, despising the shame, and is set down at the right hand of the throne of God. {12:3} For consider Him that endured such contradiction of sinners against himself, lest ye be wearied and faint in your minds. {12:4} Ye have not yet resisted unto blood, striving against sin. {12:5} And ye have forgotten the exhortation which speaketh unto you as unto children, my Son, despise not thou the chastening of the Lord, nor faint when thou art rebuked of Him: {12:6} For whom the Lord loveth He chasteneth, and scourgeth every Son whom He receiveth. {12:7} If ye endure chastening, God dealeth with you as with sons; for what Son is He whom the Father chasteneth not? {12:8} But if ye be without chastisement, whereof all are partakers, then are ye bastards, and not sons. {12:9} Furthermore we have had Fathers of our flesh which corrected [us,] and we gave [them] reverence: shall we not much rather be in subjection unto the Father of spirits, and live? {12:10} For they verily for a few days chastened [us] after their own pleasure; but He for [our] profit, that [we] might be partakers of His holiness. {12:11} Now no chastening for the present seemeth to be joyous, but grievous: nevertheless afterward it yieldeth the peaceable fruit of righteousness unto them which are exercised thereby. {12:12} Wherefore lift up the hands which hang down, and the feeble knees; {12:13} And make straight paths for your feet, lest that which is lame be turned out of the way; but let it rather be healed. {12:14} Follow peace with all [men,] and holiness, without which no man shall see the Lord: {12:15} Looking diligently lest

any man fail of the grace of God; lest any root of bitterness springing up trouble [you,] and thereby many be defiled; {12:16} Lest there [be] any fornicator, or profane person, as Esau, who for one morsel of meat sold His birthright. {12:17} For ye know how that afterward, when He would have inherited the blessing, He was rejected: for He found no place of repentance, though He sought it carefully with tears. {12:18} For ye are not come unto the mount that might be touched, and that burned with fire, nor unto blackness, and darkness, and tempest, {12:19} And the sound of a trumpet, and the voice of words; [which] voice they that heard intreated that the word should not be spoken to them any more: {12:20} (For they could not endure that which was commanded, And if so much as a beast touch the mountain, it shall be stoned, or thrust through with a dart: {12:21} And so terrible was the sight, [that] Moses said, I exceedingly fear and quake:) {12:22} But ye are come unto mount Sion, and unto the city of the living God, the heavenly Jerusalem, and to an innumerable company of angels, {12:23} To the general assembly and church of the firstborn, which are written in heaven, and to God the Judge of all, and to the spirits of just men made perfect, {12:24} And to Jesus the mediator of the new covenant, and to the blood of sprinkling, that speaketh better things than [that of] Abel. {12:25} See that ye refuse not Him that speaketh. For if they escaped not who refused Him that spake on earth, much more [shall not] we [escape,] if we turn away from Him that [speaketh] from heaven: {12:26} Whose voice then shook the earth: but now He hath promised, saying, Yet once more I shake not the earth only, but also heaven. {12:27} And this [word,] Yet once more, signifieth the removing of those things that are shaken, as of things that are made, that those things which cannot be shaken may remain. {12:28} Wherefore we receiving a kingdom which cannot be moved, let us have grace, whereby we may serve God acceptably with reverence and Godly fear: {12:29} For our God [is] a consuming fire. {32}

{13:1} Let brotherly love continue. {13:2} Be not forgetful to entertain strangers: for thereby some have entertained angels unawares. {13:3} Remember them that are in bonds, as bound with them; [and] them which suffer adversity, as being yourselves also in the body. {13:4} Marriage [is] honourable in all, and the bed undefiled: but whoremongers and adulterers God will judge. {13:5} [Let your] conversation [be] without covetousness; [and be] content with such things as ye have: for He hath said, I will never leave thee, nor forsake thee. {13:6} So that we may boldly say, The Lord [is] my helper, and I will not fear what man shall do unto me.

{13:7} Remember them which have the rule over you, who have spoken unto you the word of God: whose faith follow, considering the end of [their] conversation. {13:8} Jesus Christ the same yesterday, and to day, and for ever. {13:9} Be not carried about with divers and strange doctrines. For [it is] a good thing that the heart be established with grace; not with meats, which have not profited them that have been occupied therein. {13:10} We have an altar, whereof they have no right to eat which serve the tabernacle. {13:11} For the bodies of those beasts, whose blood is brought into the sanctuary by the high priest for sin, are burned without the camp. {13:12} Wherefore Jesus also, that He might sanctify the people with His own blood, suffered without the gate. {13:13} Let us go forth therefore unto Him without the camp, bearing His reproach. {13:14} For here have we no continuing city, but we seek one to come. {13:15} By Him therefore let us offer the sacrifice of praise to God continually, that is, the fruit of

[our] lips giving thanks to **His name**. {13:16} But to do good and to communicate forget not: for with such sacrifices **God** is well pleased. {13:17} Obey them that have the rule over you, and submit yourselves: for they watch for your souls, as they that must give account, that they may do it with joy, and not with grief: for that [is] unprofitable for you.

{13:18} Pray for us: for we trust we have a good conscience, in all things willing to live honestly. {13:19} But I beseech [you] the rather to do this, that I may be restored to you the sooner. {13:20} Now the **God** of peace, that brought again from the dead our **Lord Jesus**, that **great Shepherd** of the sheep, through the **blood** of the everlasting covenant, {13:21} Make you perfect in every good work to do **His** will, working in you that which is wellpleasing in **His** sight, through **Jesus Christ**; to **whom** [be] glory for ever and ever. Amen. {13:22} And I beseech you, brethren, suffer the word of exhortation: for I have written a letter unto you in few words. {13:23} Know ye that [our] brother Timothy is set at liberty; with whom, if He come shortly, I will see you.

{13:24} Salute all them that have the rule over you, and all the saints. They of Italy salute you.
{29}

The General Epistle of James **TOTAL 53**

{1:1} James, a servant of **God** and of the **Lord Jesus Christ**, to the twelve tribes which are scattered abroad, greeting.

{1:2} My brethren, count it all joy when ye fall into divers temptations; {1:3} Knowing [this,] that the trying of your faith worketh patience. {1:4} But let patience have [her] perfect work, that ye may be perfect and entire, wanting nothing. {1:5} If any of you lack wisdom, let him ask of **God**, that giveth to all [men] liberally, and upbraideth not; and it shall be given him. {1:6} But let him ask in faith, nothing wavering. For he that wavereth is like a wave of the sea driven with the wind and tossed. {1:7} For let not that man think that he shall receive any thing of the **Lord**. {1:8} A double minded man [is] unstable in all his ways. {1:9} Let the brother of low degree rejoice in that he is exalted: {1:10} But the rich, in that he is made low: because as the flower of the grass he shall pass away. {1:11} For the sun is no sooner risen with a burning heat, but it withereth the grass, and the flower thereof falleth, and the grace of the fashion of it perisheth: so also shall the rich man fade away in his ways. {1:12} Blessed [is] the man that endureth temptation: for when he is tried, he shall receive the crown of life, which the **Lord** hath promised to them that love **Him**. {1:13} Let no man say when he is tempted, I am tempted of **God**: for **God** cannot be tempted with evil, neither tempteth **He** any man: {1:14} But every man is tempted, when he is drawn away of his own lust, and enticed. {1:15} Then when lust hath conceived, it bringeth forth sin: and sin, when it is finished, bringeth forth death. {1:16} Do not err, my beloved brethren. {1:17} Every good gift and every perfect gift is from above, and cometh down from the **Father** of lights, with **whom** is no variableness, neither shadow of turning. {1:18} Of **His** own will begat **He** us with the word of truth, that we should be a kind of firstfruits of **His** creatures.

{1:19} Wherefore, my beloved brethren, let every man be swift to hear, slow to speak, slow to wrath: {1:20} For the wrath of man worketh not the righteousness of **God**. {1:21} Wherefore lay apart all filthiness and superfluity of naughtiness, and receive with meekness the engrafted word, which is able to save your souls. {1:22} But be ye doers of the word, and not hearers only, deceiving your own selves. {1:23} For if any be a hearer of the word, and not a doer, he is like unto a man beholding his natural face in a glass: {1:24} For he beholdeth himself, and goeth his way, and straightway forgetteth what manner of man he was. {1:25} But whoso looketh into the perfect law of liberty, and continueth [therein,] he being not a forgetful hearer, but a doer of the work, this man shall be blessed in his deed. {1:26} If any man among you seem to be religious, and bridleth not his tongue, but deceiveth his own heart, this man's religion [is] vain. {1:27} Pure religion and undefiled before **God** and the **Father** is this, To visit the **Father**less and widows in their affliction, [and] to keep himself unspotted from the world. **{16}**

{2:1} My brethren, have not the faith of our **Lord Jesus Christ**, [the **Lord**] of glory, with respect of persons. {2:2} For if there come unto your assembly a man with a gold ring, in goodly apparel, and there come in also a poor man in vile raiment; {2:3} And ye have respect to him that weareth the gay clothing, and say unto him, Sit thou here in a good place; and say to the poor, Stand thou there, or sit

here under my footstool: {2:4} Are ye not then partial in yourselves, and are become judges of evil thoughts? {2:5} Hearken, my beloved brethren, Hath not **God** chosen the poor of this world rich in faith, and heirs of the kingdom which **He** hath promised to them that love **Him**? {2:6} But ye have despised the poor. Do not rich men oppress you, and draw you before the judgment seats? {2:7} Do not they blaspheme that worthy name by the which ye are called? {2:8} If ye fulfil the royal law according to the scripture, Thou shalt love thy neighbour as thyself, ye do well: {2:9} But if ye have respect to persons, ye commit sin, and are convinced of the law as transgressors. {2:10} For whosoever shall keep the whole law, and yet offend in one [point,] he is guilty of all. {2:11} For **He** that said, Do not commit adultery, said also, Do not kill. Now if thou commit no adultery, yet if thou kill, thou art become a transgressor of the law. {2:12} So speak ye, and so do, as they that shall be judged by the law of liberty. {2:13} For **He** shall have judgment without mercy, that hath shewed no mercy; and mercy rejoiceth against judgment. {2:14} What [doth it] profit, my brethren, though a man say he hath faith, and have not works? can faith save him? {2:15} If a brother or sister be naked, and destitute of daily food, {2:16} And one of you say unto them, Depart in peace, be ye warmed and filled; notwithstanding ye give them not those things which are needful to the body; what [doth it] profit? {2:17} Even so faith, if it hath not works, is dead, being alone. {2:18} Yea, a man may say, Thou hast faith, and I have works: shew me thy faith without thy works, and I will shew thee my faith by my works. {2:19} Thou believest that there is one **God**; thou doest well: the devils also believe, and tremble. {2:20} But wilt thou know, O vain man, that faith without works is dead? {2:21} Was not Abraham our **Father** justified by works, when he had offered Isaac his Son upon the altar? {2:22} Seest thou how faith wrought with his works, and by works was faith made perfect? {2:23} And the scripture was fulfilled which saith, Abraham believed **God**, and it was imputed unto him for righteousness: and he was called the Friend of **God**. {2:24} Ye see then how that by works a man is justified, and not by faith only. {2:25} Likewise also was not Rahab the harlot justified by works, when she had received the messengers, and had sent [them] out another way? {2:26} For as the body without the spirit is dead, so faith without works is dead also. **{12}**

{3:1} My brethren, be not many masters, knowing that we shall receive the greater condemnation. {3:2} For in many things we offend all. If any man offend not in word, the same [is] a perfect man, [and] able also to bridle the whole body. {3:3} Behold, we put bits in the horses' mouths, that they may obey us; and we turn about their whole body. {3:4} Behold also the ships, which though [they be] so great, and [are] driven of fierce winds, yet are they turned about with a very small helm, whithersoever the governor listeth. {3:5} Even so the tongue is a little member, and boasteth great things. Behold, how great a matter a little fire kindleth! {3:6} And the tongue [is] a fire, a world of iniquity: so is the tongue among our members, that it defileth the whole body, and setteth on fire the course of nature; and it is set on fire of hell. {3:7} For every kind of beasts, and of birds, and of serpents, and of things in the sea, is tamed, and hath been tamed of mankind: {3:8} But the tongue can no man tame; [it is] an unruly evil, full of deadly poison. {3:9} Therewith bless we **God**, even the **Father**; and therewith curse we men, which are made after the similitude of **God**. {3:10} Out of the same mouth proceedeth blessing and cursing. my brethren, these things ought not so to be. {3:11} Doth a fountain send forth at the same place sweet [water] and bitter? {3:12} Can the fig tree, my brethren, bear olive berries? either a vine, figs? so [can] no fountain both yield salt water and fresh. {3:13} Who [is] a wise man and endued with knowledge among you? let him shew out of a good conversation his works with meekness of wisdom. {3:14} But if ye have bitter envying and strife in your hearts, glory not, and lie not against the truth. {3:15} This wisdom descendeth not from above, but [is] earthly, sensual, devilish. {3:16} For where envying and strife [is,] there [is] confusion and every evil work. {3:17} But the wisdom that is from above is first pure, then peaceable, gentle, [and] easy to be intreated, full of mercy and good fruits, without partiality, and without hypocrisy. {3:18} And the fruit of righteousness is sown in peace of them that make peace. {2}

{4:1} From whence [come] wars and fightings among you? [come they] not hence, [even] of your lusts that war in your members? {4:2} Ye lust, and have not: ye kill, and desire to have, and cannot obtain: ye fight and war, yet ye have not, because ye ask not. {4:3} Ye ask, and receive not, because ye ask amiss, that ye may consume [it] upon your lusts. {4:4} Ye adulterers and adulteresses, know ye not that the friendship of the world is enmity with **God**? whosoever therefore will be a friend of the world is the enemy of **God**. {4:5} Do ye think that the scripture saith in vain, The spirit that dwelleth in us lusteth to envy? {4:6} But **He** giveth more grace. Wherefore **He** saith, **God** resisteth the proud, but giveth grace unto the humble. {4:7} Submit yourselves therefore to **God**. Resist the devil, and he will flee from you. {4:8} Draw nigh to **God**, and **He** will draw nigh to you. Cleanse [your] hands, [ye] sinners; and purify [your] hearts, [ye] double minded. {4:9} Be afflicted, and mourn, and weep: let your laughter be turned to mourning, and [your] joy to heaviness. {4:10} Humble yourselves in the sight of the **Lord**, and **He** shall lift you up. {4:11} Speak not evil one of another, brethren. he that speaketh evil of [his] brother, and judgeth his brother, speaketh evil of the law, and judgeth the law: but if thou judge the law, thou art not a doer of the law, but a judge. {4:12} There is one **lawgiver**, who is able to save and to destroy: who art thou that judgest another?

{4:13} Go to now, ye that say, To day or to morrow we will go into such a city, and continue there a year, and buy and sell, and get gain: {4:14} Whereas ye know not what [shall be] on the morrow. For what [is] your life? It is even a vapour, that appeareth for a little time, and then vanisheth away. {4:15} For that ye [ought] to say, If the **Lord** will, we shall live, and do this, or that. {4:16} But now ye rejoice in your boastings: all such rejoicing is evil. {4:17} Therefore to him that knoweth to do good, and doeth [it] not, to him it is sin. {12}

{5:1} Go to now, [ye] rich men, weep and howl for your miseries that shall come upon [you.]{5:2} Your riches are corrupted, and your garments are motheaten. {5:3} Your gold and silver is cankered; and the rust of them shall be a witness against you, and shall eat your flesh as it were fire. Ye have heaped treasure together for the last days. {5:4} Behold, the hire of the labourers who have reaped down your fields, which is of you kept back by fraud, crieth: and the cries of them which have reaped are entered into the ears of the **Lord of sabaoth**. {5:5} Ye have lived in pleasure on the earth, and been wanton; ye have nourished your hearts, as in a day of slaughter. {5:6} Ye have condemned [and] killed the just; [and] he doth not resist you.

{5:7} Be patient therefore, brethren, unto the coming of the **Lord**. Behold, the husbandman waiteth for the precious

fruit of the earth, and hath long patience for it, until **He** receive the early and latter rain. {5:8} Be ye also patient; stablish your hearts: for the coming of the **Lord** draweth nigh. {5:9} Grudge not one against another, brethren, lest ye be condemned: behold, the **judge** standeth before the door. {5:10} Take, my brethren, the prophets, who have spoken in the **name** of the **Lord**, for an example of suffering affliction, and of patience. {5:11} Behold, we count them happy which endure. Ye have heard of the patience of Job, and have seen the end of the **Lord**; that the **Lord** is very pitiful, and of tender mercy. {5:12} But above all things, my brethren, swear not, neither by heaven, neither by the earth, neither by any other oath: but let your yea be yea; and [your] nay, nay; lest ye fall into condemnation. {5:13} Is any among you afflicted? let him pray. Is any merry? let him sing psalms. {5:14} Is any sick among you? let him call for the elders of the church; and let them pray over him, anointing him with oil in the **name** of the **Lord**: {5:15} And the prayer of faith shall save the sick, and the **Lord** shall raise him up; and if he have committed sins, they shall be forgiven him. {5:16} Confess [your] faults one to another, and pray one for another, that ye may be healed. The effectual fervent prayer of a righteous man availeth much. {5:17} Elias was a man subject to like passions as we are, and he prayed earnestly that it might not rain: and it rained not on the earth by the space of three years and six months. {5:18} And he prayed again, and the heaven gave rain, and the earth brought forth her fruit. {5:19} Brethren, if any of you do err from the truth, and one convert him; {5:20} Let him know, that he which converteth the sinner from the error of his way shall save a soul from death, and shall hide a multitude of sins.

{11}

First Epistle General of Peter   TOTAL 104

{1:1} Peter, an apostle of **Jesus Christ**, to the strangers scattered throughout Pontus, Galatia, Cappadocia, Asia, and Bithynia, {1:2} Elect according to the foreknowledge of **God** the **Father**, through sanctification of the Spirit, unto obedience and sprinkling of the **blood** of **Jesus Christ**: Grace unto you, and peace, be multiplied. {1:3} Blessed [be] the **God** and **Father** of our **Lord Jesus Christ**, which according to **His** abundant mercy hath begotten us again unto a lively hope by the resurrection of **Jesus Christ** from the dead, {1:4} To an inheritance incorruptible, and undefiled, and that fadeth not away, reserved in heaven for you, {1:5} Who are kept by the power of **God** through faith unto salvation ready to be revealed in the last time. {1:6} Wherein ye greatly rejoice, though now for a season, if need be, ye are in heaviness through manifold temptations: {1:7} That the trial of your faith, being much more precious than of gold that perisheth, though it be tried with fire, might be found unto praise and honour and glory at the appearing of **Jesus Christ**: {1:8} **Whom** having not seen, ye love; in **whom**, though now ye see [**Him**] not, yet believing, ye rejoice with joy unspeakable and full of glory: {1:9} Receiving the end of your faith, [even] the salvation of [your] souls. {1:10} Of which salvation the prophets have enquired and searched diligently, who prophesied of the grace [that should come] unto you: {1:11} Searching what, or what manner of time the Spirit of **Christ** which was in them did signify, when it testified beforehand the sufferings of **Christ**, and the glory that should follow. {1:12} Unto **whom** it was revealed, that not unto themselves, but unto us they did minister the things, which are now reported unto you by them that have preached the Gospel unto you with the **Holy Ghost** sent down from heaven; which things the angels desire to look into. {1:13} Wherefore gird up the loins of your mind, be sober, and hope to the end for the grace that is to be brought unto you at the revelation of **Jesus Christ**; {1:14} As obedient children, not fashioning yourselves according to the former lusts in your ignorance: {1:15} But as **He** which hath called you is holy, so be ye holy in all manner of conversation; {1:16} Because it is written, Be ye holy; for **I am** holy. {1:17} And if ye call on the **Father**, who without respect of persons judgeth according to every man's work, pass the time of your sojourning [here] in fear: {1:18} Forasmuch as ye know that ye were not redeemed with corruptible things, [as] silver and gold, from your vain conversation [received] by tradition from your **Fathers**; {1:19} But with the precious **blood** of **Christ**, as of a **lamb** without blemish and without spot: {1:20} **Who** verily was foreordained before the foundation of the world, but was manifest in these last times for you, {1:21} **Who** by **Him** do believe in **God**, that raised **Him** up from the dead, and gave **Him** glory; that your faith and hope might be in **God**. {1:22} Seeing ye have purified your souls in obeying the truth through the Spirit unto unfeigned love of the brethren, [see that ye] love one another with a pure heart fervently: {1:23} Being born again, not of corruptible seed, but of incorruptible, by the **word of God**, which liveth and abideth for ever. {1:24} For all flesh [is] as grass, and all the glory of man as the flower of grass. The grass withereth, and the flower thereof falleth away: {1:25} But the **word of the Lord** endureth for ever. And this is the word which by the Gospel is preached unto you. {33}

{2:1} Wherefore laying aside all malice, and all guile, and

hypocrisies, and envies, and all evil speakings, {2:2} As newborn babes, desire the sincere milk of the word, that ye may grow thereby: {2:3} If so be ye have tasted that the **Lord** [is] gracious. {2:4} To **whom** coming, [as unto] a **living stone**, disallowed indeed of men, but chosen of **God**, [and] precious, {2:5} Ye also, as lively stones, are built up a spiritual house, an holy priesthood, to offer up spiritual sacrifices, acceptable to **God** by **Jesus Christ**. {2:6} Wherefore also it is contained in the scripture, Behold, **I** lay in Sion a **chief corner stone**, elect, precious: and **he** that believeth on **Him** shall not be confounded. {2:7} Unto you therefore which believe [**He** is] precious: but unto them which be disobedient, the **stone** which the builders disallowed, the same is made the **head of the corner**, {2:8} And a **stone** of stumbling, and a **rock** of offence, [even to them] which stumble at the **word**, being disobedient: whereunto also they were appointed. {2:9} But ye [are] a chosen generation, a royal priesthood, an holy nation, a peculiar people; that ye should shew forth the praises of **Him who** hath called you out of darkness into **His** marvellous **light**: {2:10} Which in time past [were] not a people, but [are] now the people of **God**: which had not obtained mercy, but now have obtained mercy.

{2:11} Dearly beloved, **I** beseech [you] as strangers and pilgrims, abstain from fleshly lusts, which war against the soul; {2:12} Having your conversation honest among the Gentiles: that, whereas they speak against you as evildoers, they may by [your] good works, which they shall behold, glorify **God** in the day of visitation.

{2:13} Submit yourselves to every ordinance of man for the **Lord**'s sake: whether it be to the king, as supreme; {2:14} Or unto governors, as unto them that are sent by **Him** for the punishment of evildoers, and for the praise of them that do well. {2:15} For so is the will of **God**, that with well doing ye may put to silence the ignorance of foolish men: {2:16} As free, and not using [your] liberty for a cloke of maliciousness, but as the servants of **God**. {2:17} Honour all [men.] Love the brotherhood. Fear **God**. Honour the king. {2:18} Servants, [be] subject to [your] masters with all fear; not only to the good and gentle, but also to the froward. {2:19} For this [is] thankworthy, if a man for conscience toward **God** endure grief, suffering wrongfully. {2:20} For what glory [is it,] if, when ye be buffeted for your faults, ye shall take it patiently? but if, when ye do well, and suffer [for it,] ye take it patiently, this [is] acceptable with **God**. {2:21} For even hereunto were ye called: because **Christ** also suffered for us, leaving us an example, that ye should follow **His** steps: {2:22} **Who** did no sin, neither was guile found in **His** mouth: {2:23} **Who,** when **He** was reviled, reviled not again; when **He** suffered, **He** threatened not; but committed [**himself**] to **Him** that judgeth righteously: {2:24} **Who His own self** bare our sins in **His** own **body** on the tree, that we, being dead to sins, should live unto righteousness: by **whose** stripes ye were healed. {2:25} For ye were as sheep going astray; but are now returned unto the **Shepherd** and **Bishop** of your souls. {38}

{3:1} Likewise, ye wives, [be] in subjection to your own husbands; that, if any obey not the word, they also may without the word be won by the conversation of the wives; {3:2} While they behold your chaste conversation [coupled] with fear. {3:3} Whose adorning let it not be that outward [adorning] of plaiting the hair, and of wearing of gold, or of putting on of apparel; {3:4} But [let it be] the hidden man of the heart, in that which is not corruptible, [even the ornament] of a meek and quiet spirit, which is in the sight of **God** of great price. {3:5} For after this manner in the old time the holy women also, who trusted in **God**, adorned themselves, being in subjection unto their own husbands: {3:6} Even as Sarah obeyed Abraham, calling him **Lord**: whose daughters ye are, as long as ye do well, and are not afraid with any amazement. {3:7} Likewise, ye husbands, dwell with [them] according to knowledge, giving honour unto the wife, as unto the weaker vessel, and as being heirs together of the grace of life; that your prayers be not hindered. {3:8} Finally, [be ye] all of one mind, having compassion one of another, love as brethren, [be] pitiful, [be] courteous: {3:9} Not rendering evil for evil, or railing for railing: but contrariwise blessing; knowing that ye are thereunto called, that ye should inherit a blessing. {3:10} For he that will love life, and see good days, let him refrain his tongue from evil, and his lips that they speak no guile: {3:11} Let him eschew evil, and do good; let him seek peace, and ensue it. {3:12} For the eyes of the **Lord** [are] over the righteous, and **His** ears [are open] unto their prayers: but the face of the **Lord** [is] against them that do evil.

{3:13} And who [is] he that will harm you, if ye be followers of that which is good? {3:14} But and if ye suffer for righteousness' sake, happy [are ye:] and be not afraid of their terror, neither be troubled; {3:15} But sanctify the **Lord God** in your hearts: and [be] ready always to [give] an answer to every man that asketh you a reason of the **hope** that is in you with meekness and fear: {3:16} Having a good conscience; that, whereas they speak evil of you, as of evildoers, they may be ashamed that falsely accuse your good conversation in **Christ**. {3:17} For [it is] better, if the will of **God** be so, that ye suffer for well doing, than for evil doing. {3:18} For **Christ** also hath once suffered for sins, the just for the unjust, that **He** might bring us to **God**, being put to death in the flesh, but quickened by the Spirit: {3:19} By which also **He** went and preached unto the spirits in prison; {3:20} Which sometime were disobedient, when once the longsuffering of **God** waited in the days of Noah, while the ark was a preparing, wherein few, that is, eight souls were saved by water. {3:21} The like figure whereunto [even] baptism doth also now save us (not the putting away of the filth of the flesh, but the answer of a good conscience toward **God**,) by the resurrection of **Jesus Christ**: {3:22} **Who** is gone into heaven, and is on the right hand of **God**; angels and authorities and powers being made subject unto **Him**. {15}

{4:1} Forasmuch then as **Christ** hath suffered for us in the flesh, arm yourselves likewise with the same mind: for he that hath suffered in the flesh hath ceased from sin; {4:2} That he no longer should live the rest of [his] time in the flesh to the lusts of men, but to the will of **God**. {4:3} For the time past of [our] life may suffice us to have wrought the will of the Gentiles, when we walked in lasciviousness, lusts, excess of wine, revellings, banquetings, and abominable idolatries: {4:4} Wherein they think it strange that ye run not with [them] to the same excess of riot, speaking evil of [you:]{4:5} Who shall give account to **Him** that is ready to judge the quick and the dead. {4:6} For for this cause was the **Gospel** preached also to them that are dead, that they might be judged according to men in the flesh, but live according to **God** in the spirit.

{4:7} But the end of all things is at hand: be ye therefore sober, and watch unto prayer. {4:8} And above all things have fervent charity among yourselves: for charity shall cover the multitude of sins. {4:9} Use hospitality one to another without grudging. {4:10} As every man hath received the gift, [even so] minister the same one to another,

as good stewards of the manifold grace of **God**. {4:11} If any man speak, [let him speak] as the oracles of **God**; if any man minister, [let him do it] as of the ability which **God** giveth: that **God** in all things may be glorified through **Jesus Christ**, to **whom** be praise and dominion for ever and ever. Amen.

{4:12} Beloved, think it not strange concerning the fiery trial which is to try you, as though some strange thing happened unto you: {4:13} But rejoice, inasmuch as ye are partakers of **Christ**'s sufferings; that, when **His** glory shall be revealed, ye may be glad also with exceeding joy. {4:14} If ye be reproached for the **name** of **Christ**, happy [are ye;] for the spirit of glory and of **God** resteth upon you: on their part **He** is evil spoken of, but on your part **He** is glorified. {4:15} But let none of you suffer as a murderer, or [as] a thief, or [as] an evildoer, or as a busybody in other men's matters. {4:16} Yet if [any man suffer] as a Christian, let him not be ashamed; but let him glorify **God** on this behalf. {4:17} For the time [is come] that judgment must begin at the house of **God**: and if [it] first [begin] at us, what shall the end [be] of them that obey not the **Gospel** of **God**? {4:18} And if the righteous scarcely be saved, where shall the un**God**ly and the sinner appear? {4:19} Wherefore let them that suffer according to the will of **God** commit the keeping of their souls [to him] in well doing, as unto a faithful Creator. {11}

{5:1} The elders which are among you I exhort, who am also an elder, and a witness of the sufferings of **Christ**, and also a partaker of the glory that shall be revealed: {5:2} Feed the flock of **God** which is among you, taking the oversight [thereof,] not by constraint, but willingly; not for filthy lucre, but of a ready mind; {5:3} Neither as being lords over [**God**'s] heritage, but being ensamples to the flock. {5:4} And when the **chief Shepherd** shall appear, ye shall receive a crown of glory that fadeth not away. {5:5} Likewise, ye younger, submit yourselves unto the elder. Yea, all [of you] be subject one to another, and be clothed with humility: for **God** resisteth the proud, and giveth grace to the humble.

{5:6} Humble yourselves therefore under the mighty hand of **God**, that **He** may exalt you in due time: {5:7} Casting all your care upon **Him**; for **He** careth for you. {5:8} Be sober, be vigilant; because your adversary the devil, as a roaring lion, walketh about, seeking **whom** he may devour: {5:9} Whom resist stedfast in the faith, knowing that the same afflictions are accomplished in your brethren that are in the world. {5:10} But the **God** of all grace, who hath called us unto **His** eternal glory by **Christ Jesus**, after that ye have suffered a while, make you perfect, stablish, strengthen, settle [you.]{5:11} To **Him** [be] glory and dominion for ever and ever. Amen.

{5:12} By Silvanus, a faithful brother unto you, as I suppose, I have written briefly, exhorting, and testifying that this is the true grace of **God** wherein ye stand. {5:13} The [church that is] at Babylon, elected together with [you,] saluteth you; and [so doth] Marcus my **Son**. {5:14} Greet ye one another with a kiss of charity. Peace [be] with you all that are in **Christ Jesus**. Amen. {8}

Second Epistle General of Peter   TOTAL

{1:1} Simon Peter, a servant and an apostle of **Jesus Christ**, to them that have obtained like precious faith with us through the righteousness of **God** and our **Saviour Jesus Christ**: {1:2} Grace and peace be multiplied unto you through the knowledge of **God**, and of **Jesus** our **Lord**, {1:3} According as **His** divine power hath given unto us all things that [pertain] unto life and **God**liness, through the knowledge of **Him** that hath called us to glory and virtue: {1:4} Whereby are given unto us exceeding great and precious promises: that by these ye might be partakers of the **divine nature**, having escaped the corruption that is in the world through lust. {1:5} And beside this, giving all diligence, add to your faith virtue; and to virtue knowledge; {1:6} And to knowledge temperance; and to temperance patience; and to patience **God**liness; {1:7} And to **God**liness brotherly kindness; and to brotherly kindness charity. {1:8} For if these things be in you, and abound, they make [you that ye shall] neither [be] barren nor unfruitful in the knowledge of our **Lord Jesus Christ**. {1:9} But he that lacketh these things is blind, and cannot see afar off, and hath forgotten that he was purged from his old sins. {1:10} Wherefore the rather, brethren, give diligence to make your calling and election sure: for if ye do these things, ye shall never fall: {1:11} For so an entrance shall be ministered unto you abundantly into the everlasting kingdom of our **Lord** and **Saviour Jesus Christ**.{1:12} Wherefore I will not be negligent to put you always in remembrance of these things, though ye know [them,] and be established in the present truth. {1:13} Yea, I think it meet, as long as I am in this tabernacle, to stir you up by putting [you] in remembrance; {1:14} Knowing that shortly I must put off [this] my tabernacle, even as our **Lord Jesus Christ** hath shewed **me**. {1:15} Moreover I will endeavour that ye may be able after my decease to have these things always in remembrance. {1:16} For we have not followed cunningly devised fables, when we made known unto you the power and coming of our **Lord Jesus Christ**, but were eyewitnesses of **His** majesty. {1:17} For **He** received from **God** the **Father** honour and glory, when there came such a voice to **him** from the excellent glory, This is **My beloved Son**, in **whom** I **am** well pleased. {1:18} And this voice which came from heaven we heard, when we were with **Him** in the holy mount. {1:19} We have also a more sure word of prophecy; whereunto ye do well that ye take heed, as unto a light that shineth in a dark place, until the day dawn, and the **day star** arise in your hearts: {1:20} Knowing this first, that no prophecy of the scripture is of any private interpretation. {1:21} For the prophecy came not in old time by the will of man: but holy men of **God** spake [as they were] moved by the **Holy Ghost**. **{31}**

{2:1} But there were false prophets also among the people, even as there shall be false teachers among you, who privily shall bring in damnable heresies, even denying the **Lord** that bought them, and bring upon themselves swift destruction. {2:2} And many shall follow their pernicious ways; by reason of **whom** the **way of truth** shall be evil spoken of. {2:3} And through covetousness shall they with feigned words make merchandise of you: whose judgment now of a long time lingereth not, and their damnation slumbereth not. {2:4} For if **God** spared not the angels that sinned, but cast [them] down to hell, and delivered [them] into chains of darkness, to be reserved unto judgment; {2:5} And spared not the old world, but saved Noah the eighth

[person,] a preacher of righteousness, bringing in the flood upon the world of the un**God**ly; {2:6} And turning the cities of Sodom and Gomorrah into ashes condemned [them] with an overthrow, making [them] an ensample unto those that after should live un**God**ly; {2:7} And delivered just Lot, vexed with the filthy conversation of the wicked: {2:8} (For that righteous man dwelling among them, in seeing and hearing, vexed [his] righteous soul from day to day with [their] unlawful deeds;) {2:9} The **Lord** knoweth how to deliver the **God**ly out of temptations, and to reserve the unjust unto the day of judgment to be punished: {2:10} But chiefly them that walk after the flesh in the lust of uncleanness, and despise government. Presumptuous [are they,] selfwilled, they are not afraid to speak evil of dignities. {2:11} Whereas angels, which are greater in power and might, bring not railing accusation against them before the **Lord**. {2:12} But these, as natural brute beasts, made to be taken and destroyed, speak evil of the things that they understand not; and shall utterly perish in their own corruption; {2:13} And shall receive the reward of unrighteousness, [as] they that count it pleasure to riot in the daytime. Spots [they are] and blemishes, sporting themselves with their own deceivings while they feast with you; {2:14} Having eyes full of adultery, and that cannot cease from sin; beguiling unstable souls: an heart they have exercised with covetous practices; cursed children: {2:15} Which have forsaken the **right way**, and are gone astray, following the way of Balaam [the Son] of Bosor, who loved the wages of unrighteousness; {2:16} But was rebuked for his iniquity: the dumb ass speaking with man's voice forbad the madness of the prophet. {2:17} These are wells without water, clouds that are carried with a tempest; to whom the mist of darkness is reserved for ever. {2:18} For when they speak great swelling [words] of vanity, they allure through the lusts of the flesh, [through much] wantonness, those that were clean escaped from them who live in error. {2:19} While they promise them liberty, they themselves are the servants of corruption: for of whom a man is overcome, of the same is he brought in bondage. {2:20} For if after they have escaped the pollutions of the world through the knowledge of the **Lord** and **Saviour Jesus Christ**, they are again entangled therein, and overcome, the latter end is worse with them than the beginning. {2:21} For it had been better for them not to have known the **way of righteousness**, than, after they have known [it,] to turn from the holy commandment delivered unto them. {2:22} But it is happened unto them according to the true proverb, The me [is] turned to his own vomit again; and the sow that was washed to her wallowing in the mire. **{11}**

{3:1} This second epistle, beloved, I now write unto you; in [both] which I stir up your pure minds by way of remembrance: {3:2} That ye may be mindful of the words which were spoken before by the holy prophets, and of the commandment of us the apostles of the **Lord** and **Saviour**: {3:3} Knowing this first, that there shall come in the last days scoffers, walking after their own lusts, {3:4} And saying, Where is the promise of **His** coming? for since the **Father**s fell asleep, all things continue as [they were] from the beginning of the creation. {3:5} For this they willingly are ignorant of, that by the **word of God** the heavens were of old, and the earth standing out of the water and in the water: {3:6} Whereby the world that then was, being overflowed with water, perished: {3:7} But the heavens and the earth, which are now, by the same word are kept in store, reserved unto fire against the day of judgment and perdition of un**God**ly men. {3:8} But, beloved, be not ignorant of this one thing, that one day [is] with the **Lord** as a thousand years, and a thousand years as one day. {3:9} The **Lord** is not slack concerning **His** promise, as some men count slackness; but is longsuffering to us-ward, not willing that any should perish, but that all should come to repentance. {3:10} But the day of the **Lord** will come as a thief in the night; in the which the heavens shall pass away with a great noise, and the elements shall melt with fervent heat, the earth also and the works that are therein shall be burned up. {3:11} [Seeing] then [that] all these things shall be dissolved, what manner [of persons] ought ye to be in [all] holy conversation and **God**liness, {3:12} Looking for and hasting unto the coming of the day of **God**, wherein the heavens being on fire shall be dissolved, and the elements shall melt with fervent heat? {3:13} Nevertheless we, according to **His** promise, look for new heavens and a new earth, wherein dwelleth righteousness. {3:14} Wherefore, beloved, seeing that ye look for such things, be diligent that ye may be found of **Him** in peace, without spot, and blameless. {3:15} And account [that] the longsuffering of our **Lord** [is] **salvation**; even as our beloved brother Paul also according to the wisdom given unto him hath written unto you; {3:16} As also in all [his] epistles, speaking in them of these things; in which are some things hard to be understood, which they that are unlearned and unstable wrest, as [they do] also the other scriptures, unto their own destruction. {3:17} Ye therefore, beloved, seeing ye know [these things] before, beware lest ye also, being led away with the error of the wicked, fall from your own stedfastness. {3:18} But grow in grace, and [in] the knowledge of our **Lord** and **Saviour Jesus Christ**. To **Him** [be] glory both now and for ever. Amen. {17}

The First Epistle General of John **TOTAL 146**

{1:1} That which was from the **beginning**, which we have heard, which we have seen with our eyes, which we have looked upon, and our hands have handled, of the **Word** of **life**; {1:2} (For the **life** was manifested, and we have seen [**it**,] and bear witness, and shew unto you that **eternal life**, which was with the **Father**, and was manifested unto us;) {1:3} That which we have seen and heard declare we unto you, that ye also may have fellowship with us: and truly our fellowship [is] with the **Father**, and with **His Son Jesus Christ**. {1:4} And these things write we unto you, that your joy may be full.

{1:5} This then is the message which we have heard of **Him**, and declare unto you, that **God** is **light**, and in **Him** is no darkness at all. {1:6} If we say that we have fellowship with **Him**, and walk in darkness, we lie, and do not the truth: {1:7} But if we walk in the light, as **He** is in the light, we have fellowship one with another, and the **blood** of **Jesus Christ His Son** cleanseth us from all sin. {1:8} If we say that we have no sin, we deceive ourselves, and the truth is not in us. {1:9} If we confess our sins, **He** is faithful and just to forgive us [our] sins, and to cleanse us from all unrighteousness. {1:10} If we say that we have not sinned, we make **Him** a liar, and **His word** is not in us. **{20}**

{2:1} my little children, these things write I unto you, that ye sin not. And if any man sin, we have an **advocate** with the **Father**, **Jesus Christ** the righteous: {2:2} And **He** is the **propitiation** for our sins: and not for ours only, but also for [the sins of] the whole world. {2:3} And hereby we do know that we know **Him**, if we keep **His** commandments. {2:4} He that saith, I know **Him**, and keepeth not **His** commandments, is a liar, and the truth is not in Him. {2:5} But whoso keepeth **His** word, in Him verily is the love of **God** perfected: hereby know we that we are in **Him**. {2:6} He that saith he abideth in **Him** ought himself also so to walk, even as **He** walked.{2:7} Brethren, I write no new commandment unto you, but an old commandment which ye had from the beginning. The old commandment is the word which ye have heard from the beginning. {2:8} Again, a new commandment I write unto you, which thing is true in **Him** and in you: because the darkness is past, and the **true light** now shineth. {2:9} He that saith He is in the light, and hateth his brother, is in darkness even until now. {2:10} He that loveth his brother abideth in the **light**, and there is none occasion of stumbling in him. {2:11} But he that hateth his brother is in darkness, and walketh in darkness, and knoweth not whither he goeth, because that darkness hath blinded his eyes. {2:12} I write unto you, little children, because your sins are forgiven you for **His name's** sake. {2:13} I write unto you, Fathers, because ye have known **Him** [that is] from the beginning. I write unto you, young men, because ye have overcome the wicked one. I write unto you, little children, because ye have known the **Father**. {2:14} I have written unto you, Fathers, because ye have known **Him** [that is] from the beginning. I have written unto you, young men, because ye are strong, and the word of **God** abideth in you, and ye have overcome the wicked one. {2:15} Love not the world, neither the things [that are] in the world. If any man love the world, the love of the **Father** is not in him. {2:16} For all that [is] in the world, the lust of the flesh, and the lust of the eyes, and the pride of life, is not of the **Father**, but is of the world. {2:17} And the world passeth away, and the lust

thereof: but he that doeth the will of **God** abideth for ever.{2:18} Little children, it is the last time: and as ye have heard that antichrist shall come, even now are there many antichrists; whereby we know that it is the last time. {2:19} They went out from us, but they were not of us; for if they had been of us, they would [no doubt] have continued with us: but [they went out,] that they might be made manifest that they were not all of us. {2:20} But ye have an unction from the **Holy One**, and ye know all things. {2:21} I have not written unto you because ye know not the truth, but because ye know it, and that no lie is of the truth. {2:22} Who is a liar but he that denieth that **Jesus** is the **Christ**? He is antichrist, that denieth the **Father** and the **Son**. {2:23} Whosoever denieth the **Son**, the same hath not the **Father**: [(but) he that acknowledgeth the **Son** hath the **Father** also.]{2:24} Let that therefore abide in you, which ye have heard from the beginning. If that which ye have heard from the beginning shall remain in you, ye also shall continue in the **Son**, and in the **Father**. {2:25} And this is the promise that **He** hath promised us, [even] eternal life. {2:26} These [things] have I written unto you concerning them that seduce you. {2:27} But the anointing which ye have received of **Him** abideth in you, and ye need not that any man teach you: but as the same anointing teacheth you of all things, and is truth, and is no lie, and even as it hath taught you, ye shall abide in **Him**. {2:28} And now, little children, abide in **Him**; that, when **He** shall appear, we may have confidence, and not be ashamed before **Him** at **His** coming. {2:29} If ye know that **He** is righteous, ye know that every one that doeth righteousness is born of **Him**. **{34}**

{3:1} Behold, what manner of love the **Father** hath bestowed upon us, that we should be called the sons of **God**: therefore the world knoweth us not, because it knew **Him** not. {3:2} Beloved, now are we the sons of **God**, and it doth not yet appear what we shall be: but we know that, when **He** shall appear, we shall be like **Him**; for we shall see **Him** as **He** is. {3:3} And every man that hath this hope in **Him** purifieth himself, even as **He** is pure. {3:4} Whosoever committeth sin transgresseth also the law: for sin is the transgression of the law. {3:5} And ye know that **He** was manifested to take away our sins; and in **Him** is no sin. {3:6} Whosoever abideth in **Him** sinneth not: whosoever sinneth hath not seen **Him**, neither known **Him**. {3:7} Little children, let no man deceive you: He that doeth righteousness is righteous, even as he is righteous. {3:8} He that committeth sin is of the devil; for the devil sinneth from the beginning. For this purpose the **Son of God** was manifested, that **He** might destroy the works of the devil. {3:9} Whosoever is born of **God** doth not commit sin; for **His** seed remaineth in him: and he cannot sin, because he is born of **God**. {3:10} In this the children of **God** are manifest, and the children of the devil: whosoever doeth not righteousness is not of **God**, neither he that loveth not his brother. {3:11} For this is the message that ye heard from the beginning, that we should love one another. {3:12} Not as Cain, [who] was of that wicked one, and slew his brother. And wherefore slew he him? Because his own works were evil, and his brother's righteous.{3:13} Marvel not, my brethren, if the world hate you. {3:14} We know that we have passed from death unto life, because we love the brethren. He that loveth not [his] brother abideth in death. {3:15} Whosoever hateth his brother is a murderer: and ye know that no murderer hath eternal life abiding in him. {3:16} Hereby perceive we the love [of **God**,] because **He** laid down **His** life for us: and we ought to lay down [our] lives for the brethren. {3:17} But whoso hath this world's good, and seeth his brother have need, and shutteth up his bowels [of compassion] from him, how dwelleth the love of **God** in him? {3:18} my little children, let us not love in word, neither in tongue; but in deed and in truth. {3:19} And hereby we know that we are of the truth, and shall assure our hearts before **Him**. {3:20} For if our heart condemn us, **God** is greater than our heart, and knoweth all things. {3:21} Beloved, if our heart condemn us not, [then] have we confidence toward **God**. {3:22} And whatsoever we ask, we receive of **Him**, because we keep **His** commandments, and do those things that are pleasing in **His** sight. {3:23} And this is **His** commandment, That we should believe on the **name** of **His Son Jesus Christ**, and love one another, as **He** gave us commandment. {3:24} And **He** that keepeth **His** commandments dwelleth in **Him**, and **He** in **Him**. And hereby we know that **He** abideth in us, by the Spirit which **He** hath given us. {29}

{4:1} Beloved, believe not every spirit, but try the spirits whether they are of **God**: because many false prophets are gone out into the world. {4:2} Hereby know ye the Spirit of **God**: Every spirit that confesseth that **Jesus Christ** is come in the flesh is of **God**: {4:3} And every spirit that confesseth not that **Jesus Christ** is come in the flesh is not of **God**: and this is that [spirit] of antichrist, whereof ye have heard that it should come; and even now already is it in the world. {4:4} Ye are of **God**, little children, and have overcome them: because **greater** is **He** that is in you, than he that is in the world. {4:5} They are of the world: therefore speak they of the world, and the world heareth them. {4:6} We are of God: He that knoweth God heareth us; He that is not of **God** heareth not us. Hereby know we the **spirit of truth**, and the spirit of error.{4:7} Beloved, let us love one another: for love is of **God**; and every one that loveth is born of **God**, and knoweth **God**. {4:8} He that loveth not knoweth not **God**; for **God** is love. {4:9} In this was manifested the love of **God** toward us, because that **God** sent **His only begotten Son** into the world, that we might live through **Him**. {4:10} Herein is love, not that we loved **God**, but that **He** loved us, and sent **His Son** [to be] the **propitiation** for our sins. {4:11} Beloved, if **God** so loved us, we ought also to love one another. {4:12} No man hath seen **God** at any time. If we love one another, **God** dwelleth in us, and **His** love is perfected in us. {4:13} Hereby know we that we dwell in **Him**, and **He** in us, because **He** hath given us of **His Spirit**. {4:14} And we have seen and do testify that the **Father** sent the **Son** [to be] the **Saviour** of the world. {4:15} Whosoever shall confess that **Jesus is the Son of God**, God dwelleth in **Him**, and **He** in God. {4:16} And we have known and believed the love that **God** hath to us. **God** is love; and He that dwelleth in love dwelleth in **God**, and **God** in Him. {4:17} Herein is our love made perfect, that we may have boldness in the day of judgment: because as **He** is, so are we in this world. {4:18} There is no fear in love; but perfect love casteth out fear: because fear hath torment. He that feareth is not made perfect in love. {4:19} We love **Him**, because **He** first loved us. {4:20} If a man say, I love God, and hateth his brother, he is a liar: for he that loveth not his brother whom he hath seen, how can he love **God whom** he hath not seen? {4:21} And this commandment have we from **Him**, That he who loveth **God** love his brother also. {25}

{5:1} Whosoever believeth that **Jesus** is the **Christ** is born of **God**: and every one that loveth **Him** that begat loveth **Him** also that is begotten of **Him**. {5:2} By this we know that we love the children of **God**, when we love **God**,

and keep **His** commandments. {5:3} For this is the love of **God**, that we keep **His** commandments: and **His** commandments are not grievous. {5:4} For whatsoever is born of **God** overcometh the world: and this is the victory that overcometh the world, [even] our faith. {5:5} Who is **He** that overcometh the world, but **He** that believeth that **Jesus is the Son of God?** {5:6} This is **He** that came by water and blood, [even] **Jesus Christ**; not by water only, but by water and blood. And it is the Spirit that beareth witness, because the Spirit is truth. {5:7} For there are three that bear record in heaven, the **Father**, the **Word**, and the **Holy Ghost**: and these three are one. {5:8} And there are three that bear witness in earth, the spirit, and the water, and the blood: and these three agree in one. {5:9} If we receive the witness of men, the witness of **God** is greater: for this is the witness of **God** which **He** hath testified of **His Son**. {5:10} He that believeth on the **Son** of **God** hath the witness in himself: He that believeth not **God** hath made **Him** a liar; because He believeth not the record that **God** gave of **His Son**. {5:11} And this is the record, that **God** hath given to us eternal life, and this **life** is in **His Son**. {5:12} He that hath the **Son** hath **life**; [and] He that hath not the **Son of God** hath not life. {5:13} These things have I written unto you that believe on the **name** of **the Son of God**; that ye may know that ye have eternal life, and that ye may believe on the **name of the Son of God**. {5:14} And this is the confidence that we have in **Him**, that, if we ask any thing according to **His** will, **He** heareth us: {5:15} And if we know that **He** hear us, whatsoever we ask, we know that we have the petitions that we desired of **Him**. {5:16} If any man see His brother sin a sin [which is] not unto death, he shall ask, and he shall give him life for them that sin not unto death. There is a sin unto death: I do not say that he shall pray for it. {5:17} All unrighteousness is sin: and there is a sin not unto death. {5:18} We know that whosoever is born of **God** sinneth not; but he that is begotten of **God** keepeth himself, and that wicked one toucheth him not. {5:19} And we know that we are of **God**, and the whole world lieth in wickedness. {5:20} [And] we know that the **Son of God** is come, and hath given us an understanding, that we may know **Him that is true**, and we are in **Him** that is true, [even] in **His Son Jesus Christ**. This is the **true God**, and eternal life. {5:21} Little children, keep yourselves from idols. Amen.

{38}

Second Epistle of John **TOTAL 12**

{1:1} The elder unto the elect lady and her children, whom I love in the truth; and not I only, but also all they that have known the **truth**; {1:2} For the **truth**'s sake, which dwelleth in us, and shall be with us for ever. {1:3} Grace be with you, mercy, [and] peace, from **God** the **Father**, and from the **Lord Jesus Christ**, the **Son** of the **Father**, in truth and love.

{1:4} I rejoiced greatly that I found of thy children walking in **truth**, as we have received a commandment from the **Father**. {1:5} And now I beseech thee, lady, not as though I wrote a new commandment unto thee, but that which we had from the beginning, that we love one another. {1:6} And this is love, that we walk after **His** commandments. This is the commandment, That, as ye have heard from the beginning, ye should walk in it. {1:7} For many deceivers are entered into the world, who confess not that **Jesus Christ** is come in the flesh. This is a deceiver and an antichrist. {1:8} Look to yourselves, that we lose not those things which we have wrought, but that we receive a full reward. {1:9} Whosoever transgresseth, and abideth not in the doctrine of **Christ**, hath not **God**. He that abideth in the doctrine of **Christ**, he hath both the **Father** and the **Son**. {1:10} If there come any unto you, and bring not this doctrine, receive him not into [your] house, neither bid him God speed: {1:11} For he that biddeth him **God** speed is partaker of his evil deeds.

{1:12} Having many things to write unto you, I would not [write] with paper and ink: but I trust to come unto you, and speak face to face, that our joy may be full. {1:13} The children of thy elect sister greet thee. Amen.

{12}

Third Epistle of John **TOTAL 8**

{1:1} The elder unto the wellbeloved Gaius, whom I love in the truth.

{1:2} Beloved, I wish above all things that thou mayest prosper and be in health, even as thy soul prospereth. {1:3} For I rejoiced greatly, when the brethren came and testified of the **truth** that is in thee, even as thou walkest in the **truth**. {1:4} I have no greater joy than to hear that my children walk in **truth**. {1:5} Beloved, thou doest faithfully whatsoever thou doest to the brethren, and to strangers; {1:6} Which have borne witness of thy charity before the church: whom if thou bring forward on their journey after a **God**ly sort, thou shalt do well: {1:7} Because that for **His name**'s sake they went forth, taking nothing of the Gentiles. {1:8} We therefore ought to receive such, that we might be fellowhelpers to the **truth**.

{1:9} I wrote unto the church: but Diotrephes, who loveth to have the preeminence among them, receiveth us not. {1:10} Wherefore, if I come, I will remember his deeds which he doeth, prating against us with malicious words: and not content therewith, neither doth he himself receive the brethren, and forbiddeth them that would, and casteth [them] out of the church.

{1:11} Beloved, follow not that which is evil, but that which is good. He that doeth good is of **God**: but he that doeth evil hath not seen **God**. {1:12} Demetrius hath good report of all [men,] and of the **truth** itself: yea, and we [also] bear record; and ye know that our record is true.

{1:13} I had many things to write, but I will not with ink and pen write unto thee: {1:14} But I trust I shall shortly see thee, and we shall speak face to face. Peace [be] to thee. [Our] friends salute thee. Greet the friends by name.
{7}

The General Epistle of Jude **TOTAL 23**

{1:1} Jude, the servant of **Jesus Christ**, and brother of James, to them that are sanctified by **God** the **Father**, and preserved in **Jesus Christ**, [and] called: {1:2} Mercy unto you, and peace, and love, be multiplied.

{1:3} Beloved, when I gave all diligence to write unto you of the common salvation, it was needful for me to write unto you, and exhort [you] that ye should earnestly contend for the faith which was once delivered unto the saints. {1:4} For there are certain men crept in unawares, who were before of old ordained to this condemnation, un**God**ly men, turning the grace of our **God** into lasciviousness, and denying the only **Lord God**, and our **Lord Jesus Christ**. {1:5} I will therefore put you in remembrance, though ye once knew this, how that the **Lord**, having saved the people out of the land of Egypt, afterward destroyed them that believed not. {1:6} And the angels which kept not their first estate, but left their own habitation, **he** hath reserved in everlasting chains under darkness unto the judgment of the great day. {1:7} Even as Sodom and Gomorrha, and the cities about them in like manner, giving themselves over to fornication, and going after strange flesh, are set forth for an example, suffering the vengeance of eternal fire. {1:8} Likewise also these [filthy] dreamers defile the flesh, despise dominion, and speak evil of dignities. {1:9} Yet Michael the archangel, when contending with the devil he disputed about the body of Moses, durst not bring against Him a railing accusation, but said, The **Lord** rebuke thee. {1:10} But these speak evil of those things which they know not: but what they know naturally, as brute beasts, in those things they corrupt themselves. {1:11} Woe unto them! for they have gone in the way of Cain, and ran greedily after the error of Balaam for reward, and perished in the gainsaying of Core. {1:12} These are spots in your feasts of charity, when they feast with you, feeding themselves without fear: clouds [they are] without water, carried about of winds; trees whose fruit withereth, without fruit, twice dead, plucked up by the roots; {1:13} Raging waves of the sea, foaming out their own shame; wandering stars, to **whom** is reserved the blackness of darkness for ever. {1:14} And Enoch also, the seventh from Adam, prophesied of these, saying, Behold, the **Lord** cometh with ten thousands of **His** saints, {1:15} To execute judgment upon all, and to convince all that are un**God**ly among them of all their un**God**ly deeds which they have un**God**ly committed, and of all their hard [speeches] which un**God**ly sinners have spoken against **Him**. {1:16} These are murmurers, complainers, walking after their own lusts; and their mouth speaketh great swelling [words,] having men's persons in admiration because of advantage.

{1:17} But, beloved, remember ye the words which were spoken before of the apostles of our **Lord Jesus Christ**; {1:18} How that they told you there should be mockers in the last time, who should walk after their own un**God**ly lusts. {1:19} These be they who separate themselves, sensual, having not the Spirit. {1:20} But ye, beloved, building up yourselves on your most holy faith, praying in the **Holy Ghost**, {1:21} Keep yourselves in the love of **God**, looking for the mercy of our **Lord Jesus Christ** unto eternal life. {1:22} And of some have compassion, making a difference: {1:23} And others save with fear, pulling [them] out of the fire; hating even the garment spotted by the flesh.

{1:24} Now unto **Him** that is able to keep you from falling, and to present [you] faultless before the presence of **His** glory with exceeding joy, {1:25} To the only wise **God** our **Saviour**, [be] glory and majesty, dominion and power, both now and ever. Amen.

Revelation of St. John the Divine **TOTAL 396**

{1:1} The Revelation of **Jesus Christ**, which **God** gave unto Him, to shew unto His servants things which must shortly come to pass; and he sent and signified [it] by His angel unto His servant John: {1:2} Who bare record of the word of **God**, and of the testimony of **Jesus Christ**, and of all things that he saw. {1:3} Blessed [is] he that readeth, and they that hear the words of this prophecy, and keep those things which are written therein: for the time [is] at hand. {1:4} John to the seven churches which are in Asia: Grace [be] unto you, and peace, from **Him** which is, and which was, and which is to come; and from the seven Spirits which are before **His** throne; {1:5} And from **Jesus Christ**, [**who** is] the faithful witness, [and] the **first begotten** of the dead, and the **prince of the kings** of the earth. Unto **Him** that loved us, and washed us from our sins in **His own blood**, {1:6} And hath made us kings and priests unto **God** and **His Father**; to **Him** [be] glory and dominion for ever and ever. Amen. {1:7} Behold, **He** cometh with clouds; and every eye shall see **Him**, and they [also] which pierced **Him**: and all kindreds of the earth shall wail because of **Him**. Even so, Amen. {1:8} **I am Alpha** and **Omega**, the **beginning** and the **ending**, saith the **Lord**, which is, and which was, and which is to come, the **Almighty**.

{1:9} I John, who also am your brother, and companion in tribulation, and in the kingdom and patience of **Jesus Christ,** was in the isle that is called Patmos, for the word of **God**, and for the testimony of **Jesus Christ**. {1:10} I was in the Spirit on the **Lord**'s day, and heard behind me a great **voice**, as of a trumpet, {1:11} Saying, **I am Alpha** and **Omega**, the **first** and the **last**: and, What thou seest, write in a book, and send [it] unto the seven churches which are in Asia; unto Ephesus, and unto Smyrna, and unto Pergamos, and unto Thyatira, and unto Sardis, and unto Philadelphia, and unto Laodicea. {1:12} And I turned to see the **voice** that spake with me. And being turned, I saw seven golden candlesticks; {1:13} And in the midst of the seven candlesticks [one] like unto the **Son of man**, clothed with a garment down to the foot, and girt about the paps with a golden girdle. {1:14} **His** head and [**His**] hairs [were] white like wool, as white as snow; and **His** eyes [were] as a flame of fire; {1:15} And **His** feet like unto fine brass, as if they burned in a furnace; and **His** voice as the sound of many waters. {1:16} And **He** had in **His** right hand seven stars: and out of **His** mouth went a sharp twoedged sword: and **His** countenance [was] as the sun shineth in **His** strength. {1:17} And when I saw **Him**, I fell at **His** feet as dead. And **He** laid **His** right hand upon me, saying unto me, Fear not; **I am** the **first** and the **last**: {1:18} **I [am] He** that liveth, and was dead; and, behold, **I** am alive for evermore, Amen; and have the keys of hell and of death.

{1:19} Write the things which thou hast seen, and the things which are, and the things which shall be hereafter; {1:20} The mystery of the seven stars which thou sawest in **My** right hand, and the seven golden candlesticks. The seven stars are the angels of the seven churches: and the seven candlesticks which thou sawest are the seven churches. {62}

{2:1} Unto the angel of the church of Ephesus write; These things saith **He** that holdeth the seven stars in **His** right hand, **who** walketh in the midst of the seven golden candlesticks; {2:2} **I** know thy works, and thy labour, and thy patience, and how thou canst not bear them which are

evil: and thou hast tried them which say they are apostles, and are not, and hast found them liars: {2:3} And hast borne, and hast patience, and for **My name's** sake hast laboured, and hast not fainted. {2:4} Nevertheless **I** have [somewhat] against thee, because thou hast left thy first love. {2:5} Remember therefore from whence thou art fallen, and repent, and do the first works; or else **I** will come unto thee quickly, and will remove thy candlestick out of his place, except thou repent. {2:6} But this thou hast, that thou hatest the deeds of the Nicolaitanes, which **I** also hate. {2:7} he that hath an ear, let Him hear what the Spirit saith unto the churches; To Him that overcometh will **I** give to eat of the tree of life, which is in the midst of the paradise of **God**.

{2:8} And unto the angel of the church in Smyrna write; These things saith the **first** and the **last**, which was dead, and is **alive**; {2:9} **I** know thy works, and tribulation, and poverty, (but thou art rich) and [**I** know] the blasphemy of them which say they are Jews, and are not, but [are] the synagogue of Satan. {2:10} Fear none of those things which thou shalt suffer: behold, the devil shall cast [some] of you into prison, that ye may be tried; and ye shall have tribulation ten days: be thou faithful unto death, and **I** will give thee a crown of life. {2:11} he that hath an ear, let Him hear what the Spirit saith unto the churches; he that overcometh shall not be hurt of the second death.

{2:12} And to the angel of the church in Pergamos write; These things saith **He** which hath the sharp sword with two edges; {2:13} **I** know thy works, and where thou dwellest, [even] where Satan's seat [is:] and thou holdest fast **My name**, and hast not denied **My** faith, even in those days wherein Antipas [was] **My** faithful martyr, who was slain among you, where Satan dwelleth. {2:14} But **I** have a few things against thee, because thou hast there them that hold the doctrine of Balaam, who taught Balac to cast a stumblingblock before the children of Israel, to eat things sacrificed unto idols, and to commit fornication. {2:15} So hast thou also them that hold the doctrine of the Nicolaitanes, which thing **I** hate. {2:16} Repent; or else **I** will come unto thee quickly, and will fight against them with the sword of **My** mouth. {2:17} he that hath an ear, let Him hear what the Spirit saith unto the churches; To Him that overcometh will **I** give to eat of the hidden manna, and will give Him a white stone, and in the stone a new name written, which no man knoweth saving he that receiveth [it.

]{2:18} And unto the angel of the church in Thyatira write; These things saith the **Son of God, who** hath **His** eyes like unto a flame of fire, and **His** feet [are] like fine brass; {2:19} **I** know thy works, and charity, and service, and faith, and thy patience, and thy works; and the last [to be] more than the first. {2:20} Notwithstanding **I** have a few things against thee, because thou sufferest that woman Jezebel, which calleth herself a prophetess, to teach and to seduce **My** servants to commit fornication, and to eat things sacrificed unto idols. {2:21} And **I** gave her space to repent of her fornication; and she repented not. {2:22} Behold, **I** will cast her into a bed, and them that commit adultery with her into great tribulation, except they repent of their deeds. {2:23} And **I** will kill her children with death; and all the churches shall know that **I am he** which searcheth the reins and hearts: and **I** will give unto every one of you according to your works. {2:24} But unto you **I** say, and unto the rest in Thyatira, as many as have not this doctrine, and which have not known the depths of Satan, as they speak; **I** will put upon you none other burden. {2:25} But that which ye have [already] hold fast till **I** come. {2:26} And he that overcometh, and keepeth **My** works unto the end, to him will **I** give power over the nations: {2:27} And he shall rule them with a rod of iron; as the vessels of a potter shall they be broken to shivers: even as **I** received of **My Father**. {2:28} And **I** will give Him the morning star. {2:29} he that hath an ear, let him hear what the Spirit saith unto the churches. {47}

{3:1} And unto the angel of the church in Sardis write; These things saith **He** that hath the seven Spirits of **God**, and the seven stars; **I** know thy works, that thou hast a name that thou livest, and art dead. {3:2} Be watchful, and strengthen the things which remain, that are ready to die: for **I** have not found thy works perfect before **God**. {3:3} Remember therefore how thou hast received and heard, and hold fast, and repent. If therefore thou shalt not watch, **I** will come on thee as a thief, and thou shalt not know what hour **I** will come upon thee. {3:4} Thou hast a few names even in Sardis which have not defiled their garments; and they shall walk with **ME** in white: for they are worthy. {3:5} he that overcometh, the same shall be clothed in white raiment; and **I** will not blot out his name out of the book of life, but **I** will confess his name before **My Father**, and before **His** angels. {3:6} he that hath an ear, let him hear what the Spirit saith unto the churches.

{3:7} And to the angel of the church in Philadelphia write; These things saith **He** that is holy, **He** that is true, **He** that hath the key of David, **He** that openeth, and no man shutteth; and shutteth, and no man openeth; {3:8} **I** know thy works: behold, **I** have set before thee an open door, and no man can shut it: for thou hast a little strength, and hast kept **My** word, and hast not denied **My name**. {3:9} Behold, **I** will make them of the synagogue of Satan, which say they are Jews, and are not, but do lie; behold, **I** will make them to come and worship before thy feet, and to know that **I** have loved thee. {3:10} Because thou hast kept the word of **My** patience, **I** also will keep thee from the hour of temptation, which shall come upon all the world, to try them that dwell upon the earth. {3:11} Behold, **I** come quickly: hold that fast which thou hast, that no man take thy crown. {3:12} Him that overcometh will **I** make a pillar in the temple of **My God**, and he shall go no more out: and **I** will write upon Him the **name** of **My God**, and the name of the city of **My God**, [which is] new Jerusalem, which cometh down out of heaven from **My God**: and [**I** will write upon Him] **My** new **name**. {3:13} he that hath an ear, let Him hear what the Spirit saith unto the churches.

{3:14} And unto the angel of the church of the Laodiceans write; These things saith the **Amen**, the **faithful** and **true witness**, the **beginning** of the creation of **God**; {3:15} **I** know thy works, that thou art neither cold nor hot: **I** would thou wert cold or hot. {3:16} So then because thou art lukewarm, and neither cold nor hot, **I** will spue thee out of **My** mouth. {3:17} Because thou sayest, I am rich, and increased with goods, and have need of nothing; and knowest not that thou art wretched, and miserable, and poor, and blind, and naked: {3:18} **I** counsel thee to buy of **ME** gold tried in the fire, that thou mayest be rich; and white raiment, that thou mayest be clothed, and [that] the shame of thy nakedness do not appear; and anoint thine eyes with eyesalve, that thou mayest see. {3:19} As many as **I** love, **I** rebuke and chasten: be zealous therefore, and repent. {3:20} Behold, **I** stand at the door, and knock: if any man hear **My voice**, and open the door, **I** will come in to Him, and will sup with Him, and he with **ME**. {3:21} To him that overcometh will **I** grant to sit with **ME** in **My** throne, even as **I** also overcame, and **am** set down with **My Father** in **His** throne.

{3:22} he that hath an ear, let him hear what the Spirit saith unto the churches. {60}

{4:1} After this I looked, and, behold, a door [was] opened in heaven: and the first voice which I heard [was] as it were of a trumpet talking with me; which said, Come up hither, and I will shew thee things which must be hereafter. {4:2} And immediately I was in the spirit: and, behold, a throne was set in heaven, and [one] sat on the throne. {4:3} And **He** that sat was to look upon like a jasper and a sardine stone: and [there was] a rainbow round about the throne, in sight like unto an emerald. {4:4} And round about the throne [were] four and twenty seats: and upon the seats I saw four and twenty elders sitting, clothed in white raiment; and they had on their heads crowns of gold. {4:5} And out of the throne proceeded lightnings and thunderings and voices: and [there were] seven lamps of fire burning before the throne, which are the seven Spirits of **God**. {4:6} And before the throne [there was] a sea of glass like unto crystal: and in the midst of the throne, and round about the throne, [were] four beasts full of eyes before and behind. {4:7} And the first beast [was] like a lion, and the second beast like a calf, and the third beast had a face as a man, and the fourth beast [was] like a flying eagle. {4:8} And the four beasts had each of them six wings about [Him;] and [they were] full of eyes within: and they rest not day and night, saying, Holy, holy, holy, **Lord God** Almighty, which was, and is, and is to come. {4:9} And when those beasts give glory and honour and thanks to **Him** that sat on the throne, who liveth for ever and ever, {4:10} The four and twenty elders fall down before **Him** that sat on the throne, and worship **Him** that liveth for ever and ever, and cast their crowns before the throne, saying, {4:11} Thou art worthy, O **Lord**, to receive glory and honour and power: for thou hast created all things, and for thy pleasure they are and were created.

{5:1} And I saw in the right hand of **Him** that sat on the throne a book written within and on the backside, sealed with seven seals. {5:2} And I saw a strong angel proclaiming with a loud voice, Who is worthy to open the book, and to loose the seals thereof? {5:3} And no man in heaven, nor in earth, neither under the earth, was able to open the book, neither to look thereon. {5:4} And I wept much, because no man was found worthy to open and to read the book, neither to look thereon. {5:5} And one of the elders saith unto me, Weep not: behold, the **Lion of the tribe of Juda**, the **Root of David**, hath prevailed to open the book, and to loose the seven seals thereof. {5:6} And I beheld, and, lo, in the midst of the throne and of the four beasts, and in the midst of the elders, stood a **Lamb** as it had been slain, having seven horns and seven eyes, which are the seven Spirits of **God** sent forth into all the earth. {5:7} And **He** came and took the book out of the right hand of **Him** that sat upon the throne. {5:8} And when **He** had taken the book, the four beasts and four [and] twenty elders fell down before the **Lamb**, having every one of them harps, and golden vials full of odours, which are the prayers of saints. {5:9} And they sung a new song, saying, **Thou** art worthy to take the book, and to open the seals thereof: for **thou** wast slain, and hast redeemed us to **God** by **thy** blood out of every kindred, and tongue, and people, and nation; {5:10} And hast made us unto our **God** kings and priests: and we shall reign on the earth. {5:11} And I beheld, and I heard the voice of many angels round about the throne and the beasts and the elders: and the number of them was ten thousand times ten thousand, and thousands of thousands; {5:12} Saying with a loud voice, Worthy is the **Lamb** that was slain to receive power, and riches, and wisdom, and strength, and honour, and glory, and blessing. {5:13} And every creature which is in heaven, and on the earth, and under the earth, and such as are in the sea, and all that are in them, heard I saying, Blessing, and honour, and glory, and power, [be] unto **Him** that sitteth upon the throne, and unto the **Lamb** for ever and ever. {5:14} And the four beasts said, Amen. And the four [and] twenty elders fell down and worshipped **Him** that liveth for ever and ever. {12}

{6:1} And I saw when the **Lamb** opened one of the seals, and I heard, as it were the noise of thunder, one of the four beasts saying, Come and see. {6:2} And I saw, and behold a white horse: and he that sat on Him had a bow; and a crown was given unto Him: and he went forth conquering, and to conquer. {6:3} And when **He** had opened the second seal, I heard the second beast say, Come and see. {6:4} And there went out another horse [that was] red: and [power] was given to Him that sat thereon to take peace from the earth, and that they should kill one another: and there was given unto Him a great sword. {6:5} And when **He** had opened the third seal, I heard the third beast say, Come and see. And I beheld, and lo a black horse; and he that sat on Him had a pair of balances in His hand. {6:6} And I heard a voice in the midst of the four beasts say, A measure of wheat for a penny, and three measures of barley for a penny; and [see] thou hurt not the oil and the wine. {6:7} And when **He** had opened the fourth seal, I heard the voice of the fourth beast say, Come and see. {6:8} And I looked, and behold a pale horse: and His name that sat on Him was Death, and Hell followed with Him. And power was given unto them over the fourth part of the earth, to kill with sword, and with hunger, and with death, and with the beasts of the earth. {6:9} And when **He** had opened the fifth seal, I saw under the altar the souls of them that were slain for the word of **God**, and for the testimony which they held: {6:10} And they cried with a loud voice, saying, How long, O **Lord**, holy and true, dost **thou** not judge and avenge our blood on them that dwell on the earth? {6:11} And white robes were given unto every one of them; and it was said unto them, that they should rest yet for a little season, until their fellowservants also and their brethren, that should be killed as they [were,] should be fulfilled. {6:12} And I beheld when **He** had opened the sixth seal, and, lo, there was a great earthquake; and the sun became black as sackcloth of hair, and the moon became as blood; {6:13} And the stars of heaven fell unto the earth, even as a fig tree casteth her untimely figs, when she is shaken of a mighty wind. {6:14} And the heaven departed as a scroll when it is rolled together; and every mountain and island were moved out of their places. {6:15} And the kings of the earth, and the great men, and the rich men, and the chief captains, and the mighty men, and every bondman, and every free man, hid themselves in the dens and in the rocks of the mountains; {6:16} And said to the mountains and rocks, Fall on us, and hide us from the face of **Him** that sitteth on the throne, and from the **wrath of the Lamb**: {6:17} For the great day of **His** wrath is come; and who shall be able to stand? {10}

{7:1} And after these things I saw four angels standing on the four corners of the earth, holding the four winds of the earth, that the wind should not blow on the earth, nor on the sea, nor on any tree. {7:2} And I saw another angel ascending from the east, having the seal of the living **God**: and he cried with a loud voice to the four angels, to whom it was given to hurt the earth and the sea, {7:3} Saying, Hurt not the earth, neither the sea, nor the trees, till we have sealed the servants of our **God** in their foreheads. {7:4} And I heard the number of them which were sealed: [and there were] sealed an hundred [and] forty [and] four thousand of all the tribes of the children of Israel. {7:5} Of the tribe of

Juda [were] sealed twelve thousand. Of the tribe of Reuben [were] sealed twelve thousand. Of the tribe of Gad [were] sealed twelve thousand. {7:6} Of the tribe of Aser [were] sealed twelve thousand. Of the tribe of Nepthalim [were] sealed twelve thousand. Of the tribe of Manasses [were] sealed twelve thousand. {7:7} Of the tribe of Simeon [were] sealed twelve thousand. Of the tribe of Levi [were] sealed twelve thousand. Of the tribe of Issachar [were] sealed twelve thousand. {7:8} Of the tribe of Zabulon [were] sealed twelve thousand. Of the tribe of Joseph [were] sealed twelve thousand. Of the tribe of Benjamin [were] sealed twelve thousand. {7:9} After this I beheld, and, lo, a great multitude, which no man could number, of all nations, and kindreds, and people, and tongues, stood before the throne, and before the Lamb, clothed with white robes, and palms in their hands; {7:10} And cried with a loud voice, saying, Salvation to our **God** which sitteth upon the throne, and unto the **Lamb**. {7:11} And all the angels stood round about the throne, and [about] the elders and the four beasts, and fell before the throne on their faces, and worshipped **God**, {7:12} Saying, Amen: Blessing, and glory, and wisdom, and thanksgiving, and honour, and power, and might, [be] unto our **God** for ever and ever. Amen. {7:13} And one of the elders answered, saying unto me, What are these which are arrayed in white robes? and whence came they? {7:14} And I said unto Him, Sir, thou knowest. And he said to me, These are they which came out of great tribulation, and have washed their robes, and made them white in the blood of the **Lamb**. {7:15} Therefore are they before the throne of **God**, and serve **Him** day and night in **His** temple: and **He** that sitteth on the throne shall dwell among them. {7:16} They shall hunger no more, neither thirst any more; neither shall the sun light on them, nor any heat. {7:17} For the **Lamb** which is in the midst of the throne shall feed them, and shall lead them unto living fountains of waters: and **God** shall wipe away all tears from their eyes. {6}

{8:1} And when he had opened the seventh seal, there was silence in heaven about the space of half an hour. {8:2} And I saw the seven angels which stood before **God**; and to them were given seven trumpets. {8:3} And another angel came and stood at the altar, having a golden censer; and there was given unto Him much incense, that he should offer [it] with the prayers of all saints upon the golden altar which was before the throne. {8:4} And the smoke of the incense, [which came] with the prayers of the saints, ascended up before **God** out of the angel's hand. {8:5} And the angel took the censer, and filled it with fire of the altar, and cast [it] into the earth: and there were voices, and thunderings, and lightnings, and an earthquake. {8:6} And the seven angels which had the seven trumpets prepared themselves to sound.

{8:7} The first angel sounded, and there followed hail and fire mingled with blood, and they were cast upon the earth: and the third part of trees was burnt up, and all green grass was burnt up. {8:8} And the second angel sounded, and as it were a great mountain burning with fire was cast into the sea: and the third part of the sea became blood; {8:9} And the third part of the creatures which were in the sea, and had life, died; and the third part of the ships were destroyed. {8:10} And the third angel sounded, and there fell a great star from heaven, burning as it were a lamp, and it fell upon the third part of the rivers, and upon the fountains of waters; {8:11} And the name of the star is called Wormwood: and the third part of the waters became wormwood; and many men died of the waters, because they were made bitter. {8:12} And the fourth angel sounded, and the third part of the sun was smitten, and the third part of the moon, and the third part of the stars; so as the third part of them was darkened, and the day shone not for a third part of it, and the night likewise.

{8:13} And I beheld, and heard an angel flying through the midst of heaven, saying with a loud voice, Woe, woe, woe, to the inhabiters of the earth by reason of the other voices of the trumpet of the three angels, which are yet to sound!

{9:1} And the fifth angel sounded, and I saw a star fall from heaven unto the earth: and to Him was given the key of the bottomless pit. {9:2} And he opened the bottomless pit; and there arose a smoke out of the pit, as the smoke of a great furnace; and the sun and the air were darkened by reason of the smoke of the pit. {9:3} And there came out of the smoke locusts upon the earth: and unto them was given power, as the scorpions of the earth have power. {9:4} And it was commanded them that they should not hurt the grass of the earth, neither any green thing, neither any tree; but only those men which have not the seal of **God** in their foreheads. {9:5} And to them it was given that they should not kill them, but that they should be tormented five months: and their torment [was] as the torment of a scorpion, when he striketh a man. {9:6} And in those days shall men seek death, and shall not find it; and shall desire to die, and death shall flee from them. {9:7} And the shapes of the locusts [were] like unto horses prepared unto battle; and on their heads [were] as it were crowns like gold, and their faces [were] as the faces of men. {9:8} And they had hair as the hair of women, and their teeth were as [the teeth] of lions. {9:9} And they had breastplates, as it were breastplates of iron; and the sound of their wings [was] as the sound of chariots of many horses running to battle. {9:10} And they had tails like unto scorpions, and there were stings in their tails: and their power [was] to hurt men five months. {9:11} And they had a king over them, [which is] the angel of the bottomless pit, whose name in the Hebrew tongue [is] Abaddon, but in the Greek tongue hath [his] name Apollyon. {9:12} One woe is past; [and,] behold, there come two woes more hereafter.

{9:13} And the sixth angel sounded, and I heard a voice from the four horns of the golden altar which is before **God**, {9:14} Saying to the sixth angel which had the trumpet, Loose the four angels which are bound in the great river Euphrates. {9:15} And the four angels were loosed, which were prepared for an hour, and a day, and a month, and a year, for to slay the third part of men. {9:16} And the number of the army of the horsemen [were] two hundred thousand thousand: and I heard the number of them. {9:17} And thus I saw the horses in the vision, and them that sat on them, having breastplates of fire, and of jacinth, and brimstone: and the heads of the horses [were] as the heads of lions; and out of their mouths issued fire and smoke and brimstone. {9:18} By these three was the third part of men killed, by the fire, and by the smoke, and by the brimstone, which issued out of their mouths. {9:19} For their power is in their mouth, and in their tails: for their tails [were] like unto serpents, and had heads, and with them they do hurt. {9:20} And the rest of the men which were not killed by these plagues yet repented not of the works of their hands, that they should not worship devils, and idols of gold, and silver, and brass, and stone, and of wood: which neither can see, nor hear, nor walk: {9:21} Neither repented they of their murders, nor of their sorceries, nor of their fornication, nor of their thefts.

{10:1} And I saw another mighty angel come down from heaven, clothed with a cloud: and a rainbow [was] upon His head, and His face [was] as it were the sun, and His feet as pillars of fire: {10:2} And he had in His hand a little book open: and he set His right foot upon the sea, and [His] left [foot] on the earth, {10:3} And cried with a loud voice, as [when] a lion roareth: and when he had cried, seven thunders uttered their voices. {10:4} And when the seven thunders had uttered their voices, I was about to write: and I heard a voice from heaven saying unto me, Seal up those things which the seven thunders uttered, and write them not. {10:5} And the angel which I saw stand upon the sea and upon the earth lifted up His hand to heaven, {10:6} And sware by **Him** that liveth for ever and ever, **who** created heaven, and the things that therein are, and the earth, and the things that therein are, and the sea, and the things which are therein, that there should be time no longer: {10:7} But in the days of the voice of the seventh angel, when he shall begin to sound, the **mystery** of **God** should be finished, as **He** hath declared to **His** servants the prophets. {10:8} And the voice which I heard from heaven spake unto me again, and said, Go [and] take the little book which is open in the hand of the angel which standeth upon the sea and upon the earth. {10:9} And I went unto the angel, and said unto Him, Give me the little book. And he said unto me, Take [it,] and eat it up; and it shall make thy belly bitter, but it shall be in thy mouth sweet as honey. {10:10} And I took the little book out of the angel's hand, and ate it up; and it was in my mouth sweet as honey: and as soon as I had eaten it, my belly was bitter. {10:11} And he said unto me, Thou must prophesy again before many peoples, and nations, and tongues, and kings. **{5}**

{11:1} And there was given me a reed like unto a rod: and the angel stood, saying, Rise, and measure the temple of **God**, and the altar, and them that worship therein. {11:2} But the court which is without the temple leave out, and measure it not; for it is given unto the Gentiles: and the holy city shall they tread under foot forty [and] two months. {11:3} And **I** will give [power] unto **My** two witnesses, and they shall prophesy a thousand two hundred [and] threescore days, clothed in sackcloth. {11:4} These are the two olive trees, and the two candlesticks standing before the **God** of the earth. {11:5} And if any man will hurt them, fire proceedeth out of their mouth, and devoureth their enemies: and if any man will hurt them, he must in this manner be killed. {11:6} These have power to shut heaven, that it rain not in the days of their prophecy: and have power over waters to turn them to blood, and to smite the earth with all plagues, as often as they will. {11:7} And when they shall have finished their testimony, the beast that ascendeth out of the bottomless pit shall make war against them, and shall overcome them, and kill them. {11:8} And their dead bodies [shall lie] in the street of the great city, which spiritually is called Sodom and Egypt, where also our **Lord** was crucified. {11:9} And they of the people and kindreds and tongues and nations shall see their dead bodies three days and an half, and shall not suffer their dead bodies to be put in graves. {11:10} And they that dwell upon the earth shall rejoice over them, and make merry, and shall send gifts one to another; because these two prophets tormented them that dwelt on the earth. {11:11} And after three days and an half the Spirit of life from **God** entered into them, and they stood upon their feet; and great fear fell upon them which saw them. {11:12} And they heard a great voice from heaven saying unto them, Come up hither. And they ascended up to heaven in a cloud; and their enemies beheld them. {11:13} And the same hour was there a great earthquake, and the tenth part of the city fell, and in the earthquake were slain of men seven thousand: and the remnant were affrighted, and gave glory to the **God** of heaven. {11:14} The second woe is past; [and,] behold, the third woe cometh quickly. {11:15} And the seventh angel sounded; and there were great voices in heaven, saying, The kingdoms of this world are become [the kingdoms] of our **Lord**, and of **His Christ**; and **he** shall reign for ever and ever. {11:16} And the four and twenty elders, which sat before **God** on their seats, fell upon their faces, and worshipped **God**, {11:17} Saying, We give thee thanks, O **Lord God Almighty**, which **art**, and **wast**, and art to **come**; because **thou** hast taken to **thee thy** great power, and hast reigned. {11:18} And the nations were angry, and thy wrath is come, and the time of the dead, that they should be judged, and that **thou** shouldest give reward unto **thy** servants the prophets, and to the saints, and them that fear thy **name**, small and great; and shouldest destroy them which destroy the earth. {11:19} And the temple of **God** was opened in heaven, and there was seen in **His** temple the ark of **His** testament: and there were lightnings, and voices, and thunderings, and an earthquake, and great hail. **{20}**

{12:1} And there appeared a great wonder in heaven; a woman clothed with the sun, and the moon under her feet, and upon her head a crown of twelve stars: {12:2} And she being with **child** cried, travailing in birth, and pained to be delivered. {12:3} And there appeared another wonder in heaven; and behold a great red dragon, having seven heads and ten horns, and seven crowns upon His heads. {12:4} And His tail drew the third part of the stars of heaven, and did cast them to the earth: and the dragon stood before the woman which was ready to be delivered, for to devour her **child** as soon as it was born. {12:5} And she brought forth a **man child**, **who** was to rule all nations with a rod of iron: and her **child** was caught up unto **God**, and [to] **His** throne. {12:6} And the woman fled into the wilderness, where she hath a place prepared of **God**, that they should feed her there a thousand two hundred [and] threescore days. {12:7} And there was war in heaven: Michael and His angels fought against the dragon; and the dragon fought and His angels, {12:8} And prevailed not; neither was their place found any more in heaven. {12:9} And the great dragon was cast out, that old serpent, called the Devil, and Satan, which deceiveth the whole world: he was cast out into the earth, and His angels were cast out with Him. {12:10} And I heard a loud voice saying in heaven, Now is come salvation, and strength, and the kingdom of our **God**, and the power of **His Christ**: for the accuser of our brethren is cast down, which accused them before our **God** day and night. {12:11} And they overcame him by the **blood** of the **Lamb**, and by the word of their **testimony**; and they loved not their lives unto the death. {12:12} Therefore rejoice, [ye] heavens, and ye that dwell in them. Woe to the inhabiters of the earth and of the sea! for the devil is come down unto you, having great wrath, because he knoweth that he hath but a short time. {12:13} And when the dragon saw that he was cast unto the earth, he persecuted the woman which brought forth the man [child.]{12:14} And to the woman were given two wings of a great eagle, that she might fly into the wilderness, into her place, where she is nourished for a time, and times, and half a time, from the face of the serpent. {12:15} And the serpent cast out of his mouth water as a flood after the woman, that he might cause her to be carried away of the flood. {12:16} And the earth helped the woman, and the earth opened her mouth, and swallowed up the flood which the dragon cast out of his mouth. {12:17} And the dragon was wroth with the woman, and went to make war with the remnant of her seed, which keep the commandments of **God**, and have the **testimony** of **Jesus Christ**. **{13}**

{13:1} And I stood upon the sand of the sea, and saw a beast rise up out of the sea, having seven heads and ten horns, and upon His horns ten crowns, and upon His heads the name of blasphemy. {13:2} And the beast which I saw was like unto a leopard, and His feet were as [the feet] of a bear, and His mouth as the mouth of a lion: and the dragon gave Him His power, and His seat, and great authority. {13:3} And I saw one of His heads as it were wounded to death; and His deadly wound was healed: and all the world wondered after the beast. {13:4} And they worshipped the dragon which gave power unto the beast: and they worshipped the beast, saying, Who [is] like unto the beast? who is able to make war with Him? {13:5} And there was given unto Him a mouth speaking great things and blasphemies; and power was given unto Him to continue forty [and] two months. {13:6} And he opened His mouth in blasphemy against **God**, to blaspheme **His name**, and **His** tabernacle, and them that dwell in heaven. {13:7} And it was given unto Him to make war with the saints, and to overcome them: and power was given Him over all kindreds, and tongues, and nations. {13:8} And all that dwell upon the earth shall worship Him, whose names are not written in the book of life of the Lamb slain from the foundation of the world. {13:9} If any man have an ear, let Him hear. {13:10} he that leadeth into captivity shall go into captivity: he that killeth with the sword must be killed with the sword. Here is the patience and the faith of the saints. {13:11} And I beheld another beast coming up out of the earth; and he had two horns like a lamb, and he spake as a dragon. {13:12} And he exerciseth all the power of the first beast before Him, and causeth the earth and them which dwell therein to worship the first beast, whose deadly wound was healed. {13:13} And he doeth great wonders, so that he maketh fire come down from heaven on the earth in the sight of men, {13:14} And deceiveth them that dwell on the earth by [the means of] those miracles which he had power to do in the sight of the beast; saying to them that dwell on the earth, that they should make an image to the beast, which had the wound by a sword, and did live. {13:15} And he had power to give life unto the image of the beast, that the image of the beast should both speak, and cause that as many as would not worship the image of the beast should be killed. {13:16} And he causeth all, both small and great, rich and poor, free and bond, to receive a mark in their right hand, or in their foreheads: {13:17} And that no man might buy or sell, save he that had the mark, or the name of the beast, or the number of His name. {13:18} Here is wisdom. Let Him that hath understanding count the number of the beast: for it is the number of a man; and His number [is] Six hundred threescore [and] six. **{3}**

{14:1} And I looked, and, lo, a **Lamb** stood on the mount Sion, and with **Him** an hundred forty [and] four thousand, having **His Father**'s **name** written in their foreheads. {14:2} And I heard a voice from heaven, as the voice of many waters, and as the voice of a great thunder: and I heard the voice of harpers harping with their harps: {14:3} And they sung as it were a new song before the throne, and before the four beasts, and the elders: and no man could learn that song but the hundred [and] forty [and] four thousand, which were redeemed from the earth. {14:4} These are they which were not defiled with women; for they are virgins. These are they which follow the **Lamb** whithersoever **He** goeth. These were redeemed from among men, [being] the firstfruits unto **God** and to the **Lamb**. {14:5} And in their mouth was found no guile: for they are without fault before the throne of **God**.

{14:6} And I saw another angel fly in the midst of heaven, having the everlasting **Gospel** to preach unto them that dwell on the earth, and to every nation, and kindred, and tongue, and people, {14:7} Saying with a loud voice, Fear **God**, and give glory to **Him**; for the hour of **His** judgment is come: and worship **Him** that made heaven, and earth, and the sea, and the fountains of waters. {14:8} And there followed another angel, saying, Babylon is fallen, is fallen, that great city, because she made all nations drink of the wine of the wrath of her fornication. {14:9} And the third angel followed them, saying with a loud voice, If any man worship the beast and His image, and receive [His] mark in His forehead, or in His hand, {14:10} The same shall drink of the wine of the wrath of **God**, which is poured out without mixture into the cup of **His** indignation; and he shall be tormented with fire and brimstone in the presence of the holy angels, and in the presence of the Lamb: {14:11} And the smoke of their torment ascendeth up for ever and ever: and they have no rest day nor night, who worship the beast and His image, and whosoever receiveth the mark of His name. {14:12} Here is the patience of the saints: here [are] they that keep the commandments of **God**, and the faith of **Jesus**. {14:13} And I heard a voice from heaven saying unto me, Write, Blessed [are] the dead which die in the **Lord** from henceforth: Yea, saith the Spirit, that they may rest from their labours; and their works do follow them.

{14:14} And I looked, and behold a white cloud, and upon the cloud [one] sat like unto the **Son of man**, having on **His** head a golden crown, and in **His** hand a sharp sickle. {14:15} And another angel came out of the temple, crying with a loud voice to **Him** that sat on the cloud, Thrust in thy sickle, and reap: for the time is come for thee to reap; for the harvest of the earth is ripe. {14:16} And **He** that sat on the cloud thrust in **His** sickle on the earth; and the earth was reaped. {14:17} And another angel came out of the temple which is in heaven, he also having a sharp sickle. {14:18} And another angel came out from the altar, which had power over fire; and cried with a loud cry to Him that had the sharp sickle, saying, Thrust in thy sharp sickle, and gather the clusters of the vine of the earth; for her grapes are fully ripe. {14:19} And the angel thrust in His sickle into the earth, and gathered the vine of the earth, and cast [it] into the great winepress of the wrath of **God**. {14:20} And the winepress was trodden without the city, and blood came out of the winepress, even unto the horse bridles, by the space of a thousand [and] six hundred furlongs. {16}

{15:1} And I saw another sign in heaven, great and marvellous, seven angels having the seven last plagues; for in them is filled up the wrath of **God**. {15:2} And I saw as it were a sea of glass mingled with fire: and them that had gotten the victory over the beast, and over His image, and over His mark, [and] over the number of His name, stand on the sea of glass, having the harps of **God**. {15:3} And they sing the song of Moses the servant of **God**, and the song of the **Lamb**, saying, Great and marvellous [are] **thy** works, **Lord God Almighty**; just and true [are] **thy** ways, **thou King of saints**. {15:4} Who shall not fear **thee**, **O Lord**, and glorify **thy name**? for [thou] only [art] holy: for all nations shall come and worship before **thee**; for **thy** judgments are made manifest. {15:5} And after that I looked, and, behold, the temple of the tabernacle of the testimony in heaven was opened: {15:6} And the seven angels came out of the temple, having the seven plagues, clothed in pure and white linen, and having their breasts girded with golden girdles. {15:7} And one of the four beasts gave unto the seven angels seven golden vials full of the wrath of **God**, who liveth for ever and ever. {15:8} And the temple was filled with smoke from the glory of **God**, and from **His** power; and no man was able to enter into the temple, till the seven

plagues of the seven angels were fulfilled. {15}

{16:1} And I heard a great voice out of the temple saying to the seven angels, Go your ways, and pour out the vials of the wrath of **God** upon the earth. {16:2} And the first went, and poured out His vial upon the earth; and there fell a noisome and grievous sore upon the men which had the mark of the beast, and [upon] them which worshipped His image. {16:3} And the second angel poured out His vial upon the sea; and it became as the blood of a dead [man:] and every living soul died in the sea. {16:4} And the third angel poured out His vial upon the rivers and fountains of waters; and they became blood. {16:5} And I heard the angel of the waters say, **Thou** art righteous, **O Lord**, which **art**, and **wast**, and **shalt be**, because **thou** hast judged thus. {16:6} For they have shed the blood of saints and prophets, and **thou** hast given them blood to drink; for they are worthy. {16:7} And I heard another out of the altar say, Even so, **Lord God Almighty**, true and righteous [are] **thy** judgments. {16:8} And the fourth angel poured out His vial upon the sun; and power was given unto Him to scorch men with fire. {16:9} And men were scorched with great heat, and blasphemed the **name** of **God**, which hath power over these plagues: and they repented not to give **Him** glory. {16:10} And the fifth angel poured out His vial upon the seat of the beast; and His kingdom was full of darkness; and they gnawed their tongues for pain, {16:11} And blasphemed the **God** of heaven because of their pains and their sores, and repented not of their deeds. {16:12} And the sixth angel poured out His vial upon the great river Euphrates; and the water thereof was dried up, that the way of the kings of the east might be prepared. {16:13} And I saw three unclean spirits like frogs [come] out of the mouth of the dragon, and out of the mouth of the beast, and out of the mouth of the false prophet. {16:14} For they are the spirits of devils, working miracles, [which] go forth unto the kings of the earth and of the whole world, to gather them to the battle of that great day of **God Almighty**. {16:15} Behold, I come as a thief. Blessed [is] he that watcheth, and keepeth His garments, lest he walk naked, and they see His shame. {16:16} And **He** gathered them together into a place called in the Hebrew tongue Armageddon. {16:17} And the seventh angel poured out His vial into the air; and there came a great voice out of the temple of heaven, from the throne, saying, It is done. {16:18} And there were voices, and thunders, and lightnings; and there was a great earthquake, such as was not since men were upon the earth, so mighty an earthquake, [and] so great. {16:19} And the great city was divided into three parts, and the cities of the nations fell: and great Babylon came in remembrance before **God**, to give unto her the cup of the wine of the fierceness of **His** wrath. {16:20} And every island fled away, and the mountains were not found. {16:21} And there fell upon men a great hail out of heaven, [every stone] about the weight of a talent: and men blasphemed **God** because of the plague of the hail; for the plague thereof was exceeding great. {19}

{17:1} And there came one of the seven angels which had the seven vials, and talked with me, saying unto me, Come hither; I will shew unto thee the judgment of the great whore that sitteth upon many waters: {17:2} With whom the kings of the earth have committed fornication, and the inhabitants of the earth have been made drunk with the wine of her fornication. {17:3} So he carried me away in the spirit into the wilderness: and I saw a woman sit upon a scarlet coloured beast, full of names of blasphemy, having seven heads and ten horns. {17:4} And the woman was arrayed in purple and scarlet colour, and decked with gold and precious stones and pearls, having a golden cup in her hand full of abominations and filthiness of her fornication: {17:5} And upon her forehead [was] a name written, MYSTERY, BABYLON THE GREAT, THE MOTHER OF HARLOTS AND ABOMINATIONS OF THE EARTH. {17:6} And I saw the woman drunken with the blood of the saints, and with the blood of the martyrs of **Jesus**: and when I saw her, I wondered with great admiration. {17:7} And the angel said unto me, Wherefore didst thou marvel? I will tell thee the mystery of the woman, and of the beast that carrieth her, which hath the seven heads and ten horns. {17:8} The beast that thou sawest was, and is not; and shall ascend out of the bottomless pit, and go into perdition: and they that dwell on the earth shall wonder, whose names were not written in the book of life from the foundation of the world, when they behold the beast that was, and is not, and yet is. {17:9} And here [is] the mind which hath wisdom. The seven heads are seven mountains, on which the woman sitteth. {17:10} And there are seven kings: five are fallen, and one is, [and] the other is not yet come; and when he cometh, he must continue a short space. {17:11} And the beast that was, and is not, even he is the eighth, and is of the seven, and goeth into perdition. {17:12} And the ten horns which thou sawest are ten kings, which have received no kingdom as yet; but receive power as kings one hour with the beast. {17:13} These have one mind, and shall give their power and strength unto the beast. {17:14} These shall make war with the **Lamb**, and the **Lamb** shall overcome them: for **He** is **Lord of lords**, and **King of kings**: and they that are with **Him** [are] called, and chosen, and faithful. {17:15} And he saith unto me, The waters which thou sawest, where the whore sitteth, are peoples, and multitudes, and nations, and tongues. {17:16} And the ten horns which thou sawest upon the beast, these shall hate the whore, and shall make her desolate and naked, and shall eat her flesh, and burn her with fire. {17:17} For **God** hath put in their hearts to fulfil **His** will, and to agree, and give their kingdom unto the beast, until the words of **God** shall be fulfilled. {17:18} And the woman which thou sawest is that great city, which reigneth over the kings of the earth. {8}

{18:1} And after these things I saw another angel come down from heaven, having great power; and the earth was lightened with His glory. {18:2} And he cried mightily with a strong voice, saying, Babylon the great is fallen, is fallen, and is become the habitation of devils, and the hold of every foul spirit, and a cage of every unclean and hateful bird. {18:3} For all nations have drunk of the wine of the wrath of her fornication, and the kings of the earth have committed fornication with her, and the merchants of the earth are waxed rich through the abundance of her delicacies. {18:4} And I heard another voice from heaven, saying, Come out of her, **My** people, that ye be not partakers of her sins, and that ye receive not of her plagues. {18:5} For her sins have reached unto heaven, and **God** hath remembered her iniquities. {18:6} Reward her even as she rewarded you, and double unto her double according to her works: in the cup which she hath filled fill to her double. {18:7} How much she hath glorified herself, and lived deliciously, so much torment and sorrow give her: for she saith in her heart, I sit a queen, and am no widow, and shall see no sorrow. {18:8} Therefore shall her plagues come in one day, death, and mourning, and famine; and she shall be utterly burned with fire: for strong [is] the **Lord God** who judgeth her. {18:9} And the kings of the earth, who have committed fornication and lived deliciously with her, shall bewail her, and lament for her, when they shall see the smoke of her burning, {18:10} Standing afar off for the fear of her torment, saying, Alas, alas, that great city Babylon,

that mighty city! for in one hour is thy judgment come. {18:11} And the merchants of the earth shall weep and mourn over her; for no man buyeth their merchandise any more: {18:12} The merchandise of gold, and silver, and precious stones, and of pearls, and fine linen, and purple, and silk, and scarlet, and all thyine wood, and all manner vessels of ivory, and all manner vessels of most precious wood, and of brass, and iron, and marble, {18:13} And cinnamon, and odours, and ointments, and frankincense, and wine, and oil, and fine flour, and wheat, and beasts, and sheep, and horses, and chariots, and slaves, and souls of men. {18:14} And the fruits that thy soul lusted after are departed from thee, and all things which were dainty and goodly are departed from thee, and thou shalt find them no more at all. {18:15} The merchants of these things, which were made rich by her, shall stand afar off for the fear of her torment, weeping and wailing, {18:16} And saying, Alas, alas, that great city, that was clothed in fine linen, and purple, and scarlet, and decked with gold, and precious stones, and pearls! {18:17} For in one hour so great riches is come to nought. And every shipmaster, and all the company in ships, and sailors, and as many as trade by sea, stood afar off, {18:18} And cried when they saw the smoke of her burning, saying, What [city is] like unto this great city! {18:19} And they cast dust on their heads, and cried, weeping and wailing, saying, Alas, alas, that great city, wherein were made rich all that had ships in the sea by reason of her costliness! for in one hour is she made desolate. {18:20} Rejoice over her, [thou] heaven, and [ye] holy apostles and prophets; for **God** hath avenged you on her. {18:21} And a mighty angel took up a stone like a great millstone, and cast [it] into the sea, saying, Thus with violence shall that great city Babylon be thrown down, and shall be found no more at all. {18:22} And the voice of harpers, and musicians, and of pipers, and trumpeters, shall be heard no more at all in thee; and no craftsman, of whatsoever craft [he be,] shall be found any more in thee; and the sound of a millstone shall be heard no more at all in thee; {18:23} And the light of a candle shall shine no more at all in thee; and the voice of the bridegroom and of the bride shall be heard no more at all in thee: for thy merchants were the great men of the earth; for by thy sorceries were all nations deceived. {18:24} And in her was found the blood of prophets, and of saints, and of all that were slain upon the earth. {3}

{19:1} And after these things I heard a great voice of much people in heaven, saying, Alleluia; Salvation, and glory, and honour, and power, unto the **Lord** our **God**: {19:2} For true and righteous [are] **His** judgments: for he hath judged the great whore, which did corrupt the earth with her fornication, and hath avenged the blood of **His** servants at her hand. {19:3} And again they said, Alleluia. And her smoke rose up for ever and ever. {19:4} And the four and twenty elders and the four beasts fell down and worshipped **God** that sat on the throne, saying, Amen; Alleluia. {19:5} And a voice came out of the throne, saying, **Praise our God**, all ye **His** servants, and ye that fear **Him**, both small and great. {19:6} And I heard as it were the voice of a great multitude, and as the voice of many waters, and as the voice of mighty thunderings, saying, Alleluia: for the **Lord God omnipotent** reigneth. {19:7} Let us be glad and rejoice, and give honour to **Him**: for the marriage of the **Lamb** is come, and **His** wife hath made herself ready. {19:8} And to her was granted that she should be arrayed in fine linen, clean and white: for the fine linen is the righteousness of saints. {19:9} And he saith unto me, Write, Blessed [are] they which are called unto the marriage supper of the **Lamb**. And he saith unto me, These are the true sayings of **God**.

{19:10} And I fell at His feet to worship Him. And he said unto me, See [thou do it] not: I am thy fellowservant, and of thy brethren that have the testimony of Jesus: worship God: for the testimony of Jesus is the spirit of prophecy. {19:11} And I saw heaven opened, and behold a white horse; and He that sat upon Him [was] called Faithful and True, and in righteousness He doth judge and make war. {19:12} His eyes [were] as a flame of fire, and on His head [were] many crowns; and He had a name written, that no man knew, but He himself. {19:13} And He [was] clothed with a vesture dipped in blood: and His name is called The Word of God. {19:14} And the armies [which were] in heaven followed Him upon white horses, clothed in fine linen, white and clean. {19:15} And out of His mouth goeth a sharp sword, that with it He should smite the nations: and He shall rule them with a rod of iron: and He treadeth the winepress of the fierceness and wrath of Almighty God. {19:16} And He hath on [His] vesture and on His thigh a name written, KING OF KINGS, AND LORD OF LORDS.

{19:17} And I saw an angel standing in the sun; and he cried with a loud voice, saying to all the fowls that fly in the midst of heaven, Come and gather yourselves together unto the supper of the great God; {19:18} That ye may eat the flesh of kings, and the flesh of captains, and the flesh of mighty men, and the flesh of horses, and of them that sit on them, and the flesh of all [men, both] free and bond, both small and great. {19:19} And I saw the beast, and the kings of the earth, and their armies, gathered together to make war against Him that sat on the horse, and against His army. {19:20} And the beast was taken, and with Him the false prophet that wrought miracles before Him, with which he deceived them that had received the mark of the beast, and them that worshipped His image. These both were cast alive into a lake of fire burning with brimstone. {19:21} And the remnant were slain with the sword of Him that sat upon the horse, which [sword] proceeded out of His mouth: and all the fowls were filled with their flesh. {51}

{20:1} And I saw an angel come down from heaven, having the key of the bottomless pit and a great chain in His hand. {20:2} And he laid hold on the dragon, that old serpent, which is the Devil, and Satan, and bound Him a thousand years, {20:3} And cast Him into the bottomless pit, and shut Him up, and set a seal upon Him, that he should deceive the nations no more, till the thousand years should be fulfilled: and after that he must be loosed a little season. {20:4} And I saw thrones, and they sat upon them, and judgment was given unto them: and [I saw] the souls of them that were beheaded for the witness of Jesus, and for the word of God, and which had not worshipped the beast, neither His image, neither had received [His] mark upon their foreheads, or in their hands; and they lived and reigned with Christ a thousand years. {20:5} But the rest of the dead lived not again until the thousand years were finished. This [is] the first resurrection. {20:6} Blessed and holy [is] he that hath part in the first resurrection: on such the second death hath no power, but they shall be priests of God and of Christ, and shall reign with Him a thousand years. {20:7} And when the thousand years are expired, Satan shall be loosed out of His prison, {20:8} And shall go out to deceive the nations which are in the four quarters of the earth, Gog and Magog, to gather them together to battle: the number of whom [is] as the sand of the sea. {20:9} And they went up on the breadth of the earth, and compassed the camp of the saints about, and the beloved city: and fire came down from God out of heaven, and devoured them. {20:10} And the devil that deceived them was cast into the lake of fire and brimstone, where the beast and the false prophet [are,] and

shall be tormented day and night for ever and ever.

{20:11} And I saw a great white throne, and Him that sat on it, from whose face the earth and the heaven fled away; and there was found no place for them. {20:12} And I saw the dead, small and great, stand before God; and the books were opened: and another book was opened, which is [the book] of life: and the dead were judged out of those things which were written in the books, according to their works. {20:13} And the sea gave up the dead which were in it; and death and hell delivered up the dead which were in them: and they were judged every man according to their works. {20:14} And death and hell were cast into the lake of fire. This is the second death. {20:15} And whosoever was not found written in the book of life was cast into the lake of fire. {5}

{21:1} And I saw a new heaven and a new earth: for the first heaven and the first earth were passed away; and there was no more sea. {21:2} And I John saw the holy city, new Jerusalem, coming down from God out of heaven, prepared as a bride adorned for her husband. {21:3} And I heard a great voice out of heaven saying, Behold, the tabernacle of God [is] with men, and He will dwell with them, and they shall be His people, and God himself shall be with them, [and be] their God. {21:4} And God shall wipe away all tears from their eyes; and there shall be no more death, neither sorrow, nor crying, neither shall there be any more pain: for the former things are passed away. {21:5} And he that sat upon the throne said, Behold, I make all things new. And he said unto me, Write: for these words are true and faithful. {21:6} And he said unto me, It is done. I am Alpha and Omega, the beginning and the end. I will give unto Him that is athirst of the fountain of the water of life freely. {21:7} he that overcometh shall inherit all things; and I will be His God, and he shall be my Son. {21:8} But the fearful, and unbelieving, and the abominable, and murderers, and whoremongers, and sorcerers, and idolaters, and all liars, shall have their part in the lake which burneth with fire and brimstone: which is the second death.

{21:9} And there came unto me one of the seven angels which had the seven vials full of the seven last plagues, and talked with me, saying, Come hither, I will shew thee the bride, the Lamb's wife. {21:10} And he carried me away in the spirit to a great and high mountain, and shewed me that great city, the holy Jerusalem, descending out of heaven from God, {21:11} Having the glory of God: and her light [was] like unto a stone most precious, even like a jasper stone, clear as crystal; {21:12} And had a wall great and high, [and] had twelve gates, and at the gates twelve angels, and names written thereon, which are [the names] of the twelve tribes of the children of Israel: {21:13} On the east three gates; on the north three gates; on the south three gates; and on the west three gates. {21:14} And the wall of the city had twelve foundations, and in them the names of the twelve apostles of the Lamb. {21:15} And he that talked with me had a golden reed to measure the city, and the gates thereof, and the wall thereof. {21:16} And the city lieth foursquare, and the length is as large as the breadth: and he measured the city with the reed, twelve thousand furlongs. The length and the breadth and the height of it are equal. {21:17} And he measured the wall thereof, an hundred [and] forty [and] four cubits, [according to] the measure of a man, that is, of the angel. {21:18} And the building of the wall of it was [of] jasper: and the city [was] pure gold, like unto clear glass. {21:19} And the foundations of the wall of the city [were] garnished with all manner of precious stones. The first foundation [was] jasper; the second, sapphire; the third, a chalcedony; the fourth, an emerald; {21:20} The fifth, sardonyx; the sixth, sardius; the seventh, chrysolite; the eighth, beryl; the ninth, a topaz; the tenth, a chrysoprasus; the eleventh, a jacinth; the twelfth, an amethyst. {21:21} And the twelve gates [were] twelve pearls; every several gate was of one pearl: and the street of the city [was] pure gold, as it were transparent glass. {21:22} And I saw no temple therein: for the **Lord God** Almighty and the **Lamb** are the temple of it. {21:23} And the city had no need of the sun, neither of the moon, to shine in it: for the glory of **God** did lighten it, and the **Lamb** [is] the **light** thereof. {21:24} And the nations of them which are saved shall walk in the light of it: and the kings of the earth do bring their glory and honour into it. {21:25} And the gates of it shall not be shut at all by day: for there shall be no night there. {21:26} And they shall bring the glory and honour of the nations into it. {21:27} And there shall in no wise enter into it any thing that defileth, neither [whatsoever] worketh abomination, or [maketh] a lie: but they which are written in the Lamb's book of life. {3}

{22:1} And he shewed me a pure river of water of life, clear as crystal, proceeding out of the throne of **God** and of the **Lamb**. {22:2} In the midst of the street of it, and on either side of the river, [was there] the tree of life, which bare twelve [manner] of fruits, [and] yielded her fruit every month: and the leaves of the tree [were] for the healing of the nations. {22:3} And there shall be no more curse: but the throne of **God** and of the **Lamb** shall be in it; and **His** servants shall serve **Him**: {22:4} And they shall see **His** face; and **His name** [shall be] in their foreheads. {22:5} And there shall be no night there; and they need no candle, neither light of the sun; for the **Lord God** giveth them **light**: and they shall reign for ever and ever.

{22:6} And he said unto me, These sayings [are] faithful and true: and the **Lord God** of the holy prophets sent **His** angel to shew unto **His** servants the things which must shortly be done. {22:7} Behold, **I** come quickly: blessed is he that keepeth the sayings of the prophecy of this book. {22:8} And I John saw these things, and heard [them.] And when I had heard and seen, I fell down to worship before the feet of the angel which shewed me these things. {22:9} Then saith he unto me, See [thou do it] not: for I am thy fellowservant, and of thy brethren the prophets, and of them which keep the sayings of this book: worship **God**. {22:10} And he saith unto me, Seal not the sayings of the prophecy of this book: for the time is at hand. {22:11} he that is unjust, let Him be unjust still: and he which is filthy, let Him be filthy still: and he that is righteous, let Him be righteous still: and he that is holy, let Him be holy still. {22:12} And, behold, **I** come quickly; and **my** reward [is] with **ME**, to give every man according as His work shall be. {22:13} **I am Alpha** and **Omega**, the **beginning** and the **end**, the **first** and the **last**. {22:14} Blessed [are] they that do **His** commandments, that they may have right to the tree of life, and may enter in through the gates into the city. {22:15} For without [are] dogs, and sorcerers, and whoremongers, and murderers, and idolaters, and whosoever loveth and maketh a lie.

{22:16} **I Jesus** have sent **mine** angel to testify unto you these things in the churches. **I am** the **root** and the **offspring** of David, [and] the **bright and morning star**.

{22:17} And the Spirit and the bride say, Come. And let Him that heareth say, Come. And let Him that is athirst come. And whosoever will, let Him take the water of life freely.

{22:18} For I testify unto every man that heareth the words of the prophecy of this book, If any man shall add unto these things, **God** shall add unto Him the plagues that are written in this book: {22:19} And if any man shall take away from the words of the book of this prophecy, **God** shall take away His part out of the book of life, and out of the holy city, and [from] the things which are written in this book.

{22:20} He which testifieth these things saith, Surely **I** come quickly. Amen. Even so, come, **Lord Jesus**. {38}

Printed in Great Britain
by Amazon